FRANCIS of ASSISI

The Saint

Early Documents

A three-volume series

FRANCIS OF ASSISI: EARLY DOCUMENTS

Volume I	The Saint
Volume II	The Founder
Volume III	The Prophet

THE SAINT

The Writings of Francis of Assisi
The Life of Saint Francis by Thomas of Celano
The Liturgical Texts
The Life of Saint Francis by Julian of Speyer
The Versified Life of Saint Francis by Henri d'Avranches
The Sacred Exchange between Saint Francis and Lady Poverty
Related Documents

Volume I of:
Francis of Assisi: Early Documents

Edited by
Regis J. Armstrong, O.F.M. Cap.
J. A. Wayne Hellmann, O.F.M. Conv.
William J. Short, O.F.M.

New City Press
New York London Manila

Published in the United States, Great Britain, and the Philippines by
New City Press, 202 Comforter Blvd., Hyde Park, New York 12538
New City, Sovereign Park, Coronation Rd., Unit 17, London
New City Press - Manila, 4800 Valenzuela St., Sta Mesa, Manila 1016

Cover design by Nick Cianfarani
Cover art by an unknown artist of Emilia or Lombardia, Italy
in the Baptistry of the Duomo of Parma, Italy
Photograph by William R. Cook. Used with permission.
The painting offers an unusual portrait of Francis and the six-winged seraph. Since the seraph's hands are not visible and his feet show no wounds, scholars suggest that the reception of the stigmata was not intended by the artist as much as a portrait of Francis "who seemed to everyone a person of another age" (1C 36) or "like the angel ascending from the rising of the sun" (Lmj Prol 1).

Library of Congress Cataloging-in-Publication Data:
Francis of Assisi : early documents / edited by Regis J. Armstrong, J. Wayne Hellmann, William J. Short.

p. cm.
Includes bibliographical references and index.
Contents: v. 1. The saint.
ISBN 1-56548-115-1 (v. 3 : hardcover). — ISBN 1-56548-114-3 (v. 3 : pbk.)
1. Francis, of Assisi, Saint, 1182-1226. 2. Christian saints—Italy—Assisi —Biography—Early works to 1800. 3. Franciscans—History—Sources.
I. Francis, of Assisi, Saint, 1182-1226.
Works. English. 1999. II. Armstrong, Regis J. III. Hellmann, J. Wayne. IV. Short, William J.
BX4700.F6F722 1999
271'.302—dc21
[b] 99

99-18776
CIP

9th printing: August 2019

Printed in the USA

Translators:

Regis J. Armstrong, O.F.M. Cap.
Paul Barrett, O.F.M. Cap
Canisius Connors, O.F.M.
Ewert H. Cousins, Ph.D.
Edward Hagman, O.F.M. Cap.
J. A. Wayne Hellmann, O.F.M. Conv.
Serge Hughes
Claude Jarmak, O.F.M. Conv.
Jason Miskully
Dominic Monti, O.F.M.
Franco Mormando, S.J.
Peter Nickels, O.F.M. Conv.
Timothy Noone
Gregory Shanahan, O.F.M.
William J. Short, O.F.M.
Jaime Vidal, Ph.D.

Contributors and Consultants:

Joseph Chinicci, O.F.M.
Michael Cusato, O.F.M.
Lorenzo Di Fonzo, O.F.M. Conv.
Conrad Harkins, O.F.M.
Ingrid Peterson, O.S.F.
Cyprian Rosen, O.F.M. Cap.
Oktavian Schmucki, O.F.M. Cap.
Keith Warner, O.F.M.

Technical and Research Assistants:

David Chilenski
John and Vicki Chiment
Bruce Cromwell
Jay Hammond III
Eileen Haugh, O.S.F.
John Isom
Gerasimos Pagoulatos
Noel Riggs
Robert Roddy, O.F.M. Conv.

Contents

The Writings of Francis of Assisi (1205/06–1226)

The Life of Saint Francis by Thomas of Celano (1228–1229)

The Liturgical Texts (1230–1234)

The Life of Saint Francis by Julian of Speyer (1232–1235)

The Versified Life of Saint Francis by Henri d'Avranches (1232–1239)

The Sacred Exchange between Saint Francis and Lady Poverty (1237–1239)

Related Documents

Appendix

General Introduction

Appropriately Clare of Assisi, undoubtedly Francis's most faithful disciple, may have inspired this endeavor. At a celebration honoring the publication of *Clare of Assisi: Early Documents*, conversation eventually turned to the need for a new edition of *St. Francis of Assisi: Omnibus of Sources*. Published in 1973, the *Omnibus* had served the Franciscan Family of the English-speaking world for two decades. In many ways it had challenged readers to re-think the Franciscan heritage, fueled the fires of renewal, and found a place of honor in many libraries. Shortly after its appearance, however, Kajetan Esser, a renowned Franciscan scholar, published his scholarly edition of the writings of Francis, the fruit of years of research into the manuscripts of Europe's libraries. Others, such as Lorenzo di Fonzo, Théophile Desbonnets, Rosalind Brooke, and Marino Bigaroni, began to look more attentively at the tradition of Francis's companions. And Georges Maillieux and Jean-François Godet initiated the *Corpus des Sources Franciscains,* a computerized reading of the texts. A revolution had taken place, one that was accessible primarily to scholars or students struggling to understand the intricacies of the "Franciscan Question." The *Omnibus* was clearly outdated and needed to be re-done in light of contemporary scholarship.

The result of that informal discussion was this three-volume series, *Francis of Assisi: Early Documents,* a collaborative effort of English-speaking Franciscans. The editors, Regis J. Armstrong, O.F.M. Cap., J. A. Wayne Hellmann, O.F.M. Conv., and William J. Short, O.F.M., worked with translators, scholars, and technicians to publish new translations of texts about Francis in the early Franciscan tradition. Many of these texts had been published in critical, scholarly European editions, but were not available in English. In some instances, these texts are available for the first time in English translation; in all instances, they have been annotated in light of recent scholarship.

The texts of these volumes originate in the first one hundred and fifty years of the Franciscan tradition and are crucial for understanding not only Francis, but also the movement he initiated. His portrait changes in as many ways as do the circumstances of those trying to capture him in words. The writings of Thomas of Celano, Julian of Speyer, and Bonaventure define Francis in light of previous religious traditions into whose paradigms he clearly did not fit. They write not only to edify and encourage Francis's admirers, but also to defend him from the skepticism of the hierarchy and the scholastics into whose images he did not blend and whose language he did not speak. As the first generation of Francis's followers died and their successors began to struggle with his idealism, appeal to the person of Francis became a means that attempted to heal their divisions and strengthen their unity.

These volumes present texts that are hagiographical beside those that are liturgical, allegorical, anecdotal, or homiletic. Those official in nature are placed with ones that are not. Documents that provide different hues and nuances—papal decrees, liturgical texts, chronicles, writings of non-Franciscan observers, and, if appropriate, secular writers—suggest meanings initially overlooked. All of these texts—the familiar and the unfamiliar—demand their own way of interpretation. Thomas of Celano's "Second Life of Saint Francis," for example, *The Remembrance of the Desire of a Soul,* is quite different from his first. It is unique: its first section is biographical in nature, but its second, the bulk of the work, is more moral in tone as it describes the saint's virtues by use of anecdotes.

From the outset, the editors chose to present these varying texts in a chronological order. This approach revealed three underlying leitmotifs uniting the texts of each volume and, therefore, the three subtitles chosen for the series. Aside from Francis's writings, the texts of the first ten years, 1228-1238, are primarily concerned with celebrating *the saint,* Francis of Assisi. Those of the following period, 1240-1276, focus on the fundamental values or ideals of *the founder,* Francis of Assisi, while those of the last period, 1307-1365, frequently return to Francis's place in history as *the prophet.* The editors hope that this chronological arrangement will enable the reader to see more easily how portrayals of Francis changed from one generation to the next and challenge the scholar to arrive in a more critical-historical manner at a better understanding of the texts. In this light, understanding the literary genre of each text, its purpose as well as the circumstances from which it arose, should prevent using the texts uncritically. Employment of these critical translations and the tools which accompany them, the editors hope, should facilitate a study of the tradition in light of contemporary needs. The chronological presentation of the texts of these decisive one hundred and fifty years presents a challenge to re-appropriate, in ways that are critical and becoming, the tradition they contain.

Francis of Assisi: Early Documents attests to history's restless pursuit to know Francis of Assisi. After embracing a poverty that left little room for whatever he could claim as uniquely his own, the saint of universal appeal had emptied himself of everything. "There is nothing in this world we can claim as our own except our vice and sin," he maintained.[1] He developed a certain personal transparency with which future generations would be forced to struggle to grasp onto the facts in reconstructing the contours of his life. Authors, medieval and modern, have attempted to determine the basic facts, identify the social, ecclesial, and psychological influences on his actions, and define his unique enthusiasm for all that comes from God's hand. They impose different paradigms or patterns of holiness and, in the final analysis, invite others to take up the challenge anew. Thus the "Francis of legend" emerges, one who straddles the lines between projected history and scientific history, between the acts and the imagination of early thirteenth century Umbria, and between established religious structures and emerging spiritual beliefs.[2] Even a careful reading of the texts contained in these volumes will prompt the reader to wonder if it is possible to write an accurate biography of Francis or determine what precisely is at the heart of his vision.

The Writings

It would seem appropriate for Francis's own writings to be the most valuable source for discovering him. This is certainly true at the close of the twentieth century for no generation has had the same access to his writings as the present. Until the work of Esser and the proliferation of translations of his findings, however, Francis's writings had been overlooked. Beyond his *Later Rule* and *Testament,* even Franciscan writers such as Bonaventure (+1274) or Duns Scotus (+1284) rarely quote any of Francis's writings. Strange as this phenomenon may seem, the history of the Franciscan movement is one that is surprisingly devoid of an in-depth knowledge of its founder's writings. The reasons for this are difficult to ascertain. Was it the result of Francis's personality impacting the life of his followers more than his thought? Was it due to the sweeping decree of the Chapter of Paris when in 1266 the friars voted to give Bonaventure's portrait of the saint precedence over others? Or was it prompted by the simplicity of his writings or their disarming lack of sophistication? Whatever the reason, throughout their history followers of Francis have projected their own ideas and constructs onto the writings scholars have unearthed. Even with the help of a critical edition and a computerized examination of his writings, questions of interpretation abound.

When his writings are studied as a whole, they clearly reveal the depth and clarity of the saint's Gospel-centered vision and poetic sensitivity; they also manifest the limits of his education and the simplicity of his vocabulary. This makes the need more urgent for the development and acceptance of a generally objective hermeneutic for ascertaining Francis's thought, for cutting through layers of historical attachments.[3] Presenting all of his writings in a chronological manner is one step in this process, for it enables the reader to see the development of his thought and to examine that thought in light of the circumstances of his life. The rapid growth of his followers impacted the structures of the fraternity and brought about division into smaller jurisdictions. In a similar way, the influence of the Fourth Lateran Council changed his understanding of evangelization as he and his brothers became more aware of preparation for preaching. Nevertheless, the dating of a number of writings cannot be determined with certainty; others are impossible to ascertain at all. These are the writings, however, that reveal the Francis who is most in touch with the word of God and with human nature.

The Growth of the Tradition of the Saint

Within two years of his death, Francis's friend, Cardinal Hugolino, then Pope Gregory IX, canonized him. In preparation for the event, Gregory IX commissioned Brother Thomas of Celano to prepare an official account of his life, pursuit of virtue, and miraculous powers. The papal commission he received was twofold: to honor this new saint, Francis, and to instruct his readers about the importance of Francis's life and way of holiness. In the fulfillment of this mandate, Thomas unwittingly initiated a struggle that endures to this day: the attempt to capture in words the unique qualities of Francis of Assisi.

Thomas was undoubtedly inspired by the accounts of saintly men and women that were popular at the time. He refers to Sulpicius Severus's portrait of Martin of Tours, which had become a staple of Christian piety, to Bernard of Clairvaux's life of Saint Malachy, and to the early lives of Bernard himself that nourished monks searching to rejuvenate the ancient practices of monasticism. Far from being a fault, Thomas's readers undoubtedly delighted in his ability to refer to earlier patterns of holiness. These references provided more reasons to celebrate Francis's canonization and to imitate the age-old way of sanctity. Historical accuracy—in the modern sense—was not a concern for Thomas's readers.

With his canonization, Francis officially entered the catalog of saints and, according to custom, his feast day was celebrated on the day of his death, October 4. Besides his life of Francis, Thomas prepared a series of readings based on the saint's life for the liturgical celebration of the Divine Office, *The Legend for Use in the Choir.*[4] Another Brother, Julian of Speyer, composed antiphons, hymns and responsories for these liturgical celebrations between 1232 and 1235, and Pope Gregory IX himself composed a number of hymns, as did two other ecclesiastical friends of Francis, Cardinals Thomas of Capua and Ranieri Cappocci.

Within a short time other portraits of the new saint began to emerge. Julian, for example, wrote his own life of Francis relying on the writings of Thomas but employing his liturgical nuances. The result reflects images of Francis that were shaped by the prayer life of the primitive fraternity. A much more ambitious project was the work of Henri d'Avranches who, between 1232 and 1234, used Thomas's portrait as the foundation for a type of poetic literature quite popular in noble circles. Latinist in the court of Pope Gregory IX, Henri dedicated this *Versified Life of Saint Francis* to the pope and, in order to honor the pope, began each of its fourteen sections with the letters of Gregory's name. The work took the form of an epic poem in which Henri used his literary skill to describe the life of Francis in the images of the Greek and Latin classical tradition. What emerges is a portrait that is more than a poetic re-working of Thomas's writings. It underscores the heroic biblical images of the Judges used by Gregory IX in his proclamation of Francis's canonization and transforms the "little poor one" into a powerful champion of the Church.[5]

Gregory IX may well have unknowingly prompted the composition of another piece, *The Sacred Exchange between Saint Francis and Lady Poverty*. His papal decree, *Quo elongati,* September 28, 1230, was the first papal clarification of Francis's *Later Rule,* the document solemnly approved by Gregory's predecessor, Honorius III.[6] Arguing as Francis's friend and advisor, Gregory declared that Francis's *Testament,* to which many were appealing as the only true interpretation of the Rule, was not binding. When *Quo elongati* is read in the context of the increasing tensions within the fraternity, the building of the basilica in honor of Francis in Assisi, and the controversial return of Elias of Cortona as General Minister, the document challenged the foundations of the Order, especially its pursuit of poverty. *The Sacred Exchange* was not simply a response. It was an appeal to return to the lofty idealism of poverty upon which the primitive fraternity of Francis and his first brothers had been built. The identity of its author, as the date of its composition, is unknown. Yet the document eloquently expresses in an allegory rich in biblical images the principles of the first generation of Francis's followers.[7]

The Founder

A new stage of the hagiographical tradition surrounding Francis began, however, in 1243 when the newly elected General Minister, Crescentius of Iesi, ordered the collection of all available information about the saint and the early days of the fraternity. Crescentius focused his attention on Francis as the founder of an Order that was flourishing. An earlier piece may well have been an example of what he sought. *The Beginning or the Founding of the Order and the Deeds of Those Lesser Brothers Who Were the First in Religion and the Companions of the Blessed Francis* was written by a companion of Brother Giles (+1262), John of Perugia.[8] The text suggests that it was composed after the death of Brother Silvester but before that of Pope Gregory IX, that is, between March 4, 1240, and August 22, 1241. It is a work formational or educational in nature, one that deals with the primitive fraternity more than with the person of Francis himself. How widely it was known is impossible to determine. But it may have prompted the brothers to realize there were many facts about Francis of which they were ignorant.

Two highly disputed texts may reflect the contributions of brothers who identify themselves as Brothers Leo, Angelo, and Rufino or "we who were with him." The *Legend of the Three Companions* and the *Legend of Perugia* or the *Assisi Compilation* focus on the person of Francis and provide facts and insights missing from the earlier lives of Thomas and Julian. *The Legend of the Three Companions,* for example, presents a detailed exposition of Francis's early years and those of the primitive fraternity. Its authors may have had regular access to Francis himself and also to the text of John of Perugia. The other text, the *Legend of Perugia* or the *Assisi Compilation,* also presents anecdotes about Francis that could only have come from day-to-day association with him. "We who were with him" offer stories of his practice of virtue, his dealings with the brothers, and his struggles with those who found his Gospel vision difficult to understand. They provide details missing in the other portraits and do so in a way suggesting they lacked any plan or structure.

Nevertheless, both texts present external and internal problems. The earliest manuscripts of both the *Legend of the Three Companions* and the *Legend of Perugia* do not support a date close to 1244, the request of Crescentius. Although there are twenty-two manuscripts of the *Legend of the Three Companions,* the oldest comes from the early 1300's; two others come from the second half of that century. When all the manuscripts are gathered together, two different families emerge, each with its own nuances. The manuscript tradition of the *Legend of Perugia* is considerably more simple: it is found in Codex 1046 of the Biblioteca communale Augusta in Perugia, dated 1311. The dating of the manuscript has been generally accepted because of a papal declaration of 1310 by Pope Clement V that it also contains.

More difficult to resolve are the internal problems of each text. The letter attached to the *Legend of the Three Companions* is but one example.[9] To prove the historical authenticity of his presentation, the unknown author begins with a letter dated August 11, 1246, addressed to Crescentius and written by Brothers Leo, Rufino, and Angelus. In it the three companions maintain that they are not writing a *legenda* [a work intended to be read aloud], nor following a historical sequence, but are gathering "some of the more beautiful flowers . . . from a pleasant meadow." The text that follows, however, *does* follow a historical sequence by describing in detail Francis's early years until Innocent III's approval of the primitive fraternity, deals briefly with its growth and organization, and, in the later manuscripts, concludes with Francis's death and canonization. All of these difficulties raise serious questions about the date of this text. Is it a reflection of what was sent to the General Minister, Crescentius, in response to his request? Was it written in different stages? Given its authenticity, why was the Letter attached to the *Legend?* Theories abound; definite answers are lacking.

The *Legend of Perugia* has its own set of internal problems. Unfortunately, it has been published under different titles: *Legenda Antiqua* [*Ancient Legend*],[10] *I Fiori dei Tre Compagni* [*The Flowers of the Three Companions*],[11] *Scripta Leonis, Rufini et Angeli Sociorum S. Francisci* [*The Writings of Leo, Rufino and Angelo, Companions of St. Francis*],[12] *Legenda Perugina* [*Legend of Perugia*][13] and *Compilatio Assisiensis* [*The Assisi Compilation*].[14] Different scholars have presented different formats, e.g. Jacques Cambell who, in attempting to identify those who provided the material, re-ordered the text. Others, e.g. François

Delorme and Rosalind Brooke, omitted passages arguing that they could be found elsewhere. These inconsistencies have added to the failure of viewing the text from an objective perspective.

It is difficult to deny the veracity of its claims to be the anecdotes or remembrances of "we who were with him" that were submitted to Crescentius. There is little order to the text; there is a sense of personal reminiscences; and there are details mentioned that could only have been known by those who were present. However, the title suggested by Marino Bigaroni is correct in identifying the work as a compilation. And therein lies another problem.[15] Two sections of the text are made up of Leo's *Verba Sancti Francisci* [*Words of Saint Francis*] and his *Intentio Regulae* [*the Intention of the Rule*]. Both of these writings seem to have been known at the end of the thirteenth century or the beginning of the fourteenth.[16] Since the earliest known manuscript of *The Assisi Compilation* was written between March 23, 1310, and May 31, 1312, it is not difficult to see the hand of an editor in this work.

The result of Crescentius's request of the brothers was ultimately *The Remembrance of the Desire of a Soul;* its author was Thomas of Celano.[17] An examination of this text clearly shows Thomas's dependence on information sent to Crescentius by Francis's companions. This "second life" is a much fuller portrait of the saint, one that offers details of his early life which were unknown or overlooked in his *Life of Saint Francis*. The first section, for example, provides details of Francis's youth, e.g. his baptismal name, the name of his mother; it also focuses on Francis's prayerful experience before the crucifix of the church of San Damiano. The bulk of the work, however, is a thorough portrayal of the virtues of the saint's life.

After its approval by the Chapter of Lyons in 1247, the brothers prevailed upon Thomas once again. This time it was to describe in detail Francis's miracles, *The Treatise on the Miracles*. Thomas began the work in 1250, completed it three years later, and probably saw its approval at the Chapter of Metz in 1254.

The strains of the rapid growth of the Order encouraged the brothers to maintain their focus on Francis as their founder. Each Chapter or gathering of the brothers enacted legislation to safeguard his ideals.[18] By the time of the promulgation of the Constitutions of Narbonne in 1260, it was obvious that the brothers needed an interpretation of Francis's life that would address in a more consistent way the saint's pattern of holiness. At the General Chapter of Narbonne, the brothers issued the following decree: "We order that one good legend of blessed Francis be compiled from all those already in existence."[19] Three years later at the General Chapter in Pisa, Bonaventure of Bagnoreggio, the General Minister of the Order to whom the mandate was entrusted, presented not one but two works.[20] The *Legenda major* was a portrait composed of two sections, the first describing Francis's life and virtues, the second describing his miracles. The *Legenda minor* was a shorter companion piece also based on those earlier portraits, whose main purpose was liturgical in nature. In both instances,

Bonaventure relied on the works of Thomas and Julian and, as he mentions, consulted with those brothers who knew Francis and were still living, e.g. Giles (+1262) and Leo (+1268).[21] The results of his efforts, however, were those of a theologian in touch with the currents of mystical theology of his time. The virtues of Francis, while described through the anecdotes of Thomas and Julian, are presented in orderly, theological fashion. Both *legendae* reveal the hand of a teacher entrusted with the responsibility of developing in his students a love of the spiritual life of their founder.

Three years later the Chapter of Paris then made this startling decision:

> The General Chapter likewise orders under obedience that all *the legends of the Blessed Francis* that have been made should be removed. Wherever they find these outside the Order, let the brothers strive to remove them. For this *Legend* made by the general minister has been compiled as he received it from the mouth of those who were always with the blessed Francis and had certain knowledge of everything, and proven facts have been diligently placed in it.[22]

The Friars Preacher, followers of Saint Dominic, had enacted a similar measure in 1260 after Humbert of Romans had compiled from existing works a *Legend of Saint Dominic*. Their initiative was motivated by a liturgical reason: the need for a unified portrait of their founder to be read during the Divine Office. Francis's followers were far more exacting in the decree of the Chapter of Paris. They decreed that all earlier legends should be *deleantur* [removed].[23] The reasons for their initiative are unclear. Although the reference to one legend could refer to the liturgical text, the *Legenda minor,* all legends were effected. This suggests reasons other than liturgical. Was it due to the force of Bonaventure's position as General Minister or his stature as a theologian? Was it a means of reconciling the developing tensions between the more idealistic and the more moderate approaches to Francis's vision? Or was it simply a matter of poverty, that is, re-using parchment to preserve this newer text? Whatever the reasons, for the next five centuries Bonaventure's official portrait dominated the Franciscan landscape; the others written before 1266 remained hidden, presumed to have been destroyed.

The Prophet

Bonaventure's secretary and traveling companion, Bernard of Besse, was the first to sidestep the 1266 decree. *A Book of Praises of the Blessed Francis* was intended as a devotional introduction to Bernard's *Chronicle of the Fourteen or Fifteen General Ministers of the Order of Friars Minor*. The inspiration for the work was the brothers' decision to entrust Bernard with the task of writing the biographies of the General Ministers from the Order's beginning.[24] Bernard was undoubtedly influenced by his mentor, Bonaventure, in situating Francis and the three Orders he founded in the context of God's plan. The image of Francis now accentuated that of the prophet recalling his followers to an authentic way of life.

The editing and publication of the remembrances of the three companions at the beginning of the fourteenth century raise questions about the internal struggles of the friars. The intentions of the unknown editors of *The Legend of the Three Companions* and *The Assisi Compilation* may have been to correct the interpretation of Bonaventure of the material used originally by Thomas of Celano. To do so, the editor of *The Assisi Compilation* may have discovered the primitive remembrances and added to them the writings of Brother Leo. The words of Ubertino of Casale's *Declaratio* of 1311 confirm this. In citing *The Intention of the Rule,* he appeals to the authority of Brother Leo, one of those "who were with him" (i.e., Francis): ". . . all this is found, written by the hand of Brother Leo, in the book that is in Assisi."[25] Do these texts reveal the division of the Order into different camps, the Spirituals and the Moderates? Do they suggest attempts to "correct" the interpretations of Thomas of Celano, Julian, or Bonaventure? Or do they hint at continuing efforts to counteract the effects of Gregory IX's *Quo elongati?* Whatever may be the case, *The Legend of the Three Companions* and the *Assisi Compilation* represent attempts to set the record straight, that is, to rectify the mistaken interpretations of earlier portraits.

In 1318, shortly after the editing of the *Assisi Compilation,* the *Mirror of Perfection* appeared. It is clearly based on the *Compilation* but presented by an unknown author in a more pedagogical way to present "a mirror of perfection of the state of a lesser brother." Its one hundred and twenty-four sections are divided, like the *Later Rule* of Francis himself, into twelve chapters, implying that the saint's followers can discover in his life, as in his *Rule,* the way to perfection. Whereas both Thomas's *Life of Saint Francis* and Bonaventure's *legendae* were far more universal in their consideration, the editor of the *Mirror of Perfection* had only his confreres in mind. He therefore produced a work with a very limited audience, the brothers themselves.

Another attempt at "rectifying" history was Angelo Clareno's *The History of the Seven Tribulations of the Order of the Minors* written between 1323 and 1325. In it the leader of the rebel Spirituals described the first century of the Order "through the prism of the persecution suffered by the authentic heirs to the founder's evangelical ideals."[26] The work is acerbic, polemical, and representative of the tendencies of the authors of this period, many of whom were intent on purifying the Order of any aberrations that had crept into the primitive fraternity.

Much of the literature of the fourteenth century emerged in a most troubling period of the Order's history. The conflicts of the Avignon Papacy, the troublesome pontificate of John XXII, as well as the growing tensions between the Spirituals and the Moderates, caught the friars in a maelstrom that eventually brought about division.[27] The Spirituals hoped that recourse to the person of

Francis described in the writings of those "who were with him" would resolve many of the conflicts that increasingly divided the Order, especially those about poverty. At the same time, however, the reputation of the friars as extraordinary popular preachers was growing. In the midst of wars, plagues, and eroding social structures, the power of their preaching and example touched the hearts of thousands of people thirsty for a down-to-earth, optimistic spirituality. The popularity of these preachers and the curiosity of the people may well have inspired what quickly became known as *The Little Flowers of Saint Francis.*

Written between 1328 and 1343 by Hugolino of Monte Giorgio and an unknown collaborator, the *Actus Beati Francisci et sociorum ejus* [*The Deeds of Blessed Francis and His Companions*] was a collection of "little flowers" or anecdotes about Francis and his first brothers. Many of the stories were rooted in both the written and oral Franciscan tradition. They became appealing, however, because of the simple and, at times, dramatic ways in which they were written. The text became more appealing when its seventy-six chapters were reduced to fifty-three and translated into Tuscan Italian. The language of Dante, who had already dedicated a section of the *Divine Comedy* to Francis, gave the *Actus* a life of its own and gave *The Little Flowers* or *Fioretti* a popularity that has made it the best-known classic of Franciscan hagiography.

In a sense, the *Little Flowers* epitomized much of the Franciscan hagiography of the fourteenth century. It took the now popular saint and, in several stories, portrayed him as a prophet whose miraculous visions revealed the course of history, especially that of the Order. In one instance, for example, Francis foresees the apostasy and damnation of Brother Elias, who is eventually saved through the saint's prayer. While its audience may have been the people to whom they were preaching, the friars undoubtedly understood the portrayal of Francis in *The Little Flowers* as a statement about their own role in the turbulent times in which they lived.

The work also highlighted the conformity between Francis and Christ, a theme that became characteristic of the Franciscan tradition of the fourteenth century. *The Little Flowers* opens with this theme: "We must consider first of all how Saint Francis, in all the deeds of his life, conformed to the blessed Christ." This approach eventually culminated in one of the great classics of Franciscan literature, Bartholomew of Pisa's *The Conformity of the Life of the Blessed Francis to the Life of the Lord Jesus.* Written between 1385 and 1390, Bartholomew's work was an ambitious study of the life of Francis in light of that of Jesus in which it was clear that Francis was truly an *alter Christus.* Each chapter of this encyclopedic work dwells on an aspect of the life of Christ and proceeds to illustrate how it finds a parallel in that of Francis. Even Christ's birth in the straw of a manger finds a corresponding event in Francis's birth in La Stalletta, a shrine still kept in modern day Assisi.

A small work of an unknown author, *De cognatione Sancti Francisci* [*Knowledge of Saint Francis*], written in 1365, reflects perfectly this theme of conformity and provides a lens for viewing the growth of the tradition surrounding Francis. The author declares: "Saint Francis had four followers who wrote his life with great accuracy, just as Christ had four evangelists."[28] In his mind, each Franciscan evangelist shared a symbolic figure similar to his apostolic counterpart: Thomas of Celano, an angel, Matthew; Leo, a lion, Mark; Julian, an ox, Luke; and Bonaventure, an eagle, John. It is a provocative description of the ways of looking at the early biographical traditions of Francis and suggests the need of approaching them with hermeneutics similar to those used in the biblical texts.

Modern Approaches to the Tradition of Saint Francis

The dawning of the present-day approach to Franciscan hagiography began in 1625 when Luke Wadding, an Irish Franciscan, began publishing his *Annales minorum,* a chronological examination of the Order of Friars Minor until the year 1540.[29] Other chronicles of the Order had been published by Nicholas Glassberger in 1508, Mark of Lisbon in 1557, Bernardino of Colpetrazzo in 1580, Pietro Ridolfi of Tossignano in 1586, and Francesco de Gonzaga in 1587, but the historical method of Wadding left its imprint. He showed a greater desire for accuracy and for objectivity.

Forty-six years later, a Jesuit scholar, Daniel Papebroch, discovered in Perugia a manuscript of the work of John of Perugia.[30] Papebroch's search for ancient manuscripts was part of a larger project, the *Acta Sanctorum*, designed to be a historically reliable presentation of the lives of the saints.[31] A century after Papebroch's discovery, in 1768, another Jesuit scholar, Cornelius Suyskens, eventually published some selections from this work as part of the *Acta Sanctorum.* But Suyskens had a far more important text to present in that volume, arguably the most fundamental document in the Franciscan collection. He had discovered a manuscript of the *Life of Saint Francis* by Thomas of Celano. By the end of the eighteenth century a different portrait of Francis slowly began to re-emerge, one not based exclusively on that of Bonaventure.

The nineteenth century accelerated that process and eventually produced a storm of scholarly controversy about the "true" picture of the saint. In 1803 Stefano Rinaldi discovered and published a manuscript of Thomas of Celano's second portrait of Francis, *The Remembrance of the Desire of a Soul.*[32] Its publication contributed to a growing interest in the figure of Francis among scholars of very different backgrounds.[33] A few years later Niccolo Papini used the new discoveries of Papebroch, Suyskens and Rinaldi to write *La Storia di S. Francesco di Assisi* in two volumes.[34] A first attempt at providing a compilation of the newly discovered sources occurred in 1856 when Stanislao Melchiorri published *Legenda di San Francesco d'Ascesi scritta dalli suoi compagni che tutt'hora conversano con lui* [*Legend of Saint Francis of Assisi Written by His Companions Who Were Always With Him*].[35]

The Germans initiated their important Franciscan research with Joseph Göerres, the German Romantic, *Der heilige Franziskus von Assisi: Ein Troubadour* [*Saint Francis of Assisi: The Troubador*].[36] In 1856, Karl von Hase published *Franz von Assis, ein Heiligenbild* [*Francis of Assisi: An Image of a Saint*][37] and in 1885, Karl Müller published his *Die Anfänge des Minoritenordens und der Bussbruderschaft* [*The Origins of the Order of Minors and Penitents*] in which he made the first limited attempt at a historical-critical method.[38] Because of a similar approach, the 1885 work of the historian Henry Thode's *Franz von Assisi und die Anfänge der Kunst der Renaissance in Italien* [*Francis of Assisi and the Origins of the Arts of the Renaissance in Italy*] also gained recognition.[39]

By mid-century, however, French scholars were gaining importance. In 1852 Frederic Ozanam, founder of the Society of St. Vincent de Paul, wrote *Les Poétes Franciscains en Italie au Trezième Siècle, avec un choix des Petites Fleurs de Saint François Traduites de l'Italien* [*The Franciscan Poets of Italy in the Thirteenth Century with a Selection from the Little Flowers of Saint Francis Translated from the Italian*].[40] In his sixth volume of *Histoire de la France,* Jules Michelet dedicated a chapter to Francis in which he portrayed him as a poetic, thespian rebel, a precursor of the Renaissance and even of the Protestant Reformation.[41] Reacting to von Hase's *Franz von Assis,* Ernest Renan reviewed his work in the *Journal des Débats,* August 20-21, 1866, in his article "*Étude historique d'après le Dr. Karl Hase.*"[42] Renan, who had completed his controversial *Vie de Jésus* only three years earlier, portrayed Francis as a perfect mirror of Christ and as a reply of the popular conscience to a Church forgetful of spiritual values. His work undoubtedly attracted the attention of the Frenchman who was to have an enormous impact on the Franciscan studies, Paul Sabatier.[43]

Sabatier's influential 1894 study of the life of Francis and the sources, *Vie de Saint François d'Assise,* prompted Franciscan scholars to develop a more critical, objective approach.[44] This was followed in 1898 with his publication of *The Mirror of Perfection.*[45] Sabatier's interpretation of Francis as a forerunner of the Protestant Reformation, a dissenter made to conform to the plans of the Roman Church, provoked a storm of response among both Catholic and Protestant writers, both scholarly and polemical. This was the beginning of the famous "Franciscan Question," a controversy centered on which texts about Francis were the earliest and most reliable. An answer to the question would ascertain which texts provide the most reliable material for understanding the "historical Francis."

As the twentieth century began, the "Franciscan Question" dominated scholarly discussions.[46] The nineteenth century had ended with publication in the *Miscellanea Franciscana* of an open letter of Sabatier as well as response by Michele Faloci Pulignani, a noted Franciscan scholar.[47] The twentieth began with Faloci Pulignani's publication of *San Francesco d'Assisi secondo Paolo Sabatier*, a blistering attack denying the French Protestant's ability to write about the Umbrian Catholic saint.[48] In 1902 Francesco van Ortroy added to the controversy by publishing a nearly complete edition of the *Anonymous of Perugia* that Papebroch had published only in part in 1768.[49] And it revived in 1922 and again in 1926 when Ferdinand Delorme published two editions of *Legenda antiqua s. Francisci.*[50]

In a suburb of Florence, Quaracchi, a group of friars had quietly begun researching and publishing critical, scholarly editions of some early Franciscan writings in a series entitled the *Analecta Franciscana.*[51] Their desire was to publish in a scholarly way as many of the sources for the early history of the Franciscan Order as were available. Between 1926 and 1941 a number of individual texts were published. But in 1942 the friars produced the tenth volume of the *Analecta Franciscana.* It contained the "official" portraits of Thomas of Celano, Julian of Speyer, Henry d'Avranches, the liturgical documents, the two *Legendae* of Bonaventure, the *Legenda Aurea* of James of Voragine, and a variety of monastic lives. The friars had planned another volume for what they considered the "unofficial" legends, but it was never published.

While the texts of the tenth volume of the *Analecta Franciscana* assisted scholars in approaching the "official" biographies more thoroughly, questions still remained about the others. These were underscored by Arnaldo Fortini's publication of the *Nuova Vita di san Francesco* in 1959.[52] A native Assisian and a former mayor, Fortini delved into the city's archives and unearthed background material that brought Francis, his family and companions into a new light. The five-volume results of his research added significantly to an understanding of thirteenth century Assisi and, therefore, to the primitive fraternity of Francis. In 1968, Franciscan scholars gathered in Todi for a conference, *San Francesco nella ricerca storica degli anni ultimi ottanta anni* [Saint Francis in the Historical Research of the Last Eighty Years].[53] This was the first of many appeals to look more seriously at those more controversial texts that were lacking critical editions. Lorenzo di Fonzo had already begun the process of looking more seriously at these texts and, in 1972, published his thorough study of the "Anonymous of Perugia," *The Beginning or the Founding of the Order.*[54] The following year scholars gathered in Assisi to discuss: *La "questione francescana" dal Sabatier ad oggi* [The "Franciscan Question" from Sabatier to Today].[55] In the meantime, Théophile Desbonnets was preparing a critical edition of *The Legend of the Three Companions* which was published in a 1974 edition of the *Archivum Franciscanum Historicum.*[56] In addition to drawing attention to the need of scholars to look more seriously at these texts, these conferences and publications inevitably brought to the fore the work of Raoul Manselli. In 1980, Manselli published *Nos Qui Cum Eo Fuimus: Contributo alla Questione Francescana* [*We Who Were With Him: A Contribution to the*

Franciscan Question] and *S. Francesco d'Assisi*.[57] The first was more than a contribution; it was a challenge to use more critical, scientific tools in examining the texts of Francis's companions. The second was Manselli's attempt to produce a biography of the saint in a more scientific vein.[58]

In 1976 Kajetan Esser published his scholarly presentation of the writings of Saint Francis, *Die Opuscula des Hl. Franziskus von Assisi: Neue textkritische Edition* [*The Complete Works of Saint Francis of Assisi: New Critical Edition*] and, two years later, in a smaller volume, *Opuscula sancti patris Francisci Assisiensis* [*The Works of Holy Father Saint Francis of Assisi*].[59] Esser searched the libraries of Europe, consulted more than a hundred manuscripts of the writings, and published two editions, the first of which offered explanations for his varying interpretations of the texts. At the same time, George Mailleux and Jean-Francois Godet took advantage of the *Centre de Traitement Électronique des Documents* of the Catholic University of Louvain and produced a computerized analysis, not only of the Esser text, but also of all the Latin sources.[60] The seven volumes of the *Corpus des Sources Franciscaines* gradually changed the ways in which scholars examined these texts. By noting the use of words, variations in patterns and styles of writing, and providing scholars the tools to examine the different approaches of authors, knowledge of the development of the hagiographical tradition surrounding Francis became more of a critical science.

The publication of Esser's work and the *Corpus des Sources Franciscaines*—caught up as they were in the Second Vatican Council's encouragement to return to the spirit of the founder—brought a new burst of enthusiasm to Franciscan writers. Among those on the list of contributors, to mention but a few, are: Optatus van Asseldonk, Théophile Desbonnets, Kajetan Esser, David Flood, Lazaro Iriarte, Raffaele Pazzelli, and Octavian Schmucki. But the example of Raoul Manselli inspired a generation of new scholars—mostly lay persons—to approach the early Franciscan literature with a more critical, objective approach.

In 1983 Théophile Desbonnets published *De l'intuition à l'institution. Les franciscains*.[61] Not only had the French scholar painstakingly examined the texts involved in the evolution of the Franciscan movement, he thoroughly reflected on the current scholarship. In the Appendix to his conclusions, Desbonnets sketched the development of the texts as he understood it. By so doing, he—together with Manselli and DiFonzo—provided a new way of looking at this confusing collection of documents. New scholars benefited from this and approached the tradition from different perspectives. Chiara Frugoni's *Francesco e l'invenzione delle stimmate: Una storia per parole e immagini fino a Bonaventura e Giotto* addressed questions concerning the stigmata in ways much different from those used by Octavian Schmucki.[62] Attilio Bartoli Langeli raised serious questions about Esser's interpretation of the autographs of Francis, i.e., what was written with his own hand.[63] Giovanni Miccoli, Grado G. Merlo and Jacques Dalarun challenged traditional interpretations in light of the larger world of Christian hagiography.[64] Other non-Franciscans have followed the same approach: André Vauchez, Jacques LeGoff, Roberto Paccioco, Duncan Nimmo, Edith Pásztor, and Felice Accrocca. Their more objective approach is challenging members of the Franciscan family to look more critically at their heritage and translate it into more meaningful contemporary expressions.

Modern translations of these early Franciscan documents have a history of their own. As early as 1946 the Spanish initiated the practice of placing the primary texts concerning Francis in one volume.[65] In the early 1960's the German scholars, Engelbert Grau, Sophronius Classen, Kajetan Esser, and others, began to publish *Franziskanische Quellenschriften*. These formed a series of individual volumes, each dedicated to a single text. In 1968 a one-volume edition of the early documents was published in French as *Saint François d'Assise: Documents. Ecrits et premières biographies*.[66] Within a short period of time other comprehensive collections appeared. *Saint Francis of Assisi, Writings and Early Biographies: English Omnibus of Sources for the Life of St. Francis* was published in 1973.[67] Following the format of the French *Documents,* it took advantage of existing translations and introductions. The Italians published a two-volume work, *Fonti francescane,* in 1977.[68] The Spanish published a new edition of their pioneering work of 1945, *San Francisco de Asis* in 1978.[69]

The Present Edition

The translations presented in these volumes are based on the critical edition of the friars of Quaracchi whose tenth volume of the *Analecta Franciscana* was a milestone in its manner of presenting the early "official" texts concerning Francis of Assisi. For those texts which were not published in their endeavor, e.g., *The Legend of the Three Companions, The Assisi Compilation,* etc., the editors turned to labors of contemporary scholars such as Théophile Desbonnets, Marino Bigaroni, and Lorenzo di Fonzo. In all instances, these texts were examined in light of the most recent *Fontes Franciscani* in which European editors have published these medieval texts in light of most recent scholarship.[70]

During the earliest stages of planning *Francis of Assisi: Early Documents* the editors decided to present the texts touching on the life of Saint Francis written within roughly the first one hundred and fifty years of the Franciscan tradition. To go beyond this would involve translating Bartholomew of Pisa's exhaustive *The Conformity of the Life of the Blessed Francis to the Life of the Lord Jesus,* an endeavor that would clearly enlarge the scope of the project.[71] At the same time, the editors also decided to present these texts in a chronological order. In order to do so, they initially consulted Lorenzo di Fonzo, O.F.M. Conv., Conrad Harkins, O.F.M., and Octavian Schmucki, O.F.M. Cap., representing the three branches of the First Order of the Friars Minor, to obtain a scholarly consensus.

Certain texts demanded further consultation prompting discussions with Servus Gieben, O.F.M. Cap. and Michael Cusato, O.F.M. While not intending to resolve questions that surround some of these texts, the editors desired to rely upon contemporary scholarship in addressing those questions and to acknowledge that, at this point, they are unanswered.

Another decision the editors made at an early stage of the project was to place all biblical references and allusions in the outer margins. It was their judgment that the authors of these texts had been nurtured on a biblical spirituality, i.e., the *lectio divina,* and thought biblically. This fluency with Sacred Scripture, as well as the well-developed medieval sense of memory, enabled them to write texts that flowed with biblical passages, images and nuances. By noting these references and allusions in the margins, the editors hope to maintain the scriptural flow of the texts and to encourage readers to reflect as did their authors. In addition, the editors have chosen to place all references to earlier texts in the inner margins. In this way, the chronological development of the texts will be more clearly appreciated. All other references, e.g., passages from, or allusions to, other authors, have been placed in footnotes. A complete index and concordance to all the texts will be found in volume three of this series.

When appropriate the editors chose to present the translation of these texts in sense lines. Doing so enables passages to maintain their poetic and rhetorical qualities. The classical poetic style of Thomas of Celano, for example, becomes more visible and his insights into the events of Francis's life more recognizable. In all instances, the numbering found in the Latin critical editions of the paragraphs and, where appropriate, of the sentences is indicated. In this way references to the *Corpus des Sources Franciscaines* will be possible.[72]

At a very early stage of the project, Keith Warner, O.F.M., and John Isom initiated a study of the maps published in earlier works concerning Francis. As a result of their tedious research, the geographer and cartographer presented a series of comprehensive and topical maps enabling readers to discover the world of Francis and his first followers. Beginning with an overall view of present day Europe at the dawning of the thirteenth century and concluding with a detailed illustration of the small city of Umbria's Assisi, these maps offer a fresh understanding of their world.[73]

Acknowledgments

The editors are indebted to the many people who have contributed to these volumes. Those present at that celebration in honor of *Clare of Assisi: Early Documents* responded generously to the inspiration and have continually and patiently encouraged and generously supported the project. Without their enthusiasm, this work could not have moved forward. The translators of these texts quietly and unassumingly pored over the Latin or Italian texts, weighing the value of nearly every word, and, with the sensitivity of those who know their craft, presented the editors with translations that were faithful and pleasing to read. That they did this without concern for payment but as an expression of their commitment to the Franciscan heritage makes their translation more eloquent. Secondary translators, copy editors, readers, and technicians from every corner of the Franciscan Family offered their services. A large number of benefactors dedicated to the vision of Francis was always at hand to assist, as were scholars throughout the world, responding to questions or appeals for advice or critiquing interpretations or positions held. Among these benefactors, the editors of Paulist Press and Franciscan Publications were generous in freely granting permission to republish the earlier translations of Eric Doyle, O.F.M., Ewert H. Cousins, and Serge Hughes. Upon hearing of the project, the personnel of New City Press, especially Patrick Markey, not only responded to the hope of having volumes available to readers throughout the world but also unstintingly gave of their time and patience to bring the project to completion.

From the outset *Francis of Assisi: Early Documents* became an endeavor of men and women of the entire Franciscan Family, men and women enamored of the Gospel spirituality of Francis of Assisi. The manner of their giving to this project made the editors ever aware that the spirit of the thirteenth-century saint, founder, and prophet is very much alive. It has been re-assuring to know that Thomas of Celano's description of the enthusiastic, far-reaching acclaim shown at Francis's canonization continues to exist. The editors are grateful to all those assisting them in bringing this project to completion. They are even more so to the Spirit of the Lord Whose instruments they have been in attempting to follow the footsteps of Francis himself and the dedication of Thomas, Julian, Bonaventure, Leo, Angelo, Rufino and of so many articulators of the Franciscan tradition.

Notes

1. Francis of Assisi, *The Earlier Rule* XVII 7 (hereafter ER).

2. In this regard, the editors are indebted to a new generation of scholars who have approached these documents in a more objective, scientific manner, e.g. Attilio Bartoli Langeli, Giovanni Miccoli, Felice Accrocca, Duncan Nimmo, et al. Jacques Dalarun's *La Malavventura di Francesco d'Assisi: Per Uno Storico delle Leggende Francescane* (Milano: Edizioni Biblioteca Francescana, 1996), is typical of this new wave of scholarship. While not answering all the questions, it raises many new perspectives.

3. In this regard the work of David Flood is noteworthy, especially his collaboration with Willibroad VanDijk and Thadée Matura, *The Birth of a Movement* (Chicago: Franciscan Herald Press, 1976). Flood's approach prompted others to place Francis's writings in their historical contexts and consider the immediate and long-range implications of his movement.

4. The dating of *The Legend for Use in the Choir* (hereafter LCh) is debated. Because of its similarities to *The Life of Saint Francis* by Thomas of Celano (hereafter 1C), its composition between the years 1230-1232 is more commonly held. Others suggest its composition between the years 1243-1244 because of three new elements: the words of the Seraph on La Verna, the precise date of Francis's death, and the deposition of his body in San Giorgio.

5. For further information on these biblical images, see Regis J. Armstrong, *"Mira circa Nos:* Gregory IX's View of the Saint, Francis of Assisi," *Greyfriars Review* 4:1 (1990) 75-100.

6. Cf. infra pp. 570-575.

7. The editors are indebted to Michael Cusato, O.F.M., for his insights into this material. While not accepting the date of 1227 proposed by certain manuscripts for its composition, Cusato rejects that proposed by Stefano Brufani, i.e., the 1260's when poverty was challenged at the University of Paris. Cusato contends it was written between 1235 and early 1239; most likely between 1237 and 1238. Cf. infra pp. 523-528.

8. This text became known as the *Anonymous of Perugia* because of the unknown identity of its author at the time of its discovery at the Perugia friary of San Francesco al Prato.

9. To the Reverend Father in Christ, Brother Crescentius, by the grace of God Minister General, Brother Leo, Brother Rufino, and Brother Angelo, one time companions, although unworthy ones, of the Blessed Father Francis, express their due and devout reverence in the Lord.

According to your mandate, and that of the last general chapter, the brothers are to forward to Your Paternity any miracles and prodigies of our Blessed Father Francis which they know or can ascertain. We, though unworthy, who have lived with him for a long time, thought it opportune to recount truthfully to Your Holiness. Some of his many deeds we ourselves witnessed. Or we heard about them from other holy brothers, especially Brother Philip, the Visitator of the Poor Ladies, Brother Illuminato of Arce, Brother Masseo of Marignano, and a companion of the venerable Brother Giles, Brother John, who gathered much information from Brother Giles himself and from Brother Bernard of holy memory, the first companion of Blessed Francis.

We do not intend merely to relate miracles that prove but do not cause sanctity. Our intention is to show some salient aspects of his holy life and the intention of the divine will, for the praise and glory of the most high God and of the holy Father Francis, and for the edification of those who desire to follow in his footsteps.

We do not intend to write a legend, since other legends about his life and the miracles which the Lord worked through him have been written not too long ago, but rather to gather some of the more beautiful flowers, in our judgment, from a pleasant meadow. We do not follow a chronological order, omitting many things that have already been related in other legends in words as accurate as they are illustrious.

If you deem it expedient, you may insert these few things we have written into the other legend. We are convinced that if these things had been known to the venerable men who wrote these legends, they would in no way have omitted them; rather they would have embellished them, at least in part, with their own eloquent words, and transmitted them to posterity.

May Your Paternity always be well in the Lord Jesus Christ, to whom we, your devoted sons, commend Your Sanctity with humility and devotion.

Given at Greccio, August 11, in the year of Our Lord 1246.

10. "La *'Legenda Antiqua Sancti Francisci.'* Texte du Manuscripte 1046 (M. 69) de la bibliothèque communale de Pérouse," edited by François Delorme, *Archivum Franciscanum Historicum* 15 (1922) 23-70, 278-382.

11. *I Fiori dei Tre Compagni. Testi francescani latini ordinati, con introduzione e note,* edited by Jacques Cambell; Versione italiana a fronte di Nello Vian (Milan, 1966); translated into English by the title *We Were With Saint Francis: An Early Franciscan Story,* edited and translated by Salvator Butler (Chicago: Franciscan Herald Press, 1976).

12. *Scripta Leonis, Rufini et Angeli Sociorum Sancti Francisci: The Writings of Leo, Rufino and Angelo, Companions of Saint Francis*, edited and translated by Rosalind B. Brooke (Oxford: Oxford University Press, 1970).

13. *Légende de Pérouse,* translation and notes by Damien Vorreux, introduction by Théophile Desbonnets, in *Saint François d'Assise: Documents, Écrits et Premières Biographies,* rassemblés et présentés par Théophile Desbonnets et Damien Vorreux. English translation, *Legend of Perugia,* translated by Paul Oligny from the annotated French version by Damien Vorreux, with an Introduction by Théophile Desbonnets in *Saint Francis of Assisi Writings and Early Biographies: English Omnibus of the Sources for the Life of Saint Francis,* edited by Marion A. Habig (Chicago: Franciscan Herald Press, 1973).

14. *"Compilatio Assisiensis" dagli Scritti di fr. Leone e Compagni su s. Francesco d'Assisi. Dal Ms. 1046 di Perugia.* Il edizione integrale reveduta e correta con versione italiana a fronte e variazioni. Edited by Marino Bigaroni (Assisi: Publicazioni della Biblioteca Francescana di Chiesa Nuova, 1992).

15. Jacques Dalarun sees two possibilities in approaching an analysis of this work. The first, that taken by Bigaroni, consists in viewing the document as simply a compilation appearing in roughly

1311. The second, taken by Delorme, Desbonnets and Brooke, attempts to untangle the documents that make up the compilation and to study them chronologically. Cf. Jacques Dalarun, La *Malavventura di Francesco d'Assisi: Per Un Usuo Storico delle Legende Francescane* (Milano: Edizioni Biblioteca Francescana, 1996) 140-150.

16. At the beginning of the fourteenth century Angelo Clareno quoted *The Words of Saint Francis* in his *Expositio Regulae fratrum minorum* and Ubertino da Casale cites *The Intention of the Rule* in his *Arbor Vitae*.

17. The editors have chosen to maintain Thomas of Celano's original title of this work, *The Remembrance of the Desire of a Soul* (hereafter 2C) in order to highlight its unique literary character.

18. Cf. Lazaro Iriate, *Franciscan History: The Three Orders of St. Francis of Assisi,* translated by Patricia Ross. Appendix, "The Historical Context of the Franciscan Movement" by Lawrence C. Landini. (Chicago: Franciscan Herald Press: 1979)31-40.

19. *Archivum Franciscanum Historicum* 3 [1910]: 76, no. 74.

20. For a summary of Bonaventure's earlier portraits of Francis, cf. *The Disciple and The Master: St. Bonaventure's Sermons on St. Francis of Assisi,* translated and edited, with an introduction, by Eric Doyle (Chicago: Franciscan Herald Press, 1982). How well Bonaventure described Francis in his earlier writings is a subject of debate. His experience on LaVerna in 1257, the result of which was his *The Soul's Journey into God,* undoubtedly influenced the portrait that emerges in the works commissioned by the Chapter of Narbonne.

21. Cf. Bonaventure, *Major Legend* (hereafter LMj), Prologue 3.

22. *Miscellanea Franciscana* 72 [1972]: 247. This decree finds a parallel in one of the Friars Preacher.

23. According to the *Oxford Latin Dictionary,* the first meaning of the Latin verb, *delere,* is "to remove (written characters, or other marks) by wiping or scratching out, expunge, delete." The second meaning is "to destroy completely (buildings, etc.)." Since there is a question of parchment involved in this action, it is more reasonable to assume that the first meaning is more applicable. In either case, however, the result was the same: the majority of manuscripts of those earlier legends used by the brothers were obliterated.

24. The *Chronicle* may have been commissioned during the Chapter of Padua in 1276. The precise dates of its commission and its composition are debated, cf. Giuseppe Cremascoli, "Introduzione," *Fontes Francescani* (S. Maria degli Angeli: Edizioni Porziuncula, 1995) 1250-1251.

25. Ubertino da Casale, *Declaratio fratris Ubertini de Casale et sociorum eius contra falsitates datas per fratrem Raymundum procuratorem et Bonagratiam de Pergamo,* edited by F. Ehrele, *Zur Vorgeschichte des Concils von Vienne,* "Archiv für litteratur- und kirchen-Geschichte des Mitellatlers" 3 (1887), 162-195.

26. Lazaro Iriarte de Aspurz, *Franciscan History: The Three Orders of St. Francis of Assisi,* translated by Patricia Ross. Appendix, "The Historical Context of the Franciscan Movement" by Lawrence C. Landini. (Chicago: Franciscan Herald Press, 1983), xviii.

27. Cf. Duncan Nimmo, *Reform and Division in the Medieval Franciscan Order from Saint Francis to the Foundation of the Capuchins* (Roma, Biblioteca seraphico-capucina, 1987).

28. *De cognatione beati Francisci,* Assisi, Sacro Convento, Biblioteca, Ms. 558, f. 124: *Beatus enim Franciscus habuit quatuor successores qui ejus vitam magis authentice scripserunt ut Christus quatuor evangelistas.* [For Blessed Francis had four followers who wrote his life with great authenticity as Christ had four evangelists.]

29. *Annales minorum seu trium ordinum a s. Francisco institutorum,* (Lyon: 1625); 3rd ed., (Quaracchi: 1931).

30. Cf. *infra* p. 8.

31. Bollandists, *Acta Sanctorum* (Venice: S. Coleti & J.B. Albrizzi, 1734-1770), forty-three volumes.

32. *Seraphici viri Sancti Francisci Asisiatis vitae duae, auctore B. Thoma de Celano, ejus discipulo; quarum una ad fidem ms. Recensita, altera nunc primum prodit,* edited by Stefano Rinaldi (Rome: Ex Typographia S. Michaelis ad Ripam: Apud Linum Conditini, 1806).

33. *Seraphici viri s. Francisci Vitae duae auctore b. Thoma de Celano,* ed. S. Rinaldi, (Rome: 1803).

34. Nicolo Papini, *La storia di S. Francesco di Assisi* (Foligno: Giovanni Tomassini, 1825, 1827).

35. *Legenda di San Francesco d'Ascesi Scritta dalli Suoi Compagni,* edited by Stanislao Melchiorri (Rencanati, Morici e Baldaloni, 1856).

36. Joseph von Göerres, *Der heilige Franziskus von Assisi: Ein Troubadour* (Regensburg: G.J. Manz, 1879). Originally published in Strasbourg in 1826.

37. Karl von Hase, *Franz von Assis, ein Heiligenbild* (Leipzig: Breitkopf und Hartel, 1856).

38. A thorough study of the German contributions to the Franciscan literature of the nineteenth century can be found in Kaspar Elm, *"Viv Joseph Görres bis Walter Goetz: Franziskus in der deutschen Geschichts-schreibung des 19. Jahrhunderts"* in *L'Immagine di Francesco nella storiografica dall'umanesimo all'Ottocento* (Assisi 1982) 343-383.

39. Henry Thode, *Franz von Assisi und die Anfänge der Kunst der Renaissance in Italen,* (Vien: Phaidon-Verlag, 1934). Originally published in 1885.

40. Frederic Ozanam, *Les Poétes Franciscains en Italie au Trezième Siècle, avec un choix des Petites Fleurs de Saint François: Traduites de l'Italien Suivis de Recherches Nouvelles sur Les Sources Poétiques de la Divine Comedie* (Paris: V. Lecoffre, 1852).

41. Jules Michelet, *Le Moyen Âge. Histoire de France,* new edition 1981. The six volumes were originally published between 1833 and 1844, although the Preface of the definitive edition of *Histoire de France* did not appear until 1869.

42. His critique eventually became *François d'Assise* and was later published in *Nouvelles Études Religieuses* (Paris, 1884).

43. Cf. Charles-Olivier Carbonell, "De Ernest Renan à Paul Sabatier: naissance d'une historiographie scientifique de saint François en France (1864-1893)," in *L'Immagine di Francesco nella storiografica dall'umanesimo all'Ottocento* (Assisi 1982) 225-249.

44. Paul Sabatier, *Vie de Saint François d'Assise* (Paris: Libraire Fischbacher, 1894). English translation: *Life of St. Francis of Assisi,* translated by Louise Seymour Houghton (New York: Charles Scribner's Sons, 1906).

45. Paul Sabatier, *Speculum perfectionis seu S. Francisci Assisiensis legenda antiquissima auctore fratre Leon,* in *Collection d'études et de documents sur l'histoire religieuse et littérarire du Moyen Âge,* 1 (Paris, 1898).

46. Cf. Luigi Pellegrini, "A Century of Reading the Sources for the Life of Francis of Assisi," *Greyfriars Review* 7:3 (1993), 323-346.

47. Paul Sabatier, "Lettera di Paolo Sabatier," *Miscellanea Franciscana* 7 (1898) 33-35; Michele Faloci Pulignani, "Risposta alla Lettera di Paolo Sabatier," *Miscellanea Franciscana* 7 (1898) 35-51.

48. Michele Faloci Pulignani, "S. Francesco d'Assisi secondo Paolo Sabatier" (Foligno, 1902); *Miscellanea Franciscana* 9 (1902), 65-76.

49. Francesco van Ortroy, "La legenda latina di s. Francesco secondo l'Anonimo Perugino," *Miscellanea Franciscana* 9 (1902), 33-48.

50. Ferdinand M. Delorme, "La *Legenda antiqua s. Francisci* du ms. 1046 de la Bibliothèque communale de Pérouse," *Archivum Franciscanum Historicum* 15 (1922), 23-70, 278-332; *La "Legenda antiqua s. Francisci," texte du ms. 1046 (M 69),* (Paris, 1926).

51. *Analecta Franciscana sive Chronica aliaque varia documenta ad historiam fratrum minorum spectantia edita a patribus Collegii S. Bonaventuae adiuvantibus aliis eruditis viris,* I-X (Ad Aquas Claras: Florentiae, Collegium S. Bonaventurae: 1895-1941).

52. Arnaldo Fortini, *Nuova Vita di san Francesco.* Five volumes. (Assisi, 1959). Abridged English translation by Helen Moak: *Francis of Assisi* (New York: Crossroad, 1982).

53. *San Francesco nella Ricerca Storica degli Ultimi Ottanta Anni* (Todi: 1971).

54. Lorenzo di Fonzo, *"L'Anonimo Perugino tra le fonti francescane del secolo XIII. Rapporti letterari e testo critico,"* in *Miscellanea Franciscana* 72 (1972) 435-465. This text was also re-examined by Pierre Béguin in *L'Anonyme de Pérouse. Un témoin de la fraternité franciscaine primitive confronté aux autres sources contemporaines* (Paris, 1979).

55. *La "questione francescana" dal Sabatier ad oggi (Assisi: 1973)*

56. Théophile Desbonnets, *"Legenda trium Sociorum: Edition critique," Archivum Franciscanum Historicum* 67 (1974) 38-144.

57. Raoul Manselli, *Nos qui cum eo fuimus. Contributo alla questione francescana* (Roma: Biblioteca seraphico-capuccina, 1980); *S. Francesco d'Assisi,* (Roma: Biblioteca di cultura, 1980); 2nd edition, 1981; 3rd edition, 1982. English translation: *St. Francis of Assisi,* translated by Paul Duggan (Chicago: Franciscan Herald Press, 1988). *Nos qui cum eo fuimus* has yet to be translated into English.

58. Unfortunately *S. Francesco d'Assisi* was published without the footnotes to substantiate many of Manselli's interpretations. His death in November 1984 left this work incomplete.

59. *Die Opuscula des hl. Franziskus von Assisi: Neue textkritische Edition.* Edited by Kajetan Esser. (Grottaferrata: Spicilegium Bonaventurianum XIII, 1976); *Opuscula sancti patris Francisci Assisiensis: denuo edidit iuxta codices mss.* Edited by Kajetan Esser. (Grottaferrata: Editiones Collegii S. Bonaventurae, 1978).

60. *Opuscula sancti Francisci. Scripta sanctae Clarae. Concordance, Index, Listes de fréquence, Tables comparatives.* Volumes I-VII. Edited by Jean-François Godet and Georges Mailleux, (Louvain: *Corpus des Sources Franciscaines,* Centre de Traitement Électronique des Documents, Catholic University of Louvain, 1976-1990).

61. Théophile Desbonnets, *De L'Intuition à L'Institution: Les franciscains* (Paris: Editions Franciscaines, 1983). This text was translated in 1988 by Paul Duggan and Jerry DuCharme (Chicago: Franciscan Herald Press, 1988).

62. Chiara Frugoni *Francesco e l'invenzione delle stimmate. Una storia per parole e immagini fino a Bonaventura e Giotto* (Torino, 1993) Saggi, 780. Octavian Schmucki, "De Sancti Francisci Assisiensis stigmatum susceptione: Disquisitio historico-critica luce testimoniorum saeculi XIII," *Collectanea Franciscana 33* (1963): 210-66, 392-422; 34 (1964: 5-62, 241-338; English translation: *The Stigmata of St. Francis of Assisi: A Critical Investigation in the Light of Thirteenth-Century Sources,* translated by Canisius F. Connors, O.F.M. (St. Bonaventure, NY: Franciscan Institute Publications, 1991).

63. Attilio Bartoli Langeli, "Gli scritti di Francesco. L'autografia di un 'illiteratus,'" in *Frate Francesco d'Assisi* (Spoleto, 1994) 101-159).

64. E.g., Giovanni Miccoli, *Francesco d'Assisi. Realtà e memoria di un'esperienza cristiana* (Torino, 1991); Grado G. Merlo, *Tra eremo e città. Studi su Francesco d'Assisi e sul francescanesimo* (Assisi, 1991) Saggi, 2; Jacques Dalarun, *Donna e donne negli scritti e nelle legende di Francesco d'Assisi* (Roma: Viella, 1994); *La malavventura di Francesco d'Assisi: per un uso storico delle legende francescane* (Milano: Edizioni Biblioteca Francescana, 1996).

65. *San Francisco de Asis. Sus escritos. Las Florecillas. Biografias del Santo por Celano, San Buenaventura y los Tres Compañeros. Espejo de Perfección,* edited by Juan R. Legísima and Lino Gómez Cañedo (Madrid, Editorial Catolica, 1946).

66. *Saint François d'Assise: Documents. Ecrits et premières biographies,* edited by Théophile Desbonnets, OFM, and Damien Vorreux, OFM, (Paris: Editions franciscaines, 1968).

67. *Saint Francis of Assisi, Writings and Early Biographies: English Omnibus of Sources for the Life of St. Francis,* edited by Marion Habig (Chicago: Franciscan Herald Press, 1973).

68. *Fonti francescane. Scritti e biografie di san Francesco d'Assisi. Cronache e altre testimonianze del primo secolo francescano. Scritti e biografie di santa Chiara d'Assisi.* 2 vols, (Assisi: Movimento francescano,1977).

69. *San Francisco de Asís: Escritos, Biografías, Documentos de la época,* 2nd Edition, edited by Jose Antonio Guerra (Madrid: Editorial Catolica, 1978).

70. *Fontes Franciscani,* a cura di Enrico Menestò e Stefano Brufani, e di Giuseppe Cremascoli, Emore Paoli, Luigi Pellegrini, Stanislao da Campagnola; apparati di Giovanni M. Boccali (Sta. Maria degli Angeli: Edizioni Porziuncula, 1995).

71. The editors hope that after the publication of the three volumes, *Francis of Assisi: Early Documents,* a translation of Bartholomew's work will be undertaken since it is one of the most important—and more neglected—texts of the Franciscan tradition.

72. This decision was not followed in the text of *The Sacred Exchange between Saint Francis and Lady Poverty* (hereafter ScEx). While following the critical edition of Stefano Brufani in the translation of the work, the manner of numbering the text adopted by Brufani is considerably different from that of the editors of the Quaracchi edition followed in the *Corpus des Sources Franciscaines.*

73. Cf. infra pp. 200, 208, 211, 232, 233, 237, 268, 613-635.

Abbreviations

Writings of Saint Francis

Adm	The Admonitions	LtMin	A Letter to a Minister
BIL	A Blessing for Brother Leo	LtOrd	A Letter to the Entire Order
CtC	The Canticle of the Creatures	LtR	A Letter to Rulers of the Peoples
CtExh	The Canticle of Exhortation	ExhP	Exhortation to the Praise of God
1Frg	Fragments of Worchester Manuscript	PrOF	A Prayer Inspired by the Our Father
2Frg	Fragments of Thomas of Celano	PrsG	The Praises of God
3Frg	Fragments from Hugh of Digne	OfP	The Office of the Passion
LtAnt	A Letter to Brother Anthony of Padua	PrCr	The Prayer before the Crucifix
1LtCl	First Letter to the Clergy (Earlier Edition)	ER	The Earlier Rule (*Regula non bullata*)
2LtCl	Second Letter to the Clergy (Later Edition)	LR	The Later Rule (*Regula bullata*)
1LtCus	The First Letter to the Custodians	RH	A Rule for Hermitages
2LtCus	The Second Letter to the Custodians	SalBVM	A Salutation of the Blessed Virgin Mary
1LtF	The First Letter to the Faithful	SalV	A Salutation of Virtues
2LtF	The Second Letter to the Faithful	Test	The Testament
LtL	A Letter to Brother Leo	TPJ	True and Perfect Joy

Franciscan Sources

1C	The Life of Saint Francis by Thomas of Celano	HTrb	The History of the Seven Tribulations by Angelo of Clareno
2C	The Remembrance of the Desire of a Soul	ScEx	The Sacred Exchange between Saint Francis and Lady Poverty
3C	The Treatise on the Miracles by Thomas of Celano	AP	The Anonymous of Perugia
		L3C	The Legend of the Three Companions
LCh	The Legend for Use in the Choir	AC	The Assisi Compilation
Off	The Divine Office of Saint Francis by Julian of Speyer	1-4 Srm	The Sermons of Bonaventure
		LMj	The Major Legend by Bonaventure
LJS	The Life of Saint Francis by Julian of Speyer	LMn	The Minor Legend by Bonaventure
		BPr	The Book of Praises by Bernard of Besse
VL	The Versified Life of Saint Francis by Henri d'Avranches	ABF	The Deeds of Saint Francis and His Companions
1-3JT	The Praises by Jacopone da Todi		
DCom	The Divine Comedy by Dante Alighieri	LFl	The Little Flowers of Saint Francis
		KnSF	The Knowing of Saint Francis
TL	Tree of Life by Ubertino da Casale	ChrTE	The Chronicle of Thomas of Eccleston
1MP	The Mirror of Perfection, Smaller Version	ChrJG	The Chronicle of Jordan of Giano
2MP	The Mirror of Perfection, Larger Version		

Other Sources

AFH	Archivum Franciscanum Historicum
BFr	Bullarium Franciscanum
DEC	Decrees of the Ecumenical Councils
DMA	Dictionary of the Middle Ages
LdM	Lexikon des Mittelalters
PL	Patrologia Latina
RBC	Robert Burchard Constantijn Huygens

Scripture abbreviations are from *The New American Bible*; the Psalms follow the modern numbering sequence. Scripture references accompanying non-italicized text imply *confer,* or cf.

THE WRITINGS

OF

FRANCIS OF ASSISI

(1205/06–1226)

Introduction

Until the late 1970's, the fundamental source for the life and mind of Saint Francis came not from writings by him but from those about him. With the exception of the *The Later Rule* and *The Testament,* little attention was paid to the writings of Francis that we now realize clearly reveal his spirit, such as *The Admonitions,* the exhortations to the faithful, or the letters to his brothers. Instead focus was on works such as *The Little Flowers of Saint Francis* or, in a more serious vein, Saint Bonaventure's *Major Legend* or the works of Thomas of Celano. The reasons for this neglect are undoubtedly caught in the web of Franciscan history. The transparent simplicity of Francis, so obviously challenging, prompted a variety of interpretations which were best expressed by attempts to understand his life and thought and to articulate that understanding in a more sophisticated vocabulary. Thus the Gospel vision of Francis's writings was caught up, not only in the hagiographical style of Thomas of Celano and Henri d'Avranches, and the mystical, scholastic constructs of Bonaventure, but also in the editorial tendencies of the friars of the fourteenth and fifteenth centuries, influenced as they were by the *devotio moderna.*

In attempting to understand the rediscovery of Francis's writings, it is important to review the history of the tradition, that is, of the passing of these writings from one generation to another. At the very heart of this history is the question of literary criticism or the struggle to examine critically the texts which our generation has received in order to determine their authenticity. These are questions or struggles reflecting those of biblical scholars who exert enormous time and energy in the pursuit of accuracy and interpretation. The history of this Franciscan tradition embraces four different stages: from the actual composition of Francis's writings to their contemporary analysis through the prisms of our technological advances.

The First Stage

While Francis's writings clearly reveal his poetic sensitivity, they also manifest the limits of his education and the simplicity of his vocabulary. In a description of his burial in the church of Saint George, Bonaventure tells us that it was there that Francis *litteras didicit* [learned letters] or, as Thomas of Celano describes it, *didicerat legere* [learned to read]. Since there are no records of how well he succeeded, we must rely on his writings to tell us. Thomas of Eccleston, the thirteenth century English chronicler, suggests that he did poorly when he writes of Francis's *falsum latinum* [crude Latin]. Were we to judge by Francis's simple and brief letter to Brother Leo, one of the few originals we have, that indictment would be confirmed for it contains mistakes in both spelling and grammar.[1]

Nevertheless, his writings suggest that Francis was someone who had great respect for the written word. Thomas of Celano tells us in *The Life of Saint Francis* the saint's respect for the written word. ". . . [W]henever [Francis] would find anything written about God or anyone, along the way, or in a house, or on the floor, he would pick it up with the greatest reverence and put it in a sacred or decent place" (1C 82). We see this in his *Letter to the Entire Order* as he insists that his writings be held onto and preserved (cf. LtOrd 48). In his exhortations to the faithful and to the clergy he promises blessings for those who copy, pass on, or study his words (cf. 2LtF 88; 1LtCl 15). It is not surprising, then, that he took advantage of those who could write to take down his words. Bonizzo of Bologna, Benedict of Pirato, Caesar of Speyer and, most especially, Leo of Assisi appear among those who took dictation from Francis or, in the case of Caesar, who embellished his thought.

Curiously there are only two examples of Francis's own writings. The first is a small piece of parchment, written on both sides, that Francis gave to Leo of Assisi while they were on LaVerna. It contains his Praises of God and, on the opposite side, his blessing of Leo. The other is a brief personal letter which he wrote to Brother Leo to resolve some of the scruples which Leo experienced interpreting Francis's vision of gospel life. Our knowledge of his other writings is dependent upon what has been given to us through the manuscripts of his first followers. And here we are presented with one of our most fundamental difficulties: these are pieces written by hand, *manu scripta.* They are susceptible to the idiosyncrasies of those responsible for copying the original. While Francis insists in two instances that his words be copied exactly and without any additions or subtractions (cf. Test 35; ER XXIV 4), a study of the earliest manuscripts suggests that his desires were not followed. Words were changed to "polish" the image of Francis or to make his thought more acceptable. Grammatical mistakes were corrected, or images of God were embellished. Despite his eagerness that his words be preserved, there were writings that were lost: a letter to Elizabeth of Hungary, another to a woman looking for a cure for her son, and letters to both the Poor Ladies of Saint Damian and to Cardinal Hugolino.

The Second Stage

By the middle of the thirteenth century, the friars began to collect Francis's writings. The earliest collection is preserved in the library of the Basilica of Saint Francis in Assisi. Others are scattered throughout Italy in libraries in Florence, Volterra, and the Vatican; one is in London, England. Although there are differences in many of the writings of these collections, what is missing in them is striking. The only writing that is consistently present in these collections is the *Admonitions*. Copies of *The Earlier Rule* and *The Letter to a Minister* do not appear until the next century.

The friars of the fourteenth century seem to have been far more zealous in preserving Francis's writings. Three large collections of manuscripts exist. The Portiuncula collection contains manuscripts that were gathered together by friars who were neither scholars nor professional scribes, for they made many mistakes. The Avignon Collection, on the other hand, is composed of manuscripts that follow a model, thus the prefix found in many manuscripts: *fac secundum exemplar* [Make according to exemplar]. The consistency and accuracy of these manuscripts suggest a more professional approach in their transmission and the influence of curial officials. Finally, the Northern Low Countries Collection encompasses manuscripts found through Germany and present day Belgium, Holland, Poland, etc. These collections became the basis for those eighty-one manuscripts produced in the fifteenth century and the twenty-nine that appeared before the use of the printing press in the sixteenth.

The Third Stage

With the invention of the printing press, distribution of Francis's writings became more common. Within eight years of the first publications in Italy and Germany, editions appeared in Spain and France. It was not until the following century, however, that the Irish friar, Luke Wadding, attempted to produce a thorough edition of Francis's writings.

It is difficult to know what Wadding used as his criteria for publishing the writings. He divided his edition into three parts. The first contained seventeen letters and thirteen prayers; the second, four rules, twenty-eight "conferences," forty-one sayings, and the Office of the Passion; and the third, Bonaventure's *Major Legend.* Wadding may have been influenced by the monastic literature when he published what he entitled Francis's "ascetical teachings" or "conferences" akin to those of John Cassian or other monastic writers. He freely used the words or sayings of Francis found in Bonaventure's work; in some instances he changed them. Nonetheless, his 1623 work, *Opuscula Beati Francisci Assisiensis,* was a landmark and remained the standard work until the beginning of the twentieth century.

Four hundred years after the first printed edition, three editions appeared in Italy, Switzerland, and Germany. Leonard Lemmens's *Opuscula* dramatically reduced the number of writings offered by Wadding. There were only six letters, one "conference," two rules and one blessing. The number of prayers was significantly reduced and the forty-one sayings were completely dropped.

Boehmer, editor of the Swiss *Analekten zur Geschichte des Franziskus von Assisi,* followed suit, as did Goetz, editor of the German *Die Quellen zur Geschichte des hl. Franziskus von Assisi.*

As these editions were becoming known, however, Paul Sabatier wrote an essay calling for a serious study of Francis's writings. In his *Examen de Quelques Travaux Recents sur les Opuscules de Saint François,* Sabatier was the first to call for a critical edition, that is, one based on an objective study of the existing manuscripts, established criteria, and the desire to determine the authentic text regardless of the outcome. Sabatier was far ahead of his time with this proposal. It seemed to be influenced by the Protestant biblical scholars who were calling for the same approach to the scriptures. In 1954 and again in 1965, Jacques Cambell revived Sabatier's thought by showing how a critical edition of the writings was badly needed. Shortly thereafter, Kajetan Esser and Rémy Oliger began the tedious task of examining the manuscript tradition, a task which took them throughout Europe and more than ten years to complete.

The Fourth Stage

In 1972 Esser and Oliger published *La Traditione Manuscrite des Opuscules de Saint François d'Assise: Preliminaires de l'Édition Critique.* It was a work which provided a key to understanding the enormous work they had undertaken in identifying and classifying the earliest manuscripts of Francis's writings. The following year, Esser articulated his own guidelines and criteria in *Studien zu den Opuscula des hl. Franziskus von Assisi* and prepared his readers for what he proposed as a critical text. Throughout the next three years, the scholarly German friar published a number of articles reflecting his research and discoveries of manuscripts and texts that had been overlooked. Since the Franciscan world continued to respond to the Second Vatican Council's call to explore the charism of its founder, Esser's work became pivotal.

Although Giovanni Boccali published an edition of the writings of Francis as well as a concordance of those writings, Esser's text attracted the most attention. Boccali had consulted only eleven manuscripts, whereas Esser and Oliger had pored over one hundred and eighty-one. While Boccali provided a wider variety of biblical references, Esser offered nuanced readings and interpretations of variant texts, as well as explanations for the rejection of writings long held to be those of Francis. A major difficulty of the Esser edition, its readability, was overcome two years later when a small edition, written only in Latin, appeared. It corrected the errors and lacunae of the 1976 edition and satisfied many of Esser's critics. Both editions, however, became the fundamental source for all future publications of the writings and the means by which they became accessible to readers throughout the world. Within a short time, translations of Esser's critical edition appeared in the European languages and then in many of those of Asia.

One of the primary tools enabling better use of the Esser editions, however, was the publication of a computerized concordance. Two friars in Belgium, Jean-François Godet and George Mailleux, took the critical edition of the writings and entered it into a data base. The result was the fifth volume of the *Corpus des Sources Franciscaines* that provided a detailed analysis of Francis's words. Scholars quickly had access to the nuances of his thought and unleashed a tidal wave of articles and books that offered new insights. By the time of Esser's death, two years after the publication of his critical edition, Francis's writings entered profoundly into the consciousness of men and women all over the world.

For the most part, this edition of Francis's writings follows the Esser edition. Where changes have been made to the text, such as changes in the titles suggested by Esser or scriptural passages or allusions different from those he noted, footnotes offer explanations. A significant difference, however, is the omission of the *opuscula dictata* [dictated works] which Esser maintained were "rough drafts of sayings about whose written form nothing can be said, but whose existence is attested by various sources." The editors have chosen to publish only one of these, *True and Perfect Joy,* that may be more available to the ordinary reader. Furthermore, the editions of those texts written in Francis's own hand have been published in two editions. In the case of the parchment given to Brother Leo on LaVerna containing *The Praises of God* and *The Blessing*, the edition of Duane Lapsanski, with the additions made by Esser, and that of Attilio Bartoli Langeli have been presented. *The Letter to Brother Leo* is presented in the editions of Esser and Bartoli Langeli. In both instances, differences are present that may suggest various interpretations.

Finally, in keeping with the editorial decision to present the texts of *Francis of Assisi: Early Documents* in a chronological manner, the editors have attempted to do so with the writings of Francis. This has been a difficult undertaking since, given the current state of research, many of the writings have been difficult to date. A separate set of writings have been left as simply undated. Nevertheless, viewing the writings in a chronological manner enables the reader to see the development of Francis's Gospel vision, while viewing those that are undated enhances the timeless character of many of his insights.

Notes

1. Attilio Bartoli Langeli maintains: "Francis's training in writing proves . . . that he is an *illiteratus,* in other words, that his educational level lies somewhere between illiteracy and full and complete literacy." Cf. Attilio Bartoli Langeli, "Gli scritti da Francesco: l'autografia di un 'illiteratus,' " in *Francesco d'Assisi* (Spoleto: 1994) 101-159.

The Prayer before the Crucifix
(1205/06)

While Thomas of Celano and Saint Bonaventure characterize the early years of Francis's life as a struggle to discern God's will, the author of *The Legend of the Three Companions*, according to two manuscripts, summarizes Francis's yearnings in this simple prayer and places it on his lips as he kneels before the Crucifix of the crumbling church of San Damiano in Assisi.[a] The prayer may have been influenced by the liturgical opening prayer of the Eucharistic liturgy. This version of the prayer is based on the simple text found in the majority of Latin manuscripts. As it became more popular, the prayer was embellished and lost some of its simplicity.[b]

Most High,
glorious God,
enlighten the darkness of my heart
and give me
true faith,
certain hope,
and perfect charity,
sense and knowledge,
Lord,
that I may carry out
Your holy and true command.

a. Cf. L3S 13 in a manuscript in the Barcelona's Biblioteca Central, Codex 665, which is dated 1405, and the Fribourg Biblioteque des Cordeliers, Codex 23J60, which is dated 1406.

b. Cf. Kajetan Esser, *Die Opuscula des Hl. Franziskus von Assisi* (Grottaferrata-Rome: Editiones Collegii S. Bonaventurae ad Aquas Claras, 1976) 354—362; *Opusucla Sancti Patris Francisci Assisiensis* (Grottaferrata-Rome: Editiones Collegii S. Bonaventurae ad Aquas Claras, 1978) 223-224.

Earlier Exhortation
To the Brothers and Sisters of Penance[a]
(The First Version of the Letter to the Faithful)
(1209-1215)

The earliest manuscript of this writing, located in the Guarnacci Library in the Italian city of Volterra, introduces it with these words: "These are words of life and salvation. Whoever reads and follows them will find life and draw from the Lord salvation." While Kajetan Esser entitled it "The First Version of the Letter to the Faithful," it has been more correctly seen as an exhortation given to those first penitents who came to Francis desiring to share in his Gospel way of life. Since 1976, when Kajetan Esser brought the text into prominence, it has served as the Prologue to the Rule of the Secular Franciscan Order.

In the Name of the Lord!

[Chapter One]
Those Who Do Penance

[1]All those who love the Lord *with their whole heart, with their*
whole soul and mind, with their whole strength and love their neigh- Mk 12:30
bors as themselves, [2]who hate their bodies with their vices and sins, Mt 22:39
[3]who receive the Body and Blood of our Lord Jesus Christ, [4]and who
produce worthy fruits of penance. [5]O how happy and blessed are these Mt 22:39
men and women while they do such things and persevere in doing
them,[b] [6]because *the Spirit of the Lord will rest upon them* and *make* Its Is 11:2
home and *dwelling place* among them, [7]and they are children of the Jn 14:23

a. In light of the scholarship of Raffaele Pazzelli, the editors have chosen to propose this as the basic title of this work. Pazzelli argues convincingly that Esser erred in seeing this document as simply an earlier version of the Letter to the Faithful. Cf. Raffaele Pazzelli, "The Title of the 'Recensio Prior of the Letter to the Faithful:' Clarifications regarding Codex 225 of Volterra (cod. Vo)," translated by Nancy Celaschi, *Greyfriars Review*, 4:3 (1990), pp. 1-6.

b. Francis uses the term *beatus* (in this instance *beati*) within an eschatological perspective, analogous to the use of "blessed" in the Beatitudes of the Gospels. Moreover, he makes explicit reference to both men and women by using *illi et illae*.

Mt 5:45 heavenly Father Whose works they do, and they are spouses, brothers,
Mt 12:50 and mothers of our Lord Jesus Christ.[a]

[8]We are spouses when the faithful soul is joined by the Holy Spirit to
our Lord Jesus Christ. [9]We are brothers to Him when we do *the will of the*
Mt 12:50 *Father who is in heaven.* [10]We are mothers when we carry Him in our
1 Cor 6:20 heart and body through a divine love and a pure and sincere conscience
and give birth to Him through a holy activity which must shine as an ex-
Mt 5:16 ample before others.[b]

[11]O how glorious it is to have a holy and great Father in heaven![c]
[12]O how holy, consoling to have such a beautiful and wonderful
Spouse! [13]O how holy and how loving, gratifying, humbling,
peace-giving, sweet, worthy of love, and, above all things, desirable: to
have such a Brother and such a Son, our Lord Jesus Christ, Who laid
Jn 10:15 down His life for His sheep and prayed to His Father, saying:

Jn 17:11; •Jn 17:6 [14]*Holy Father, in your name, save those •whom you have given me*
•Jn 17:8 *in the world; they were yours and you gave them to me.* •[15]The *words*
that you gave to me I have given to them, and they accepted them and
have believed *in truth that I have come from you and* they have known
that you have sent me.

Jn 17:9; •Jn 17:17 [16]I pray for them *and not for the world.* •[17]Bless and *sanctify them; •I*
•Jn 17:19 *sanctify myself for them.* •[18]*I pray not only for them, but for those who*
•Jn 17:20; •Jn 17:23 *will believe in me through their word •that they might be* sanctified *in*
•Jn 17:11 *being one •as we are.*

Jn 17:24 [19]*I wish, Father, that where I am, they also may be with me that they*
•Mt 20:21 *may see my glory •in your kingdom.* Amen.

---

a. Francis frequently uses the title "Spirit of the Lord" to refer to the Third Person of the Trinity (*Admonitions* I 12 [hereafter Adm]; Adm XII 1; *First Letter to the Faithful* I 6 [hereafter 1LtF]; *Second Letter to the Faithful* 48 [hereafter 2LtF]; *Later Rule* X 9 [hereafter LR]). While in this instance the biblical reference is to Isaiah 11:2, in most instances there is a reflection of a Pauline pneumatology in which the Holy Spirit is described as "the Spirit of Christ" (Rom 8:9) "the Spirit of His Son" (Gal 4:6), and "the Spirit of Jesus Christ" (Phil 1:19). Since the saint perceives the Spirit of the Lord as the dynamic principle of the life of his followers, it is helpful to understand the Christological implications of these passages.

b. Francis frequently uses the phrase *sancta operatio,* holy activity, (cf. 1LtF II 21; 2LtF 53; LR X 8; *Testament* 39 [hereafter Test]). It is used most frequently in conjunction with the Spirit of the Lord or the words of Francis himself which echo those of Jesus and are "spirit and life" (cf. Jn 6:64). Thus, Francis underscores the dynamic principle of the spiritual life, the Holy Spirit, which must be ever operative in the life of a Christian.

c. The Latin text contains an ambiguous grammatical construction: *O quam gloriosum est, sanctum et magnum in caelis habere patrem!* If we take *sanctum* and *magnum* as neuter and not masculine, the phrase could be translated: "how glorious it is, how holy and great, to have a Father in heaven!" However, if *sanctum* and *magnum* are masculine accusatives agreeing with Father, we would translate the phrase: "how glorious it is to have in heaven a holy and great Father!" In view of the parallel constructions of sentences 11, 12 and 13, it seems best to follow the latter translation.

[Chapter Two]
Those Who Do Not Do Penance

[1]All those men and women who are not living in penance, [2]who do not receive the Body and Blood of our Lord Jesus Christ, [3]who practice vice and sin and walk after the evil concupiscence and the evil desires of their flesh, [4]who do not observe what they have promised to the Lord, [5]and who in their body serve the world through the desires of the flesh,[a] the concerns of the world and the cares of this life: [6]They are held captive by the devil, whose children they are, and whose works
they do. [7]They are blind because they do not see the true light, our Lord Jn 8:41
Jesus Christ. [8]They do not possess spiritual wisdom because they do
not have the Son of God, the true wisdom of the Father. [9]It is said of
them: *Their wisdom has been swallowed up* and *Cursed are those who* Ps 107:27
turn away from your commands. [10]They see and acknowledge, know Ps 119:21
and do evil, and knowingly lose their souls.

[11]See, you blind ones, deceived by your enemies: the flesh,[b] the world, and the devil, because it is sweet for the body to sin and it is bitter to serve God, [12]for every vice and sin flow and *proceed from the human heart* as the Lord says in the Gospel. [13]And you have nothing in Mt 15:19; Mk 7:21
this world or in that to come. [14]And you think that you will possess this world's vanities for a long time, but you are deceived because a day and an hour will come of which you give no thought, which you do not know, and of which you are unaware when the body becomes weak, death approaches, and it dies a bitter death. [15]And no matter where, when, or how a person dies in the guilt of sin without penance and satisfaction, if he can perform an act of satisfaction and does not do so, the devil snatches his soul from its body with such anguish and distress that no one can know [what it is like] except the one receiving it.[c]

[16]And every talent, ability, *knowledge, and wisdom* they think they 2 Chr 1:12
have will be taken away from them. [17]And they leave their wealth to Lk 8:18; Mk 4:25
their relatives and friends who take and divide it and afterwards say: "May his soul be cursed because he could have given us more and acquired more than what he distributed to us." [18]Worms eat his body and

a. The term "bodily" (*corporaliter*) should not be understood in the narrow sense of "physically." Rather, it signifies in a fuller sense "completely or actually with body and soul" serve the world.

b. It is significant that Francis places the flesh in the first place among the three enemies of the soul.

c. While Francis does not generally distinguish clearly between *suus* and *eius*, in this case he does. The phrase, *rapit animam suam de corpore eius*, denotes that the devil snatches or takes what is his own. The soul submerged in sin, by definition, belongs to the devil. Thus, the soul, which because of sin already belongs to the devil, is taken by the devil from the body of the sinner.

so body and soul perish in this brief world and they will go to hell where they will be tortured forever.

1 Jn 4:16) [19]In the love which is God we beg all those whom these words reach to receive those fragrant words of our Lord Jesus Christ written above with divine love and kindness. [20]And let whoever does not know how to read have them read to them frequently. [21]Because *they are spirit*
Jn 6:63 *and life,* they should preserve them together with a holy activity to the end.

[22]And whoever has not done these things will be held accountable
Rm 14:10; Mt 12:36 *before the tribunal of* our Lord Jesus *Christ on the day of judgment.*

Later Admonition and Exhortation To the Brothers and Sisters of Penance
(Second Version of the Letter to the Faithful)[a]
(1220?)

This writing may have been written upon Francis's return from his journey to the Middle East in the Spring of 1220, for not only does it speak of his weakened condition but also suggests the post-conciliar concerns of Pope Honorius III. At the same time, it recalls Francis's earlier exhortation to the Brothers and Sisters of Penance and encourages its observance in light of many of the teachings of the Fourth Lateran Council.

[1]In the name of the Father and of the Son and of the Holy Spirit. Amen.

Brother Francis, their servant and subject, sends esteem and reverence, true peace from heaven and sincere love in the Lord to all Christian religious people: clergy and laity, men and women, and to all who live in the whole world.[b]

[2]Because I am the servant of all, I am obliged to serve all and to administer the fragrant words of my Lord to them.[c] [3]Therefore, realizing that I could not visit each one of you personally because of sickness and the weakness of my body, I decided to offer you in this letter and message the words of our Lord Jesus Christ, Who is the Word of the Father, and the words of the Holy Spirit, which *are spirit and life.*[d] Jn 6:63

a. The titles of this particular text suggest that it is a *commonitorium* and an exhortation, a work reminding and encouraging its recipients to fulfill a commitment previously undertaken. While Kajetan Esser's critical edition of the text identifies this work by the more generic title, *Letter to All the Faithful*, this designation does not appropriately indicate either the recipients or the contents of the texts.

b. It is difficult to identify the recipients of this work since the earliest manuscripts read: *Universis christianis religiosis clericis et laicis masculis et feminis omnibus qui habitant in universo mundo.* Since these manuscripts contain no punctuation, the meaning of the sentence is unclear. In his critical edition, Kajetan Esser placed a comma after *Universis christianis religiosis* and argued that Francis was addressing not all Christians but rather "all Christian religious: clergy and laity, men and women . . .", that is, Christians who had committed themselves to living more intensely their baptismal commitment through a life of penance.

c. A special bond of union between Francis and the recipients of this exhortation is expressed in this paragraph, an interpretation which is strengthened in verse 40 when the saint writes of "the yoke of service and holy obedience," as well as the special love and responsibility which characterize their relationships. This bond is further underscored in Francis's repeated use of the first person plural throughout verses 19 to 47.

d. Offhanded comments of Francis's biographers suggest that the deterioration of his health was a long process aggravated by his imprisonment in Collestrada (1202) and in San Damiano (1207-1208). Prior to his journey to the Middle East, illness struck Francis in Spain (1214/15) and in Assisi (1216/17). After his return from the Middle East, the infirmity of his eyes began to intensify.

4 The most high Father made known from heaven through His holy
angel Gabriel this Word of the Father—so worthy, so holy and glorious—in the womb of the holy and glorious Virgin Mary, from whose
womb He received the flesh of our humanity and frailty.[a] 5 Though He
2 Cor 8:9 was rich, He wished, together with the most Blessed Virgin, His
mother, to choose poverty in the world beyond all else.[b]

6 And as His Passion was near, He celebrated the Passover with His
disciples and, taking bread, gave thanks, blessed and broke it, saying:
Mt 26:26 *Take and eat: This is My Body.* 7 And taking the cup He said: *This is My*
Blood of the New Covenant which will be poured out for you and for
Mt 26:28 *many for the forgiveness of sins.* 8 Then He prayed to His Father, say-
Lk 22:42 ing: *Father, if it can be done, let this cup pass from me.* 9 *And His sweat*
Lk 22:44 *became as drops of blood falling on the ground.* 10 Nevertheless, He
placed His will in the will of His Father, saying: *Father, let Your will be*
Mt 26:42; Mt 26:39 *done; not as I will, but as You will.* 11 His Father's will was such that His
blessed and glorious Son, Whom He gave to us and Who was born for
us, should offer Himself through His own blood as a sacrifice and obla-
tion on the altar of the cross: 12 not for Himself through Whom all
Jn 1:3 things were made, but for our sins, 13 leaving us an example that we
1 Pt 2:21 might follow His footprints.

14 And He wishes all of us to be saved through Him and receive Him
with our heart pure and our body chaste. 15 But, even though His *yoke is*
Mt 11:30 *easy* and His *burden light,* there are few who wish to receive Him and
be saved through Him. 16 Those who do not wish to taste how sweet the
Ps 34:9; Jn 3:19 Lord is and who love *the darkness more than the light,* not wishing to
fulfill God's commands, are cursed; 17 it is said of them by the prophet:
Ps 119:21 *Cursed are those who stray from your commands.*

18 But how happy and blessed are those who love God and do as the
Lord Himself says in the Gospel: *You shall love the Lord your God with*
Mt 22:37, 39 *all your heart* and all *your mind,* and *your neighbor as yourself.* 19 Let
us love God, therefore, and adore Him with a pure heart and a pure
mind, because He Who seeks this above all things has said: *True ador-*
Jn 4:23 *ers adore the Father in Spirit and Truth.* 20 For all *who adore Him must*

a. In these verses, 4-13, Francis presents a catechetical tool against the Christological teachings of the Cathars who viewed matter and the flesh as evil. Thus he accentuates the central mysteries of Christian belief in graphically concrete incarnational expressions, leading to the conclusion that Christians are called to follow the footsteps of the Word made flesh, a fundamental concern of the saint.

b. The phrasing of this passage, "*cum dives esset, super omnia voluit,*" makes its interpretation difficult. It could be translated "Though He was rich beyond all things . . ." or, as in this edition, "He wished . . . to choose . . . beyond all else . . ."

adore Him *in the Spirit* of truth.[a] 21 And *day and night* let us direct Jn 4:24
praises and prayers to Him, saying: *Our Father, Who art in heaven . . .* Ps 32:4; Mt 6:9
for we *should pray always and not become weary.* Lk 18:1

22 We must, of course, confess all our sins to a priest and receive the
Body and Blood of our Lord Jesus Christ from him.[b] 23 Whoever does
not eat His flesh and drink His blood *cannot enter the kingdom of God.* Jn 6:54,57; Jn 3:5
24 But let him eat and drink worthily because anyone who receives *unworthily, not distinguishing,* that is, not discerning, *the Body of the
Lord, eats and drinks judgment on himself.* 1 Cor 11:29

25 In addition, let us produce worthy fruits of penance. Lk 3:8

26 And let us love our neighbors as ourselves. 27 And if anyone does Mt 22:39
not want to love them as himself, let him at least not do them any harm,
but let him do good.

28 Let whoever has received the power of judging others pass judgment with mercy, as they would wish to receive mercy from the Lord.
29 For *judgment will be without mercy* for those *who have not shown
mercy.* Jas 2:13

30 Let us, therefore, have charity and humility and give alms because
it washes the stains of our sins from our souls. 31 For, although people Tb 4:11; 12:9
lose everything they leave behind in this world, they, nevertheless,
carry with them the rewards of charity and the alms they have given for
which they will receive a reward and a fitting repayment from the Lord.

32 We must also fast and abstain from vices and sins and from an ex- Sir 3:32
cess of food and drink and be Catholics.[c]

33 We must also frequently visit churches and venerate and revere
the clergy not so much for themselves, if they are sinners, but because
of their office and administration of the most holy Body and Blood of
Christ which they sacrifice upon the altar, receive and administer to
others. 34 And let all of us know for certain that no one can be saved except through the holy words and Blood of our Lord Jesus Christ which

a. This passage begins a series of ten commands, all of which contain the word *debere,* and explanations of what is implied in each command.

b. This emphasis of the role of the priest may well be directed against the Waldensians who embraced the principle that their system of life made them the real depositories of the Gospel and gave them the right to preach. The confession of sins to a priest, and the reception of the Eucharist, became primary concerns of the IV Lateran Council, canon 21, cf. infra, ER XX, p. 7, b.

c. In this and the following verses, Francis addresses abuses found in the Cathars and the Waldensians who maintained that fasting and abstaining should be practiced because of a dualistic concept of the world which sees the body and material things as evil. The penitents should fast and abstain according to the directives of the Church. The insistence on being Catholic also reflects a concern of the IV Lateran Council which addressed the theme in its first three canons, cf. infra ER XIX, p. 77, a.

the clergy pronounce, proclaim and minister.[a] 35And they alone must minister and not others.[b] 36Religious, however, who have left the world, are bound to do more and greater things, but not to overlook these.

Mt 15:18-19; Mk 7:23 37We must hate our bodies with their vices and sins because the Lord says in the Gospel: All evils, vices and sins *come from the heart.*

Mt 5:44; Lk 6:27 38We must love our *enemies* and do good *to those who* hate us.

39We must observe the commands and counsels of our Lord Jesus Christ.

Mt 16:24; Mk 8:34; Lk 9:23 40We must also deny ourselves and place our bodies under the yoke of servitude and holy obedience as each one has promised to the Lord.[c] 41And let no one be bound to obey another in anything in which a crime or sin would be committed. 42Instead, let the one to whom obedience has been entrusted and *who is* considered *the greater* be *the lesser* and
Mt 20:26-27; Mk 10:43-44; Lk 22:26 the servant of the other brothers.[d] 43And let him have and show mercy to each of his brothers as he would want them to do to him were he in a
Mt 7:12; Lk 6:31 similar position. 44Let him not become angry at the fault of a brother but, with all patience and humility, let him admonish and support him.

1 Cor 1:26 45We must not be wise and prudent according to the flesh, but, instead, we must be simple, humble and pure. 46And let us hold our bodies in scorn and contempt because, through our own fault, we are all wretched and corrupt, disgusting and worms, as the Lord says through the prophet: *I am a worm and not a man, the scorn of men and the out-*
Ps 22:7 *cast of the people.*[e]

47We must never desire to be above others, but, instead, we must be
1 Pt 2:13 servants and subject *to every human creature for God's sake.*

48And *the Spirit of the Lord will rest* upon all those men and women
Is 11:2; cf. Lk 4:18 who have done and persevered in these things and It will make a home
Jn 14:23 and *dwelling place in them.* 49And they will be the children of the heav-

---

a. By using these three verbs, "*dicunt, annuntiant et ministrant,*" Francis emphasizes the role of the priest as the only ordained minister able to consecrate the Eucharist, preach the Word, and administer the sacraments.

b. This emphasis clearly addresses the position of the Waldensians who maintained that the power to consecrate the Eucharist and to administer the sacraments was based not upon ordination but on the worthiness of the person.

c. Body here signifies the whole person. The penitents must place themselves under the yoke of service and holy obedience, that is, they must overcome self-centeredness.

d. The *nullus homo* of this text is stronger than *nemo* found in verse 34. This text also suggests a development in the organizational structure of the penitential communities. While the 1LtF speaks only of a promise (cf. 1LtF 2:4), this text presupposes communities which are structured with a vow of obedience and which need, therefore, to guard against abuses of obedience and of authority.

e. *Corpora nostra* [our bodies] signifies the personal "I," the egotistical self.

enly Father, Whose works they do. [50]And they are spouses, brothers Mt 5:45
and mothers of our Lord Jesus Christ. Mt 12:50; Mk 3:35; Lk 8:21

[51]We are spouses when the faithful soul is united by the Holy Spirit
to our Lord Jesus Christ. [52]We are brothers, moreover, when we do *the*
will of His *Father Who* is in heaven; [53]mothers when we carry Him in Mt 12:50; Mk 3:35
our heart and body through love and a pure and sincere conscience; and 1 Cor 6:20
give Him birth through a holy activity, which must shine before others
by example. Mt 5: 16

[54]O how glorious and holy and great to have a Father in heaven![a]
[55]O how holy, consoling, beautiful and wonderful to have such a
Spouse! [56]O how holy and how loving, gratifying, humbling,
peace-giving, sweet, worthy of love, and above all things desirable it is
to have such a Brother and such a Son: our Lord Jesus Christ, Who laid
down His life for His sheep and prayed to His Father, saying: Jn 10:15

Holy Father, save in your name those whom you have given me. Jn 17:11
•[57]Father, all those *whom you have given me in the world were yours*
and you have given them to me. [58]*The words that you gave me, I have* •Jn 17:6
given to them; they have accepted them and known in truth that I have
come from you and they have believed that you have sent me. Jn 17:8

I pray for them and *not for the world;* •bless and sanctify them.[b] •[59]*I* Jn 17:9; •Jn 17:17
sanctify myself for them that they may be sanctified in •being one as we •Jn 17:19
are one. •Jn 17:11

[60]And I wish, Father, *that where* I am, *they may be with me that they*
may see my glory •in your kingdom. Jn 17:24; •Mt 20:21

[61]Let *every creature*
in heaven, on earth, in the sea and in the depths,
give praise, *glory, honor and blessing* Rv 5:13
To Him Who suffered so much,
Who has given and will give in the future every good,
[62]for He is our power and strength,
Who *alone is good,* Mk 10:18; Lk 18:19
Who alone is almighty,
Who alone is omnipotent, wonderful, glorious

a. Cf. infra, 1LtF 1:11 p. 42, c.

b. The omission of John 17:20, "Not only for these do I pray, but for those who through their words will believe in me . . .", is significant. It may have been prompted by the numerous questions and conflicts concerning the role of lay preachers within the penitential movement and the right to preach. Thus this Johannine passage may have been omitted to avoid its possible interpretation as a support of non-authorized lay preaching. This may also explain Francis's insistence on the unique role of the clergy in this regard as we can see in this document, verses 34-35.

and Who alone is holy,
worthy of praise and blessing
through endless ages.
Amen.

[63]All those, however, who are not living in penance, who do not receive the Body and Blood of our Lord Jesus Christ, [64]who practice vice
and sin and walk after evil concupiscence and wicked desires, who do
not observe what they have promised, [65]and who serve the world with
their bodies, the desires of the flesh, the cares and anxieties of this
world, and the preoccupations of this life [66][all these] are deceived by
Jn 8:41 the devil whose children they are and whose works they do.[a] They are
blind because they do not see the true light, our Lord Jesus Christ.
[67]They do not have spiritual wisdom because they do not possess the
Son of God, the true wisdom of the Father, within them. It is said of
Ps 107:27 them: *Their wisdom has been swallowed up.* [68]They see, recognize,
know, and do evil; and, knowingly, they lose their souls.

[69]See, you blind ones, deceived by your enemies, that is, the flesh,
the world, and the devil, for it is sweet for the body to commit sin and
bitter to serve God, because every evil, vice and sin flow and *proceed*
Mk 7:21//Mt 15:19 *from people's hearts,* as the Lord says in the Gospel. [70]And you have
nothing in this world or in that to come. [71]You think you possess the
vanities of the world for a long time, but you are deceived because a
day and an hour are coming of which you do not think, do not know,
and are not aware.

[72]The body becomes weak, death approaches, relatives and friends
come saying: "Put your affairs in order." [73]Look, his wife and children,
relatives and friends pretend to cry. [74]Glancing about, he sees them
weeping and is moved by an evil impulse. He says, thinking to himself,
"See, I place my soul and body, all that I have in your hands." [75]In fact,
that man is cursed who entrusts and places his soul and body and all he
has in such hands; [76]for, as the Lord says through the prophet, *Cursed*
Jer 17:5 *is the one who trusts in another.* [77]And immediately they make a priest
come. The priest says to him: "Do you want to receive penance for all
your sins?" [78]"I do," he responds. "Do you wish to make satisfaction,
as far as you can, out of your wealth, for what you have done and the

a. The word *detenti* found in the 1LtF 2:6 has been changed to *decepti*. While *detenti* may be understood as a variation of the Italian *detenere* meaning to imprison or to hold prisoner, it follows the sense of the general concept of being possessed. However such a meaning might have seemed too severe in this context and was perhaps theologically unsatisfactory. Its force, then, was weakened to the more acceptable *decepti*.

ways in which you have cheated and deceived people?" [79]"No," he responds. [80]"Why not?" the priest asks. "Because I have placed everything in the hands of my relatives and friends." [81]And the wretched man begins to lose his speech and so dies.

[82]But let everyone know that whenever and however someone dies in mortal sin without making amends when he could have [done so] and did not, the devil snatches his soul from his body with such anguish and distress that no one can know [what it is like] except the one experiencing it.

[83]And every talent and power and knowledge that he thought he had
will be taken away from him.[a] [84]And he leaves his relatives and friends Mk 4:25
and they take and divide his wealth and, afterwards, they say: "Let his soul be cursed because he could have given us more and acquired more than he distributed to us!" [85]Worms eat his body and so he loses his body and soul in this brief world and goes to hell where he will be tortured without end.

[86]In the name of the Father and of the Son and of the Holy Spirit. Amen.

[87]I, brother Francis, your lesser servant, with a wish to kiss your
feet, beg and implore you in the love that is God, to receive, to put into 1 Jn 4:16
practice, and to observe, as you should, these words and the others of our Lord Jesus Christ with humility and love.[b] [88]And may the Father and the Son and the Holy Spirit bless all those men and women who receive them with kindness, understand them and send copies of them to
others, if *they have persevered to the end* in them. Mt 24:13

Amen.

a. Francis's use of this threefold formula, "every talent and power and knowledge," may well suggest a symbolism highlighting the total loss of all things.

b. A number of manuscripts contain an additional sentence at this point, one which parallels the conclusion of the 1LtF: "Let those who cannot read have [this letter] read to them frequently and, with a holy activity, preserved among them to the end for [its words] are *spirit and life*." (cf. Jn 6:63)

Exhortations to the Clergy
(Letters to the Clergy)[a]

These exhortations reflect Francis's encouragement of the clergy to exercise solicitude ". . . in keeping the churches and altars and everything used in the celebration of the divine mysteries clean" (*Assisi Compilation* 60). Two versions exist, the second of which suggests influences of the Fourth Lateran Council and, more specifically, accentuates the concerns of Pope Honorius III whose exhortation, *Sane cum olim* or *Expectavimus hactenus* expresses similar exhortations.

Earlier Edition
(before 1219)[b]

[1]Let all of us, clergymen, consider the great sin and the ignorance some have toward the most holy Body and Blood of our Lord Jesus Christ and His most holy names and written words that consecrate His Body.[c] [2]We know It cannot be His Body without first being consecrated by word. [3]For we have and see nothing bodily of the Most High
1 Jn 3:14 in this world except His Body and Blood, His names and words
through which we have been made and redeemed *from death to life.*

[4]Let all those who administer such most holy mysteries, however, especially those who administer them illicitly, consider how very dirty are the chalices, corporals and altar-linens upon which HIS Body and Blood are sacrificed. [5]It is placed and left in many dirty places, carried about unbecomingly, received unworthily, and administered to others

a. Since both editions of this text are exhortatory in nature and lack the customary epistolary introductions, the editors believe it more appropriate to call them exhortations.

b. A missal in the Benedictine monastery of Subiaco contains this earlier edition which was copied between 1229 and 1238 to commemorate a visit of the saint at an earlier time. It was embellished with the sign of the Tau with which Francis frequently ended his writings.

c. The Latin phrase *nomina et verba* appears several times in the writings of Francis (*First Letter to the Clergy* 1,3,6,12 [hereafter 1LtCl]; *First Letter to the Custodians* 2,5[hereafter 1LtCus]; Test 14). In this context, the phrase occurs within the context of seeing the Most High "bodily" and suggests Francis's understanding not only of the connectedness between the Eucharist and the Word but also of the sacramental meaning of both.

without discernment.[a] [6]Even His written names and words are at times left to be trampled under foot; [7]*for the carnal person does not perceive the things of God.* 1 Cor 2:14

[8]Are we not moved by piety at these things when the pious Lord puts Himself into our hands and we touch Him and receive Him daily with our mouth?[b] [9]Do we refuse to recognize that we must come into His hands? [10]Let us, therefore, amend our ways quickly and firmly in these and all other matters. [11]Wherever the most holy Body and Blood of our Lord Jesus Christ has been illicitly placed and left, let It be moved from there, placed in a precious place and locked up.[c] [12]Likewise, wherever the names and written words of the Lord may be found in unclean places, let them be gathered up and put in a becoming place.

[13]All the clergy are forever bound to observe all these things above everything else. [14]And whoever *does not do so, let him know he must render an accounting on the day of judgment* before our Lord Jesus Christ. [15]Let those who make copies of this writing in order that it might be better observed, know they have been blessed by the Lord God. Mt 12:36

---

a. *Indiscrete*, the negative form of *discrete*, is best translated as "without discernment" rather than "without discretion." *Discernere* has the meaning of separating or distinguishing by knowing. Francis may well have been influenced by 1 Corinthians 11:29 in which Paul writes of discerning the Body of the Lord.

b. In this passage Francis is obviously accentuating *pietas*, the ancient Roman virtue of showing respect towards one's parents, family, or neighbor. From Francis's perspective, the Lord is pious and, in the Eucharist, becomes the model of piety for us.

c. This verse reflects Canon 20 of the Fourth Lateran Council: "We decree that in all churches the chrism and the Eucharist are to be kept in properly protected places provided with locks and keys, so that they may not be reached by rash and undiscerning persons and used for impious and blasphemous purposes."

Later Edition
(1220)[a]

[1]Let all of us, clergymen, consider the great sin and the ignorance some have toward the most holy Body and Blood of our Lord Jesus Christ and His most holy names and written words that consecrate His Body. [2]We know It cannot be His Body without first being consecrated by word. [3]For we have and see nothing corporally of the Most High in this world except [His] Body and Blood, [His] names and words
1 Jn 3:14 through which we have been made and redeemed *from death to life.*

[4]Let all those who administer such most holy ministries, however, especially those who administer them without discernment, consider how very dirty the chalices, corporals and altar-linens are upon which the Body and Blood of our Lord are sacrificed. [5]It is left in many dirty places, carried about unbecomingly, received unworthily, and administered to others without discernment. [6]Even His names and written words are at times left to be trampled under foot; [7]*for the carnal person*
1 Cor 2:14 *does not perceive the things of God.*

[8]Are we not moved by piety at these things when the pious Lord offers Himself into our hands and we touch Him and receive Him daily with our mouth? [9]Do we refuse to recognize that we must come into His hands? [10]Let us, therefore, amend our ways quickly and firmly in these and all other matters. [11]Wherever the most holy Body and Blood of our Lord Jesus Christ has been illicitly placed and left, let It be moved from there, placed in a precious place and locked up. [12]Likewise, wherever the names and written words of the Lord may be found in unclean places, let them be gathered up and placed in a becoming place.

[13]We know that we are bound to observe above all else all of these matters according to the precepts of the Lord and the constitutions of

a. Kajetan Esser found the text of this later exhortation in a number of manuscripts but noted that there were different incipits, e.g. "Reverence for the Body of the Lord (or, 'of Christ') and the Cleanliness of the Altar;" "A Letter and Admonition of the Holy Father to All Brothers, Especially Those Who Are Priests, Concerning Reverence for the Body of the Lord and Reverence for the Altar;" "An Admonition of Our Blessed Father Francis to All Clerics Concerning Reverence for the Body of Our Lord Jesus Christ and Especially for Reverence for the Altar."

holy mother Church.[a] [14]Whoever does not do this, let him know that, *on the day of judgment,* he will be bound *to render an account* of himself before our Lord Jesus Christ. Mt 12:36

[15]Let whoever makes copies of this writing so that it may be better observed know that they will be blessed by the Lord God.

a. A direct reference to the decree *Sane cum olim* or *Expectavius hactenus* of Pope Honorius III, November 22, 1219, *Bullarium Romanum,* Honorius III, n. XL, tom. III, pages 366a-366b. "Since in times past the golden vessel full of manna prefigured the Body of Christ that contained the Godhead and since this vessel was placed below the Holy of Holies in the gold-covered Ark of the Covenant in order that it might be preserved decently in a holy place, we deplore and are grieved that in several provinces priests who are ignoring canonical sanctions and the judgment of God are carelessly reserving and irreverently touching, with unclean hands, the Sacred Eucharist. [And they do this] so that they neither fear the Creator nor love the Life-Giver, nor tremble before the Judge of all, even though the Apostle sternly threatens that whoever disdains *the Son of God* or *considers the covenant-blood to be ordinary* or insults *the Spirit of grace* (cf. Heb 10:29) will merit a worse punishment than one who transgresses the Law of Moses for which the penalty is the sentence of death. Therefore, lest the wrath of God blaze up in the future against the irreverent because of the carelessness of priests, We strictly enjoin by precept that the Eucharist be reserved always devotedly and faithfully in a place of honor that is clean and designated for It alone. Every priest should teach his people frequently that they should bow in reverence whenever the Life-Giving Host is elevated at the celebration of Mass and that each one should do the same when the priest is carrying It to the sick. At the same time, the priest should carry It in becoming apparel covered with a clean veil and should bring It back opening at his breast and with respect. The priest should be preceded by a torch, since the Eucharist is the radiance of Eternal Light, so that the faith and devotion of everyone be increased. If Prelates desire to escape the vengeance of God and Ours, they should not delay in punishing seriously transgressors of this precept. You should see that the foregoing is so observed that you may be made partakers not of punishment but of reward. Given as above, at Viterbo, on the twenty-second day of November in the fourth year of our pontificate. Honorius III, Pope."

The First Letter to the Custodians
(1220)[a]

This inspiration for this letter also expresses Francis's concern for reverence for the Eucharist and the Word of God as well as his awareness of the post-conciliar exhortations of Pope Honorius III. Thus it was probably written after Francis's return from the Middle East.

[1]To all the custodians of the Lesser Brothers whom this letter reaches,[b] Brother Francis, your servant and little one in the Lord God, sends a greeting together with new signs of heaven and earth which are great and extraordinary in the sight of God yet regarded as of little importance by many religious and others.[c]

[2]With all that is in me and more I beg you that, when it is fitting and you judge it expedient, you humbly beg the clergy to revere above all else the most holy Body and Blood of our Lord Jesus Christ and His holy names and the written words that sanctify His Body. [3]They should hold as precious the chalices, corporals, appointments of the altar, and everything that pertains to the sacrifice. [4]If the most holy Body of the Lord is very poorly reserved in any place, let It be placed and locked up in a precious place according to the command of the Church. Let It be carried about with great reverence and administered to others with discernment. [5]Let the names and written words of the Lord, whenever

a. Codex 225 in the Guarnacci Library, Volterra, Italy, contains the text of this letter. It was discovered by Paul Sabatier in 1902 and, although we can only find it in that manuscript, its authenticity has not been questioned since it clearly shows the spirit of Francis's *Exhortations to the Clergy.*

b. Throughout this translation, the phrase *Fratres Minores* will be translated as "Lesser Brothers" as opposed to "Friars Minor." While traditionally the more accepted phrase, the latter is an early English translation which has become the standard and official way of identifying members of the First Order of Saint Francis. However, as other texts will show, the phrase is one which received considerable attention as it is rich in identifying Francis's followers as "brothers" whose primary characteristic was that of being "less than others." For its origins, cf. ER VI, p. 68, b.

c. This letter marks the first use of the term *custos* [custodian], brothers designated to serve their confreres in a sub-division of a province. It entered the vocabulary of Francis's followers through the papal document *Cum secundum consilium,* November 22, 1220, in which Pope Honorius III addresses both "priors" and "custodians." Various interpretations of the *nova signa caeli et terrae* [new signs of heaven and earth] exist seeing in the phrase a rebuttal of the Eucharistic teaching of the Cathari or an influence of the followers of Joachim of Fiore. While it is difficult to arrive at a definitive interpretation, it seems best to understand the phrase in the context of the entire letter which calls for the proclamation of penance, the reception of the Word of God and the Eucharist at the sound of a bell, that is, at a new call to worship.

they are found in dirty places, be also gathered up and kept in a becoming place.

[6]In every sermon you give, remind people about penance and that no one can be saved unless he receives the most holy Body and Blood of the Lord. [7]When It is sacrificed on the altar by a priest and carried anywhere, let all peoples praise, glorify and honor on bended knee the Lord God living and true.[a] [8]May you announce and preach His praise to all nations in such a way that praise and thanks may always be given to the all-powerful God by all people throughout the world at every hour and whenever bells are rung.

Jn 6:54

1 Thes 1:9

[9]Let my brother custodians who have received this writing, who have made copies of it and kept it for themselves and for the brothers who have the responsibility of preaching and the care of the brothers, and who have made known and preached about everything contained in it, know that they have God's blessing as well as my own. [10]Let these be matters of true and holy obedience for them.

a. Although the influence of *Sane cum olim* can be seen in these verses, it is interesting to note the differences: Whereas the papal document exhorts priests to teach the people to "bow in reverence," Francis encourages the people to ". . . praise, glorify and honor . . . on bended knee."

A Letter to the Rulers of the Peoples
(1220)[a]

This text exemplifies Francis's practice of encouraging civil authorities to be mindful of Gospel truths, a practice described by Thomas of Celano in *The Life of Saint Francis* 43 in which Emperor Otto IV was reminded of the brevity of his glory and in *The Remembrance of the Desire of a Soul* 200 in which emperors were encouraged to enact laws for the feeding of animals on Christmas Day. The introduction of seemingly Islamic practices suggests the composition of this text after Francis's return from the Middle East.

[1]Brother Francis, your little and looked-down-upon servant in the
Lord God, wishes health and peace to all mayors and consuls, magistrates and governors throughout the world and to all others to whom
these words may come.[b]

Gn 47:29 [2]Reflect and see that the day of death is approaching. [3]With all possible respect, therefore, I beg you not to forget the Lord because of this
world's cares and preoccupations and not to turn away from His commandments, for all those *who* leave Him in oblivion and *turn away*
Ps 119:21; Ez 33:13 *from His commandments are cursed* and *will be left in oblivion* by Him.

[4]When the day of death does come, everything they think they have
Mt 13:12; Mk 4:25; Lk 8:18 shall be taken from them.[c] [5]The wiser and more powerful they may
have been in this world, the greater will be the punishment they will en-
Wis 6:7 dure in hell.

[6]Therefore I strongly advise you, my Lords, to put aside all care and
preoccupation and receive the most holy Body and Blood of our Lord
Jesus Christ with fervor in holy remembrance of Him.[7]May you foster

a. A copy of this letter was discovered by Luke Wadding in the *De origine seraphicae religionis franciscanae* of Francisco Gonzaga, General Minister from 1579 to 1587. According to Gonzaga, John Parenti, the first Provincial Minister of Spain, brought a copy of this letter to Spain.

b. The delineation of the rulers—*potestatibus et consulis, iudicibus atque rectoribus* [mayors and consuls, magistrates and governors]—reflects a more Italian medieval understanding of government, one that seems more particular to the area of Assisi. *Potestatibus* or *podestà*, mayor, presides over citizens in matters of war and civic functions; *consulibus*, consuls, generally offered counsel to those involved in business or shipping and, in some cases, were also civil magistrates; *judicibus*, judges, were government officials who held great power; *rectoribus*, governors, were responsible for shipping, territorial, and as time progressed, property in general.

c. Francis's reminder of death prompts the interpretation of some authors that this letter was written as a result of his presence in the Battle of Damiata, August 29, 1219.

such honor to the Lord among the people entrusted to you that every evening an announcement may be made by a messenger or some other sign that praise and thanksgiving may be given by all people to the all-powerful Lord God.[a] [8]If you do not do this, know that, *on the day of judgment,* you must render *an account* before the Lord Your God, Jesus Christ. Mt 12:36

[9]Let those who keep this writing with them and observe it know that they will be blessed by the Lord God.

a. This advice also suggests the influence of the Islamic world and the call to worship, the *sâlat,* proclaimed five times throughout the day.

The Second Letter to the Custodians
(1220)[a]

The contents to this simple letter echo those of the other writings of this period; in fact, we can find references to the *Exhortation of the Clergy* and the *Letter to the Rulers of the People.* Of these letters written after Francis's visit to the Middle East, the reference to "the other letter" suggests that Francis wrote this letter last.

[1]Brother Francis, the least of the servants of God, sends greetings and holy peace in the Lord to all the custodians of the Friars Minor whom this letter reaches.

[2]Know that there are certain very lofty and sublime things in the sight of God that people sometimes think of as worthless and contemptible; [3]there are others that are esteemed and remarkable to people that God considers extremely worthless and contemptible.

[4]In the sight of our Lord God, I beg you, as much as I can, to give to bishops and other members of the clergy those letters treating of the most holy Body and Blood of our Lord; [5]and to keep in mind what we have recommended to you about these things.

[6]Make many copies of the other letter I am sending you, in which it is written that the praises of God be proclaimed among the peoples and in the piazzas, to give to mayors, consuls and rulers, [7]and distribute them with great zeal to those to whom they should be given.[b]

---

a. Luke Wadding discovered this text in the archives of a friary in Saragossa, Spain. It has been preserved there since the time of John Parenti, the first Provincial Minister of the Province of Spain and General Minister of the Order from 1227-1232. Since Wadding put the text in a new Latin translation, it is difficult to identify many of the stylistic idiosyncrasies of the saint; nevertheless, the context of the letter confirms its authenticity.

b. Francis's advice to proclaim God's praises suggest the influence of the Islamic *sâlat*, the prayer that every adult Muslim says five times daily.

A Rule for Hermitages
(1217–1221)

This text can be found in the oldest manuscript collection of the writings of Francis, the Assisi Codex 338, and in the manuscript tradition of the fourteenth and fifteenth centuries. Names of hermitages are spread throughout the early biographies of the saint suggesting that the eremitical spirit of the primitive fraternity was quite strong. While reflecting many of the expressions of the monastic hermitage, e.g., separation from the world, private cells, the tradition of Martha and Mary, this text expresses a distinctly Franciscan character, i.e., the fraternal dimension, the begging of alms, the role and visit of the provincial minister and the custodian.

[1]Let those who wish to stay in hermitages in a religious way be three brothers or, at the most, four; let two of these be "the mother" and have two "sons" or at least one.[a] [2]Let the two who are "mothers" keep the life of Martha and the two "sons" the life of Mary and let one have one enclosure in which each one may have his cell in which he may pray and sleep.[b] Lk 10:38-42

[3]And let them always recite Compline of the day immediately after sunset and strive to maintain silence, recite their Hours, rise for Matins, and *seek first the kingdom of God and His justice.* [4]And let them recite Prime at the proper hour and, after Terce, they may end their silence, speak with and go to their mothers. [5]And when it pleases them, they can beg alms from them as poor little ones out of love of the Lord God.[c] [6]And afterwards let them recite Sext, None and, at the proper hour, Vespers. Mt 6:33

a. *Stare* [to stay] is a difficult word to translate with accuracy since it has a sense of permanence as well as transience. Thus the practice of staying in hermitages may be interpreted in terms of a vocation in itself or of a period of recollection. *Religiose* [in a religious way] suggests monastic terminology which, in the twelfth century, speaks of *eremitica conversatio* or *rigor eremiticae conversationis* and called for a) physical distance from centers of urban activity; b) distinctive architecture keeping the "world" at a distance and minimizing interaction among those within; and c) rules imposing and maintaining silence.

b. This Lucan imagery can also be found in the Cistercian texts, *De institutione inclusarum* of Aelred of Rievaulx (1110-1167).

c. The opportunity to beg alms is an important expression of the bond of poverty and fraternity found in Francis's thought, cf. ER IX 1-9; LR VI.

[7]And they may not permit anyone to enter or eat in the enclosure where they dwell. [8]Let those brothers who are the "mothers" strive to stay far from everyone and, because of obedience to their minister, protect their "sons" from everyone so that no one can speak with them. [9]And those "sons" may not talk with anyone except with their "mothers" and with the minister and his custodian when it pleases them to visit with the Lord's blessing.

[10]The "sons," however, may periodically assume the role of the "mothers," taking turns for a time as they have mutually decided.[a] Let them strive to observe conscientiously and eagerly everything mentioned above.

a. The exchange of roles was an important aspect of the fraternity of the eremitical life referring more to life within hermitage than to that of the larger fraternity.

The Earlier Rule
(The Rule Without a Papal Seal)[a]
(1209/10-1221)

This document has its origins in the simple form of life which Francis brought to Pope Innocent III for his approval in 1209 or 1210. During the following years it developed in light of the experiences of the brothers, the teaching of the Church, especially the decrees of the Fourth Lateran Council, and the teachings of Francis himself. The final stage of its composition occurred at the Chapter of 1221, the last Pentecost Chapter at which all the brothers gathered together.

[Prologue]

[1]In the name of the Father and of the Son and of the Holy Spirit.

[2]This is the life of the Gospel of Jesus Christ that Brother Francis petitioned the Lord Pope to grant and confirm for him; and he did grant and confirm it for him and his brothers present and to come.

[3]Brother Francis—and whoever is head of this religion—promises obedience and reverence to the Lord Pope Innocent and his successors.[b] [4]Let all the brothers be bound to obey Brother Francis and his successors.

[Chapter I: The Brothers must live without anything of their own and in chastity and in obedience]

[1]The rule and life of these brothers is this, namely: "to live in obedience, in chastity, and without anything of their own,"[c] and to follow the

a. David Flood's study of this document, *Die Regula non bullata der Minderbrüder,* initiated a series of studies including that of Kajetan Esser which formed the basis of this translation, cf. David Flood, *Die Regula non bullata der Minderbrüder, Franziskanische Forschungen, Heft* 19 (Werl i. W. 1967); Kajestan Esser, *Textkritische Untersuchungen zur Regula non bullata der Minderbrüder, Spicilegium Bonaventuianum* 9, (Grottaferrata: 1974).

b. *Religio* [religion] refers to any religious community yet implies less of a sense of a religious *Ordo* [Order] as that of Saint Benedict or that of the Cistercians. The reference to Pope Innocent III (+July 16, 1216) suggests that the roots of this document are the *propositum vitae,* the primitive document, which the Pope approved orally in 1209.

c. Innocent III used this formula in approving the Rule of the Trinitarians, December 17, 1198, cf. PL 214, 445; 217, 1137.

teaching and footprints of our Lord Jesus Christ, Who says: [2]*If you*
Mt 19:21; Lk 18:22 *wish to be perfect, go, sell everything you have and give it to the poor,*
Mt 19:21 *and you will have treasure in heaven; and come, follow me.* [3]And: *If*
anyone wishes to come after me, let him deny himself and take up his
Mt 16:24 *cross and follow me.* [4]Again: *If anyone wishes to come to me and does*
not hate father and mother and wife and children and brothers and sis-
Lk 14:26 *ters, and even his own life, he cannot be my disciple.* [5]And: *Everyone*
who has left father or mother, brother or sisters, wife or children,
Mt 19:29; Mk 10:29 *houses or lands because of me, will receive a hundredfold and will pos-*
Mt 19:29//Mk 10:29// Lk 18:30 *sess eternal life.*

[Chapter II: The Reception and the Clothing of the Brothers][a]

[1]If anyone, wishing by divine inspiration to accept this life, comes to our brothers, let him be received by them with kindness.[b] [2]If he is determined to accept our life, let the brothers be very careful not to become involved in his temporal affairs but present him to their minister as quickly as possible. [3]On his part, let the minister receive him with kindness, encourage him and diligently explain the tenor of our life to him.

[4]When this has been done, let the above-mentioned person—if he
wishes and is capable of doing so spiritually without any difficulty—sell all his belongings and be conscientious in giving every-
Mt 19:21; Lk 18:22 thing to the poor. [5]Let the brothers and the minister of the brothers be
careful not to interfere in any way in his temporal affairs, [6]nor to accept
money either by themselves or through an intermediary.[c] [7]Neverthe-
less, if the brothers are in need, they can accept, like other poor people,
whatever is needed for the body excepting money.

[8]When he has returned, the minister may give him the clothes of probation for a year, that is, two tunics without a hood, a cord, trousers,

a. Three stages of development appear in this chapter: a) verses 1 and 14 suggest the *propositum vitae* of 1209/1210; b) verses 2 and 4, which speak of the role of a minister, suggest the period after 1217 when the fraternity was divided into provinces; and c) verses 8, 11-13, which show the influence of the papal decree *Cum secundum consilium,* thus a period after November 22, 1220, cf. infra pp. 560-561.

b. The phrase, divine inspiration, suggests the dynamic principle of vocation and can also be found in the LR II 1 in this same context and in ER XVI and LR XII 11 in the context of those going among the Saracens. It may well be a biblical allusion to 2 Tm 3:16, a text which was used concerning the inspiration of Sacred Scripture: "All Scripture is inspired by God and is useful for teaching the truth, rebuking error, correcting faults, and giving instruction for right living."

c. At this period of history money was seen as a medium of exchange which represented concentrated, mobile wealth or wealth in safekeeping. Because it created tensions between morality and behavior, religion and life itself, many moralists of the early generations of the profit-seeking monetary economy advocated its avoidance by anyone seeking to live a spiritual life.

and a small cape reaching to the cord. [9]When the year and term of probation has ended, he may be received into obedience. [10]After this it will be unlawful for him to join another Order or to "wander outside obedience" according to the decree of the Lord Pope and the Gospel, for *no one putting his hand to the plow and looking to what was left behind is fit for the kingdom of God.*[a] Lk 9:62

[11]However, if anyone comes who cannot give away his belongings without difficulty and has the spiritual will to do so, let him leave them behind, and it will suffice for him.

[12]No one may be received contrary to the rite and practice of the Holy Church.

[13]All the other brothers who have already promised obedience may have one tunic with a hood and, if it is necessary, another without a hood and a cord and trousers. [14]Let all the brothers wear poor clothes and, with the blessing of God, they can patch them with sackcloth and other pieces, for the Lord says in the Gospel: *Those who wear expensive clothing and live in luxury* and *who dress in fine garments are in* Lk 7:25
the houses of kings. [15]Even though they may be called hypocrites, let Mt 11:8
them nevertheless not cease doing good nor seek expensive clothing in this world, so that they may have a garment in the kingdom of heaven. Mt 22:11

[Chapter III: The Divine Office and Fasting][b]

[1]The Lord says: *This kind* of devil *cannot come out except* through fasting and prayer; [2]and again: *When you fast do not become gloomy* Mk 9:28
like the hypocrites. [3]For this reason let all the brothers, whether clerical Mt 6:16
or lay, recite the Divine Office, the praises and prayers, as is required of them.

[4]Let the clerical brothers recite the Office and say it for the living and the dead according to the custom of clerics. [5]Every day let them say the *Have mercy on me, O God* with the *Our Father* for the failings Ps 51; Mt 6:9-13
and negligence of the brothers; [6]and let them say the *Out of the depths* Ps 130
with the *Our Father* for the deceased brothers. [7]They may have only the books necessary to fulfill their office.

[8]The lay brothers who know how to read the psalter may have one. [9]Those who do not know how to read, however, may not be permitted

a. Cf. Honorius III, *Cum secundum consilium*, cf. infra pp. 560-561.

b. This chapter seems to have two stages of development: a) verses 1-3, 11-13 which may have been part of the *propositum vitae;* and b) verses 4-10 which may have been added at a later date.

to have any book. [10]Let the lay brothers say the *Creed* and twenty-four *Our Fathers* with the *Glory to the Father* for Matins; for Lauds, let them say five; for Prime, the *Creed* and seven *Our Fathers* with the *Glory to the Father*; for each of the hours, Terce, Sext and None, seven; for Vespers, twelve; for Compline, the *Creed* and seven *Our Fathers* with the *Glory to the Father;* for the deceased, seven *Our Fathers* with the *Eternal Rest;* and for the failings and negligence of the brothers three *Our Fathers* each day.[a]

[11]Similarly, let all the brothers fast from the feast of All Saints until the Nativity, and from the Epiphany, when our Lord Jesus Christ began to fast, until Easter. [12]However, at other times, according to this life, let them not be bound to fast except on Fridays. [13]In accordance with the Gospel, it may be lawful for them to eat of all the food that is placed be-
Lk 10:8 fore them.

[Chapter IV: The Ministers and the Other Brothers and How They Are Related][b]

[1]In the name of the Lord![c]

[2]Let all the brothers who have been designated the ministers and servants of the other brothers assign their brothers in the provinces and places where they may be, and let them frequently visit, admonish and encourage them spiritually. [3]Let all my other brothers diligently obey them in those matters concerning the well-being of their soul and which are not contrary to our life.

[4]Let them behave among themselves according to what the Lord
Mt 7:12 says: *Do to others what you would have them do to you;* [5]and "Do not do to another what you would not have done to you."[d]

[6]Let the ministers and servants remember what the Lord says: I have
Mt 20:28 *not* come *to be served, but to serve;* and because the care of the brothers' souls has been entrusted to them, if anything[e] is lost on account of

a. The directives offered for those lay brothers who are unable to read show the influence of the *Propositum Humiliatorum* 10, 13 which received papal approval on June 7, 1201.

b. The following three chapters clearly come from a period after 1217 when the primitive fraternity was divided into geographical jurisdictions or provinces in which ministers were appointed to serve the brothers.

c. A traditional formula used at the beginning of legal documents suggesting the insertion of this lengthy section into the *propositum vitae.*

d. Benedict, *Rule* LXI 14; LXX 7; cf. Tb 4:16.

e. Esser notes that the majority of the manuscripts, following the lead of Angelo of Clareno, contain *aliquis*/anyone. He choses, however, to follow the more ancient manuscript tradition which has *aliquid*/anything.

their fault or bad example, they will have *to render an account* before
the Lord Jesus Christ *on the day of judgment.* Mt 12:36

[Chapter V: The Correction of the Brothers at Fault]

[1]Keep watch over your soul, therefore, and those of your brothers,
because *it is a fearful thing to fall into the hands of the living God.* [2]If Heb 10:31
anyone of the ministers commands one of the brothers something con-
trary to our life or to his soul, he is not bound to obey him because obedience is not something in which a fault or sin is committed.

[3]On the other hand, let all the brothers who are under the ministers
and servants consider the deeds of the ministers and servants reason-
ably and attentively. [4]If they see any of them walking according to the
flesh and not according to the Spirit in keeping with the integrity of our
life, if he does not improve after a third admonition, let them inform the Rom 8:4
minister and servant of the whole fraternity at the Chapter of Pentecost
regardless of what objection deters them.

[5]Moreover, if, anywhere among the brothers, there is a brother who
wishes to live according to the flesh and not according to the Spirit, let Rom 8:4
the brothers with whom he is living admonish, instruct and correct him
humbly and attentively. [6]If, however, after the third admonition he refuses to improve, let them send or report him to their minister and ser- Mt 18:15-17
vant as soon as they can; and let the minister and servant deal with him
as he considers best before God.

[7]Let all the brothers, both the ministers and servants as well as the
others, be careful not to be disturbed or angered at another's sin or evil
because the devil wishes to destroy many because of another's fault.
[8]But let them spiritually help the one who has sinned as best they can,
because *those who are well do not need a physician, but the sick do.* Mt 9:12 // Mk 2:17

[9]Likewise, let all the brothers not have power or control in this instance, especially among themselves; [10]for, as the Lord says in the
Gospel: *The rulers of the Gentiles lord it over them and the great ones*
make their authority over them felt; it shall not be so among the broth- Mt 20:25
ers. [11]Let whoever *wishes to be the greater* among them *be* their *minis-* Mt 20:26a
ter and *servant.* [12]*Let whoever is the greater among them become the* Mt 20:26b; Mt 20:27
least. Lk 22:26

[13]Let no brother do or say anything evil to another; [14]on the contrary, *through the charity of the Spirit, let them serve* and obey *one an-*

Gal 5:13; 1 Pt 1:22; 2:13-15 *other* voluntarily. [15]This is the true and holy obedience of our Lord
Jesus Christ.

[16]As often as *they have turned away from the commands of the Lord*
and "wandered outside obedience,"[a] let all the brothers know, as the
Prophet says, they are cursed outside obedience as long as they know-
Ps 119:21 ingly remain in such a sin. [17]When they have persevered in the Lord's
commands—as they have promised by the Holy Gospel and their life,
let them know they have remained in true obedience and are blessed by
the Lord.

[Chapter VI: The Recourse of the Brothers to the Minister; Let No Brother Be Called "Prior"]

[1]If the brothers, wherever they may be, cannot observe this life, let
them have recourse to their minister as soon as they can, making this
known to him. [2]Let the minister, on his part, endeavor to provide for
them as he would wish to be provided for him were he in a similar posi-
Mt 7:12 tion.

Mt 20:27 [3]Let no one be called "*prior,*" but let everyone in general be called a
Mt 23:8; Lk 22:26; Jn 13:14 lesser brother.[b] [4]Let one wash the feet of the other.

[Chapter VII: The Manner of Serving and Working][c]

[1]None of the brothers may be treasurers or overseers in any of those
places where they are staying to serve or work among others. They may
not be in charge in the houses in which they serve nor accept any office
Mk 8:36 which would generate scandal or *be harmful to their souls;* [2]Let them,
Lk 22:26; 1 Pt 2:13 instead, be the lesser ones and be subject to all in the same house.

[3]Let the brothers who know how to work do so and exercise that
trade they have learned, provided it is not contrary to the good of their
souls and can be performed honestly. [4]For the prophet says: *You shall*
Ps 128:2 *eat the fruit of your labors; you are blessed and it shall be well for you.*

---

a. Honorius III, *Cum secundum consilium*, cf. infra pp. 560-561.

b. "Prior" was a term used in the earlier tradition of religious life for one who was a vicar or a delegate of a monastery which had no abbot. At the time of Francis, a prior was the superior of a small house and in this sense was adopted by the Friars Preachers, the Augustinians, et al. Apart from this reference, the oldest acknowledgment of the title, "Friars Minor" or "Lesser Brothers," appears in the Chronicles of the Premonstratensian Burchard of Urspurg (+1230) who encountered the brothers in 1210 and writes of a change in their name from "Poor Minors" to "Friars Minor," cf. infra pp. 593-594.

c. While many commentators suggest that this chapter formed part of the *propositum vitae*, others see verses 1-2 coming at a later stage of development, that is, after the brothers had been achieving success in their work.

[5]The Apostle says: *Whoever does not wish to work shall not eat.* [6]and 2 Thes 3:10
Let everyone remain in that trade and office *in which he has been*
called. 1 Cor 7:24

[7]And for their work they can receive whatever is necessary excepting money. [8]And when it is necessary, they may seek alms like other poor people. [9]And it is lawful for them to have the tools and instruments suitable for their trades.[a]

[10]Let all the brothers always strive to exert themselves in doing good works, for it is written: "Always do something good that the devil may find you occupied."[b] [11]And again: "Idleness is an enemy of the soul."[c] [12]Servants of God, therefore, must always apply themselves to prayer or some good work.

[13]Wherever the brothers may be, either in hermitages or other places, let them be careful not to make any place their own or contend with anyone for it. [14]Whoever comes to them, friend or foe, thief or robber, let him be received with kindness.

[15]Wherever the brothers may be and in whatever place they meet,[d]
they should respect spiritually and attentively one another, and *honor*
one another without complaining. [16]Let them be careful not to appear 1 Pt 4:9
outwardly as sad and gloomy hypocrites but show themselves *joyful,*
cheerful and consistently gracious *in the Lord.* Phil 4:4

[Chapter VIII: Let the Brothers Not Receive Money]

[1]The Lord teaches in the Gospel: *Watch, beware of all* malice and
greed. [2]*Guard yourselves* against the anxieties of this world and the Lk 12:15
cares of this life. Lk 21:34; Mt 13:22

[3]Let none of the brothers, therefore, wherever he may be or go, carry, receive, or have received in any way coin or money, whether for clothing, books, or payment for some work—indeed, not for any reason, unless for an evident need of the sick brothers; because we should

a. While all the early manuscripts contain the word *necessaria* [necessary], in preparing his critical edition of the text Esser chose to follow the earliest edition of this document, Angelo Clareno's *Expositio Regulae Fratrum Minorum,* c. 1321-1323, which has *opportuna* [suitable]. Cf. Angelo Clareno, *Expositio Regulae Fratrum Minorum,* edited by Livarius Oliger (Quaracchi Ad Aquas Claras, Collegium S. Bonaventurae, 1912).

b. Francis alludes to the teachings of Saint Gregory the Great, *Homilia XIII in Evangelica* (PL 76:1123); Saint Jerome, *Epistola* 125 (PL 22:1078); Ionae Aureliano, *Institutito Laicalis* 3:6 (PL 106:2450); and Saint Anselm, *Epistola* 3:49 (PL 159:81A).

c. Cf. Saint Benedict, *Rule,* Chapter XLVIII:1.

d. Francis uses an unusual word in this passage, *revidere,* to indicate the encounters of the brothers. It has the sense of seeing one another anew and may have been intended to emphasize the new appreciation of one brother for another after an absence.

not think of coin or money having any greater usefulness than stones.[a]
[4]The devil wants to blind those who desire or consider it better than
Mt 19:27 stones. [5]May we who have left all things, then, be careful of not losing
the kingdom of heaven for so little.

[6]If we find coins anywhere, let us pay no more attention to them
than to the dust we trample underfoot, for *vanity of vanities and all is*
Eccl 1:2 *vanity.* [7]If by chance, which God forbid, it happens that some brother is
collecting or holding coin or money, unless it is only for the aforesaid
needs of the sick, let all the brothers consider him a deceptive brother,
Jn 12:6 an apostate, a thief, a robber, and as the one who held the money bag,
unless he has sincerely repented.

[8]Let the brothers in no way receive, arrange to receive, seek, or arrange to seek money for leper colonies or coins for any house or place;[b] and let them not accompany anyone begging money or coins for such places. [9]However, the brothers can perform for those places other services not contrary to our life with the blessing of God. [10]Nevertheless, the brothers can beg alms for a manifest need of the lepers. [11]But let them beware of money. [12]Similarly, let all the brothers be careful of going throughout the world for filthy gain.

[Chapter IX: Begging Alms]

[1]Let all the brothers strive to follow the humility and poverty of our
Lord Jesus Christ and let them remember that we should have nothing
else in the whole world except, as the Apostle says: *having food and*
1 Tm 6:8 *clothing, we are content with these.*

[2]They must rejoice when they live among people considered of little value and looked down upon, among the poor and the powerless, the sick and the lepers, and the beggars by the wayside.

[3]When it is necessary, they may go for alms. [4]Let them not be
ashamed and remember, moreover, that our Lord Jesus Christ, *the Son of*
Jn 11:27; Is 50:7 *the* all powerful *living God, set His face like flint* and was not ashamed.
[5]He was poor and a stranger and lived on alms—He, the Blessed Virgin,
and His disciples. [6]When people revile them and refuse to give them
alms, let them thank God for this because they will receive great honor
before the tribunal of our Lord Jesus Christ for such insults. [7]Let them

a. Cf. supra ER II, p.64, c.

b. This verse suggests three locations in need of alms: hospices for the poor or for lepers are particularly singled out.

realize that a reproach is imputed not to those who suffer it but to those who caused it. [8]Alms are a legacy and a justice due to the poor that our Lord Jesus Christ acquired for us. [9]The brothers who work at acquiring them will receive a great reward and enable those who give them to gain and acquire one; for all that people leave behind in the world will perish, but they will have a reward from the Lord for the charity and almsgiving they have done.

[10]Let each one confidently make known his need to another that the other might discover what is needed and minister to him. [11]Let each one love and care for his brother as a mother loves and cares for her son in those matters in which God has given him the grace. [12]*Let the one* 1 Thes 2:7
who does not eat not judge the one who does. Rom 14:3b

[13]Whenever a need arises, all the brothers, wherever they may be, are permitted to consume whatever food people can eat, as the Lord says of David who ate *the loaves of offering that only the priests could* Mt 12:4
lawfully eat. Mk 2:26

[14]Let them remember what the Lord says: *Be careful that your hearts do not become drowsy from carousing, drunkenness and the anxieties of daily life, and that the day catches you by surprise;* [15]*for that day will assault everyone who lives on the face of the earth like a trap.* [16]Similarly, in time of an obvious need, all the brothers may do as Lk 21:34-35
the Lord has given them the grace to satisfy their needs, because necessity has no law.[a]

[Chapter X: The Sick Brothers][b]

[1]If any of the brothers falls sick, wherever he may be, let the other brothers not leave him behind unless one of the brothers, or even several of them, if necessary, is designated to serve him as "they would want to be served themselves."[c] [2]In case of the greatest need, however, they can entrust him to someone who should do what needs to be done for his sickness.

[3]I beg the sick brother to thank God for everything and to desire to be whatever the Lord wills, whether sick or well, because God teaches all those He *has destined for eternal life* "by the torments of punish- Acts 13:48

a. *Decretum Gratiani* P. II, C.q.1 glossa ante c.40.

b. The following chapters, X-XIII, seem to offer clarifications or warnings which were added at a later date. They flow from the material contained in Chapter VII.

c. Augustine, *Epistola* Cl. II, 40, IV, 4; cf. Mt 7:12.

ments," sicknesses, "and the spirit of sorrow," as the Lord says: *Those*
Rv 3:19 *whom I love, I* correct *and chastise.*[a]

[4]If anyone is disturbed or angry at either God or his brothers, or perhaps anxiously and forcefully seeks medicine with too much of a desire to free the flesh that is soon to die and is an enemy of the soul: this comes to him from the Evil One and is carnal. He does not seem to be one of the brothers because he loves his body more than his soul.

[Chapter XI: The Brothers Should Not Revile or Detract, But Should Love One Another]

2 Tm 2:14 [1]Let all the brothers be careful not to slander or engage in disputes;
[2]let them strive, instead, to keep silence whenever God gives them the
grace. [3]Let them not quarrel among themselves or with others but
Lk 17:10 strive to respond humbly, saying: *I am a useless servant.* [4]Let them not
become angry because *whoever is angry with his brother is liable to*
judgment; whoever says to his brother "fool" shall be answerable to
Mt 5:22 *the Council; whoever says "fool" will be liable to fiery Gehenna.*

[5]Let them love one another, as the Lord says: *This is my command-*
Jn 15:12 *ment: love one another as I have loved you.* [6]Let them express the love
Jas 2:18 they have for one another by their deeds, as the Apostle says: *Let us not*
1 Jn 3:18 *love in word or speech, but in deed and truth.*

Ti 3:2 [7]*Let them revile no one.* [8]Let them not grumble or detract from oth-
Rom 1:29-30 ers, for it is written: *Gossips* and *detractors* are *detestable* to God. [9]Let
Ti 3:2 them be *modest by showing graciousness toward everyone.* [10]Let them
Mt 7:1 not judge or condemn. [11]As the Lord says, let them not consider the
Mt 7:3; Lk 6:41 least sins of others; [12]instead, let them reflect more upon their own sins
Is 38:15 *in the bitterness of their soul.* [13]Let them struggle *to enter through the*
Lk 13:24 *narrow gate,* for the Lord says: *The gate is narrow and the road that*
Mt 7:14 *leads to life constricted; those who find it are few.*

[Chapter XII: Impure Glances and Frequent Association with Women]

[1]Wherever they may be or may go, let all the brothers avoid evil glances and association with women. [2]No one may counsel them, travel alone with them or eat out of the same dish with them. [3]When giving penance or some spiritual advice, let priests speak with them in

a. Cf. Gregory the Great, *Homilia in Evangelia* XVIII 18; PL 76, 1148. This is a homily on Luke X 1-10, the missionary discourse. Francis adds "sicknesses" to the text.

a becoming way. [4]Absolutely no woman may be received to obedience by any brother, but after spiritual advice has been given to her, let her do penance wherever she wants.

[5]Let us all keep close watch over ourselves and keep all our members clean, for the Lord says: *Whoever looks at a woman with lust has already committed adultery with her in his heart;* [6]and the Apostle: *Do you not know that your members are a temple of the Holy Spirit?* Therefore, whoever *violates God's temple, God will destroy.*

Mt 5:28
1 Cor 6:19
1 Cor 3:17

[Chapter XIII: Avoiding Fornication]

[1]If, at the instigation of the devil, any brother commits fornication, let him be deprived of the habit he has lost by his wickedness, put it aside completely, and be altogether expelled from our Order.[a] [2]Afterwards he may do penance.[b]

1 Cor 5:4-5

[Chapter XIV: How the Brothers Should Go Through the World]

[1]When the brothers go through the world, let them take *nothing* for the journey, *neither knapsack, nor purse, nor bread, nor money, nor walking stick.* [2]*Whatever house they enter,* let them first say: Peace to this house. [3]They may eat and drink *what is placed before them* for as long as they stay *in that house.* [4]Let them not resist anyone evil, but whoever strikes them on one cheek, let them offer him the other as well. [5]*Whoever takes their cloak, let them not withhold their tunic.* [6]*Let them give to all who ask of them and whoever takes what is theirs, let them not seek to take it back.*

Lk 9:3; 10:4; Mt 10:10
Lk 10:5
Lk 10:7
Mt 5:39; Lk 6:29; Lk 6:29
Lk 6:30

[Chapter XV: The Brothers May Not Ride Horses]

[1]I command all my brothers, both cleric and lay, that when they go through the world or dwell in places they in no way keep any animal either with them, in the care of another, or in any other way. [2]Let it not be lawful for them to ride horseback unless they are compelled by sickness or a great need.[c]

a. The only use of *habitus* [habit] suggests that this chapter was written after November 22, 1220, the promulgation of *Cum secundum consilium* which contains the phrase *habitus vitae vestrae* [the habit of your life], cf. infra pp. 560-561.

b. The harsh, juridical tone of this chapter reflects Paul's reproach of similar sins in 1 Corinthians 5: 1b-2: "It is widely reported that there is fornication among you . . . The one who did this deed should be expelled from your midst."

c. These pieces of legislation were also found in the other itinerant forms of life of this period, e.g. the Humiliati, for traveling on horseback or keeping pets were seen as signs of affluence.

[Chapter XVI: Those Going Among the Saracens and Other Nonbelievers][a]

[1]The Lord says: *Behold I am sending you like sheep in the midst of*
Mt 10:16 *wolves.* [2]Therefore, *be prudent as serpents and simple as doves.* [3]Let
any brother, then, who desires by divine inspiration to go among the
Saracens and other nonbelievers, go with the permission of his minister and servant.[b] [4]If he sees they are fit to be sent, the minister may give
them permission and not oppose them, for he will be bound to render an
Lk 16:2 accounting to the Lord if he has proceeded without discernment in this
and other matters.

[5]As for the brothers who go, they can live spiritually among the Saracens and nonbelievers in two ways. [6]One way is not to engage in argu-
Ti 3:2; 2 Tm 2:14 ments or disputes but to be subject *to every human creature for God's*
1 Pt 2:13 *sake* and to acknowledge that they are Christians. [7]The other way is to
announce the Word of God, when they see it pleases the Lord, in order
that [unbelievers] may believe in almighty God, the Father, the Son
and the Holy Spirit, the Creator of all, the Son, the Redeemer and Savior, and be baptized and become Christians because *no one can enter*
Jn 3:5 *the kingdom of God without being reborn of water and the Holy Spirit.*

[8]They can say to them and the others these and other things which
please God because the Lord says in the Gospel: *Whoever acknowl-*
Mt 10:32 *edges me before others I will acknowledge before my heavenly Father.*
[9]*Whoever is ashamed of me and of my words, the Son of Man will be*
Lk 9:26 *ashamed of when he comes in his glory and in the glory of the Father.*

[10]Wherever they may be, let all my brothers remember that they have
given themselves and abandoned their bodies to the Lord Jesus Christ.
[11]For love of Him, they must make themselves vulnerable to their ene-
mies, both visible and invisible, because the Lord says: *Whoever loses his*
Lk 9:24; Mt 25:46 *life because of me will save it* in eternal life.[c] [12]*Blessed are they who suffer*
Mt 5:10 *persecution for the sake of justice, for theirs is the kingdom of heaven.* [13]*If*
Jn 15:20 *they have persecuted me, they will also persecute you.* [14]*If they persecute*
Mt 10:23; Mt 5:11; Lk 6:22 *you in one town, flee to another.* [15]*Blessed are you when people hate you,*

a. The inspiration for the following initiative is the urging of Pope Innocent III whose letter, *De negotio Terrae Sanctae* in 1213, and exhortation at the beginning of the Fourth Lateran Council encouraged "the recovery of the Holy Land for the reformation of the Universal Church."

b. Esser chose to follow the edition of Angelo Clareno which does not contain this phrase "divine inspiration."

c. Prince Peter of Portugal notes that the desire for martyrdom characterized the lives of the early brothers who were initially received with kindness by the Muslims and were martyred mainly because of their unbending zeal. "Therefore, according to the form of their Rule, they requested permission to go among the Saracens so that, if possible, they might be able to bring forth fruit among them." Cf. Peter of Portugal, *Martyrum quinque fratrum;* also Roger of Wendover, *Chronicle,* and the *Gesta Senonensis ecclesiare.*

speak evil of you, persecute, expel, and abuse you, denounce your name Mt 5:11
as evil and utter every kind of slander against you because of me. [16]*Re-* Lk 6:22; Mt 5:11
joice and be glad on that day because your reward is great in heaven. Lk 6:23; Mt 5:12

[17]*I tell you, my friends, do not be afraid of them* [18]*and do not fear* Lk 12:4
those who kill the body and afterwards have nothing more to do. [19]*See* Mt 10:28; Lk 12:4
that you are not alarmed. [20]*For by your patience, you will possess your* Mt 24:6
souls; [21]*whoever perseveres to the end will be saved.* Lk 21:19; Mt 10:22//24:13

[Chapter XVII: Preachers]

[1]Let no brother preach contrary to the rite and practice of the Church or without the permission of his minister. [2]Let the minister be careful of granting it without discernment to anyone. [3]Let all the brothers, however, preach by their deeds. [4]No minister or preacher may make a ministry of the brothers or the office of preaching his own, but, when he is told, let him set it aside without objection.[a]

[5]In the love that is God, therefore, I beg all my brothers—those who 1 Jn 4:16
preach, pray, or work, cleric or lay—to strive to humble themselves in everything, [6]not to boast or delight in themselves or inwardly exalt themselves because of the good words and deeds or, for that matter, because of any good that God sometimes says or does or works in and through them, in keeping with what the Lord says: *Do not rejoice be-*
cause the spirits are subject to you. [7]We may know with certainty that Lk 10:20
nothing belongs to us except our vices and sins. [8]We must rejoice, instead, when we fall *into various trials* and, in this world, suffer every Jas 1:2
kind of anguish or distress of soul and body for the sake of eternal life.

[9]Therefore, let all the brothers, beware of all pride and vainglory. [10]Let us guard ourselves from the wisdom of this world and the prudence of the flesh. [11]Because the spirit of the flesh very much desires Rm 8:6
and strives to have the words but cares little for the activity; it does not seek a religion and holiness in an interior spirit, [12]but wants and desires to have a religion and a holiness outwardly apparent to people. [13]They are the ones of whom the Lord says: *Amen, I say to you, they have re-*
ceived their reward. Mt 6:2

[14]The Spirit of the Lord, however, wants the flesh to be mortified and looked down upon, considered of little worth and rejected. [15]It

a. These opening three verses are probably the result of the Fourth Lateran Council which attempted to restrict the office of preaching to those who were qualified. The remaining section of this chapter may have been written at an earlier period when Francis was eager to teach his brothers how they should react to the successful unfolding of their ministries.

strives for humility and patience, the pure, simple and true peace of the spirit. [16]Above all, it desires the divine fear, the divine wisdom and the divine love of the Father, Son and Holy Spirit.

[17]Let us refer all good
to the Lord, God Almighty and Most High,
acknowledge that every good is His,
and thank Him,
"from Whom all good comes,
for everything."[a]
[18]May He,
the Almighty and Most High,
the only true God,
have, be given, and receive
all honor and respect,
all praise and blessing,
all thanks and glory,
to Whom all good belongs,
Lk 18:19 He Who alone is good.
[19]When we see or hear evil spoken or done
or God blasphemed,
let us speak well and do well
and praise God
Rom 12:21; 1:25 *Who is blessed forever.*[b]

[Chapter XVIII: How the Ministers Should Meet One Another][c]

[1]Once a year on the feast of Saint Michael the Archangel, each minister can come together with his brothers wherever they wish to treat of those things that pertain to God.

[2]All the ministers who are in regions overseas and beyond the Alps may come to the Chapter of Pentecost in the church of Saint Mary of the Portiuncula once every three years, and the other ministers once a

a. Oration of Fifth Sunday after Easter.

b. Many manuscripts conclude this chapter with "Amen" suggesting that ER, in one of its earlier forms, came to an end at this point.

c. This chapter shows the influence of the Fourth Lateran Council, 1215, which, in its twelfth canon, ordained: "In every ecclesiastical province there shall be held every three years, saving the rights of the diocesan ordinaries, a general chapter of abbots and priors having no abbots, who have not become accustomed to celebrate such chapters." Cf. Herbert J. Schroeder, *Disciplinary Decrees of the General Councils* (St. Louis: Herder and Herder, 1938), page 253.

year, unless it has been decreed otherwise by the minister and servant of the entire fraternity.

[Chapter XIX: That the Brothers Live as Catholics][a]

[1]Let all the brothers be, live, and speak as Catholics.

[2]If someone has strayed in word or in deed from Catholic faith and life and has not amended his ways, let him be expelled from our brotherhood.

[3]Let us consider all clerics and religious as our masters in all that pertains to the salvation of our soul and does not deviate from our religion, and let us respect their order, office, and administration in the Lord.

[Chapter XX: Penance and the Reception of the Body and Blood of Our Lord Jesus Christ][b]

[1]Let all my blessed brothers, both clerics and lay, confess their sins to priests of our religion.[c] [2]If they cannot, let them confess to other discerning and Catholic priests, knowing with certainty that, when they have received penance and absolution from any Catholic priest, they are without doubt absolved from their sins, provided they have humbly and faithfully fulfilled the penance imposed on them.

[3]If they have not been able to find a priest, however, let them confess to their brother, as the Apostle James says: *Confess your sins to one another.*[d] [4]Nevertheless, because of this, let them not fail to have Jas 5:16

a. The following directive also reflects the influence of the Fourth Lateran Council: in this instance, canon 1 which speaks of the "Catholic faith," canon 2 of the errors of Joachim of Fiore, and canon 3 which excommunicated and condemned ". . . everyone professing heresy against the holy, orthodox, catholic faith . . ."

b. Canon 21 of the Fourth Lateran Council prescribed: "All the faithful of both sexes, after they have reached the age of discerning, shall faithfully confess all their sins to their own priest at least once a year and perform the penance imposed to the best of their abilities, receiving reverently at least at Easter the sacrament of the Eucharist, unless perchance, at the advice of their priest, they may abstain for a time after its reception for a good reason; otherwise, they shall be cut off from the Church during life and deprived of Christian burial at death. Wherefore, let this salutary decree be published frequently in the churches that no one may find in the pleas of ignorance a shadow of excuse. Let the priest be discerning and cautious that he may pour wine and oil into the wounds of the one injured after the manner of a skillful physician, carefully inquiring into the situation of the sinner and the sin, from the nature of which he may understand what kind of advice to give and what remedy to apply, making use of different experiments to heal the sick one."

c. The need for priests of one's religion inevitably led to the gradual clericalization of the primitive fraternity, a refinement of the Fourth Lateran Council, Canon 21.

d. The practice of confessing sins to another Christian in the absence of a priest was common in the Middle Ages. It was seen as a means of expressing reconciliation among the community of the faithful.

Mt 18:18 recourse to a priest because the power of binding and loosing is granted only to priests.

[5]Contrite and having confessed in this way, let them receive the Body and Blood of our Lord Jesus Christ with great humility and respect remembering what the Lord says: *Whoever eats my flesh and*
Jn 6:54; Lk 22:19 *drinks my blood has eternal life* [6]and *Do this in memory of me.*

[Chapter XXI: The Praise and Exhortation That All the Brothers Can Make][a]

[1]Whenever it pleases them, all my brothers can announce this or similar exhortation and praise among all peoples with the blessing of God:

[2]Fear and honor,
praise and bless,
1 Thess 5:18 *give thanks* and adore
the Lord God Almighty in Trinity and in Unity,
Father, Son, and Holy Spirit,
the Creator of all.
Mt 3:2 [3]Do penance,
Lk 3:8 performing worthy fruits of penance
because we shall soon die.
Lk 6:38 [4]*Give and it will be given to you.*
Mt 6:14 [5]*Forgive and you shall be forgiven.*
[6]*If you do not forgive people their sins,*
Mk 11:25 the Lord *will not forgive you yours.*
Jas 5:16 *Confess all your sins.*
[7]Blessed are those who die in penance,
for they shall be in the kingdom of heaven.
[8]Woe to those who do not die in penance,
1 Jn 3:10 for they shall be *children of the devil*
Jn 8:41 whose works they do
Mt 18:8; 25:41 and they shall go *into everlasting fire.*
[9]Beware of and abstain from every evil
and persevere in good till the end.

a. The nature and origin of these verses have been interpreted in a variety of ways. Most authors agree, however, that they suggest the influence of the Fourth Lateran Council's concern for orthodox preaching as well as Francis's own eagerness to promote the embrace of a life of penance.

[Chapter XXII: An Admonition to the Brothers][a]

[1]All my brothers: let us pay attention to what the Lord says: *Love your*
enemies and *do good to those who hate you* [2]for our Lord Jesus Christ, Mt 5:44
Whose footprints we must follow, called His betrayer a friend and will- 1 Pt 2:21; Mt 26:50
ingly offered Himself to His executioners. Jn 10:18

[3]Our friends, therefore, are all those who unjustly inflict upon us
distress and anguish, shame and injury, sorrow and punishment, martyrdom and death. [4]We must love them greatly for we shall possess
eternal life because of what they bring us.

[5]And let us hate our body with its vices and sins, because by living
according to the flesh, the devil wishes to take away from us the love of Rom 8:4
Jesus Christ and eternal life and to lose himself in hell with everyone
else. [6]Because, by our own fault, we are disgusting, miserable and opposed to good, yet prompt and inclined to evil, for, as the Lord says in
the Gospel: [7]*From the heart proceed and come evil thoughts, adultery,* Mk 7:21; Mt 15:19
fornication, murder, theft, greed, malice, deceit, licentiousness, envy, Mk 7:21-22
false witness, blasphemy, foolishness. [8]*All these evils come from* Mt 15:19; Mk 7:23
within, from a person's heart, and these are what defile a person. Mk 7:23; Mt 15:20

[9]Now that we have left the world, however, we have nothing else to
do but to follow the will of the Lord and to please Him. [10]Let us be careful that we are not earth along the wayside, or that which is rocky or full
of thorns, in keeping with what the Lord says in the Gospel: [11]*The word*
of God is a seed. Lk 8:11

[12]What *fell along the wayside and was trampled under foot, how-* Lk 8:5
ever, •*are those who hear the word* and do not understand it. •[13]*The* •Lk 8:12; •Mt 13:19
devil comes •*immediately* •*and snatches* •*what was planted in their* •Lk 8:12; •Mk 4:15; •Mt 13:19
hearts •*and takes the word from their hearts that they may not believe* •Mk 4:15
and be saved. •Lk 8:12

[14]What *fell on rocky ground, however,* •*are those who, as soon as* Mt 13:20
they hear the word, receive it at once with joy. •[15]*But when tribulation* •Mk 4:16
and persecution come because of the word, they immediately fall away. Mt 13:21
These have no roots in them; they last only for a time, •because *they be-*
lieve only for a time •*and fall away in time of trial.* •Mk 4:17; •Lk 8:13

[16]What *fell among thorns, however, are those* •*who hear the word of* Lk 8:14
God •*and the anxiety* •*and worries of this world,* •*the lure of riches,* •*and* •Mk 4:18; •Mt 13:22; •Mk 4:19; •Mt 13:22

a. Although some authors see this chapter as a "testament" which Francis left his followers prior to his departure for the Middle East in the later summer of 1219, others maintain that it is a statement or synthesis of his understanding of Gospel discipleship or a "catechism" of prayer and, in this context, a summary of Franciscan life.

other inordinate desires intrude and choke the word and they remain
•Mk 4:19 *without fruit.*
Mt 13:23; •Lk 8:15 17 *But what was sown •in good soil •are those who hear the word with*
•Mt 18:23; •Mt 13:23 *a good and excellent heart,* •understand •*and preserve it and bear fruit*
•Lk 8:15 *in patience.*
18 Therefore, as the Lord says, brothers, let us let *the dead bury their*
Mt 8:22 *own dead.* 19 And let us beware of the malice and craftiness of Satan,
who does not want anyone to turn his mind and heart to God. 20 And
1 Pt 5:8 prowling around he wants to ensnare a person's heart under the guise of
some reward or assistance, to choke out the word and precepts of the
Mk 4:19 Lord from our memory, and, desiring a person's heart, [he wants] to
blind it through worldly affairs and concerns and to live there, as the
Lord says: 21 *When an unclean spirit goes out of a person, it roams*
Mt 12:43; Lk 11:24 *through arid and waterless regions seeking rest;* 22 *and not finding any,*
Lk 11:24 *it says: "I will return to my home from which I came."* 23 And *coming*
Mt 12:44 *upon it, it finds it empty, swept, clean and tidied.* 24 And *it goes off and*
brings seven other spirits more wicked than itself, who move in and
Lk 11:26 *dwell there, and the last state of that person is worse than the first.*
25 Therefore, all my brothers, let us be very much on our guard that,
under the guise of some reward or assistance, we do not lose or take our
1 Jn 4:16 mind away from God. 26 But, in the holy love which is God, I beg all my
brothers, both the ministers and the others, after overcoming every impediment and putting aside every care and anxiety, to serve, love,
honor and adore the Lord God with a clean heart and a pure mind in
whatever way they are best able to do so, for that is what He wants
above all else.
Jn 14:23 27 Let us always make a home and a dwelling place there for Him
Who is the Lord God Almighty, Father, Son and Holy Spirit, Who
says: *Be vigilant at all times and pray that you have the strength to es-*
cape the tribulations that are imminent and to stand before the Son of
Lk 21:36; Mk 11:25; Lk 11:2; Mt 6:9 *Man.* 28 *When you stand to pray say: Our Father in heaven.* 29 And let us
adore Him with a pure heart, *because it is necessary to pray always and*
Lk 18:1; Jn 4:23 *not lose heart;* 30 *for the Father seeks such* people who adore Him.
31 *God is Spirit and those who adore Him must adore Him in Spirit and*
Jn 4:24 *truth.* 32 Let us have recourse to Him as *to the Shepherd and Guardian*
1 Pt 2:25 *of our souls,* Who says: "I am the Good Shepherd Who feeds My sheep
Jn 10:14-15 and I lay down My life for my sheep."
33 *All of you are brothers.* 34 *Do not call anyone on earth your father;*
you have but one Father in heaven. 35 *Do not call yourselves teachers;*

you have but one Teacher in heaven. [36]*If you remain in me and my* Mt 23:8-10
words remain in you, ask for whatever you want and it will be done for
you. [37]*Wherever two or three are gathered together in my name, there* Jn 15:7
am I in the midst of them. [38]*Behold I am with you until the end of the* Mt 18:20
world. [39]*The words I have spoken to you are spirit and life.* [40]*I am the* Mt 28:20; Jn 6:63
Way, the Truth, and the Life. Jn 14:6

[41]Let us, therefore, hold onto the words, the life, the teaching and
the Holy Gospel of Him Who humbled Himself to beg His Father for us
and to make His name known saying: *Father, glorify Your name* •*and* Jn 12:28a
glorify Your Son that Your Son may glorify You. •Jn 17:1b

[42]Father, *I have made Your name known to those whom You have*
given me. •*The words You gave to me I have given to them, and they* Jn 17:6
have accepted them and truly have known that I came from You and
they have believed that You sent me. [43]*I pray for them, not for the*
world, [44]*but for those You have given me, because they are Yours and*
everything of mine is Yours. •[45]Holy Father, *keep in Your name those* •Jn 17:8-10
You have given me that they may be one as We are. •[46]*I say this while in* •Jn 17:11b
the world that they may have joy completely. [47]*I gave them Your word,*
and the world hated them, because they do not belong to the world as I
do not belong to the world. [48]*I do not ask you to take them out of the*
world but that you keep them from the evil one. •[49]*Glorify them in truth.* •Jn 17:13b-15
[50]*Your word is truth.*

[51]*As You sent me into the world, so I sent them into the world.* [52]*And*
I sanctify myself for them that they also may be sanctified in truth. [53]*I*
ask not only for them but also for those who will believe in me through
them, •*that they may be brought to perfection as one, and the world may* •Jn 17:17-20
know that You have sent me and loved them as You loved me. •[54]*I shall* •Jn 17:23
make known to them Your name, that the love with which You loved me
may be in them and I in them. •[55]*Father, I wish that those whom You* •Jn 17:26
have given me may be where I am that they may see Your glory •*in Your* •Jn 17:24
kingdom. •Mt 20:21

[Chapter XXIII: Prayer and Thanksgiving]

[1]All-powerful, most holy,
Almighty and supreme God,
Holy and just *Father,* Jn 17:11
Lord King *of heaven and earth* Mt 11:25
we thank You for Yourself

for through Your holy will
and through Your only Son
with the Holy Spirit
You have created everything spiritual and corporal
and, after making us *in Your own image and likeness,*
Gn 1:26; 2:15 *You placed us in paradise.*

[2]Through our own fault we fell.

[3]We thank You
for as through Your Son You created us,
so through Your holy love
Jn 17:26 *with which You loved us*
You brought about His birth
as true God and true man
by the glorious, ever-virgin, most blessed, holy Mary
and You willed to redeem us captives
through His cross and blood and death.

[4]We thank You
for Your Son Himself will come again
in the glory of His majesty
to send into the eternal fire
the wicked ones
who have not done penance
and have not known You
and to say to all those
who have known You, adored You and served You in penance:
"*Come, you blessed of my Father,*
receive *the kingdom prepared for you*
Mt 25:34 from the beginning *of the world.*"

[5]Because all of us, wretches and sinners,
are not worthy to pronounce Your name,
we humbly ask
our Lord Jesus Christ,
Your *beloved Son,*
Mt 17:5 *in Whom You were well pleased,*
together with the Holy Spirit,

the Paraclete,
to give You thanks,
for everything
as it pleases You and Him,
Who always satisfies You in everything,
through Whom You have done so much for us.
Alleluia!

[6]Because of Your love,
we humbly beg
the glorious Mother, the most blessed, ever-virgin Mary,
Blessed Michael, Gabriel, and Raphael,
all the choirs of the blessed
seraphim, cherubim, thrones, dominations,
principalities, powers, virtues, Col 1:15
angels, archangels,
Blessed John the Baptist,
John the Evangelist,
Peter, Paul,
the blessed patriarchs and prophets,
the innocents, apostles, evangelists, disciples,
the martyrs, confessors and virgins,
the blessed Elijah and Henoch,
all the saints who were, who will be, and who are
to give You thanks for these things,
as it pleases You,
God true and supreme,
eternal and living,
with Your most beloved Son,
our Lord Jesus Christ,
and the Holy Spirit,
the Paraclete,
world without end.
Amen.
Alleluia! Rv 19:3,4

[7]All of us lesser brothers, *useless servants,* Lk 17:10
humbly ask and beg
those who wish to serve the Lord God

within the holy Catholic and Apostolic Church
and all the following orders:
priests, deacons, subdeacons,
acolytes, exorcists, lectors, porters, and all clerics,
all religious men and women,
all penitents and youths,[a]
the poor and the needy,
kings and princes,
workers and farmers,
servants and masters,
all virgins, continent and married women,
all lay people, men and women,
all children, adolescents, young and old,
the healthy and the sick,
all the small and the great,
Rv 7:9 all peoples, races, tribes, and tongues,
all nations and all peoples everywhere on earth,
who are and who will be
to persevere in the true faith and in penance
for otherwise no one will be saved.

8 *With our whole heart,*
our whole soul,
our whole mind,
with our whole strength and fortitude
Lk 10:27//Mk 12:30-33 *with our whole understanding*
with all our powers
with every effort,
every affection,
every feeling,
every desire and wish
Mk 12:30 let us all love *the Lord God*
Who has given and gives to each one of us
our whole body, our whole soul and our whole life,
Tb 13:5 Who has created, redeemed and will save us by His mercy alone,
Who did and does everything good for us,
miserable and wretched,

a. The word here is *conversi* [penitents], those lay penitents who became associated with Cistercian monasteries in positions of service.

rotten and foul,
ungrateful and evil ones.

[9]Therefore,
let us desire nothing else,
let us want nothing else,
let nothing else please us and cause us delight
except our Creator, Redeemer and Savior,
the only true God,
Who is the fullness of good,
all good, every good, the true and supreme good,
Who alone is good, Lk 18:19
merciful, gentle, delightful, and sweet,
Who alone is holy,
just, true, holy, and upright,
Who alone is kind, innocent, clean,
from Whom, *through Whom* and in Whom Heb 2:10
is all pardon, all grace, all glory
of all penitents and just ones,
of all the blessed rejoicing together in heaven.

[10]Therefore,
let nothing hinder us,
nothing separate us,
nothing come between us.

[11]Wherever we are,
in every place,
at every hour,
at every time of the day,
every day and continually,
let all of us truly and humbly believe,
hold in our heart and love,
honor, adore, serve,
praise and bless,
glorify and exalt,
magnify and give thanks
to the Most High and Supreme Eternal God
Trinity and Unity,

Mt 18:19 *Father, Son and Holy Spirit,*
Creator of all,
Savior of all
Who believe and hope in Him,
and love Him, Who,
without beginning and end,
is unchangeable, invisible,
indescribable, ineffable,
Rom 11:33 *incomprehensible, unfathomable,*
blessed, praiseworthy,
Dn 3:52 *glorious, exalted,*
sublime, most high,
gentle, lovable, delightful,
and totally desirable above all else
for ever.
Amen.

[Chapter XXIV: Conclusion][a]

Col 3:17 [1]*In the name of the Lord!*

I ask all my brothers to learn and frequently call to mind the tenor and sense of what has been written in this life for the salvation of our souls. [2]I beg God, Who is All-powerful, Three and One, to bless all who teach, learn, retain, remember, and put into practice these things, each time they repeat and do what has been written there for the salvation of our soul, [3]and, kissing their feet, I implore everyone to love, keep, and treasure them greatly.

[4]On behalf of Almighty God and of the Lord Pope, and by obedience, I, Brother Francis, firmly command and decree that no one *delete*
Dt 4:2; 12:32 or *add* to what has been written in this life.

The brothers may have no other Rule.

[5]Glory be to the Father, and to the Son, and to the Holy Spirit. As it was in the beginning, is now, and will be forever. Amen.

a. The presence of this chapter in the *propositum vitae* or in a very early edition of *The Earlier Rule* has been widely debated.

Fragments
(1209-1223)

A manuscript of the Worchester Cathedral in England and the passing comments of Thomas of Celano and Hugh of Digne present formative exhortations or quotations from what might have been other versions of an early form of life or rule. While not definitive, these texts or fragments offer insights into not only Francis's understanding of the Gospel life but also those of his early followers.

I. Fragments Found in a Manuscript in the Worchester Cathedral:[a]

[1] [All my brothers: let us pay attention to what the Lord says: *Love your*
enemies and *do good to those who hate you* for our Lord Jesus Christ, Mt 5:44
Whose footprints we must follow, called His betrayer a friend and will- 1 Pt 2:21; Mt 26:50
ingly offered Himself to His executioners. [2] Our friends, therefore, are Jn 10:18
all those who unjustly bring us distress and anguish, shame and][b] injury, sorrow and punishment, martyrdom and death; we must love them greatly for we will possess eternal life because of what they bring us.

[3] Let us CHASTISE our body CRUCIFYING IT with its vices, CONCUPIS-
CENCE and sins, because by living according to the flesh, the devil Rom 8:4
wishes to take away from us the love of Jesus Christ and eternal life and
to lose himself in hell with everyone else.[c] [4] Because, by our own fault,
we are disgusting, miserable and opposed to good, yet prompt and inclined to evil, [5] for, as the Lord says in the Gospel: *From the heart pro-*
ceed and come evil thoughts ET CETERA. Mk 7:21

[6] Now that we have left the world, however, we have nothing else to
do but BE EAGER to follow the will of the Lord and to please Him. [7] Let
us be careful that we are not earth on the path, or that which is rocky or
full of thorns, in keeping with what the Lord says in the Gospel: *The*

a. These fragments can be found in a manuscript of the Library of the Worchester Cathedral, Worchester, England, Codex Q 27, dated in the early part of the fourteenth century. It contains various treatises on penance, e.g., in the school of Augustine, Dominic, and Francis. Along with these fragments there is also a copy of Francis's *Testament*.

b. This and future lengthy bracketed passages are interpolations of Esser as the manuscript is difficult to decipher.

c. Those passages placed in capital letters indicated new words or phrases not found in *The Earlier Rule*.

Lk 8:11 *word of God is a seed.* [8]What *fell on the path and was trampled under*
Lk 8:5; Lk 8:15 *foot,* ET CETERA UNTIL: *and bear fruit in patience.*[a]

Mt 8:22 [9]Therefore, as the Lord says, brothers, let us let *the dead* . . . [10]Let us
beware of the malice and skill of Satan, who does not want someone to
1 Pt 5:8 turn his strength or heart to the Lord God. [11]As he prowls about he
wants to ensnare a person's heart under the guise of some reward or assistance, to choke out the word and precepts of the Lord from our mem-
Mk 4:19 ory, and, desiring a person's heart, to blind it through worldly affairs
and concerns and to live there, as the Lord says: [12]*When an unclean*
Mt 12:43 *spirit* . . . ET CETERA UNTIL: [13]*the last state of that person is worse than*
Lk 11:26 *the first.*

[14]Therefore, all my brothers, let us be very much on our guard that,
under the guise of some reward or assistance, we do not lose or take our
1 Jn 4:16 mind away from God. [15]But, in the holy love that is God, I beg all my
brothers, both the ministers and the others, after overcoming every impediment and putting aside every care and anxiety, to serve, love,
honor and adore the Lord God with a clean heart and a pure mind in
whatever way they are best able to do so for that is what He wants
Jn 14:23 above all else. [16]Let us always make a home and a dwelling place for
Him Who is the Lord God Almighty, Father, Son and Holy Spirit, Who
says: *Be vigilant at all times and pray that you have the strength to es-*
cape the tribulations that are imminent and to stand before the Son of
Lk 21:36; Mk 11:25; Lk 11:2; Mt 6:9 *Man. When you stand to pray, say: Our Father in heaven.* [17]Let us
adore Him with a pure heart, *because it is necessary to pray always and*
Lk 18:1; Jn 4:23 *not lose heart; for the Father seeks such* people who adore Him. [18]*God*
Jn 4:24 *is Spirit and those who adore Him must adore Him in Spirit and truth.*
[19]Let us have recourse to Him as *to the Shepherd and Guardian of our*
1 Pt 2:25; Jn 10:11 *souls,* Who says: *"I am the Good Shepherd . . ."* ET CETERA UNTIL: "I
Jn 10: 15 lay down My life for my sheep." [20]*All of you are brothers. Do not call*
Mt 23: 8-9 *anyone on earth your father,* ET CETERA. [21]*Do not call yourselves*
Mt 23:8-10 *teachers,* ET CETERA. [22]*If you remain in me and my words remain in*
Jn 15:7 *you, ask for whatever you want and it will be done for you.* [23]*Wherever*
Mt 18:20 *two or three are gathered together in my name,* ET CETERA. [24]*Behold I*
Mt 28:20 *am with you always,* ET CETERA. [25]*The words I have spoken to you are*
Jn 6:63; Jn 14:6 *spirit and life.* [26]*I am the Way, the Truth, and the Life.*

---

a. The *Worchester Fragment* frequently begins a Scripture passage and leaves off with *et cetera.* This causes difficulties in interpreting the text because of a temptation to exaggerate the interpretation of the biblical passage when scribes may well have been using shorthand.

[27]Let us, therefore, hold onto the words, the life, the teaching and
the Holy Gospel of our Lord Jesus Christ Who humbled Himself to beg
His Father for us and to make His name known saying: Father, *I have
made Your name known to those whom You have given me.* ET CETERA Jn 17:6
UNTIL: [28]*Father, I wish that those whom You have given me may be
where I am that they may see Your glory in Your kingdom.* [29]Glory to Jn 17:24; Mt 20:21
the Father and to the Son and to the Holy Spirit. As it was in the beginning, is now, and will be forever. Amen.

[30]Let them express the delight for the poor that they have for one another as the Apostle says: *Let us not love in word or speech,* ET CETERA. 1 Jn 3:18

[31]Let all the brothers, wherever they may be or may go, avoid evil
glances and association with women. Let no one counsel them.
FURTHER ON: [32]Let us all keep close watch over ourselves and keep all
our members clean, for the Lord says: *Whoever looks at a woman with
lust,* ET CETERA. Mt 5:28

FURTHER ON:

[33]When the brothers go through the world, let them take *nothing* for
the journey, *neither knapsack nor purse, nor bread, nor money,* nor Lk 10:4; Lk 9:3
walking stick. FURTHER DOWN: [34][Let them not resist anyone evil, but Mt 10:10
whoever strikes them on one cheek, let them offer] him the other as
well. [35][*Whoever takes their cloak and tunic, let them not withhold,*] Mt 5:39; Lk 6:29
and whoever [*takes*] *what is* [*theirs, let them not take it back.* Lk 6:30

[36]The brothers who] go with the permission of their minister can
live spiritually among nonbelievers in two ways. [37]One way is not to
engage in arguments or disputes but to be subject *to every human creature for God's sake* and to acknowledge they are Christians. [38]The 1 Pt 2:13
other way is to announce the Word of God, when they see it pleases
God, in order that they may believe in the all-powerful God, the Father,
the Son and the Holy Spirit. FURTHER ON:

[39]Let all my brothers, wherever they may be, remember that they
have given themselves and abandoned their bodies to the Lord Jesus
Christ. [40]For love of Him, they must endure persecution and death
from their enemies, both visible and invisible, ET CETERA.

FURTHER ON:

[41]Let the brothers preach in every way. [42]No minister or preacher
may make a ministry of the brothers or the office of preaching his own,
but, when he is told, let him set it aside without objection. [43]In the love
that is God, therefore, I beg all my brothers—those who preach, pray, 1 Jn 4:16
or work, cleric or lay—to strive to humble themselves in everything,

[44]not to glory or delight in themselves or inwardly exalt themselves in
the good words and deeds or, for that matter, in any good that God says
or does or at times works in and through them, in keeping with what the
Lk 10:20 Lord says: *Do not rejoice because the spirits are subject to you,* ET CET-
ERA.

[45]We may know with certainty that nothing belongs to us except our
vices and sins. [46]We must rejoice, instead, when we fall *into various*
Jas 1:2 *trials* and, in this world, suffer every kind of anguish or distress of soul
and body for the sake of eternal life.

[47]Let all the brothers, therefore, beware of all pride and vainglory.
Let us guard ourselves from the wisdom of this world and the prudence
Rm 8:6 of the flesh. [48]Because the spirit of the flesh very much wants and
strives to have the words but cares little for the manner of working; it
does not seek a religion and holiness in an interior spirit, [49]but wants
and desires to have a religion and holiness outwardly apparent to people. [50]They are the ones of whom the Lord says: *Amen, I say to you,*
Mt 6:2 *they have received their reward.* [51]The Spirit of the Lord, however,
wants the flesh to be mortified and despised, considered of little worth,
rejected and insulted. [52]It strives for humility and patience, PURE SIM-
PLICITY and true peace of the spirit. [53]Above all, it desires the divine
fear, the divine wisdom and the divine love of the Father, Son and Holy
Spirit.

[54]Let us refer all good to the Lord, God Almighty and Most High,
acknowledge that every good is His, and thank Him "from Whom all
Rom 1:25 good comes for everything." [55]May He, the Almighty and Most High,
the only true God, have, be given, and receive all honor and respect, all
praise and blessing, all thanks and glory, to Whom all good belongs,
He Who alone is good.

[56]When we see or hear evil spoken or done or God blasphemed, let
us speak well and do well and praise THE LORD *Who is blessed forever.*

[57]Let us consider all clerics and religious as our lords in all that pertains to the salvation of our soul and does not deviate from MY religion,
and let us respect their order, office, and administration in the Lord.[a]
FURTHER ON:

[58]Whenever it pleases them, all my brothers, INASMUCH AS GOD IN-
SPIRES THEM, can announce this or similar exhortations and praise
among all peoples with the blessing of God: [59]Fear and honor, praise

a. This passage presents a curious use of personal pronouns and the only first person singular possessive pronoun in these texts.

and bless, *give thanks* and adore the Lord God Almighty in Trinity and
in Unity, Father, Son, and Holy Spirit, the Creator of all. [60]Do penance,
performing fitting fruits of penance because YOU KNOW THAT we shall
soon die. [61]*Give and it will be given to you.* [62]*Forgive* and you will be
forgiven. [63]*If you do not forgive people their sins,* the Lord *will not forgive you yours.* Confess all your sins. [64]Blessed are those who die in
penance, for they shall be in the kingdom of heaven. [65]Woe to those
who do not die in penance, for they shall be *children of the devil* whose
works they do and they shall go *into everlasting fire.* [66]Beware of and
abstain from every evil and persevere till the end in good.

[67]Let the brothers, wherever they may be, either in hermitages or
other places, be careful not to make any place their own OR CONTEND
WITH ANYONE FOR IT. [68]Whoever comes to them, friend or foe, thief or
robber, let them in no way contend with him. [69]Wherever the brothers
may be and in whatever [place they may meet, they should see one another anew, spiritually and attentively, and *honor one another without
complaining.* [70]Let them be careful not to appear outwardly as sad and 1 Pt 4:9
gloomy hypocrites; but let them show themselves *joyful,* cheerful] and
consistently gracious *in the Lord.*[a] Phil 4:4

[71]I beg the sick brother to thank God for everything and to desire to
be whatever the Lord wills, whether sick or well, because God teaches
all those He *has destined for eternal life* "by the torments of punish- Acts 13:48
ments," sicknesses, "and the spirit of sorrow," as the Lord says: *Those
whom I love.* ET CETERA. Rv. 3:19

[72]THEREFORE I BEG ALL MY SICK BROTHERS not to be disturbed or
angry in their infirmities at either God or their brothers, or perhaps anxiously and forcefully seek medicine with too much of a desire to free
the flesh that is soon to die and is an enemy of the soul.

[73]Let all the brothers strive to follow the humility and poverty of our
Lord Jesus Christ and remember that we should have nothing else in
the whole world except, as the Apostle says: *having food and clothing,
we are content with these.* [74]They must rejoice when they live among 1 Tm 6:8
people considered of little value and looked down upon, among the
poor and the powerless, the sick and the lepers, and the beggars by the
wayside. [75]When it is necessary, let them go for alms. [76]Let them not
be ashamed and remember, moreover, that our Lord Jesus Christ, *the
Son of the* all powerful *living God, set His face like flint* and was not

a. This lengthy bracketed passage is again an interpolation of Esser as the manuscript is difficult to decipher.

Jn 11:27; Is 50:7 ashamed. [77]He was poor and a stranger and lived on alms, He, the Blessed Virgin, HIS HOLY MOTHER MARY, and His disciples. [78]When people MAKE THEM ASHAMED and refuse to give them alms, let them thank God for this because they will receive great honor before the tribunal of our Lord Jesus Christ for such insults.

[79]Let them know that reproach is charged not to those who suffer it but to those who caused it [80]BECAUSE alms are a legacy and a justice due to the poor that our Lord Jesus Christ acquired for us. [81]The brothers who work to acquire them will receive a great reward and enable those who grant them to gain and acquire one, for all that people leave behind in the world will perish, but they will have a reward from the Lord for the charity and almsgiving they have done.

II. Fragments Inserted into the *Exposition of the Rule of the Friars Minor* by Hugh of Digne (1245–1255)[a]

[1]Wherefore the saint used to speak in this way in the Rule that had not yet received the papal seal: "Let the brothers and the brothers' ministers be careful that they do not in any way enter into their affairs." ER II 5

[2]Before the Rule received the papal seal the saint added: "And although they may be called hypocrites, they shall not cease doing good." ER II 15

[3]Wherefore before it received the papal seal the Rule used to contain: "But at other times they may not be bound to fast according to this life except on Fridays." ER III 12

[4]. . . as the saint at first said in the Rule: "Let the ministers remember—he said—that the care of the brothers' souls has been entrusted to them; if anyone of them is lost because of their fault or bad example, it will be necessary for them to render an account for them before our Lord Jesus Christ." ER IV 6

[5]The Saint used to speak thus in the original Rule: "All the brothers, the ministers as well as the others, should be careful that they do not become disturbed or angry because of the sin of another or because of his bad example since the devil wishes to corrupt many because of the sin of one; but spiritually, as they can, they should help the one who has

a. Whereas the fragments from the *Worchester Fragment* treat of spiritual themes, those of Hugh of Digne are more juridical interpretations of *The Earlier Rule*.

sinned since it is not the healthy who need a physician but those who
ER 7-8 are sick."

[6]According to that word of the Lord that the blessed Francis also
said to the brothers: "*The leaders of the nations lord it over them, and
those who are greater exercise power over them;* it shall not be that Mt 20:25-26a
ER V 10 way among you."

[7]The saint used to exhort them in the Rule before it had received the
papal seal: "Through the love of the Spirit, let them willingly serve and
obey one another. This is," he said, "the true and secure obedience of
ER V 14b-15 our Lord Jesus Christ."

[8]Wherefore he used to say at first in the Rule: "In whatever place
they may be, the brothers who may not observe our life spiritually shall
indicate this to their ministers. But let the ministers so provide for them
ER VI 1-2 as they would wish to be done for themselves."

[9]. . . or according to the first Rule, as it was said: "In whatever place
ER VI 1 the brothers are . . ."

[10]Wherefore the Rule at first used to contain: "In whatever place
they are staying, all the brothers may not be the chief stewards or ad-
ministrators nor may they be placed before others with the honors of
those they serve; nor may they receive any office which engenders
scandal or causes any harm to their souls; but let them be minors and Mk 8:36
ER VII 1-2 subject to everyone who is in the same house."

[11]Wherefore at first it was said in the Rule: "Let the brothers who
know how to work do so and exercise the skill they know if it is not con-
ER VII 3 trary to their salvation."

[12]And after a few [words]: "Each one may remain in that employment and position in which he has been called according to the determi- 1 Cor 7:24
ER VII 6 nation of the minister."

[13]Wherefore he placed in the Rule before it received the papal seal:
"The servants of God must always insist upon prayer or some good
ER VII 12 work."

[14]These words were in the Rule before it received the papal seal:
"Let the brothers be careful they do not appropriate or defend any place
ER VII 13 or anything."

[15]The saint originally used to speak in this way in the Rule . . . and
again: "Wherever the brothers may be and whatever place they find
themselves, let them consider one another spiritually and diligently,
and honor one another without murmuring. And let them be careful 1 Pt 4:9
that they do not show themselves outwardly as sad and depressed

hypocrites, but let them show themselves as rejoicing in the Lord and
fittingly grateful." ER VII 15-16

[16]The saint used to speak in this way concerning money that was
discovered: "If we find money, let us treat it as only dust that is trampled under foot." ER VIII 6

[17]Francis maintained that the brothers could seek alms for lepers
who were in great need; even so, let them be careful of money. And
even though he loved the holy places in which the brothers were given
hospitality and rest, nevertheless he did not allow them to seek money
for some place or cause it to be sought after or go with those seeking it. ER VIII 10-11; 8

[18]And the letter of the first Rule used to have this: "When it is necessary, the brothers may go for alms." ER IX 3

[19]He used to place these things more diffusely in the original Rule:
"When it is necessary, the brothers may go for alms. Let them not be
ashamed but rather remember that our Lord Jesus Christ, Son of the liv-
Jn 11:27; Is 50:7 ing and omnipotent God, set his face like flint and was not ashamed. He
was a poor man and a transient and lived on alms, as did his disciples.
When men would bring shame upon them and would be unwilling to
give to them, they would then give thanks to God since they would receive a great honor before the judgment seat of our Lord Jesus Christ
because of these insults. And let them know that shame will be placed
not on those who suffer it, but on those who cause it; and alms are an inheritance and right that is due to the poor which our Lord Jesus Christ
won for us. We brothers who work to procure them will receive a great
reward and will enable their donors to receive the same reward, since
everything people leave behind them in the world perishes, but the
charity and almsgiving they do will receive a reward from the Lord." ER IX 3-9

[20]The saint spoke in this way in the first Rule: "Let each one express
his need confidently to another so that the other may discover his need
and minister to him." ER IX 10

[21]The saint used to admonish in the Rule before it received the papal
seal: "I beg the sick brother, thanking the Creator for every grace, to desire to be whatever the Lord wants him to be, well or sick." ER X 3

[22]And after a few words: "I beg all my brothers in their infirmities
not to be angry or disturbed at God or their brothers, nor to seek medicine very eagerly, nor to desire excessively to free the flesh that is soon
to die and is the enemy of the soul." ER X 4

[23]Let them never lead a brother to call another "fool" or some type
Mt 5:22 of insult since the first Rule and the words of the Gospel express this. ER XI 4

[24]The Gospel teaches not to dispute, nor strike, nor resist evil—all
of which the Rule, before it received the papal seal, especially ex-
ER XI 1; XIV 4-7 pressed; but now it includes everything in precise and general words.

[25]The saint spoke in the first Rule of the two ways of behaving
among non-believers: "The brothers can behave among them spiritually in two ways. One way is not to engage in arguments or disputes but
to be subject to every creature for God's sake and to acknowledge they 1 Pt 2:13
are Christians. The other way is, when they see that it pleases God, to
announce the word of God, that they might believe in God the Father
almighty, His Son and the Holy Spirit, the creator of everything, the redeemer and savior of all the faithful, and might be baptized and become
Christians, because they cannot be saved unless they are baptized and
be true and spiritual Christians, because, unless someone has been reborn from water and the Holy Spirit, he cannot enter the kingdom of
ER XVI 5-7 God." Jn 3:5

[26]And he later added: "Let the brothers remember that they have
given themselves and left their bodies for God's sake to the Lord Jesus
Christ. For his love they must endure tribulation, persecution and
death, because the Lord says: 'Whoever loses his life for my sake will
save it.' 'I say to you, my friend, do not be afraid of those who kill the Lk 9:24
R XVI 10-11, 17, 14 body.' 'If they persecute you in one city, flee to another.' " Lk 12:4; Mt 10:23

[27]. . . as the saint encouraged in the first Rule: "Let all the brothers
ER XVII 3 preach with their deeds."

[28]In a marvelous way the saint wanted to defer to ecclesiastical persons: "Let us hold all clergy and religious as our Lord in those matters
that do not deviate from our religion and respect their order and admin-
ER XIX 3 istration in the Lord."

[29]I remind all the brothers of the tenor and spirit of what is written in
this Rule and ask the Lord to bless those who teach, learn and examine
ER XXIV 1-3 it . . .

III. Fragments found in the *Remembrance* of Thomas of Celano (1247)

[1]Let [the ministers] be bound to render an account before you, Lord,
on judgment day, if any of their brothers perishes because of their neg-
ER IV 6 ligence, example or harsh correction.

[2]Let the brothers beware that they do not show themselves outwardly gloomy and sad hypocrites, but let them show themselves joyful in the Lord, cheerful and appropriately gracious. ER VII 6; 2

[3]. . . and he quoted to the rash brother the words of the rule from which it is very clear that a coin that is found is to be trampled upon as if it were dust. ER VIII 6

[4]Wherefore in one of his rules he had these words set down; "I beg all my sick brothers that they do not become angry in their infirmities or disturbed either at God or at their brothers. Let them not be too solicitous in asking for medicines, nor too desirous that the flesh which is soon to die and which is the enemy of the soul be delivered. let them
1 Thes 5:18 give thanks in all things, so that they may desire to be as God wants
Acts 13:48 them to be. For whom God has destined for eternal life, he instructs by the goads of scourging and sicknesses, as he himself said those whom i
Rv 3:19 love, i correct and chastise." ER X 3-4

A Letter to a Minister
(1221-1223)[a]

Although there is little doubt about the authenticity of this letter, two of its earliest manuscripts only present its first twelve lines underscoring that there are two distinct approaches to the brothers who sin, one which is personal, the other legal. Many attempts have been made to identify the recipient of this letter: all have been in vain. The mention of custodian and guardian in the context of re-writing of the Rule suggests that the date of the letter's composition was between 1221 and 1223.

[1]To Brother N., minister: *May the Lord bless you.*[b] Nm 6:24a

[2]I speak to you, as best I can, about the state of your soul. You must consider as grace all that impedes you from loving the Lord God and whoever has become an impediment to you, whether brothers or others, even if they lay hands on you. [3]And may you want it to be this way and not otherwise. [4]And let this be for you the true obedience of the Lord God and my true obedience, for I know with certitude that it is true obedience. [5]And love those who do those things to you [6]and do not wish anything different from them, unless it is something the Lord God shall have given you. [7]And love them in this and do not wish that they be better Christians. [8]And let this be more than a hermitage for you.

[9]And if you have done this, I wish to know in this way if you love the Lord and me, His servant and yours: that there is not any brother in the world who has sinned—however much he could have sinned—who, after he has looked into your eyes, would ever depart without your mercy, if he is looking for mercy. [10]And if he were not looking for mercy, you would ask him if he wants mercy. [11]And if he would sin a thousand times before your eyes, love him more than me so that you may draw him to the Lord; and always be merciful with brothers such

a. The manuscripts offer a variety of titles for this text: (a) "A Letter of Saint Francis to a Certain Minister;" (b) "A Letter Which Saint Francis Sent to the General Minister, i.e., Brother Elias;" (c) "A Letter Sent to Brother Elias;" (d) "A Letter Saint Francis Sent to the General Minister about the Manner of Serving the Brothers Who Sin Mortally and Venially." Kajetan Esser chose this simple title because of the anonymity of the minister to whom the letter is addressed.

b. Since the manuscripts contain no name to designate the recipient of this letter, scholars have suggested different friars: Peter Catanii, Elias, or simply a provincial minister.

as these. [12]And you may announce this to the guardians, when you can, that, for your part, you are resolved to act in this way.[a]

[13]During the Chapter of Pentecost, with the help of God and the advice of our brothers, we shall make one chapter such as this from all the chapters of the Rule that treat of mortal sin:[b]

> [14]If any one of the brothers, at the instigation of the enemy, shall have sinned mortally, let him be bound by obedience to have recourse to his guardian. [15]Let all the brothers who know that he has sinned not bring shame upon him or slander him; let them, instead, show great mercy to him and keep the sin of their brother very secret because *those who are well do not need a physician,*
> Mt 9:12; Mk 2:17; Lk 5:31 *but the sick do.* [16]In a similar way let them be bound by obedience to send him to his custodian with a companion. [17]And let that custodian provide for him with mercy as he would wish to be
> Mt 7:12; Lk 6:31 provided for were he in a similar position. [18]If he falls into some venial sin, let him confess to his brother who is a priest. [19]If there is no priest there, let him confess to his brother until he has a
> Jas 5:16 priest who may canonically absolve him, as it has been said. [20]And let them not have the power to impose any other penance
> Jn 8:11 on them except this: *Go and sin no more.*[c]

[21]May you keep this writing with you until Pentecost so that it may be better observed, when you will be with your brothers. [22]With the help of the Lord God, you will take care of these and everything else that is not clear in the Rule.

---

a. "Guardian" was an expression which the friars used initially to describe a quality of ministry rather than a specific ministry. Thus the function of a minister was that of protecting or guarding the brothers from temptation or evil (cf. ER IV-V). As the brothers settled down in residence, a practice that became more common after Francis's death, the local minister received the title "guardian."
Fifteen manuscripts conclude with this sentence. The majority, however, continue with the concern for appropriate legislation concerning the brothers who sin, legislation which was eventually incorporated into LR.

b. Concerning the Chapter of Pentecost see ER XVIII 2; Chapters V, XIII, and XX of the same document treat the brothers who sin. The need to simplify the directives of these chapters is obvious.

c. This concise statement was incorporated in a modified way in LR VII and X.

The Later Rule
(1223)

The Earlier Rule of Francis's brothers had its origins in the statement presented to and approved by Pope Innocent III in 1209/10. It grew as the experiences and structures of the brothers became more complex. The Rule which received its final redaction at the Chapter of 1221, inspirational as it may have been, received a re-working that its vision would be more succinct and forthright. This later description of the Gospel life became a papal document on November 29, 1223, when Pope Honorius III placed the papal seal on it. Since that time it has been the foundational document forming and inspiring the Gospel vision of Franciscans of the First Order (Conventual, Capuchin Friars as well as those of the Leonine Union), of the Sisters of Saint Clare whose Rule incorporates many of its passages, and of the Religious and Secular Third Order. While some of the language of this document seems foreign to that of Francis himself and thus suggests the presence of canonists or other religious, e.g. the Cistercians, who helped with its composition, there is no doubt that it expresses his Gospel vision.

Bull of Pope Honorius III

Honorius,
Bishop, Servant of the servants of God,
to His Beloved Sons,
Brother Francis and the other brothers
of the Order of the Lesser Brothers,
Health and Apostolic Benediction.

The Apostolic See is accustomed to grant the pious requests and favorably to accede to the laudable desires of its petitioners. Therefore, beloved sons in the Lord, attentive to your pious prayers, We confirm with Our Apostolic Authority, and by these words ratify, the Rule of your Order, herein outlined and approved by Our predecessor, Pope Innocent of happy memory, which is as follows:

[Chapter I][a]
In the Name of the Lord! The Life of the Lesser Brothers Begins

[1]The Rule and Life of the Lesser Brothers is this: to observe the Holy Gospel of Our Lord Jesus Christ by living in obedience, without anything of one's own, and in chastity.

[2]Brother Francis promises obedience and reverence to our Lord Pope Honorius and his successors canonically elected and to the Roman Church. [3]Let the other brothers be bound to obey Brother Francis and his successors.

[Chapter II]
Those Who Wish to Adopt This Life, and How They Should Be Received

[1]If there are any who wish to accept this life and come to our brothers, let them send them to their provincial ministers, to whom alone and not to others is permission granted to receive the brothers. [2]Let the ministers examine them carefully concerning the Catholic faith and the sacraments of the Church. [3]If they believe all these things, will faithfully profess them, and steadfastly observe them to the end; [4]and if they have no wives, or if they have wives who have already taken a vow of continence and are of such an age that suspicion cannot be raised about them, and who have already entered a monastery or have given their husbands permission by the authority of the bishop of the diocese,[b] [5]let the ministers speak to them the words of the holy Gospel that they go
Mt 19:21//Mk 10:21 Lk 18:22 and sell all they have and take care to give it to the poor. [6]If they cannot do this, their good will may suffice. [7]Let the brothers and the minister be careful not to interfere with their temporal goods that they may dispose of their belongings as the Lord inspires them. [8]If, however, coun-

a. Unlike ER, this document contains titles for each section. They may have been imposed by a curial official who desired to divide the document into twelve parts to signify its apostolic foundations. However, there are no indications of chapters as suggested by the brackets.

b. This is taken literally from the *Decretum Gratiani* 22, CXXVII, q.2: "If a married man wishes to enter a monastery, he is not to be received unless he has first been freed from his marriage by a profession of chastity on the part of his wife." Innocent III echoed this teaching in 1198 : "Nor may one party turn to the Lord and the other party remain in the world; moreover, one of the spouses may not be received to regular observance unless the other spouse has made a promise of perpetual continence. The other partner must also change his or her way of life, unless perhaps due to his or her age, that partner can remain in the world without suspicion of incontinence." Honorius III, speaking of women entering religious life, declared: ". . . and is of such age that no suspicion can be raised against her, but you shall not allow her to be forced against her will to enter a convent and observe a vow of continence." All of these were incorporated into the *Decretals* of Pope Gregory IX, c. 13, III 32, 18.

sel is sought, the minister may send them to some God-fearing persons according to whose advice their goods may be distributed to the poor.

[9]Then they may be given the clothes of probation, namely, two tunics without a hood, a cord, short trousers, and a little cape reaching to the cord, [10]unless, at times, it seems good to these same ministers, before God, to act otherwise. [11]When the year of probation has come to an end, they may be received to obedience promising always to observe this rule and life. [12]On no account shall it be lawful for them to leave this Order, according to the decree of our Lord the Pope, [13]for, according to the Gospel: *no one who puts a hand to the plow and looks to what was left behind is fit for the kingdom of God.* Lk 9:62

[14]Those who have already promised obedience may have one tunic with a hood and another, if they wish, without a hood. [15]And those who are compelled by necessity may wear shoes. [16]Let all the brothers wear poor clothes and they may mend them with pieces of sackcloth or other material with the blessing of God. [17]I admonish and exhort them not to look down upon or judge those whom they see dressed in soft and fine clothes and enjoying the choicest food and drink, but rather let everyone judge and look down upon himself.

[Chapter III]
The Divine Office, Fasting and How the Brothers Should Go About in the World

[1]Let the clerical [brothers] recite the Divine Office according to the rite of the holy Roman Church excepting the psalter, [2]for which reason they may have breviaries.[a] [3]The lay [brothers], however, may say twenty-four *Our Fathers* for Matins, and five for Lauds; seven for each of the Hours of Prime, Terce, Sext, and None, twelve for Vespers, and seven for Compline. [4]Let them pray for the dead.

[5]Let them fast from the feast of All Saints until the Lord's Nativity. [6]May those be blessed by the Lord who fast voluntarily during that holy Lent that begins at the Epiphany and lasts during the forty days which our Lord consecrated by His own fast; but those who do not wish Mt 4:2; Lk 4:2
to keep it will not be obliged. [7]Let them fast, however, during the other [Lent] until the Lord's Resurrection. [8]At other times they may not be

a. When examined in light of the ER III 4 which spoke of celebrating "according to the custom of the clergy," "according to the rite of the holy Roman Church" is a change in the phrasing of this passage. This indicates the changes that had taken place in legislation concerning the Divine Office.

bound to fast except on Fridays. [9]During a time of obvious need, however, the brothers may not be bound by corporal fast.

[10]I counsel, admonish and exhort my brothers in the Lord Jesus
Christ not to quarrel or argue or judge others when they go about in the
2 Tm 2:14 world; [11]but let them be meek, peaceful, modest, gentle, and humble,
speaking courteously to everyone, as is becoming. [12]They should not
ride horseback unless they are compelled by an obvious need or an infirmity. [13]Into whatever house they enter, let them first say: "Peace be
Lk 10:5 to this house!" [14]According to the holy Gospel, let them eat whatever
Lk 10:8 food is set before them.

[Chapter IV]
Let the Brothers Never Receive Money

[1]I strictly command all my brothers not to receive coins or money in any form, either personally or through intermediaries.[a] [2]Nevertheless, the ministers and custodians alone may take special care through their spiritual friends to provide for the needs of the sick and the clothing of the others according to places, seasons and cold climates, as they judge necessary,[b] [3]saving always that, as stated above, they do not receive coins or money.

[Chapter V]
The Manner of Working

[1]Those brothers to whom the Lord has given the grace of working may work faithfully and devotedly [2]so that, while avoiding idleness, the enemy of the soul, they do not extinguish the Spirit of holy prayer and devotion to which all temporal things must contribute.[c]

[3]In payment for their work they may receive whatever is necessary for the bodily support of themselves and their brothers, excepting coin

---

a. An important shift in Francis's thought can be found in his firm prohibition against accepting money. In ER VIII, this prohibition followed Francis's encouragement to work and his subsequent warning to avoid money as a payment for that work. In this instance, however, Francis strongly commands his brothers to reject the security represented by money.

b. Cf. Benedict, *Rule* LV 1-4 which speaks of changes in religious garb according to "local conditions and climate."

c. This phrase summarizes ideas found throughout the earlier writings, e.g. ER XXII, by seeing prayer and devotion fundamentally as activities of the Holy Spirit. The use of the word "devotion" in this context points to an experience of desire or a fervor expressed in a certain enthusiasm for or focus on the Lord.

or money, [4]and let them do this humbly as is becoming for servants of God and followers of most holy poverty.

[Chapter VI]
Let the Brothers Not Make Anything Their Own; Begging Alms, the Sick Brothers[a]

[1]Let the brothers not make anything their own, neither house, nor
place, nor anything at all. [2]As pilgrims and strangers in this world, 1 Pt 2:11
serving the Lord in poverty and humility, let them go seeking alms with
confidence, [3]and they should not be ashamed because, for our sakes,
our Lord made Himself poor in this world. [4]This is that sublime height 2 Cor 8:9
of most exalted poverty which has made you, my most beloved brothers, heirs and kings of the Kingdom of Heaven, poor in temporal things
but exalted in virtue. [5]Let this be your portion which leads into the land Jas 2:5
of the living. [6]Giving yourselves totally to this, beloved brothers, never Ps 142:6
seek anything else under heaven for the name of our Lord Jesus Christ.

[7]Wherever the brothers may be and meet one another, let them show
that they are members of the same family. [8]Let each one confidently
make known his need to the other, for if a mother loves and cares for
her son according to the flesh, how much more diligently must some- 1 Thes 2:7
one love and care for his brother according to the Spirit! [9]When any
brother falls sick, the other brothers must serve him as they would wish
to be served themselves. Mt 7:12

[Chapter VII]
The Penance To Be Imposed on the Brothers Who Sin[b]

[1]If any brother, at the instigation of the enemy, sins mortally in regard to those sins concerning which it has been decreed among the brothers to have recourse only to the provincial ministers, let him have recourse as quickly as possible and without delay. [2]If these ministers

a. The teachings on fraternity and poverty which are scattered throughout the ER are brought together in this synthesis underscoring the interconnection found between the two concepts.

b. Cf. the second section of the *Letter to A Minister* 13-20 (hereafter LtMin) in which Francis presents a first draft of this legislation. Its incorporation into this papal document and the distinction of ministers who may not be priests underscores the mixed clerical and lay nature of the Order.

are priests, with a heart full of mercy[a] let them impose on him a penance; but, if the ministers are not priests, let them have it imposed by others who are priests of the Order, as in the sight of God appears to them more expedient. [3]They must be careful not to be angry or disturbed at the sin of another, for anger and disturbance impede charity in themselves and in others.

[Chapter VIII]
The Election of the General Minister of This Fraternity and the Chapter of Pentecost

[1]Let all the brothers always be bound to have one of the brothers of this Order as general minister and servant of the whole fraternity and let them be strictly bound to obey him. [2]When he dies, let the election of his successor be made by the provincial ministers and custodians in the Chapter of Pentecost, at which all the provincial ministers are bound to assemble in whatever place the general minister may have designated. [3]Let them do this once in every three years, or at other longer or shorter intervals, as determined by the aforesaid minister.

[4]If, at any time, it appears to the body of the provincial ministers and custodians that the aforesaid general minister is not qualified for the service and general welfare of the brothers, let the aforesaid brothers, to whom the election is committed, be bound to elect another as custodian in the name of the Lord.

[5]Moreover, after the Chapter of Pentecost, the provincial ministers and custodians may each, if they wish and it seems expedient to them, convoke a Chapter of the brothers in their custodies once in the same year.

[Chapter IX]
Preachers

[1]The brothers may not preach in the diocese of any bishop when he has opposed their doing so. [2]And let none of the brothers dare to preach in any way to the people unless he has been examined and approved by

a. The translator has taken the liberty of translating *misericordia* more freely as "a heart full of mercy." This translation follows the more etymological sense of the word, *miser* + *cor*, that is, a heart sensitive to misery.

the general minister of this fraternity and the office of preacher has been conferred upon him.

[3]Moreover, I admonish and exhort those brothers that when they preach their *language be well-considered and chaste* for the benefit Ps 13:7; 19:13
and edification of the people, announcing to them vices and virtues, punishment and glory, with brevity, because our Lord when on earth kept his word brief. Rom 9:28; Is 10:22ff

[Chapter X] The Admonition and Correction of the Brothers

[1]Let the brothers who are the ministers and servants of the others visit and admonish their brothers and humbly and charitably correct them, not commanding them anything that is against their soul and our rule. [2]Let the brothers who are subject, however, remember that, for God's sake, they have renounced their own wills. [3]Therefore, I strictly command them to obey their ministers in everything they have promised the Lord to observe and which is not against their soul or our Rule.

[4]Wherever the brothers may be who know and feel they cannot observe the Rule spiritually, they can and should have recourse to their ministers. [5]Let the ministers, moreover, receive them charitably and kindly and have such familiarity with them[a] that these same brothers may speak and deal with them as masters with their servants, [6]for so it must be that the ministers are the servants of all the brothers.

[7]Moreover, I admonish and exhort the brothers in the Lord Jesus Christ to beware of all pride, vainglory, envy and greed, of care and solicitude for the things of this world, of detraction and murmuring. Let Mt 13:22; Lk 12:15
those who are illiterate not be anxious to learn, [8]but let them pay attention to what they must desire above all else: to have the Spirit of the Lord and Its holy activity, [9]to pray always to Him with a pure heart, to have humility and patience in persecution and infirmity, [10]and to love those who persecute, rebuke and find fault with us, because the Lord says: *Love your enemies and pray for those who persecute and calumniate you.* [11]*Blessed are those who suffer persecution for the sake of* Mt 5:44
justice, for theirs is the kingdom of heaven. [12]*But whoever perseveres* Mt 5:10
to the end will be saved. Mt 10:22

a. *Familiaritas* is a difficult word to translate, containing a wide variety of nuances: that of a family, of a servant, of familiarity or intimacy, or of solidarity. All of these nuances can be read into this sentence in which Francis attempts to describe a fundamental characteristic of a minister.

[Chapter XI]
The Brothers May Not Enter the Monasteries of Nuns[a]

[1]I strictly command all the brothers not to have any suspicious dealings or conversations with women, [2]and they may not enter the monasteries of nuns, excepting those brothers to whom special permission has been granted by the Apostolic See; [3]and they may not be godfathers to men or women, so that scandal may not arise among the brothers or concerning them on account of this.

[Chapter XII]
Those Going Among the Saracens and Other Non-Believers

[1]Let those brothers who wish by divine inspiration to go among the Saracens or other non-believers ask permission to go from their provincial ministers. [2]The ministers, however, may not grant permission except to those whom they see fit to be sent.

[3]In addition to these points, I command the ministers through obedience to petition from our Lord the Pope for one of the Cardinals of the Holy Roman Church, who would be the governor, protector and corrector of this fraternity, [4]so that, being always submissive and subject at the feet of the same Holy Church and steadfast in the Catholic Faith, we may observe poverty, humility, and the Holy Gospel of our Lord Jesus Christ as we have firmly promised.

It is forbidden, therefore, for anyone to tamper with this decree which we have confirmed, or rashly dare to oppose it. If anyone presume to attempt this, let him know that he shall incur the anger of Almighty God and of His blessed Apostles Peter and Paul.

Given at the Lateran, the twenty-ninth day of November, in the eighth year of Our pontificate.

a. This entire paragraph is reflective of Cistercian and Premonstratentian influences. Both religious communities had attracted many female followers, struggled to establish monasteries or religious houses for them close to their own, and thus became increasingly more obligated to minister to their needs. As a result of these developments, legislation on the enclosure became more defined at this period of history as the *Form and Manner of Life* imposed by Cardinal Hugolino on the Poor Ladies of San Damiano in 1219 indicates. Cf. *Clare of Assisi: Early Documents*, edited and translated by Regis J. Armstrong (St. Bonaventure: Franciscan Institute, 1993), page 92ff.

A Letter to Brother Anthony of Padua[a]

In his *Chronicle of the Twenty-Four Generals,* Arnold of Arrant states that Anthony of Lisbon was an Augustinian religious who became a follower of Francis of Assisi after learning of the martyrdom of Brother Berard and his companions. After his entrance into the Fraternity, the Brothers asked him to accept the responsibility of teaching them. "He did not presume to teach," the Chronicle maintains, "no matter how urgent the brothers' request without first obtaining the permission of the blessed Francis."[b] The date of this letter, granting Anthony permission, is some time after the papal seal was placed on the Rule, that is, after November 29, 1223.

[1]Brother Francis sends greetings to Brother Anthony, my Bishop.[c]

[2]I am pleased that you teach sacred theology to the brothers providing that, as is contained in the Rule, you "do not extinguish the Spirit of prayer and devotion" during study of this kind.[d]

---

a. Although born in Lisbon, Portugal, Anthony is commonly identified by the place of his death and burial, Padua, Italy. He was canonized on May 30, 1232.

b. Cf. Arnold of Sarrant, "Chronica XXIV Generalium Ordinis Minorum," *Analecta Franciscana sive Chronica aliaque varia Documenta ad Historiam Fratrum Minorum spectantia* III 132 (Quaracchi, Ad Aquas Clara: 1897)

c. *Episcopus,* bishop, literally means inspector or supervisor, a term Francis transfers in this instance to theologians, who minister spirit and life (cf. Test 13). It suggests the concept that preachers and theologians when receiving episcopal approval share in their office of preaching and teaching.

d. The incorporation of this phrase found in the LR V into the teaching and implied study of theology places those ministries within the framework of prayer and devotion. Thus Francis describes the environment of Franciscan theology and study.

The Praises of God and the Blessing
(The Parchment Given to Brother Leo on LaVerna)[a]
(1224)

Leo of Assisi, who was with Francis on LaVerna in the Fall of 1224, wrote in red ink on one side of this piece of parchment: "Two years before his death, the blessed Francis spent forty days on Mount LaVerna from the Feast of the Assumption of the holy Virgin Mary until the September Feast of Saint Michael, in honor of the Blessed Virgin Mary, the Mother of God, and the blessed Michael the Archangel. And the Lord's hand was upon him. After the vision and message of the Seraph and the impression of Christ's stigmata upon his body, he composed these praises written on the other side of this page and wrote them in his own hand, thanking God for the kindness bestowed on him."

On the other side of the same parchment Brother Leo wrote: "The blessed Francis wrote this blessing for me with his own hand." Then: "In a similar way he made with his own hand this sign TAU together with a skull."

The original parchment is now preserved in the Basilica of Saint Francis in Assisi. In preparing his edition of these texts, Kajetan Esser relied on the work of Duane Lapsanski who had examined the original parchment with the help of infra-red technology and was able to read passages now illegible to the naked eye.[b] Even with the aid of technology, the parchment was still illegible in certain places, particularly at the edges and on the folds, Lapsanski then had recourse to early manuscript copies of the texts. These supplemental readings will be indicated by placing the text in bold print. Esser, relying on a broader examination of those manuscripts, changed some of Lapsanski's readings. These variants will be noted in the footnotes.

a. The original text of these writings can be found in a small piece of parchment on which Francis wrote on both sides. It is one of the two autographs of Francis which remain.

b. Cf. Duane Lapsanski, "The Autographs of the 'Chartula' of St. Francis of Assisi," AFH 67 (1967) 18-37.

A: The Praises of God

(Edition of Duane Lapsanski and Kajetan Esser)

[1]You are the **holy** Lord God *Who does* **wonderful things.**[a] Ps 77:15

[2]You are strong. *You are great.* You are the most high. Ps 86:10
You are the almighty king. You *holy Father,* Jn 17:11
King of *heaven and* **earth.** Mt 11:25

[3]You are three and one, the Lord *God of gods;* Ps 136:2
You are the good, all good, the highest good,
Lord God *living and true.* 1 Thes 1:9

[4]You are love, charity; You are wisdom, You are humility,
You are **patience, You are beauty, You are meekness,** Ps 71:5
You are security, You are rest,
You are gladness and joy, You are our hope, You are justice,
You are moderation, You are all our riches to sufficiency.

[5]You are beauty, You are meekness,
You are the protector, You are our custodian and defender, Ps 31:5
You are strength, You are refreshment. [6]You are our hope, Ps 43:2
You are our faith, You are our charity,
You are all our sweetness, **You are our eternal life:**
Great and wonderful Lord, Almighty God, Merciful Savior.

---

a. Passages in italics indicate scriptural quotations or allusions found in Kajetan Esser's edition.

(Edition of Attilio Bartoli Langeli)[a]

Attilio Bartoli Langeli offers an alternate edition of this parchment. It too is based on the 1974 study of Duane Lapsanski as well as personal examination of the manuscript in the glass enclosed reliquary of Assisi's Basilica of Saint Francis. In this instance, however, there is no attempt to supply the illegible and missing words or the missing capitalization and punctuation. Thus this edition, while less polished, presents more accurately what Francis wrote on the small piece of parchment he gave to and preserved by Brother Leo.

1 ______________________________

2 _____ are great you are the most high

3 _____ are the almighty king you holy father king of heaven and

4 _____you are three and one the lord g___[b]

5 of __ods you are the good all good the highest good

love

6 lord god living and true you are charity[c]

h

7 ________dom you are umility[d] you are pa

you are_______[e]

8 tience, you are security, You are the qui

you are our hope,

9 et you are joy and happiness you are justice,

all our[f]

10 ____temperance______e riches to sufficiency.

11 You are beaut__ you are meekness

12 you are protector you are custodian and defender

13 you are strength you are refuge[g] you are our hope

14 you are our faith, you are char___

---

a. Attilio Bartoli Langeli, "Gli scritti da Francesco. L'autografo di un 'illiteratus,' " *Frate Francisco d'Assisi* (Spoleto: 1994) 101-159.

b. The letters close to the edge of the parchment are illegible. Thus *deus* (god) and the following word *deorum* (of gods) can only be partially seen, a phenomenon difficult to capture in translation.

c. Slightly above the word *caritas* (charity) Francis inserted the word *amor* (love).

d. The parchment indicates that Francis himself corrected the spelling of *umilitas* (humility) by the superscripted "h."

e. The parchment contains the words *tu es* (you are) but nothing is legible. At this point, Esser added a phrase found in one fourteenth century manuscript: "You are patience, You are beauty, You are meekness," cf. Naples, Biblioteca Nazionale, codex XIII.C.98.

f. This phrase, *omnia nostra* (all our), is also written slightly above *divitia* (riches).

g. Attilio Bartoli Langeli sees the word *refugium* (refuge) not *refrigerium* (refreshment) as seen by Lapsanski and Esser.

15 ______[a] you are all our sweetness, ______________

16 ____[b]

a. As in other instances this word is illegible. The assumption of Lapsanski and Esser is that it was *nostra* (our) as in "our hope" and "our faith."

b. Although Attilio Bartoli Langeli discovered some mark here, he did not consider it sufficient to propose the interpretation of earlier manuscripts, *vita nostra eterna* (our eternal life). Nor did he find justification for adding what others consider the last verse: *magnus et admirabilis Dominus, Deus omnipotens, misericors Salvator* (great and wonderful Lord, Almighty God, Merciful Savior).

B: A Blessing for Brother Leo

(Edition of Duane Lapsanski and Kajetan Esser)

[1]*May the Lord bless you and keep you.*
May He show His face to you and be merciful to you.

Nm 6:24-26 [2]*May He turn His countenance to you and give you peace.*

Nm 6:27 [3]*May the Lord bless you,* Brother Leo.

(Edition of of Attilio Bartoli Langeli)

[1]May the lord bless you and keep
[2]you may He show His face
[3]to you and be merciful to you.
[4]may he turn his countenance to you
[5]and give you peace.[a]

a. Contrary to the opinions of Lapsanski and Esser, Attilio Bartoli Langeli does not see the words written with the TAU and the drawing of a profile, etc., as forming a final blessing of Brother Leo, i.e., "Dominus benedicat te, f. Leo (May the Lord bless you, brother Leo)." The words, Attilio Bartoli Langeli maintains, are written in a manner that do not suggest the reading traditionally held. Thus at the left is *D(omi)n(u)s*, at the right *bene*, below at the left *te*, at the right *dicat*.

The Canticle of the Creatures
(1225)

Chronologically, there are three stages to consider in the development of this poetic praise of God, each of which reveals a side of Francis's vision of God, creation, and the human soul. Francis's companions tell us of the composition of the first part of this piece, verses 1-9, in which the saint sings the praises of creation in glorifying God. While suffering intensely from his physical infirmities, he announced: "I wish to compose a new hymn about the Lord's creatures, of which we make daily use, without which we cannot live, and with which the human race greatly offends its Creator."[a] A short while later, after hearing of a quarrel that had broken out between the civil and religious authorities of Assisi, Francis asked the brothers to go before them singing these verses, but added two more, verses 10-11.[b] He composed the final verses 12-13 on his death bed.[c] Verse 14 may well be a refrain used after each verse of the entire Canticle.

1 Most High, all-powerful, good Lord,
Yours are *the praises, the glory,* and *the honor,* and all *blessing,* Rv 4:9,11
2 To You alone, Most High, do they belong,
and no human is worthy to mention Your name.[d]
3 Praised be You, my *Lord,* with all *Your creatures,* Tb 8:7
especially Sir Brother Sun,
Who is the day and through whom You give us light.[e]
4 And he is beautiful and radiant with great splendor;
and bears a likeness of You, Most High One.
5 *Praised* be You, my Lord, through Sister *Moon* and *the stars,* Ps 148:3

a. Cf. *The Assisi Compilation,* 83 (hereafter AC).

b. Cf. AC 84.

c. Cf. AC 7.

d. It would seem that in these first nine verses Francis envisioned this as a song of God's creatures in which human beings, because of sin, had no part, a theme about which he hints in other writings, e.g. Adm II, ER XIII. While the first verse directs praise, glory, honor and blessing to God alone, a sentiment underscored in the first part of this second verse, its second part is quite clear in denying any role to a human being.

e. In Francis's use of the passive voice, "Praised be you . . .", and his linking the praise of the Lord with that of creatures, this verse provides many insights into the interpretation of the entire Canticle. While the sun, moon and stars, wind, water, fire, and earth may be seen as instruments of praise or as reasons for praise, praising them also implies praising the God Who created them and acknowledging that they are symbols of their Creator. Thus Francis's poetic use of adjectives is important to comprehend his images of God.

in heaven You formed them clear and precious and beautiful.[a]
[6]Praised be You, my Lord, through Brother Wind,
and through the air, cloudy and serene, and every kind of weather,
through whom You give sustenance to Your creatures.
Ps 148:4,5 [7]*Praised* be You, my Lord, through Sister *Water,*
who is very useful and humble and precious and chaste.
Dn 3:66 [8]*Praised* be You, my Lord, through Brother *Fire,*
Ps 78:14 through whom *You light the night,*
and he is beautiful and playful and robust and strong.
Dn 3:74 [9]*Praised* be You, my Lord, through our Sister Mother *Earth,*
who sustains and governs us,
Ps 104:13, 14 and who produces various *fruit* with colored flowers and *herbs.*

[10]Praised be You, my Lord, through those who give pardon for Your
Mt 6:12 love,
and bear infirmity and tribulation.[b]
[11]Blessed are those who endure in peace
for by You, Most High, shall they be crowned.

[12]Praised be You, my Lord, through our Sister Bodily Death,
from whom no one living can escape.[c]
[13]Woe to those who die in mortal sin.
Blessed are those whom death will find in Your most holy will,
Rv 2:11; 20:6 for *the second death* shall do them no harm.[d]

Dn 3:85 [14]*Praise* and *bless* my *Lord* and give Him thanks
and serve Him with great humility.

---

a. *Per* suggests a variety of meanings: (a) a corruption of the Latin *per,* (b) the French *pour,* or (c) the developing Italian *par.* Thus it may be translated "for" offering an attitude of thanksgiving; "by," expressing a sense of instrumentality; or "through," suggesting instrumentality and, at the same time, a deeper sense of praising God's presence in the creatures mentioned. This translation follows the last possibility based on verse 3, "Praised be you, my Lord, with all your creatures . . ."

b. The second section of the Canticle introduces humanity into the praise of God. However, such praise is only achieved through identifying with the suffering Servant of God, Jesus, who endured weakness and tribulation in peace. In this way, reconciliation is achieved in light of the Paschal Mystery.

c. These two verses, 12 and 13, composed in Francis's last hours, indicate an understanding of death much different from that of 1Ltf 2:14ff, 2LtF 72ff, and *Letters to the Rulers of the Peoples* 2-4 [hereafter LtR]. Rather than fearing death, Francis greets it as yet another expression of God's presence.

d. Fulgentius of Ruspe comments on these verses in his treatise on forgiveness: "Here on earth they are changed by the first resurrection, in which they are enlightened and converted, thus passing from death to life, sinfulness to holiness, unbelief to faith, and evil actions to holy life. For this reason the second death has no power over them . . . As the first resurrection consists of the conversion of the heart, so the second death consists of unending torment (cf. Fulgentius of Ruspe, *On Forgiveness,* Liber 2, 11, 1-2,1. 3-4; *Corpus Christianorum* 91A, 693-695).

The Canticle of Exhortation for the Ladies of San Damiano
(1225)

At the same time of his composition of the *Canticle of the Creatures,* Francis wrote another canticle for the Poor Ladies of San Damiano's who, according to the author of *The Assisi Compilation,* were suffering at knowledge of his ailments.[a]

[1]Listen, little poor ones called by the Lord,
who have come together from many parts and provinces.[b]
[2]Live always in truth, Jn 17:17; 2 Jn 4; 3 Jn 3
that you may die in obedience.
[3]Do not look at the life without,
for that of the Spirit is better.[c]
[4]I beg you out of great love,
to use with discernment
the alms the Lord gives you.
[5]Those weighed down by sickness
and the others wearied because of them,
all of you: bear it in peace.
[6]For you will sell this fatigue at a very high price
and each one will be crowned queen
in heaven with the Virgin Mary.[d]

---

a. The text of this piece seemed to have been lost until 1941 when it was published with the *Rule and Constitutions of the Nuns of the Order of Saint Clare.* In 1976, however, Giovanni Boccali discovered it in a fourteenth century manuscript which, he maintained, proved its authenticity. The text, like CtC, is written in Umbrian dialect. Cf. Giovanni Boccali, "Parole di esortazione alle 'poverelle' di San Damiano," *Forma Sororum* 14 (1977) 54-70; idem, "Canto di esortazione di san Francesco per le 'poverelle' di San Damiano," *Collectanea Franciscana* 48 (1978): 5-29.

b. In addition to being the introduction to this song, the encouragement to listen may well be a reflection on a biblical and monastic emphasis expressed throughout the Old Testament, e.g. Isaiah 1:2,10; Proverbs 1:8; 4:1,10; 8:6,32ff, and in the opening of the Benedictine Rule. By this time some of the Poor Ladies of San Damiano's came from the provinces of Perugia, Spello, Pisa, and Rome, as well as from a number of different towns.

c. This verse may be referring to two realities, the enclosure or the interior life. In both instances, Francis encourages the Poor Ladies to pay attention to the life of the Spirit within rather than that of the external work.

d. The translation offered is based upon Oktavian Schmucki's interpretation of the text in which he reads the Umbrian dialect differently from Giovanni Boccali. In Boccali's interpretation, the passage should read: "You will see that such fatigue is precious . . ." Cf. supra.

A Letter to the Entire Order
(1225-1226)

The promulgation of the papal document, *Quia populares tumultus,* December 3, 1224, granting the friars permission to celebrate the Eucharist in their churches and oratories, may well have occasioned this letter.[a] At the same time, its themes reflect many of the concerns of *The Testament* which was written during the last days of Francis's life.[b] While a number of manuscripts entitle the work "A Letter to a General Chapter," others prefer the present title since it reflects more accurately the universal audience of all the brothers mentioned in verse 2.

[1] In the name of the most high Trinity and holy Unity: the Father and the Son and the Holy Spirit.

[2] To all my reverend and dearly beloved brothers: to Brother A.,[c] the
General Minister of the Order of Friars Minor, its lord, and the other
general ministers who will come after him, and to the ministers, custodians, humble priests of this same brotherhood in Christ, and to all simple and obedient brothers, from the first to the last: [3] Brother Francis, a
worthless and weak man, your very little servant sends his greetings in
Rv 1:5 Him Who has redeemed and *washed us in His* most precious blood.
Lk 1:32 [4] When you hear His name, the name of that *Son of the Most High,* our
Rm 1:25 Lord Jesus Christ, *Who is blessed forever,* adore His name with fear
2 Ezr 8:6 and reverence, *prostrate on the ground!*

[5] Listen, sons of the Lord and my brothers, *pay attention to my*
Acts 2:14; Is 55:3 *words.*[d] [6] *Incline the ear* of your heart and obey the voice of the Son of

a. Cf. Infra, pp. 561-563.

b. Ubertino da Casale indicates that the letter was written "at the end of [Francis's] days" in his *Arbor vitae crucifixae Iesu Christi.*

c. It is difficult to identify the friar referred to in this passage. The majority of the manuscripts simply refer to him as unknown, although they do suggest his being the General Minister of the Order. Since Peter Catanii had died in March 1221, Elias, who was appointed at that time, is most likely the recipient of this letter. This may well be confirmed by the further reference in lines 38, 40 and 47 to Brother H (Latin [H]elias). A number of manuscripts indicate Elias as the name that should be inserted in these places.

d. This is a difficult phrase to translate because of the obscurity of the Latin text: *Audite domini filii et fratres mei . . .* The comma may be placed in different places: *Audite, domini filii et fratres mei . . .* or *Audite, domini, filii et fratres mei . . .* Thus the passage has been translated: "Listen, my lord, sons and brothers . . ."; "Listen, sons of the Lord and my brothers . . ."; and "Listen, lords, sons and my brothers . . ." All are acceptable.

God. [7]Observe His commands with your whole heart and fulfill His
counsels with a perfect mind. [8]*Give praise* to Him *because He is good;* Ps 136:1
exalt Him *by your deeds;* [9]for this reason He has sent you into the Tb 13:6
whole world: that you may bear witness to His voice in word and deed
and bring everyone to know that there is *no one who is all-powerful* except Him. [10]Persevere *in discipline* and holy obedience and, with a Tb 13:4; Heb 12:7
good and firm purpose, fulfill what you have promised Him. [11]The
Lord *God* offers *Himself* to us as to His *children.* Heb 12:7

[12]Kissing your feet, therefore, and with all that love of which I am
capable, I implore all of you brothers to show all possible reverence
and honor to the most holy Body and Blood of our Lord Jesus Christ
[13]in Whom that which is in heaven and on earth has been brought to
peace and reconciled to almighty God. Col 1:20

[14]I also beg in the Lord all my brothers who are priests, or who will
be, or who wish to be priests of the Most High that whenever they wish
to celebrate Mass, being pure, they offer the true Sacrifice of the most
holy Body and Blood of our Lord Jesus Christ with purity and reverence, with a holy and unblemished intention, not for any worldly reason or out of fear or love of anyone, as if they were pleasing people. Eph 6:6; Col 3:22
[15]But let all their will, as much as grace helps, be directed to God, desiring, thereby, to please only the Most High Lord Himself because He
alone acts there as He pleases, [16]for He Himself says: *Do this in mem-
ory of me.* If anyone acts differently, he becomes Judas the traitor and Lk 22:19; 1 Cor 11:24
guilty of the Body and Blood of the Lord. 1 Cor 11:27

[17]My priest brothers, remember what is written in the law of Moses:
whoever committed a transgression against even externals died without mercy by a decree of the Lord. [18]*How much greater* and *more se-* Heb 10:28
*vere will the punishment be of the one who tramples on the Son of God,
and who treats the Blood of the Covenant in which he was sanctified as
unclean and who insults the Spirit of grace*?[a] [19]For a person looks Heb 10:29
down upon, defiles and tramples upon the Lamb of God when, as the
Apostle says, not distinguishing and discerning the holy bread of 1 Cor 11:29
Christ from other foods or actions, he either unworthily or, even if he is
worthy, eats It in vain and unworthily since the Lord says through the
prophet: The person *is cursed who* does the work of the Lord *deceit-
fully.* [20]He will, in truth, condemn priests who do not wish to take this Jer 48:10
to heart, saying: *I will curse your blessings.* Mal 2:2

a. This passages reflects the influence of Honorius III, *Sane cum olim*, cf. supra p. 55, a.

[21]Listen, my brothers: If the Blessed Virgin is so honored, as is becoming, because she carried Him in her most holy womb; if the Baptist
trembled and did not dare to touch the holy head of God;[a] if the tomb in
which He lay for some time is held in veneration, [22]how holy, just and
fitting must be he who touches with his hands, receives in his heart and
mouth, and offers to others to be received the One Who is not about to
die but Who is to conquer and be glorified, upon Whom *the angels*
1 Pt 1:12 *longed to gaze.*[b]
1 Cor 1:26 [23]*See your* dignity, [my] priest *brothers,* and be holy because He is
Lv 19:2 holy. [24]As the Lord God has honored you above all others because of
this ministry, for your part love, revere and honor Him above all others.
[25]It is a great misery and a miserable weakness that when you have
Him present in this way, you are concerned with anything else in the
whole world!

[26]Let everyone be struck with fear,
let the whole world tremble,
and let the heavens exult
when Christ, the Son of the living God,
is present on the altar in the hands of a priest!
[27]O wonderful loftiness and stupendous dignity!
O sublime humility!
O humble sublimity!
The Lord of the universe,
God and the Son of God,
so humbles Himself
that for our salvation
He hides Himself
under an ordinary piece of bread!
[28]Brothers, look at the humility of God,
Ps 62: 9 and *pour out your hearts before Him!*
Humble yourselves
1 Pt 5:6; Jas 4:10 that you may be exalted by Him!
[29]Hold back nothing of yourselves for yourselves,
that He Who gives Himself totally to you
may receive you totally!

a. A reference to the work of Psuedo-Bernard of Cluny, *Tractatus de Corpore Domini* (PL 183:146A).

b. This passage shows the influence of Bernard of Clairvaux, *Sermo I, Epiphania Domini* (PL 183:146A) as well as the Psuedo-Bernard of Cluny, *Instructio sacerdotis, seu praeparations eius ad digne celebrandum tantum mysterium* (PL 184:787a).

[30]I admonish and exhort you in the Lord, therefore, to celebrate only one Mass a day according to the rite of the Holy Church in those places where the brothers dwell. [31]But if there is more than one priest there, let the other be content, for the love of charity, at hearing the celebration of the other priest;[a] [32]because our Lord Jesus Christ fills those present and absent who are worthy of Him. [33]Although He may seem to be present in many places, nevertheless, He remains, undivided and knows no loss; but One everywhere, He acts as He pleases, with the Lord God the Father and the Holy Spirit the Paraclete for ever and ever. Amen.

[34]Because *whoever belongs to God hears the words of God,* we who are more especially charged with divine responsibilities must not only listen to and do what the Lord says but also care for the vessels and other liturgical objects that contain His holy words in order to impress on ourselves the sublimity of our Creator and our subjection to Him. [35]I, therefore, admonish all my brothers and encourage them in Christ to venerate, as best as they can, the divine written words wherever they find them. [36]If they are not well kept or are carelessly thrown around in some place, let them gather them up and preserve them, inasmuch as it concerns them, honoring in the words the Lord *Who spoke them.* [37]For many things are made holy by the words of God and the sacrament of the altar is celebrated in the power of the words of Christ.

Jn 8:47

3 Kgs 2:4

1 Tm 4:5

[38]Moreover, I confess all my sins to the Lord God, Father, Son, and Holy Spirit, to the blessed ever Virgin Mary, all the saints in heaven and on earth, to Brother H.,[b] the Minister of our Order as my venerable lord, to the priests of our Order and all my other blessed brothers. [39]I have offended the Lord in many ways by my serious faults especially in not observing the Rule that I have promised Him and in not saying the Office as the Rule prescribes either out of negligence or by reason of my weakness or because I am ignorant and stupid.

[40]Therefore, I beg by all means, as best I can, Brother H., the General Minister, my lord, to have the Rule observed inviolably by everyone, [41]to have the clerics say the Office with devotion before God not concentrating on the melody of the voice but on the harmony of the mind, that the voice may be in harmony with the mind, the mind truly in

a. While questions arise concerning the interpretation of this passage, it should be remembered that the rite of concelebration was not practiced at this point of history and private mass was only beginning to be a common occurrence. Thus Francis encourages the social or communal character of the Eucharist as the center of Gospel life.

b. Cf. supra p. 116, c.

harmony with God.[a] [42][Let them do this] that they may be able to please God by their purity of heart and not just charm the ears of people by their sweetness of voice.

[43]For my part, I firmly promise to observe these things, as God shall give me the grace, and I pass them on to the brothers who are with me to be observed in the Office and the other prescriptions of the Rule.

[44]I do not consider those brothers who do not wish to observe these things Catholics or my brothers; I do not even wish to see or speak with them until they have done penance. [45]I even say this about all those who wander about, having put aside the discipline of the Rule, [46]for our Lord Jesus Christ gave His life that He would not lose the obedience of
Phil 2:8 His most holy Father.

[47]I, Brother Francis, a useless man and an unworthy creature of the Lord God, speak through the Lord Jesus Christ to Brother H., the General Minister of our entire Order and to all the general ministers who will come after him, and to the other custodians and guardians of the brothers, who are and who will be, that they might keep this writing with them, put it into practice and eagerly preserve it. [48]I exhort them to guard what is written in it carefully and to have it observed more diligently according to the pleasure of the all-powerful God, now and forever, as long as the world lasts.

[49]Blessed by the Lord are you who do these things and may the Lord be with you forever. Amen.

[Prayer][b]

[50]Almighty, eternal, just and merciful God,
give us miserable ones
the grace to do for You alone
what we know you want us to do
and always to desire what pleases You.
[51]Inwardly cleansed,
interiorly enlightened
and inflamed by the fire of the Holy Spirit,

a. This passage parallels the *Benedictine Rule* XIX: "Let us, therefore, consider in what state one must be in the sight of God and his angels; we shall, then, stand while chanting, so that our hearts will be in harmony with our voices." It also resonates with this sentiment of Saint Augustine: "While you are praying to God during the chanting of the psalms and hymns, what you express on your lips should also be alive in your hearts" (*Epistola* 48:3; *Epistola* 221:7). For the meaning of "devotion" see supra p. 102, c.

b. Although the Assisi Codex 338, the oldest collection of Francis's writings, places this prayer at the end of this letter, many manuscripts consider it a separate piece.

may we be able to follow
in the footprints of Your beloved Son,
our Lord Jesus Christ,
52 and, by Your grace alone,
may we make our way to You,
Most High,
Who live and rule
in perfect Trinity and simple Unity,
and are glorified
God almighty,
forever and ever.
Amen.

A Letter to Brother Leo
(1224-1226)[a]

This short letter was written on a small piece of parchment. Worn spots suggest that Brother Leo must have kept it with him as a precious relic. Although scholars do not agree, a comparison of Francis's handwriting in this parchment with that given to Leo on LaVerna indicates that he may have been suffering from the stigmata at the time of offering him this piece of advice.[b]

Edition of Kajetan Esser

[1]Brother Leo, health and peace from Brother Francis![c]

[2]I am speaking, my son, in this way—as a mother would—because I am putting everything we said on the road in this brief message and advice.[d] If, afterwards, you need to come to me for counsel, I advise you thus: [3]In whatever way it seems better to you to please the Lord God and to follow His footprint[e] and poverty, do it with the blessing of the Lord God and my obedience. [4]And if you need and want to come to me for the sake of your soul or for some consolation, Leo, come.

---

a. The history of this original manuscript, written by Francis himself, is filled with mystery. It is missing from any list of Francis's writings until 1604 when the Poor Clares gave it to the Conventual Friars in Spoleto. It then disappeared until 1895 when Clito Cardinale, a parish priest of Spoleto, brought it to Michele Faloci-Pulignani, a church official, to determine its authenticity. Faloci-Pulignani brought it to Pope Leo XIII who entrusted it to the care of the canons of the Duomo of Spoleto who still maintain its care.

b. See A. Pratesi, "Autografo di San Francesco nel Duomo si Spoleto," *San Francesco e i Francescani a Spoleto*, (Spoleto: Accademia Spoletina 1984) 17-26; and Attilio Bartoli Langeli, "Gli scritti da Francesco. L'autografo di un 'illiteratus,'" *Frate Francesco d'Assisi.* Atti del XXI Convegno Internazionale, Spoleto: Centro Italiano di Studi sull'Alto Medievo, 1994, 101-159.

c. The Latin text of this autograph is *f leo f francissco tuo salutem et pacem.* Two points have puzzled scholars: its grammatical construction, suggesting that Leo is sending this to Francis, and the misspelling of the saint's name. In the first instance, the greeting may be an example of the saint's poor grasp of Latin. In the second, some have suggested that *Sco,* as is *francis-sco,* may have been the saint's nickname, its use suggesting the close bond of friendship that existed between the two.

d. The concept of relationships qualified by motherhood is undoubtedly intertwined in Francis's concept of bringing others to life through the word of God, an image found in Paul, e.g., 1 Corinthians 4:6 and I Thessalonians 2:7. It is found elsewhere in Francis's writings, e.g. ER IX 11, LR VI 8, *Rule for Hermitages* 1-2,10 (hereafter RH), and in the testimony of Odo of Cheriton who, in 1219, maintained that he heard Francis reply to a question of how the fraternity came to be: "I became like a woman impregnated by the word of God." The stimulus for this writing is a discussion both men were having while traveling. In this regard, it is similar to the *True and Perfect Joy* (hereafter TPJ) (cf. infra). In both instances, Leo appears as being troubled or disturbed by questions of the essence of Francis's view of Gospel life.

e. No explanation has been found for Francis's unusual use of the singular case in this reference to the footprints of Jesus.

Edition of Attilio Bartoli Langeli

Bartoli Langeli studied the manuscript of this autograph of Francis and offered a significantly different edition of the text,[a] one which suggests that not only was he not accustomed to writing, but that his educational level may well have been "somewhere between illiteracy and full and complete literacy."[b]

1 Brother Leo, your brother Francis
2 health and peace. I am speaking to you,
3 my son, in this way as a mother—because
4 all the words that we spoke
5 on the road I place and advise
6 briefly in this message[c] and
7 afterwards, it is not necessary
8 to come to me for counsel.
9 Because I advise you thus: In what-
10 ever way it seems better
11 to you to please the Lord
12 God and to follow His footprints[d] and
13 poverty, you may do it
14 with the blessing of the Lord
15 God and my obedience.
16 And if it is necessary for you[e]
17 for your soul for some
18 consolation to you,[f] and you want
19 to come back to me, come.

---

a. Attilio Bartoli Langeli, "Gli scritti da Francesco. L'autografo di un 'illitertus,'" *Frate Francesco d'Assisi.* Atti del XXI Convegno Internazionale, Spoleto: Centro Italiano di Studi sull'Alto Medievo, 1994, 101-159.

b. Cf. Bartoli Langeli, p. 122, n. 4.

c. The editor has taken the liberty of re-arranging the text for the sake of readability. The Bartoli Langeli text reads literally: "4 all the words that we spoke 5 on the road briefly in this message 6 I place and advise . . ."

d. Whereas Esser read *vestigiam* (singular), sensing that the final mark indicated an abbreviation, Bartoli Langeli sees it as a characteristic of Francis's way of dotting an "i."

e. Bartoli Langeli believes that these last four lines were added later for there is an obvious change of pen. Accordingly, he suggests that Francis ended his letter with *obedientia* and then added the last four lines.

f. This phrase is difficult to interpret. According to Bartoli Langeli the parchment reads: "17 . . . propter ali*am* 18 *con*solationem tua *et* uis." (Italics indicate letters that have been abbreviated or replaced by signs.)

The Testament
(1226)[a]

Those "who were with him," the brothers who write in *The Assisi Compilation,* tell of a number of documents or "testaments" which Francis dictated as his health deteriorated and death drew near: that of Siena in which he outlined the basic principles of his Gospel vision, that concerning the Portiuncula in which he asked his brothers to care for this special symbol of their life, and another in which he provided guidelines for building new dwellings.[b] This document, which has come to be known as "The Testament," has remained a primary expression of Francis's profound wisdom and vision. While popular tradition maintains that it was written at the Portiuncula while he was dying, the document's different styles of writing suggest that it was written at different moments of those final days and was prompted by different questions swirling around his simple Gospel vision.

[1]The Lord gave me, Brother Francis, thus to begin doing penance in this way: for when I was in sin, it seemed too bitter for me to see lepers.
Sir 35:4 [2]And the Lord Himself led me among them and *I showed mercy* to them.[c] [3]And when I left them, what had seemed bitter to me was turned into sweetness of soul and body. And afterwards I delayed a little and left the world.

[4]And the Lord gave me such faith in churches that I would pray with simplicity in this way and say: [5]"We adore You, Lord Jesus Christ, in

a. It is difficult to determine the meaning of *testamentum* (testament) as the title of this work. Its profane or legal sense suggests a last will and "testament" concerning one's goods or possessions. Pope Gregory IX, in the papal document, *Quo elongati* (1230), suggests this meaning when he states: "Toward the end of his life [Francis] made a command, which is called a 'Testament.' " In 1295 Peter Olivi in a letter to Conrad of Offida claims the title was given by others and calls it simply a letter. A short time later, Ubertino da Casale reflects upon the tension between the title and the text when he writes: ". . . in his *Testament,* as he himself calls the document . . ." In recent times, Auspicius van Corstanje has suggested a biblical interpretation and interpreted the work as an expression of God's covenant (*testamentum*) with the poor Francis and his brothers, cf. *The Covenant with God's Poor,* (Chicago: Franciscan Herald Press, 1966).

b. Cf. AC 59, 56, 106, 23.

c. The phrase *feci misericordiam* [I showed mercy] has a rich biblical tradition, one that is frequently associated with penance. Forms of the phrase *facere misericordiam* appear almost fifty times in the Vulgate edition, most of them in the Old Testament. Of these the editors have chosen to suggest a reference to Sirach 35:4 "*qui faciet misericordiam offert sacrificum* [whoever shows mercy offers sacrifice]."

all Your churches throughout the whole world and we bless You because by Your holy cross You have redeemed the world."[a]

[6]Afterwards the Lord gave me, and gives me still, such faith in
priests who live according to the rite of the holy Roman Church because of their orders that, were they to persecute me, I would still want
to have recourse to them. [7]And if I had as much *wisdom* as *Solomon* and 1 Kgs 4:30-31
found impoverished priests of this world, I would not preach in their
parishes against their will. [8]And I desire to respect, love and honor
them and all others as my lords. [9]And I do not want to consider any sin
in them because I discern the Son of God in them and they are my lords.
[10]And I act in this way because, in this world, I see nothing corporally
of the most high Son of God except His most holy Body and Blood
which they receive and they alone administer to others. [11]I want to
have these most holy mysteries honored and venerated above all things
and I want to reserve them in precious places. [12]Wherever I find our
Lord's most holy names and written words in unbecoming places, I
want to gather them up and I beg that they be gathered up and placed in
a becoming place. [13]And we must honor all theologians and those who
minister the most holy divine words and respect them as those who
minister to us *spirit and life.* Jn 6:63

[14]And after the Lord gave me some brothers, no one showed me
what I had to do, but the Most High Himself revealed to me that I
should live according to the pattern of the Holy Gospel. [15]And I had
this written down simply and in a few words and the Lord Pope confirmed it for me. [16]And those who came to receive life gave *whatever*
they had to the poor and were content with one tunic, patched inside Tb 1:3
and out, with a cord and short trousers. [17]We desired nothing more.
[18]We clerical [brothers] said the Office as other clerics did; the lay
brothers said the *Our Father;* and we quite willingly remained in Mt 6:9-13
churches. [19]And we were simple and subject to all.

[20]And *I worked with* my *hands,* and I still desire to work; and I ear- Acts 20:34
nestly desire all brothers to give themselves to honest work. [21]Let those
who do not know how to work learn, not from desire to receive wages,
but for example and to avoid idleness. [22]And when we are not paid for
our work, let us have recourse to the table of the Lord, begging alms

a. This prayer is made up of a liturgical formula recited on the feast of Good Friday and the Exaltation of the Cross: "We adore you, O Christ, and we bless you, because by your cross you have redeemed the world." To this formula, however, Francis made three additions: (a) the name, Jesus Christ; (b) the phrase, in all your churches throughout the world; and (c) the adjective, holy, to describe the cross.

from door to door. [23]The Lord revealed a greeting to me that we should say: "*May the Lord give* you *peace.*"

[24]Let the brothers be careful not to receive in any way churches or poor dwellings or anything else built for them unless they are according to the holy poverty we have promised in the Rule.[a] *As pilgrims and strangers,* let them always be guests there.

[25]I strictly command all the brothers through obedience, wherever they may be, not to dare to ask any letter from the Roman Curia, either personally or through an intermediary, whether for a church or another place or under the pretext of preaching or the persecution of their bodies.[b] [26]But, wherever they have not been received, *let them flee into another* country to do penance with the blessing of God.

[27]And I firmly wish to obey the general minister of this fraternity and the other guardian whom it pleases him to give me. [28]And I so wish to be a captive in his hands that I cannot go anywhere or do anything beyond obedience and his will, for he is my master.

[29]And although I may be simple and infirm, I nevertheless want to have a cleric always with me who will celebrate the Office for me as it is prescribed in the *Rule.*

[30]And let all the brothers be bound to obey their guardians and to recite the Office according to the Rule. [31]And if some might have been found who are not reciting the Office according to the Rule and want to change it in some way, or who are not Catholics, let all the brothers, wherever they may have found one of them, be bound through obedience to bring him before the custodian of that place nearest to where they found him.[c] [32]And let the custodian be strictly bound through obedience to keep him securely day and night as a man in chains, so that he cannot be taken from his hands until he can personally deliver him into

---

a. *The Testament* takes a decidedly different direction at this point as Francis ceases to reminisce about the early days of his life and those of his brothers and begins a series of exhortations and commands. This change has led some to conclude that the document was written at different times and, perhaps, with the assistance of different brothers who took his dictation. In this instance, while recognizing the gradual development of accepting churches and residences, a step away from his original view of poverty introduced by the papal document *Cum secondum consilium* (1220) which established the year of probation, Francis encourages the brothers to keep the ideal of poverty before them. Cf. infra pp. 560-561.

b. The encouragement of the previous section becomes a strong command prohibiting the active search for churches or residences regardless of the reason. The papal document, *In eo quod audivimus,* sent to the Archbishop of Pisa and the Abbot of Saint Paul's on October 4, 1225, provides some insight into the persecution encountered by religious and the protection promised by the Holy See. Three papal documents written during the last years of Francis's life, *Vineae Domini custodes* (October 7, 1225), *Urgenti officii nostri* (February 20, 1226) and *Ex parte vestra* (March 17, 1226) promise the itinerant brothers the same type of protection and threaten sanctions on those who persecute them. Cf. infra. *Related Documents,* p. 563.

c. This passage parallels Francis's *Letter to the Entire Order* 44-46 (hereafter LtOrd) and accentuates his insistence that the Liturgy of the Hours forms a strong link binding the brothers to one another and to the Church.

the hands of his minister. [33]And let the minister be bound through obedience to send him with such brothers who would guard him as a prisoner until they deliver him to the Lord of Ostia, who is the Lord, the Protector and the Corrector of this fraternity.

[34]And the brothers may not say: "This is another rule."[a] Because this is a remembrance, admonition, exhortation, and my testament, which I, little brother Francis, make for you, my blessed brothers, that we might observe the Rule we have promised in a more Catholic way.

[35]And let the general minister and all the other ministers and custodians be bound through obedience not *to add to* or *take away* from these words. [36]And let them always have this writing with them together with the Rule.[37]And in all the chapters which they hold, when they read the Rule, let them also read these words. [38]And I strictly command all my cleric and lay brothers, through obedience, not to place any gloss upon the Rule or upon these words saying: "They should be understood in this way." [39]But as the Lord has given me to speak and write the Rule and these words simply and purely, may you understand them simply and without gloss and observe them with a holy activity until the end.

Dt 4:2; 12:32

[40]And whoever observes these things, let him be blessed *in heaven with the blessing* of the Most High Father, and *on earth* with the blessing of His Beloved Son with the Most Holy Spirit, the Paraclete, and all the powers of heaven and with all the saints. [41]And, as far as I can, I, little brother Francis, your servant, confirm for you, both within and without, this most holy blessing.

Gn 27:27-28

a. This passage introduces the question of the nature of this document, a question which Francis himself must have suspected would arise in light of the exhortations and commands contained in its final paragraphs. The answer to the question is found in Francis's calling to mind the ideals of the primitive fraternity in light of the reality of its growth. Thus, rather than establish new legislative positions, he strongly re-interprets many of the ideals articulated in the Rule.

The Undated Writings

The Admonitions

A medieval admonition was more than a warning or a calling to mind; it had more of a religious sense in which a biblical passage or image was presented and, in light of it, a practical application was made. Thus these twenty-eight teachings of Francis offer insights into his biblical thought and the ways in which he translated them into the ordinary experiences of daily life. Although some of these pieces offer clues as to their composition or deliverance, they are difficult to date. The five manuscript collections of the thirteenth century contain only one consistent document: the following twenty-eight pieces or admonitions. This attests to their importance in the early Franciscan tradition and to their place as Francis's "Canticle of Minority."

[I. The Body of Christ]

[1]The Lord Jesus says to his disciples: *I am the way, the truth and the
life; no one comes to the Father except through me.* [2]*If you knew me,
you would also know my Father; and from now on, you do know him
and have seen him.* [3]*Philip says to him: Lord, show us the Father and it
will be enough for us.* [4]*Jesus says to him: Have I been with you for so
long a time and you have not known me? Philip, whoever sees me sees*
Jn 14:6-9 *my Father as well.*
1 Tm 6:16; Jn 4:24 [5]The Father dwells *in inaccessible light,* and *God is spirit,* and *no*
Jn 1:18 *one has ever seen God.* [6]Therefore He cannot be seen except in the
Spirit because *it is the Spirit that gives life; the flesh has nothing to of-*
Jn 6:63 *fer.* [7]But because He is equal to the Father, the Son is not seen by any-
one other than the Father or other than the Holy Spirit.

[8]All those who saw the Lord Jesus according to the humanity, therefore, and did not see and believe according to the Spirit and the Divinity that He is the true Son of God were condemned. [9]Now in the same way, all those who see the sacrament sanctified by the words of the Lord upon the altar at the hands of the priest in the form of bread and wine, and who do not see and believe according to the Spirit and the Divinity that it is truly the Body and Blood of our Lord Jesus Christ, are condemned.[10][This] is affirmed by the Most High Himself Who says:

*This is my Body and the Blood of my new covenant [which will be shed
for many];* [11]and *Whoever eats my flesh and drinks my blood has eter-* Mk 14:22,24
nal life. [12]It is the Spirit of the Lord, therefore, That lives in Its faithful, Jn 6:55
That receives the Body and Blood of the Lord. [13]All others who do not
share in this same Spirit and presume to receive Him eat and drink
judgment on themselves. 1 Cor 11:29

[14]Therefore: *children, how long will you be hard of heart?* [15]Why Ps 4:3
do you not know the truth and believe *in the Son of God?* [16]Behold, Jn 9:35
each day He humbles Himself as when He came *from the royal throne* Phil 2:8
into the Virgin's womb; [17]each day He Himself comes to us, appearing Wis 18:15
humbly; [18]each day He comes down *from the bosom of the Father* upon Jn 1:18
the altar in the hands of a priest.[a]

[19]As He revealed Himself to the holy apostles in true flesh, so He reveals Himself to us now in sacred bread. [20]And as they saw only His flesh by an insight of their flesh, yet believed that He was God as they contemplated Him with their spiritual eyes, [21]let us, as we see bread and wine with our bodily eyes, see and firmly believe that they are His most holy Body and Blood living and true. [22]And in this way the Lord is always with His faithful, as He Himself says: *Behold I am with you
until the end of the age.* Mt. 28:20

[II. The Evil of Self-Will][b]

[1]The Lord said to Adam: *Eat of every tree; you may not eat, however, of the tree of the knowledge of good and evil.* Gn 2:16,17

[2]He was able to eat of every tree of paradise, because he did not sin as long as he did not go against obedience. [3]For that person eats of the tree of the knowledge of good who makes his will his own and, in this way, exalts himself over the good things the Lord says and does in him. [4]And so, through the suggestion of the devil and the transgression of the command, it became the apple of the knowledge of evil. [5]Therefore it is fitting that he suffer the punishment.

---

a. These verses reflect the influence of the *Tractatus de Corpore Domini* written by the anonymous Cistercian, the Pseudo-Bernard. (cf. PL 184:1149-1150).

b. The theology of this admonition can be found in the writings of Augustine (*Ennarationes in Psalmos* 70, 7, PL 36, 896ff) and in the tradition of the Cistercians Pseudo-Bernard (*Tractatus de statu virtutum*, PL 184:805, 799) and Godfrey of Amont (*Homilia Domincae* XXII, PL 174, 150), et al. Yet the view of this sin as one against poverty, i.e., making his will his own, is unique to Francis.

[III. Perfect Obedience]

[1]The Lord says in the Gospel: *Whoever does not renounce all that he*
Lk 14:33 *possesses cannot be my disciple;* [2]and: *Whoever wishes to save his life*
Lk 9:24 *must lose it.*

[3]That person who offers himself totally to obedience in the hands of his prelate leaves all that he possesses and loses his body.[a] [4]And whatever he does and says which he knows is not contrary to his will is true obedience, provided that what he does is good.

[5]And should a subject see that some things might be better and more useful for his soul than what a prelate commands, let him willingly offer such things to God as a sacrifice; and, instead, let him earnestly strive to fulfill the prelate's wishes. [6]For this is loving obedience be-
1 Pt 1:22 cause it pleases God and neighbor.

[7]If the prelate, however, commands something contrary to his conscience, even though he may not obey him, let him not, however, abandon him. [8]And if he then suffers persecution from others, let him love
1 Jn 3:15-16 them all the more for the sake of God. [9]For whoever chooses to suffer
persecution rather than wish to be separated from his brothers truly remains in perfect obedience because he lays down *his life* for his broth-
Jn 15:13 ers. [10]In fact, there are many religious who, under the pretext of seeing
Lk 9:62 things better than those which the prelate commands, look back, and
Prv 26:11; 2 Pt 2:22 return to the vomit of their own will. [11]These people are murderers and,
because of their bad example, cause many to lose their souls.[b]

[IV. Let No One Make Being Over Others His Own]

Mt 20:28 [1]*I did not come to be served, but to serve, says the Lord.*

[2]Let those who are placed over others boast about that position as
much as they would if they were assigned the duty of washing the feet
of their brothers. [3]And if they are more upset at having their place over
others taken away from them than at losing their position at their feet,
Jn 12:6 the more they store up *a money bag* to the peril of their soul.[c]

a. The term "prelate" was one used in the Cistercian tradition for one who was a "superior," i.e., an abbot or prior. It can be found only seven times in Francis's writings; five of these are in this admonition. The other two instances come from the biographical tradition, i.e., the *Siena Testament* (AC 59) and TPJ (Acts 7). Thus the presence of a Cistercian at the utterance of this admonition is quite possible.

b. Once again the influence of the *Tractatus de status virtutum* of the Cistercian, the Pseudo-Bernard, can be found (PL 184, 80).

c. The reference is to the treachery of Judas, a frequent allusion found in monastic literature, e.g. Godfrey of Auxerre (PL 185, 446), *Declarationes 14, De loculis Judae.*

[V. Let No One Be Proud, but Boast in the Cross of the Lord]

[1]Consider, O human being, in what great excellence the Lord God has placed you, for He created and formed you *to the image* of His beloved Son according to the body and *to His likeness* according to the Spirit. 1 Gn 1:26

[2]And all creatures under heaven serve, know, and obey their Creator, each according to its own nature, better than you. [3]And even the demons did not crucify Him, but you, together with them, have crucified Him and are still crucifying Him by delighting in vices and sins.

[4]In what, then, can you boast? [5]Even if you were so skillful and wise that you possessed *all knowledge,* knew how to interpret every *kind of* 1 Cor 13:2 *language,* and to scrutinize heavenly matters with skill: you could not 1 Cor 12:28 boast in these things. [6]For, even though someone may have received from the Lord a special knowledge of the highest wisdom, one demon knew about heavenly matters and now knows more about those of earth than all human beings.[a]

[7]In the same way, even if you were more handsome and richer than everyone else, and even if you worked miracles so that you put demons to flight: all these things are contrary to you; nothing belongs to you; you can boast in none of these things.

[8]But we can boast *in* our *weaknesses* and in carrying each day the 2 Cor 12:5 holy cross of our Lord Jesus Christ. Lk 14:27

[VI: Imitation of Christ]

[1]Let all of us, brothers, consider the Good Shepherd Who bore the suffering of the cross to save His sheep.

[2]The Lord's sheep followed Him in tribulation and persecution, in shame and hunger, in weakness and temptation, and in other ways; and for these things they received eternal life from the Lord.

[3]Therefore, it is a great shame for us, the servants of God, that the saints have accomplished great things and we want only to receive glory and honor by recounting them.

---

a. The pursuit of wisdom or knowledge is a prominent theme in *The Admonitions* as is seen in this passage. Adm VII points out the dangers of knowledge of Sacred Scripture without possessing its Spirit. Adm X 3 speaks of the wisdom of keeping our enemy in control, while Adm XXI of the person who wisely keeps his counsel. The presence of words such as *sapiens, sapientiores, sapienter* and *sapientia* confirm the belief that the pursuit of knowledge and the risks it presents is one of the strong themes of *The Admonitions.*

[VII: Let Good Action Follow Knowledge]

2 Cor 3:6 1 The apostle says: *The letter kills, but the spirit gives life.*
2 Those people are put to death by the letter who only wish to know
the words alone, that they might be esteemed wiser than others and be
able to acquire great riches to give to their relatives and friends.
3 And those religious are put to death by the letter who are not willing to follow the spirit of the divine letter but, instead, wish only to
know the words and to interpret them for others.
4 And those people are brought to life by the spirit of the divine letter
who do not attribute every letter they know, or wish to know, to the
body but, by word and example, return them to the most high Lord God
to Whom every good belongs.

[VIII. Avoiding the Sin of Envy]

1 The apostle says: *No one can say: Jesus is Lord, except in the Holy*
1 Cor 12:3; Rom 3:12 *Spirit;* 2 and: *There is not one who does good, not even one.*
3 Therefore, whoever envies his brother the good that the Lord says
or does in him incurs a sin of blasphemy because he envies the Most
Mt 20:15 High Himself Who says and does every good thing.

[IX. Love]

1 The Lord says: *Love your enemies [do good to those who hate you*
Mt 5:44 *and pray for those who persecute and slander you].*
2 For that person truly loves his enemy who is not hurt by an injury
done to him, 3 but, because of love of God, is stung by the sin of his soul.
4 Let him show him love by his deeds.

[X. Castigating the Body]

1 There are many people who, when they sin or are injured, fre-
Gn 3:12-13 quently blame the enemy or their neighbor. 2 But it is not so, because
each one has the enemy in his power, that is his body through which he
sins.
Mt 24:46 3 *Blessed is the servant,* then, who always holds captive the enemy
delivered into his power and wisely safeguards himself from him; 4 because, as long as he does this, no other enemy visible or invisible will
be able to harm him.

[XI: Let No One Be Corrupted by the Evil of Another]

[1]Nothing should displease a servant of God except sin. [2]And no matter how another person may sin, if a servant of God becomes disturbed and angry because of this and not because of charity, he is storing up guilt for himself. [3]That servant of God who does not become angry or disturbed at anyone lives correctly without anything of his own.[a] [4]Blessed is the one for whom nothing remains except for him *to return to Caesar what is Caesar's and to God what is God's.*

Rom 2:5

Mt 22:21

[XII: Knowing the Spirit of the Lord]

[1]A servant of God can be known to have the Spirit of the Lord in this way: [2]if, when the Lord performs some good through him, his flesh does not therefore exalt itself, because it is always opposed to every good. [3]Instead he regards himself the more worthless and esteems himself less than all others.

[XIII: Patience]

[1]*Blessed are the peacemakers, for they will be called children of God.* Mt 5:9

A servant of God cannot know how much patience and humility he has within himself as long as he is content. [2]When the time comes, however, when those who should make him content do the opposite, he has as much patience and humility as he has at that time and no more.

[XIV: Poverty of Spirit]

[1]*Blessed are the poor in spirit, for theirs is the kingdom of heaven.* Mt 5:3

[2]There are many who, while insisting on prayers and obligations, inflict many abstinences and punishments upon their bodies. [3]But they are immediately offended and disturbed about a single word which seems to be harmful to their bodies or about something which might be taken away from them. [4]These people are not poor in spirit, for some-

a. The phrase *sine proprio* [without anything of his own] is the same as that found in the formula of the three vows, cf. ER I 1; LR I 1. It was used as a technical form to describe the vow of poverty. Yet Francis extends its meaning, as this text suggests, and implies that poverty is much more than a material concern. As the doctrine of a life "without anything of one's own" unfolds in *The Admonitions*, poverty touches on poverty in relationship to (a) one's brothers, (b) one's inner self, and (c) God.

one who is truly poor in spirit hates himself and loves those who strike
Mt 5:39 him on the cheek.

[XV: Peace]

[1]*Blessed are the peacemakers, for they will be called children of*
Mt 5:9 *God.*

[2]Those people are truly peacemakers who, regardless of what they suffer in this world, preserve peace of spirit and body out of love of our Lord Jesus Christ.

[XVI: Cleanness of Heart]

Mt 5:8 [1]*Blessed are the clean in heart, for they will see God.*

[2]The truly clean of heart are those who look down upon earthly things, seek those of heaven, and, with a clean heart and spirit, never cease adoring and seeing the Lord God living and true.

[XVII: The Humble Servant of God]

Mt 24:46 [1]*Blessed is that servant* who no more exalts himself over the good the Lord says or does through him than over what He says or does through another.

[2]A person sins who wishes to receive more from his neighbor than what he wishes to give of himself to the Lord God.

[XVIII: Compassion for a Neighbor][a]

[1]Blessed is the person who supports his neighbor in his weakness as
Gal 6:2; Mt 7:12 he would want to be supported were he in a similar situation.

[2]Blessed is the servant who returns every good to the Lord God be-
cause whoever holds onto something for himself *hides the money of his*
Mt 25:18 *Lord* God within himself, and *what* he thinks *he has will be taken away*
Lk 8:18 *from* him.

a. Kajetan Esser breaks with the more customary division of *The Admonitions* and follows the more solid manuscript tradition in joining Adm XVIII and Adm XIX, and in dividing Adm XXV into two separate pieces.

[XIX: A Humble Servant of God]

[1]Blessed is the servant who does not consider himself any better when he is praised and exalted by people than when he is considered worthless, simple, and looked down upon, [2]for what a person is before God, that he is and no more.

[3]Woe to that religious who has been placed in a high position by others and [who] does not want to come down by his own will.

[4]*Blessed is that servant* who is not placed in a high position by his Mt 24:46
own will and always desires to be under the feet of others.

[XX: The Good and the Vain Religious]

[1]Blessed is that religious who has no pleasure and delight except in the most holy words and deeds of the Lord [2]and, with these, leads people to the love of God with gladness and joy. Ps 51:10

[3]Woe to that religious who delights in idle and empty words and leads people to laughter with them.

[XXI: The Frivolous and the Talkative Religious]

[1]Blessed is the servant who, when he speaks, does not disclose everything about himself under the guise of a reward and is not quick to speak, but who is wisely cautious about what he says and how he responds. Prv 29:20

[2]Woe to that religious who does not hold in his heart the good things the Lord reveals to him and does not reveal them by his behavior, but, under the guise of a reward, wishes instead to reveal them with his words. [3]He receives *his reward* and his listeners carry away little fruit. Lk 2:19, 51; Mt 6:2, 16

[XXII: Correction]

[1]Blessed is the servant who endures discipline, accusation, and reprimand from another as patiently as he would from himself.

[2]Blessed is the servant who, after being reprimanded, agrees courteously, submits respectfully, admits humbly, and makes amends willingly.

[3]Blessed is the servant who is not quick to excuse himself, and endures with humility, shame, and reprimand for a sin, when he did not commit the fault.

[XXIII: Humility]

[1]Blessed is the servant who has been found as humble among his subjects as he was among his masters.

[2]Blessed is the servant who always remains under the rod of correction.

Mt 24:45 [3]*Faithful and prudent is the servant* who does not delay in punishing himself for all his offenses, inwardly through contrition and outwardly through confession and penance for what he did.

[XXIV: True Love]

Blessed is the servant who loves his brother as much when he is sick and cannot repay him as when he is well and can repay him.

[XXV: The Same Point]

Blessed is the servant who loves and respects his brother as much when he is far away from him as when he is with him, and who would not say anything behind his back that he would not say with charity in his presence.

[XXVI: Let Servants of God Honor the Clergy]

[1]Blessed is the servant who has faith in the clergy who live uprightly according to the rite of the Roman Church.

[2]Woe to those who look down upon them; for even though they be sinners, no one should judge them because the Lord alone reserves judgment on them to Himself. [3]For just as their ministry is greater in its concerns for the most holy Body and Blood of our Lord Jesus Christ, which they receive and they alone administer to others, [4]so those who sin against them commit more of a sin than [if they had sinned] against all other persons in this world.

[XXVII: Virtue Puts Vice to Flight]

[1]Where there is charity and wisdom,
there is neither fear nor ignorance.

[2]Where there is patience and humility,
there is neither anger nor disturbance.

3Where there is poverty with joy,
there is neither greed nor avarice.[a]

4Where there is rest[b] and meditation,
there is neither anxiety nor restlessness.

5Where there is fear of the Lord to guard an entrance, Lk 11:21
there the enemy cannot have a place to enter.

6Where there is a heart full of mercy[c] and discernment,
there is neither excess nor hardness of heart.

[XXVIII: Hiding the Good That It Not Be Lost]

1Blessed is the servant who stores up in heaven the good things which the Lord shows to him and does not wish to reveal them to people under the guise of a reward, 2because the Most High Himself will reveal His deeds to whomever He wishes. Mt 6:20

3Blessed is the servant who safeguards the secrets of the Lord in his heart. Lk 2:19,51

---

a. Whereas these first three verses contain many words and themes frequently present in Francis's writings, e.g. charity, patience, humility, poverty and joy, the following three verses are filled with hapaxlogomena, words which are used only once, e.g., meditation, restlessness, *superfluitas* (excess) and *induratio* (hardness of heart). These first three verses describe the fundamental characteristics of the servant of God; the final three present more specific characteristics involving and flowing from prayer.

b. *Quies* is used only in this instance in Francis's writings and may be interpreted in different ways as in the Cistercian tradition of the period: the *quies claustri* expressions of solitude and the discipline of the enclosure; the *quies mentis* which considered virtues such as silence, mortification, and inner peace; and the *quies contemplationis* themes such as idleness, free time or resting in God. Since the word is linked with meditation and restlessness, this latter concept is seen as more appropriate, i.e., resting in God. Curiously, Clare of Assisi never uses the term; instead she prefers the term contemplation which may suggest the differences between the monastic and itinerant expressions of prayer.

c. The translator has again taken the liberty of translating *misericordia* more freely as "a heart full of mercy." This translation follows the more etymological sense of the word, *miser* + *cor*, that is, a heart sensitive to misery. In this instance, there seems to be a connection between discernment, excess, and hardness of heart.

Exhortation to the Praise of God

Although the manuscript for this collage of biblical and liturgical praises comes from a sixteenth century friar, Marianus of Florence, he attributes it to a wooden panel that formed the antependium of an altar in the hermitage chapel, Saint Mary of the Angels, of Cesi di Terni in the Spoleto Valley.[a]

Rv 14:7 — 1 *Fear the Lord and give Him honor.*
Rv 4:11 — 2 *Worthy is the Lord to receive praise and honor.*
Ps 22:24 — 3 All you *who* fear *the Lord praise Him.*
Lk 1:28 — 4 *Hail Mary, full of grace, the Lord is with you.*
Ps 69:35 — 5 *Heaven and earth, praise Him.*
Dn 3:78 — 6 All you rivers, *praise the Lord.*
Dn 3:82 — 7 *All you children of God, praise the Lord.*
Ps 118:24 — 8 *This is the day the Lord has made, let us rejoice and be glad in it!*
Ps 105:1; Jn 12:23 — *Alleluia, alleluia, alleluia! The King of Israel!*
Ps 150:6 — 9 *Let every spirit praise the Lord.*
Ps 147:1 — 10 *Praise the Lord because He is good;*
Ps 103:21 — *all you who read this, bless the Lord.*
Ps 103:22 — 11 *All you creatures, bless the Lord.*
Dn 3:80 — 12 *All you birds of heaven, praise the Lord.*
Ps 113:1 — 13 All you *children,* praise *the Lord.*
Ps 148:12 — 14 *Young men and virgins, praise the Lord.*
15 *Worthy is the Lamb Who was slain to receive praise, glory, and*
Rv 5:12 — *honor.*
16 Blessed be the Holy Trinity and Undivided Unity.[b]
17 Saint Michael the Archangel, defend us in battle.[c]

---

a. For further information concerning the authenticity of this document consult Kajetan Esser, " *'Exhortatio ad laudem Dei.'* Ein wenig beachtetes Loblied des hl. Franziskus," *Archivum Franciscanum Historicum* 67 (1974): 3-17.

b. Taken from the Introit of the Liturgy of the Feast of the Holy Trinity.

c. Taken from the Liturgy of the Feast of Saint Michael the Archangel which, at the time of Francis, was celebrated on May 8 and September 28.

The Office of the Passion

Devotional Offices dedicated to the Passion or to the Blessed Virgin have their roots in the *Liber Precum* (Book of Prayers) of the monastic tradition. Until the thirteenth century such Offices were recited in connection with the Liturgy of the Hours. At the time of Francis, however, these more devotional offices became increasingly independent and were seen as private prayers. Although it is difficult to date its composition, Francis's Office of the Passion seems to have been composed at different times, a theory confirmed by his use of both the Gallican and Roman Psalters.

[Introduction]

These are the psalms which our most holy Father Francis composed in reverence, memory and praise of the Passion of the Lord. They should be said during each of the hours of the day and the one hour of the night. They begin with Compline of Holy Thursday, for on that night our Lord Jesus Christ was betrayed and taken captive. Note that Saint Francis used to recite this office in this way:

- At the beginning he used to say the prayer that the Lord and Master taught us: O OUR FATHER MOST HOLY, etc., with the Praises, that is, HOLY, HOLY, HOLY, etc., as they are written above.
- At the end of the Praises with the prayer, he used to begin this antiphon: HOLY MARY.
- First he used to say the Psalms of Saint Mary; afterward he used to recite the other psalms which he had chosen, and at the end of the psalms he had recited, he said the psalms of the Passion.[a]
- At the end of the psalm he used to recite the antiphon: HOLY VIRGIN MARY.
- At the end of the antiphon the Office was finished.

a. This is a reference to the Little Office of the Blessed Virgin, a devotion begun in the ninth century and, by the twelfth, one which was obligatory for secular and religious clergy. It was based upon the psalms of the liturgical Office of the Blessed Virgin Mary.

[Part One: For the Sacred Triduum of Holy Week and for Weekdays Throughout the Year][a]

At Compline[b]
Antiphon: Holy Virgin Mary
Psalm [I]

1 God, I have told you of my life;*
Ps 56:8b-9 you have placed all my tears in your sight.
Ps 41:8 2 All my enemies were plotting evil against me;*
Ps 71:10 they took counsel together.
3 They repaid me evil for good*[c]
Ps 109:5 and hatred for my love.
4 They slandered me in return for my love,*
Ps 109:4 but I continued to pray.
Jn 17:11; Mt 11:25 5 My holy Father, King of heaven and earth, do not leave me*
Ps 22:12 for trouble is near and there is no one to help.
6 Let my enemies be turned back+
on whatever day I shall call upon you;*
Ps 56:10 for now I know that you are my God.
7 My friends and my neighbors have drawn near
and have stood against me;*
Ps 38:12 those who were close to me have stayed far away.
8 You have driven my acquaintances far from me;*
they have made me an abomination to them.+
Ps 88:9 I have been handed over and did not escape.
Jn 17:11; Ps 22:20 9 Holy Father, do not remove your help from me;*
Ps 71:12 my God, look to my aid.
10 Come to my help,*
Ps 38:23 Lord, God of my salvation.
Glory to the Father, and to the Son, and to the Holy Spirit.
As it was in the beginning, is now, and will be forever. Amen.

---

a. The collage of psalm verses which make up the hours of this first part form not only the prayer of Holy Thursday, Good Friday, and the Easter Vigil; they more importantly shape the prayer of the greater part of the year, i.e., those periods outside of the seasons of Advent, Christmas and Easter, as well as outside of Sunday and principal feasts.

b. The opening directive of the Office of the Passion indicates the reason for its beginning with Compline of Holy Thursday: "For on that night our Lord Jesus Christ was betrayed and taken captive." Thus the verses chosen by Francis for this hour reflect the prayers of Jesus in Gethsemani.

c. Although Esser chose to interpret the manuscript tradition as favoring *vobis*, others prefer *bonis*, the word contained in the Latin Vulgate.

Antiphon[a]

[1] Holy Virgin Mary,
among the women born into the world,
there is no one like you.
[2] Daughter and servant
of the most high and supreme King
and of the Father in heaven,
Mother of our most holy Lord Jesus Christ,
Spouse of the Holy Spirit,
[3] pray for us
with Saint Michael the Archangel,
all the powers of heaven
and all the saints,
at the side of your most holy beloved Son,
our Lord and Teacher.
Glory to the Father, and to the Son, and to the Holy Spirit.
As it was in the beginning, is now, and will be forever. Amen.

[Note: the preceding antiphon is recited at all hours and is said in place of the antiphon, chapter, hymn, versicle and prayers, both at Matins and, likewise, at all the hours. Francis did not say anything else in these hours except this antiphon with its psalms. At the conclusion of the office, Francis used to say:]

Prayer

Let us bless
the Lord God *living and true!* 1 Thes 1:9
Let us always render Him
praise, *glory, honor, blessing* and every good. Rv 4:9
Amen. Amen.
So be it. So be it. Ps 41:14

a. It is helpful to note that this antiphon was used at the beginning and end of each hour. Thus these images of Mary are brought to mind fourteen times throughout the day, a practice which is bound to influence one's theology of the Mother of God.

At Matins[a]
Antiphon: Holy Virgin Mary
Psalm *[II]*

1 *Lord, God of my salvation,**
Ps 88:2 *I cry day and night to you.*
2 *Let my prayer enter into your sight;**
Ps 88:3 *incline your ear to my prayer.*
3 *Attend to my soul and free it;**
Ps 69:19 *set me free because of my enemies.*
4 *For it was you who took me out of the womb,+*
*you, my hope from my mother's breasts.**
Ps 22:10 *I have been cast upon you from the womb.*
5 *From my mother's womb you have been my God;**
Ps 22:11 *do not depart from me.*
6 *You know my disgrace, my confusion**
Ps 69:20 *and my reverence.*
7 *All those who trouble me are in your sight;**
Ps 69:21 *My heart has expected abuse and misery.*
8 *I looked for someone to grieve together with me+*
*and there was none,**
Ps 69:21 *for someone to console me and I found none.*
9 *God, the wicked have risen against me,**
*the assembly of the powerful has sought my life;**
Ps 86:14 *they have not placed you in their sight.*
10 *I am numbered among those who go down into the pit.**
Ps 88:5-6 *I have become as someone without help, cut off among the dead.*
11 You are my most Holy Father,*
Ps 44:5 *my King and my God.*
12 *Come to my aid,**
Ps 38:23 *Lord God of my salvation.*

a. The psalm verses chosen for Matins cannot be related easily to a single scene of the Passion. While verses 4 and 5 suggest Christ's uninterrupted self-emptying in obedience to His Father, the introductory verses 1, 2 and 3 form a prayer for deliverance. Verses 6 through 10 conjure up images of Jesus' capture and trial and the final verses, 11 and 12, His utter confidence in a loving Father.

At Prime[a]
Antiphon: Holy Virgin Mary
Psalm *[III]*

[1]*Have mercy on me, O God, have mercy on me**
because my soul places its trust in you. Ps 57:2
[2]*I will hope in the shadow of your wings**
until wickedness pass by. Ps 57:2
[3]*I will cry to the Most High God,* my most holy Father,*
who has done good to me. Ps 57:3
[4]*He has sent from heaven and delivered me;**
He has disgraced those who have trampled upon me. Ps 57:4
[5]*God has sent His mercy and His truth;** Ps 57:4
He has snatched my life from the strongest of my enemies + Ps 57:5
and from those who hated me for they were too powerful for me. Ps 18:18
[6]*They prepared a trap for my feet**
and bowed down my soul. Ps 57:7
[7]*They dug a pit before my face**
and fell into it themselves! Ps 57:7
[8]*My heart is ready, O God, my heart is ready;**
I will sing and chant a psalm. Ps 57:8
[9]*Arise, my glory, arise psalter and harp,**
I will arise at dawn. Ps 57:9
[10]*I will praise you among the peoples, O Lord,**
I will chant a psalm to you among the nations. Ps 57:10
[11]*Because your mercy is exalted even to the skies,**
and your truth even to the clouds. Ps 57:11
[12]*Be exalted above the heavens, O God,**
and may your glory be over all the earth. Ps 57:12

[Note that the preceding psalm is always recited at Prime]

a. The people of the Middle Ages commonly held that the setting of Prime was the hour when Christ was brought before Pilate. While the first eight psalm verses form a prayer for strength, the final four express one of praise. Thus Prime becomes for Francis the hour recalling both Christ's appearance before Pilate and His resurrection.

At Terce[a]
Antiphon: Holy Virgin Mary
Psalm *[IV]*

1 *Have mercy on me, O God, for people have trampled me underfoot;**
Ps 56:2 *all day long they have afflicted me and fight against me.*
2 *All day long my enemies trampled upon me**
Ps 56:3 *for there were many waging war against me.*
Ps 41:8 3 *All my enemies have been thinking evil things against me;**
Ps 41:9 *they made an evil plot against me.*
4 *Those who were guarding my life**
Ps 71:10 *have conspired together.*
5 *They went out**
Ps 41:7; Ps 41:8 *and spread it everywhere.*
6 *Seeing me everyone laughed at me;**
Ps 22:8 *they whispered and shook their heads.*
7 *I am a worm and no human.**
Ps 22:7 *the scorn of men and the outcast of the people.*
8 *I have been made despicable to my neighbors;+*
*far beyond all my enemies,**
Ps 31:12 *a thing of fear to all my acquaintances.*
Jn 17:11 9 *O holy Father, do not keep your help from me**
Ps 22:20 *but look to my defense.*
10 *Come to my aid,**
Ps 38:23 *Lord, God of my salvation.*

At Sext[b]
Antiphon: Holy Virgin Mary
Psalm *[V]*

1 *I cried to the Lord with all my voice;**
Ps 142:2 *with all my voice I begged the Lord.*
2 *I pour out my prayer in His sight**
Ps 142:3 *and I tell the Lord of all my trouble.*
3 *When my spirit failed me**
Ps 142:4 *you knew my ways.*

a. The verses chosen for Terce form the prayers of Jesus at the hour of the scourging, the crowning with thorns, and the mockery and abuse of the crowd.

b. Sext was seen as the hour of the crucifixion, noon, in which Christ was totally abandoned and "zeal for [the Father's] house" had completely consumed Him.

4 *On the path where I walked,**
the proud hid a trap for me. Ps 142:4
5 *I looked to my right and saw:**
there was no one who knew me. Ps 142:5
6 *I have no means of escape:**
there is no one who cares for my life. Ps 142: 5
7 *I have borne abuse because of you**
and confusion covers my face. Ps 69:8
8 *I have become an outcast to my brothers,**
a stranger to the children of my mother. Ps 69:9
9 *Holy Father, zeal for your house has consumed me;** Jn 17:11
and the insults of those who blasphemed you have fallen on me. Ps 69:10
10 *They rejoiced and united together against me.**
Blows were heaped on me and I knew not why. Ps 35:15
11 *More numerous than the hairs of my head**
are those who hate me without cause. Ps 69:5
12 *My enemies, who persecuted me unjustly, have been strengthened;* *
I then repaid what I did not steal. Ps 69:5
13 *The wicked witnesses who rise up*
asked me about things of which they are ignorant. Ps 35:11
14 *They repaid me evil for good and harassed me** Ps 35:12
because I pursued good. Ps 38:21
15 *You are* my most holy Father*
my King and my God. Ps 44:5
16 *Come to my aid,**
Lord, God of my salvation. Ps 38:23

At None[a]
Antiphon: Holy Virgin Mary
Psalm *[VI]*

[1]*O all you who pass along the way**
Lam 1:12 *look and see if there is any sorrow like my sorrow.*
[2]*For many dogs surrounded me**
Ps 22:17 *a pack of evildoers closed in on me.*
[3]*They looked and stared at me;**
they divided my garments among them+
Ps 22:18-19 *and they cast lots for my tunic.*
[4]*They pierced my hands and my feet**
Ps 22:17-18 *they counted all my bones.*
[5]*They opened their mouth against me**
Ps 22:14 *like a raging and roaring lion.*
[6]*I have been poured out like water**
Ps 22: 15 *and all my bones have been scattered.*
[7]*My heart has become like melting wax**
Ps 22:15 *in the midst of my bosom.*
[8]*My strength has been dried up like baked clay**
Ps 22:16 *and my tongue clings to my jaws.*
[9]*They gave me gall as my food**
Ps 69:22 *and, in my thirst, vinegar to drink.*
Ps 22:16 [10]*They led me into the dust of death**
Ps 69:27 *and* added sorrow to my wounds.
Ps 3:6 [11]*I have slept and risen**
Ps 73:24 *and* my most holy Father *has received me with glory.*
Jn 17:11 [12]*Holy Father, you held my right hand**
led me with your counsel+
Ps 73:24 *and have taken me up with glory.*
[13]*For what is there in heaven for me**
Ps 73:25 *and what do I want on earth besides you?*
[14]See, *see that I am God,* says the Lord*
I shall be exalted among the nations+
Ps 46:11 *and exalted on the earth.*

a. The verses of None, the hour of Christ's death on the cross, express, in the words of the psalmist, Christ's attitudes. While they express the depth of depression, the last six verses also express the hope of the resurrection.

15 *Blessed be the Lord, the God of Israel** Lk 1:68
Who has redeemed the souls of His servant
with His very own most holy Blood+
and Who will not abandon all who hope in Him. Ps 34:23
16 And we know that *He is coming**
that He will come to judge justice. Ps 96:11

Vespers[a]
Antiphon: Holy Virgin Mary
Psalm *[VII]*

1 *All you nations clap your hands**
shout to God with a voice of gladness. Ps 47:2
2 *For the Lord, the Most High,**
the Awesome, is the Great King over all the earth. Ps 47:3
3 For the Most Holy Father of heaven, *our King before all ages** Ps 74:12
sent His Beloved *Son* from on high+ 1 Jn 4:9
and has brought salvation in the midst of the earth. Ps 74:12
4 *Let the heavens rejoice and the earth exult**
let the sea and all that is in it be moved+
let the fields and all that is in them be glad. Ps 96:11-12
5 *Sing a new song* to Him*
Sing to the Lord all the earth. Ps 96:1
6 *Because the Lord is great and highly to be praised,**
awesome beyond all gods. Ps 96:4
7 *Give to the Lord, you families of nations,+*
*Give to the Lord glory and honor**
Give to the Lord the glory due His name. Ps 96:7-8
8 Take up your bodies and *carry* His holy *cross** Lk 14:27; Jn 19:17
and *follow* His most holy commands even to the end.[b] 1 Pt 2:21
9 *Let the whole earth tremble before His face**
tell among the nations that the Lord has ruled from a tree. Ps 96:9-10

[The Office is recited daily from Good Friday to the Feast of the Ascension till this point. On the Feast of the Ascension, however, these versicles are added:]

---

a. These verses express the victory of the Risen Lord whose resurrection was traditionally celebrated during Vespers. They contain sentiments of wonder and an eagerness to share the good news of salvation with all creation.

b. Even in the midst of these declarations of joy, Francis returns to his central theme of entrance into the mystery of Christ's Passion, the only path leading from death to life.

[10]He ascended into heaven+
and is seated at the right hand of the most holy Father in heaven*
O God, be exalted above the heavens+
Ps 57:12 *and above all the earth be your glory.*
[11]We know that *He is coming**
Ps 96:13 *that He will come to judge* justice.

[Note: from the Ascension to the Lord's Advent this psalm is said each day in the same way, that is: "All you nations" with the preceding verses; the "Glory to the Father" is said at the end of the Psalm, that is: "that He will come to judge justice."
Note: the preceding psalms are recited from Good Friday until Easter Sunday. They are said in the same way from the Octave of Pentecost until the Lord's Advent and from the Octave of Epiphany until Easter Sunday, excepting for Sunday and the principal feasts when they are not said; on other days, however, they are said each day.]

[Part Two: The Easter Season]
On Holy Saturday,
that is, at the end of the day

Compline
Antiphon: Holy Virgin Mary
Psalm *[VIII]*

[1]*O God, come to my assistance,**
Ps 70:2 *Lord, make haste to help me.*
[2]*Let those who seek my life**
Ps 70:3 *be put to shame and confounded.*
[3]*Let those who wish me evil**
Ps 70:4 *be put to flight and disgraced.*
[4]*Let those who say to me: "Well done! Well done!"**
Ps 70:4 *be turned back in shame.*
[5]*May all those who seek you exult and be glad in you**
may those who love your salvation always say:+
Ps 70:5 *"May the Lord be glorified!"*
[6]*But I am afflicted and poor;**
Ps 70:6 *help me, O God.*
[7]*You are my help and my deliverer;**
Ps 70:7 *Lord, do not delay.*

[This is recited each day at Compline until the octave of Pentecost]

Matins of Easter Sunday
Antiphon: Holy Virgin Mary
Psalm *[IX]*

1 *Sing a new song to the Lord**
for He has done wonderful things. Ps 98:1
2 His *right hand and holy arm**
have sacrificed his beloved Son. Ps 98:1
3 *The Lord has made His salvation known;**
has revealed his justice in the sight of the nations. Ps 98:2
4 *On that day the Lord has sent his mercy,**
and at night his song. Ps 42:9
5 *This is the day the Lord has made;**
let us rejoice and be glad in it. Ps 118:24
6 *Blessed is the one who comes in the name of the Lord,**
the Lord is God, and has enlightened us. Ps 118:26, 27
7 *Let the heavens rejoice and the earth exult**
let the sea and all that is in it be moved+
let the fields and all that is in them be glad. Ps 96:11-12
8 *Give to the Lord, you families of nations,+*
*Give to the Lord glory and honor**
Give to the Lord the glory due His name. Ps 96:7-8

[From Easter Sunday to the Feast of the Ascension, the Office is recited at all hours each day to this point except for Vespers, Compline and Prime. On the night of the Ascension these verses are added:]

9 *Sing to the Lord, kingdoms of the earth,**
sing psalms to the Lord. Ps 68:33
10 *Sing psalms to God Who ascends above the heights of the heavens**
to the rising of the sun. Ps 68:33-34
11 *Behold, the Lord will give his voice the voice of power;+*
*give glory to God!**
Whose greatness is over Israel;+
Whose power is in the skies. Ps 68:34-35
12 *God is marvelous in his holy ones;**
the God of Israel himself will give power and strength to his peo-
ple.+
Blessed be God! Ps 68:36

Glory be to the Father and to the Son and to the Holy Spirit.
As it was in the beginning, is now and will be forever.

[Note: from the Ascension until the octave of Pentecost, this psalm is recited each day with the preceding verses at Matin, Terce, Sext, and None; the Glory to the Father is recited where "Blessed be God" is recited and not elsewhere.
Also note: on Sundays and principal feasts, from the octave of Pentecost until Holy Thursday, for on that day the Lord ate the Passover meal with His disciples, this psalm is recited in the same way only at Matins. From Easter Sunday until the Feast of the Ascension, but not beyond, another psalm, i.e., "I will praise you, O Lord" (Ps 29) as in the Psalter, can be said at Matins or Vespers.]

Prime
Antiphon: Holy Virgin Mary
Psalm *[III]* as above

Terce, Sext, None
Antiphon: Holy Virgin Mary
Psalm *[IX]* as above

Vespers
Antiphon: Holy Virgin Mary
Psalm *[VII]* as above

[Part Three: Sundays and Principal Feasts]

[The other psalms that our most blessed Father arranged begin at this point. They are to be recited in place of the preceding psalms of the Lord's Passion on Sunday and principal feasts from the Octave of Pentecost until Advent and from the Octave of the Epiphany until Holy Thursday. And, as you will clearly understand, they are to be recited on that day, i.e., Holy Thursday, for it is the Passover of the Lord.]

Compline
Antiphon: Holy Virgin Mary
Psalm *[VIII]* as above

Matins
Antiphon: Holy Virgin Mary
Psalm *[IX]* as above

Prime
Antiphon: Holy Virgin Mary
Psalm *[III]* as above

Terce
Antiphon: Holy Virgin Mary
Psalm *[X]*

[1] *Cry out with joy* to the Lord, *all the earth,**
Chant a psalm to his name+
give glory to his praise. Ps 66:1-2
[2] *Say to God: How awesome are your works, O Lord**
your enemies shall fawn upon you in the greatness of your strength. Ps 66:3
[3] *Let all the earth adore you and sing a psalm to you,**
let us chant a psalm to your name. Ps 66:4
[4] *Come, listen and I will tell you, all you who fear God,**
how much he has done for my soul. Ps 66:16
[5] *I cried with my mouth to him,**
and I have exulted with my tongue. Ps 66:17
[6] *From his holy temple, he heard my voice**
and my cry reached His ears. Ps 18:7
[7] *Bless our* Lord, *you peoples**
make the voice of his praise *heard.* Ps 66:8
[8] *May all the tribes of the earth be blessed in him**
and all nations will glorify him. Ps 72:17
[9] *Blessed be the Lord, the God of Israel,**
Who alone does great wonders. Ps 72:18
[10] *Blessed forever be the name of his majesty,**
and may all the earth be filled with his majesty.+
So be it. So be it. Ps 72:19

Sext
Antiphon: Holy Virgin Mary
Psalm *[XI]*

1 *May the Lord hear you on the day of your distress,+*
Ps 20:2 *may the name of the God of Jacob protect you.*
2 *From the sanctuary, may He send you help,**
Ps 20:3 *and from Sion, may He sustain you*
3 *May He remember all your sacrifices**
Ps 20:4 *and may your burnt offering be fruitful.*
4 *May He grant you your heart's desires,**
Ps 20:5 *and fulfill your every plan.*
5 *We will rejoice in your salvation,**
Ps 20:6 *and be glorified in the name of the Lord our God.*
6 *May the Lord fulfill all your requests,+*
Ps 20:7; 1 Jn 4:9 *now I have known that* the Lord has sent Jesus Christ *His Son,**
Ps 9:9 *and He will judge the peoples with justice.*
7 *The Lord has become the refuge of the poor+*
*their help in times of trial**
Ps 9:10 *let those who know your name trust you.*
8 *Blessed be the Lord my God**
Who has become my stronghold and refuge on the day of my dis-
Ps 59:17 *tress.*
9 *My help, I will sing a psalm to you+*
*because you, God, are my stronghold**
Ps 59:18 *my God, my mercy!*

None
Antiphon: Holy Virgin Mary
Psalm *[XII]*

1 *In you, Lord, I have hoped, let me not be put to shame**
Ps 71:1 *in your justice, free me and rescue me.*
2 *Incline your ear to me**
Ps 71:2 *and save me.*
3 *God be my protector and my stronghold**
Ps 71:3 *that you may save me.*
4 *Because you are my patience, Lord**
Ps 71:5 *Lord, my hope from my youth.*

[5] *From the womb I have been strengthened in you+*
*from my mother's womb you are my protector.**
my song will always be to you. Ps 71:6
[6] *May my mouth be filled with praise+*
*that I may sing of your glory**
and all day long of your greatness. Ps 71:8
[7] *Hear me, Lord, because your mercy is kind**
look upon me according to the greatness of your mercies. Ps 69:17
[8] *Do not turn your face from your child;**
because I am afflicted, quickly hear me. Ps 69:18
[9] *Blessed be the Lord my God+* Ps 144:1
*Who has become my protector and my refuge**
on the day of distress. Ps 59:18
[10] *O my helper I will chant a psalm to you, because you, O God, are my protector,**
My God, my mercy. Ps 59:18

Vespers
Antiphon: Holy Virgin Mary
Psalm *[VII]* as above

[Part Four: The Time of the Lord's Coming]

[The other Psalms that our most blessed Father Francis likewise arranged begin here. They are to be said in place of the preceding psalms of the Lord's Passion from His Coming until the Vigil of the Nativity inclusively.]

Compline:
Antiphon: Holy Virgin Mary
Psalm *[XIII]*

[1]*How long, Lord, will you forget me forever?**
Ps 13:1 *How long will you turn your face from me?*
[2]*How long will I place doubts in my soul**
Ps 13:2 *sorrow in my heart day after day?*
[3]*How long will my enemy exult over me?**
Ps 13:3 *Look upon me and hear me, Lord, my God.*
Ps 13:4 [4]*Give light to my eyes that I may never sleep in death**
Ps 13:5 *so that my enemy may never say: I have overcome him!*
[5]*Those who afflict me would rejoice if I stumble**
Ps 13:5 *but I have hoped in your mercy.*
[6]*My heart shall rejoice in your salvation;+*
*I will sing to the Lord Who gives me good things.**
Ps 13:6 *I will chant a Psalm to the name of the Lord the Most High.*

Matins
Antiphon: Holy Virgin Mary
Psalm *[XIV]*

Is 12:1; Mt 11:25 [1]*I will praise you, Lord,* Most Holy Father, King *of heaven and earth,**
Is 12:1 *because you have consoled me.*
[2]You are *God, my Savior,**
Is 12:2 *I will act with confidence and not be afraid.*
[3]*The Lord is my strength and my glory,**
Is 12:2 *He has become my salvation.*

[4]Your right hand, Lord, has been glorified in strength+
*your right hand, Lord, has struck my enemy**
and in the greatness of your glory+
you have deposed my adversaries. Ex 15:6-7
*[5]May the poor see and rejoice,**
seek God and your soul shall live. Ps 69:33
*[6]Let heaven and earth praise Him,**
the sea and every living thing in them. Ps 69:35
*[7]Because God will save Sion,**
the cities of Judah will be rebuilt. Ps 69:35
*[8]They will dwell there**
and acquire it by inheritance. Ps 69:36
*[9]The descendants of God's servants will possess it**
and those who love God's name will dwell there. Ps 69:37

Prime
Antiphon: Holy Virgin Mary
Psalm *[III]*

Terce
Antiphon: Holy Virgin Mary
Psalm *[X]*

Sext
Antiphon: Holy Virgin Mary
Psalm *[XI]*

None
Antiphon: Holy Virgin Mary
Psalm *[XII]*

Vespers
Antiphon: Holy Virgin Mary
Psalm *[VII]*

[Note: this psalm is recited only to the verse "Let the whole earth tremble before His face" (verse 9) and the entire verse "Offer your bodies" is recited. At the end of this verse "Glory to the Father . . ." is recited. Each day at Vespers from Advent until the Vigil of the Nativity, it is recited in this way.]

[Part Five: The Time of the Lord's Birth
until the Octave of the Epiphany]

Vespers of the Lord's Birth
Antiphon: Holy Virgin Mary
Psalm *[XV]*

Ps 81:2 1 *Exult in God our help!**
Ps 47:2 *Shout* to the Lord God living and true *with cries of gladness!*
2 *Because the Lord, the Most High,**
Ps 47:3 *the Awesome, is the Great King over all the earth.*
Ps 74:12 3 Because the Most Holy Father of heaven, *our King before all ages,*+
sent His Beloved Son from on high*
and He was born of the Blessed Virgin Holy Mary.
Ps 89:27 4 *He called to me: You are my Father**
and I will place Him, my firstborn, as the Highest,+
Ps 89:28 *above all the kings of the earth.*
5 *On that day the Lord sent His mercy**
Ps 42:9 *and at night His song.*
6 *This is the day the Lord has made**
Ps 118:24 *let us rejoice and be glad in it.*
7 For the Most Holy Child has been given to us+
Is 9:6 and has been born for us on the way*
Lk 2:7 and placed in a manger
because he did not have a place in the inn.
8 *Glory to* the Lord *God in the highest**
Lk 2:14 *and peace on earth to those of good will.*
9 *Let the heavens rejoice and the earth exult,*+
*let the sea and its fullness resound,**
Ps 96:11-12 *let the fields and all that is in them be joyful.*
10 *Sing a new song to the Lord,**
Ps 96:1 *sing to the Lord all the earth.*
11 *Because the Lord is great and worthy of praise**
Ps 96:4 *He is awesome beyond all gods.*
12 *Give to the Lord, you families of nations,*+
*give to the Lord glory and praise,**
Ps 96:7-8 *give to the Lord the glory due His name.*

[13]Take up your bodies and carry His holy cross* Lk 14:27; Jn 19:17
And follow His most holy commands even to the end.[a] 1 Pt 2:21

[Note: from the Lord's Birth until the Octave of the Epiphany, this psalm is recited at every hour.
If anyone wishes to recite this Office of Saint Francis, it may be said in this way: first say the "Our Father" with its praises, i.e., "Holy, Holy, Holy." At the end of the praises with the prayer, as it is written above, say the antiphon Holy Virgin Mary with the psalm that has been arranged for each hour of the day and night. May this Office be recited with great reverence.]

a. Once again Francis returns to that central theme of carrying the cross or entering into the mystery of Christ's passion. Even in celebrating His birth, Francis does not neglect to reflect upon the perfection of God's love found in the cross.

A Prayer Inspired by the Our Father

(Expositio in Pater Noster)

Two thirteenth-century examples of this type of commentary on the Lord's Prayer suggest that this style of prayer forms a "catechism of prayer" offering strong attitudes toward, as well as images of, God. In fact, this writing is perhaps the only instance in which we find an example of how Francis responded to his brothers' request to teach them how to pray.

Mt 6:9 [1]O *Our Father* most holy:
Our Creator, Redeemer, Consoler, and Savior:

Mt 6:9 [2]*Who are in heaven:*
In the angels and the saints,
1 Jn 1:5 enlightening them to know, for *You, Lord, are light;*
inflaming them to love, for You, Lord, are love;
dwelling in them and filling them with happiness,
for You, Lord, are Supreme Good, the Eternal Good,
from Whom all good comes
without Whom there is no good.

Mt 6:9 [3]*Holy be Your Name:*
May knowledge of You become clearer in us
that we may know
the breadth of Your blessings,
the length of Your promises,
the height of Your majesty,
Eph 3:18 *the depth* of Your judgments.

Mt 6:10 [4]*Your kingdom come:*
That You may rule in us through Your grace
Lk 23:42 and enable us *to come* to *Your kingdom*
where there is clear vision of You,
perfect love of You,
blessed companionship with You,
eternal enjoyment of You.

Mt 6:10 [5]*Your will be done on earth as in heaven:*
That we may love You

with our whole heart by always thinking of You, Dt 6:5
with our whole soul by always desiring You,
with our whole mind by always directing all our intentions to You,
and by seeking Your glory in everything,
with all our whole strength by exerting
all our energies and affections of body and soul Lk 10:27
in the service of Your love and of nothing else;
and we may love our neighbor as ourselves
by drawing them all to Your love with our whole strength,
by rejoicing in the good of others as in our own,
by suffering with others at their misfortunes,
and by giving offense to no one. 2 Cor 6:3

[6]*Give us this day:* Mt 6:11
in remembrance, understanding, and reverence
of that love which [our Lord Jesus Christ] had for us
and of those things that He said and did and suffered for us.

our daily Bread: Mt 6:11
Your own beloved Son, our Lord Jesus Christ.

[7]*Forgive us our trespasses:* Mt 6:12
through Your ineffable mercy
through the power of the passion of Your beloved Son
and through the merits and intercession
of the ever blessed Virgin and all Your elect.

[8]*As we forgive those who trespass against us:* Mt 6:12
And what we do not completely forgive,
make us, Lord, forgive completely
that we may truly love our enemies because of You
and we may fervently intercede for them before You,
returning no one evil for evil 1 Thes 5:15
and we may strive to help everyone in You.

[9]*And lead us not into temptation:* Mt 6:13
hidden or obvious,
sudden or persistent.

Mt 6:13 [10]*But deliver us from evil:*
past,
present,
and to come.

Glory to the Father, and to the Son, and to the Holy Spirit.
As it was in the beginning, is now, and will be forever. Amen.

The Praises To Be Said at All the Hours

Three sets of rubrics or directives which accompany this text in the manuscript tradition suggest that these were biblical passages used by the brothers before each hour of the Office.

1 *Holy, holy, holy Lord God Almighty,* Is 6:3
Who is, and Who was, and Who is to come:[a] Rv 4:8
And *let us praise and glorify Him forever.* Dn 3:57
2 *O Lord our God, You are worthy to receive*
praise, *glory and honor* and blessing. Rv 4:11
And *let us praise and glorify Him forever.* Rv 4:8
3 *The Lamb Who was slain is worthy to receive*
power and divinity, wisdom and strength,
honor and glory and blessing. Rv 5:12
And *let us praise and glorify Him forever.* Rv 4:8
4 Let us bless the Father and the Son with the Holy Spirit:[b]
And *let us praise and glorify Him forever.* Rv 4:8
5 *Bless the Lord, all you works of the Lord.* Dn 3:57
And let us praise and glorify Him forever. Rv 4:8
6 *Sing praise to our God, all you His servants*
and you who fear God, the small and the great. Rv 19:5
And *let us praise and glorify Him forever.* Rv 4:8
7 *Let heaven and earth praise Him Who is* glorious. Ps 69:35
And *let us praise and glorify Him forever.* Rv 4:8
8 Every creature *in heaven, on earth and* under the earth;
and in the sea and *those which* are *in it.* Rv 5:13
And *let us praise and glorify Him forever.* Rv 4:8
9 Glory to the Father and to the Son and to the Holy Spirit.
And *let us praise and glorify Him forever.* Rv 4:8
10 As it was in the beginning, is now, and will be forever.
And *let us praise and glorify Him forever.* Rv 4:8

---

a. Curiously none of the manuscripts attempt to correct this mistaken quotation in which Francis inverts the time sequence of the Book of Revelation.

b. This phrase is taken from the Canticle of Lauds for Easter Sunday.

[11]Prayer

All-powerful, most holy, most high, supreme God: all good, su-
Lk 18:19 preme good, totally good, You Who *alone are good,* may we give You
Rv 5:12 all praise, all *glory,* all thanks, all *honor,* all *blessing,* and all good. So
be it! So be it! Amen.

A Salutation of the Blessed Virgin Mary

This simple collection of titles forms a litany of greetings describing Mary's role in the plan of salvation. The manuscript tradition suggests a close tie between this piece and the following, the *A Salutation of the Virtues,* and, therefore, presents the Virgin Mary as the model for every Christian who responds to God's virtuous presence in his or her life.

1 Hail, O Lady,
Holy Queen,
Mary, holy Mother of God,
Who are the Virgin made Church,[a]
2 chosen by the most Holy Father in heaven
whom he consecrated with His most holy beloved Son
and with the Holy Spirit the Paraclete,
3 in whom there was and is
all fullness of grace and every good.

4 Hail His Palace!
Hail His Tabernacle!
Hail His Dwelling!
5 Hail His Robe!
Hail His Servant!
Hail His Mother!

6 And hail all You holy virtues
which are poured into the hearts of the faithful
through the grace and enlightenment of the Holy Spirit,
that from being unbelievers,
You may make them faithful to God.[b]

a. While Saint Ambrose writes of Mary as a type of the Church, cf. *Expositio Lucae* II 7, PL 15, 1555, and others have seen her as a pattern, type or model of the Church, Francis is quite unique in calling her the "Virgin made Church."

b. Cf. infra, *A Salutation of the Virtues* (hereafter SalV) p, 164, a.

A Salutation of the Virtues[a]

As suggested in the introduction to *A Salutation of the Blessed Virgin Mary,* the manuscript tradition suggests that Francis saw these virtues as hers; yet they are clearly those of any Christian who has died to sin. Francis greets each virtue in a fashion typical of a medieval troubadour, describes the predisposition which each Christian must have before possessing them, and concludes by interpreting the function of each.

[1]Hail, Queen Wisdom![b]
May the Lord protect You,
with Your Sister, holy pure Simplicity!
[2]Lady holy Poverty,
may the Lord protect You,
with Your Sister, holy Humility!
[3]Lady holy Charity,
may the Lord protect You,
with Your Sister, holy Obedience.
[4]Most holy Virtues,
may the Lord protect all of You
from Whom You come and proceed.

[5]There is surely no one in the whole world
who can possess any one of You
without dying first.
[6]Whoever possesses one
and does not offend the others
possesses all.
Jas 2:10 [7]Whoever *offends one*
does not possess any
and offends all.[c]
[8]And each one confounds vice and sin.

a. The titles found in the early manuscripts suggest that this salutation was closely linked with that of the Blessed Virgin. In fact, two of the manuscripts consider them one document; others reflect the same unity as can be seen in these titles: "The virtues possessed by the holy Virgin and which should be present in a holy soul"; "The Salutation of the Virtues with which the Blessed Virgin was clothed and which should be present in a holy soul." Others contain these more simple titles: "The Salutation of the Virtues and their efficacy in confounding vices"; "The Linking of the Virtues."

b. The pursuit of wisdom or knowledge is a prominent theme throughout Francis's writings, cf. Adm XXVII.

c. Cf. Jas 2:10.

[9]Holy Wisdom confounds
Satan and all his cunning.
[10]Pure holy Simplicity confounds
all *the wisdom of this world* 1 Cor 2:6
and the wisdom of the body.
[11]Holy Poverty confounds
the desire for riches,
greed,
and the cares of this world.
[12]Holy Humility confounds
pride,
all people who are in the world
and all that is in the world.[a]
[13]Holy Charity confounds
every diabolical and carnal temptation
and every carnal *fear.* 1 Jn 4:18
[14]Holy Obedience confounds
every corporal and carnal wish,
binds its mortified body
to obedience of the Spirit
and obedience to one's brother,
so that it is
subject and submissive
to everyone in the world,
not only to people
but to every beast and wild animal as well
that they may do whatever they want with it
insofar as it *has been given* to them
from above by the Lord. Jn 19:11

a. In this verse a number of manuscripts read *honores* for *homines*. This would render the text: "Holy Humility confounds pride, all the honors which are in the world and all that is in the world." The translation presented in this edition reflects that of the critical edition of Kajetan Esser.

True and Perfect Joy

The fourteenth century biographical tradition is the source of this piece which has always been considered authentic. Kajetan Esser placed this text in a section entitled "Dictated Writings" and relied on the research of Benvenutus Bughetti whose convincing arguments placed it among the writings of Francis.[a] While it parallels *Admonition* V and Thomas of Celano's *The Remembrance of the Desire of a Soul,* 125 and 145, it reflects the letter which Francis sent to Brother Leo which was the result of a conversation on the road and the resolution of a question about Gospel life. It is impossible to date this incident with any certainty.

[1]The same [Brother Leonard] related in the same place that one day at Saint Mary's, blessed Francis called Brother Leo and said: "Brother Leo, write." [2]He responded: "Look, I'm ready!" [3]"Write," he said, "what true joy is."

[4]"A messenger arrives and says that all the Masters of Paris have entered the Order. Write: this isn't true joy! [5]Or, that all the prelates, archbishops and bishops beyond the mountains, as well as the King of France and the King of England [have entered the Order]. Write: this isn't true joy! [6]Again, that my brothers have gone to the non-believers and converted all of them to the faith; again, that I have so much grace from God that I heal the sick and perform many miracles. I tell you true joy doesn't consist in any of these things."

[7]"Then what is true joy?"

[8]"I return from Perugia and arrive here in the dead of night. It's winter time, muddy, and so cold that icicles have formed on the edges of my habit and keep striking my legs and blood flows from such wounds. [9]Freezing, covered with mud and ice, I come to the gate and, after I've knocked and called for some time, a brother comes and asks: 'Who are you?' 'Brother Francis,' I answer. [10]'Go away!' he says. 'This is not a decent hour to be wandering about! You may not come in!' [11]When I insist, he replies: 'Go away! You are simple and stupid! Don't come back to us again! There are many of us here like you—we don't need you!' [12]I stand again at the door and say: 'For the love of God, take me

a. Kajetan Esser, *Die Opuscula des Hl. Franziskus Von Assisi: Neue Textkritische Edition* (Grottaferrata [Rome]: Collegii S. Bonaventura Ad Claras Aquas, 1976) 459-461; *Opuscula Sancti Patris Francisi Assisiensis, editio minor* (Grottaferrata [Rome]: Colegii S. Bonaventurae Ad Clara Aquas, 1976) 324-326.

in tonight!' [13]And he replies: 'I will not! [14]Go to the Crosiers' place and ask there!'

[15]"I tell you this: If I had patience and did not become upset, true joy, as well as true virtue and the salvation of my soul, would consist in this."

THE LIFE OF SAINT FRANCIS

BY

THOMAS OF CELANO

(1228–1229)

Introduction

Brother Thomas of Celano (d. 1260) was the first to write a life of Saint Francis and the first to describe the earliest days of the life of his followers. With his masterful pen he laid the foundation for the rich Franciscan literary tradition of the 13th century by composing two major works: *The Life of Saint Francis,* commonly referred to as *The First Life* [*Vita Prima*], in 1229 and *The Remembrance of the Desire of a Soul,* commonly referred to as *The Second Life* [*Vita Secunda*] in 1247.[1] Thomas also wrote two other works on Saint Francis, *The Legend for Use in the Choir* [*Legenda ad Usum Chori*] in 1230 and *The Treatise on the Miracles* [*Tractatus de Miraculis B. Francisci*] in 1254. Except for his presence at the Pentecost Chapter at the Portiuncula in 1221 and for his part in the subsequent mission of the friars to Germany, there is little other known evidence about Thomas's life. No scholarly biography of his life has ever been written.[2]

Thomas's birth, into the noble family of the Conti dei Marsi, occurred sometime between 1185-1190. The city of his birth, Celano, is a small city in the Abruzzi, twenty miles southeast of Aquila in the mountains southeast of Rome.[3] His exceptional writing ability indicates Thomas received a solid liberal arts education in the basic curriculum of study in the Middle Ages, the *trivium* and *quadrivium,* possibly at the Benedictine monastery of Saint John the Baptist near Celano. His knowledge of the monastic literary tradition as well as his theological acumen supports the opinion that he studied theology, perhaps at Monte Cassino, Rome or Bologna.[4] Thomas probably includes himself in the remark he makes in *The Life of Saint Francis* that, at the Portiuncula, after Saint Francis returned from Spain in 1215 "some literate men and nobles gladly joined him."[5] Thomas prefaces this comment in a rare autobiographical reference by indicating that the God who brought Francis back from Spain to Italy "was pleased to be mindful of me and many others."[6]

During the Chapter of 1221 Thomas was among the brothers chosen for the mission to Germany.[7] After arrival in Germany, he was elected to the office of custodian to lead the friars of Worms, Speyer, and Cologne. Later, on the recommendation of Brother Caesar of Speyer, Thomas became the vicar of all the brothers of Germany. It is not known why he returned to Italy, but by July 16, 1228, he was most likely back in Assisi for the canonization of Saint Francis. His vivid and dramatic narration of the canonization event in Book Three of *The Life of Saint Francis* suggests an eyewitness account.[8]

Shortly before the July 1228, canonization and shortly after Pope Gregory IX's decree, *Recolentes qualiter,* of April 29, 1228, calling for a burial church to be built for Francis in Assisi, Gregory IX conferred upon Thomas the distinguished task of writing a life of the new saint.[9] Thomas, it would seem, was to complement the architectural celebration of Francis with the composition of a new literary monument. Both contributions, requested by Gregory IX within months of each other, were to help preserve the memory of the life and example of the Poverello.

Unlike the new burial church, *The Life of Saint Francis* was quickly completed, within six to eight months. On February 25, 1229, Gregory IX had already approved, confirmed and declared it official. By the next year, 1230, Thomas finished his second work on the life of Saint Francis, *The Legend for Use in the Choir.*[10] This second work was for use within the celebration of the Divine Office. It was written at the request of Brother Benedict of Arezzo, Minister of Romania and Greece.[11] In composing *The Legend for Use in the Choir* Thomas selected material from *The Life of Saint Francis* and divided it into nine lessons or selections so that it could be included among the readings of the breviary.[12] It is a shortened and concise version of *The Life of Saint Francis,* condensing certain sections for the readings on the feast of Saint Francis and during the octave, the eight days following the feast.

Fourteen years later, at the Chapter of Genoa in 1244, Thomas was again called. This time, it was not the pope but the brothers who sought his assistance. The General Minister, Crescentius of Jesi (1244-1247), acting on the direction of the General Chapter, called for a collection of the stories circulating about Francis and commissioned Thomas to capture those memories in his classical style of writing. Thomas dedicated his collection, *The Remembrance of the Desire of a Soul,* to Crescentius.[13]

Crescentius's successor, Brother John of Parma, further commissioned Thomas to write his fourth and final work on Francis, *The Treatise on the Miracles.* Although Thomas had reported on miracles in his earlier writings on Francis, he was asked to produce a systematic collection of all accounts of these extraordinary events during and after Francis's life that were circulating. Evidently, Thomas did not respond quickly to the request. According to the *Chronicle of the Twenty-Four Generals,* John had to make several requests.[14] The *Treatise on the Miracles* was finally confirmed by John of Parma at the General Chapter of Metz on May 31, 1254, twenty-five years after Gregory IX had confirmed and approved *The Life of Saint Francis.*[15]

It is not certain where Thomas was residing during these years. His literary activity provides clues. During the writing of *The Life of Saint Francis* and *The Legend for Use in the Choir,* Thomas probably lived in or near Assisi, where he could find the witnesses he needed. It is certain that he was living in Assisi in 1230 when Jordan of Giano visited there. Jordan reports that he "went to Brother Thomas of Celano, who gave him some relics of The Blessed Father Francis."[16] Fourteen years later, when commissioned by the Chapter of Genoa in 1244 the already famous writer would have returned to Assisi for the composition of *The Remembrance of the Desire of a Soul.* In the latter years of his life he would again have been in Assisi for the composition of *The Treatise on the Miracles.*[17] Some authors maintain that Thomas may be the author of *The Legend of Saint Clare,* who was canonized on August 15, 1255. Were this the case, he would again have found himself in Assisi where he could find the sources, witnesses and oral tradition he needed.[18]

Most likely Thomas lived his life between Assisi and Tagliacozzo, a town about fifteen miles west of his hometown of Celano. In Tagliacozzo, Thomas spent the last years prior to his death as chaplain to the Poor Ladies, the followers of Saint Clare, at the convent of San Giovanni di Val dei Varri.

Thomas died on October 4, 1260 in Tagliacozzo and was buried in the monastery of the Poor Ladies.[19] In 1516, long after the monastery was abandoned in 1476, the brothers transferred his bones to the church of Saint Francis in Tagliacozzo where his bones presently rest. Locally, Thomas continues to be honored as the saint who wrote about a saint.

The Life of Saint Francis (1229)

As the first written account of the life of Saint Francis, Thomas's work holds a place of honor. It holds a unique place in the historical sequence of the many other lives which would subsequently be written. This is not to argue that this text is more "historical" in the contemporary sense of that concept. More importantly, *The Life of Saint Francis* captures the first burst of enthusiasm in the new religious movement of the Lesser Brothers. It expresses the joy of the canonization and celebrates Saint Francis's memory. Its author is convinced that through Francis something new and refreshing entered into the spiritual communion of saints and into the visible life of the Church. In fact, Francis is the preeminent saint: "That is why every order, sex, and age finds in him a clear pattern of the teaching of salvation and an outstanding example of holy deeds."[20]

The Life of Saint Francis and the Early Development of the Order

Besides Francis, three other historical figures find an honored place within the pages of *The Life of Saint Francis.* They are: Clare of Assisi (1194-1253), Elias Buonbarone (1180-1253) and Hugolino dei Conti di Segni, who reigned as Pope Gregory IX from 1227-1241. At various points within the narrative Thomas accents their relationship to Francis and sings their praises.

Clare, still a relatively young woman while Thomas was writing in 1228, is praised as "bright in name, more brilliant in life, most brilliant in character." Numbers 18,19 and 20 in the First Book are dedicated to her and to her sisters at San Damiano. Again, after Francis's death near the end of Book Two, it is Clare and her sisters "who kissed his most splendid hands."[21] Clare and her sisters embody the grief of the whole church at the saint's death.

Thomas describes Brother Elias as "the one he chose for the role of mother to himself and had made a father of the other brothers."[22] Elias, appointed by Francis in 1217 as the first minister in the Holy Land, was already well known as a leader of the expansion of the Order. He led the Chapter of 1221 and organized the second and successful mission to Germany. Under his direction, the Order also spread to France, Spain, and in 1223 to England. Understandably, Thomas writes eloquently of the affectionate relationship between Elias and Francis. Elias hurries to Francis in his illness and receives an extraordinary blessing from his dying father: "I bless you, my son, in all and through all and just as the most High has increased my brothers in your hands, so too upon you and in you, I bless them all." Elias, like the biblical Jacob, becomes an instrument of Francis's blessing for all of the brothers.

Finally, Hugolino dei Conti di Segni is presented as the choice of Francis to be "father and lord over the whole religion and order of his brothers." Thomas writes that Hugolino "conformed himself to the ways of the brothers," was "humble with the humble and poor with the poor," and "a brother among brothers." This was the man, Thomas acknowledges, who "helped greatly to spread the Order."[23] Hugolino, born in 1155 at Anagni, son of the count of Segni and nephew of Pope Innocent III, had excelled in theology and canon law at Paris and Bologna. As cardinal bishop of Ostia, he gave proof of his great political skills as papal legate in southern Italy, Germany, Lombardy and Tuscany. He was also known to be intensely religious and in touch with contemporary spiritual movements. After he became cardinal protector of the Lesser Brothers in 1220, he threw his exceptional political weight behind the faltering fraternity. After Francis's first vicar, Peter di Catanio, died suddenly within a year of his appointment, it may have been Cardinal Hugolino who suggested that Elias become the new vicar.

The Life of Saint Francis in Service of the Church

The Life of Saint Francis, like the basilica raised in his honor, was a work intended by Pope Gregory for the whole Church. After Francis's canonization on July 19,1228, Gregory exhorted the bishops of the world to promote the cult of the new saint in a letter dated February 21, 1229.[24] Only four days later, on February 25, Gregory officially approved and promulgated *The Life of Saint Francis*. This context gives it an official ecclesial character.[25] Designed to appeal to the rich tradition of holiness manifested in the lives of the saints, it reaches beyond the particular interests of Francis's followers to inspire men and women everywhere. Therefore, Thomas situates the saint, Francis, within the ancient Christian tradition and brings the freshness of his example into the life of the Church.

Unlike Thomas's later works on Francis, *The Life of Saint Francis* is not written about Francis for the brothers at the request of the brothers. Only about a fourth of the text treats Francis and his relationship with the brothers. The rest is dedicated to conversion, promotion of the gospel, and his example and teaching of Christian holiness.

In this context, the success of *The Life of Saint Francis* was important for Gregory, not only for the promotion of the memory of Saint Francis and the strengthening of the Franciscan Order in the Church, but also as a part of his effort to promote spiritual renewal within the life of the Church. At a time when heresies abounded, crusades failed and the struggle for power between the Holy Roman Empire and the Papacy intensified, the poor and humble follower of the gospel, Francis of Assisi, offered an alternative way of Christian living.

The Life of Saint Francis as Hagiography

To accomplish his purpose, Thomas draws from the memory of the martyrs, the ascetics and the monks to illustrate that Francis is a saint rooted in the tradition of the Church. Thomas explains that Francis's participation in the same holiness as that of the great saints of memory is based on a conversion that frees him from many burdensome cares and leads him into the life of the Church where he hears the Word of God.

In his conversion Francis no longer lives as a "deaf hearer" of the gospel but he becomes instead a bold proclaimer of the Word of God.[26] The gospel he proclaims makes his hearers "children of peace."[27] Promoting the gospel message of peace, Francis spends his life rebuilding the life of the Church upon its solid and ancient foundation. His work of rebuilding three churches, ones dedicated to the Virgin (Saint Mary of the Angels), to the apostles (Saint Peter) and to a martyr (Saint Damian), renews the life of the Church on its ancient foundations of the Virgin, the apostles and the martyrs.

Although there are canonical and hagiographical aspects to the text of *The Life of Saint Francis*, these are not the only dimensions or perspectives from which Thomas writes. He includes specific biographical and historical data. In these specifics about Francis and his early followers, Thomas appeals to his own experience of Francis and, as he writes in the prologue, to "trustworthy witnesses" who also would have themselves been readers of his final text. Clearly, he had access to important textual sources within the Order: the *Earlier Rule,* the *Later Rule,* the *Testament,* the *Admonitions,* and *The Canticle of Creatures.*

The official canonical purposes and hagiographical elements Thomas utilized to construct his text do not lessen the value of *The Life of Saint Francis* as a primary source for historical elements of Francis's life and of the early life of the new fraternity. Thomas still presents a Francis situated in real places and connected to his concrete historical contemporaries, including early followers and many friends among ecclesiastical and lay persons with authority and influence.

However, narrating historical events about Francis and the early brothers is not his primary purpose. The canonized Francis is no longer a simple companion to his brothers. Now Francis is for the Church. For his sources, therefore, Thomas went beyond the brothers to Pope Gregory IX, to Bishop Guido II of Assisi, and certainly also to Clare. Although there is no process of canonization extant, Thomas had access to the catalogue of miracles which were read aloud at Francis's canonization, and these probably make up a good portion of Book Three.

The Life of Saint Francis is a grand tapestry of "trustworthy witnesses," varying literary and liturgical sources, multiple hagiographical traditions and several ecclesial purposes. Although Thomas included historical data, he intended primarily to announce Francis to the world. In the development of his text, he presents Francis as a model of conversion in order to express the unique gospel message of Francis's life. Finally he captures the moment of Francis's reception of the stigmata on La Verna. Thomas wrote to increase the joy among the Christians of his day over Francis's canonization. Likewise, it seems he hoped to solidify the spiritual identity and mission of the Order in service of the life of the universal Church.

The Life of Saint Francis: A Mirror of Incarnation, Passion and Resurrection

The Life of Saint Francis can be read from any of the perspectives mentioned above: historical, canonical or official, hagiographical, as well as formational or pastoral. Structurally, it is divided into three books. Traditionally, this three-fold division is accented as chronological: 1) from his youth to Christmas of 1223; 2) the last two years of his life from early 1224 to his death on October 4, 1226; 3) the canonization and the catalogue of miracles read at the canonization on July 16, 1228.

The first two books differ in tone and purpose, but they are complementary treatises. Between the first two books there is a close thematic relationship. The third and last book, which narrates the celebration of Francis's 1228 canonization, appears to be an eyewitness account. This third book has a function different from that of the first two books. It is written in a different literary genre, that of miracle accounts, and differs in style from the other two. While the first and second books focus on Francis's life, the third recounts events in the Church after the death of Francis.

The theme of "the humility of the incarnation" uniquely identifies Book One, as Thomas summarizes the conversion, life, teaching and example of Francis. Humility enabled Francis to celebrate the birth of the Incarnate Word that he heard, preached, and lived throughout his life. Book One concludes with a vivid description of the great midnight Christmas liturgy of the cave at Greccio in which there is a wondrous vision: ". . . a little child lying lifeless in the manger . . . is awakened and impressed on their loving memory by His own grace through His holy servant Francis."[28] The gospel word heard and proclaimed through Francis's life of conversion brought about a marvelous vision of the Incarnation. Thomas explains through the life of Francis, how the Church, with all of creation, is renewed because the Word made flesh, long forgotten, comes to life again.

In Book Two the "charity of the Passion" predominates. The gospel word is no longer the commission to sell and give all goods to the poor. Rather, the Word is Christ on the Cross. This Word is experienced in a vision on La Verna. Francis sees what he hears. He comes to the mystical experience of both, the Word and the vision, in his own flesh, the stigmata. By the Word and the vision, Francis is transformed into the Incarnate and Crucified Christ. By employing the biblical image of the Seraph, an image rich in the contemplative tradition, Thomas identifies Francis's transformative experience as one of burning and intimate love.[29] The "charity of the Passion" is incarnated in Francis's own flesh, transporting him into the heavenly liturgy. In the prayer that concludes Book Two, Francis places his stigmata before Jesus Christ, Son of the most high Father. This is a form of intimate intercessory prayer that has salvific significance for all. In response, Christ Crucified is moved to "bear his own wounds to the Father, and because of this the Father will ever show us in our anguish His tenderness."[30]

Book Three, in the account of the canonization and the miracles, describes the liturgy of Francis that continues to be celebrated on earth. It captures that exuberance: "a new spirit was placed in the hearts of the elect and a holy anointing has been poured out in their midst."[31] There is new joy and power among those Francis left behind. As Francis is canonized, Christians of every vocation rejoice and the whole region is filled with new life and enthusiasm. At his tomb there is new life. Many people are healed and find consolation. The third book is a "Pentecost" experience. From this perspective, it flows from the first two books. After celebration of Francis's conversion leading to renewal of the Incarnation in Greccio and after the celebration of new life in the transformation of Francis in his stigmata and his *transitus* to the heavenly throne, there is new faith, healing and life in the community left behind. In the third book, the Church reaps the fruit of Francis's conversion and conformity to Christ Crucified. Even in that time of crisis, a new grace of the Spirit is alive in the Church.

Conclusion

Thomas of Celano's *The Life of Saint Francis* is a master's tapestry interweaving multiple colored threads of hagiography, historical data, invitation toward gospel and ecclesial renewal, and identification of the mission and formation of the brothers after Francis. The frame of this tapestry, holding all together, is a profound theology of the Word and of the Cross, fused into a Christology of Incarnation and Passion. Ultimately, the story of Francis is an invitation to experience a love that radically transforms the human person into the image of Christ Crucified, in intimate union with an all-loving and merciful God. The differing threads within this tapestry provide multiple ways to understand, remember and celebrate Saint Francis.

There are many ways of approaching Thomas's portrait. While Augustinian in nature, Thomas's anthropology draws the reader into a rich symbolic theology in which image, experience, and mysticism blend. His theology of conversion and grace reveal themselves at every turn.[32] Thomas describes Francis as God's instrument of ecclesial renewal and reform and, in doing so, develops a strong theology of the Church upon which later authors will build.[33] *The Life of Saint Francis* is a text that demands the active cooperation of a reader. Not simply an encomium for the newly proclaimed saint, Thomas's work is a stimulus for the ever-struggling sinner—a testament of hope focused, as Francis would have it, on the Christ he knew so intimately.

Notes

1. The editors have chosen to use the title used by Thomas in describing his major works. Since there was no question of his writing a "second life" of Saint Francis at the time he wrote his "first life," Thomas entitled his work, simply *The Life of Saint Francis.* When asked to supplement that work with remembrances unknown or overlooked at the time, Thomas entitled his second work *The Remembrance of the Desire of a Soul.* It is a title inspired by Isaiah 26: 8, "your name and your remembrance are the desire of my soul." Since the majority of this work is dedicated to Francis's pursuit of virtues—only the first twenty-five numbers of Thomas's work are "biographical" in nature—Thomas's title expresses more fully its nature.

2. Studies on Thomas's life are few. The following are available: Sophronius Clasen, "Vom Franziskus der Legende zum Franziskus der Geschicthe," *Wissenschaft und Weisheit,* 29 (1966):15-29; Engelbert Grau, "Thomas of Celano: Life and Work," trans. Xavier John Seubert, *Greyfriars Review* v.8, 2 (1994): 177-200; Giovanni Odoardi, "Tommaso da Celano e S. Francesco," in *Tommaso da Celano e la sua opera di biografo di S. Francesco.* Atti del Convegno di studio: Celano, Novembre 29-30,1982 (Celano,1985), 105-23; N. Petrone, "Note biografiche su fra Tommaso da Celano," in *Fra Tommaso da Celano storico-poeta e santo,* a cura di N. Petrone, Tagliacozzo 1992, 9-15.

3. Cf. Odoardi, Giovanni, *Fra Tommaso da Celano, storico letterato poeta uomo di virtù* (Tagliacozzo: S. Francesco)1969.

4. Cf. Odoardi, *Fra Tommaso,* 10.

5. Thomas of Celano, *The Life of Saint Francis,* 57 (hereafter 1C).

6. 1C 56.

7. In naming those who were chosen to embark on a mission to Germany, Jordan lists in fourth place "Thomas of Celano, who later wrote both the first and the second legends of Saint Francis." Cf. Jordan of Giano, *Chronicle* 19 (hereafter ChrJG).

8. 1C 124-126.

9. It is interesting to note that Gregory's commission for the writing of a life of Francis followed the commission for the new basilica in Francis's honor. Both were commissioned shortly before Francis's can-

onization. Cf. W.R. Thomson, *Checklist of Papal Letters Relating to the Three Orders of Saint Francis: Innocent III-Alexander IV, AFH 64 (1971)* 367-580, specifically pages 383-384.

10. Chiara Frugoni has suggested that *The Legend for Use in the Choir* (hereafter LCh) was written later, after the Treatise on the Miracles, that is, after 1253. She argues that the description of the stigmata indicates a later development. Cf. Chiara Frugoni, *Francesco e l'invenzione delle stimmate. Una storia per parole e immagini fino a Bonaventura e Giotto* (Torino 1993)171-173, 198-199.

11. Cf. LCh 1 ; Michael Bihl, "De S. Francisci Legenda ad usum chori auctore Fr. Thoma celanensi, iuxta novum codicem senensem" in *Archivum Franciscanum Historicum* 26 (1933) 343-389.

12. LCh has a few differences from 1C: in n. 11 the Seraph takes a more active role in the stigmata event, in n. 13 there is mention of placing Francis's body in the tomb; in nos. 14-16 new miracles are mentioned; in n. 17 there is allusion to Francis's death on a Sunday and there is allusion to the new church as Francis's burial place.

13. Since Crescentius was replaced on July 13, 1247, the work was completed earlier in that year of 1247.

14. Cf. *Chronica XXIV Generalium Ordinis Minorum, Analecta Francescana* III, 276.

15. For the sake of completeness, it can here be mentioned that Thomas is also considered the poet of liturgical sequences, *Sanctitatis nova signa* and *Fregit victor.* Cf. *Analecta Francescana* X, 402-04 and pages 355-360 below. Also, since the 14th century, Thomas has been considered the poet of the sequence, *Dies Irae.* This, however, is doubtful. Cf. M. Inguanez and A. Amelli, "Il Dies irae in un codice del secolo XII," *Miscellanea Cassinese* 9 (1931) 5-11; K. Vellekoop, *Dies irae. Studien zur Frugeschichte einer Sequenz* (Bilthoven, 1978).

16. Cf. ChrJG 59.

17. Cf. *Preface* in *Analecta Franciscana* X, pp. v, xxiv-xxvi, xxxvi-xxxix.

18. Cf. Francesco Pennacchi, *Legenda Sanctae Clare Virginis* (Assisi, 1910). Pennacchi, in the first publication of *The Legend of Saint Clare,* which was based upon the Assisi Codex 338, attributed the authorship to Thomas of Celano. Subsequent publications by other scholars have suggested other authors, both named and anonymous. A critical edition of the text is necessary before the question can be resolved. For a summary of the scholarship on *The Legend of Saint Clare* see Regis J. Armstrong, *Clare of Assisi: Early Documents* (St. Bonaventure, NY: Franciscan Institute Publications, 1993) 246-249.

19. The tradition for the date of his death is October 4. In listings of the death dates of martyrs and saints used in the Franciscan Order, Thomas is listed under October 4. See *Martyrologium Franciscanum,* auctore Arturo a Monasterio, recognitum et auctum a Ignatio Beschin et Juliiene Palazzolo (Roma, Librariam Collegi S. Antonii, 1938) under October 4.

20. Cf. 1C 90,119.

21. Cf. 1C 117.

22. Cf. 1C 98.

23. Cf. 1C 99.

24. Cf. *Sicut phialae aureae,* BF I 49.

25. Because 1C was commissioned by a pope for purposes of church renewal, it is often called canonical. This does not mean the text is simply a tool for furthering church politics. It means the text emerges out of specific context for a specific purpose, in this case the promotion of a saint worthy of imitation by all people.

26. Cf. 1C 22.

27. Cf. 1C 23.

28. Cf. 1C 86.

29. Cf. J.A. Hellmann, "The Seraph in Thomas of Celano's *Vita Prima*" in *That Others May Know and Love: Essays in Honor of Zachary Hayes,* ed. Michael Cusato and F. Edward Coughlin (St. Bonaventure, NY: Franciscan Institute 1997) 23-41.

30. Cf. 1C 118.

31. Cf. 1C 89.

32. Cf. François de Beer, *La Conversion de Saint François* (Paris: Editions Franciscaines, 1963).

33. Cf. Regis J. Armstrong, "Clare of Assisi, the Poor Ladies, and Their Ecclesial Mission in the First Life of Thomas of Celano," *Greyfriars Review* 5:3 (1991) 389-424.

Prologue

IN THE NAME OF THE LORD. AMEN.
HERE BEGINS THE PROLOGUE TO THE LIFE OF THE BLESSED FRANCIS

[1]It is my desire to explain in orderly detail the acts and life of our most blessed father Francis: pious devotion and truth will always be
Acts 1:1 my guide and instructor.[a] Since everything which *he did and taught* is retained fully in the memory of none, I have endeavored to set forth, insofar as I was able, though with unskilled words, at least those things which I heard from his own mouth or I learned from trustworthy and esteemed witnesses, just as the illustrious lord Pope Gregory has commanded.[b] But how I wish I were deserving to be a disciple of him who always avoided the obscurities of expression and the embellishments of language!

[2]I have divided everything that I was able to gather together about the blessed man into three books, and I have separated each book into individual chapters.[c] In this way the sequence of his various exploits will not be confused nor their truthfulness be brought into doubt. Accordingly, the first book follows an historical sequence and is devoted principally to the purity of his blessed way of life, to his virtuous conduct and his wholesome teaching. In this book I have also introduced a few of the many miracles which our Lord God deemed worthy to per-
Phil 1:22 form through him while he was *living in the flesh.* The second book, on the other hand, tells of his deeds from the next to last year of his life up to his happy death. The third book contains many miracles, while passing over in silence many others, which our most glorious Saint per-
Rv 20:4 formed on earth while reigning *with Christ* in the heavens. Also recorded in this section are the veneration, honor, praise and glory paid

a. At the very outset, Thomas begins to follow the lines of traditional hagiography, in this instance, *The Life of Saint Martin of Tours* (+397) by Sulpicius Severus (+ c. 420).

b. The reference is to Pope Gregory IX, Hugolino dei Conti di Segni, whose papacy extended from March 19, 1227, until August 22, 1241. Born in 1170, he was a nephew of Pope Innocent III into whose service he entered after completion of his studies in Paris and Bologna. In 1217 Hugolino became the Papal Legate for Lombardy and Tuscany, and encountered Francis, Clare and their followers. Eventually he became their official protector.

c. The individual chapter is further divided into numbered subsections. All references to this text are to these numbered subsections.

to him by the blessed Pope Gregory, together with all the cardinals of the holy Roman Church, when they enrolled him in the catalogue of the saints. Thanks be to Almighty God, who always displays Himself *in His saints* as worthy of admiration and love. Ps 68: 36

End of the Prologue.

The First Book

TO THE PRAISE AND GLORY OF GOD ALMIGHTY,
THE FATHER AND THE SON AND THE HOLY SPIRIT. AMEN.
HERE BEGINS THE LIFE OF OUR MOST BLESSED FATHER FRANCIS.

Chapter I
HOW HE LIVED IN THE CLOTHING AND SPIRIT OF THE WORLD

[1]In the city of Assisi, which is located in the confines of the Spoleto
Jb 1:1 valley, *there was a man* named Francis. From the earliest years of his life his parents reared him to arrogance in accordance with the vanity of the age.[a] And by long imitating their worthless life and character he himself was made more vain and arrogant.[b]

A most wicked custom has been so thoroughly ingrained among those regarded as Christians, and this pernicious teaching has been so universally affirmed and prescribed, as though by public law, that, as a result, they are eager to bring up their children from the very cradle too indulgently and carelessly. For when they first begin to speak or babble, little children just born are taught shameful and detestable things by gestures and utterances. And when the time of weaning arrives, they are compelled not only to say but to devote themselves to things full of excess and lewdness. Compelled by the anxiety of youth, they are not bold enough to conduct themselves honorably, since in doing so they would be subject to harsh discipline. A secular poet puts it eloquently:

> Since we have grown up with the training of our parents,
> all sorts of evils pursue us from our childhood.[c]

a. Thomas does not give us a date for Francis's birth, but elsewhere he writes that Francis died in the twentieth year of his conversion (cf. n. 119), or twenty years after he had given himself perfectly to Christ (cf. n. 88). Since Francis's conversion took place when he was about 25 years old (cf. n. 2), and since he died on October 3, 1226, he must have been born in 1181 or 1182. Gregory the Great (+604), whose second book of his *Dialogues* is dedicated to a life of Benedict of Nursia (+546), treats the birth of Benedict in the same way, that is, without a date, cf. Gregory the Great, *Dialogue* II, Introduction.

b. The literary tradition of the Middle Ages and the strong influence of Saint Augustine of Hippo (+430) on medieval hagiography prompted Thomas to stress the power of evil operative upon the young Francis.

c. Seneca, *Ad Lucilium epistulae morales*, v 1, ep. 60, 1. The philosopher Seneca (+85 C.E.) enjoyed great popularity in the Middle Ages as a moralist and presumed correspondent of Saint Paul. Thomas calls him a poet because of several plays attributed to him. The quotation here is from his letters.

This is quite true, for the desires of parents are more injurious to their children, the more they yield gladly to lax discipline.

But even when the children advance a little more in age, they always fall into more ruinous actions by their own choice. For a flawed tree grows from a flawed root; and what was once badly corrupted can only with difficulty be brought back to the norm of justice.

But when they begin to enter the gates of adolescence, what sort of individuals do you imagine they become? Then, without question, flowing on the tide of every kind of debauchery, since they are permitted to fulfill everything they desire, they surrender themselves with all their energy to the service of outrageous conduct. For having become *slaves of sin* by a voluntary servitude, all the members of their body Rom 6: 20
display the *weapons of iniquity,* and, displaying nothing of the Chris- Rom 6: 13
tian religion in their own lives and conduct, they content themselves with just the name of Christian. These wretched people generally pretend that they have done more wicked things than they actually have, so that they do not appear despicable by seeming innocent.[a]

[2]This is the wretched early training in which that man whom we today venerate as a saint—for he truly is a saint—passed his time from childhood and miserably wasted and squandered his time almost up to the twenty-fifth year of his life. Maliciously *advancing beyond* all of
his *peers* in vanities, he proved himself a more excessive *inciter of evil* 2 Mc 4:1
and *a zealous imitator* of foolishness. He was an object of admiration Gal 1: 14
to all, and he endeavored to surpass others in his flamboyant display of vain accomplishments: wit, curiosity, practical jokes and foolish talk, songs, and soft and flowing garments. Since he was very rich, he was not greedy but extravagant, not a hoarder of money but a squanderer of
his property, a prudent dealer but a most unreliable steward.[b] He was, Lk 19:20
nevertheless, a rather kindly person, adaptable and quite affable, even though it made him look foolish.[c] For this reason more than for any-

a. Cf. Saint Augustine, *The Confessions:* "I pretended to obscenities I had not committed, lest I might be thought less courageous for being more innocent, and be accounted cheaper for being more chaste" (II, 3, 7). [This and all future quotations from *The Confessions* have been taken from: Augustine, *The Confessions*, translated with an introduction and notes by Maria Boulding, O.S.B. (Hyde Park, New York: New City Press,1997).]

b. Thomas returns to the examples of the earlier hagiographical tradition in which highlighting the goodness of a person before his conversion can be found. In this case there is a possible allusion to *The Life of Saint Anselm of Canterbury* (+1109) by Eadmer of Canterbury (+1124) in which he describes the saint as generous and reliable. Cf. Eadmer, *Life of Anselm* I, 1.

c. Sulpicius Severus described Martin as being "kept completely free from those vices in which that class of men [soldiers] become too frequently involved." *The Life of Martin* 2. [This and all future quotations from *The Life of Martin* have been taken from: "The Works of Sulpicius Severus," translated with Preface and Notes by Alexander Roberts, in *A Select Library of Nicene and Post-Nicene Fathers of the Christian Church*, Second Series, Volume XI, (New York: The Christian Literature Company, 1894).]

thing else, many went over to him, partisans of evil and inciters of crime. Thus with his crowded procession of misfits he used to strut about impressively and in high spirits, making his way through the streets of Babylon.[a]

Ps 33:13 Then *the Lord looked down from the heavens*
and *for the sake* of His own *name*
He removed His own *anger far* from him,
and for His own *glory He bridled* Francis's mouth
Is 48:9 so that he would *not perish* completely.
Ez 1:3 *The hand of the Lord was upon him,*
Ps 77:11 *a change of the right hand of the Most High,*
that through him the Lord might give sinners confidence
in a new life of grace;
and that of conversion to God
he might be an example.[b]

Chapter II
HOW GOD VISITED HIS HEART THROUGH A BODILY ILLNESS AND A VISION IN THE NIGHT

[3]That man was still boiling in the sins of youthful heat, and his unstable time of life was driving him without restraint to carry out the laws of youth. At the very time when he, not knowing how to become
Rv 20:2 tame, was aroused by the venom of the *ancient serpent,* the divine vengeance, or rather the divine anointing, came upon him.[c] This aimed, first of all, at recalling his erring judgment by bringing distress to his mind and affliction to his body, according to that prophecy: *Behold I*
Hos 2:6 *will hedge up your path with thorns, and I will stop it with a wall.*

Thus worn down by his long illness, as human obstinacy deserves since it is rarely remedied except through punishment, he began *to mull*

a. *The Confessions* (II, 3, 8): "With companions like these I roamed the streets of Babylon and wallowed in its filth as though basking amid cinnamon and precious ointments." See also *Lives of the Desert Fathers* VIII, 3, and Eadmer, *The Life of Anselm* II, 24 both of which refer to a pre-conversion state by the image of the "streets of Babylon."

b. In order to express the rhetorical and poetic quality of Thomas's work, the translators have broken the text into sense lines. By doing so they break with the customary way of presenting Thomas's work in order to express in a clearer way the beauty of the text. Cf. Introduction for explanation of sense lines.

c. Thomas uses the Latin word, *fervescere*, which literally means "to boil" to highlight the "boiling" passions of the adolescent Francis. In this sentence Thomas plays on two Latin words, *divina ultio* [divine vengeance] and *divina unctio* [divine anointing].

over within himself things that were not usual for him.[a] When he had recovered a little and, with the support of a cane, had begun to walk about here and there through the house in order to regain his health, he went outside one day and began to gaze upon the surrounding countryside with greater interest. But the beauty of the fields, the delight of the vineyards, and whatever else was beautiful to see could offer him no delight at all.[b] He wondered at the sudden change in himself, and considered those who loved these things quite foolish. Lk 12:17

[4]From that day he began to regard himself as worthless and to hold in some contempt what he had previously held as admirable and lovable, though not completely or genuinely. For he had not yet been freed from the *bonds of vanities* nor *had he thrown off from his neck the yoke* of degrading servitude. It is difficult to leave familiar things behind, and things once instilled in the spirit are not easily weakened. The spirit, even a long time after its early training, reverts to them; and vice, with enough custom and practice, becomes second nature.[c] Is 5:18; Gn 27:40

Thus Francis still tried to avoid the divine grasp, and, for a brief time losing sight of the Father's reproach while good fortune smiled upon him, *reflected upon worldly matters.* Ignoring *God's plan,* he vowed, out of vainglory and vanity, to do great deeds. A certain nobleman from the city of Assisi was furnishing himself on a large scale with military weaponry and, swollen by the wind of *empty glory,* he asserted solemnly that he was going to Apulia to enrich himself in money or distinction.[d] When Francis heard of this, because he was whimsical and overly daring, he agreed to go with him. Although Francis did not equal him in nobility of birth, he did outrank him in graciousness; and though poorer in wealth, he was richer in generosity. 1 Cor 7:34; Wis 9:13 Gal 5:26

[5]One night, after Francis had devoted himself with all of his determination to accomplish these things and was eager, seething with de-

a. Medieval hagiography frequently describes illness as providing the occasion for conversion. In *The Life of Anselm* I,3, for example, Anselm actually prays for an illness in order to be received into the monastic way of life.

b. Gregory the Great writes of the early years of Benedict in a similar way: "While still living in the world, free to enjoys its earthly advantages, he saw how barren it was with its attractions and turned from it without regret." Cf. Gregory the Great, *Dialogue II,* Prologue. [This and all subsequent quotations will be taken from the following text: Gregory the Great, *Dialogues,* translated Odo John Zimmerman, O.S.B., *The Fathers of the Church,* vol. 39 (New York: Fathers of the Church, Inc., 1959).]

c. Cf. Cicero (+43 B.C.E.), *De finibus bonorum* V 25 74: "Even the votaries of pleasure take refuge in evasions: the name of virtue is on their lips all the time, and they declare that pleasure is only at first the object of desire, and that later habit produces a sort of second nature, which supplies a motive for many actions not aiming at pleasure at all." Cf. Macrobius, *Saturnalia* VII 9 7; Augustine, *Contra Julianum opus imperfectum* IV 103.

d. Apulia is located in the southeastern part of the peninsula. It is the place where Walter of Brienne, head of Innocent III's papal militia, was fighting against Markwald of Anweiler, seneschal of the German Empire. The latter claimed tutelage over the young Frederick II, who had been entrusted to the pope.

sire, to make the journey, the One who had struck him with the *rod of*
Is 10:24; Jb 4:13; 33:15 *justice* visited him in a *vision during the night* in the sweetness of
grace.[a] Because he was eager for glory, the Lord exalted and enticed
him to its pinnacle. For it seemed to him that his whole house was filled
with soldiers' arms: saddles, shields, spears and other equipment.
Though delighting for the most part, he silently wondered to himself
about its meaning. For he was not accustomed to see such things in his
house, but rather stacks of cloth to be sold. He was greatly bewildered
at the sudden turn of events and the response that all these arms were to
be for him and his soldiers. With a happy spirit he awoke the next
morning. Considering his vision a prediction of great success, he felt
sure that his upcoming journey to Apulia would be successful. *In fact*
Mk 9:5 *he did not know what he was saying,* and as yet he did not at all understand the gift sent to him from heaven. He should have been able to see
that his interpretation of it was mistaken. For, although the vision bore
some semblance of great deeds, his spirit was not moved by these
things in its usual way. In fact, he had to force himself to carry out his
plans and undertake the journey he had desired.

It is a fine thing
that at the outset mention be made of arms,
and very fitting
that arms be handed over
to a soldier about to do battle
Lk 11:21 *with one strong and fully armed.*
Thus,
like a second David
1 Sm 17:45 *in the name of the Lord God of hosts*
from the long-standing abuse of its enemies,
1 Sm 17:26 he might *liberate Israel.*

a. The phenomenon of dreams, frequently found in medieval hagiography, is present throughout the Bible (e.g., Gn 28:12; 41:5; 47:7; 1 Kgs 3:15). Further information can be found in Martin Dulaey, "*Sognes-Reves*", in *Dictionnaire de Spiritualité Ascetique et Mystique XIV* (Beauchesne: Paris, 1990) 1054-1066. For other examples in medieval hagiography, cf. Eadmer, *The Life of Anselm* I,2; *Lives of the Desert Fathers* X:4.

Chapter III
How, changed in mind but not in body, Francis talked allegorically about the treasure he had found and about his bride

[6]Changed in mind but not in body, he now refused to go to Apulia and was anxious to direct his will to God's. Thus he retired for a short time from the tumult and business of the world and was anxious to keep Jesus Christ in his inmost self. Like an experienced merchant, he concealed *the pearl he had found* from the eyes of mockers and *selling all he had,* he tried to buy it secretly. Mt 13:46

Now there was in the city of Assisi a man he loved more than all the rest. They were of the same age and the constant intimacy of their mutual love made him bold to share his secrets with him. He often brought him to remote places suitable for talking, asserting that he had found a great and valuable treasure. This man was overjoyed, and since he was so excited about what he heard, he gladly went with him whenever he was summoned. There was a cave near the city where they often went and talked together about the treasure.[a] The man of God, who was already holy because of his holy intention, was accustomed to enter the cave, while his companion waited outside, and inspired by a new and extraordinary spirit he would pray to his *Father in secret.* He acted in Mt 6:6
such a way that no one would know what was happening within. Wisely taking the occasion of the good to conceal the better, he consulted God alone about his holy purpose. He prayed with all his heart that the eternal and true God guide his way and *teach him to do His will.* Ps 143: 10
He endured great suffering in his soul, and he was not able to rest until he accomplished in action what he had conceived in his heart. Different thoughts followed one after another, and their relentlessness severely disturbed him. He was burning inwardly with a divine fire, and he was unable to conceal outwardly the flame kindled in his soul. He repented that he had sinned so grievously and that he had offended *the eyes of majesty.* While his past and present transgressions no longer delighted Is 3:8
him, he was not yet fully confident of refraining from future ones. Therefore, when he came back out to his companion, he was so ex-

a. Gregory the Great had described this period of Benedict's conversion in a similar way when writing of his flight to a "lonely wilderness" where he made his home in a "narrow cave." Cf. Gregory, *Dialogue* II 1. Thomas uses the word *crypta* to describe that place of solitude. It is translated in this instance as "cave." Its location and nature remain problematic.

hausted from his struggle that one person seemed to have entered, and another to have come out.

[7]One day, when he had invoked the Lord's mercy with his whole
heart, the Lord showed him what he must do. *He was filled with* such
Ps 126:2 *great joy* that, failing to restrain himself in the face of his happiness,
he carelessly mentioned something to others. Even though he could
not remain silent because of the greatness of the love inspired in him,
he nevertheless spoke cautiously and in riddles. Just as he spoke to his
Mt 13:44 special friend about a *hidden treasure,* so he endeavored to talk to
others in figures of speech. He said that he did not want to go to Apulia, but promised to do great and noble deeds at home. People thought he wanted to get married, and they would ask him: "Do you want to get married, Francis?" He replied: "I will take a bride more noble and more beautiful than you have ever seen, and she will surpass the rest in beauty and excel all others in wisdom."

Indeed
the *unstained bride* of God is
Jas 1:27 the true *religion* that he embraced,
Mt 13:44 and the hidden treasure *the kingdom of heaven,*
that he sought with great longing.
For it had to be that the gospel call be fulfilled
in the one who was to be
1 Tm 2:7 *in faith and truth*
Eph 3:7 *a minister of the gospel.*

Chapter IV
How after he sold all his belongings, he despised the money he received

[8]Ah! Inclined and strengthened by the Holy Spirit the blessed ser-
Jb 12:5 vant of the Most High, seeing that the *appointed time* was at hand, fol-
lowed that blessed impulse of his soul. Thus, as he trampled upon worldly things, he made his way to the greatest good. He could no longer delay, for by then a fatal disease had spread everywhere and infected the limbs of so many that, were the doctor to delay just a little, it would stifle breath and snatch life away.

After fortifying himself with the sign of the holy cross, he arose, and when his horse was made ready, he mounted it. Taking with him scarlet cloth to sell, he quickly came to a city called Foligno.[a] There after selling everything he brought in his usual way, this successful merchant even left behind the horse he was riding, when he had obtained his price. Starting back, he put down his bags and pondered conscientiously what to do about the money. In a wonderful way, in an instant, he turned completely to the work of God. Feeling the heavy weight of carrying that money even for an hour, and reckoning all its benefit to be like so much sand, he hurried to get rid of it. Returning toward the city of Assisi, he came across a church on the side of the road. It had been built in ancient times in honor of Saint Damian and was threatening to collapse because of age.[b]

[9]Arriving at this church, the new *soldier of Christ,* aroused by piety 2 Tm 2:3
at such a great need, entered it with awe and reverence.[c] He found a poor priest there, kissed his holy hands with great devotion, offered him the money he was carrying and explained his purpose in great detail.[d]

The priest was astounded and, surprised at this sudden conversion in incredible circumstances, he refused to believe what he was hearing. Because he thought he was being mocked, he refused to keep the money offered to him. It seemed to him that Francis, just the day before, was living outrageously *among his relatives and acquaintances* Lk 2:44
and *exalting his stupidity* above others. But Francis stubbornly per- Prv 14:29
sisted and endeavored to create confidence in his words. He pleaded, begging the priest with all his heart to allow him to stay with him for the

a. Foligno is located about 15 km or 9 miles east of Assisi. In modern use the term "scarlet" describes a vivid shade of red. Prior to the 16th century it referred to a bright dye, white, blue or green. The taste for the exotic that influenced Western fashion at the time of the Crusades brought from the East its first samples of damask, scarlet and crimson. All these rare fabrics were prized and very expensive.

b. The church of San Damiano was built in 1103 by a consortium of noble families that later entrusted it to the prior of San Rufino in Assisi and later to the city's bishop. It is difficult to know the condition of the church when Francis first entered it. For information concerning the origins and questions of the Church of San Damiano, see Marino Bigaroni, "San Damiano-Assisi: The First Church of Saint Francis," *Franciscan Studies* (1986) 45-97; Arnaldo Fortini, *Francis of Assisi,* translated by Helen Moak (New York: Crossroad, 1981), p. 215, j.

c. Thomas uses the word *pietas* here, a word he employs nineteen times in 1C. It is a difficult word to translate since our modern English word, piety, does not fully express the richness of a word that classical Roman writers associated with humility, religion and spirituality, and viewed as the bedrock of all social relationships. Cf. H. Hagenvoort, *Pietas: Selected Studies in Roman Religion,* (Leiden, E.J. Brill: 1980). For a thorough study of the word in the history of spirituality, see Irénée Noye, *"Piété," Dictionnaire de la Spiritualité Ascetique et Mystique.*

d. *Propositum,* a word Thomas uses twenty-two times in this work, does not always have the same meaning, cf. *Corpus des Sources Franciscaines I, Thesaurus Celanensis,* edited Georges Mailleux, (Louvain: Publications du CETEDOC, 1974). At times it refers to purpose, as in this instance, while at other times it suggests a plan or a proposal. The word takes on a technical sense when it refers to the *propositum vitae,* the primitive "rule," which Francis and his first brothers presented to Pope Innocent III. Cf. 1C 33.

sake of the Lord.[a] Finally the priest agreed to let him stay, but out of fear of Francis's parents did not accept the money. The true scorner of wealth threw it onto a window opening, since he cared for it as much as he cared for dust.[b]

For he desired
to possess wisdom, which *is better than gold,*
Prv 16:16 and *to acquire understanding,* which *is more precious than silver.*

Chapter V

How his Father persecuted and bound him

Acts 16:17; Mt 25:5 10 While the *servant of the most high God was staying* there, his father went around everywhere like a diligent spy, wanting to know what
had happened to his son. When he had learned that Francis was living
in that place in such a way, he was *touched inwardly with sorrow of*
Gn 6:6; Ps 6:4 *heart* and *deeply disturbed* by the sudden turn of events. *Calling to-*
Lk 15:6 *gether his friends* and *neighbors*, he raced to the place where the servant of God was staying.

The new athlete of Christ,[c] when he heard the threats of his pursuers
and learned in advance of their coming, lowered himself into a hiding
place, which he had prepared for himself for this very purpose, wanting
Rom 12:19 *to leave room for their anger.* That pit was in the house and was known
to only one person.[d] He hid in it for one month continually and scarcely
dared to come out even for human needs. Whenever food was given he

a. Bernard of Clairvaux (+1153) writes of a similar desire expressed by Saint Malachy (+1148). Cf. Bernard, *The Life and Death of Saint Malachy the Irishman* 4. This text is important because it provides an example of the hagiographic style of Bernard of Clairvaux whose influence on the spiritual literature of the early thirteenth century—and hence on Thomas—was significant.

b. In the changing economy of the twelfth and thirteenth centuries, such an attitude toward money was common. Money was "portable" wealth and concern for it presented new temptations to greed and exploitation. Cf. Lester K. Little, *Religious Poverty and the Profit Economy in Medieval Europe* (Ithaca, NY: Cornell University Press, 1978), especially pp. 35-41; George Duby, *William Marshal: The Flower of Chivalry*, translated by Richard Howard (New York: Pantheon Books, 1985), pp. 87-90.

c. The image of a trained athlete appears in hagiography from the time of the martyrs to describe one involved in the struggle of the spiritual life. As one had to practice physical asceticism or self-discipline to be a strong athlete, so one had to do the same in the spiritual life. Bernard of Clairvaux portrays Malachy as an "athlete of the Lord," cf. Bernard of Clairvaux, *The Life and Death of Saint Malachy the Irishman* VIII, 16. [All passages from this text are taken from Bernard of Clairvaux, *The Life and Death of Saint Malachy the Irishman*, translated and annotated by Robert Meyer, (Kalamazoo: Cistercian Publications, 1978).] Felix, a monk of the eighth century, described the Anglo-Saxon saint, Guthlac (+714), as an "athlete of Christ," cf. Felix, *The Life of Saint Guthlac* 33. [All passages from this text are taken from: *Felix's The Life of Saint Guthlac*, text, translation and notes by Bertram Colgrave, (Cambridge: Cambridge University Press, 1985).]

d. This passage raises questions: the nature of the *fovea* [pit], its location, and the identity of the one person who knew of its existence. Subsequent writers attempt to bring clarity to these issues in their biographies of Francis.

ate it in the secrecy of the pit, and every service was provided to him in secret. He prayed with flowing tears[a] *that the Lord would free* him *from the hands of those persecuting* his *soul* and that he could favorably fulfill his fervent wishes. *Fasting and weeping,* he earnestly prayed for the Savior's mercy, and, lacking confidence in his own efforts, *he cast his care upon the Lord.* Though staying *in a pit and in darkness,* he was imbued with an indescribable happiness never before experienced. Then totally on fire, he abandoned the pit and openly exposed himself to the curses of his persecutors.

Ps 142:7; Jl 2:12; Ps 55: 23; Dn 2:22

[11]He rose, therefore, swift, energetic and eager, carrying *the shield of faith* for the Lord, and strengthened with the armor of great confidence, he set out for the city.[b] Burning with holy fervor, he began to accuse himself of idleness and sloth.

Eph 6:16

When all those who knew him saw him, they compared his latest circumstances with his former and they began to reproach him harshly.[c] Shouting that he was insane and out of his mind, *they threw mud from the streets and stones* at him. They saw him as changed from his earlier ways and weakened by starving his body. They blamed everything he did on starvation and madness.

Ps 18:43; Jn 8:59

But since *the patient person is better than the proud*, God's servant showed himself deaf to all of them, and neither broken nor changed by any wrong to himself he gave thanks to God for all of them.

Eccl 7:9

For in vain do the wicked persecute those striving for virtue,
for the more they are stricken, the more fully will they triumph.
As someone says, "Disgrace makes a noble mind stronger."[d]

[12]For some time rumor and gossip of this sort raced *through the streets* and *quarters of the city*, and the noise of that ridicule echoed here and there. The report of these things reached the ears of many, finally reaching his father. When he heard the name of his own son men-

Sg 3:2

a. For similar descriptions see Alan, Bishop of Auxerre, *Vita secunda s. Bernardi* 4; Eadmer, *The Life of Anselm* II,53; and Gregory the Great, *Dialogue II* 17.

b. Once again Thomas uses military images which were frequently used in medieval hagiography. Cf. Felix, *The Life of Saint Guthlac* 27: "Then girding himself with spiritual arms . . . he took the shield of faith." See also, Bernard of Clairvaux, *The Life and Death of Saint Malachy the Irishman* 26: "He puts on the weapons so mighty with God."

c. Geoffrey of Auxerre, author of Book Four of the *Vita prima s. Bernardi,* writes: "When his brothers and close relatives saw that [Bernard] was considering leaving the world and adopting this way of life, they began to use every means in their power to try and make Bernard change his mind."

d. Thomas seems to refer to Seneca's *Epistola Morales* 4, n.10:2: *Habet enim hoc optimum in se generosus animus, quod concitatur ad honestia* [For this is the best that the generous spirit has within itself, that it is urged toward honorable things].

tioned and that the commotion among the townspeople swirled around him, he immediately arose, not to free him, but rather to destroy him. With no restraint, he pounced on Francis like a wolf on a lamb and, glaring at him fiercely and savagely, he grabbed him and shamelessly dragged him home. With no pity, he shut him up for several days in a dark place.[a] Striving to bend Francis's will to his own, he badgered him, beat him, and bound him.

As a result of this Francis became more fit and eager to carry out his holy plan. Neither the reproach of words nor the exhaustion of chains eroded his patience.

Those taught to rejoice in suffering
will not deviate from an upright intention and way of life
nor be stolen from Christ's flock
because of beatings and chains.
Ps 32:6 Nor will they fear *in the flood of many waters*
whose refuge from oppression is the Son of God,
who always shows them his sufferings,
greater than those they endure.

Chapter VI

How his mother freed him and how he stripped himself before the bishop of Assisi

[13]When his father had left home for a little while on pressing family business, the man of God remained bound in the prison of his home.[b] His mother, who had remained at home alone with him, did not approve of her husband's action and spoke to her son in gentle words. After she saw that she could not dissuade her son from his intention, *she*
1 Kgs 3:26 *was moved by* maternal *instinct.* She broke his chains and let him go free. Thanking Almighty God, he quickly returned to the place he had

a. The same spirit of persecution by one's father appears elsewhere in hagiography. Cf. Eadmer, *The Life of Anselm* I,4: "That is to say, he stirred up in his father's mind so keen a hatred against him that he persecuted him as much, or even more, for the things he did well as for those which he did ill." [This and all future references are taken from: Eadmer of Canterbury, *The Life of Saint Anselm, Archbishop of Canterbury*, edited with introduction, notes by Richard Southern, (London, New York:Thomas Nelson and Sons Ltd, 1962).]

b. As a merchant in the cloth trade, Pietro di Bernardone may have traveled to cloth fairs in Champagne. He would have taken the usual trade route from the Mediterranean to the North Sea. Since the end of the 12th century Champagne had been the main center for trade between East and West. Trade fairs traveled from city to city: Troyes, Provins, Bar-sur-Aube and Lagny. Generally Italian businessmen were the driving force and the masters of trade travelling the passes of the Alps and Apennines, at times in harsh weather. They traveled alone or, because the road was dangerous, in caravans. Cf. Map B, p. 208.

been before. Since he had passed the test of temptations, he now enjoyed greater freedom. Throughout these many struggles, he began to exhibit a more joyful appearance. From the injuries inflicted he received a more confident spirit and, now free to go anywhere, he moved about with even greater heart.

Meanwhile, the father returned and, not finding him and heaping sin upon sin, he turned to reviling his wife. He raced to the place, shaking and screaming, so that if he could not call his son back, he might at least drive him from the area. But since *the fear of the Lord is the assurance of fortitude,* when the child of grace heard that his father in the flesh Prv 14:26
was coming to him, he went out on his own to meet his father crying out loudly that binding and beating lead to nothing. In addition, he declared he would gladly suffer anything for the name of Christ.

14 When the father saw that he could not recall him from the journey he had begun, he became obsessed with recovering the money. The man of God had desired to spend it on feeding the poor and on the buildings of that place. But the one who did not love money could not be deceived even by this appearance of good, and the one who was not bound by any affection for it was not disturbed in any way by its loss. The greatest scorner of the things of earth and the outstanding seeker of heavenly riches had thrown it into the dust on the windowsill. When the money was found, the rage of his angry father was dampened a little and his thirsty greed was quenched a bit by its discovery. Then he led the son to the bishop of the city to make him renounce into the bishop's hands all rights of inheritance and return everything that he had.[a] Not only did he not refuse this, but he hastened joyfully and eagerly to do what was demanded.

15 When he was in front of the bishop, he neither delayed nor hesitated, but immediately took off and threw down all his clothes and returned them to his father. He did not even keep his trousers on, and he was completely stripped bare before everyone. The bishop, observing his frame of mind and admiring his fervor and determination, got up and, gathering him in his own arms, covered him with the mantle he was wearing. He clearly understood that this was prompted by God and

a. This is a reference to Bishop Guido II, who was bishop of Assisi from 1204 until his death, July 30, 1228. A papal decree of May 12, 1198 addressed to his predecessor, Guido I, confirmed the many episcopal privileges by the bishop of Assisi. At the time of these events, Guido II possessed broad powers in both the ecclesiastical and civil worlds. Cf, *Regesta Honorii Papae III*, ii, P. Pressutti, Rome, 1895, n. 4958, p. 242 NV. I, p. 323. For information on the juridical procedures for bringing an accused person before the consuls or bishop, cf. Arnaldo Fortini, *Francis of Assisi*, translated by Helen Moak (New York: Crossroad, 1981), 222-230.

he knew that the action of the man of God, which he had personally ob-
Ps 30:11 served, contained a mystery. After this *he became* his *helper.* Cher-
Col 3:12 ishing and comforting him, he embraced him in the depths of charity.

Look!
Now he wrestles naked with the naked.
1 Cor 7: 33 After putting aside all that is *of the world,*
he is mindful only of divine justice.[a]
Now he is eager to despise his own life,
by setting aside all concern for it.
Thus
there might be peace for him,
a poor man on a hemmed-in path,
and only the wall of the flesh would separate him
from the vision of God.

Chapter VII
How, when captured by bandits, he was thrown into the snow, and how he served lepers

[16]He who once enjoyed wearing scarlet robes now traveled about half-clothed. Once while he was singing praises to the Lord in French in a certain forest, thieves suddenly attacked him.[b] When they savagely demanded who he was, the man of God answered confidently and
Ps 48:3; Mt 27:4 forcefully: "I am the herald *of the great King!* What is it to you?" They beat him and threw him into a ditch filled with deep snow, saying: "Lie there, you stupid herald of God!" After they left, he rolled about to and fro, shook the snow off himself and jumped out of the ditch. Exhilarated with great joy, he began in a loud voice to make the woods resound with praises to the Creator of all.

a. The theme of nudity entered the language of spirituality through the literature of the early Christian martyrs, as can be seen in the *The Life of Polycarp* 13; *Acts of the Martyrdom of Perpetua and Felicitas* 10, 20; *Martyrdom of SS. Carpus, Papylus, and Agathonice.* It entered into medieval literature through Saint Jerome, *The Life of Paula* and Saint Gregory the Great, *Homilia in Evangelium* 32 n. 2 (PL 76, 1233). Cf. Michel Mollat, *The Poor in the Middle Ages: An Essay in Social History*, translated by Arthur Goldhammer (New Haven and London: Yale University Press, 1986); Margaret Miles, *Carnal Knowing: Female Nakedness and Religious Meaning in the Christian West* (Boston, MA: Beacon Press, 1989).

b. The expression *lingua francigena,* translated in this text "French," refers to the language of Champagne. Francis may have learned French from his father or from accompanying him on his journeys to the trade fairs, cf. p. 193, a.

Eventually he arrived at a cloister of monks, where he spent several days covered with only a cheap shirt, serving as a scullery boy in the kitchen.[a] He wanted to be fed at least some soup. No mercy was shown him and he was not even able to get some old clothes. Not moved by anger but forced by necessity, he moved on to the city of Gubbio, where he obtained a cheap tunic from an old friend. Shortly afterward, when the fame of the man of God had grown far and wide and *his name was spread* among the people, the prior of that monastery, when he recalled 2 Chr 26:8; Lk 4:37
the event and understood what had been done to the man of God, came to him and, out of reverence for the Savior, begged forgiveness for himself and his monks.

17 Then the holy lover of profound humility moved to the lepers and stayed with them.[b] For God's sake he served all of them with great love. He washed all the filth from them, and even cleaned out the pus of their sores, just as he said in his *Testament:* "When I was in sin, it seemed too bitter for me to see lepers, and the Lord led me among them
Test 2 and I showed mercy to them." For he used to say that the sight of lepers was so bitter to him that in the days of his vanity when he saw their houses even two miles away, he would cover his nose with his hands.

When he started thinking of holy and useful matters with the grace and *strength of the Most High*, while still in the clothes of the world, he Lk 1:35
met a leper one day. Made stronger than himself, he came up *and kissed him.*[c] He then began to consider himself less and less, until by the Mk 14:45
mercy of the Redeemer, he came to complete victory over himself.

While staying in the world and following its ways, he was also a helper of the poor. He extended a hand of mercy to those who had nothing and he poured out compassion for the afflicted. One day, contrary to his custom (since he was very polite), he rebuked a poor person seeking alms from him, and he was immediately *led to penance.* He began Mt 27:3
to say *to himself* that to refuse what was asked by someone begging in Lk 7:49
the name of such a great King would be both a shame and a disgrace.

---

a. This may have been the monastery of *San Verecondo,* today *Vallingegno,* located just south of Gubbio. The Latin word, *garcio* [scullery boy], is a term of contempt for a certain class of workers regarded as unskilled and uncouth.

b. This may be the leper hospital of San Rufino dell'Arce near the Portiuncula or that of San Lazaro close to the Rivo Torto, or that of San Salvatore delle Mura, site of the present day Casa Gualdi which lies below Assisi and halfway to Saint Mary of the Angels. The precise location is still contested. In Assisi, as in other communes, harsh rules governed the whereabouts and movements of lepers. They were forbidden to enter the city.

c. Association with lepers and outcasts was seen as part of the life of Martin of Tours and, through him, entered into the pattern of medieval spirituality. Cf. Sulpicius Severus, *The Life of Martin* 18: "At Paris, again, when Martin was entering the gate of the city, with large crowds attending him, he gave a kiss to a leper, of miserable appearance, while all shuddered at seeing him do so."

Ps 14:1; Acts 5:4 And so he fixed this *in his heart:* to the best of his ability, never to deny anything to anyone begging from him for God's sake. This he did and with such care that he offered himself completely, in every way, first practicing before teaching the gospel counsel:[a] *"Give to the one who begs from you, and do not turn away from the one who wants to borrow*
Mt 5: 42 *from you."*

Chapter VIII
How he built the church of San Damiano, and of the way of life of the Ladies living in that place[b]

[18]The first work that blessed Francis undertook,
after he had gained his freedom
from the hands of his carnally-minded father,
was to build a house of God.
He did not try to build a new one,
but he repaired an old one,
restored an ancient one.[c]
He did not tear out the foundation,
but he built upon it,
always reserving to Christ his prerogative,
although unaware of it,
for no one can lay another foundation,
but that which has been laid,
1 Cor 3:11 *which is Christ Jesus.*

When he had returned to the place mentioned where
the church of San Damiano had been built in ancient times,
he repaired it zealously within a short time,

---

a. The practice and the teaching of the gospel is a prominent theme of Christian hagiography. This can be seen in Gregory of Nyssa's (+394) *The Life of Moses,* II, 55: "The history all but cries out to you not to be presumptuous in giving advice to your hearers in your teaching unless the ability for this has been perfected in you by a long and exacting training such as Moses had." [This and all future passages from this text are taken from: Gregory of Nyssa, *The Life of Moses,* edited with translations, introductions, and notes by Abraham Malherbe and Everett Ferguson, (Paulist Press, NY, 1978).] Cf. Carolyn Walker Bynum, *Docere Verbo et Exemplo: An Aspect of Twelfth-Century Spirituality,* (Missoula, MT: Scholars Press, 1978).

b. Thomas uses the title, *Domina* [Lady] which traditionally referred either to princesses of blood or to nuns and canonesses. (See Du Cange, Glossarium mediae et infimae latinitatis, ed. L. Favre, (Graz,1883-1887). *Domina* 5, and *Domicellae* 2).

c. Thomas uses the adjective *novus* [new] thirty-nine times in this work emphasizing Francis as a "new soldier of Christ" (n. 9), a "new athlete of Christ" (n. 10), and a "new evangelist" (n. 89). Integrally associated with him are a new: mystery (n. 85), song (n. 126), Bethlehem (n. 85), miracles (nn. 119, 121), vine (n. 74), light (nn. 119, 123), order (n. 74), joy (n. 119), waters (n. 151), teachings (n. 26), spirit (n. 6) and rite (n. 89).

aided by the grace of the Most High.[a]
This is the blessed and holy place where
the glorious religion and most excellent Order
of Poor Ladies and holy virgins
had its happy beginning,
about six years after the conversion of the blessed Francis
and through that same blessed man.

The Lady Clare,[b]
a native of the city of Assisi,
the most precious and strongest stone of the whole structure,
stands as the foundation for all the other stones.[c]
For
after the beginning of the Order of Brothers,
when this lady was converted to God
through the counsel of the holy man,
she lived for the good of many
and as an example to countless others.
Noble by lineage, but more noble by grace,[d]
chaste in body, most chaste in mind,
young in age, mature in spirit,
steadfast in purpose and most eager in her desire for divine love,
endowed with wisdom and excelling in humility,
bright in name, more brilliant in life, most brilliant in character.[e]
19 A noble structure of precious pearls arose above this woman,
whose praise comes not from mortals but from God, Rom 2:29
since our limited understanding is not sufficient to imagine it,
nor our scanty vocabulary to utter it.

---

a. Rebuilding churches was a medieval expression of piety. The eighth century author, Eddius Stephanus, for example, writes of the English saint Wilfrid (+710), that he first rebuilt a church at York and subsequently another in honor of Saint Peter and, finally, one in honor of Saint Mary. Cf. Eddius Stephanus, *The Life of Bishop Wilfrid,* text, translation and notes by Bertram Colgrave (Cambridge, New York: Cambridge University Press, 1985). Similar examples may be found in the following: Theodore of Cyrus, *A History of the Monks of Syria,* "Life of Julian," 13, translated by R.M. Price,(Kalamazoo: Cistercian Publications, 1985); Bernard of Clairvaux, *The Life of Saint Malachy the Irishman* VI, 12.

b. For further information on the life of Clare of Assisi, see *Clare of Assisi: Early Documents,* translated and edited by Regis J. Armstrong, (St. Bonaventure, NY: Franciscan Institute, 1993); Ingrid Peterson, *Clare of Assisi: A Biographical Study* (Quincy: Franciscan Press, 1993).

c. This may allude to 1 Kgs 7:9-10, a description of Solomon's temple, and Rv 21:19, a description of the city walls of the heavenly Jerusalem and thus would refer to the temples of the historical and the heavenly Jerusalem.

d. Cf. Jerome, *Paula* 1, "Noble in family, she was nobler still in holiness."

e. This is the earliest instance of the play on the name Clare or *Chiara* which is translated as "bright." Thus the Latin text: *Clara nomine, vita clarior, clarisima moribus.*

First of all,
the virtue of mutual and continual charity
that binds their wills together
flourishes among them.
Forty or fifty of them can dwell together in one place,
wanting and not wanting the same things
forming one spirit in them out of many.[a]
Second,
the gem of humility,
preserving the good things bestowed by heaven
so sparkles in each one
that they merit other virtues as well.[b]
Third,
the lily of virginity and chastity
diffuses such a wondrous fragrance among them
that they forget earthly thoughts
and desire to meditate only on heavenly things.
So great a love of their eternal Spouse arises in their hearts
that the integrity of their holy feelings keeps them
from every habit of their former life.
Fourth,
all of them have become so distinguished
by their title of highest poverty
that their food and clothing
rarely or never
manage to satisfy extreme necessity.[c]
[20]Fifth,
they have so attained the unique grace
of abstinence and silence
that they scarcely need to exert any effort

a. "*Idem velle atque idem nolle, ea demum firma amicitia est* [Wanting and not wanting the same thing—this is the foundation of a firm friendship]." This is a proverbial saying that Sallust places in the mouth of Cataline who urges his fellow conspirators in the name of friendship to join him in revolt, cf. Caius Crispus Sallust, *Bellum Catilinarium,* XX 4 (The Loab Classical Library) 33-34.

b. The monastic tradition presented humility as the foundation of all virtue, e.g. Bernard of Clairvaux, *Sermo I in Nativitate Domini* (PL 183:115): "Be eager to humble yourselves, for [humility] is the foundation and guardian of the virtues." "No gem," writes Bernard, "is more resplendent . . . than humility." Cf. Bernard, *De Consideratione ad Eugenium papam tertiam libri quinque* II 13. "What is as pure," he asks, "or as perfect as humility of heart?" Bernard, *In Annuntiatione, Sermo* III, 9. Thomas, however, places it in the second position in the life of the Poor Ladies even though he echoes the earlier approach in suggesting that humility "preserves the good things bestowed by heaven" and enables them to "merit other virtues as well."

c. In this instance the Latin *titulus* [title] is a canonical term signifying the source of one's adequate support. In the phrase *altissimae paupertatis titulo* [the title of the highest poverty] Thomas uses the term in a paradoxical way to indicate that the source of support of the Poor Ladies is poverty.

to check the prompting of the flesh
and to restrain their tongues.[a]
Sixth,
they are so adorned with the virtue of patience
in all these things,
that adversity of tribulation,
or injury of vexation
never breaks or changes their spirit.[b]
Seventh,
and finally,
they have so merited the height of contemplation
that they learn in it everything they should do or avoid,
and they know how to go beyond the *mind to God* with joy, 2 Cor 5:13
persevering night and day
in praising Him and praying to Him.

For the moment
let this suffice
concerning these virgins dedicated to God
and most devout servants of Christ.
Their wondrous life
and their renowned practices received from the Lord Pope Gregory,[c]
at that time Bishop of Ostia,
would require another book
and the leisure in which to write it.

a. The vast amount of medieval literature on silence flows from the monastic tradition in which it was viewed as a form of abstinence. Cf. Carolyn Walker Bynum, *Holy Feast and Holy Fast: The Religious Significance of Food to Medieval Women* (Berkeley: University of California, 1987); Rudolph Bell, *Holy Anorexia* (Chicago: University of Chicago Press, 1985).

b. The cultivation of patience was seen as a primary means of identification with Christ. While strongly present in the literature of martyrdom, it entered into that of monasticism through the Desert tradition and became a prerequisite for the quiet of contemplation.

c. *Institutio* [practices] refers to the *Form of Life* given by Cardinal Hugolino to the Poor Ladies of San Damiano in 1219, cf. Hugolino "The Form and Manner of Life Given by Cardinal Hugolino (1219)" in *Clare of Assisi: Early Documents*, translated and edited by Regis J. Armstrong (St. Bonaventure: Franciscan Institute Publications, 1993) 89-100.

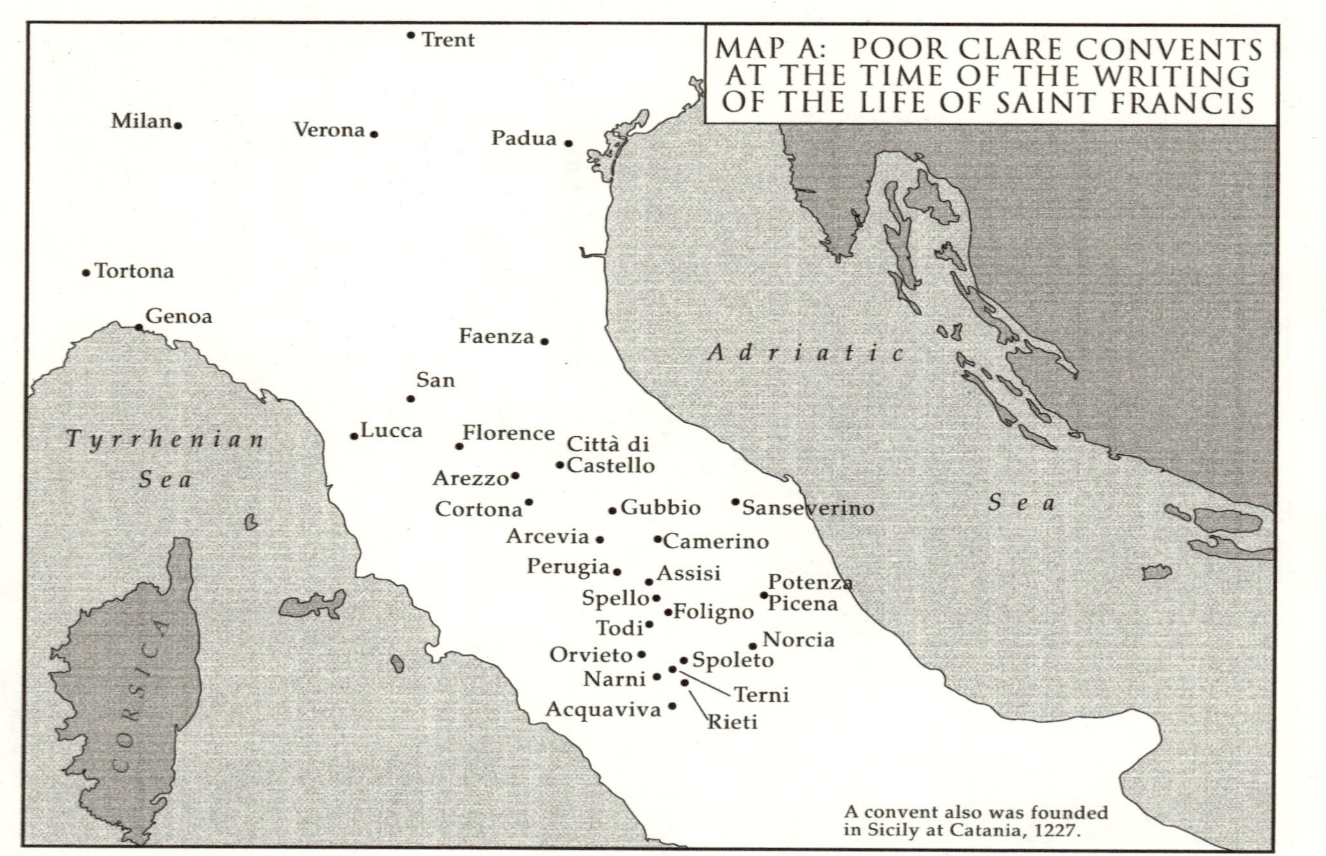
MAP A: POOR CLARE CONVENTS AT THE TIME OF THE WRITING OF THE LIFE OF SAINT FRANCIS
Trent
Milan
Verona
Padua
Tortona
Genoa
Faenza
San
Lucca
Florence
Città di Castello
Arezzo
Cortona
Gubbio
Sanseverino
Arcevia
Camerino
Perugia
Assisi
Potenza Picena
Spello
Foligno
Todi
Norcia
Orvieto
Spoleto
Narni
Terni
Acquaviva
Rieti
Adriatic Sea
Tyrrhenian Sea
CORSICA
A convent also was founded in Sicily at Catania, 1227.

Chapter IX

HOW, WHEN HE HAD CHANGED HIS HABIT, HE REBUILT THE CHURCH OF SAINT MARY OF THE PORTIUNCULA, AND HOW, WHEN HE HAD HEARD THE GOSPEL AND LEFT BEHIND EVERYTHING, HE DESIGNED AND MADE THE HABIT WORN BY THE BROTHERS

[21]Meanwhile, the holy man of God, having changed his habit and rebuilt that church, moved to another place near the city of Assisi, where he began to rebuild a certain church that had fallen into ruin and was almost destroyed. After a good beginning he did not stop until he had brought all to completion.[a]

From there he moved to another place, which is called the "Portiuncula," where there stood a church of the Blessed Virgin Mother of God built in ancient times. At that time it was deserted and no one was taking care of it.[b] When the holy man of God saw it so ruined, he was moved by piety because he had a warm devotion to the Mother of all good and he began to stay there continually.[c] The restoration of that church took place in the third year of his conversion. At this time he wore a sort of hermit's habit with a leather belt. He carried a staff in his hand and wore shoes.

[22]One day the gospel was being read in that church about how the Lord sent out his disciples to preach. The holy man of God, who was attending there, in order to understand better the words of the gospel, humbly begged the priest after celebrating the solemnities of the Mass to explain the gospel to him. The priest explained it all to him thoroughly line by line. When he heard that Christ's disciples should not *possess gold* or *silver* or *money,* or *carry on their journey a wallet or a*
sack, nor bread nor a staff, nor *to have shoes* nor *two tunics*, but that Mt 10:9-10
they should preach *the kingdom of God* and *penance*, the holy man, Lk 9:2; Mk 6:12
Francis, immediately *exulted* in the *spirit of God.*[d] "This is what I Lk 1:47

a. While Thomas uses the Latin word, *habitus*, taken here in the material sense of habit as clothing, it implies also a juridical change: Francis is now under Church protection. The church is probably the church of Saint Pietro della Spina, in the fields beyond Assisi not far from the Rivo Torto. It was cared for by the Benedictines.

b. The first mention of this church in the archives of Assisi occurs in 1045, although it is not listed until 1150 as among the churches of the area. There is a legend that it was built at the direction of Pope Liberius (352-366) by some hermits who upon their arrival from the Holy Land placed a "little piece [*portiuncula*]" of stone there from the place of the Dormition of the Blessed Virgin. Another legend maintains that Saint Benedict enlarged it in 516. The present building, however, dates from the 10th century. At the time of Francis, this church was also dependent on the Benedictine abbey of Mt. Subasio.

c. For Thomas's use of *pietas* [piety] cf. p. 189, c.

d. Rather than a single gospel text, this is a collection of phrases borrowed from the three Synoptics. Traditionally it is held that this event took place on the feast of the apostle, Saint Matthias, February 24.

want," he said, "this is what I seek, this is what I desire with all my
2 Cor 7:4 heart." The holy father, *overflowing with joy*, hastened to implement the words of salvation, and did not delay before he devoutly began to put into effect what he heard.[a] Immediately, *he took off the shoes from*
Ex 3:5 *his feet*, put down the staff from his hands, and, satisfied with one tunic, exchanged his leather belt for a cord. After this, he made for himself a tunic showing the image of the cross, so that in it he would drive off every fantasy of the demons.[b] He made it very rough, so that in it he might
Gal 5:24 *crucify the flesh with its vices* and sins. He made it very poor and plain, a thing that the world would never covet. As for the other things he heard, he set about doing them with great care and reverence. For he was no deaf hearer of the gospel; rather he committed everything he heard to his excellent memory and was careful to carry it out to the letter.[c]

Chapter X

HIS PREACHING THE GOSPEL AND ANNOUNCING PEACE AND THE CONVERSION OF THE FIRST SIX BROTHERS

[23]He then began to preach penance to all with a fervent spirit and joyful attitude. He inspired his listeners with words that were simple
Sir 23:22 and a heart that was heroic. His word was like *a blazing fire*, reaching the deepest parts of the heart, and filling the souls of all with wonder. He seemed entirely different from what he had been, and *looking up to*
Mk 6:41 *heaven* he refused to look down upon earth. It is truly amazing that he
Mt 4:17 first *began to preach* where he had learned to read as a little boy, and where at first he was reverently buried.

---

a. Thomas now relies upon Athanasius's (+373) *The Life of Antony* (+356), a text which not only established the framework of Christian hagiography but also had an enormous influence on the development of religious life. "[Antony] went into the church pondering these things, and just then it happened that the gospel was being read, and he heard the Lord saying to the rich man, 'If you would be perfect, go, sell what you possess and give to the poor, and you will have treasure in heaven.' It was as if by God's design he held the saints in his recollection and as if the passage were read on his account. Immediately Antony went out from the Lord's house and gave to the townspeople the possessions he had from his forebears." Athanasius, *The Life of Antony* 2. [This and all further quotations are taken from *Athanasius: The Life of Antony and the Letter to Marcellinus*, translation and introduction by Robert C. Gregg, preface by William A. Clebsch (New York, Ramsey, Toronto: Paulist Press, 1980).]

b. Throughout his writings Thomas frequently refers to struggles with demons, a theme that was expressed throughout medieval hagiography because of the influence of Athansius's *The Life of Antony* in which demons occupy an important place.

c. Cf. Sulpicius Severus, *The Life of Martin*, 2: ". . . *iam tum Evangelii non surdus auditor* [He was no deaf hearer of the gospel]." For the important role of memory in ancient and medieval learning, see Mary Carruthers, *The Book of Memory: A Study of Memory in Medieval Culture* (Cambridge: Cambridge University Press, 1990).

Thus;
a blessed beginning was confirmed
by a more blessed end.[a]
Where he learned, there he also taught;
and where he began, there he blessedly ended.

In all of his preaching, before he presented the word of God to the assembly, he prayed for peace saying, *"May the Lord give you peace."* 2 Thes 3:16
He always proclaimed this to men and women, to those he met and to those who met him. Accordingly, many *who hated peace* along with Ps 120:7
salvation, *with the Lord's help* wholeheartedly embraced peace. They Mk 16:20
became themselves *children of peace,* now rivals for eternal salvation.[b] Lk 10:6

[24] Among these there was a man from Assisi with a holy and simple character, who was the first to follow devoutly the man of God.[c]

After him, brother Bernard, embracing *the delegation of peace,* eagerly ran after *the holy man of God* to gain *the kingdom of heaven.*[d] He had often received the blessed father as a guest, had observed and tested his life and conduct. Refreshed by the fragrance of his holiness, he conceived fear and gave birth to the spirit of salvation. He used to see him praying all night long, sleeping rarely, praising God and the glorious Virgin, His mother. He was amazed and said, "*This man truly is from God.*" So he hurried *to sell all* he had and distributed it to the poor, not to his relatives. Grasping the title of a more perfect way, he fulfilled the counsel of the holy gospel: *"If you wish to be perfect, go and sell* all *you own, and give to the poor, and you will have treasure in heaven; then come, follow me."* When he had done this, he joined the holy man, Francis, in the same life and habit, and was always with him, until the brothers increased in number and he, with the obedience of his devoted father, was sent to other regions.[e]

Lk 14:32; Lk 4:34; Mt 13:44-46; Lk 23:47; Mt 13:46; Mt 19:21

a. The church of Saint George, which stood on the site of the present Blessed Sacrament Chapel in the basilica of Saint Clare, was near the house of Pietro Bernardone and included a school which Francis attended. Clare went to the church to hear him preach and it was there that he was first buried in 1226 and there that his canonization took place in 1228.

b. The proclamation or greeting of peace is a theme frequently present in medieval hagiography. Cf. William of Saint Thierry, Arnold of Bonval, Geoffrey of Auxerre, *Vita prima s. Bernardi* XXIII; Cf. Bernard, *The Life of Malachy* VIII.17

c. The identity of this first companion remains unknown. He is never mentioned again in any writing, not even by Thomas himself. It has been suggested that after his initial enthusiasm he left Francis's company.

d. This is a reference to Bernard, son of Quintavalle di Berardello, a wealthy, educated noble and a member of a family that was prominent in Assisi.

e. *Sanctus* can mean "saint" and, as such, refer to the title conferred by canonization. It may also simply mean "holy" and, thus, refer more generally to a holy person.

His conversion to God stood out as a model
for those being converted
in the way he sold his possessions
and distributed them to the poor.
Mt 2:10 The holy man Francis *rejoiced with very great joy*
over the arrival and conversion of such a man,
because the Lord seemed to be caring for him,
giving him a needed companion
Sir 6:14 and a *faithful friend.*

[25]Immediately another man from the city of Assisi followed him. This man was highly respected in his way of life, and what he began in a holy fashion he completed within a short time in an even holier way.[a]
Mt 25:19 Not *much later,* brother Giles followed, *a simple and upright man who*
Jb 2:3 *feared God.*

[He lived for a long time:
Ti 2:12 he was holy, living *justly* and *piously.*
He left us examples of perfect obedience,
work, including work with his hands,
solitary life, and holy contemplation.][b]

When one other, brother Philip, joined them, he brought their num-
Is 6:6-7 ber to seven.[c] The Lord touched his *lips with the coal* that cleanses, so that he might speak of Him in words that were sweet and flowing with honey.[d] Understanding and interpreting the holy Scriptures, *although*
Jn 7:15 *he had not studied,* he became an imitator of those whom the Jewish
Acts 4:13 leaders considered *ignorant* and *without learning.*

a. This may be Peter di Catanio di Guiduccio, who joined Francis with Bernard on April 16, 1208. He served as vicar during Francis's early absences and later accompanied him to Egypt and Syria in 1219. When Francis resigned his office in 1220, Peter was named his vicar. He died on March 10, 1221, at the Portiuncula where he is buried.

b. Giles was received into the Order on April 23,1208, and died on April 27, 1262. This sentence, then, is an interpolation. Thomas could not have written in 1229 about Brother Giles's long life at this early date.

c. Philip the Tall, *Filippo Longo,* accompanied Francis to the Rieti Valley and, in 1209, to Rome. He served as Visitator of the Poor Ladies of Saint Damian in 1219 and again from 1228 to 1246. He died in 1259.

d. The Latin word *mellifluous,* flowing with honey, appears three times in the 1C: in this paragraph, in referring to Francis's words at Greccio (n. 86) and in those of Pope Gregory IX at Francis's canonization (n. 125). It is used frequently in Cistercian literature, especially by Bernard of Clairvaux, the "Mellifluous" Doctor.

Chapter XI
THE SPIRIT OF PROPHECY AND THE ADMONITIONS OF SAINT FRANCIS

[26]Day by day the blessed father Francis was being *filled* with the *consolation* and the grace of the *Holy Spirit*, and, with all vigilance and concern, he was forming his new sons with new instruction, teaching them to walk with steady steps the way of holy poverty and blessed simplicity.[a] Acts 9:31

One day he was marveling at the Lord's mercy in the kindness shown to him. He wished that the Lord would show him the course of life for him and his brothers, and he went to a place of prayer, as he so often did.[b] He remained there a long time *with fear and trembling* before *the Ruler of the whole earth.* He recalled *in the bitterness of* his *soul the years* he spent badly, frequently repeating this phrase: *"Lord, be merciful to me, a sinner."* Gradually, an indescribable joy and tremendous sweetness began to well up deep in his heart. Tb 13:6 Zec 4:14 Is 38:15 Lk 18:13

He began to lose himself;
his feelings were pressed together;
and that darkness disappeared
which fear of sin had gathered in his heart.
Certainty of the forgiveness of all his sins poured in,
and the assurance of being revived in grace was given to him.
Then he was caught up above himself and totally engulfed in light,
and, with his inmost soul opened wide,
he clearly saw the future.
As that sweetness and light withdrew,
renewed in spirit,
he now seemed to be *changed into another man.*[c] 1 Sm 10:6; Ps 51:12

[27]He returned and said to the brothers with joy: *"Be strong,* dear brothers, and *rejoice in the Lord.* Do not be sad, because you seem so few, and do not let my simplicity or yours discourage you. The Lord has shown me that God will make us grow into a great multitude, and will spread us to the ends of the earth. I must also tell you what I saw Eph 6:10 Phil 3:1

a. Cf. p.196, c.

b. This place of prayer was probably Poggio Bustone in the Rieti Valley. Francis passed this area on his way to or from Rome.

c. The language here is reminiscent of Gregory the Great whose theology of compunction and contemplation influenced much of the later tradition. Cf. Gregory, *Dialogue* II 35: ". . . the light of holy contemplation enlarges and expands the mind in God until it stands above the world."

about your future, though it would please me more to remain silent, if
Rv 7:9 charity did not compel me to tell you. *I saw a great multitude* of people
coming to us, wishing to live with us in the habit of a holy way of life
and in the rule of blessed religion. Listen! The sound of them is still *in*
Sg 2:14; Gn 8:3 *my ears*, their *coming and going* according to the command of holy
obedience. I seemed to see highways filled with this multitude gather-
Acts 2:5 ing in this region *from* nearly *every nation.* Frenchmen are coming,
Spaniards are hurrying, Germans and Englishmen are running, and a
huge crowd speaking other languages is rapidly approaching."[a]

When the brothers heard this, they were filled with wholesome joy, either because of the grace which the Lord God had conferred on His holy one, or because they eagerly thirsted for the profit of their neighbors, whom they wanted to increase in number daily in order to *be*
Acts 2:47 *saved.*

[28]And the holy man said to them: "So that we may give thanks LR V1
◦faithfully and devotedly◦[b] to the Lord our God for all His gifts and that you may know how our present and future brothers should live, understand this truth about the course of things to come. In the beginning of our way of life together we will find fruit that is very sweet and pleasant. A little later fruit that is less pleasant and sweet will be offered.
Lam 1:20 Finally, fruit *full of bitterness* will be served, which we will not be able to eat. Although displaying some outward beauty and fragrance, it will be too sour for anyone to eat. As I told you, the Lord certainly will make
Gn 12:2 us grow into *a great nation.* But in the end it will turn out as follows: it is like a man who tosses his nets into the sea or a lake and catches *a*
Lk 5:6 *great number of fish.* When he has loaded them all into his boat, he is reluctant to carry them all because of their great number. So *he would pick out* for his *baskets* the larger ones and those he likes, but the others
Mt 13:47-48 he would *throw out.*"

All these things the holy man of God predicted.
How brightly their truth shines!
How they came true in events is clear

a. A similar vision can be found in the *Vita prima s. Bernardi* IX in which the universal appeal to and attraction of many followers demonstrate the fruits of holiness and confirm credibility. The author writes of Bernard: "Longing for his work to bear rich fruit filled his heart and, as he stood still and closed his eyes in prayer, he saw coming down the mountains round about and down into the valley below such a great company of men of every type and standing that the valley could not hold them all."

b. References on the inside margin point out passages found in other writings that influenced Thomas in the composition of this work. Direct references are indicated in the text with an open bullet.

to those who reflect in the spirit of truth.
See how *the spirit of prophecy rested* on Saint Francis! Is 11:2

Chapter XII

How he sent them in pairs through the world, and how they came together again in a short time

29 At that same time, another good man entered their religion, and they increased their number to eight.[a] Then the blessed Francis called them all to himself and told them many things about *the kingdom of God,* contempt of the world, denial of their own will, and subjection of the body. He separated them into four groups of two each. Acts 1:3

"Go, my dear brothers," he said to them, "*two by two* through different parts of the world, *announcing peace* to the people and *penance for the remission of sins.* Be *patient in trials,* confident that the Lord will fulfill His plan and promise. Respond humbly to those who question you. *Bless those who persecute you.* Give thanks to those who harm you and bring false charges against you, for because of these things an *eternal kingdom is prepared* for us." Lk 10:1 Acts 10:36 Mk 1:4; Rom 12:12 LR III 10-14 Rom 12:14 Mt 25:34

Accepting the command of holy obedience *with* much *joy and gladness,* they humbly prostrated themselves on the ground before Saint Francis. Embracing them, he spoke sweetly and devotedly to each one: *"Cast your care upon the Lord, and he will sustain you."* He used to say this phrase whenever he transferred brothers by obedience. 1 Mc 5:54 Ps 55:23

30 Then brother Bernard with brother Giles hastened on the way to Santiago;[b] Saint Francis with one companion chose another part of the world.[c] The other four, two by two, went to other regions.

Only a short time had passed when Saint Francis began desiring to see them all. *He prayed to the Lord,* who *gathers the dispersed of Israel,* mercifully to bring them together soon. So it happened in a short time: they came together at the same time according to his desire, without any human summons, *giving thanks to God.* Ex 8:30 Ps 147:2 Col 3:17

a. It is difficult to establish the identity of the individual brothers as they appear in Thomas's account. Leaving aside the anonymous man (cf. n. 24), there are now seven companions—Bernard, Giles and Philip, whom Thomas identifies, and four unidentified brothers, who, together with Francis, make eight.

b. This is Santiago de Compostela, the shrine to Saint James the Apostle, in northwestern Spain. After Jerusalem it was the most popular place of pilgrimage in the Middle Ages.

c. Francis may have gone to the Rieti Valley. His companion seems to have been Philip the Tall.

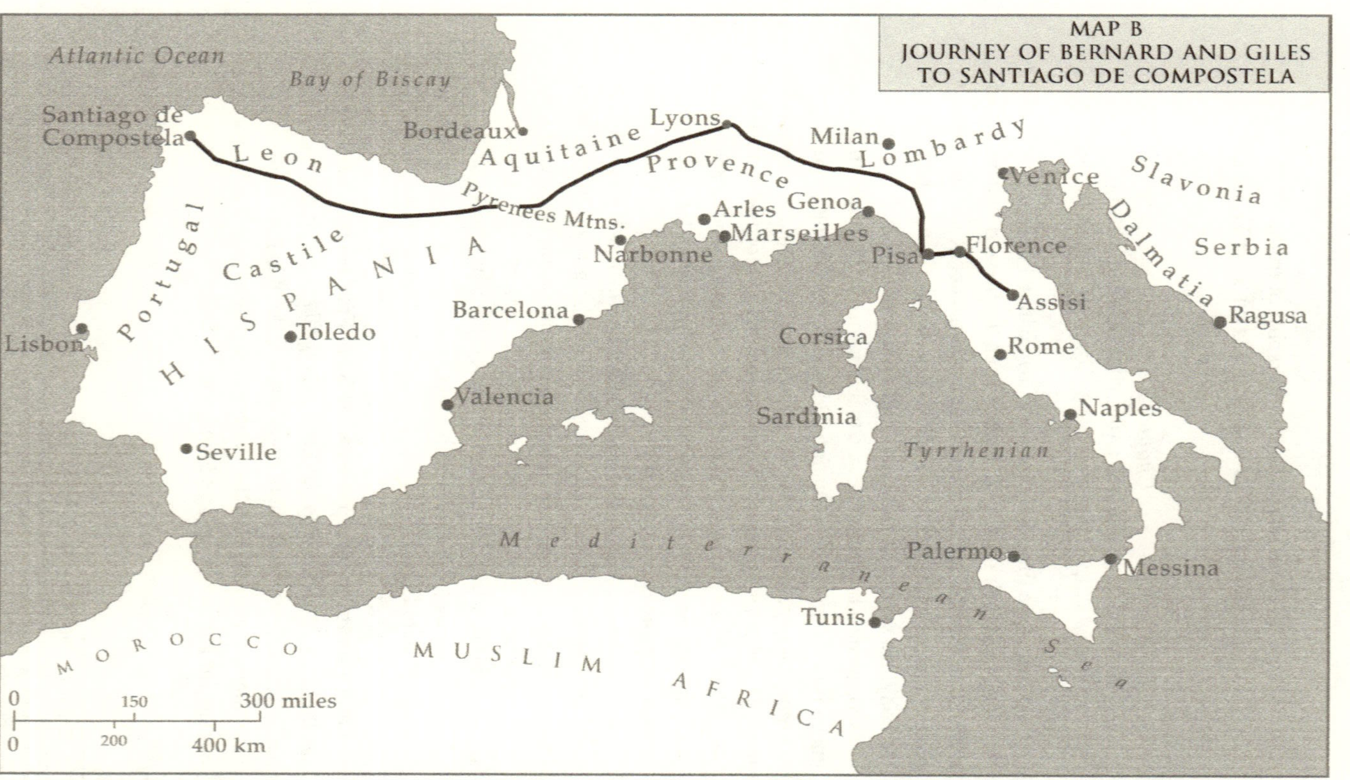

The route shown on this map is that followed by the majority of pilgrims from Italy over the Alps and through Provence to Hispania (Spain), and it is most likely that Bernard and Giles would have travelled this route (1C 30). It is also likely that Francis would travelled part of this route when he tried to reach Morocco and the Miramamolin in 1213 or 1214 (1C 56).

ER XVIII

Coming together in one place, 1 Cor 11:20
they celebrate with great joy on seeing their devoted shepherd,
and they are amazed that
the same desire to come together moved all of them in this way.
They report the good things
which *the merciful Lord* was doing for them, Ps 115:5
and if they had been somewhat negligent and ungrateful,
they humbly ask and carefully accept
correction and punishment from the holy father.[a]

They always acted in this way when they came to him, and they did not hide from him the least of their thoughts or even immediate impulses of their souls. When they had fulfilled *everything which* had been *commanded,* they regarded themselves as *useless servants.* For a pure spirit so possessed that whole first school of blessed Francis that, though they knew how to carry out things that were useful, *holy* and *just,* they were completely ignorant of how to rejoice over them with vanity. The blessed father, embracing his sons with unbounded love, began to open up to them his proposal and to show them what the Lord had revealed to him.

Lk 17:10; Phil 4:8-9

[31]Immediately four other good and sound men *were added* to them as followers of the holy man of God. On that account, a loud cry began among the people and the fame of the man of God began to spread far and wide. At that time Saint Francis and his brothers felt great *gladness and* unique *joy* whenever one of the faithful, *led by the Spirit* of God, came and accepted the habit of holy religion, whoever the person might be: rich or poor, noble or insignificant, wise or simple, cleric or illiterate, a layman of the Christian people. This was a great wonder to those of the world and an example of humility, challenging them to the way of a more reformed life and to penance for sins.

Acts 2:41; Lk 1:14; Mt 4:1

No lowliness of birth,
no weakness of poverty
stood in the way of building up in God's work
the ones *God* wanted *to build up,* Acts 20:32

a. Through a curious shift into the present tense, Thomas seems to suggest that what he describes in this passage became the "ritual" of the chapters celebrated by the early fraternity. The "chapter" comes out of the earlier monastic tradition in which monks gathered together to hear a reading of a "chapter" of the monastic rule, confessed their faults and received correction.

a God who delights to be
Prv 3:32 with *the simple* and those rejected by the world.

Chapter XIII
HOW HE FIRST WROTE A RULE WHEN HE HAD ELEVEN BROTHERS, AND HOW THE LORD POPE INNOCENT CONFIRMED IT, AND ABOUT THE VISION OF A TREE

Acts 2:47 32When blessed Francis saw that the Lord God was *daily increasing* their numbers, he wrote for himself and his brothers present and future, simply and in few words, a form of life and a rule.[a] He used primarily words of the holy gospel, longing only for its perfection. He inserted a few other things necessary for the practice of a holy way of life. Then he went to Rome with all his brothers, since he greatly desired that the Lord Pope Innocent the Third confirm for him what he had written. There was in Rome at this time the venerable bishop of Assisi, Guido by name, who honored Saint Francis and all the brothers in everything and revered them with special love. When he saw Saint Francis and his brothers, he reacted strongly at their arrival, as he did not know the reason for it. He feared they wanted to leave their homeland, where the Lord had begun to perform great things through his servants. He greatly rejoiced to have such men in his diocese, for he relied most of all on their life and character. But when he heard the cause and understood their plan, *he rejoiced*
Phil 4:10 *greatly in the Lord* and promised to give them advice and to offer his support. Saint Francis also approached the reverend lord bishop of Sabina, named John of Saint Paul, who, among the other princes and great men at the Roman Curia, seemed to look down on the things of earth and love the things of heaven.[b] The bishop received him °kindly LR X 5
and charitably°[c] and praised highly his wish and plan.

a. These are the very terms used by Francis in The *Testament* to describe the document, the *propositum vitae*, presented by the first brothers to Pope Innocent III.

b. Giovanni de Colonna was known as John of Saint Paul since he was a Benedictine monk of the Monastery of Saint Paul Outside the Walls. A personal friend of Bishop Guido and a confidant of Pope Innocent III and knowledgeable and active in the apostolic movements of the period, he became Cardinal Bishop of Sabina in 1204. He died in 1215. The quotation is taken from the medieval Postcommunion Prayer for the Second Sunday of Advent.

c. Thomas describes John of Saint Paul receiving Francis *benigne et caritative* [kindly and charitably], in other words, with the same dispositions Francis demands of a minister responding to a brother who is experiencing difficulties, cf. LR X 5.

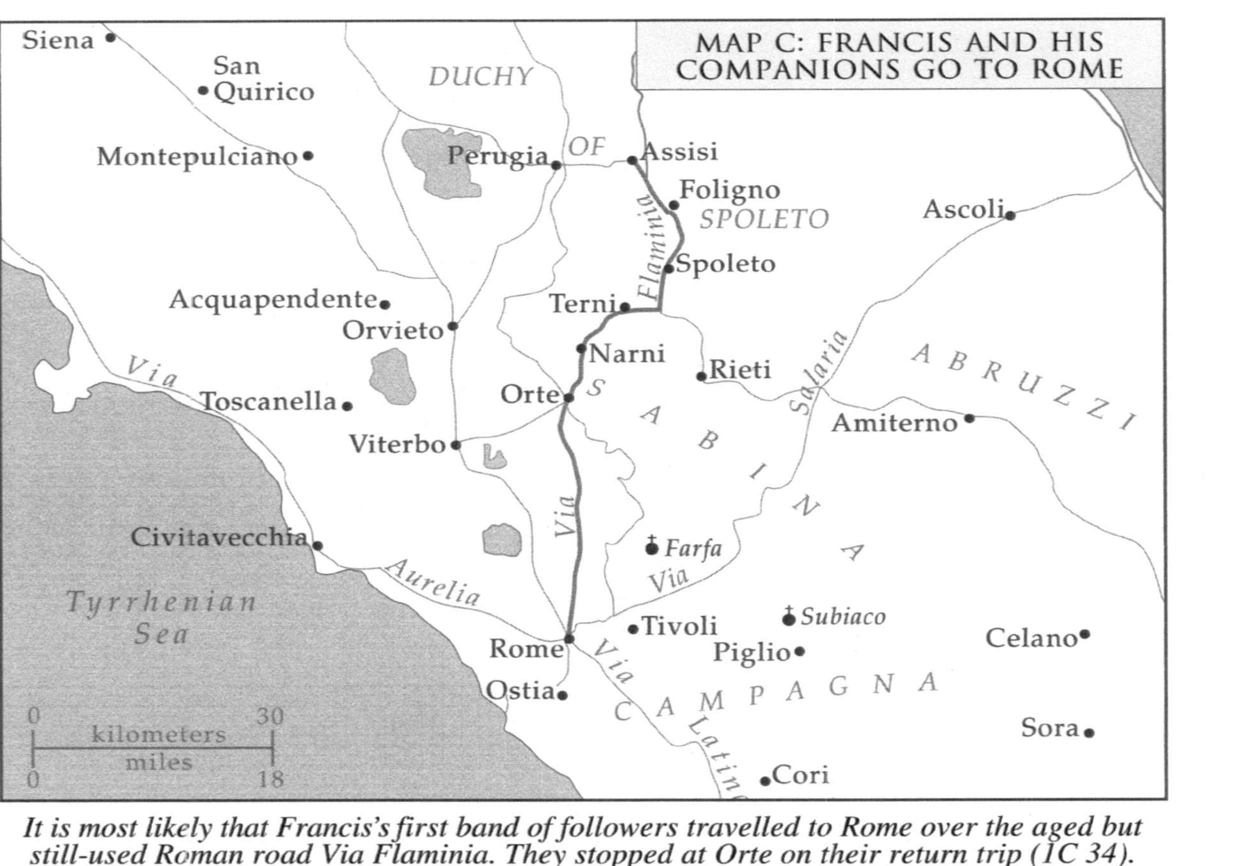

It is most likely that Francis's first band of followers travelled to Rome over the aged but still-used Roman road Via Flaminia. They stopped at Orte on their return trip (1C 34).

[33]The bishop of Sabina, a far-sighted and discerning man, questioned him about many things, urging him to turn to the monastic or eremitical life. But Saint Francis, as much as he could, humbly refused his urging. He did not despise what was urged on him, but he was intently seeking other things, moved by a loftier desire. That lord marveled at his enthusiasm and, fearful that the holy man might fail in such a lofty proposal, he pointed out smoother paths. Finally, won over by his perseverance, the bishop agreed to his pleas and from then on strove to promote his interests before the lord pope.

1 Cor 1:2 Presiding over *God's Church* at that time was the lord Pope Innocent the Third, a glorious man, prolific in learning, brilliant in speech, burning with zeal for justice in matters which the cause of the Christian faith demanded. When he recognized the wish of the men of God, he first considered the matter and then gave his assent to their request, something he completed by a subsequent action. Exhorting and then warning them about many things, he blessed Saint Francis and his brothers and said to them: "Go with the Lord, brothers, and as the Lord will see fit to inspire you, preach penance to all. When the almighty
Dt 7:12,13; Lk 10:17 *Lord increases* you in numbers and grace, come back to me *with joy*, and I will grant you more things than these and, with greater confidence, I will entrust you with greater things."[a]

1 Sm 3:19 *The Lord was* truly *with* Saint Francis
Gn 20:16 *wherever he went*,
gladdening him with revelations and encouraging him with gifts.
For when he had gone to sleep one night,
he seemed to be walking down a road,
and alongside it stood *a tree of great height.*
That *tree was lovely and strong,*
Dn 4:7-8 thick and *exceedingly high.*
Lk 7:11-12 *It came about* that when he *approached* the tree
Jdt 10:14 and stood under it and *marveled at its beauty* and height,
the holy man himself rose to so great a height
that he touched the top of the tree.
Taking it into his hand, he easily bent it to the ground.
It really happened this way,
when the lord Innocent,

a. Thus Pope Innocent III gave oral approval to the document or *propositum vitae* that Francis and his brothers brought him. This event took place in either 1209 or 1210.

a very high and lofty tree in the world,
bent himself so kindly to his wish and request.

Chapter XIV
His return from the city of Rome to the Spoleto Valley and of a stop along the way

[34]Saint Francis with his brothers
rejoiced greatly at the task and the favor
given by so great a father and lord.
They *gave thanks* to Almighty *God,* Acts 27:35
who places the lowly on high
and raises up mourners to health. Jb 5:11

He immediately went to visit the tomb of Saint Peter, and after praying there he left the city. Setting out with his companions, he took the road to the Spoleto Valley. As they were going, *they discussed among themselves* the many gifts of different kinds the merciful God granted them. (Lk 24:17) They had been graciously received by Christ's vicar, the lord and father of the whole Christian nation. How could they carry out his advice and commands? How could they sincerely keep the rule they had accepted and steadfastly safeguard it? How could they walk before the Most High in all holiness and religion? Finally, how could their life and conduct, by growth in the holy virtues, be an example to their neighbors?

By the time Christ's new students in the school of humility had finished their disputation, the day was far spent *and the hour was late.* They arrived at *a deserted place.* (Mt 14:15) They were hungry and exhausted from the weariness of their journey and could not find any food, as that place was far removed from people's homes. But God's grace was looking after them, for suddenly they met a *man* carrying *bread in his hand,* and *he gave it* to them and left.[a] (1 Kgs 10:3, 4; Mk 14:13) They honestly did not recognize him and, marveling in *their hearts*, they all eagerly encouraged each other to a greater trust in divine mercy. (Ps 35:25)

After eating the food and being much strengthened by it, they went on to a place near the city of Orte, where they stayed for about fifteen

a. The conviction that God provides for the journey of those dedicated to him is another frequent theme in hagiography. Cf. *Desert Fathers* I 47; II 9; VIII 5, 6, 38-41, 44-47; X 8; XII 4, 14-15.

days. Some of them went into the city to acquire the necessary food. They brought back to the other brothers the small amount they managed to obtain by going door-to-door and they ate together *with* Acts 24:3; Is 30:29 *gratitude* and *joyful hearts.* If anything remained, since they could not give it to anyone, they stored it in a tomb, which had once held the bodies of the dead, so they could eat it at another time. The place was deserted and abandoned, and hardly anyone ever visited it.

[35]They had great joy, because they saw nothing and had nothing that could give them empty or carnal delight.[a] There, they began to have commerce with holy poverty.[b] Greatly consoled in their lack of all 1 Cor 7:33 *things of the world,* they resolved to adhere to the way they were in that place always and everywhere. Only divine consolation delighted them, 1 Pt 5:7 having put aside all *their cares* about earthly things. They decided and resolved that even if buffeted by tribulations and driven by temptations Eccl 3:5 they would not withdraw *from* its *embrace.*

Even though the delight of that place could have greatly spoiled true spiritual vigor, it did not capture their affection. They left the place, so the continuity of a longer stay would not tie them even by appearance to some kind of ownership. Then following their blessed father, they entered the Spoleto Valley. These true proponents of justice conferred together about whether they should live among people or go off to solitary places. Saint Francis did not put his trust in his own efforts, but Ps 88:14 with holy *prayer coming before* any decision, he chose not *to live for* 2 Cor 5:15 *himself* alone, but for the one *who died for all.* For he knew that he was sent for this: to win for God souls which the devil was trying to snatch away.

Chapter XV
On the Fame of Blessed Francis and of the Conversion of Many to God, and How the Order Was Named the Lesser Brothers and How Blessed Francis Formed Those Entering Religion

[36]Francis, Christ's bravest soldier,
Mt 9:35 *went around the cities and villages,*

---

a. A possible allusion to Seneca, *Epistolae morales*, Liber 1, epistola 2,6: *Honesta res laeta paupertas* [An upright thing is joyful poverty]. As frequently in the writings of Francis, poverty is here linked with joy. Cf. Adm XXVII.

b. The Latin text reads: *Coeperunt propterea cum sancta paupertate ibidem habere commercium.* Thomas uses the word *commercium* to evoke the ideas of contract and covenant.

proclaiming the kingdom of God
and *preaching peace* Mt 9:35; Acts 10:36
and penance *for the remission of sins,* Mk 1:4
not in the persuasive words of human wisdom
but in the learning and *power of the Spirit.* 1 Cor 2:4

He *acted confidently* in all matters because of the apostolic authority granted him. He did not use fawning or seductive flattery. He did not smooth over but cut out the faults of others. He did not encourage but struck at the life of sin with a sharp blow, because he first convinced himself by action and then convinced others by words. Not fearing anyone's rebuke, he spoke the truth boldly, so that even well-educated men, distinguished by fame and dignity, were amazed at his words and were shaken by a healthy fear in his presence. Acts 9:28

Men ran, women also ran,
clerics hurried,
and religious rushed to see and hear the holy one of God,
who seemed to everyone a person of another age.[a]
People of all ages and both sexes hurried to behold the wonders
which the Lord worked anew in the world through his servant.

At that time,
through the presence of Saint Francis and through his reputation,
it surely seemed a new light had been sent from heaven to earth,
driving away all the darkness
that had so nearly covered that whole region
that hardly anyone knew where to turn.
Deep forgetfulness of God
and lazy neglect of his commandments
overwhelmed almost everyone,
so that they could barely be roused from old, deep-seated evils.
[37] He gleamed
like a shining *star in the darkness of night* Sir 50:6; Prv 7:9
and *like the morning spread over* the darkness.[b] Jl 2:2

---

a. Eadmer of Canterbury offers a similar picture of people of all ways of life coming to Anselm. Cf. Eadmer, *The Life of Anselm,* I, 22.

b. These images, inspired by Gregory IX's proclamation, *Mira circa nos,* issued at Francis's canonization, reflect Thomas's theology of reform in which images of light-darkness, fertility-aridity, death-life were so prominent. Thomas raises Francis to the level of a theological-historical exemplar who begins a reform of the Church during his earthly life and who leaves behind a *forma* or model by which this reform is to be continued.

Thus, in a short time,
the appearance of the entire region was changed
and, once rid of its earlier ugliness,
it revealed a happier expression everywhere.
The former dryness was put to rout
and a crop sprang up quickly in the untilled field.
Zec 8:12 Even the uncultivated *vine* began
Lv 1:9 to produce buds with a *sweet-smell* for the Lord,
and when it had produced *flowers of sweetness,*
Sir 24:23 it brought forth equally *the fruit of honor and respectability.*
Is 51:3 *Thanks and the voice of praise* resounded everywhere,
as many,
casting aside earthly concerns,
gained knowledge of themselves
in the life and teaching of the most blessed father Francis
and aspired to love and reverence for their Creator.

Many people,
well-born and lowly, cleric and lay,
driven by divine inspiration,
began to come to Saint Francis,
for they desired to serve
under his constant training and leadership.[a]
All of these
the holy one of God,
like a fertile stream of heavenly grace,
watered with showers of gifts
and he adorned the field of their hearts
with the flowers of perfection.

Ex 38:23 He is without question an *outstanding craftsman*,
for through his spreading message,
the Church of Christ is being renewed in both sexes
according to his form, rule and teaching,
and there is victory for the triple army of those being saved.[b]
Furthermore,

a. Cf. Eadmer of Canterbury, *The Life of Anselm* 1, 22, 31.

b. This may be an allusion either to the three ranks in the church (clergy, religious, laity) or to the three Franciscan Orders (Lesser Brothers, Poor Ladies, and Lay Penitents).

to all he gave a norm of life
and to those of every rank
he sincerely pointed out the way of salvation.

[38]But the subject at hand is primarily the Order that he accepted and retained as much out of love as out of profession. What was that Order? He himself originally planted the Order of Lesser Brothers and on the occasion of its founding gave it this name.[a] For when it was written in the Rule, "Let them be lesser . . . ," at the uttering of this statement, at that same moment he said, "I want this fraternity to be called the Order of Lesser Brothers."

Test 19 They were truly lesser who, by being °subject to all,° always sought the position of contempt, performing duties which they foresaw would be the occasion of some affront. In this way they might merit to be grounded on the solid rock of true humility and to have the well-designed spiritual structure of all the virtues arise in them.

Yes, the noble building of charity rises
upon the foundation of perseverance; Eph 2:20
and in it *living stones,* 1 Pt 2:5
gathered from every part of the world,
have been built into a dwelling place of the Holy *Spirit.* Eph 2:22
What a great flame of charity burned in the new disciples of Christ!
What great love of devout company flourished in them![b]
When they all gathered somewhere
or met each other on the road (which frequently happened),
in that place a shoot of spiritual love sprang up,
scattering over all love the seeds of real delight.

What more can I say?
There were
chaste embraces, delightful affection, a holy kiss,
sweet conversation,
modest laughter, joyful looks, *a clear eye,* Mt 6:22

a. *Ordo Fratrum Minorum* is translated as Order of Lesser Brothers. "Friars Minor," the commonly accepted title of the First Order of Saint Francis, reflects the early English translations of *frater* as "friar" and the diminutive *minor* as "minor."

b. A spirituality of mutual love and affection characterizes the monastic tradition especially in the literature of the twelfth century Cistercian reform. Cf. *Lives of the Desert Fathers*, XX, 8 and *The Life of Bernard*, 14.

Prv 15:4-1 a supple spirit, *a peaceable tongue, a mild answer,*
a single purpose, prompt obedience, and untiring hands.

[39]Since they looked down on all earthly things and never loved themselves selfishly, they poured out all their loving affection in common, hiring themselves out for wages to provide for their brothers' needs. They gathered together out of desire and were delighted to stay together; but they found being apart a burden, parting bitter, and separation hard.

But these obedient soldiers never dared to put anything before the orders of obedience: before the word of obedience was uttered, they prepared themselves to carry out the order. They almost ran headlong to carry out what they were asked with no thought of contradicting it, knowing nothing about distinguishing precepts.[a]

As °followers of most holy poverty,° since they had nothing, they loved nothing; so they feared losing nothing. They were satisfied with a single tunic, often patched both inside and out. Nothing about it was refined, rather it appeared lowly and rough so that in it they seemed completely *crucified to the world.* They wore crude trousers with a cord for a belt. They held firmly to the holy intention of remaining this way and having nothing more. So they were safe wherever they went. Disturbed by no fears, distracted by no cares, they awaited the next day without any worry.[b] Though frequently on hazardous journeys, they were not anxious about where they might stay the next day. Often they needed a place to stay in extreme cold, and a baker's oven would receive them; or they would hide for the night humbly in caves or crypts.

LR V 4
Test 16
Gal 6:14

During the day those who knew how worked with their own hands, staying in the houses of lepers or in other suitable places, serving everyone humbly and devoutly. They did not want to take any job that might give rise to scandal;[c] but rather always doing what was holy and just, honest and useful, they inspired all they dealt with to follow their example of humility and patience.

ER VII

a. This comment suggests that, already at the time of Thomas's writing, the Order had a number of brothers who argued about the prescriptions of LR and Test. The lack of legal precision in the document approved by Pope Innocent III and the ambiguous nature of Test confirm that, as many maintain, the Founder saw commitment to the gospel life as a work of the Holy Spirit. Cf. LR X 8.

b. Cf. Seneca, *Epistulae morales* I ep. 12 n. 9: *Ille beatissimus est et securus sui possessor, qui crastinum sine sollicitudine expectat* [That person is most happy and in secure possession of his self who awaits the next day without great concern].

c. ER VII prohibits them from being treasurers, overseers, or having any kind of supervisory position in a house. It adds: "Let them be subject to all in the same house."

[40]The virtue of patience so enveloped them that they sought to be where they would suffer persecution of their bodies rather than where their holiness would be known and praised, lifting them up with worldly favor. Often mocked, objects of insult, stripped naked, beaten, bound, jailed,[a] and not defending themselves with anyone's protection, they endured all of these abuses so bravely that from their mouths came only the *sound of praise and thanksgiving.* Is 51:3

They never or hardly ever stopped praying and praising God. Instead, in ongoing discussion, they recalled what they had done. They gave thanks to God for the good done and, with groans and tears, paid for what they neglected or did carelessly. They would have thought themselves abandoned by God if they did not experience in their ordinary prayers that they were constantly visited by the spirit of devotion. For when they felt like dozing during prayer, they would prop themselves up with a stick, so that sleep would not overtake them. Some anchored themselves with cords, so furtive sleep would not disturb prayer. Some bound themselves with irons; and others shut themselves in wooden cells.

Whenever their moderation was upset, as normally happens, by too much food or drink, or if they went over the line of necessity because of weariness from travel, they punished themselves severely with many days of fasting. They strove to restrain the burning of the flesh by such harsh treatment that they did not hesitate to strip themselves on freezing ice, and to cover themselves in blood from gashing their bodies with sharp thorns.[b]

[41]They so spurned earthly things that they barely accepted the most basic necessities of life; and, as they were usually far from bodily comfort, they did not fear hardship. In all these things, they sought *peace* and meekness *with all.* Always doing what was *modest and peaceful,* Heb 12:14; Jas 3:17
they scrupulously avoided all scandal. For they hardly spoke even when necessary; nor did anything harmful or useless *come out of their mouth,* so that in all their life and action nothing immodest or unbe- Mt 4:4
coming could be found. Their every act was disciplined, their bearing modest. With eyes fixed on the ground and their minds set on heaven,

a. This passage is reminiscent of Paul's Second Letter to the Corinthians 11:23-27 in which he reflects on his sufferings for the gospel.

b. In his description of the brothers throwing themselves into freezing water or into thorn bushes, Thomas combines accounts of the actions of Benedict and of Bernard. Cf. Gregory the Great, *Dialogue* II 2; Alan, Bishop of Auxerre, *Vita secunda s. Bernardi* III.

all their senses were so subdued that they scarcely allowed themselves to hear or see anything except what their holy purpose demanded.

Among them there was
no envy, no malice, no rancor,
no mocking, no suspicion, no bitterness.
Instead, there was
great harmony, constant calm,
Is 51:3 *thanksgiving, and songs of praise.*
These are the lessons by which the devoted father
instructed his new sons
not so much *in words* and *speech*
1 Jn 3:18 *but in deed and truth.*

Chapter XVI
CONCERNING THEIR STAY IN RIVO TORTO AND ABOUT SAFEGUARDING POVERTY

[42]Blessed Francis gathered with the others in a place called Rivo Torto near the city of Assisi.[a] In this place there was an abandoned hut. Under its cover lived these despisers of great and beautiful houses, protecting themselves from the torrents of rain. As the saint said, "It is easier to get to heaven from a hut than from a palace."[b] All his sons and brothers were living in that same place with the blessed Father, *with*
2 Cor 11:27 *great labor*, and lacking everything. Often they were deprived of the comfort of bread, content with turnips they begged in their need here and there on the plain of Assisi. The place in which they were staying was so narrow that they could barely sit or sleep in it.

Yet there was no complaining about this,
no grumbling;
but with peaceful heart,
the soul filled with joy
preserved the virtue of patience.[c]

a. Rivo Torto, a crooked, snake-like stream below the road from Assisi to Panzo, flows down into the Umbrian Valley not far from San Damiano.

b. A similar saying is attributed to "a certain hermit" by Peter Cantor (+1197): "*Melius et tutius prosilitur in caelum de turgurio quam de palatio* [It is better and safer to proceed into heaven from a simple hut than from a palace]" Cf. Peter Cantor, *Verbum abbreviatum* 86.

c. These words are taken from the hymn from the Common of Several Martyrs, *Sanctorum Meritis: Non murmur resonat, non querimonia/Sed corde tacito, mens bene conscia/Conservat patientiam* [No grumbling resounds, no complaint/But with silent heart, the mind well attuned/Preserves patience].

Saint Francis used to engage carefully in a daily, or rather, constant examination of himself and his followers. Allowing nothing dangerous to remain in them, he drove from their hearts any negligence. Unbending in his discipline, he *was* watchful *of his guard* at every hour. Is 21:8
For if, as happens, any temptation of the flesh struck him, he would immerse himself in a ditch filled in winter with ice, remaining in it until every seduction of the flesh went away. The others avidly followed his example of mortifying the flesh.[a]

[43]He taught them to mortify not only vices and to check the promptings of the flesh, but also to check the external senses, through which death enters the soul. At that time the emperor Otto passed through that area, traveling in great pomp and circumstance to receive the crown of an earthly empire. The most holy father and his followers were staying in that small hut next to the very parade route. He did not go outside to look and did not allow the others to do so, except for one who, without wavering, proclaimed to the emperor that his glory would be short-lived.[b] The glorious holy one, living within himself and walking in *the breadth of his heart,* prepared in himself a worthy *dwell-* Ps 119:45
ing place of God.[c] That is why the uproar outside did not seize his ears, Eph 2:22
nor could any cry intrude, interrupting the great enterprise he had in hand. Apostolic authority resided in him; so he altogether refused to flatter kings and princes.

[44]He always strove for holy simplicity, refusing to allow the narrow place to restrict *the breadth of his heart.* For this reason, he would write Ps 119:45
the names of the brothers on the beams of that little house so that each would know his place when he wished to pray or rest, and the confines of the place would not disturb the silence of the spirit.

One day while they were staying there, a man came leading an ass to the little shelter where the man of God and his companions were staying. To avoid being sent away, the man urged the ass to enter by saying,

a. The mortification of the flesh is a prominent theme throughout medieval hagiography and Thomas's descriptions of these practices of Francis are not unlike those described by *Vita prima s. Bernardi* III or recommended by Bernard himself, *On Consideration* IV 6, 21.

b. The emperor Otto IV (1198-1218) passed through the duchy of Spoleto at the end of September 1209, but the event related here probably took place in 1210 during another of Otto's passages. In Roman triumphal processions, a slave would whisper into a general's ear admonishing him that the glory of his triumph would be brief. Francis's refusal to flatter the emperor is reminiscent of Saint Martin of Tours: "It is almost a miracle that a bishop should not have succumbed to the temptation of flattering an emperor." Cf. Sulpicius Severus, *The Life of Martin* 20.

c. Gregory writes of Benedict in similar terms: *solus habitavit secum* [alone he lived with himself], thus accentuating the strong place of solitude in the monastic tradition. Cf. Gregory, *Dialogue* II 3. The same is written of Bernard: *libere secum habitans et deambulans in latitudine cordis sui* [living freely with himself and walking in the broad expanse of his heart] Cf. *Vita prima s. Bernardi* III 1, 2.

"Get inside, for we shall do well for this place!" When the holy Francis
heard this statement, he took it seriously, since he knew the man's intention: the man thought that the brothers wanted to stay there to ex-
Is 5:8 pand the place by *joining house to house.* Immediately Saint Francis 1C 21
left the place, abandoning it because of what the peasant had said. He
moved to another place, not far away, which was called "Portiuncula,"
where, as told above, he had repaired the church of Saint Mary a long
time before. He wanted *to own nothing* so that he could *possess every-*
2 Cor 6:10 *thing* more fully in the Lord.

Chapter XVII
How Blessed Francis taught the brothers to pray and about the obedience and purity of the brothers

Lk 11:1 45 The brothers at that time begged him *to teach* them *how to pray,*
Prv 20:7 because, *walking in simplicity* of spirit, up to that time they did not
know the Church's office. Francis told them: *"When you pray, say* Test 5
Mt 6:9 *'Our Father'* and 'We adore you, O Christ, in all your churches
throughout the whole world, and we bless you, for by your holy cross
you have redeemed the world.' " The brothers, devout disciples of their
master, strove diligently to observe this. For they attempted to fulfill
completely not only the things he told them as brotherly advice or fatherly commands, but even those things he thought or meditated upon,
if they could know them by some indication. The blessed father told
them that true obedience is not about just what is spoken but also about
what is thought, not just what is commanded but what is desired, that is:
"If a brother subject to a prelate not only hears his words but under- Adm III
stands his will, he should immediately ready himself fully for obedience, and do whatever by some sign he knows the other wants."

For this reason, in whatever place a church had been built, even when they were not near it, but could glimpse it from a distance, they would turn toward it. Prostrate on the ground, bowing inwardly and outwardly, they would adore the Almighty saying, "We adore you, O Christ, in all your churches . . ." just as their holy father taught them. What is just as striking is that wherever they saw a cross or the sign of a cross, whether on the ground, on a wall, in the trees or roadside hedges they did the same thing.

[46]In this way holy simplicity filled them,
innocence of life taught them,
and purity of heart so possessed them
that they were completely ignorant of duplicity of heart.
For just as there was in them *one faith,*
so there was *one spirit,* Eph 4:3-5
one will, one charity, continual unity of spirit,
harmony in living, cultivation of virtues,
agreement of minds, and loyalty in actions.

For example, they often used to confess their sins to a certain secular priest, even when his wickedness had been reported to them by many people. He had a very bad reputation and was despised by everyone else because of the enormity of his misdeeds. But they did not wish to believe it; so they did not stop confessing their sins to him as usual, nor stop showing him proper reverence.

One day he, or another priest, said to one of the brothers, "Watch out, brother, don't be a hypocrite!" The brother immediately believed that he was a hypocrite because of the priest's statement. For this reason, he was crying and weeping day and night, moved by deep sorrow. When the brothers asked him what caused such grief and unusual gloom, he answered, "A priest told me something that has upset me so much that I can hardly think about anything else." The brothers kept trying to console him and urged him not to believe it. But he said, "How can you say that, brothers? A priest told me this. Could a priest lie? Since a priest does not lie, we must believe what he said." Remaining for a long time in this simplicity, he finally gave in to the words of the blessed father who explained to him the priest's statement and wisely excused his intention. For in almost any case of disturbance of mind in one of the brothers, at his *burning words* the clouds would break up and Ps 119: 140
clear weather would return.

Chapter XVIII
About the Fiery Chariot and the Knowledge that Blessed Francis Had of Those Absent

Gn 17:1 47 *Walking before God with simplicity*
Prv 10:9 *and among people with confidence,*
the brothers merited at that time to rejoice in a divine revelation.
They were on fire with the Holy Spirit
Mt 6:9 and with prayerful voices sang the "*Our Father*"
in the melody of the Spirit.
They did this at all hours and not simply those assigned,
since earthly concerns and the nagging anxiety of cares
troubled them little.

One night the blessed father Francis was away from them in body.
About midnight, some of the brothers were sleeping and others were
praying in silence with deep feeling, when a brilliant *fiery chariot* en-
2 Kgs 2:11-14 tered through the little door of the house, and moved *here and there*
through the little house two or three times. On top of it sat a large ball
that looked like the sun, and it made the night bright as day.[a] *Those who*
were awake were dumbfounded, while those sleeping woke up *in a*
Lk 2:8; Mt 24:4 *fright*, for they sensed the brightness with their hearts as much as with
their bodies. *They gathered together* and *began to ask each other* what
1 Cor 11:20; Lk 22:23 all this *meant.* From the strength and grace of such great light, the conscience of each was revealed to the others.

At last they understood, realizing that the soul of the holy father radiated with great brilliance. Thus, thanks to the gift of his outstanding purity and his deep concern for his sons, he merited the blessing of such a gift from the Lord.

48 They learned time and again by clear signs and their own experi-
1 Cor 14:25 ence that the hidden *recesses of their hearts* were not hidden from their
most holy father.

How often he knew the deeds of absent brothers,
not by human teaching but the revelation of the Holy Spirit!

---

a. Light expresses the splendor and glory of God in which saints, after the example of Elijah, are frequently bathed after long periods of prayer. Cf. *Lives of the Desert Fathers*, II, 9; *Guthlac* 50; *The Life of Anselm*, I, 16; *The Life of Malachy the Irishman* XXIX 65.

He opened up the hidden *recesses of their hearts*, 1 Cor 14:25
and examined their consciences![a]
How many he warned in their dreams,
both ordering what they should do
and forbidding what they should not!
How many future evil deeds he foretold
of those whose present deeds seemed so good in appearance!
So too did he announce
the future grace of salvation to many,
since he foresaw the ending of their misdeeds.
In fact, if someone in a spirit of purity and simplicity
merited enlightenment,
he would gain a singular consolation from a vision of him,
something not experienced by others.

I shall report just one of the many stories that I have learned from the reports of reliable witnesses. At one time, brother John of Florence was appointed by Saint Francis as minister of the brothers in Provence. He celebrated a chapter of the brothers in that province, and the Lord God with his usual favor opened the *door of eloquence* for him and made all (Col 4:3) the brothers willing and attentive listeners. Among them was a certain brother priest named Monaldo, distinguished by a brilliant reputation and by an even more brilliant life. His virtue was grounded in humility, aided by frequent prayer, and preserved by the shield of patience.

Also at that chapter was brother Anthony whose *mind* the Lord *had opened to understand the Scriptures* and *who poured forth* among all (Lk 24:45) the people *sweet words* about Jesus, *sweeter than milk and honey.*[b] He (Ps 45:2; Ps 19:11) was preaching to the brothers fervently and devoutly on the verse, "*Jesus of Nazareth, king of the Jews.*" Brother Monaldo glanced at the (Jn 19:19) door of the house in which the brothers *were all gathered.* He saw there (Jos 9:2) with his bodily eyes blessed Francis lifted up in the air with his hands extended as if on a cross, blessing the brothers. *All of them* seemed *filled with the consolation of the Holy Spirit* and were so taken with the (Acts 9:31) joy of salvation that they believed readily what they heard regarding the vision and the presence of the glorious father.

---

a. Throughout the hagiographic tradition the texts frequently speak of the saint's ability to read hearts. Cf. *Lives of the Desert Fathers*, XII, 10; Gregory, *Dialogue* II 20; Eadmer of Canterbury, *The Life of Anselm* I,8; Alan, Bishop of Auxerre, *Vita secunda s. Bernardi* XII; and Bernard, *The Life of Saint Malachy*, XV, 35.

b. A reference to Brother Anthony of Lisbon or Padua. He was born in Lisbon, Portugal, in 1195. Inspired by the news of the first Franciscan martyrs in Morocco, Anthony left the Canons Regular and joined the Order in 1220. He died in 1231 and was canonized in the following year.

[49]I shall relate only one account, undoubtedly true, about how he knew the hidden recesses of troubled hearts, something that many often experienced.

There was a certain brother named Riccerio, noble by birth but more noble in character, a lover of God and despiser of himself. With a devout spirit he was led wholeheartedly to attain and possess the favor of
Jdt 8:8 the blessed father Francis. He *was quite fearful* that the holy man Francis would detest him for some secret reason and thus he would become
Lk 2:25 a stranger to the gift of his love. That brother, since *he was fearful,* thought that any person the holy man Francis loved intimately was also worthy to merit divine favor. On the other hand, he judged that someone to whom he did not show himself kindly and pleasant would incur the wrath of the supreme Judge. This brother turned these matters over
Gn 24:45 in his heart; he *silently* spoke *of these matters* to himself, but revealed to no one else his secret thoughts.

[50]One day the blessed father was praying in his cell and that brother
Lk 4:34 came to the place disturbed by his usual thoughts. *The holy one of God* knew both that the brother had come and understood what was twisting in his heart. So the blessed father immediately called him to himself. "Let no temptation disturb you, son," he said to him, "and do not be troubled by any thought. You are very dear to me and you should know that, among those dearest to me, you are worthy of my love and intimacy. Come to me confidently whenever you want, knowing you are welcome, and, in this intimacy, speak freely." That brother was amazed and from then on became even more reverent. The more that he grew in the holy father's grace, the more he began to enjoy God's mercy with confidence.

How bitterly they feel your absence, holy father,
who completely despair
of ever finding anyone like you on earth!
We ask you, through your intercession,
help those covered by the harmful stain of sin.
Though you were already filled
with the spirit of all the just,[a]
foreseeing the future

a. Cf. Gregory the Great, "Dialogue" II 8: "*Vir iste spiritu iustorum omnium plenus fuit* [that man was filled with the spirit of all the just]." Also, *The Life* of William the Great (+1157), *Acta Santorum*, 3rd Edition (Paris, Rome: 1863-1870), February 10 II, p. 464: "*omnium iustorum spiritu plenus fuit* [he was filled with the spirit of all the just]."

and knowing the present,
to avoid all boasting
you always displayed the image of holy simplicity.
But let us return now to the matters mentioned above,
following again the order of our story.

Chapter XIX

HIS WATCHFULNESS OVER THE BROTHERS, SCORN FOR HIMSELF, AND TRUE HUMILITY

[51]Blessed Francis returned in body to his brothers, whom, as was said above, he never left in spirit. Asking carefully and in detail about all their doings, he was always moved by a wholesome curiosity about those in his charge. If he found something inappropriate was done, he did not leave it unpunished. He first discerned any spiritual vices. Then he judged those of the body, and finally uprooted any occasions that might open the way to sin.

He zealously and carefully safeguarded Lady Holy Poverty. In order to avoid the superfluous, he would not even permit a small plate to remain in the house if, without it, he could avoid dire need. He said it was impossible to satisfy necessity without bowing to pleasure. He rarely or hardly ever ate cooked foods, but if he did, he would sprinkle them with ashes or dampen the flavor of spices with cold water.[a] Often,
when he was wandering through the world to preach *the gospel of God,* Rom 1:1
he was called to a dinner given by great princes who venerated him
ER XIV,3; LR III,14 with much fondness. He would taste some meat in order to observe the
holy gospel.[b] The rest, which he appeared to eat, he put in his lap, rais- Lk 10:7-8
ing his hand to his mouth so that no one could know what he was doing. What shall I say about drinking wine, when he would not allow himself to drink even enough water when he was burning with thirst?

[52]Now as to *his bed:* wherever he received hospitality, he refused to Sg 1:11
use a straw mattress or blankets. The naked ground received his naked body, with only a thin tunic between them. Sometimes when he would refresh his small body with sleep, he would often sleep sitting up, not lying down, using a stone or a piece of wood as a pillow.

a. This approach to food reflects the early Christian ascetical tradition. Cf. Marcianus, 21 in *History of the Monks of Syria.*

b. Francis placed this teaching in both rules. This distinguishes Francis from the Cathars who refused to touch meat.

As normally happens, sometimes the craving to eat something came
upon him, but afterwards he would barely allow himself to eat it. Once,
because he was ill, he ate a little bit of chicken. When his physical
strength returned, he entered the city of Assisi. When he reached *the*
Lk 7:12 *city gate,* he commanded the brother who was with him to tie a cord
around his neck and drag him through the whole city as if he were a
thief, loudly crying out: "Look! See this glutton who grew fat on the
flesh of chickens that he ate without your knowledge." Many people
ran to see this grand spectacle and, groaning and weeping, they said:
"Woe to us! We are wretches and our whole life is steeped in blood!
With excess and drunkenness we feed our hearts and bodies to over-
Acts 2:37 flowing!" *They were touched in their hearts* and were moved to a better
way of life by such an example.

[53]He often did things in this way both to despise himself fully and to
invite others to everlasting honors. Toward himself *he had become like*
Ps 31:13 *a broken vessel,* burdened by no fear or concern for his body. He would
zealously expose himself to insults so that he would not be forced by
self-love to lust for anything temporal. A true scorner of himself, he
taught others to despise themselves by word and example. To what Adm V, XIII, XVI XX, XXIII, XXIV
Lk 4:15 end? He was *honored by all* and merited high marks from everyone. He
alone considered himself vile and was the only one to despise himself
fervently. Often honored by others, he suffered great sorrow. Shunning Adm XII, XIX
human praise, he had someone, as an antidote, revile him. He would
call one of the brothers to him, saying, "I command you under obedience to insult me harshly and speak the truth against their lies." When
the brother, though unwilling, called him a boor and a useless
hired-hand, he would smile and clap loudly, saying: "*May the Lord*
Nm 6:24; Ps 128:5 *bless you,* for you are really telling the truth; that is what the son of
Pietro Bernardone needs to hear." Speaking in this fashion, he called to
mind the humble origins of his birth.

[54]In order to show himself contemptible and to give others an example of true confession, when he did something wrong he was not
ashamed to confess it in his preaching before all the people. In fact, if he
had perhaps thought ill of someone or for some reason let slip a harsh
word, he would go with all humility to the person of whom he had said or
thought something wrong and, confessing his sin, would ask forgiveness. His conscience, a witness of total innocence, guarding itself with
2 Cor 8:7 *all care,* would not let him rest until it gently healed the wound of his

heart. In every type of praiseworthy deed he wished to be outstanding, but to go unnoticed. In every way he fled praise to avoid all vanity.

Woe to us who have now lost you,
O worthy father,
model of all kindness and humility!
Since we did not strive to know you when we had you,
we have lost you by *a just judgment!* Dt 16:18

Chapter XX
THE DESIRE TO UNDERGO MARTYRDOM WHICH TOOK HIM FIRST TO SPAIN AND THEN JOURNEYING TO SYRIA; AND HOW GOD SAVED SAILORS FROM DANGER, MULTIPLYING THEIR SUPPLY OF FOOD

[55]Burning with divine love,
the blessed father Francis was always eager
to *try his hand at brave deeds*, Prv 31:19
and walking *in the way of* God's *commands* Ps 115:32
with heart wide-open,
he longed to reach the summit of perfection.

In the sixth year of his conversion, burning with the desire for holy martyrdom, he wished to take a ship to the region of Syria to preach the Christian faith and repentance to the Saracens and other unbelievers.[a] But after he had boarded a ship to go there, contrary winds started blowing, and he found himself with his fellow travelers on the shores of Slavonia.[b]

When he realized that he had been cheated of what he desired, after a little while he begged some sailors going to Ancona to take him with them, since there were hardly any ships that could sail that year to Syria. But the sailors stubbornly refused to do so since he could not pay them. The holy one of God, trusting God's goodness, secretly boarded the ship with his companion. By divine providence, a man arrived unknown to anyone, who brought the food needed. He called over a per-

a. Probably in 1212. The desire for martyrdom is a theme at the very heart of the pursuit of religious life. Thus hagiography is filled with examples of men and women who desired to give their lives for Christ. Cf. Athanasius, *The Life of Antony*, 46; *Vita prima s. Bernardi* X.

b. Present day Dalmatia, it was called Slavonia at the time. It is east of Italy, across the Adriatic Sea. Since he left from Ancona, Francis would not have covered more than 150 km/95 mi.

Jb 1:1; Tb 11:4 son from the ship, *a God-fearing man. "Take with you* all these things,"
Sir 8:12 he said, "and in their *time of need* faithfully give them to those poor
men hiding on your ship."

A great storm arose and they had to spend many days *laboring at the*
Mk 6:48 *oars.* They had used up all their food. Only the food of the poor Francis
remained. Owing to divine grace and power, his food multiplied so
much that, although there were still many days of sailing remaining, it
fully supplied the needs of them all until they reached the port of
Ancona. When the sailors realized that they had escaped the dangers of
the sea through God's servant Francis, they gave thanks *to almighty*
Sir 50:19 *God,* who is always revealed through his servants as awesome and loving.

Dn 3:93 56Francis, *the servant of the most high,* left the sea and began to
Dt 21:3 walk *the earth. Furrowing with the plough* of the word, *he sowed the*
Mt 13:3 *seed* of life, bearing blessed *fruit.* Soon many good and suitable men,
2 Pt 1:4 cleric and lay, *fleeing the world* and courageously escaping the devil,
by the grace and will of the Most High, followed him devoutly in his
life and proposal.

Though the shoot of the gospel was producing choice fruit in abundance, it did not stifle his highest purpose, the burning desire for mar-
Mt 25:19 tyrdom. Not *too long after* this, he began to travel towards Morocco[a] to
preach the gospel of Christ to the Miramamolin and his retinue.[b] He
was so carried away with desire that he would sometimes leave behind
2 Cor 8:19 *his companion on the journey* and hurry ahead, intoxicated in spirit, in
order to carry out his purpose. But the good God, out of pure kindness,
was pleased to be mindful of me and many others.[c] After he reached
Gal 2:11 Spain God *withstood him to his face,* striking him with illness, and
called him back from the journey he had begun.[d]

---

a. To go to Morocco, Francis most likely followed the route to Santiago de Compostella. See Map B, p. 208. Morocco, during Francis's time, was ruled by the reformist movement of the al-Muwahhidun. From this Arabic term is derived the name "Almohads" by which they are designated in western literature. Their military occupation of North Africa was begun in 1129. They seized Tunis and Tripoli in 1159 and created for the first time in North Africa a single state. During these years of Francis's life, under the reign of Muhammad al Nasir (1199-1213), the Almohad army was invincible and the empire at its zenith of material and cultural success.

b. "Miramamolin" refers to "Amir al-Mu'minin," which translates as "Commander of the Believers." It is a religious title somewhat parallel to "sultan," which is a title for one who holds political power. "Miramamolin" can serve as a protocol title for a caliph.

c. In this passage Thomas makes a rare, personal reference to himself and to his own relationship to Francis.

d. Thomas does not provide information about the nature of this illness. Later, in *The Treatise on the Miracles* 34 (hereafter 3C), he says that it was "a very grave illness." "For after suffering privation and weakness," he writes, "and having been driven from a lodging place by the incivility of the host, he lost his speech for three days." But Thomas says little else.

[57]Shortly afterwards when Francis returned to the Church of Saint Mary of the Portiuncula, some literate men and nobles gladly joined him.[a] He received such men with honor and dignity, since he himself was very noble and distinguished in spirit, and respectfully gave to each his due. In fact, since he was endowed with outstanding discernment, he wisely considered in all matters the dignity of rank of each one.

But still he would not rest from carrying out fervently the holy impulse of his spirit. Now in the thirteenth year of his conversion, he journeyed to the region of Syria, while bitter and long battles were being waged daily between Christians and pagans.[b] Taking a companion with him, he was not afraid to present himself to the sight of the Sultan of the Saracens.[c]

Who is equal to the task of telling this story?
What great firmness he showed standing in front of him!
With great strength of soul he spoke to him,
with eloquence and confidence
he answered those who insulted the Christian law.

Before he reached the Sultan, he was captured by soldiers, insulted and beaten, but was not afraid. He did not flinch at threats of torture nor was he shaken by death threats. Although he was ill-treated by many with a hostile spirit and a harsh attitude, he was received very graciously by the Sultan. The Sultan honored him as much as he could, offering him many gifts, trying to turn his mind to worldly riches. But when he saw that he resolutely scorned all these things like dung, the Sultan was overflowing with admiration and recognized him as a man unlike any other. He was moved by his words *and listened to him very willingly.* Mk 6:20

In all this, however,
the Lord did not *fulfill* his *desire,* Ps 127:5
reserving for him the prerogative of a unique grace.[d]

---

a. Thomas may have been among some of the educated noblemen to receive the habit from Francis himself.

b. The journey to Syria took Francis to Damietta (Dimyat), a town in Lower Egypt situated on the eastern arm of the Nile near its mouth. This was an important town even before the Muslim conquest. As key to Egypt, it was the object of frequent naval raids, at first from the Byzantines and subsequently from Crusaders. Curiously, Thomas uses the word *paganos* [pagans], while Francis uses *infideles* [non-believers].

c. The Sultan whom Francis met was Malik al-Kamil (1180-1238). In 1218, upon the death of his father al-Adil, al-Kamil became Sultan of Egypt and supreme head of the Ayubid realm. In 1219 the Fifth Crusade succeeded in capturing the town of Damietta. For two years, al-Kamil was able to hold them at bay from his new camp, al-Marssura, south of Damietta, until the combined forces of other Ayubid princes reached Egypt in August 1221. They completely circled the crusaders and after heavy fighting the crusaders were forced to surrender on August 27, 1221. This brought the Fifth Crusade to an inglorious end. Francis visited al-Kamil at his camp Al-Marssura before the arrival of the other Ayyubid forces. Cf. H. L. Gottschalk, *Al-Malik al Kamil von Egypten und seine Zeit,* Wiesbaden, 1958. Cf. Historia Occidentalis, 593ff.; 617ff.

d. An allusion to the reception of the stigmata as a different martyrdom.

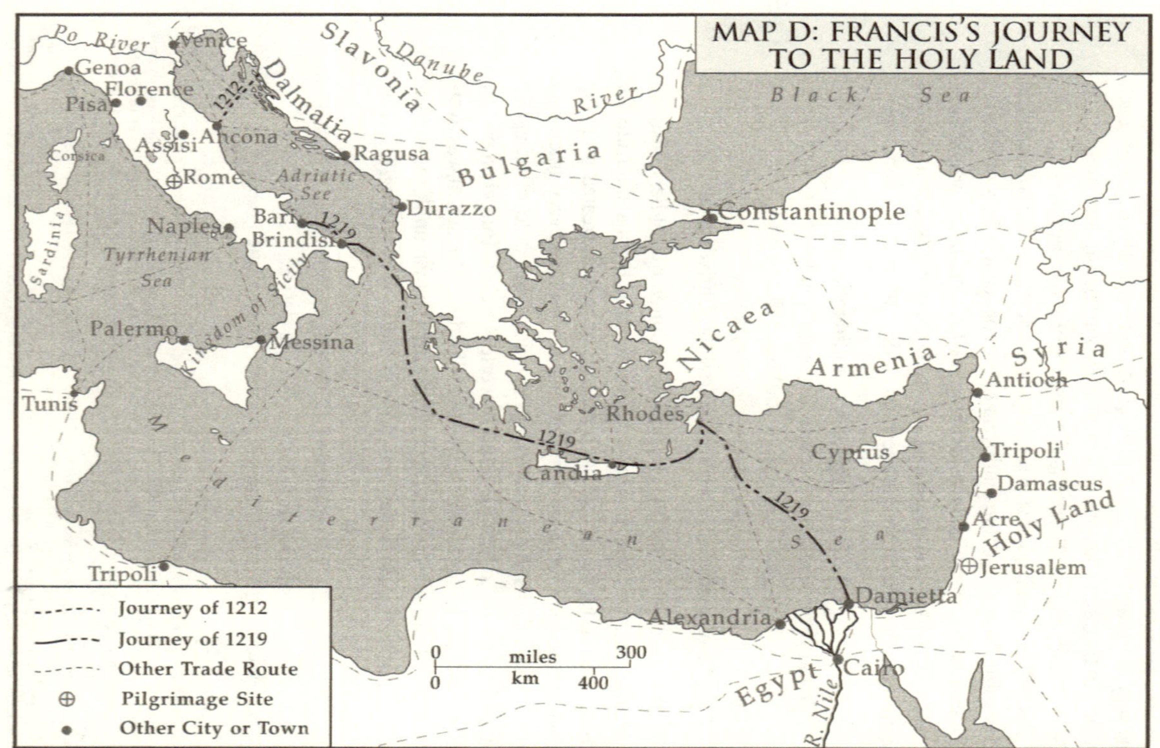

Francis's first efforts to travel to the Holy Land failed when his ship was blown ashore at Dalmatia and the winds for continuing were not favorable (probably in late 1212). He was finally successful in joining the Fifth Crusade at Damietta in the summer of 1219. He probably left from Bari or Brindisi in a ship which hugged the shoreline as far as Rhodes and then crossed the Eastern Mediterranean.

MAP E: FRANCIS & THE FIFTH CRUSADE AT DAMIETTA

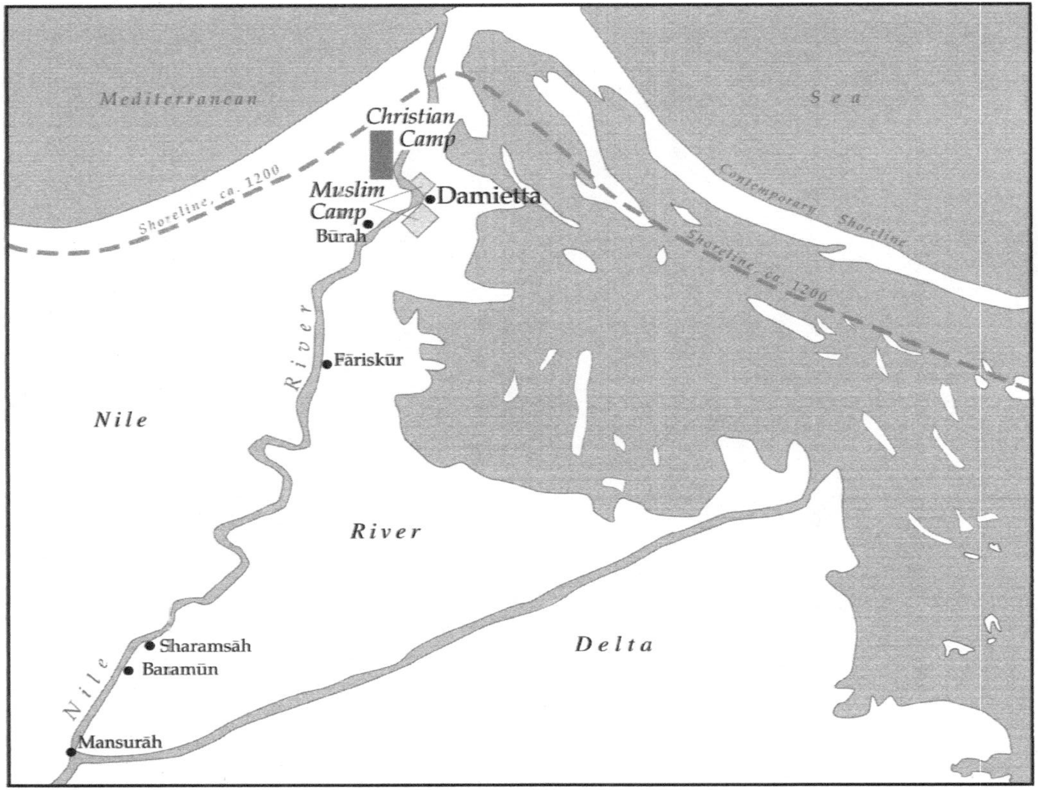

Mediterranean
Sea
Shoreline, ca. 1200
Contemporary Shoreline
Shoreline, ca. 1200
Christian Camp
Muslim Camp
Damietta
Būrah
Fāriskūr
River
Nile
River
Delta
Sharamsāh
Baramūn
Nile
Mansurāh

Area of Detail Shown at Right
Damietta
Alexandria
Nile
River
Delta
Cairo

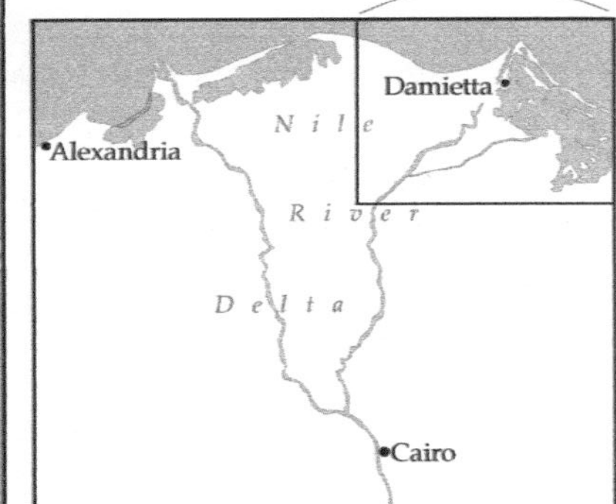

1C 57 narrates Francis's journey to the Fifth Crusade and his dramatic crossing of the battle lines in order to visit to the Sultan.

Chapter XXI

PREACHING TO THE BIRDS AND THE OBEDIENCE OF CREATURES

Acts 2:41 [58]While many *were joining* the brothers, as already related, the blessed father Francis was travelling through the Spoleto valley. He reached a place near Bevagna, in which a great multitude of birds of different types gathered, including doves, crows, and others commonly called *monaclae.*[a] When Francis, the most blessed servant of God, saw them, he ran swiftly toward them, leaving his companions on the road. He was a man of great fervor, feeling much sweetness and tenderness even toward lesser, irrational creatures. When he was already very close, seeing that they awaited him, he greeted them in his usual way.[b] He was quite surprised, however, because the birds did not 1C 23 take flight, as they usually do. Filled with great joy, he humbly requested that they listen to the word of God.

Among many other things, he said to them: "My brother birds, you should greatly praise your Creator, and love Him always. He gave you feathers to wear, wings to fly, and whatever you need. God made you noble among His creatures and gave you a home in the purity of the air, Lk 12:24 so that, though you neither *sow nor reap,* He nevertheless protects and governs you without your least care." He himself, and those brothers who were with him, used to say that, at these words, the birds rejoiced in a wonderful way according to their nature. They stretched their necks, spread their wings, opened their beaks and looked at him. He Lk 4:30 *passed through their midst,* coming and going, touching their heads and bodies with his tunic. Then he blessed them, and having made the sign of the cross, gave them permission to fly off to another place. The blessed father, *however, went* with his companions along their way *re-* Acts 8:39; Acts 27:35 *joicing* and *giving thanks to God,* Whom all creatures revere by their devout confession.

He was already simple by grace, not by nature. After the birds had listened so reverently to the word of God, he began to accuse himself of negligence because he had not preached to them before. From that day on, he carefully exhorted all birds, all animals, all reptiles, and also insensible creatures, to praise and love the Creator, because daily, *invok-* Acts 22:16 *ing the name* of the Savior, he observed their obedience in his own experience.

---

a. These are shiny black crows tinged with purple. The various manuscript readings for the name of this bird leave us only three choices: the jackdaw, the "grolle" or the magpie.

b. That is, with the greeting: "The Lord give you peace," cf. 1C 23, p. 203

59 One day he came to a village called Alviano to preach the word of
God. *Going up to a higher place* where all could see him, he called for Jgs. 13:16
silence. All remained silent and stood reverently. But a large number of
swallows nesting there were shrieking and chirping. Since blessed
Francis could not be heard by the people, he said to the noisy birds:
"My sister swallows, now *it is time* for me also to speak, since you have Tb 12:20
already said enough. *Listen to the word of the Lord* and stay quiet and Is 1:10
calm until *the word of the Lord is completed."* Immediately those little 2 Chr 36:21
birds fell silent — to the amazement and surprise of all present — and
did not move from that place until the sermon was over. Those men
who *saw* this *sign* were filled with great wonder, saying: *"Truly, this* Mt 12:38
man is holy, and a friend of the Most High."[a] Lk 23:47

With great devotion they hurried to touch at least his clothes, while
praising and blessing God. It was certainly a marvel that even Lk 24:53
irrational creatures recognized his feeling of tenderness toward them,
and sensed the sweetness of his love.

60 Once while he was staying near the town of Greccio, a certain
brother brought him a live rabbit caught in a trap. Seeing it, the most
blessed man was moved with tenderness. "Brother rabbit," he said,
"come to me. Why did you let yourself get caught?" As soon as the
brother holding it let go, the rabbit, without any prompting, took shelter
with the holy man, as in a most secure place, resting *in his bosom.* After 2 Sm 12:3; Lk 16:23
it had rested there for a little while, the holy father, caressing it with
motherly affection, let it go, so that now free it would return to the
woods. As often as it was put on the ground, it rushed back to the holy
man's lap, so he told the brothers to carry it away to the nearby forest.
Something similar happened with another little rabbit, a wild one,
when he was on the island in the Lake of Perugia.[b]

61 He had the same tender feeling toward fish. When he had the chance he would throw back into the water live fish that had been caught, and he warned them to be careful not to be caught again. One time while he was sitting in a little boat at the port on the Lake of Rieti, a fisherman caught a large fish, commonly called a *tinca,* and reverently offered it to him.[c] He accepted it gladly and gratefully, calling it

---

a. Suetonius, "Life of Julius Caesar," Book 2, 94:10 in *The Lives of the Caesars* in which Caesar silences noisy frogs so that he can speak. Cf. *Suetonius,* Vol. I, The Loeb Classical Library translated by J.C. Rolfe, (Cambridge: Harvard University Press, 1950).

b. This lake is also known as Lake Trasimene, cf. Map D, p. 232. Not far from Cortona, it is the largest lake found in the peninsula of Italy. On its largest island, Isola Maggiore, Francis spent the Lent of 1211 or 1213.

c. A *tinca* or "tench" is a common European freshwater fish of the carp family.

"brother." He put it back in the water next to the little boat, and with de-
Ps 113:2 votion blessed *the name of the Lord.* For some time that fish did not leave the spot but stayed next to the boat, playing in the water where he put it until, at the end of his prayer, the holy man of God gave it permission to leave.

Thus the glorious father Francis,
walking in the way of obedience,
and embracing the yoke of complete submission to God,
was worthy of the great honor before God
of having the obedience of creatures.[a]

Water was changed into wine for him once at the hermitage of Sant'Urbano when he was suffering from a severe illness. Once he tasted it, he recovered so easily that everyone believed it was a divine miracle, as it indeed was.

He is truly a saint,
whom creatures obey in this way:
at his wish
the very elements convert themselves
to other uses.[b]

Chapter XXII

His Preaching at Ascoli and How the Sick Were Healed, Even When He Was Away, by Items He Had Touched with His Hand

[62] At the time the venerable father Francis preached to the birds, as
Mt 9:35 reported above, he went around *the towns and villages,* sowing the
seed of divine blessings everywhere, until he reached the city of
Ascoli. There he spoke the word of God with his usual fervor. By a
Ps 77:11 change *of the right hand of the Most High,* nearly all the people were
filled with such grace and devotion that they were *trampling each*
Lk 12:1 *other* in their eagerness to hear and see him. Thirty men, cleric and lay,
at that time received the habit of holy religion from him.

a. The obedience of animals is considered a sign of holiness in the *Dialogues* of Sulpicius Severus, PL 20:193.

b. Bede, *The Life of Cuthbert:* "If someone serves the Creator of all creatures, faithfully and wholeheartedly, it is no wonder that every creature should serve his commands and desires." Cf. B. Colgrave, *Two Lives of Saint Cuthbert* (Cambridge Harvard University Press, 1940), 224.

1C speaks specifically of Francis preaching in only five places: Bevagna (1C 58), Alviano (1C 59), Ascoli (1C 62) Ancona (1C 77), and Gubbio (1C 86).

So great was the faith of men and women
and so great the devotion of their hearts
towards the holy one of God,
that a person was considered fortunate
Mt 9:21 who was able to touch *at least his clothing.*
When he entered a city,
clergy rejoiced, bells rang,
men exulted, women rejoiced, and children clapped.
Often taking branches from trees and singing psalms,
they went out to meet him.

The perversity of heretics was shamed,
the faith of the Church was extolled
and, as believers rejoiced, heretics hid.[a]

The marks of his holiness were so clear in him that no one dared to
Nm 27:22 speak against him, as *the assembly of the people* paid attention to him alone. He put the faith of the Holy Roman Church above and beyond all things, preserving, honoring and following it, since the salvation of all who would be saved was found in it alone. He honored priests and affectionately embraced every ecclesiastical order.

63 The people used to bring him loaves of bread to bless, which they kept for a long time, and, on tasting them, they were cured of various diseases.

Driven by great faith, people often tore his habit until sometimes he was left almost naked. Even more remarkable is that health was restored to some people through some thing that the holy father had touched with his hands.

There was a pregnant woman living on a small farm in the Arezzo area. At the time of childbirth she was in labor with such excruciating pain that she hovered between life and death. *Her neighbors and rela-*
Lk 1:58 *tives heard* that the blessed Francis was going to pass by there on his
Acts 28:6 way to a hermitage.[b] *While they were waiting* the blessed Francis went
Mt 2:12 to that place *by another route.* He had gone on horseback because he

a. This paragraph interrupts the narrative sequence or "historical order" of Thomas's portrait in order to extol the magnificence of Francis's moral virtues. In doing so Thomas goes beyond the first of two requirements for canonization established by Pope Innocent III: "virtue of behavior and the virtue of signs, that is, works of mercy during life and miraculous signs after death". Cf. Innocent III, Letter of Canonization, January 12, 1199, in *Regesta Pontificium Romanorum,* vol. I (Berlin, 1874), p. 55, no. 573. The narration of these miracles performed by Francis during life will continue until paragraph 71.

b. The city of Arezzo is on the way to the hermitage at La Verna. Cf. Map F. p. 237.

was weak and sick. When he reached that place, he sent one of the brothers, named Peter, to return the horse to the man who had lent it to him out of sincere charity.

When returning the horse brother Peter went down the road near the house where the woman was suffering. The men of that area saw him and raced to meet him, thinking that he was blessed Francis. When they realized that he was not, *they were sorely disappointed. They began to* Mt 18:31
inquire among themselves if they could find some item that blessed Lk 22:23
Francis's hand had touched. *They had spent* quite a bit of time in this Mt 24:45
search, when they finally discovered the bridle reins which he had held in his hand while riding. Pulling the bridle from the horse's mouth, they placed on the woman the reins which he had held in his very hands. At this, the danger passed, and the woman gave birth in great joy and good health.

[64]Gualfreduccio was an inhabitant of Città della Pieve, a man who
was *religious, worshiping and fearing God with all his household.* He Acts 10:2
had a cord at his home that blessed Francis once used as a belt. Many men and not a few women in that area suffered from various diseases and fevers. That man went to the houses of the sick and gave the sufferers water to drink which had been touched by the cord or mixed with its
threads. And in this way all of them *in the name of Christ* regained their 1 Pt 4:14
health.

These things happened, moreover, in the absence of blessed Francis. There are so many others that they could not all be mentioned even briefly in a very long story. But we shall now include in this book a
brief mention of those things that *the Lord our God* worked through his Ps 99:9
presence.

Chapter XXIII
How He Healed a Lame Man at Toscanella and a Paralyzed Man at Narni

[65]Once when the holy man of God, Francis, was travelling far and wide through the land, proclaiming *the good news of the kingdom of*
God, he came to a city called Toscanella. As he was sowing the seed of Lk 4:43
life as usual, a knight of that same city took him in as his guest. The man
had only one son, who was lame and had no bodily strength. Although Lk 7:12
the young boy was no longer being breast-fed, he was still sleeping in a cradle. The father of the boy, seeing the man of God was endowed with

Ru 3: 7-8 such holiness, humbly *fell down at his feet,* begging him for his son's
health. For a long time the holy man Francis refused to comply, considering himself useless and unworthy of such power and grace. But at
last, overcome by the persistence of the father's entreaties, Saint Fran-
Acts 3:7 cis prayed, laid hands on the boy and, blessing him, *lifted him up.* Im-
Acts 4:19 mediately the boy, *in the name of our Lord Jesus Christ* stood up
healed and, with the onlookers rejoicing, began to walk all around the
house.

1 Kgs 9:6 66 Once the *man of God* Francis came to Narni and remained there
for several days. A man of that city named Pietro was *bedridden as a*
Mt 9:2 *paralytic.* Over a five-month period this man had been so deprived of
the use of all his members that he could not get up at all or even move.
He had completely lost the use of his feet, hands, and head. He could
only move his tongue and blink his eyes. Hearing that Saint Francis had
come to Narni, he sent a message to the bishop of the city requesting
him, for the sake of divine mercy, to send the servant of *the most High*
Lk 8:28 *God* to him. He believed that seeing him and being in his presence
would free him from the bonds of that paralysis. And so it did! The
blessed Francis came to him, made the sign of the cross over him from
head to toe, and, as the affliction vanished, immediately *restored* him
Mt 12:13 to *his earlier health.*

Chapter XXIV

How he gave sight to a blind woman at Narni and healed a crippled woman at Gubbio

67 A woman of that same city, afflicted with blindness, received the sign of the cross made by the blessed Francis over her eyes. She merited to receive immediately the sight for which she longed.

At Gubbio, there was a woman with both hands so crippled that she was unable to handle anything with them. When she heard that Saint Francis had entered the city, she immediately ran to him. With a sad and mournful face she showed him her crippled hands and begged him to touch them. He was moved with great pity. He touched her hands and healed them. The woman immediately returned home full of joy, made a cheesecake with her own hands, and offered it to the holy man.[a]

a. The scene recalls the cure of Peter's mother-in-law. Cf. Mk 1:31.

He kindly took a little of that cake and told her to eat the rest of it with her family.

Chapter XXV
How he freed a brother from a falling sickness or a demon and how he freed a possessed woman at San Gemini

[68]One of the brothers often suffered from a terrible affliction, dreadful to see. I do not know quite what I should call it, since there are some who believe it was an evil demon. He would often fall, looking around with a pitiful expression, and *roll around foaming at the mouth.* Sometimes his limbs would contract and then stretch out; sometimes they would be bent and twisted and, at other times, rigid and hard. Sometimes, when he was completely stretched out and rigid with his feet level with his head, he would be lifted into the air as high as a man stands and then suddenly bounce back to the ground. The holy father Francis took pity upon his serious condition, went to see him and, after praying, signed him and blessed him. The man was suddenly healed. Afterwards he never had any trouble from that illness. Mk 9:19

[69]One day the most blessed father Francis was passing through the diocese of Narni. He came to a village called San Gemini. While he was proclaiming there the *good news of the kingdom of God*, he, along with three of the brothers, received hospitality from a man *fearing and serving God.* This man enjoyed a very good reputation in the area. His wife, however, was *troubled by a demon,* as all the people living in the area were aware. Her husband pleaded with blessed Francis for her, trusting that through his merits she would be set free. But since the blessed Francis preferred in his simplicity to be held in contempt rather than to be lifted up by worldly honor for some display of holiness, he refused to do it. Yet God was involved in the case! Since so many people kept asking, he gave in to their pleas. He called over the three brothers who were with him. He set one in each corner of that house. "Brothers," he said to them, "let us pray to the Lord for this woman, that God may *shake off* the devil's *yoke* from her 'to His praise and glory.' "[a] He added: "Let us stand apart in the corners of the house to prevent the evil spirit from fleeing or deceiving us by trying to hide in the corners." Lk 4:43 Acts 10:2 Mt 15:22 Gn 27:40

a. A reference to the *Suscipiat* response of the Liturgy of the Eucharist.

Jdt 6:16 When *the prayer was finished,* blessed Francis, *in the power of the*
Rom 15:13, 19 *Spirit,* approached the woman, who was twisting miserably and
screaming horribly. "*In the name of our Lord Jesus Christ,*" he said, "*I*
Acts 16:18 *command you,* demon, under obedience, *to come out from her* and not
trouble her any more." He had scarcely uttered the words when the
Gn 39:12 demon *went out.* It did so with such swiftness and with such a furious
roar, that on account of the sudden cure of the woman and the immediate obedience of the demon, the holy father thought he was deceived. So he left that place right away, ashamed. Divine Providence arranged it that way so he could not boast vainly.

That is why when blessed Francis passed through that same place on
another occasion and brother Elias was with him, that woman, hearing
Acts 9:34 of his arrival, *got up immediately,* ran down the street, and *cried out af-*
Mt 15:23 *ter him,* asking him to speak to her. But he refused to do so, knowing
that she was the woman from whom he had once, by divine power,
Est 13:13 driven out a demon. She *kissed his very footprints, giving thanks to*
Acts 28:15 *God* and his holy servant Francis, who had *freed her from the hand of*
Hos 13:14 *death.* At last, brother Elias forced him by his pleas; and blessed Francis spoke to her after being reassured by many about the affliction that was mentioned and her deliverance.

Chapter XXVI
HOW HE ALSO DROVE OUT A DEMON AT CITTÀ DI CASTELLO

[70]At Città di Castello also there was a woman who was possessed by a
demon.[a] When the most blessed father Francis was in that city, the
woman was led to the house where he was staying. But the woman *stood*
Jn 20:11 *outside* and began to gnash her teeth and howl in a horrible voice with a
Mt 10:1; Jn 19:40 twisted face, which is *usual with unclean spirits.* Many people from the city, both women and men, came to plead with Saint Francis on the woman's behalf. That evil spirit had troubled her for a long time by twisting her body and disturbed the people themselves with its howling. The holy father sent out to her the brother who was with him, since he wished to check whether it was a demon or the woman's deception. When that woman saw the brother, she began to mock him, since she knew that he was hardly the holy man, Francis. Meanwhile, Francis had

a. Città di Castello was an important center of the Tiber Valley. It is situated on the most convenient and direct route from Saint Mary of the Angels to La Verna. Francis must have passed this way frequently. Cf. Map F, p. 237.

been praying and once his prayer was finished he came outside. The woman started to shake and roll on the ground, since she could not bear his power. Saint Francis called her to himself, saying: "In virtue of obedience, I command you, *evil spirit: come out* of her." The evil spirit released her immediately without harm, and departed, furious. Mk 5:8

Thanks be *to almighty God* who *works all things* in everyone. But we have not chosen to describe miracles — they do not make holiness but show it—but rather to describe the excellence of his life and the honest form of his manner of living. Passing over the miracles, because they are so numerous, let us return to narrating the works *of eternal salvation.*[a] Sir 50:19; 1 Cor 12:11 Heb 5: 9

Chapter XXVII

THE PURITY AND STEADFASTNESS OF HIS MIND, HIS PREACHING IN FRONT OF THE LORD POPE HONORIUS; AND HOW HE COMMITTED BOTH HIS BROTHERS AND HIMSELF TO THE PROTECTION OF THE LORD HUGO, BISHOP OF OSTIA

71 *The man of God,* the blessed Francis, 1 Sm 9:6, 10
had been taught not to seek his own salvation,
but what he discerned would help the salvation of others.
More than anything else he desired
to be set free and to be with Christ. Phil 1:23
Thus his chief object of concern was
to live free from all things *that are in the world,* 1 Jn 2:15
so that his inner serenity would not be disturbed
even for a moment
by contact with any of its dust.[b]
He made himself insensible to all outside noise,
gathering his external senses into his inner being
and checking the impetus of his spirit,
he emptied himself for God alone.

In the clefts of the rock he would build his nest
and *in the hollow of the wall* his dwelling. Sg 2:14

a. At this point Thomas leaves his narration of Francis's miracles and virtues.

b. Thomas uses the image of dust to describe money (n. 9) and, in this instance, worldly distractions. Cultivation of a serene interior peace is the reason for seeking solitary places. Cf. Gregory the Great, *Dialogue* II 3.

With blessed devotion he visited the heavenly mansions;
Phil 2:7 and, totally *emptied* of *himself*,
he rested for a long time in the wounds of the Savior.
That is why he often chose solitary places
to focus his heart entirely on God.

But he was not reluctant,
when he discerned the time was right,
to involve himself in the affairs of his neighbors,
and attend to their salvation.
For his safest haven was prayer;
not prayer of a fleeting moment, empty and proud,
but prayer that was prolonged,
full of devotion, peaceful in humility.
If he began at night,
he was barely finished at morning.
Walking, sitting, eating, drinking,
he was focused on prayer.
He would spend the night alone praying
in abandoned churches and in deserted places
where,
with the protection of divine grace,
he overcame his soul's many fears and anxieties.[a]

Ez 21:24 [72]He used to struggle *hand to hand* with the devil who, in those places, would not only assault him internally with temptations but also frighten him externally with ruin and undermining.[b] The brave soldier of God knew that his Lord could do all things in all places; thus he did not give in to the fears but said in his heart: "You, evil one! You cannot strike me with your evil weapons here any more than if we were in front of a crowd in a public place."

He was extremely determined and paid no attention to anything be-
1 Cor 7:32; Acts 13:5 yond *what was of the Lord.* Though he often preached *the word of God*
among thousands of people, he was as confident as if he were speaking

a. Unceasing prayer and all night vigils characterize the prayer of the saints in the hagiographic tradition. For example, Sulpicius Severus describes the prayer of Martin of Tours: "In fact he did not indulge either in food or sleep, except insofar as the necessities of nature required. . . . Never did a single hour or moment pass in which he was not either actually engaged in prayer; or, if it happened that he was occupied with something else, still he never let his mind loose from prayer." Cf. Sulpicius Severus *The Life of Martin* 26.

b. This experience of temptation is also common among the saints and is described as direct and immediate. Once again the examples of Antony, Martin, and Benedict are paramount. Cf. *The Life of Antony*, 9; *The Life of Martin* 22; and *Dialogue* II 8.

with a close friend. He used to view the largest crowd of people as if it were a single person, and he would preach fervently to a single person as if to a large crowd. Out of the purity of his mind he drew his confidence in preaching and, even without preparation, he used to say the most amazing things to everyone. Sometimes he prepared for his talk with some meditation, but once the people gathered he could not remember what he had meditated about and had nothing to say. Without any embarrassment he would confess to the people that he had thought of many things before, but now he could not remember a thing. Sometimes he would be filled with such great eloquence that he moved the hearts of his hearers to astonishment. When he could not think of anything, he would give a blessing and send the people away with this act alone as a very good sermon.

73 Once he came to the city of Rome on a matter concerning the Order, and he greatly yearned to speak before the Lord Pope Honorius and the venerable cardinals.[a] Lord Hugo, the renowned bishop of Ostia, venerated the holy man of God with special affection. When he learned of his arrival, Lord Hugo was filled with fear and joy, admiring the holy man's fervor yet aware of his simple purity. *Trusting* to the mercy *of the Almighty* that never fails the faithful *in time of need,* he led 2 Mc 8:18; Sir 8:12
the holy man before the Lord Pope and the venerable cardinals.

As he stood in the presence of so many princes of the Church, blessed Francis, after receiving permission and a blessing, fearlessly *began to speak.* Lk 7:15

He was speaking with such fire of spirit
that he could not contain himself for joy.
As he brought forth the word from his mouth,
he moved his feet as if dancing,
not playfully but burning with the fire of divine love,
not provoking laughter but moving them to tears of sorrow.
For many of them *were touched in their hearts,* Acts 2: 37
amazed at the grace of God
and the great *determination* of the man. Acts 4:13

The venerable lord bishop of Ostia was waiting fearfully, praying to God that they would not despise the blessed man's simplicity; for both

a. A reference to Honorius III, immediate successor to Innocent III, and pope from July 18, 1216, to March 8, 1227.

the glory and the disgrace of the holy man would reflect on himself,
Lk 12: 42 since he was the father set *over the* saint's *household.*

[74]For Saint Francis clung to the bishop
as *a son* does to his father
Lk 7:12 and *an only child to its mother,*
2 Sm 12:3 safely resting and *sleeping in the lap* of his kindness.
The bishop filled the role and did the work of a shepherd,
but left the name of shepherd to the holy man.
Blessed Francis would foresee needs,
but that blessed lord would deliver
what was foreseen.
There were many who plotted to destroy
Ps 144:12 *the new planting* of the Order at its beginning.
Jer 2:21 There were many trying to suffocate the *chosen vineyard*
which the Lord's hand had so kindly planted anew in the world.
There were many trying to steal and eat its first fresh fruit.
But all of these opponents were *slain with the sword*
of the venerable father and lord
Acts 5:36 *and their efforts came to naught.*
For he was a river of eloquence,
a wall of the Church,
a spokesman for truth,
and a lover of the humble.

That was a memorable and blessed day when the holy man of God committed himself to such a venerable lord. Once this lord was acting in Tuscany as legate of the Apostolic See, as he frequently did. Blessed Francis, not yet having many brothers and intending to go to France,[a] reached Florence where the bishop was then staying. At that time the two of them were not yet joined by close friendship, but their shared reputation for holy living joined them in mutual and affectionate charity.

[75]Upon entering a city or area, it was blessed Francis's custom to visit the priests or bishops. Upon hearing there was such a great pontiff in Florence, he presented himself to the bishop's kindness with great reverence. When the lord bishop saw him, he received him humbly and

a. Here *France* refers to the property of the kings of France, which after the 15th century came to be called Ile-de-France: Paris and a broad area around it.

devoutly, just as he always did for those professing holy religion, especially those carrying the noble banner of blessed poverty and holy simplicity. Now the bishop was concerned *to provide for the needs* of the poor and to handle their affairs in a special way. So he carefully inquired the reason for the blessed man's arrival there and graciously understood his plan. He perceived in the holy man someone who, more than others, spurned all earthly things, one who was burning with the fire which Jesus *sent down to the earth.* From that moment, his soul *was joined to the soul* of the holy man.[a] Sincerely asking for his prayers, the bishop freely offered the holy man his protection in all things. Then, the lord bishop advised him not to complete the journey he had begun, but rather to be vigilant, to care for and protect those whom the Lord God had entrusted to him.

2 Cor 8:14

Lk 12: 49

1 Sm 18:1

When the holy man Francis saw that this revered lord had such a devout attitude, sweet affection, and powerful words, he *rejoiced greatly. Falling at his feet,* he handed over and entrusted himself and his brothers wholeheartedly to the bishop.

Mt 2:11

Acts 10:25

Chapter XXVIII
THE SPIRIT OF CHARITY AND THE FEELING OF COMPASSION FOR THE POOR THAT GLOWED IN HIM AND WHAT HE DID WITH THE SHEEP AND THE LAMBS

76 *The father of the poor,*
the poor Francis,
conforming himself to the poor in all things,
was distressed to see anyone poorer than himself,
not out of any desire *for empty glory,*
but from a feeling of simple compassion.
Though he was content with a ragged and rough tunic,
he often wished to divide it with some poor person.

Jb 29:16

Gal 5:26

This richest poor man, moved by a great feeling of pity, in order to help the poor in some way, used to approach the rich people of this world during the coldest times of the year, asking them to loan him

a. As the Scriptural allusion suggests, Thomas likens the friendship between Francis and Hugolino to that of David and Jonathan. "When David had finished speaking, the soul of Jonathan was bound to the soul of David, and Jonathan loved him as his own soul," (1 Sm 18:1).

their cloaks or furs. As they responded even more gladly than the blessed father asked, he used to say to them, "I shall accept this from you only on the condition that you never expect to have it returned." The first poor man who happened to meet him, he would then clothe with whatever he had received, exulting and rejoicing.

He was deeply troubled whenever he saw one of the poor insulted or
Jos 8:34 heard *a curse* hurled at any creature. It happened that a certain brother
insulted a poor man begging alms, saying: "Are you sure that you are
not really rich and just pretending to be poor?" When Saint Francis, *the*
Jb 29:16 *father of the poor,* heard this, he was deeply hurt and he severely rebuked the brother who had said these things. Then he ordered the
brother to strip naked in front of the poor man and to kiss his feet, to beg
his forgiveness. He used to say: "Anyone who curses the poor insults
Christ whose noble banner the poor carry, since Christ *made himself* LR VI 3
2 Cor 8:9 *poor for us in this world."* That is also why, when he met poor people
burdened with wood or other heavy loads, he would offer his own weak
shoulders to help them.

77 The holy man overflowed with the spirit of charity, bearing within himself a deep sense of concern not only toward other humans in need but also toward mute, brute animals: reptiles, birds, and all other creatures whether sensate or not. But among all the different kinds of creatures, he loved lambs with a special fondness and spontaneous affection, since in Sacred Scripture the humility of our Lord Jesus Christ is frequently and rightly compared to the lamb. He used to embrace more warmly and to observe more gladly anything in which he found an allegorical likeness to the Son of God.

Once he was making a journey through the Marches of Ancona and
Acts 15:36 *preached the word of the Lord* in the city. Then he took the road toward
Acts 26:16 Osimo, with lord Paul, the one whom he had *appointed minister* of all
the brethren in that province. He came upon a shepherd in the fields
pasturing a flock of goats. There was one little sheep walking humbly
and grazing calmly among these many goats. When blessed Francis
Gn 6:6 saw it, he stopped in his tracks, *and touched with sorrow in his heart,* he
groaned loudly, and said to the brother accompanying him: "Do you
see that sheep walking so meekly among those goats? I tell you, in the
Mt 11:29 same way our Lord Jesus Christ, *meek and humble,* walked among the
Pharisees and chief priests. So I ask you, my son, in your love for Him
to share my compassion for this little sheep. After we have paid for it,
Ps 136:11 let us *lead* this little one *from the midst* of these goats."

78 Brother Paul was struck by his sorrow and also began to feel that sorrow himself. They had nothing except the cheap tunics they wore and they were concerned about how to pay for the sheep, when suddenly a traveling merchant arrived and offered to pay for what they
wanted. Taking up the sheep, they *gave thanks to God* and after reach- Col 3: 17
ing Osimo made their way to the bishop of the city, who received them with great reverence. Now the lord bishop was surprised both at the
sheep *the man of God* was leading and at the affection for it that was 2 Kgs 24:9
leading him to do this. But when the servant of Christ recounted the
long parable of the sheep, the bishop *was touched in his heart* by the Acts 2:37
purity of the man of God, and *gave thanks to God.* Acts 27:35

The next day, on leaving the city, the man of God began to wonder what to do with the sheep. On the advice of his companion and brother, he entrusted it to the care of the maidservants of Christ in the cloister of San Severino. The venerable servants of Christ gladly received the little sheep as a great *gift from God.* They devotedly cared for the sheep 2 Mc 15:16
for a long time and made a tunic from its wool, a tunic they sent to the blessed father Francis at the church of Saint Mary of the Portiuncula at the time of a chapter meeting. The holy man of God received the tunic with great reverence and high spirits, hugging and kissing it, and invited all those around him to share this great joy.

79 On another occasion he was traveling through the Marches and the same brother was gladly accompanying him when he came across a man on his way to market. The man was carrying over his shoulder two little lambs bound and ready for sale. When blessed Francis heard the
bleating lambs, *his innermost heart was touched* and, drawing near, he 1 Kgs 3:26
touched them as a mother does with a crying child, showing his compassion. "Why are you torturing my brother lambs," he said to the man, "binding and hanging them this way?" "I am carrying them to market to sell them, since I need the money," he replied. The holy man asked: "What will happen to them?" "Those who buy them will kill them and eat them," he responded. At that, the holy man said: "No, this must not happen! Here, take my cloak as payment and give me the lambs." The man readily gave him the little lambs and took the cloak since it was much more valuable. The cloak was one the holy man had borrowed from a friend on the same day to keep out the cold. The holy man of God, having taken the lambs, now was wondering what he should do with them. Asking for advice from the brother who was with him, he gave them back to that man, ordering him never to sell them or allow

any harm to come to them, but instead to preserve, nourish, and guide them carefully.

Chapter XXIX
THE LOVE THAT HE HAD TOWARD ALL CREATURES FOR THE SAKE OF THE CREATOR AND A DESCRIPTION OF BOTH ASPECTS OF HIS PERSON

[80]To enumerate and recount all the things
our glorious father Francis did
Phil 1:22 and taught while *living in the flesh*
would be a lengthy or an even impossible task.
Who could ever express the deep affection he bore
Mt 22:21 for all things *that belong to God?*
Sir 18:2 *Or who would be able to tell*
of the sweet tenderness he enjoyed
while contemplating in creatures
the wisdom, power, and goodness of the Creator?
From this reflection
he often overflowed
with amazing, unspeakable joy
as he looked at the sun,
gazed at the moon, or observed the stars in the sky.
What simple piety!
What pious simplicity!

Even for worms he had a warm love, since he had read this text
Ps 22:7 about the Savior: *I am a worm and not a man.* That is why he used to pick them up from the road and put them in a safe place so that they would not be crushed by the footsteps of passersby.

What shall I say about the other lesser creatures? In the winter he had honey or the best wine put out for the bees so that they would not perish from the cold. He used to extol the artistry of their work and their remarkable ingenuity, giving glory to the Lord. With such an outpouring, he often used up an entire day or more in praise of them and other
creatures. Once the three young men *in the furnace of burning fire* in- CtC
vited all the elements *to praise and glorify* the Creator of all things, so this *man, full of the spirit of God* never stopped *glorifying, praising,*

and blessing the Creator and Ruler of all things in all the elements and creatures. Dn 3:17;3:51

[81]How great do you think was the delight the beauty of flowers brought to his soul whenever he saw their lovely form and noticed their sweet fragrance? He would immediately turn his gaze to the beauty of that flower, brilliant in springtime, sprouting *from the root of Jesse.* By its *fragrance* it raised up countless thousands of the dead. Whenever he found an abundance of flowers, he used to preach to them and invite them to praise the Lord, just as if they were endowed with reason. Is 11:1 2 Cor 2:14

Fields and vineyards,
rocks and woods,
and all *the beauties of the field,* Sir 24:19
flowing springs and blooming gardens,
earth and fire, air and wind:
all these he urged to love of God and to willing service.
Finally, he used to call all creatures
by the name of "brother" and "sister"
and in a wonderful way, unknown to others,
he could discern the *secrets of the heart* of creatures 1 Cor 14:25
like someone who has already passed
into the freedom of the glory of the children of God. Rom 8:21

O good Jesus,
with the angels in heaven
he now praises you as wonderful,
who, when *placed on earth,* Jb 20:4
preached you as lovable to all creatures.

[82]Whenever he used to say *your name, O holy Lord,* he was moved in a way beyond human understanding. He was so wholly taken up in joy, filled with pure delight, that he truly seemed a new person of another age.[a] Ps 8:2; Is 6:3

For this reason he used to gather up any piece of writing, whether divine or human, wherever he found it: on the road, in the house, on the floor. He would reverently pick it up and put it in a sacred or decent Test 12; 1LtCl 12; LtOrd 35; 1LtCus 5

a. In this paragraph, Thomas underscores Francis's reverence not only for the written word of Scripture, a theme frequently offered in his writings, cf. 1LtCl 6; 2LtCl 6; 1LtCus 5; LtOrd 35-37; but for any written articulation of God's name. At the same time, he draws attention to the medieval custom of preserving Sacred Scripture in a special place of honor in each church, i.e., the aumbry.

place because the name of the Lord, or something pertaining to it, might be written there.

Once a brother asked why he so carefully gathered bits of writing, even writings of pagans where the name of the Lord does not appear. He replied: "Son, I do this because they have the letters which make the
Dt 5:11 glorious *name of the Lord God.* And the good that is found there does not belong to the pagans nor to any human being, but to God alone 'to whom belongs every good thing.' "[a]

What is even more amazing is this: when he had letters written as greetings or admonitions he would not allow a single letter or syllable to be erased from them even when they included a repetition or mistake.

83 How handsome,
how splendid!
2 Sm 6:22 How *gloriously he appeared*
in innocence of life,
in simplicity of words,
in purity of heart,
in love of God,
in fraternal charity,
in enthusiastic obedience,
in agreeable compliance,
Jgs 13:6 *in angelic appearance.*

Friendly in behavior,
serene in nature,
affable in speech,
generous in encouragement,
Prv 11:13 *faithful in commitment,*
prudent in advice,
efficient in endeavor,[b]
Est 2:15 he was *gracious in everything!*

Tranquil in mind,
pleasant in disposition,

a. Although the statement is an echo of ER XVII 18, it also resonates with the long-standing tradition of Christian education and the appropriation of pagan language and learning found in the practices of the Middle Ages. This is expressed in Saint Augustine's *On Christian Doctrine* and Hugh of Saint Victor's *Didiscalion.*

b. These two attributes, "*in consiliis providus, in negotiis efficax* [prudent in advice, efficient in endeavor]" are taken from William of Saint Thierry, Arnold of Bonval, Geoffrey of Auxerre, *Vita prima s. Bernardi* III 1,1. In this same passage, William, author of the First Book, also describes, as does Thomas, Bernard's physical appearance and inner strengths. Cf. PL 185: 303.

sober in spirit, 2 Tm 1:7
lifted in contemplation,
tireless in prayer,
he was fervent in everything!

Firm in intention,
consistent in virtue,
persevering in grace,
he was the same in everything!

Swift to forgive, Jas 1:19
slow to grow angry,
free in nature,
remarkable in memory,
subtle in discussing, Wis 7:22; 7:23
careful in choices,
he was simple in everything!

Strict with himself,
kind with others,
he was discerning in everything!

He was very eloquent, with a cheerful appearance and a kind face; free of laziness and arrogance. He was of medium height, closer to short,[a] his head was of medium size and round. His face was somewhat long and drawn, his forehead small and smooth, with medium *eyes* black and *clear.* His hair was dark; his eyebrows were straight, and his nose even and thin; his ears small and upright, and his temples smooth. *His tongue was peaceable,* fiery and sharp; *his voice* was powerful, but *pleasing,* clear, and musical.[b] His teeth were white, well set and even; his lips were small and thin; his beard was black and sparse;[c] his neck was slender, his shoulders straight; his arms were short, his hands slight, his fingers long and his nails tapered. He had thin legs, small feet, fine skin and little flesh.[d] His clothing was rough, his sleep was short, his hand was generous.

Mt 6:22
Prv 15:4
Sg 2:14

a. A similar description can be found of Bernard of Clairvaux, cf. *Vita prima s. Bernardi* III 1,1.

b. The same adjectives are used again in Thomas's description of Francis proclaiming the gospel of the Nativity at Greccio. Cf. n. 86 below.

c. For a similar passage see *Vita prima s. Bernardi* III 1,1.

d. Another passage similar to the *Vita prima s. Bernardi* III 1,1. Although Thomas knew this work, as is obvious from the similar pattern Thomas provides in describing Francis's appearance and inner strengths, a comparison of both texts shows that Thomas portrays Francis differently.

Ti 3:2 Because he was very humble, he showed *meekness to all people,* and duly adapted himself to the behavior of all. Holy among the holy,
Wis 4:10; Gn 3:22 *among sinners he was like one of them.*

Help sinners,
O lover of sinners,
most holy father.
We beg you,
by your glorious prayers,
raise up mercifully
those you see miserable in the filth of misdeeds!

Chapter XXX
THE MANGER HE MADE IN CELEBRATION OF THE LORD'S BIRTHDAY

[84]His highest aim, foremost desire, and greatest intention was
to pay heed to the holy gospel in all things and through all things,
to follow the teaching of our Lord Jesus Christ
and to retrace His footsteps completely
with all vigilance and all zeal,
all the desire of his soul
and all the fervor of his heart.

Francis used to recall with regular meditation the words of Christ
and recollect His deeds with most attentive perception.
Indeed, so thoroughly did the humility of the Incarnation
and the charity of the Passion
occupy his memory
that he scarcely wanted to think of anything else.

We should note then, as matter worthy of memory and something to be recalled with reverence, what he did, three years prior to his death, at the town of Greccio, on the birthday of our Lord Jesus Christ. *There was*
Jb 1:1; Phil 4:8 *a certain man in that area* named John who *had a good reputation* but an even better manner of life. Blessed Francis loved him with special affection, since, despite being a noble in the land and very honored in human society, he had trampled the nobility of the flesh under his feet and pursued instead the nobility of the spirit. As usual, blessed Francis had John summoned to him some fifteen days prior to the birthday of the Lord. "If

you desire to celebrate the coming feast of the Lord together at Greccio," he said to him, "hurry before me and *carefully make ready* the things I tell you. For I wish to enact the memory of that babe *who was born in Bethlehem:* to see as much as is possible with my own bodily eyes the discomfort of his infant needs, how he *lay in a manger,* and how, with an ox and an ass standing by, he rested on hay." Once the good and faithful man had heard Francis's words, *he ran quickly* and prepared in that place all the things that the holy man had requested.[a]

Prv 24:27
Mt 2: 1,2
Lk 2:7
Jn 20:4

[85]Finally, *the day of joy* has drawn near,
the time of exultation *has come.*
From many different places the brethren have been called.
As they could,
the men and women of that land with exultant hearts
prepare candles and torches to light up that night
whose shining star has enlightened every day and year.
Finally, the holy man of God comes
and, finding all things prepared,
he saw them and was glad.
Indeed, the manger is prepared,
the hay is carried in,
and the ox and the ass are led to the spot.
There simplicity is given a place of honor,
poverty is exalted,
humility is commended,
and out of Greccio is made a new Bethlehem.

Tb 13:10; Sg 2:12
Jn 8:56

The night is lit up like day,
delighting both man and beast.
The people arrive, ecstatic at this new mystery of new joy.
The forest amplifies the cries
and the boulders echo back the joyful crowd.
The brothers sing, giving God due praise,
and the whole night abounds with jubilation.
The holy man of God stands before the manger,
filled with heartfelt sighs,

Ps 139:12
Mk 1:24

a. At this point Thomas once again makes an unexpected shift into the present tense, suggesting that what had happened at Greccio had become an annual event. This text could be a description of the ceremony repeated each Christmas at Greccio in memory of Francis's action.

contrite in his piety,
and overcome with wondrous joy.[a]
Over the manger the solemnities of the Mass are celebrated
and the priest enjoys a new consolation.

[86]The holy man of God is dressed in the vestments of the Levites, since he was a Levite, and with full voice sings the holy gospel.[b] Here is
Sg 2:14 his voice: a powerful voice, *a pleasant voice,* a clear voice, a musical voice, inviting all to the highest of gifts. Then he preaches to the people standing around him and pours forth sweet honey about the birth of the poor King and the poor city of Bethlehem. Moreover, burning with excessive love, he often calls Christ the "babe from Bethlehem" whenever he means to call Him Jesus. Saying the word "Bethlehem" in the manner of a bleating sheep, he fills his whole mouth with sound but even more with sweet affection. He seems to lick his lips whenever he uses the expressions "Jesus" or "babe from Bethlehem," tasting the word on his happy palate and savoring the sweetness of the word. The gifts of the Almighty are multiplied there and a virtuous man sees a wondrous vision.[c] For the man saw a little child lying lifeless in the manger and he saw the holy man of God approach the child and waken him from a deep sleep. Nor is this vision unfitting, since in the hearts of
Ps 31:13 many the child Jesus has been *given over to oblivion.* Now he is awakened and impressed on their loving memory by His own grace through His holy servant Francis. At length, the night's solemnities draw to a close and everyone went home with joy.

[87]The hay placed in the manger there was preserved afterwards so that, through it, the Lord might restore to health the pack animals and
Ps 36:7-8 the other *animals* there, as He *multiplied his* holy *mercy.* It came to pass in the surrounding area that many of the animals, suffering from various diseases, were freed from their illnesses when they ate some of this hay. What is more, women who had been suffering with long and hard labor had an easy delivery after they placed some of this hay upon

a. This description of Francis's experience at Greccio is reminiscent of one of Bernard of Clairvaux on Christmas eve. Cf. *Vita secunda s. Bernardi* 2.

b. With this description of Francis in the vestments of a Levite, Thomas is the first to suggest that Francis was a deacon. *Levita* [Levite or deacon] refers to the Old Testament Levite, one set aside for service within the Temple. Thus the text is ambiguous in nature. Later texts, e.g. Julian of Speyer's *The Life of Saint Francis* 55 (hereafter LJS), and Bonaventure's *Major Legend* X, 7 (hereafter LMj) are more precise in identifying Francis as a deacon. How and when he was ordained is not known.

c. This may possibly be John of Greccio himself about whose background nothing is known.

themselves. Finally, an entire group of people of both sexes obtained much-desired relief from an assortment of afflictions.

At last, the site of the manger was consecrated as a temple to the Lord. In honor of the most blessed father Francis, an altar was constructed over the manger, and a church was dedicated.

This was done
so that where animals *once ate the fodder of the hay,* Dn 5:21
there humans henceforth
for healing of body and soul
would eat the flesh
of the immaculate and spotless lamb,
our Lord Jesus Christ,
who *gave Himself for us* Ti 2:14
with supreme and indescribable love,
who lives and rules with the Father and the Holy Spirit as God,
eternally glorious forever and ever.
Amen.
Alleluia, Alleluia.

Here ends the first book of the life and deeds of blessed Francis.

The Second Book

HERE BEGINS THE SECOND BOOK
REGARDING JUST TWO YEARS
OF THE LIFE AND THE HAPPY DEATH OF OUR BLESSED FATHER FRANCIS

Chapter I

[THE CHARACTER OF THIS BOOK, THE TIME WHEN SAINT FRANCIS BLESSEDLY DIED, AND HIS ACHIEVEMENTS][a]

88 In the previous book, which by the Savior's grace we have brought to a fitting conclusion, we have written down the story of the life and deeds of our blessed father Francis up to the eighteenth year of his conversion. In this book, we shall add a brief account of his remaining deeds, beginning with the next to last year of his life, as we have been able to determine them. For now we intend to note only those things that seem more important so that those who wish to say more about them may always find something to add.

For in the one thousandth, two hundredth, and twenty-sixth year
of the Incarnation of the Lord,
in the fourteenth year of the indiction,[b]
on the fourth day before the Nones of October,[c]
a Sunday,
our most blessed father Francis
departed from the prison of the flesh
and soared to the dwellings of the heavenly spirits.
This happened in the city of Assisi where he was born
at Saint Mary of the Portiuncula
where he first planted the Order of Lesser Brothers,

a. In a number of manuscripts this explanatory heading is missing.

b. An indiction was a recurring cycle of fifteen years and was spoken of as "a cycle of indiction." The number attached to it indicated the specific year within the cycle, as in this instance, the 14th year within the indiction. Thomas follows the Roman or Papal indiction according to which an indiction is determined by adding 3 to the year in question, that is, 1226 plus 3. The sum is then divided by 15. The number of the indiction, then, was 82 and within that 82nd cycle, it was the 14th year.

c. Nones was the ninth day before the Ides, hence the fifth day of every month except for March, May, July and October, when it was the seventh; in this case, then, the fourth day before the Nones would be October 4. Since each day began at sunset, our modern calendar would consider it October 3.

twenty years after he embraced Christ completely
following the life and *footsteps* of the Apostles, 1 Pt 2:21
bringing to perfect completion what he had begun.
In that city,
with hymns and praises,
his holy and sacred body was laid to rest
and honorably enclosed.
There it glitters
with many miracles
to the glory of the Almighty.
Amen.

89 From the first flower of his youth, he was given little or no instruction *in the way of God* or knowledge of Him. He remained for quite some time in natural simplicity and the heat of vices. By the *change* brought about in him by the power of *the right hand of the Most High he was justified from sin.* And by the grace and *power of the Most High* he was filled with divine *wisdom* beyond all others of his time. As the teachings of the gospel had declined seriously in practice—not just in some cases but in general everywhere—*this man was sent* from God so that everywhere, throughout the whole world, after the example of the Apostles, *he might bear witness to the truth.* And so it was, *with the Christ leading,* that his teaching showed clearly that all *the wisdom of the world* was *foolish,* and quickly, he turned all toward the true *wisdom of God through the foolishness of his preaching.*

Bar 3:13; Rom 6:7; Lk 1:35; Dt 34: 9; Jn 1:6:7; Dn 9:25; 1 Cor 1: 21

In these last times, 1 Pt 1:5
a new Evangelist,
like one of the rivers of Paradise, Gn 2:10
has poured out Is 44:3
the streams of the gospel
in a holy flood over the whole world.[a] Est 13:4
He preached the way of the Son of God
and the teaching of truth in his deeds.
In him and through him

a. These passages are indicative of the renewal theme in Thomas's portrait. In addition to repeating the theme of newness (cf. 196, c), Thomas now introduces an apocalyptic tone by referring to "these last times" and to many prophetic themes. The inspiration for these passages may come from Pope Gregory IX's *Mira circa nos*, the papal decree of canonization, in which Francis is portrayed as God's instrument "at the eleventh hour." Cf. infra pp. 565 -569.

an unexpected joy and a holy newness
came into the world.
A shoot of the ancient religion
suddenly renewed the old and decrepit.
A new spirit was placed in the hearts of the elect
Ez 11:19; 36:26 and a holy anointing *has been poured out in* their *midst.*
Gal 1:1:0 This holy *servant of Christ,*
Gn 1:14 like one of the *lights of heaven,*
shone from above with a new rite and new signs.
The ancient miracles have been renewed through him.
In the desert of this world
a fruitful vine has been planted
in a new Order but in an ancient way,
bearing *flowers, sweet*
Sir 24:23; Ps 52:10 with the *fragrance* of holy virtues
Ez 17:6,7 and *stretching out* everywhere *branches* of holy religion.

Jas 5:17 90 Although *like us, subject to suffering,* he was not satisfied with observing the ordinary precepts. Rather, overflowing with burning charity, he set out on the way of full perfection, reached out for the peak
Ps 119:96 of perfect holiness, and *saw the goal of all perfection.* That is why every order, sex, and age finds in him a clear pattern of the teaching of salvation and an outstanding example of holy deeds. If people intend to
Prv 31:19; 1 Cor 12:31 put *their hand to difficult things,* and strive *to seek the higher gifts* of a more excellent way, let them look into the mirror of his life, and learn all perfection.[a] There are some who tend to lower, more level paths, fearing to walk the steep route and climb to the summit of the mountain: they too shall find in him suitable reminders. Finally, those who
1 Cor 1:22 *seek signs* and miracles, let them ask his holiness, and they will receive what they request.

Yes, his glorious life reveals in even brighter light
the perfection of earlier saints;
the passion of Jesus Christ proves this,
and His cross shows it clearly.
For the venerable father was in fact marked in five parts of his body
with the marks of the passion and the cross,

a. In this passage Francis is proposed for the first time as a mirror for those seeking perfection, an image that develops in importance in subsequent Franciscan literature.

as if he had hung on the cross with the Son of God.
This is a great sacrament, Eph 5:32
and evidence of the grandeur of a special love.
But there is hidden here some secret;
here is concealed some awesome mystery,
one we believe is known to God alone,
though it was partly revealed by the Saint to one person.
For this reason it is useless to try to praise him,
whose praise is from the One Who is
the praise of all, their origin and greatest honor,
the giver of the gifts of light.
Now *blessing God, holy, glorious,* and true, Lk 24:53; Is 58:13
let us return to our story.

Chapter II
THE HIGHEST DESIRE OF BLESSED FRANCIS AND HOW IN OPENING THE BOOK HE UNDERSTOOD THE LORD'S WILL FOR HIM

[91]At one time the blessed and venerable father Francis, with worldly crowds gathering eagerly every day to hear and see him, sought out a place of rest and secret solitude. He desired to free himself for God and *shake off any dust that clung to him* from the time spent (Lk 10:11) with the crowds.[a] It was his custom to divide the time given him to merit grace and, as seemed best, to spend some of it to benefit his neighbors and use the rest in the blessed solitude of contemplation. *He took with him* only a few companions—who knew his holy way of living better than others—so that they could shield him *from the interruption and disturbance of people,* respecting and protecting his silence in every way. (Lk 9:28; Mk 14:33; Ps 91:6; 30:21)

After he had been there for some time, through unceasing prayer and frequent contemplation, he reached intimacy with God in an indescribable way. He longed to know what in him and about him was or could be most acceptable to the *Eternal King.* He sought this diligently and devoutly longed to know in what manner, in what way, and with what desire he would be able to cling more perfectly to the *Lord God,* according to His *counsel* and the *good pleasure* of His will. This was (Ps 29:10; Ps 73:28; Sir 40:25)

a. Cf. Gregory the Great, *Diaolgues*, Prologue (PL 77:152A).

always his highest philosophy; this was the highest *desire* that always
Nm 11:4 *burned* in him as long as he lived. He asked the simple and the wise, the
Ps 119:30 perfect and the imperfect, how he could reach the *way of truth* and ar-
rive at his great goal.

92 Since he was the most perfect among the perfect, he refused to
think he was perfect and thought himself wholly imperfect. He could
Ps 34:9 *taste and see* how pleasing, *sweet and good* the God of Israel is to those
Ps 73:1 who are of sincere heart and who *seek Him* in true purity and *in* pure
Wis 1:1 *simplicity.*

He felt pouring down on him from above a sweetness and delight
rarely given to even a few, and it made him lose himself completely. He 1C 26
was filled with such joy that he wished by any means to pass over entirely to that place where, in passing out of himself, he had already par-
1 Cor 7:40 tially gone. This man, having *the spirit of God,* was ready to endure any
suffering of mind and bear any affliction of the body, if at last he *would*
Jos 24:15 *be given the choice* that the *will of the heavenly Father* might be *ful-*
Mt 6:14 *filled* mercifully in him. So one day he approached the sacred altar
which had been built in the hermitage where he was staying and, taking
up the volume where the holy Gospels were written, he placed it reverently upon the altar.

Then he prostrated himself with his heart as much as his body *in*
Lk 6:12; Jl 2:13 *prayer to God,* asking in humble prayer that *God in His kindness—the*
2 Cor 1:3 *Father of mercies and the God of all consolation*—be pleased to show
him His will. He prayed earnestly that at the first opening of the book
he would be shown what was best for him to do, so that he could bring
to complete fulfillment what he had earlier simply and devotedly begun. In this he was led by the spirit of the saints and holy ones, as we
read they did something similar with sincere devotion in their desire
for holiness.[a]

Lk 22:45; Dn 3:39 93 *Rising from prayer in a spirit of humility and with a contrite heart,*
he prepared himself with the sign of the holy cross. He took the book
from the altar, and *opened it with reverence* and fear. *When he opened*
Rv 5:7; 5:8 *the book,* the first passage that met his eye was the passion of our Lord
Jesus Christ that tells of the suffering he was to endure. To avoid any
suspicion that this was just a coincidence, he opened the book a second
and a third time. Every time he found either the same text or one that

a. This approach to the Scriptural text has its roots in Saint Augustine. Cf. *The Confessions* VIII, 12, 29: "For on leaving it I had put down there the book of the apostle's letters. I snatched it up, opened it and read in silence the passage on which my eyes first lighted."

was similar. This *man filled with the spirit of God* then understood that he would *have to enter into the kingdom of God through many trials,* difficulties and struggles. Gn 41:38 Acts 14:21

The brave soldier *was not disturbed by oncoming battles,* nor was he downcast in his spirit as he was about to *fight the wars of the Lord* in the camps of this world. Eccl 8:8 1 Sm 25:28

He was not afraid that he would yield to the enemy
since he had long struggled beyond human strength
not even to give in to himself.
He was so filled with fire that,
even if in preceding ages
there had been someone with a purpose equal to his,
no one has been found whose desire was greater than his.
He found it easier to do what is perfect
than to talk about it;
so he was constantly active
in showing his zeal and dedication in deeds, not in words,
because words do not do what is good,
they only point to it.
Thus he remained undisturbed and happy,
singing *songs of joy in his heart* to himself and to God. Eph 5:19
For this reason he was found worthy of a greater revelation,
since he rejoiced over a small one;
faithful in a small thing, Lk 19:17
he was placed over greater ones. Mt 25:21

Chapter III

THE VISION OF A MAN HAVING THE IMAGE OF A CRUCIFIED SERAPH

94While he was staying in that hermitage called La Verna, after the place where it is located, two years prior to the time that he returned his soul to heaven, he saw *in the vision of God* a man, *having six wings like a Seraph, standing over* him, *arms extended and feet joined,* affixed to a cross. *Two of his wings* were raised up, *two were stretched out over his head as if for flight,* and *two covered his* whole *body.* When the blessed servant of the most High saw these things, he was filled with the greatest awe, but could not decide what this vision meant for him. Moreover, he greatly rejoiced and was much delighted by the kind and Ez 1:1; 8:1 Is 6:2

gracious look that he saw the Seraph gave him.[a] The Seraph's beauty was beyond comprehension, but the fact that the Seraph was fixed to the cross and the bitter suffering of that passion thoroughly frightened him. Consequently, he got up both sad and happy as joy and sorrow took their turns in his heart. Concerned over the matter, he kept think-
Ps 143:4 ing about what this vision could mean and his *spirit was anxious* to discern a sensible meaning from the vision.

While he was unable to perceive anything clearly understandable from the vision, its newness very much pressed upon his heart. Signs of the nails began to appear on his hands and feet, just as he had seen them a little while earlier on the crucified man hovering over him.

95 His hands and feet seemed to be pierced through the middle by nails, with the heads of the nails appearing on the inner part of his hands and on the upper part of his feet, and their points protruding on opposite sides. Those marks on the inside of his hands were round, but rather oblong on the outside; and small pieces of flesh were visible like the points of nails, bent over and flattened, extending beyond the flesh around them. On his feet, the marks of nails were stamped in the same way and raised above the surrounding flesh. His right side was marked with an oblong scar, as if pierced with a lance, and this often dripped blood, so that his tunic and undergarments were frequently stained with his holy blood.[b]

Sadly, only a few merited seeing the sacred wound in his side during the life of the crucified servant of the crucified Lord. Elias was fortunate and did merit somehow to see the wound in his side.[c] Rufino was
1 Jn 1:1 just as lucky: he *touched it with his own hands*. For one time, when the same brother Rufino put his hand onto the holy man's chest to rub him,

---

a. The "seraph" or "seraphim" belong to the highest choir of angels. These angels, most intimately present to God, are found in the biblical tradition, especially in visions of God. Cf. Is 6:1-13; Ez 1:5-14, 1:22-25; and Rv 4:6-9.

b. For extensive study on the stigmata see Octavian Schmucki, *The Stigmata of Saint Francis of Assisi: A Critical Investigation in the Light of Thirteenth-Century Sources*. Translated by Canisius Connors. (St. Bonaventure, NY: The Franciscan Institute, 1991).

c. In Book Two, Thomas gives importance to Elias Buonbarone (+1253), who was born in either Assisi or in Cortona. Shortly after the first missionary Chapter in 1217, Elias departed for the Holy Land to serve as Minister for the new venture. Later, during his own 1219-1220 visit in the East, Francis met Elias and brought him back to Italy. In 1221, after the death of his first vicar, Francis appointed Elias. Elias presided at the Chapter of Mats in 1221, which furthered the missionary activity of the Order into Germany. After Francis's death, the Pentecost Chapter of 1227 elected John Parenti, Minister from Spain, to be the Minister General. Elias was engaged by Gregory IX to oversee the building of a new basilica in honor of the new saint. In 1232, Elias was elected to succeed John Parenti. During his tenure as Minister General, Elias promoted theological studies and missionary expansion into Asia and Africa. In 1239, the brothers, distressed by his abuse of authority and his autocratic use of visitators, requested Pope Gregory IX to depose Elias from his office. After he was removed, Elias sided with the Emperor Frederick II in his political dispute with Gregory IX. Gregory IX excommunicated him. Elias died reconciled and absolved in Cortona on April 22, 1253.

his hand slipped, as often happens, and it chanced that he touched the
precious scar in his right side. As soon as he had touched it, the holy
one of God felt great pain and pushed Rufino's hand away, crying out
for the Lord to spare him. Gn 19:16

He hid those marks carefully from strangers, and concealed them
cautiously from people close to him, so that even the brothers at his side
and his most devoted followers for a long time did not know about them.

Although the servant and friend of the Most High saw himself
adorned with such magnificent pearls, like *precious stones,* and mar- 2 Chr 9:9
velously decorated *beyond the glory and honor of all others,* still his Sir 3:19; Ps 8:6
heart did not grow vain. *He did* not *seek* to use this to *make himself ap-*
pealing to anyone in a desire for vainglory. Rather in every way possi- Gal 1:10
ble he tried to hide these marks, so that human favor would not *rob him*
of the grace *given* him. Mt 6:18; 6:19

[96]He would never or rarely reveal his great secret to anyone. He
feared that his special friends would reveal it to show their intimacy
with him, as friends often do, and he would then lose some of *the grace*
given to him. He always carried in his heart and often had on his lips the Rom 12:3; 2 Cor 7:9
saying of the prophet: *"I have hidden your words in my heart to avoid*
any sin against You." Ps 119:11

Whenever some people of the world approached him and he did not
wish to speak with them, he would give this sign to the brothers and
sons staying with him: if he recited the verse mentioned above, immediately they would dismiss politely those who had gathered to see him.
He had learned through experience that one cannot be a spiritual person unless one's secrets are deeper and more numerous than *what can*
be seen on the face and by their appearance can be judged in different 2 Cor 10:7
ways by different people. For he had met some people who agreed with
him outwardly but inwardly disagreed, applauding him to his face but
laughing behind his back. These brought *judgment upon themselves* 1 Cor 11:29
and made honest people seem somewhat suspect to him.

So it is that malice often attempts to smear sincerity
and because of the lies of many,
the truth of the few *is not believed.* 2 Thes 2:11

Chapter IV
THE FERVOR OF BLESSED FRANCIS AND THE DISEASE OF HIS EYES

[97]During this same period his body began to be afflicted with different kinds of illness, and more severe than usual. Since he had *over many*
Rom 15:23; 1 Cor 9:27 *years chastised his body and brought it into subjection,* he suffered infirmities often. During the course of the eighteen years which by then had
2 Cor 7:5 passed, his *flesh* rarely or never *had any rest,* as he traveled through
Gn 41:46 many *distant regions,* so that the *willing spirit,* the devout spirit, and the
Acts 18:25; Rom 8:11 *fervent spirit which dwelt within him* might scatter everywhere the *seed*
Lk 8:11 Mt 26:41; Wis 1:7 *of the word of God. He filled the* whole *world* with the gospel of Christ;
Mk 6:6 in the course of one day often *visiting* four or five *towns and villages,*
Lk 8:1 proclaiming to every one the *good news of the kingdom of God,* edifying his listeners by his example as much as by his words, as he made of his whole body a tongue.

There was in him such harmony of flesh with spirit
and such obedience that,
as the spirit strove to reach all holiness,
the flesh did not resist
but even tried to run on ahead,
according to the saying:
For you my soul has thirsted;
Ps 63:2 *and my flesh in so many ways!*
Repeated submission became spontaneous,
as the flesh, yielding each day,
reached a place of great virtue,
for habit often becomes nature.[a]

[98]According to the laws of nature and the human condition *day by*
2 Cor 4:16 *day* the body must *decay* though *the inner being is renewed.* So the pre-
Mt 13:44 cious *vessel* in which the heavenly *treasure was hidden* began to shatter all over and lose all its strength. Yet *when a man has finished, then*
Sir 18:6 *he will begin* and when he has finished, then he will start to work. And
Mt 26:41 so the *spirit* became *willing* in the *flesh that was weak.* He so desired the salvation of souls and longed to benefit his neighbors that, even

a. Cf. n. 4 above; Augustine, *Treatise on John's gospel,* Tract 44 n. 1 (PL 35, 1744); Cicero, *De Finibus bonorum* V 25 74; Macrobius, *Saturnalia* VII 9 7. The passage also appears in *Vita prima s. Bernardi* IV 20 and Alan, Bishop of Auxerre, *Vita secunda s. Bernardi* IV 16 [PL 185, 238, 479].

though he could no longer walk on his own, *he went through the towns* riding on a little donkey. Lk 9:6

The brothers often advised him, urging him to give some relief to his frail and weakened body through the help of doctors. But he absolutely refused to do this. His noble spirit was aimed at heaven and he only *desired* to be set free and *to be with Christ.* But he had not yet *filled* Phil 1:23
up in his *flesh what is lacking in the sufferings of Christ,* even though *he* Col 1:24
bore the marks on his *body.* So *God multiplied* his *mercy* on him, and Gal 6:17; Ps 36:8
he contracted a serious disease of the eyes.[a] Day after day the disease grew worse and seemed to be aggravated daily from lack of treatment. Brother Elias, the one he chose for the role of mother to himself and had made a father of the other brothers,[b] finally forced him not to refuse medicine but to accept it *in the name of the Son of God.* Through Him it 1 Jn 5:13
was created, as it is written: *The Most High created* medicine *from the earth and the wise will not refuse it.* The holy father then gladly agreed Sir 38:4
with him and humbly accepted his direction.

Chapter V
How he was received at the city of Rieti by the Lord Hugolino, Bishop of Ostia, and how the holy man declared that he would be bishop of the whole world

[99]Many came with their medicines to help him but no remedy could be found. So he went to the city of Rieti where a man was staying who was said to be the greatest expert in curing that disease. When he arrived there he was received kindly and respectfully by the whole Roman Curia, which was then staying in that city. He was especially well received by Lord Hugolino, the bishop of Ostia, who was renowned for his upright conduct and holy life.

Blessed Francis, with the consent and approval of the Lord Pope Honorius, chose this man as father and lord over the whole religion and order of his brothers because blessed poverty greatly pleased him and holy simplicity received his greatest reverence.

a. The disease has been diagnosed as ophthalmia, a severe inflammation of the eyeball or the mucous membrane lining the inner surface of the eyelids and covering the front part of the eyeball.

b. Placing Elias in the role of "mother" is consistent with Francis's understanding of the way in which each of the brothers should "love and care" for one another, cf. ER IX 11; LR VI 8; RH 1, 2, 10.

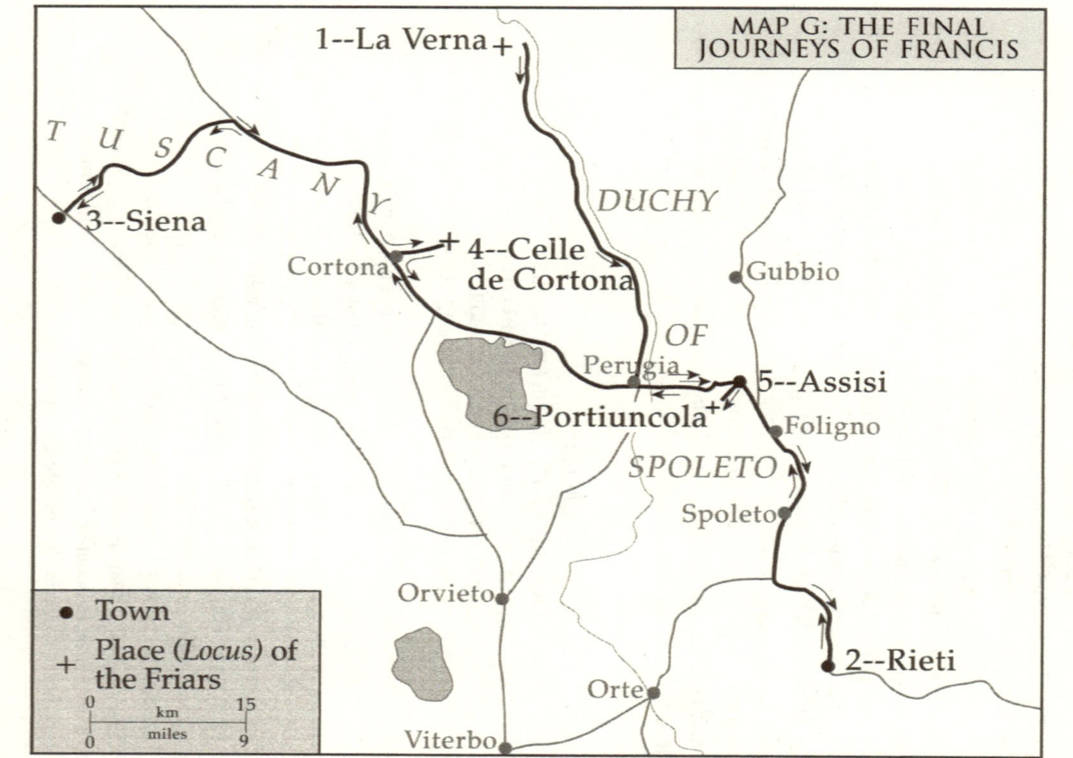

1C 99-108 relate that at the end of his life Francis travelled through Tuscany and the Duchy of Spoleto. After receiving the stigmata on Mt. LaVerna (1), Francis travelled to several places in the region: to Rieti (2), then north and west to Siena (3), then back to Celle de Cortona (4), on to Assisi (5), and finally to the Portiuncula (6).

That lord conformed himself to the ways of the brothers.
In his desire for holiness
he was simple with the simple,
humble with the humble,
and poor with the poor.
He was a brother among brothers,
the least among the lesser,[a]
and in his life and habits strove to behave
as one of them
as much as was possible.

He took care to plant this holy religion everywhere
and in faraway places his glowing reputation,
from an even more glowing life,
helped greatly to spread the Order.
The Lord *gave* him *a learned tongue.* Is 50:4
With it he confounded the opponents of truth,
refuted *the enemies of the cross of Christ,* Phil 3:18
led the strangers back to the way, Dt 22:1
made peace between those in conflict,
and bound together those in peace
in a stronger *bond of love.* Hos 11:4
In the Church of God
he *was a lamp burning and shining,* Jn 5:35
a *chosen arrow* Is 49:2
ready *at the right time.* Ps 32:6
Many times he took off his fine clothes
and, dressed in rough garments
and with bare feet,
like one of the brothers,
he went *asking for terms of peace.* Lk 14:32
He used to do this with great care whenever necessary
between neighbor and neighbor, Jer 7:5
and always between God and the people.
For this reason
God *chose him* Sir 45:4

a. The phrase "the least among the lesser" is a play on words since the comparative form of the adjective "*minores*" is also used as a noun to designate the followers of Francis. The idea here is that the bishop was more a lesser brother than the other brothers.

Acts 5:11 to be the pastor *of all His* holy *church*
Ps 110:7; Rv 13:7 and *lifted up his head among the tribes of the people.*

[100]The blessed father Francis foretold this in words and foreshad-
2 Tm 3:16 owed it in action so that it would be recognized as *inspired by God* and
done by the will of Christ Jesus. It happened in this way. The Order and
religion of the brothers had begun to spread by the grace of God. Like a
Ez 31:8; Ps 110:3 *cedar in the garden of God* it lifted its crown of merit *into the heavens,*
Jer 2:21 and like *a chosen vineyard* it stretched out its holy *branches to the ends*
Ps 80:12; 18:20 *of the earth.*[a]

At that time Saint Francis approached the lord Pope Honorius, who was then at the head of the Roman Church, humbly asking him to appoint the lord Hugolino, bishop of Ostia, as father and lord for him and his brothers. The lord Pope bowed to the holy man's request, and kindly agreeing, entrusted to the bishop his authority over the Order of the brothers. Like *a prudent and faithful servant set over the family* of the
Lord, the bishop accepted it reverently and devoutly. He strove in every
Mt 24:45; Ps 145:15 way to administer the *food* of eternal life *in due season* to those entrusted
to him. The holy father for this reason subjected himself to him in every
way and venerated him with wonderful and reverent affection.

Mt 4:1 Blessed Francis was *led by the Spirit* of God with which *he was*
Acts 13:9 *filled.* Therefore he saw long before what was later to appear *in the*
Is 52:10 *sight of all.* For whenever he wanted to write to him, impelled by the
needs of the Order they both served, or, more often, moved *by the love*
2 Cor 5:14 *of Christ* which he felt so strongly toward him, he would never allow
him to be called in his letters "Bishop of Ostia and Velletri" as others did in customary greetings. Instead, taking up the topic, he used to say; "To the Most Reverend Father, Lord Hugolino, Bishop of the Whole World."

Often he would greet him with unheard-of blessings, and although he was a son in his loyal submission, he would sometimes console him with a fatherly word at the prompting of the Spirit so that he could *strengthen* him *with the blessings of the fathers until the desire of the*
Gn 49:26 *everlasting hills should come.*

[101]That same lord also felt great love for the holy man and therefore was pleased with whatever the blessed man did or said, and was deeply moved at the mere sight of him. He swears that no matter how dis-

a. In order to experience the fullness of affective, poetic and religious power conveyed by a simple biblical allusion, see the beautiful allegory of the cedar, (Ez 31:9) to which Thomas alludes here.

turbed or troubled he became, when he saw or talked to Saint Francis the clouds inside him would break up and clear weather would return; his depression would vanish and joy would pour down over him.

This man *ministered* to blessed Francis, *as a servant to his lord,* and, Lk 12:37
whenever he saw him, he offered the reverence due to *an apostle of Christ.* Bowing before him both outwardly and inwardly, he would of- 1 Cor 1:1
ten kiss his hand with his consecrated lips.

With devotion and care, he tried to find a way for the blessed father
to regain the earlier health of his eyes, knowing he was *a holy and just* Acts 3:14
man, *very much* needed and useful to the Church of God. He shared in Neh 2:2
worrying about him with the whole assembly of the brothers, *pitying the sons* because *of their father.* Then he advised the holy father to take Ps 103:13
care of himself and not to refuse the things needed to treat his illness, because neglecting them would not be considered praiseworthy but sinful. Saint Francis humbly observed what such a revered lord and a beloved father told him. From then on he more carefully and freely did what was needed for his treatment. But now the illness had grown so bad that any relief at all required the greatest expertise and demanded the most bitter medicine. This is what was done: his head was cauterized in several places, his veins opened, poultices applied, and drops poured into his eyes. Yet *he had no improvement but kept getting* Ps 89:23
steadily worse. Mk 5:26

Chapter VI
THE CONDUCT OF THE BROTHERS ATTENDING SAINT FRANCIS AND THE WAY HE DECIDED TO LIVE

102 For nearly two years he endured these things
with complete patience and humility,
in all things giving thanks to God. Tb 2.14, 1 Thes 5.18
But in order to be able
to devote his attention to God more freely,
he entrusted his own care to certain brothers,
who with good reason were very dear to him.
Thus he could more freely explore in frequent *ecstasy of Spirit* 2 Cor 5:13
the blessed dwelling places of heaven,
and, in the abundance of grace,
stand *in heavenly places* Eph 1:3
before the gentle and serene *Lord of all things.* 2 Mc 14:35

1 Mc 5:50 These brothers were *men of virtue,* devoted to God,
pleasing to the saints, and well-liked by people.
The blessed Father Francis *rested* upon them
Jgs 16:29 as a *house* upon four *pillars.*[a]
I omit their names for the present, out of regard for modesty,
which is a close friend of these spiritual men.
Modesty is the beauty of all ages,
a witness of innocence,
the sign of a pure mind,
Prv 22:15 *the rod of correction,*
the special glory of conscience,
the protector of reputation,
and the mark of thorough integrity.

This virtue graced those men and made them loveable and kind to
Acts 2:44 people. This grace *they all held in common*, but a particular virtue also adorned each one. One had outstanding discernment, another had extraordinary patience, one was famous for his simplicity, and the last had great physical strength along with gentleness of spirit. These men vigilantly, zealously, and eagerly protected the peace of mind of the blessed father, cared for him in his illness, and spared no pain or labor in offering themselves completely to the saint's service.

Jn 11:9 [103]In the sight of God and the people *of this world*
the glorious father had been made perfect in grace.
In all that he did he glowed brilliantly,
yet he always kept thinking
about how to undertake even more perfect deeds.
Gn 32:2 Like a soldier, well-trained in *the battle camps of God,*
challenging the enemy,
he wanted to stir up fresh battles.
Dn 9:25 With *the Christ as leader,* 1C 7
he resolved "to do great deeds,"
and with weakening limbs and dying body,
he hoped for victory over the enemy in a new struggle.

a. The four pillars refer to the four brothers who nursed Francis. Traditionally, these brothers are identified as Angelo Tancredi, Rufino, Leo, and either Bernard or John.

True bravery knows no real limits of time,
for its hope of reward is eternal.

He burned with a great desire to return to his earliest steps toward humility; *rejoicing in hope* because of his boundless love, he planned to call his body back to its original servitude, although it had now reached its limit. He cut away completely the obstacle of all cares and silenced the noise of all concerns. When he had to relax this rigor because of illness, he used to say: "Let us begin, brothers, to serve the Lord God, for up until now we have done little or nothing." *He did not consider that he had already attained* his goal, but tireless in pursuit of holy newness, he constantly hoped to begin again.

Nm 11:4; Mt 2:10

Rom 12:12

Phil 3:13

He wanted to return to serving lepers
and to be held in contempt, just as he used to be.
He intended to flee human company
and go off to the most remote places,
so that,
letting go of every care
and putting aside anxiety about others,
for the time being
only the wall of the flesh would stand between him and God.[a]

104 He saw many rushing for positions of authority. Despising their arrogance, he strove by his own example to call them back from such sickness. Indeed, he used to say that it was a good and acceptable thing in God's sight to take care of others. He held it was appropriate for some to take on the care of souls as long as in this *they sought* nothing *of their own will,* but in all things constantly obeyed God's will. Such people should consider in the first place their own salvation and aim for the growth of their subjects, not their applause. They should seek *glory* before *God,* not honor from people, never desiring but fearing the office of prelate. If given to them it would humble them, not exalt them; were it taken away, it would not leave them dejected, but uplifted.

Phil 2:21

Rom 4:2

Adm IV; ER XVII

He maintained it was dangerous to direct others and better to be directed, especially in these times when malice is *growing so much* and wickedness *is increasing.* It hurt him that some had abandoned their

2 Thes 1:3

a. This passage is reminiscent of the vocabulary of monasticism which viewed the practice of prayer and asceticism in terms of the angelic life, that is, in terms of sharing in the angelic ministry of adoration and of serving those in need of God's mercy. Cf. 1C 15.

Rv 2:5 *early deeds* and, in the midst of new discoveries, had forgotten their original simplicity. That is why he grieved over those who now sank to the level of what was low and cheap, although they once had striven for higher things with all their desire. They had abandoned true joy and were running here and there, wandering through the fields of an empty freedom. So he prayed for God's mercy to set his sons free and fer-
Rom 12:3 vently begged that they be preserved in the *grace given to them.*

Chapter VII
How he came to Assisi from Siena and concerning the Church of Saint Mary of the Portiuncula and the blessing of the brothers

105 Six months before the day of his death, he was staying in Siena for treatment of his eye disease. But then all the rest of his body started to show signs of serious illness. His stomach had been destroyed, and his liver was failing. He was vomiting a lot of blood, so much that he seemed close to death. On hearing of this in a place far away, brother Elias rushed to his side. At his arrival the holy father had recovered so much that they left that area and went together to Le Celle near
Mt 25:5 Cortona.[a] After reaching the place he *stayed for a while,* but then the swelling began in his abdomen, his legs, and his feet. His stomach became so weak that he could hardly eat any food at all. At that point, he asked brother Elias to have him carried to Assisi. The good son did what the kind father commanded and, when everything was ready, led
Est 8:15; 2 Cor 7:6 him to the place he longed for. *The city rejoiced at the arrival* of the
Dn 3:51 blessed father and all the people with one voice *praised God,* since *the*
Lk 1:10; Mk 1:24 *whole multitude of the people* hoped that *the holy one of God* would die close to them, and this was the reason for such great rejoicing.

Jb 26:11 106 And so it was also the *will of God*
that his holy soul, freed from the flesh,
Mt 3:2 would pass over to *the kingdom of heaven*
from that place
Phil 1:24 where, while *still living in the flesh,*
he had first been given the knowledge of higher things
and had the oil of salvation poured out upon him.

a. Francis first came to "Le Celle" of Cortona in 1211. At that time it was probably the site of some small buildings [*celle*], most likely mills harnessing the stream of water that flows beside them.

He knew that the *kingdom of heaven* Mt 5:3
was established in every *corner of the earth* Ez. 34:13
and he believed that divine grace was given
to God's chosen ones in every place. Rom 8:33
Yet he knew from his own experience
that the place of the church of Saint Mary of the Portiuncula
was especially full of grace
and filled with visits of heavenly spirits.
So he often told the brothers:
"See to it, my sons, that you never abandon this place.
If you are driven out from one side,
go back in from the other,
for this *is truly a holy place* Ez 42:13
and *the dwelling place of God.* 1 Chr 29:1
Here the Most High increased our numbers
when we were only a few; 1 Chr 16:19
here He *enlightened the hearts* of his poor ones Eph 1:18
with the light of His wisdom;
here He kindled our wills with the fire of His love;
here all who pray wholeheartedly will receive what they ask,
while offenders will be severely punished.
Therefore, my sons, hold this place, *God's dwelling,* 1 Kgs 8:30; 8:33
as worthy of all honor
and *here praise God* Jer 29:13
in cries of joy and praise Ps 42:5
with your whole heart." Jer 29:13

[107]As his illness grew worse, he lost all bodily strength, and deprived of all his powers, he could not even move. One of the brothers asked him what he would prefer to endure: this long-lasting illness or suffering a martyr's cruel death at the hands of an executioner. "My son," he replied, "whatever is *more pleasing to the Lord my God* to do (Dt 13:18; Rom 12:1) with me and in me has always been and still is dearer, sweeter, and more agreeable to me. I desire to be found always and completely in harmony with and obedient to God's will alone in everything. But to suffer this illness, even for three days, would be harder for me than any martyrdom. I am not speaking about its reward but only of the *pain* and suffering *it causes.*" Dn 3:50

O martyr,
martyr laughing and rejoicing,
who endured so gladly
what was bitter and painful
for others to see!

Not one of his members remained without great pain and suffering;
his bodily warmth gradually diminished, and each day he drew closer
to his end. The doctors were amazed and the brothers were astonished
that the spirit could live in flesh so dead, since with *his flesh all con-*
Jb 19:20 *sumed* only skin *clung to his bones.*

108 When he saw his final day drawing near,
as shown to him two years earlier by divine revelation,
Mk 3:13 he *called to him* the brothers he *chose.*
Jn 19:11 He blessed each one as it was *given* to him *from above,*
just as Jacob of old, the patriarch, blessed his sons.
He was like another Moses
about *to ascend the mountain*
Dt 32:49 *that the Lord had shown* him,
when imparting blessings on the children of Israel.

When brother Elias sat down on his left side with the other brothers
around him, the blessed father crossed his arms and *placed his right*
Gn 48:14 *hand on* Elias' *head.* He had lost the sight and use of his bodily eyes, so
he asked: "Over whom am I holding my right hand?" "Over brother
Elias," they replied. "And this is what I wish to do," he said, "I bless
Eph 4:6 you, my son, *in all and through all,* and just as the most High has increased my brothers and sons in your hands, so too, upon you and in
you, I bless them all. May the king of all *bless you in heaven and on*
Ps 113:6; Tb 9:9 *earth.* I bless you as I can, and more than I can, and what I cannot do
Dn 14:37 may the One who can do all things do in you. *May God remember* your
work and labors, and may a place be reserved for you among *the re-*
Heb 2:2 *wards of the just.* May you receive every blessing you desire and may
your every worthy request be fulfilled."

Eccl 9:22 "Good-bye, all my sons. Live *in the fear of God* and remain in Him
Sir 27:6; Ps 22:12 always, for a great *test* will come upon you and tribulation is drawing
Mt 10:22 near! Happy are those *who will persevere* in what they have begun:
many will be separated from them by the scandals that are to come. But

now I am hurrying to the Lord *and I am confident that I am going to my God whom I have served in my spirit."* Ps 30:9; Rom 1:19

He was staying then in the palace of the bishop of Assisi, and he asked the brothers to carry him quickly to the place of Saint Mary of the
1C 88,106 Portiuncula. For he wanted to give back his soul to God in that place where, as noted above, he first came to know perfectly *the way of truth.* Ps 19:30

Chapter VIII
WHAT HE DID AND SAID AT HIS BLESSED DEATH

109 Twenty years had now passed since his conversion, and his time was ending just as it had been shown to him by God's will. For, once the blessed father and brother Elias were staying at Foligno, and one night while they were sleeping, a priest of venerable appearance and great age dressed in white clothing appeared to brother Elias. "Get up, brother," he said, "and tell brother Francis that eighteen years have passed since he renounced the world and clung to Christ. He will remain in this life only two more years; then he will go *the way of all flesh when the Lord calls* Jos 23:14; Gn 3:9
him to Himself." So it came to pass that, at the established time, the *word of the Lord* spoken long before now *was fulfilled.* 2 Chr 36:21

After he had rested a few days in that place he so longed for, knowing *the time* of his death *was close at hand,* he called to him two broth- Heb 9:9
ers, his special sons, and told them to sing *The Praises of the Lord* with a loud voice and joyful spirit, rejoicing at his approaching death, or rather at the life that was so near.[a] He himself, as best he could, broke into that psalm of David: *"With a loud voice I cried to the Lord; with a loud voice I beseeched the Lord."* Ps 142:2-8

There was a brother there whom the holy man loved with great affection. Seeing what was happening and realizing the saint was nearing the end, he grew very concerned about all the brothers and said: "Oh, kind father, your sons will now be *without a father,* and will be de- Lam 5:3
prived *of the true light* of their eyes! Remember the orphans you are 1 Jn 2:8
leaving behind;[b] forgive all their faults, and gladden them all, whether present or absent, with your holy blessing." The holy man answered: "See, my son, I am being called by God. I forgive all my brothers, pres-

a. This refers to the CtC to which Francis added, on his deathbed, the verse: "Praised be You, my Lord, through our sister Bodily Death . . ."

b. Cf. Sulpicius Severus, *Letter* II, *To the Deacon Aurelius,* 10. This is in reference to the death of Saint Martin of Tours.

ent and absent, all their faults and offenses, and I absolve them insofar
as I am able. When you give them this message, bless them all for me."
110 Then he ordered the book of the Gospels to be brought in. He
asked that the Gospel according to John be read to him, starting with
Jn 12:1 the passage that begins: *Six days before the Passover,* Jesus, knowing
Jn 13:1 that the hour had come for him to pass from this world to the Father.[a]
This was the very gospel his minister had planned to read, even before
he was told to do so; that was the passage that met his eye as he first
opened the book, although he had the complete Bible from which to
read the gospel. Then he told them to cover him with sackcloth and to
Sir 10:9; 17:27 sprinkle him with ashes, as he was soon to become *dust and ashes.*
Dt 31:11 *Many* brothers *gathered* there, for whom *he was* both father and
Acts 14:11 *leader.* They stood there reverently, all awaiting his blessed *departure*
Sir 33:24 and happy *end.* And then that most holy soul was released from the
flesh, and as it was absorbed into the abyss of light, his body *fell asleep*
Acts 7:60 *in the Lord.*

One of his brothers and followers, a man of some fame, whose name
I will conceal for now since he does not wish to glory in such fame
Gal 2:20 while still *living in the flesh,* saw the soul of the most holy father *rise*
Jos 8:20; Ps 29:3; Sir 50:6 *straight to heaven over many waters.* It was *like a star* but as big as the
1 Cor 15:41 moon, with *the brilliance of the sun,* and *carried up* upon *a small white*
Rv 14:14 *cloud.*[b]

111 Let me cry out therefore:
"O what a glorious saint he is!
His disciple saw his soul *ascending into heaven:*
beautiful as the moon,
Acts 2:34; Sg 6:9 *bright as the sun,*
Rv 14:14; Sg 3:6 *glowing* brilliantly as *it ascended* upon *a white cloud!*
O true *lamp* of the world,
Mt 5:15; Rom 16:16 *shining* more brilliantly than the sun in the *Church of Christ!*
Now, you have withdrawn the rays of your light,
as you withdraw into that luminous homeland.

a. Thomas creates some confusion here. The first words of the quotation are from Jn 12:1, whereas what follows is from Jn 13:1ff. It is difficult to know if Francis wanted his brothers to read only the pericope of Jesus washing the feet of the Apostles or that which follows. Since Francis quotes John's Last Supper discourse so frequently in his writings, it seems plausible that he wanted to hear it during his last moments.

b. The soul of a saint in death moves to heaven in light. Cf. Gregory the Great, *Dialogue* II, 35: "In the dead of night he suddenly beheld a flood of light shining down from above more brilliant than the sun, and with it every trace of darkness cleared away. As he gazed at all this dazzling display, he saw the soul of Germanus, the Bishop of Capua, being carried by angels up to heaven in a ball of fire."

You have exchanged our poor *company*
for that *of the angels* and saints! Heb 12:22
In your glorious goodness and great renown,
do not put aside care for your sons,
though you have put aside flesh like theirs.
You know, you truly know,
the danger in which you have left them;
for it was your blessed presence alone
that always mercifully relieved
their countless labors and frequent troubles!
O truly merciful and most holy father,
you were always kind and ready
to show mercy and forgive your sinful sons!
We bless you therefore, worthy father,
as you *have been blessed* by the Most High, Tb 8:17; Gn 27:27
Who *is God over all things blessed forever. Amen."* Rom 9:5

Chapter IX

THE LAMENT OF THE BROTHERS AND THEIR JOY WHEN THEY PERCEIVED THAT FRANCIS BORE THE SIGNS OF THE CROSS IN HIS BODY AND ABOUT THE WINGS OF THE SERAPH

[112]At Francis's death,
a whole crowd of people praising God
came together and said: Acts 21:30; Mi 5:7; Lk 2:13
"You, *our Lord and God, be praised and blessed,* Dn 3:57; Ps 41:14
for you have given us unworthy ones so precious a remnant!
Praise and glory to you, O ineffable Trinity!"

The whole city of Assisi rushed down *as a group* and *the entire region* hurried to see *the wonderful works of God* which *the Lord of majesty* gloriously displayed in his holy servant. Each person burst into a song of joy at the urging of a *joyful heart,* and all of them had their *desire fulfilled* and blessed the almighty Savior. Still his sons were mourning, bereft of so great a father, and showed the deep feeling of their hearts in groaning and tears.

Mt 8:34; Mt 3:5; Acts 2:11; Is 2:10; Lam 5:15; Phil 4:19

Then incredible joy lightened their grief!
A new miracle
turned their minds to amazement.
Est 13:17 *Their mourning turned* into song,
their weeping to jubilation.
For they had never heard or read in Scripture
about what their eyes could see:
they could not have been persuaded to believe it
if it were not demonstrated by such clear evidence.
In fact,
there appeared in him
the form of the cross and passion
1 Pt 1:19 *of the spotless lamb*
Rv 1:5 *who washed away* the sins *of the world.*
It seemed
he had just been taken down from the cross,
his hands and feet pierced by nails
and his right *side*
Jn 19:34 wounded *by a lance.*

They looked at his skin which was black before but now shining white in its beauty, promising the rewards of the blessed resurrection.
Acts 6:15 They saw *his face* like *the face of an angel,* as if he were not dead, but alive. All his limbs had become as soft and moveable as in childhood innocence. His muscles were not taut, as they usually are in the dead, his skin was not hard, his limbs were not rigid but could be easily moved back and forth.

Ex 33:10 113 *All the people saw* him glowing with remarkable beauty and his flesh became even whiter than before. It was even more wonderful for them to see in the middle of his hands and feet not just the holes of the nails, but the nails themselves formed by his own flesh, retaining the dark color of iron, and his right side red with blood. These signs of martyrdom did not provoke horror, but added great beauty and grace, like little black stones in a white pavement.

His brothers and sons hurried to him and, weeping together, kissed the hands, the feet, and the right side of their dear father who had left them. The wound in his side made them remember the One who poured
Jn 19:34; 2 Cor 5:19 out *blood and water* from His own side and *reconciled the world* to the Father.

People considered it a great gift to be allowed to kiss or even to see the sacred *marks of Jesus* Christ which Saint Francis *bore in* his own *body.* Gal 6:17

And seeing them,
who would not be moved to joy rather than tears?
And if moved to tears,
would that not be more
from gladness than sadness?
Whose heart would be so iron-hard
that it would not be moved to groan?
Whose *heart* would be so much *like stone* Ez 11:19
that it would not break with sorrow,
that it would not burn with divine love
or would not be strengthened with good will?
Who would be so dull-witted and senseless
as not to realize the obvious truth?
He is a saint!
If he was so honored with a unique gift on earth,
he must *be exalted* with unspeakable glory *in heaven.* Is 33:5
[114]This is a unique gift,
a sign of special love:
1C 5 to decorate the soldier with the same arms of glory
that in their great dignity belong to the King alone![a]
This is a miracle worthy of *everlasting remembrance* Ps 112:7
and a sacrament to be remembered
with unceasing and wondering reverence.
It presents to the eyes of faith
that mystery in which *the blood of the spotless lamb,* 1 Pt 1:19
flowing abundantly through the five wounds,
washed away the sins *of the world.* Rv 1:5
O sublime splendor of the living cross,
giving life to the dead!
Its burden presses so lightly and hurts so sweetly
that through it dead flesh lives
and the weak spirit grows strong.

a. These "arms of glory," now identified with the stigmata, were foreseen in Francis's dream at the outset of his journey to Apulia.

You have made radiantly beautiful
Lk 7:47 this man who *loved* You *so much!*
Glory and blessing to God,
Rv 5:13; Rom 16:27 *who alone is wise,*
Sir 36:6 and *gives new signs and works new wonders*
to console the weak with revelations
and to raise their hearts to the love of things unseen
Ps 139:14 through *wonderful works* that are seen.[a]
O wonderful and loving plan of God!
To allay suspicion about the newness of this miracle,
Jn 3:13; 3:31 there first appeared mercifully in the One *from heaven*
what later appeared wondrously in the one who lived on earth.
2 Cor 1:3 The true *Father of mercies*
wanted to show how worthy of reward is the one
Mt 22:37 who strives *to love* Him *with his whole heart;*
worthy to be placed closer to Himself
in the highest order of supercelestial spirits.[b]

We too will certainly be able to reach these heights if, like the Ser-
Ez 1:22; 1:23 aphim, we *spread two wings over our heads:* that is, following blessed Francis's example, in every good work we have a pure intention and upright conduct, and, directing these to God, we strive untiringly to please God alone in all things.[c] These two wings must be joined for us
Jas, 1:17 to cover our heads because *the Father of lights* will not accept our activity as upright without a pure intention nor vice versa, since He says: *If your eye is sound, your whole body will be full of light; but if your eye*
Mt 6:22-23 *is evil, your whole body will be full of darkness.* That *eye* is *not sound* if it does not see what should be seen, because it does not know the truth, or if it looks at what should not be seen, because it does not have a pure

a. This echoes the Preface for Christmas: *Per hunc in invisibilium amorem rapiamur* [Through this we are lifted up into an invisible love].

b. The seraphim are found in the highest choir of angels, the choir closest to the divine majesty of God. Here Thomas places the life of Francis and especially the manifestation of the stigmata into the broader context of salvation history by showing how his life and its events participate in the mystery of divine love.

c. Thomas follows an allegorical and pedagogical explanation of the visions in Is. 6:1-13; Ez 1:5-14; 1:22-25; and Rv 4:6-9. Here at the end of Book Two, Thomas returns to comment on the significance of the seraph which, within the description of Francis's reception of the stigmata, he had introduced in n. 94 above. With the words, "We too will certainly be able to reach these heights . . ." Thomas proceeds to apply an allegorical interpretation of the seraph's six wings which invites the reader to follow Francis and to participate in the mystery of communion with Christ's passion and Cross. The allegorical interpretation of the seraph's wings originated with Pseudo-Dionysius, *Celestial Hierarchy* 7.1; 13.1; 15.2; in *Pseudo-Dionysius: The Complete Works*, translated by Colm Luibheid (New York: Paulist Press, 1987). It was continued in the West by Gregory the Great, *Homilia 34 in Evangelia, PL* 76:1246-49, 1252-53; Allan of Lille, *De Sex Alis Cherubim PL* 210:266-80, esp. 267-268; and Richard of Saint Victor, *The Mystical Ark* 1. 10, in *Richard of Saint Victor: The Twelve Patriarchs, The Mystical Ark, Book Three of the Trinity*, translated by Grover Zinn, (New York: Paulist Press, 1979).

intention. An open mind will judge neither as sound; the first is blind and the second evil. *The feathers* of *the wings* are the love of the saving and merciful Father and the *fear of the Lord*, the terrible judge. These lift the souls of the chosen above things of earth while restraining evil thoughts and ordering chaste affections. Ez 1:23-24 Sir 1:11

The *other two wings* are for flying: showing a double charity to our neighbor, refreshing the soul with the *word of God* and nourishing the body with material aid. These *wings* are rarely *joined together,* since one person could hardly do both. The *feathers* of these wings are varied works of counsel and help offered to our neighbor. Is 6:2 Lk 4:4 Ez 1:11

The last *two wings* are *to cover the body* that is bare of merits. This happens regularly as it is stripped naked whenever sin breaks in, but is then clothed again in innocence through contrition and confession. The feathers of these wings are the wide range of affections arising from hatred of sin and developing a longing for justice. Ez 1:11

115 Our blessed father Francis fulfilled all these things completely: he had both the image and the form of the Seraph and, remaining on the cross, he merited to fly away to the highest order of spirits. He was always upon his cross, never shirking labor or pain, fulfilling to the utmost the Lord's will in and about himself.

The brothers who lived with him know
that daily, constantly, talk of Jesus was always on his lips,
sweet and pleasant conversations about Him, Ez 33:32
kind words full of love.
Out of the fullness of the heart his mouth spoke. Mt 12:34
So the spring of radiant love
that filled his heart within
gushed forth.
He was always with Jesus:
Jesus in his heart,
Jesus in his mouth,
Jesus in his ears,
Jesus in his eyes,
Jesus in his hands,
he bore Jesus always in his whole body.
Often he sat down to dinner
but on hearing or saying or even thinking "Jesus"
he forgot bodily food,

as we read about another saint:
"Seeing, he did not see; hearing, he did not hear."[a]
Often as he walked along a road,
thinking and singing of Jesus,
he would forget his destination
and start inviting all the elements
to praise Jesus.
With amazing love he bore
Lk 2:19 *in his heart and always held onto*
1 Cor 2:2 *Christ Jesus and Him crucified.*
For this reason,
he, above others, was stamped with Christ's brilliant seal
2 Cor 5:13 as, in *rapture of spirit,*
he contemplated in unspeakable and incomprehensible glory
the One sitting "at the right hand of the Father,"
Lk 1:32 the Most High *Son of the Most High,*
Who, with the Father, "in the unity of the Holy Spirit,
lives and reigns," conquers and commands,
God eternally glorified *throughout all the ages.*
Dn 3:52; 3:90 *Amen.*

Chapter X

THE MOURNING OF THE LADIES AT SAN DAMIANO AND HOW HE WAS BURIED WITH PRAISE AND GLORY

[116]His brothers and sons had assembled with *the whole multitude of*
Ez 27:33 *people* from the neighboring cities, rejoicing to take part in such solemn rites. They spent that entire night of the holy father's death in the praises of God. The sweet sound of jubilation and the brightness of the lights made it seem that angels were keeping vigil.

Jn 21:4; Acts 2:6 *When day was breaking,* the multitude of the city of Assisi *gathered* with all the clergy. They lifted his sacred body from the place where he had died and carried it with great honor to the city, singing hymns and
Jos 6:20 praises *with trumpets blaring. They all took branches* of olive and
Jn 12:13; Mt 21:8 *other trees* and solemnly followed the funeral procession, bringing even more candles as they sang songs of praise in loud voices.

a. Similar descriptions can be found describing Bernard of Clairvaux, cf. *Vita prima s. Bernardi* IV, *Vita secunda s. Bernardi* IV.

With the sons carrying their father and the flock following the shepherd who was hastening to *the Shepherd of them all,* he arrived at the place where he first planted the religion and the Order of the consecrated virgins and Poor Ladies. They laid him out in the church of San Damiano, home to those daughters he gained for the Lord. The small window was opened, the one used by these servants of Christ *at the appointed time* to receive the sacrament of the Lord's body. The coffin was also opened: in it lay hidden the treasure of supercelestial powers; in it he who had carried many was now carried by a few. Ez 37:24 2 Sm 24:15

The Lady Clare!
Clearly a woman of true brilliance and holiness,
the first mother of all the others,
the first plant of that holy Order:
she comes with her daughters
to see the father
who would never again
speak to them or return to them,
as he was quickly going away.
[117]They looked upon him,
groaning and weeping with great *anguish of heart.* Ps 38:9

"Father, O father, what shall we do?" they *began to cry out.* "Why are you abandoning us poor women? We are forsaken! To whom are you entrusting us?[a] Why didn't you send us ahead of you in joy to the place you are going, instead of leaving us behind in sorrow? What would you have us do, enclosed in this cell, without your usual visits? *All consolation* ebbs away along with you, just as no solace remains for us who are buried to the world! Who will comfort us in so great a poverty, poverty of merit as much as of goods? Jos 3:3 2 Cor 1:5

"*O father of the poor!* O lover of poverty! Who will help us in temptation? You, who experienced so many temptations! You, who were such a careful judge of temptations! Who will comfort us in the midst of distress? *You, who were so often our help in times of distress!* What bitter separation, what painful absence! Jb 29:16 Ps 46:2

"O death, dreadful death! You are killing thousands of his sons and daughters by taking away their father! *Our* poor *efforts* bore fruit through him, and you rush to tear him far from us, beyond recall!" Jer 7:3,5

a. Cf. Sulpicius Severus, *Letter* III 10. "Before the death of Saint Martin, the monks cry out: 'Why are you abandoning us, father? To whom have you left your forsaken?' "

The virgins' modesty overcame their tears.
Zec 12:10 *To grieve* too much *over him* was unbecoming,
for at his passing
a host of angels rushed to greet him,
and *the citizens of heaven*
Eph 2:19 *and members of God's household* rejoiced.[a]
Thus,
torn between sorrow and joy,
they kissed his most splendid hands
that glittered with rare jewels and shining pearls.[b]
Once he was taken away,
the door
that never again will suffer such pain,
Mt 25:10 *was closed* on them.

O how great was the grief of all at the misery of these women!
How full was their mourning and the devotion of their outcry!
Above all how great was the wailing of his grieving sons![c]
The sadness of each was shared by all,
since no one could keep from crying
Is 33:7 when even *the angels of peace wept bitterly.*

118Finally all reached the city
Bar 3:35; Ps 45:16 and *with* great *joy and gladness*
Mt 27:59 *laid* the most holy *body* in a sacred place
about to become even more sacred.[d]
In the past he had brightened that place wonderfully
with instruction by his holy preaching.
Jn 1:9 There he now *enlightens the world*
with a multitude of new miracles
Rv 16:14 glorifying the Most High *God Almighty.*
Thanks be to God.
Amen.

---

a. A phrase borrowed from the seventh responsory for Matins of the Feast of Saint Martin of Tours, November 11, "at whose passing the corps of saints sings, the choir of angels rejoices, the host of all the heavenly virtues and worshippers gather to meet him."

b. This is a passage taken from the second responsory and the second antiphon of the third nocturn for the feast of Saint Agnes, Virgin and Martyr: "rare jewels . . . glittering and shining, precious pearls."

c. Sulpicius Severus, *Letter* III 18: "How great was the grief of all, above all how great was the wailing of the grieving monks."

d. The holy place where he was buried was the church of Saint George.

Now look at what I have done, most holy and blessed father,
I have seen you through to the end with fitting and worthy praises,
inadequate though they be,
and I have written down your deeds
telling the story as well as I could.
Please allow me,
pitiful as I am,
to follow you worthily in the present,
that I may mercifully merit joining you in the future.

O loving one,
bear in mind your poor sons
for whom, without you,
their one and only consolation,
there is little comfort.
Even though you,
their primary and prized portion,
have joined the choirs of angels,
and are seated with the apostles on a *throne of glory,* Dn 3:53,54
they still lie *in a muddy swamp,* Ps 40:3
enclosed in a dark cell,
tearfully crying out to you:
"O father,
place before Jesus Christ, son of the Most High Father,
His sacred stigmata;
and show Him the signs of the cross on your hands, feet, and side,
that He may mercifully bare His own wounds to the Father,
and because of this
the Father *will ever show us* in our anguish
His tenderness. Jb 33:26
Amen.
So be it, so be it."[a] Ps 72:19

Here Ends the Second Book.

a. Except for the last words—"the Father will ever show us in our anguish His tenderness," which replaces "He will give us one who is able to take the place of such a father," this prayer of Francis's orphaned followers is copied from an antiphon, *Plange turba paupercula,* composed by Gregory IX immediately after the saint's death. Luke Wadding, following Salimbene, thought the antiphon was written in 1239 for the chapter that was convened to choose a successor to Brother Elias. It dates from 1227 and preceded the election of John Parenti, the first successor of Francis.

The Third Book

HERE BEGINS THE THIRD BOOK WHICH TREATS OF THE CANONIZATION OF OUR BLESSED FATHER FRANCIS AND HIS MIRACLES

[119]Francis, the most glorious father,
in the twentieth year of his conversion,
Lk 23:45 as he most blessedly *commended his spirit* to heaven,
brought a blessed beginning to an even more blessed end.
Ps 8:6 There, *crowned with honor and glory*
Ez 28:14 and granted a place *among the stones of fire,*
he stands by the throne of God,
devoted to dealing effectively with the concerns
of those he left on earth.
What could be denied him?
Stamped with the holy stigmata,
he reflects the image of the One,
co-equal with the Father,
Who *is seated at the right hand of the majesty on high,*
the brightness of his glory and the image of the divine *substance,*
Heb 1:3 Who *cleanses us from all sin.*
Why would he not be heard?
Conformed to the death of Christ Jesus
Phil 3:10 *by sharing in His sufferings,*
he displays His sacred wounds in his hands, feet, and side.
He gladdens the whole world
with the gift of new joy,
and offers to all the benefits of true salvation.
He floods the world with the brilliant light of miracles,
a true star glowing brightly over the whole earth.
The world once mourned when robbed of his presence
Ps 50:1 and saw itself overwhelmed by the dark abyss *at his setting,*
Is 16:3 but now it seems like the *light of midday.*

With new light rising,
the world is growing bright in these shining rays[a]
and feels all the darkness leave.
Now, all its complaints have stopped;
Blessed be God! Ps 66:20

Everyday, everywhere people rejoice anew
as the world is filled to overflowing with holy gifts from him.
From East and West they come, Mt 8:11
from North and South: Gn 13:3; Ez 48:31
those helped by his patronage come
to attest to these things in *witness to the truth.* Jn 5:33
While he *lived in the flesh,* Phil 1:22; 1 Pt 4:2
this great lover of the things of heaven
held nothing of the world as his own,
so that he could possess the greatest good of all
more fully and more joyfully.
For this reason he has become in all things
what he did not want to be in few things,
and has exchanged time for eternity.
He helps everyone, everywhere.
He is near to everyone, everywhere.
Yet this lover of true unity
is not divided by being shared.[b]
120 *While he still lived among sinners,* Wis 4:10
he traveled the whole world preaching;
but now reigning with the angels on high, Ps 149:1
he flies quicker than a thought as the herald of the Great King,
bringing wonderful gifts to all peoples.
For this reason,
all peoples honor, venerate, glorify and praise him.
They all share now a common good.
Who can estimate the quantity

a. This is a clear reference to the hymn of praise of the Easter Mystery at the paschal candle, the *Exultet.*

b. This is reference to the medieval liturgy of Holy Saturday in which a rod with three tapers was carried in procession into the church. During the procession, the Deacon would chant *Lumen Christi* three times and each time would light one of the tapers. At a certain point in chanting the *Exsultet,* the Deacon lit the paschal candle with one of these candles and chanted: "*Qui licet sit divisus in partes, mutuati tamen luminis detrimenta non novit* [This (triple candle) although it might be divided in parts, does not suffer loss through sharing its light].

or tell the quality of the miracles
the Lord has chosen to work everywhere through him?

Just in France, Francis has worked so many miracles that the Frankish king and queen and all the nobility hasten to kiss and venerate the pillow that Saint Francis used during his illness.[a] There also the world's wise and literate, whom Paris usually produces more abun-
Jer 1:18 dantly than the whole world, humbly and devotedly venerate, admire, and revere Francis, an uneducated man, a friend of true simplicity and whole-hearted sincerity.

He is truly "France-ish" whose heart was so frank and free.[b] Those who experienced the greatness of his soul know well how free and freeing he was in everything, how intrepid and fearless in all circumstances.[c] With great strength and bravery he trampled upon every worldly thing.

And what can I say of other parts of the world? Disease disappears and illness flees simply by means of his cord, and both men and women are freed from distress merely by invoking his name.

121 At his tomb new miracles occur constantly
and, as the prayers increase,
remarkable aid is given to body and soul.
The blind recover sight,
the deaf regain hearing,
the lame walk again,
the mute speak,
those with gout jump,
Mt 11:5 *lepers are cleansed,*
those with swelling see it reduced,
and those suffering the burden of many different diseases

---

a. The king of France here is probably Saint Louis IX (+1270) and the "queen" Blanche of Castille, his mother (+1252). At the time Thomas was writing in 1228, the king was no more than fourteen years old. The text seems to say that the relic was kept in France and exposed for the veneration of the faithful. According to 3C 37-39, Lady (Brother) Jacopa dei Settesoli came to see Francis as he lay dying. Among the things she brought him was a pillow for his head.

b. Thomas engages in a wordplay here that is nearly impossible to translate. The word for Francis in Latin, *Franciscus*, is closely related to the word for a Frenchman in medieval Latin, *Francus*, as in the phrase *rex Francorum*, and literally translates as the diminutive "little Frenchman." But the adjectival form *francus* means "noble" and "free." Hence there are four meanings being put into play here: French, noble, free, and Francis. One could translate this opening line as "Truly was he French," "Truly was he free," and "Truly was he noble." The meaning of a name was extremely important in the Middle Ages. Here, as earlier in the case of Clare, Thomas surely sees more than a fanciful etymology.

c. In Francis's name, Thomas sees two qualities, namely independence with regard to himself and discernment with regard to the initiatives of his neighbor. In the Latin text these two qualities are *liber* [free] and *liberalis* [freeing].

obtain the relief for which they have longed.
His dead body heals living bodies,
just as when living it raised dead souls.

The Roman Pontiff heard of these things and understood:
he, chief pontiff of all,
leader of Christians,
lord of the world,
shepherd of the Church,
the anointed of the Lord, 1 Sm 24:11
and the Vicar of Christ.
He rejoiced and exulted, dancing with joy,
for in his own day he was seeing
1C 18 the Church of God being renewed
with new mysteries that were ancient wonders.
This was happening because of his own son,
the one he had
carried in his sacred womb,
held in his lap,
nursed with the word,
nurtured on the food of salvation.
The other keepers of the Church also heard this,
those who are
the shepherds of the flock,
defenders of the faith,
friends of the bridegroom, Jn 3:29
his supporters,
the poles of the earth,
the venerable Cardinals.
They rejoiced with the Church and shared the Pope's delight,
giving glory to the Savior who chose
with supreme, unfathomable wisdom,
supreme, incomprehensible grace,
and supreme, boundless goodness,
the foolish and lowly of the world 1 Cor 1:27; 1:28
in order *to draw* the strong *to Himself.* Jn 12:32
The entire world heard of this and applauded,
and every realm subject to the Catholic faith,

overflowed *with joy,*
2 Cor. 7:4 flooded with holy *comfort.*

122 But then there came a rapid change in events, as a new problem rose up in the world.[a] The joyful peace was quickly shaken as the torch of envy was lit and the Church was torn apart by internal warfare among its members. The Romans, that fierce and rebellious people, struck with their usual savagery against their neighbors and boldly
1 Mc 14:31 *stretched forth their hands against the holy places.*[b] The great Pope Gregory tried to restrain this rising evil, to control the savagery, and to stop the attacks, to safeguard the Church of Christ like a fortified tower. Danger multiplied, destruction increased, and in the rest of the world
Ps 129:4 sinners *lifted up their necks* in rebellion against God. What could he do? With great experience, he gauged the future and assessed the present, deciding to abandon the City to the rebels so as to free the world and defend it from more rebellion. He went to the city of Rieti, where he was received with fitting honor. From there he continued on to Spoleto, where everyone honored him with great reverence. He stayed there for several days to organize the Church's cause. Then, accompanied by the venerable cardinals, he kindly paid a visit to the handmaids of Christ, dead and buried to the world.[c] Their holy way of life, their
2 Cor 8:2 *highest poverty,* and their renowned way of living moved him to tears along with his companions, encouraging them to despise worldly things and enkindling in them love for the life of chastity.

O lovable humility, nurse of all graces!
The prince of the whole world,
successor of the prince of the Apostles,
visits the poor women,
going to the lowly, humble and enclosed!

---

a. The German emperor Frederick II controlled northern Italy and, through his mother, the Kingdom of the Two Sicilies; he exercised a vise-like grip on the Papal States. He invaded the Papal States and from a distance exercised his influence on the people of Rome, who revolted on Easter Monday 1228 during the papal Mass in Saint Peter's Basilica. Gregory IX did not return to Rome until 1230. Thus, Thomas refers to the people stretching "forth their hands against the holy places."

b. This passage is reminiscent of Bernard of Clairvaux's comments to Pope Eugene III about the Romans in his work *De consideratione ad Eugenium III,* IV c. 2, n.2. "What shall I say of the people? They are Romans. I could say nothing more concise or express anything more openly than what I feel about your parishioners. What is better known to the world than the impudence and arrogance of the Romans! They are a nation hostile to peace, one that is merciless and unmanageable, completely ignorant of what it means to be subject unless they are incapable of resisting." Elsewhere he writes: "These people are hateful of heaven and earth, for they raise their hands against both: disrespectful toward God, irreverent toward the sacred, rebellious toward one another, envious toward their neighbors, inhumane toward foreigners."

c. A reference to the Poor Ladies of the monastery of Saint Paul, near Spoleto.

Worthy of *a good judgment,* Dt 16:18
an example of this humility is rare,
not seen for many ages.

123 After that he hurried on, he hurried to Assisi, where a glorious treasure was being kept for him, to make all his suffering and pressing trials disappear. On his arrival, the whole region rejoiced, the city *was filled with gladness,* a great crowd of people joined the joyful celebration, and the bright day grew brighter with new lights. Everyone went forth *to meet him* and joined in solemn vigil. The devoted group of poor brothers went out to meet him, each one singing sweet songs to *the Lord's anointed.* The Vicar of Christ reached the place and first going down to the tomb of Saint Francis, he eagerly paid his respects with great reverence. Groaning deeply, he struck his breast, and breaking into tears, he bowed his venerable head in an outpouring of devotion.

Ps 126:2

2 Kgs 4:26

1 Sm 24:11

Meanwhile, a solemn assembly was called for the canonization of the saint and the eminent body of cardinals met frequently to consider the matter.[a] Many who had been freed from their illnesses through the holy man of God came from far and wide, and from here and there countless miracles gleamed: these miracles were heard, verified, accepted, and approved.

But then a new problem arose and, obliged by the duties of office, the blessed Pope had to go to Perugia, only in order to be able to return once again to Assisi with *more abundant* and special *grace* for the most important task.[b] Another meeting was called in Perugia. The sacred consistory of cardinals met in the chambers of the Lord Pope to consider the cause. All were in agreement. They read the miracles with great reverence; they extolled the life and conduct of the holy man with the highest praise.

Rom 5:20

124 "The holy life of this holy man," they said, "does not require the evidence of miracles *for we have seen it with our eyes and touched it with our hands* and tested it with truth as our guide." They all leapt to their feet with tears of joy; and in their *tears* there was a great *blessing.* They immediately fixed the blessed date when they would fill the whole world with blessed joy.[c]

1 Jn 1:1

Heb 12:17

a. Gregory continued the work of his predecessors, Innocent III and Honorius III by further revising the canonization process. All three insisted on two things: virtue of behavior and the virtue of signs, that is, works of mercy during life and miraculous signs after death. Undoubtedly Gregory gathered the cardinals to consider these two requirements.

b. From June 13 to July 13, 1228, Gregory continued to be involved in matters of state.

c. The day of the canonization was set for July 16, 1228.

The solemn day arrives, "A day held in reverence by every age,"[a]
showering the earth and even the heavenly mansions with ecstatic rejoicing. Bishops gather, abbots arrive, prelates from the most remote
areas appear; a king's presence is noticed, with a noble crowd of counts
and dukes.[b] All accompany the lord of the whole earth, and with him enter the city of Assisi in a happy procession. They come to the place prepared for this solemn meeting and the glorious crowd of cardinals,
bishops, and abbots gathers around the blessed pope.[c] A distinguished
assembly of priests and clerics is there, a happy and sacred gathering of
religious men, and the modest presence of veiled consecrated women, a
2 Chr 4:18 great crowd from every people: an almost *numberless multitude of both*
Jgs 16:27 *sexes.* They are running from all over, and in this crowd every age is represented enthusiastically. *The small and the great are there; the servants*
Jb 3:19 *and those freed from their masters.*

125 The supreme pontiff,
bridegroom of the Church of Christ *is standing,*
Ps 45:10 surrounded *with* such *variety* of children,
Is 62:3; Rv 14:14 *a crown of glory* on his head
Sir 45:14 *marked with the sign of holiness.*
He stands adorned with the pontifical regalia
Ex 40:13 and clothed in *holy vestments*
Sir 45:13 with *settings of gold, the work of a jeweler.*
1 Sm 24:11 He stands there, *the Lord's anointed,*
Ps 45:10; Is 4:2 *gilded in magnificence and glory*
Sir 45:13 and covered *with precious stones* cut and sparkling,
catching the eyes of all.
Cardinals and bishops surround him,
Is 61:10 *clothed* with *jewels* glittering
on garments gleaming white as snow,
offering an image of the beauty of heaven,
displaying the joy of the glorified.
1 Sm 12:19 *All the people* are waiting for *the cry of joy,*
Jer 25:10 *the song of gladness,*

a. This phrase, *Toto venerabilis aevo,* is another echo of the Easter liturgy, which is taken from the hymn *Salve festa dies* by Venantius Fortunatus, bishop of Poitiers in 599. In this passage Thomas shifts again to the present tense for dramatic narrative.

b. John of Brienne was crowned king of Jerusalem on October 3, 1210. Toward the end of his life, he became a disciple of Francis and was buried in the basilica dedicated to the saint.

c. The canonization took place near the church of Saint George.

a new song,
a song full of sweetness,
a song of praise, Ps 26:7
a song of everlasting blessing.

Pope Gregory first preaches *to all the people* with deeply felt words sweeter than honey, proclaiming the praises of God in a resonant voice. He praises the holy father Francis in noble words. Recalling his way of life and speaking of his purity, he is drenched in tears. His sermon begins with the text: *"Like the morning star in the midst of clouds, like the full moon, like the shining sun, so in his days did he shine in the temple of God."*[a]

Heb 9:19 Sir 50:6-7

At the end of this *speech, so true and worthy of complete acceptance,* one of the subdeacons of the lord Pope, Ottaviano by name, reads in a loud voice the miracles of the Saint to the whole assembly.[b] Lord Ranieri, a Cardinal-deacon, a man of keen intelligence, of outstanding devotion and conduct, speaks about them with sacred eloquence, his eyes welling with tears.[c] The shepherd of the Church is overcome with joy, with deep sighs rising from the bottom of his heart and, often sobbing, breaks out in tears. The other prelates of the Church were also pouring out a flood of tears that dripped onto their sacred vestments. Then all *the people are weeping,* tired out with eager expectation.

1 Tm 1:15 1 Sm 11:5

126 At that moment the blessed Pope cries out in a ringing voice, and *raising* his hands *to heaven* proclaims: "To the praise and glory of God almighty, Father, Son, and Holy Spirit, the glorious Virgin Mary, the blessed Apostles Peter and Paul, to the honor of the glorious Roman Church! On the advice of our brothers and other prelates, we decree that the most blessed father Francis, whom the Lord has glorified in heaven and we venerate on earth, shall be enrolled in the catalogue of saints, and his feast is to be celebrated on the day of his death." At this

2 Mc 3:20

a. Anonymous, *The Life of Gregory IX* which provides a further description of the pope's role in the canonization of Francis, cf. Infra, pp. 603-604. The biblical reference is to Simon the High Priest in whose days the temple was renewed, cf. Sir 50:1-23. It is used in the papal declaration of Francis's canonization, *Mira circa nos*, cf.

b. Ottaviano degli Ubaldini di Mugello was a cousin of Innocent III, and was later made cardinal by Innocent IV. Salimbene writes that Gregory IX held him in high regard. Cf. *Chronicle of Salimbene of Adam* translated by Joseph L. Baird, Giuseppe Baglivi, and John Robert Kane (Binghamton, NY: Center for Medieval and Renaissance Studies, 1986), 386.

c. The Cistercian Ranieri Capocci of Viterbo, made cardinal in 1216, was a good friend of the Order. He is the author of the hymn *Plaude turba paupercula* and the antiphon *Caelorum candor splenduit* in honor of Francis.

announcement, the reverend cardinals join the pope in singing the *Te Deum laudamus* in a loud voice.

Is 17:12; Lk 2:13 And there rises the cry of *many peoples* praising God;
the earth echoes the booming sound,
the air is filled with jubilation,
and the ground is soaked with tears.
Ps 33:3 *They sing new songs*
Jb 38:7 and the servants *of God rejoice*
in the melody of the Spirit.[a]
Sweet sounding instruments are playing
as hymns are sung with musical voices.
Ex 29:18 A *very sweet fragrance is flowing there*
and an even more pleasant melody is echoing there,
moving everyone deeply.
The day is breaking, colored with radiant sunbeams.
There are green *branches* of olive
Mt 21:8 and fresh boughs *of other trees.*
There all are dressed in festive clothing, shining brightly,
while the blessing of peace gladdens the spirits of all.

Is 6:1 The blessed Pope Gregory then comes down from the *high throne,*
Ps 73:17 and by the lower steps *enters the sanctuary to offer prayers and sacri-*
Nm 29:39 *fices,* and with his blessed lips kisses the tomb holding the sacred body
Jb 40:22; Is 1:15 dedicated to God.[b] *He offers many prayers* and celebrates the sacred
Sir 50:13 mysteries. Around him stands *a ring of brothers, praising, adoring and*
Lk 24:52,53; 2 Mc 3:22 *blessing almighty God, who has done wondrous things through all the*
Sir 50:22 *earth.*

All the people
Mt 27:25; Lk 18:43 *echoed the praise of God,*
offering gifts of thanks to Francis
in honor of the Most High Trinity.
Amen.

---

a. The use of a biblical expression (Ps 33:3; 96:1; 98:1) may be no more than a rhetorical device here. This does not necessarily exclude the hypothesis that we have an allusion to the pieces composed by Gregory IX himself for the canonization. These were later incorporated into the Office for the Feast of Saint Francis: the hymn *Proles de caelo,* the responsory *De paupertatis horreo,* and the prose composition *Caput draconis.*

b. This sanctuary is the church of Saint George. Thomas states that the pope entered *per inferiores gradus* (by the lower steps). The author's care for detail and his keen interest in each scrap of information suggest his presence at the ceremonies he describes.

These things happened in the city of Assisi, in the second year of the pontificate of the Lord Pope Gregory the Ninth, on the seventeenth day of the calends of the month of August.[a]

a. That is, July 16, 1228.

The Miracles of Saint Francis

IN THE NAME OF CHRIST
HERE BEGIN THE MIRACLES OF OUR MOST HOLY FATHER FRANCIS

2 Cor 8:9; 13:13 [127]Humbly calling upon *the grace of Jesus Christ our Lord,* we shall briefly but accurately describe the miracles that were read in the presence of the Lord Pope and announced to the people, both in order
Dn 9:25 to arouse *fitting devotion* among those living and to strengthen the faith of those to come.

Chapter I
THE CRIPPLED WHO WERE HEALED

The very same day on which the sacred and holy body of the blessed father was laid away as a most precious treasure, anointed with heavenly ointments rather than with those found on earth, a young girl was brought there who, for over a year, had suffered a deformity in her neck so hideous that her head rested on her shoulder and she could only look up sideways. She put her head for a little while beneath the coffin in which the precious body of the saint rested, and through the merits of that most holy man she was immediately able to straighten her neck, and her head was restored to its proper position. At this the girl was so overwhelmed at the sudden change in herself that she started to run away and to cry. There was a depression in her shoulder where her head had been when it was twisted out of position by her prolonged affliction.

[128]In the district of Narni there was a boy whose leg was bent back so severely that he could not walk at all without the aid of two canes. He made his living by begging; he had been burdened with that affliction for many years, and he had no idea who his father and mother were. This boy was completely freed from his affliction by the merits of our blessed father Francis so that he could walk about freely without any support from the canes and did so praising and blessing God and His saint.

[129]A certain Nicolò, a citizen of Foligno, was so crippled in his left leg that it caused him extreme pain; as a result he spent so much on doctors in his endeavor to restore his health that he went more deeply into debt than he could ever hope to pay. Finally, when the help of physicians had proven worthless, he was suffering such extreme pain that his neighbors could not sleep at night because of his moaning cries. Then dedicating himself to God and to Saint Francis, he had himself carried to the tomb of the saint. After spending a night in prayer at the saint's tomb, his crippled leg was cured and, overflowing with joy, he returned home without a cane.

[130]A boy had one leg so deformed that his knee was pressed against his chest and his heel against his buttocks. He came to the tomb of the blessed Francis, while his father was mortifying his own flesh with a hair shirt and his mother was performing severe penance for him. Suddenly the boy had his health so fully restored that he could run through the streets, healthy and happy, *giving thanks to God* and Saint Francis. Acts 28:15

[131]In the city of Fano there was a man who was crippled with his legs doubled-up under him. They were covered with sores that gave off such a foul odor that the hospice staff refused to take him in or keep him. But then he asked the blessed father Francis for mercy and, through his merits, in a short time he rejoiced in being cured.

[132]There was also a little girl in Gubbio; her hands and all her limbs were so crippled that for over a year she was totally unable to use them. Carrying a wax image, her nurse brought her to the tomb of the blessed father Francis to seek the favor of a cure.[a] After she had been there for eight days, on the last day all her limbs were restored to their proper functions so that she was considered well enough to return to her activities.

[133]There was a boy from Montenero lying for several days in front of the doors of the church where the body of Saint Francis rested. He could not walk or sit up, since he was completely paralyzed from the waist down. One day he got into the church and touched the tomb of the blessed father Francis. When he came back outside, he was completely cured. Moreover, the young boy himself reported that while he was lying in front of the tomb of the glorious Saint, a young man was there with him clothed in the habit of the friars, on top of the tomb. The young man was carrying some pears in his hands, and he called the boy.

a. In the Middle Ages there was a widespread custom that people who visited a shrine would offer an amount of wax, metal, bread or oil equal to the weight of the sick person for whom they were praying. The weighing was even accompanied by a special ritual. The same custom is mentioned in 1C 140, 146, 149.

Offering him a pear, he encouraged him to get up. The boy took the pear from the young man's hand, and answered: "See, I am crippled and cannot get up at all!" He ate the pear given to him, and then started to put out his hand for another pear that the young man offered him. The young man again encouraged him to stand up, but the boy, feeling weighed down with his illness, did not get up. But while the boy reached out his hand, the young man holding out the pear took hold of his hand and led him outside. Then he vanished from sight. When the boy saw that he was cured, he began to cry out at the top of his voice, telling everyone what had happened to him.

[134]There was a woman from the village of Coccorano who was brought to the tomb of the glorious father on a stretcher; for, except for her tongue, all her limbs were totally paralyzed. After *she stayed a*
Mt 25:5 *while* before the tomb of the most holy man, she stood up, entirely cured.

After another citizen from Gubbio brought his crippled son on a stretcher to the tomb of the holy father, he received him back whole and sound, though before he had been so crippled and deformed that his legs were completely withered and drawn up under him.

[135]Bartolomeo from the city of Narni was poverty-stricken and indigent. One day after he had been sleeping in the shade of a nut-tree he awoke to find himself so crippled he could not walk at all. As the disease spread, his leg and foot wasted away; they grew crooked and withered and he could not feel the cutting of a knife, nor was he afraid of burns from a fire. One night the saintly Francis, the true lover of the
Dn 2:19 poor and the father of all the needy, appeared to him *in a dream.* He ordered him to go to a certain bathing pool, because, moved by pity at the man's misery, he wanted to free him there from his illness. When he
Lk 9:33; Acts 5:7 awoke, *he did not know what to do,* so he told the whole story of the vision to the bishop of the city. The bishop urged him to hurry to the pool as he was ordered and, making the sign of the cross, blessed him. Leaning on a stick, he set out to drag himself to the place as best he could. As he moved along sadly, worn out by great effort, *he heard a voice saying*
Acts 9:4 *to him:* "Go on in the peace of the Lord. I am the one to whom you vowed yourself." When the man drew near to the pool, it was night and
Acts 9:4 he took the wrong road. *He heard a voice again telling him* that he was not on the right road, and it directed him to the pool. When he reached the place and entered the pool, he felt a hand placed upon his foot and another that gently pulled his leg. He was immediately freed, and he

jumped out of the pool, praising and blessing the all-powerful Creator and His servant, blessed Francis, who had received such grace and power from Him. That man, who was already mature, had been crippled and begging for six years.

Chapter II
THE BLIND WHO RECEIVED THEIR SIGHT

136 A woman named Sibilla suffered from blindness in her eyes for many years. She was led to the tomb of the man of God, blind and dejected. She recovered her sight and, rejoicing and exulting, returned home.

At the tomb of the holy body, a blind man from Spello recovered his sight, which he had lost long before.

Another woman, from Camerino, was totally blind in her right eye. Her parents covered the damaged eye with a cloth that the blessed Francis had touched. After making a vow, they gave thanks to the Lord God and Saint Francis for restoring her sight.

A similar thing happened to a woman from Gubbio who, after making a vow, rejoiced on recovering her vision.

A citizen of Assisi was blind for five years. While the blessed Francis was still living, he was friendly to him, so whenever he prayed to the blessed man, he would recall their former friendship. He was cured as soon as he touched his tomb.

Albertino from Narni was totally blind for about a year, for his eyelids hung down over his eyes. Vowing himself to the blessed Francis, his sight was immediately restored; then he prepared himself and went to his glorious tomb.

Chapter III
THOSE POSSESSED BY DEMONS

137 *There was a man* in the city of Foligno named Pietro, who, either Jb 1:1
to fulfill a vow or as a penance imposed on him for his sins, went one time on a pilgrimage to the shrine of Blessed Michael the Archangel.[a] He stopped at a fountain, and since he was thirsty and weary from his journey, he had started to drink the water of that fountain when he saw

a. At Monte Gargano in the province of Foggia, Apulia.

himself drinking up demons. He was possessed by them for three years, and he used to do things dreadful to see and worse to tell. When he came to the sepulcher of the most holy Father, the demons were furious and mauled him savagely. By an outstanding miracle, he was marvelously delivered from them when he touched the tomb.

[138]A woman in the city of Narni was driven by a most violent madness, and since she was out of her mind, would do dreadful things and say very inappropriate things. Blessed Francis appeared to her in a vi-
Nm 12:6 sion and said: "Make the sign of the cross!" "I can't," she replied. The Saint himself made the sign of the cross on her and drove out all trace of her insanity and the phantoms of the demons.

Many other men and women who were harassed by torments of evil spirits and led astray by their tricks were rescued from their power through the outstanding merits of the holy and glorious father.

However, since deception frequently comes into question with people of this kind, we shall pass them by with this brief account, and go on to the most impressive cases.

Chapter IV
THOSE SICK UNTO DEATH WHO RECOVERED, A MAN WITH SWELLING, ONE MAN WITH DROPSY, AN ARTHRITIC, THE PARALYZED, AND THOSE AFFLICTED WITH VARIOUS OTHER ILLNESSES

Mt 9:2 [139]A little boy named Matteo, from the city of Todi, *lay on his bed* for eight days as if dead. His mouth was tightly closed; he could see nothing, the skin on his face and hands and feet became as black as a kettle, and everyone despaired of his life. But when his mother made a vow, he recovered with amazing speed. He had been throwing up putrid blood from his mouth so that it seemed as if he were losing his intestines. His mother immediately knelt down and humbly called on Saint Francis. As soon as she arose from prayer, the little boy opened his eyes, looked around, and took his mother's breast. In a little while the black skin peeled off, his flesh returned to the way it was, and he was once again strong and healthy. As soon as he started to improve, his mother asked him: "Who cured you, my son?" In answer he lisped: "Cecco, Cecco." Again she asked him: "Whose servant are you?" Again he answered: "Cecco, Cecco." Since he was just a baby, he could not speak distinctly, and so in trying to pronounce the name of "Francesco," he left out half of it.

140 There was a young man who had been up on a very high place and fell from there and lost the use of all his limbs as well as his ability to speak. For *three days he neither ate nor drank* nor felt anything, so that they thought he was dead. His mother, without even seeking the aid of a doctor, asked blessed Francis to cure him. After she had made a vow the young man was restored to her, alive and sound, and she began to praise the all-powerful Savior. Acts 9:9; Mt 11:18

Another man by the name of Mancino was so sick and so near death that everyone gave up all hope for him. But he invoked as well as he could the name of the blessed Francis and he was immediately restored to health.

A boy from Arezzo by the name of Gualtiero was suffering from prolonged fever and so tormented by a multiple abscess that all the doctors gave up hope for him. But his parents made a vow to blessed Francis, and he recovered the health they so longed for.

Another man, who was near death, made a wax image, and before it was even finished, he was entirely relieved of his unbearable pain.[a]

141 A woman was confined to bed for many years by illness, unable to turn or move at all. She vowed herself to God and the blessed Francis. She was freed from her illness and resumed her usual activities. In the city of Narni, there was a woman who for eight years had a hand so withered that she could not use it at all. The blessed Francis appeared to her *in a vision,* stretching out his hand to her, and thereby made her withered hand able to work as well as her other one. Acts 18:9

A young man in the same city was in the grip of a very serious illness for ten years; his whole body was so swollen that no medicine brought him any relief. After his mother made a vow, he received the relief of health through the merits of blessed Francis.

There was a man in the city of Fano suffering from dropsy, whose limbs were horribly swollen. Through blessed Francis he obtained a complete cure of his illness.

A citizen of Todi suffered from such an acute arthritic condition that he could neither sit nor lie down at all. The severity of the affliction grew so serious as to cause ever-increasing stiffness and it seemed he would become entirely helpless. He called doctors and took baths. He

a. A person unable to visit a shrine would have a wax image made as a substitute to stand near the saint's tomb, a practice reflected in the "vigil light" candles in churches.

tried all kinds of medicines, but none of these brought him any relief. One day while the priest was visiting, he made a vow to Saint Francis, asking to be restored to health. Soon after finishing his prayers to the Saint, he realized that he had been restored to health.

142 There was a woman in the city of Gubbio who lay paralyzed. After she invoked the name of blessed Francis three times, she was freed from her infirmity and cured.

A man by the name of Bontadoso suffered such agonizing pains in his feet and toes that he could not walk or bend over and could neither eat nor sleep. A woman visited him one day and suggested that he vow himself to the blessed Francis with all his heart, if he wished to find quick relief from his sufferings. But that man, beside himself with pain, cried: "I do not believe that he is a saint!" But the woman stubbornly insisted that he make the vow. He finally vowed himself in this way: "I vow myself to Saint Francis and I believe he is a saint, if he frees me from this illness in three days." Through the merits of the Saint of God, he was soon cured, and was able to eat and sleep, *giving glory to al-*
Jn 9:24; Rom 4:20 *mighty God.*

143 A man was seriously wounded in the head by a metal arrow that had gone through his eye socket and lodged in his head. He could get no relief from the doctors. So with humble devotion he vowed himself to the Saint of God, Francis, hoping to be helped by the Saint's intercession. He then lay down to rest a little, and *while he was sleeping,* he *was*
Gn 31:24 *told* by Saint Francis to have the arrow pulled out through the back of his
Gn 31:10 head. The next day he did *as he was told in the dream,* and without great difficulty he obtained relief.

144 A man from the village of Spello, named Imperatore, suffered for two years with such a severe rupture that all his intestines protruded through the side of his body. He could not keep them in place for any length of time so he had to wear a truss to hold them in. He went to doctors to seek relief, but they kept asking for more than he could afford to pay; in fact, he did not have enough left to live on or to eat for more than a day, so he gave up all hope of getting any help from them. Then he turned to seek divine help, and while on the road or at home or wherever he was, he humbly called upon blessed Francis. After a short time, it turned out that through the grace of God and the merits of blessed Francis he was restored to full health.

145 A brother in the March of Ancona, who had vowed obedience in the ranks of our Order, suffered so greatly from a painful ulcer in his

side that all hope of a cure had been given up by his physicians because the infection had spread so far.[a] So he asked his minister, under whose obedience he lived, for permission to visit the place where the body of the most blessed Father rested, for he was confident that he would obtain the favor of a cure through the merits of the Saint. But his minister forbade him to go for fear his condition would grow worse from the hardships of the journey, for it was the season of rain and snow. Since the brother felt badly about not receiving permission to go, the holy Father Francis one night stood by him. "My son," he said, "do not worry about such things any more. Take off that fur you are wearing, remove that dressing and the bandages holding it, and keep your Rule; then you will be cured.[b] When he arose in the morning he did just as he was told, and *gave thanks to God* for his immediate cure. Acts 27:35

Chapter V
THE LEPERS WHO WERE CLEANSED

[146] At San Severino in the March of Ancona there was a young man named Atto who was covered with leprosy; everyone was convinced he was a leper, for such was the opinion of the doctors. All his limbs were swollen and distended, and, since his blood vessels were protruding, he looked at everything with an unpleasant expression. He could not walk, but spent all his time in misery upon his sickbed, a cause of great sorrow and pain to his parents. His father, torn with unremitting grief, did not know what to do for him. Finally he felt in his heart that he should dedicate him completely to the blessed Francis. So he said to his son: "My son, do you want to vow yourself to Saint Francis, who is famous everywhere for his many miracles, that he may be pleased to deliver you from this suffering?" He answered: "Yes, I want to, father." Immediately the father had them fetch a piece of paper and he took measurements of his son's height and width. He then said: "Sit up, my son, and vow yourself to blessed Francis. When you are cured, you will take him a candle as large as you are every year as long as you live." At his father's bidding he sat up as best he could and, folding his hands, he humbly begged blessed Francis for mercy. After the measurements

a. He is the only brother who appears in this series of miracles. Another was the object of a miracle in those occurring during Francis's life, cf. 1C 68.

b. This admonition to keep the Rule is probably based on the fact that the brother was wearing a fur which would be considered a *vestis mollis* [soft garment] rather than a *vestis vilis* [coarse garment] contrary to LR II 13-15.

had been taken and he had finished his prayers, he was cured of his lep-
Jn 9:24; Rom 4:20 rosy on the spot. He got up, *giving glory to God* and to blessed Francis,
Col 1:10;1:11 and *joyfully* started *to walk about.*

In the city of Fano there was a young man named Buonuomo whom all the doctors claimed was a paralytic and a leper. He was devoutly offered to blessed Francis by his parents, and he was cured of his leprosy and the paralysis vanished; he recovered his health completely.

Chapter VI
THE MUTE WHO BEGAN TO SPEAK AND THE DEAF WHO BEGAN TO HEAR

[147]At Città della Pieve there was a boy who was very poor and a
Jn 9:1 beggar. *From birth* he had been completely mute and deaf. His tongue
was so short and stubby that, to those who many times examined it, the
tongue seemed to be completely cut out. Late one evening the boy went
to the house of a man named Marco, who lived in the same village.
Using the signs the mute ordinarily use, the boy begged Marco to take
him in; he inclined his head to one side, and put his hands under his
cheek to indicate that he wanted to sleep there that night. That man
Jude 6:19 gladly *received him into his house,* and was happy to keep him, for he
found the young man to be a great help around the house. The boy had a
1 Kgs 11:28 *good disposition,* and although he was deaf and mute from infancy, he
understood orders by means of signs. One evening that man was dining
with his wife, while the boy stood by. The man said to his wife: "I
would consider it the greatest miracle if blessed Francis were to give
back to this boy his speech and hearing."

2 Sm 15:7 [148]He added: "*I vow to the Lord* God that if blessed Francis in his
goodness will do this, for the love of him I will always hold this boy dear
and support him all the days of his life." A marvelous promise indeed!
Gn 8:15 When he had finished, the boy immediately *spoke up:* "Long live Saint
Francis!" Then, looking up, he said: "I see Saint Francis standing above
me here; he came to give me speech." Then the boy added: "What will I
Ps 69:31 tell the people?" The man answered: "*You shall praise God* and *you*
Ps 36:7; Is 14:7 *shall save* many *people.*" The man, *happy and joyful,* got up and told ev-
eryone what had happened. All the people came running, for they had
seen the boy many times before when he was unable to speak. *Filled*
Acts 3:10 *with wonder* and amazement, they humbly sang praise to God and to

blessed Francis. The boy's tongue had grown so that he could use it to speak; and he began to form words as if he had been talking all his life.

[149]There was another boy, named Villa, who could neither speak nor walk. His mother made a wax image for him and carried it with great reverence to the resting place of the blessed father Francis. When she returned home, she found her son walking and talking.

There was a man in the diocese of Perugia who was unable to utter a word. His mouth was always open, and he gaped and gasped horribly, for his throat was swollen and inflamed. When he came to the place where the most holy body rested and started going down the steps to the tomb, he vomited much blood. And he was entirely cured and began to speak, opening and closing his mouth in a normal way.

[150]A woman suffered great pains in her throat. Due to a violently feverish condition, her tongue stuck to her palate and withered. She could neither talk, nor eat, nor drink. Although poultices were applied and various medicines were tried, they gave her no relief from her illness. Finally she vowed herself to Saint Francis in her heart, since she could not speak. Suddenly there was a rattling noise and a small round stone came out of her throat; this she took in her hand and showed to everyone and soon she was entirely well.

In the town of Greccio there was a young man who had lost his speech and hearing and even his memory, so that he neither understood nor grasped anything. His parents had great faith in Saint Francis, and they vowed the boy to him with humble devotion. After they made this vow, through the favor of the most holy and glorious Father Francis, he was richly blessed with the use of all the faculties of which he had been deprived.

To the praise, glory and honor of Our Lord Jesus Christ, whose kingdom and empire remains firm and immovable forever and ever. Amen.

End.

[Epilogue]

[151]We have said a little about the miracles of our blessed father Francis, and have left out much, to inspire in those who wish *to follow*
his footsteps an eagerness to seek the grace of new blessings. Thus he, 1 Pt 2:21
who so magnificently renewed the whole world by word and example,

life and teaching, might always graciously water the souls of those *who*
Ps 119:132 *love the name of the Lord* with new showers of heavenly gifts.

For the love of the Poor Crucified, and by His sacred *stigmata*
Gal 6:17 which the blessed Father Francis *bore in* his *body*, I ask all those who
Gal 1:20; Lk 18:13 read, see or hear these words, to remember *me, a sinner, before God.*
Amen.

Rv 5:13 *Blessing and honor* and all praise
Rom 16:27 *to the only wise God,*
Who always with great wisdom
1 Cor 12:6 *works all things in all* to His glory.
Amen. Amen. Amen.

THE LITURGICAL TEXTS

(1230–1234)

Introduction

The canonization of Francis of Assisi demanded the development of new liturgical texts for both the Divine Office and for the Mass so that Francis could be fittingly honored on his feast day, October 4. While the texts for the celebration of the Eucharist were taken—according to the practice of the time—from the Common of a Confessor-non-Pontiff, those for the Divine Office were developed with far more flexibility and creativity. The development of these liturgical texts is significant for two reasons. In the first place, it shows the earliest stages through which the memory of Francis was incorporated into the prayer life of the brothers and of the Church. Secondly, it shows how the theological interpretation of Saint Francis moved forward in the first years after his death. While these liturgical texts draw from Thomas of Celano's *The Life of Saint Francis,* they in turn would serve as liturgical sources and inspiration for subsequent lives as the images and symbols they contained influenced the thought of his followers.

Thomas of Celano composed *The Legend for Use in the Choir* in 1230.[1] Julian of Speyer completed the text for *The Divine Office of Saint Francis* before 1235.[2] Several other liturgical pieces were later inserted into *The Divine Office of Saint Francis* and added as Sequences or amplifications of the Alleluia of the Mass,[3] contributions suggesting the interest and involvement of the papal court in the formation of the liturgical cult in honor of Saint Francis. Pope Gregory IX wrote the hymn for First Vespers *Proles de caelo prodiit,* as well as antiphons for the *Office* for the Octave of the feast of Saint Francis.[4] Cardinal Thomas of Capua (+1243), a curial official in the service of both Honorius III and Gregory IX, composed the responsory for the third nocturn of Matins and a hymn for Second Vespers.[5] The Cistercian Cardinal Ranieri Capocci, also a curial official of Honorius III and Gregory IX, created a hymn for Lauds, *Plaude, turba paupercula.*[6]

Early Franciscan Liturgical Developments: The Divine Office

The second chapter of the *Earlier Rule* offers the first indication of the early development of a liturgical life among the brothers: ". . . all the brothers, whether clerical or lay, should celebrate the Divine Office, the praises and prayers, as is required of them. The clerical [brothers] should celebrate the office and say it for the living and the dead according to the custom of the clergy."[7] The "custom of the clergy" at that time varied from church to church even within the city of Rome. Thus the form of the Divine Office used by the brothers may have remained free-flowing and open-ended. The significance of this directive of the *Earlier Rule,* however, lies in the fact that Francis chose the Office found in the churches of the clergy rather than in the choirs of the monks.

With the promulgation of the *Later Rule* in 1223, the liturgical life of the brothers took a new turn: "The clerical [brothers]," the third chapter states, "shall celebrate the Divine Office according to the rite of the holy Roman Church, except for the Psalter, for which reason they may have breviaries." This new insertion into the *Rule* was in many ways an important change. One form of the Divine Office from among the many, that "according to the rite of the holy Roman Church," required uniformity and specifically of the clerical brothers.[8] Developed during the time of Innocent III and distinct from the Divine Office celebrated in the Lateran Basilica and other churches in Rome, it was abridged and simplified for the convenience of the papal household.[9] Unlike other forms, it consisted of one portable volume, the "breviary."[10]

The process of implementing this prescription of the *Later Rule,* however, required several years. By the time of the General Chapter of 1230, a sufficient number of copies of the breviary had been produced at the new scriptorium in Assisi. The General Chapter ordered them sent out to the nearly twenty provinces in order to be further copied and distributed throughout the Order.[11] These breviaries became known as the *Regula breviaries* or *Breviaries of the Rule.*[12] The brothers, however, found the *Regula breviaries* with rubrics intended for the papal household too hard to copy and too complicated to use. The attempt at uniformity also caused confusion. Later, after the General Chapter of 1239, four masters of theology,[13] in their *Exposition of the Rule,* lament that liturgical texts were scarce and in disarray. The four masters insisted that the missal should be in agreement with the breviary and believed that liturgical confusion was one of the disciplinary problems of the Order.

This prompted the Minister General Haymo of Faversham[14] at the General Chapter of Bologna in 1243 to bring some order into the liturgical practice of the brothers. He presented a new *Ordinal,* a ceremonial that in the ritual of the Divine Office and the Mass gave order to both the "action" to be performed and the "speech" or texts to be read; and these rites and texts were "in accordance with the custom of the Roman Church."[15] However, unlike the earlier *Ordinal* drawn up at the papal curia upon which the *Regula breviary* was based, that produced by Haymo was more in accord with the simpler needs of the brothers. Into this *Ordinal* Haymo inserted *The Divine Office of Saint Francis* by Julian of Speyer together with the compositions of Gregory IX, Thomas of Capua and Ranieri Capocci. However, he did not insert a choir legend for matins on the feast of Saint Francis. Some suggest Haymo was waiting for the choir legend by Thomas of Celano, but it did not arrive before his death early in 1244, less than a year after the General Chapter of 1243 that had approved his *Ordinal.* This suggests that *The Legend for Use in the Choir* was not used as widely as Julian of Speyer's Office. However, *The Divine Office of Saint Francis,* as well as the other texts included in it, because of the promotion in Haymo's *Ordinal,* received widespread use.[16]

In *The Legend for Use in the Choir,* Thomas of Celano distributes the story of Francis's life over nine lessons, following very closely the form and textual development of *The Life of Saint Francis.*[17] In *The Divine Office of Saint Francis,* however, a new literary genre appears. His "rhymed" or "rhythmic" Office was written with musical notation and was intended to be sung according to the tradition of literary and musical composition of late eleventh and early twelfth century France.[18]

As these rhymed offices developed in the thirteenth century, they generally celebrated the memory of a saint. Often the whole life of the saint was distributed over the nine lessons (twelve in the monasteries) of Matins. The sung parts of the office (antiphons, responsories, and hymns) were normally drawn from a "life" of the saint, paraphrased and condensed into a poetic form. The text of each antiphon and responsory formed a single stanza of poetry.

As the memory of the saint became transferred from hagiographical texts into the poetic liturgical texts of antiphons and responsories, the use of symbolism and allegory, appropriate for poetic style increased. Because these liturgical texts, formed from the texts of the lives of saints, connected with and introduced a theme already contained with the ancient poetry of the Psalter, new literary expressions about the saint were formed.

Julian of Speyer was educated in this rhythmic tradition and employed it in composing *The Divine Office of Saint Francis.* He thereby brought the interpretation of Francis to another level. His liturgical text of the Office is intentionally poetic and conditioned by theological, liturgical and biblical interpretations. The images of Francis are framed either to introduce the theme of a psalm or to respond to Scriptural or other readings. Although Julian of Speyer uses *The Life of Saint Francis* by Thomas of Celano as a source, he adjusts or explicates the significance of Francis according to his own purposes.

The first antiphon of First Vespers (Evening Prayer) places Francis squarely within the context of the Roman Church, while the second traces his papal mentors, Innocent, Honorius and Gregory. He is the "valiant catholic . . . perfectly apostolic" adhering to the "faith of the Roman Church," docile and respectful to its teachers.[19] The other antiphons of First Vespers further this ecclesial vision and view it as the context of his Gospel life and of his relationship to all creatures. Church, Gospel and all of creation are interwoven. Gregory IX takes up this refrain in his hymn, *Proles de caelo prodiit,* by viewing his life in the context of the Transfiguration and the apostolic initiative to build three tabernacles.

The nine psalms of Matins are individually encased by nine antiphons, which progressively describe Francis's life, beginning with his youth and concluding with his simple way of Gospel life. These antiphons are placed in a marvelous harmony with the nine responsories to the readings of Matins narrating the life of Francis. The three movements or nocturns of Matins unfold, therefore, accenting through antiphons, psalms, lessons and responsories Francis's youthful struggles, his conversion, and his Spirit-filled life. At their heart, the fifth responsory, the ecclesial theme of Gregory's hymn of First Vespers is re-introduced: "Foreshadowing his Orders three/ From God the inspiration came/ Francis built up churches three." [20] Julian sees the mission of the three orders of the Brothers, the Poor Ladies, and the Penitents rooted in Francis's work of rebuilding the three churches.

Lauds (Morning Prayer) continues the presentation of Francis's life of virtue. The first antiphon begins by focusing on his prayer, the fifth concludes the hour's psalms by accentuating his characteristic praise of the Savior and Creator. The hour's other antiphons highlight Francis's preaching, his role in the three Orders, and the spiritual teachings he gave to his followers. The hymn of the Cistercian Cardinal Ranieri Capocci, *Plaude, turba paupercula,* is a richly textured praise of Francis's living and teaching poverty, echoes of which will fill the pages of Franciscan spirituality.[21] Zachary's Canticle, the *Benedictus,* which traditionally brings the hour to a close, introduces the theme of Francis's desire for martyrdom and, in so doing, recalls the stigmata.

The stigmata of Saint Francis appears four times in the course of the texts of the Divine Office. The first is in the Invitatory antiphon for Matins: "The marks of whose redeeming wounds/ In Saint Francis are renewed"[22] and the second is in the *Benedictus* antiphon: "The Seraph on the cross you saw . . ."[23] In both of these, Julian of Speyer goes beyond Thomas of Celano's description of the stigmata in *The Life of Saint Francis.*[24] In Julian of Speyer's texts, the stigmata becomes a sign of the renewal of Christ's presence in Francis and in the world, not just a sign of Francis's intimate contemplative union with Christ on the cross. Furthermore, Julian of Speyer places the Seraph "on the cross," a new feature beyond "a man . . . like a Seraph" in *The Life of Saint Francis* by Thomas of Celano.

The more significant theological and symbolic development concerning the stigmata in the Divine Office is found in Thomas of Capua's hymn for Second Vespers: "Regal seals on our worthy guide/ Are imprinted on hand and side . . ."[25] and in Ranieri Capocci's antiphon for the Octave: "To him the Seraph did appear/ Who marked him with his sacred seal . . ."[26] The stigmata authenticates Francis as a trustworthy teacher and guide for the Christian life: it is safe to follow him. The Cardinals extend the symbol and significance of the stigmata to confirm Francis's teaching authority. The seraph, beyond its role in Thomas of Celano's text, here takes on an active role. The seraph becomes the agent actually "marking" Francis with the wounds. In the liturgical texts of the Divine Office, the already highly symbolic nature of the stigmata and the seraph first presented in *The Life of Saint Francis* by Thomas of Celano received greater emphasis. Julian of Speyer took liberty with Thomas of Celano's narration of the stigmata to foster more pastoral and liturgical applications. In this respect, he likely took cues from the hymns earlier composed by Cardinals Thomas of Capua and Ranieri Capocci.

These liturgical texts are highly significant for the religious, cultural, and literary formation of the first generation of brothers after the death of Saint Francis. These texts offer insight into the importance the early brothers of the Order placed on poetry, music and liturgical formation. They offer an important example of medieval liturgy and they provide a foundation for understanding how the symbolic and spiritual role of Saint Francis initially influenced the brothers.

On the feast of Saint Francis and throughout the octave of this feast, *The Divine Office of Saint Francis* continued to be widely used throughout the Latin Church until the new *Breviarium Romanum* of Pius V in the sixteenth century, and throughout the Order until the eighteenth century. It served as a model for writing other offices in rhythmic and musical form. Julian of Speyer composed the musical notation that accompanied the office, and throughout the centuries composers have set Julian of Speyer's text to their own music.[27] *The Divine Office of Saint Francis* must be ranked among the very finest literary treasures of the liturgy of the thirteenth century.

Early Franciscan Liturgical Developments: The Mass

The liturgical directives of both Francis's *Earlier* and *Later Rules* treat only the Divine Office. There is nothing said about the celebration of the Eucharist. This does not suggest that it did not have an important role in the spiritual lives of the brothers; the *Exhortations to the Clergy*, the *First Admonition* and, above all, the *Letter to the Entire Order* draw attention to the central place the Eucharist held. It is important to recall, however, that the number of priest brothers was small and that the brothers in general frequented parish churches. It was not until the General Chapter of 1230 that a statute concerning the reservation of the Eucharist was enacted. This suggests a new development: the residences of some of the brothers had chapels. With the advent of chapels and more priests among the brothers, the question of missals could hardly be avoided. Thus, together with the *Regula breviary*, the General Chapter of 1230 approved a *Regula missal* for the brothers' use. The earliest Franciscan liturgical calendar, which appeared in 1230, indicates three feasts honoring Saint Francis: his feast day, October 4; the commemoration of the translation (transferral) of his body from the Church of Saint George to the newly built basilica, May 25; and the commemoration of his canonization, July 25. In addition, there is the celebration of an octave, eight days of celebration after his feast day.

The manuscripts of the thirteenth and fourteenth centuries contain three Masses, each identified by the first words of the Introit or entrance antiphon.[28] Of these three, the earliest formula, *Dilectus Deo* [Beloved by God], may have been composed by Gregory IX and may have been among the "new songs" sung by the people at Francis's canonization.[29] The other two formulas were traditionally used for celebrations of Confessors-non-Pontiffs, *Os justi* [The mouth of the just], and for celebrations of great solemnities *Gaudeamus* [Let us rejoice].

The thirteenth century, however, was a time when liturgical Sequences were popular for major celebrations. These were rhymed poetry with paired lines generally set to music and sung after the Alleluia and before the Gospel.[30] There were four Sequences sung in the celebration of Francis's feast.[31] Cardinal Thomas of Capua, an expert in the art of poetry, is the author of *Laetabundus,* a clever re-wording of a Sequence of the same name sung on the Nativity. In his *Chronicle,* Salimbene of Parma maintains that Gregory IX is the author of the second Sequence, *Caput draconis.*[32] And Luke Wadding attributes the final two Sequences, *Sanctitatis Nova Signa* and *Fregit Victor,* to Thomas of Celano.[33] Beyond their presence in early manuscripts, there is no clear indication of when these Sequences were introduced.

While the Mass formulas reflect the more traditional approach of the Church in honoring the male saints who were not bishops, the Sequences reveal the creativity of those who knew Francis more intimately, Gregory IX and Thomas of Celano; or of members of the papal court, who realized his importance. Gregory clearly describes Francis as a militant agent or legate of Christ sent to crush the seven-headed dragon and to convert the people. Thomas of Celano continues Gregory's theme in *Fregit Victor* [Valiant Victor] as he describes Francis in the same bellicose imagery, but in twelve rhetorical questions repeatedly draws attention to the Cross, the sign of victory, with which Francis was armed. As his *Sanctitatis Nova Signa* [Sanctity's New Signs] clearly suggests, Thomas of Celano saw Francis in the same terms as Gregory: as a strong force of renewal and reform in the Church. This may also be said of Cardinal Thomas of Capua. Although avoiding the militaristic vocabulary of both Gregory IX and Thomas of Celano, the very motif of Thomas of Capua's Sequence, that of Christmas, suggests Thomas of Capua's sensitivity to the role of Francis in renewing the signs of Christ's presence on earth. The repetition of *novus* [new], the accentuation of miracles reflecting those of Christ, and, in conclusion, the striking reference to the stigmata, "Gifts of a newer kind/Bestowed by that Son/The Virgin bore:" underscore Francis's unique role in the Church's mission.

The liturgical texts composed within a short time of Francis's canonization clearly reveal the depth of the impression the new saint had made on his contemporaries. The images, figures and symbols used by Thomas of Celano, Julian of Speyer and by those of the papal court, Gregory IX, Cardinal Thomas of Capua and Cardinal Ranieri Capocci, entered deeply into the consciousness of Francis's early followers. As they celebrated his feasts, the literature they produced often echos these early liturgical prayers.

Notes

1. The Latin text of LCh can be found in *Analecta Franciscana sive Chronica Aliaque Varia Documenta ad Historiam Fratrum Minorum Spectantia edita a patribus Collegii S. Bonaventurae adjutantibus aliis eruditis viriis,* Tomus X (Ad Claras Aquas, Florentiae: Collegium S. Bonaventurae, 1895-1946) 119-126; *Fontes Franciscani,* edited by Enrico Menestò and Stefano Brufani (Sta. Maria degli Angeli: Edizioni Porziuncula: 1995) 427-439.

2. The Latin text of *The Divine Office of Saint Francis* (*Officium Rhythmicum Sancti Francisci*) can be found in *Analecta Franciscana* Tomus X 375-404; *Fontes Franciscani,* 1105-1121. Thomas of Eccleston writes that Gregory IX was present in Assisi for the feast of Saint Francis in 1235 when the brothers chanted *The Divine Office of Saint Francis* composed by Julian of Speyer (hereafter Off). Cf. *Tractatus de Adventu Fratrum Minorum in Angliam,* ed. Andrew Little (Manchester: Manchester University Press, 1951) 90.

3. Bernard of Besse indicates that the hymns of Gregory IX and the cardinals were composed before Off, cf. *Liber de Laudibus,* Prologue, *Analecta Franciscana* III 666. See Hilarin Felder, *Die Liturgischen Reimofficien auf die heiligen Franciscus und Antonius gedichtet und componiert durch Fr. Julian von Speier* (+c.1250) (Freiburg, Schweiz: Universitäts Buchhandlung, 1901) 64. For further references within the manuscript tradition that attest to the authorship of these hymns inserted into Off, see Felder, 49-52.

4. Cf. *Proles de caelo prodiit* [A scion blest came from the skies . . .] Off 3, *Sancte Francisce, propere* [Saint Francis, come, do not delay . . .] Off 26, I and *Plange, turba paupercula* [Lament, poor little company . . .] Off 26, III.

5. Thomas of Capua (+1243), cardinal of Santa Sabina, was "dictator" at the papal court and wrote an *ars dictamini,* the art of letter writing. Cf. *In caelesti collegio* [In that celestial company. . .] Off 8 and *Decus morum* [Flower of Virtue, chief Friar Minor . . .] Off 24.

6. Ranieri Capocci of Viterbo (+1250), was a notary for Innocent III and Gregory IX, served as legate for Innocent IV to Emperor Frederick II, and led the military initiative against Frederick. He was made cardinal of Santa Maria in Cosmedin in 1216. According to Thomas of Celano, he took a prominent part in the celebration of Francis's canonization. Cf. 1C 125; *Plaude, turba paupercula* [Poor little cluster, clap your hands . . .] Off 19. See also an antiphon, *Caelorum candor splenduit* [The skies above in splendor gleamed . . .], for use within the octave and for the commemoration of Saint Francis which is attributed to Ranieri Capocci, Off 26, IV.

7. Cf. LR III.

8. Saint Francis's acceptance of the shortened Divine Office used in the papal court thereby gave this form of the breviary a very wide diffusion, making it quasi-official throughout Europe. See Stephen J.P. Van Dijk and J. Hazelden Walker, *The Origins of the Modern Liturgy,* (Newman Press: Westminster, Md.1960) 237.

9. See Hyacinth Workman, "Liturgy and the Franciscan Order" in *The Franciscan Educational Conference* 21 (1939) 11-15. While the rule states the Divine Office is to be celebrated "according to the rite of the holy Roman Church" there were at that time diverse rites of the Divine Office even within the various churches of Rome. What is intended here is the rite of the Roman Curia. On this point, see Giuseppe Abate, "Il Primitivo Breviario Francescano (1224-1227)" in *Miscellanea Francescana* 60 (1960) 65. Earlier in 1213, the liturgy of Innocent III's chapel had been adopted by the Order of the Holy Spirit. Cf. *Regula,* cap. 27; PL 217, 1143.

10. The "breviary" was a portable volume that contained all the elements of the canonical hours of prayer until then distributed among several books: the psalter, the antiphonary, the hymnal, the lectionary, the responsorial, the book of the Gospels, and the book of homilies. Breviaries began to be developed already in the late eleventh century. See Dom Pierre, *The Breviary through the Centuries* tr. Sister David Mary, S.N.J.M (Collegeville, MN: Liturgical Press 1962).

11. In commenting on this General Chapter of 1230, Jordan of Giano also noted: "In the same general chapter breviaries and antiphonaries according to the usage of the Order were sent to the provinces." Cf. Jordan of Giano, *Chronica* in *Collection d'études et de documents sur l'histoire religieuse et littéraire du Moyen Age* edited Henricus Boehmer (Paris, 1908) 57.

12. In the various studies, the *Regula breviaries* are also known as the "Breviaries of Honorius III" or as the "Pre-Haymonian Breviaries."

13. The four masters were Alexander of Hales, John of La Rochelle, Robert of Bassee, and Eudes Rigaud. All taught theology at the University of Paris.

14. Haymo of Faversham was General Minister of the Order from 1240 until his death in 1244.

15. For this reference and for further information on Haymo's liturgical activity, see Van Dijk and Walker, *The Origins*, 292-320.

16. The editors of the *Analecta Franciscana* list ten manuscripts of LCh, (Cf. AF X, 118); and an additional twenty-seven for the hymns for Off; they list fifty-five for the whole office (Cf. AFX 372-374). For the earliest known copy of Julian of Speyer's Office, see Codex A, *Fratrum Minorum Monachii. Breviarium Franciscanum* (1227-34).

17. This work was intended for public reading in the Divine Office during the night hour of matins. During this hour there were readings from the Bible, from patristic writings and from the lives of saints. In the thirteenth century, the readings about the saints were taken from two types of lectionaries, the *Passionale* and the *Legendarium*, the former giving accounts of the suffering of martyrs and the later giving lives of other saints. This work was intended as the *legenda* to be used in a choir or community celebration of matins. From this, it gets its name.

18. Adam of Saint Victor's (+ c.1180) sequences may have provided the model for Julian of Speyer's rhymed offices. Julian of Speyer was also a contemporary of Perotin (+1236), a noted composer at Notre Dame. For musical aspects, see Eliseus Bruning, "Giuliano da Spira e l'officio ritmico de S. Francesco," *Note d'archivio per la Storia Musicale* 4 (1927):129-202, rpt. (Rome: Edizione "Psalterium"). See also "Rhymed Offices" in *Dictionary of the Middle Ages* v 10, edited by Joseph R. Strayer (New York: Charles Schribner's Sons 1988) 366-377.

19. Cf. Off 1.

20. Cf. Off 14, V.

21. It is interesting to note that most of the references to Francis as poor and to the brothers living poorly are found in the hymns or antiphons by Gregory IX, Thomas of Capua, and Ranieri Capocci rather in the texts of Julian of Speyer. Cf. nos. 3, 8 VI & VII, 19 V & VI.

22. Cf. Off 7.

23. Cf. Off 21.

24. Cf. 1C 94.

25. Cf. Off 24.

26. Cf. Off 26, IV.

27. For musical notation, as found in the earliest of manuscripts of Off, see Felder, appendix. For the significance of this text for subsequent Franciscan musicians, see Giuseppe Abate, "La Leggenda Napoletana di S. Francesco e L'Ufficio Rimato di Giuliano da Spira Secondo un Codice Umbro" in *Miscellanea Franciscana* 30 (1930) 146-148.

28. All of these liturgical texts may be found in *Analecta Franciscana*, Tomus X, 375-396.

29. This is the suggestion of Stephen J.P. Van Dijk and Walker, cf. *Origins*, 378-382.

30. A study of the Sequence together with an informative bibliography can be found in E. Leahy, "Sequence," *New Catholic Encyclopedia*, Volume XIII (Washington, D.C: The Catholic University of America, 1967) 100-104.

31. These Sequences can be found in *Analecta Franciscana*, Tomus X, 400-404.

32. Cf. Salimbene of Parma, *Chronica* 383.

33. Cf. Luke Wadding, *Annales Ordinis Minorum*, ad an. 1228, n. 78.

The Legend for Use in the Choir
by
Thomas of Celano
(1230–1232)

[1]You asked me, Brother Benedict, to make excerpts from the Legend of our most blessed father Francis and put them into the order required for the series of nine readings, so that they could be put into
breviaries where all could have them at hand because of their brevity. I
have done what I could and *since you are a man of desires* I have duti- Dn 9:23
fully, although unworthily, tried to please you. I ask, as the price for
this short bit of work, the lasting fruit of your holy prayer.

[I][a]

1C 1 [2]Blessed Francis, born in the city of Assisi, was raised from his ear-
1C 2 liest youth to be arrogant. He became a man of business and used up his
time with vain living until he was twenty-five years of age. But while
he was involved in the goings-on of this world with no concern for the
1C 3 exercise of virtue, the Lord struck him with the whip of illness. And so,
at the change of the right hand of the most High, Francis was suddenly Ps 77:11
changed *into a different man* and gave himself over, with full delibera- 1 Kgs 10:6
tion, to becoming a merchant for *the kingdom of heaven* by rejecting all Mt 13:44-46
1C 8 the riches of this world. *He sold* all *that he had* and offered the money Mt 19:21
1C 9 gained thereby to a certain poor priest. But the priest refused to take the
money because of his fear of Francis's parents; at this, Francis immediately threw the money down at the priest's feet since he considered it to
be so much dirt. Then he was bound by his earthly father, enclosed in
1C 12 their house, beaten by him, and put into chains; but for the name of the
Savior he utterly looked down upon the health of his body.

a. This division of LCh into nine sections or lessons attempts to replicate what may have been the usual practice with the Office of Matins at this period of history. Unfortunately, none of the manuscripts suggest a similar division.

[3]He was then rejected by his own fellow citizens who threw mud at 1C 11
him; he was struck by stones, but fixing his mind on God alone, he
made himself deaf to all these events. On a certain day, when he heard 1C 22
in the gospel what our Lord had said to his disciples when they were
sent to preach, he rose from his place, vowing immediately to put into
practice all the Lord's words with all his might. He took the shoes from
his feet, kept only the one coarse tunic he had, and used only a cord to
gird his waist; for the rest of his life, he took great care to fulfill literally
all the rest of what he had heard.

He left his native land, dead to the world, and walked about fear- 1C 16
lessly. Once in the winter he was taken captive by some robbers, who
threw him naked into the snow. He then went to a monastery, but was
scorned there, and left once again hungry and naked. In the meantime, 1C 4
he began to humble himself more and more and finally took himself to 1C 17
the lepers and lovingly cared for those whom he had previously heart-
ily despised; he wiped their sores, washed their bleeding wounds, and
embraced in them whatever others loathed.

[II]

Prv 31:20 [4]Meanwhile, the Lord *opened His hand* to fill others with this blessing. He gave Francis companions and followers whom the blessed fa- 1C 24-26
ther formed with sound morals; he taught them to follow the way of
evangelical perfection, to take up the title of complete poverty, and to
walk the way of holy simplicity. He proclaimed the word of repentance 1C 23
Lk 5:1 to all and announced *the word of God* in simple words, but with a great
heart. At the outset of all his addresses, he proclaimed peace and pre-
fixed all of his letters with a salutation using the word of peace. On account of these things, many people *who had* previously *hated both*
Ps 120:7; Mk 16:20 *peace* and salvation, *with the Lord's cooperation,* came to embrace
Lk 10:6 peace with all their heart; they became themselves *children of peace*
and ardent seekers of eternal salvation. Thereafter many men—nobles 1C 37
and commoners, clergy and lay—clung to his footsteps and, rejecting
Sir 51:34 all the world's false airs, *they submitted their necks to the yoke* of God. 1C 57

[5]The affection of dutiful love burned brightly in the holy man of 1C 26
God; he applied himself ever more diligently to progressing toward
higher things, deeply desiring to learn what was useful for himself and
his brothers. He prayed earnestly, was inspired with holy sorrow, lulled
Ps 73:17 his flesh to sleep, and was led *into the holy place of God;* he was

1C 27,28 thereby able to see clearly that his flock would increase. He gave
thanks to God and revealed this and many other things he had seen to
1C 32,33 his sons. Thereafter he wrote down a gospel rule —a rule confirmed by
the Lord Pope Innocent at the urging of divine grace—for himself and
1C 36 those with him as well as those to come. And so *he went* out more confidently into the world to do *the work* of the gospel; using flattering Lk 2:47
words with no one, he rejected fancy speeches, yet even the most
learned men *were amazed at the prudence of his replies.* Following the Lk 2:47
1C 29 gospel, he joined his brothers *two by two* and sent them out into the Lk 10:1
1C 38 whole world. He called them the Lesser Brothers so that they would
mark the profession of their name chiefly with the virtue of humility.

1C 43 [6]He taught them to eliminate their vices, to repress urgings of the
flesh, and to render their exterior senses insensitive to all things that
clamor for attention. For as often as he himself felt the tickling of the
flesh—as often happened—he used to immerse himself into a ditch
filled with ice and snow. All of the others with him used to imitate this
1C 51 example of mortification. He used to examine carefully the deeds of
the brothers: leaving nothing unpunished, he made them entirely obedient. Since he was graced with a geat abstinence, he used to alter the
flavor of his food, rarely take wine, and even drink water in meager
1C 52 quantities; the bare ground served as his bed and he slept more often
1C 53 sitting up than lying down. He performed many deeds of simplicity in
order to be thought to be lowly and ordinary and always avoided praise
1C 62 so as to avoid the risk of becoming vain. He held in special honor
priests and venerated the teachers of the divine law with remarkable affection.

[III]

1C 47 [7]As he was rendered more and more worthy of receiving divine grace,
he was soon overflowing with the dew of the Holy Spirit. For example,
appearing as the sun, borne by a chariot, he visited the brothers in the dark-
1C 48 ness of the middle of the night, examining their consciences, opening up
the hidden recesses of their hearts; he knew the deeds of the brothers who 1 Cor 14:25
were absent and foretold what good deeds they would perform in the fu-
1C 58 ture. Since this holy man attained the very summit of perfection and was
filled *with the simplicity of the dove,* he urged all creatures toward the love Mt 10:16
of the Creator. He used to preach to the birds, which heard him and allowed him to touch them; nor would they leave until he dismissed them.

Once there were swallows chattering so much that they would not allow 1C 59
him to preach to the people; he told them to keep quiet and they immediately fell silent. The wild beasts harmed by others used to flee to him and 1C 60
they received the love of piety from him, finding in his presence solace
amidst their trials. What love do you think he bore towards the salvation of 1C 77
human beings, since he was so compassionate towards even the lower
creatures? For example, he often freed lambs and sheep from the threat of 1C 79
slaughter because of the graciousness he felt towards the simplicity of
their nature; he even picked worms out of the roadway so that they would 1C 80
not be harmed by passers-by.

8 He was filled with a wonderful and unspeakable love owing to his
love of the Creator whenever he used to gaze upon the sun, the moon,
and the stars. In fact, he used to urge earth and heaven, fire and air, to 1C 81
love of God with the most refined purity of heart. He found the name of 1C 82
our Lord sweeter than honey whenever he pronounced it with his
mouth, in a manner that exceeded what people could understand. Because of his love for the Lord's name, he loathed the world and wished 1C 55
Phil 1:23 *to be released* through the grace of martyrdom *and to be with Christ.*
He undertook a journey towards Morocco in order to preach the gospel
of Christ to Miramolin, but he was called back to Italy by the divine 1C 57
will. In the thirteenth year of his conversion he traveled to the region of
Syria, hurrying to the Sultan. Assaulted and beaten he preached Christ;
and was sent back by the infidels to the camp of the faithful.

Lk 4:15 9 *He was made much of by everyone* and daily the devotion and faith 1C 53,62
of the people increased in him through God's will; everyone used to 1C 63
run to see him, sometimes even cutting off part of his clothing because
of their love and devotion. The conversion of many to God came about 1C 62
through him and the enormous number of his brothers *increased every*
Acts 2:47 *day.* People used to come to meet him along the road before he could
even enter a city and then would receive him solemnly, carrying the
Mt 21:8 *branches of trees* and filling the countryside and trampling the growth
on both sides of the road. Through his preaching the depravity of heresy was confounded and the Catholic faith was strengthened. He used 1C 82
to find assurance for giving his sermons from the purity of his heart and
would address many or few with the same constancy of mind. People 1C 63
used to offer him bread to bless and then preserve it for long periods of
time; for they found that sick people would grow well again upon tasting it.

[IV]

1C 61,65 [10]Shining with the light of miracles, he turned *water* into *wine;* re- Jn 2:9
1C 66,67 stored the ability to walk to a lame man in Tuscany; at Narni he cured a
paralytic and gave back sight to a blind woman there after driving off
1C 68 the ancient darkness; at Gubbio he healed a woman who was crippled.
He made whole another man, struck down by the devil; then restored
1C 69,70 certain other women, *troubled by evil spirits,* to their senses and to sal- Lk 6:18; 8:2
1C 63,64; 55 vation. Various diseases were cured through his cord. He multiplied
1C 84 food for sailors on a ship and guided the shipwrecked to port. He zealously strove with tremendous devotion to call to mind all the things that
Christ *did while in the flesh* and became so intent on these things that Acts 1:1; I Pt 4:1
none of them escaped his attention.

1C 94 [11]Two years before the servant and friend of God, Francis, gave
back his spirit to heaven, in the vision of God, he saw above him a crucified Seraph who clearly impressed on him the signs of the crucifixion
1C 95 so that Francis, too, appeared crucified. Francis's hands, feet, and side
were marked with the stamp of the cross and there appeared clearly on
1C 90 him the marks of Christ. Insofar as he could, however, he tried to hide
1C 96 these marks from the eyes of people, so that he would not suffer any
loss in the grace that had been given to him. Rom 12:3; 2 Cor 7:9

[V]

1C 97 [12]Throughout this period, his body suffered from illness more se-
1C 108 verely than it had previously; and when he approached his last day and
had by then been completely deprived of the light and use of his out-
1C 109 ward eyes, *he blessed his sons with* crossed *hands,* just as long ago the Gn 48:14-15
patriarch Jacob did. Then the day of his release came and he ordered
the brothers to sing joyfully the Praises of the Lord at his passing. He
himself broke into the song of the psalmist, saying: *"With my voice I
cried to the Lord; with my own voice I beseeched the Lord,"* and so he Ps 142:2-8
continued with the rest of the psalm. Then the gospel was read, a sackcloth was placed over him, and he bade farewell to his sons. His most
holy soul was released from the flesh and taken up into the abyss of
light, and his body *fell asleep in the Lord.* Acts 7:60

1C 110 [13]His soul was seen by one person in a vision: it was rising to
1C 112 heaven, carried on *a little white cloud* and shone like a star. People Rv 14:14
came rushing in large groups from all around; the whole city of Assisi

rejoiced and the whole area hurried there. His sons cried because of the 1C 113
joy in their hearts and kissed the marks of the Great King left on their
father. The most holy body was buried in peace and the holy funeral 1C 116
concluded with many hymns and praises.

[VI]

[14]On the very day that he was buried, Francis scattered signs daz- 1C 127
zling as lightning. He restored to her regular height a young girl whose body had been bent and severely twisted. Thereafter, he poured out everywhere the grace of health on those afflicted with grave illness, but especially on those who came to his memorial shrine. Many cripples he restored to their ordinary height: some had their legs bent curled up under their buttocks; others were lying twisted with their knees pressing upon their chests and their legs broken; others were lying on stretchers and were unable to move without being carried by others; still others, bereft of all consolation, had crippled hands and withered limbs.

[VII]

[15]Francis restored sight to many blind people: he gave sight for the first time to a man who had never had it; another man's eyes were popped out and dangling on thin veins down to his jaw: he returned
them to their proper place. *He* also *made the deaf hear and the mute*
Mk 7:37 *speak.* He gave a tongue to one who, if he had a tongue, it was so short
Lk 7:22 that it could barely be seen; *he cleansed* two *lepers* —one of them was
also a paralytic, and he received healing from both afflictions. He drove demons out of many who were possessed; he healed those afflicted with dropsy, paralytics, and others suffering various diseases—an untold number of people—all through the power of Christ.

Indeed, in the city of Capua he raised a little boy from the dead: he had fallen into a river while playing with other boys and the river mud had covered his body as if it were entombed. In the city of Sessa, a house had suddenly fallen down, killing a young man. At the invocation of the name of the holy father Francis, he not only revived, but even appeared to be unharmed. In Sicily, he gloriously restored to life another young man who had suffered a similar death; in Germany, he restored yet another young man to life. In Germany he also raised another person who had died. And he rescued from the jaws of death another seven who were approaching their end.

[VIII]

[16]Francis healed certain men who suffered a great weight on their genitals as their intestines were slipping into the lower parts of their bodies. This happened with such speed that they were dumbfounded; they thought that they were deluded by a dream rather than experiencing a true cure, so quickly were they healed. He also mercifully freed a
woman who had *suffered* from a *flow of blood* for twenty-three years; Mt 9:20
another woman was healed from the same affliction who had been worn out by suffering the disease for seven years. A certain clergyman
had drunk something deadly and vomited up the poison upon invoking Mk 16:18
his name. Francis was kind liberator of many captives: he opened prisons and loosed chains, allowing them to go free.

And so in all parts of the world, Francis has brought about genuine miracles and freed many people from various misfortunes through the power of Him Whom he always loved, Whom he loved *with all his
mind,* and Whom he always bore in his heart. Lk 10:27

[IX]

1C 88 [17]Freed from the fetters of this mortal life, he blessedly departed to Christ in the year of the Incarnation of Our Lord 1226, on the fourth day of the Nones of October, a Sunday; by then he had spent twenty years
1C 121 perfectly adhering to Christ. Since, moreover, he shone with the new light of miracles after his death, the supreme pontiff, the blessed Pope
1C 123-126 Gregory, along with the whole Church enrolled him in the catalogue of the saints and ordered that his feast be solemnly celebrated on the day of his death.

And he added many favors for him: he ordered that a church should be built in the saint's honor, and donated a large sum; he laid the church's foundation stone, and exempted the church from any jurisdiction beneath his. He sent a golden cross, decorated with precious gems, in which was enclosed a piece of the wood from the Lord's cross. He also sent vestments, vessels pertaining to the ministry of the altar, including some ceremonial vestments which were very expensive. He

made the place outstanding by granting many indulgences and remissions of sin for those who visited. Through these the faith and devotion
Rv 16:14 of the people increased daily, to the praise and glory *of God almighty,*
Rv 4:9; 11:15 *who lives and reigns forever and ever. Amen.*

The Divine Office of Saint Francis
by
Julian of Speyer
and Others
(1228–1232)

First Vespers[a]

1. Antiphons[b]

I. Francis, the valiant catholic
And perfectly apostolic,
Did instruct us to adhere
To the faith of the Roman Church,
And those who were her priests, he'd urge
We should most of all revere.[c]

II. Innocent set him on the course
That in the reign of Honorius
Splendidly achieved its aim.
Succeeding these, Pope Gregory
Heaped on him honors greater yet,
When miracles brought him fame.[d]

III. This man the saint had selected
As His father and protector,
While prelate of a lower see,

a. First Vespers, the evening prayer which initiated the celebration of the feast of Saint Francis, followed the practice of the Church by having a twofold purpose. It marked the ending of the day and, as such, was laudatory or thankful in nature. At the same time, however, it anticipated the feast that was about to be celebrated and was, therefore, caught up in the themes of the following day.

b. Antiphons had a twofold purpose in the Divine Office: (a) musically, they indicated the tone upon which a psalm should be chanted; (b) liturgically, they suggested the dominant thought or theme with which a psalm should be prayed.

c. Whereas antiphons were traditionally scriptural in nature, i.e., echoing a passage from the psalm itself or highlighting a Gospel interpretation of the psalm, others possessed an historical character. In this instance, the antiphons reflected some aspect of the saint's life which exemplifies the psalm in question, Psalm 109 *Dixit Dominus Domino meo* [The Lord said to my lord]. In keeping with the sacerdotal accent of the psalm, Julian of Speyer crafts an antiphon from 1C 62 which offers an interpretation of the psalm from the perspective of Francis's life.

d. The second psalm is Psalm 110 *Confiteor tibi, Domine, in toto corde meo* [I will praise You, Lord, with all my heart].

Endowed with prophetic spirit,
He foretold he would by merit
Apostolic Shepherd be.[a]

IV. Francis, taking up the Gospel,
Not a single dot or morsel
Mt 5:18 Nor a jot did he transgress.
No sweeter yoke than Christ's he owned,
Mt 11:30 No lighter load than His he found
That could this life's wheel possess.[b]

V. Over creatures this man held sway,
Yet wholly did the will obey
Of the God who creatures made;
The delight found in every thing
He stored as an offering
To its Maker's glory paid.[c]

2. Short Scripture Reading

But God forbid that I should glory save in the cross of our Lord Je-
Gal 6:14 sus Christ: by whom the world is crucified to me and I to the world.

R/ Thanks be to God.

3. Hymn[d]
(composed by Pope Gregory IX)

I. A scion blest came from the skies
And worked for us new prodigy,
Uncovered bliss for blinded eyes;
Unhindered and dry shod, the sea,

a. The third psalm is Psalm 111, *Beatus vir qui timet Dominum* [Blessed is the man who fears the Lord] which Julian of Speyer uses to highlight the role of the Pope, that is, when Hugolino who, as Cardinal, was like a father and was protector of Francis and his brothers. Thomas of Eccleston narrates that when Gregory IX, Hugolino, went to Assisi in 1235 to celebrate the Feast of Saint Francis, the friars sang this antiphon as he went to the pulpit to preach, cf. Thomas of Eccleston, *The Coming of the Friars Minor to England,* 15. Julian of Speyer refers to 1C 99-100.

b. The fourth psalm is Psalm 112 *Laudate pueri, Dominum* [Praise the Lord, you children] which Julian of Speyer interprets through 1C 84.

c. The fifth psalm is Psalm 116 *Laudate Dominum, omnes gentes* [Praise the Lord, all you nations] which Julian of Speyer interprets 1C 58, 80.

d. This hymn, as the others in these liturgical texts, followed the strict metrical form required in such chants, thus it is a piece of poetry as well as of music. Gregory's hymn of praise is typical in its weaving biblical images together with those of Francis's life.

II. With Egypt's spoils enriched, Ex 3:22; 12:36
Yet the true nature and the name
Of Poverello never lost;
Fruit-bearing to his poor he came.

III. Like those Apostles, led to climb
The mountain of the bright new day, Mt 17:1
In fields of poverty sublime
Francis spoke, and to Christ did say:

IV. "Three little dwellings let us make," Mt 17:4
Just as had Simon vowed,
Whose name he did not now forsake
But whose example he obeyed.[a]

V. The Law, the Prophets and Grace Mt 5:17; 7:12; 22:40; Lk 16:16,31; Jn 1:17, 45
Were honored by him graciously;
The Trinity's office of praise
He celebrated on a solemn feast.[b]

VI. That time he worthily restored
Three havens where as guest he stayed,
And the temple of those blessed
Spirits to Christ did consecrate.[c]

VII. At "house," at "gate," at "tomb,"[d]
Father Francis, visit us, come,
And to the sorry race of Eve
From mortal slumber bring reprieve. Amen

4. V/ Pray for us, O blessed Francis
R/ That we may be made worthy of the promises of Christ.

---

a. Gregory IX is playing with Peter's name and is obviously accentuating Simon whose name, according to Jerome could be interpreted as *Pone moerorem*, literally "He builds walls," or, according to others, e.g. Isidore of Spain, "Obedient," cf. Jerome, *De nominis hebraicis*, PL XXIII 1163; Isidore of Spain, *Etymologia* VII 9, 3-6, PL LXXXII 287.

b. While the opening verses of this strophe refer back to the previous reference to the building of three tabernacles, the last two verses obviously point to Francis's devotion to the Trinity. Thus Gregory brings together two important aspects of Francis's spirituality: devotion to the Trinity and to the Church.

c. The reference here to the "blessed spirits" echoes the language of the Psuedo-Dionysius who, in the John Scotus Eurigena translation of *The Celestial Hierarchy*, saw the angels as *beatae mentes*, thus a reference to Saint Mary of the Angels, the Portiuncula, the third church which Francis restored.

d. A possible reference to the new and magnificent friary [*domus*] built by Gregory IX beside the Basilica of Saint Francis; to the fortified entrance to the city of Assisi [*portam*] near which the Basilica was built; and, to the tomb of Saint Francis [*tumulum*] over which the Basilica was built; or to domestic life [*domus*], civic, public life [*porta*], and life after death [*tumulus*] represented by the tomb or sarcophagus.

5. Magnificat Antiphon[a]

O wonderment and joy combined!
Human arbiter of the mind:
You it is who to our trainband
Are chariot and its reinsman;
4 Kgs 2:11, 12 A fiery team once carried you,
Transfigured into presence new,
While gathered brothers stood amazed,
Mt 17:2 As though upon the sun they gazed.
On you, wonders radiating,
Future things annunciating,
Came to rest the spirit's unction,
4 Kgs 2:9, 15 Prophecy in double portion.[b]
Succor now your poor descendants,
Father Francis, and defend us,
For grief increases sign and groan
Ps 38:10; 79:13 Among the sheep that are your own.

6. Prayer

God, by the merits of blessed Francis you enlarge your Church with the birth of new offspring. Grant, that by imitating him we may look away from everything on earth, in order to enjoy forever sharing the gifts of heaven. Through our Lord . . .

a. Mary's canticle, the *Magnificat,* held a place in the Evening Prayer of the Church from ancient times since it was seen as the ideal expression of New Testament praise.

b. Julian of Speyer's antiphon uses 1C 47-50, the prophetic description of Francis as another Elijah.

Matins[a]

7. Invitatory [Antiphon][b]

Of His doing let everything
Pay tribute to Christ the King, Ps 145:10
The marks of whose redeeming wounds
In Saint Francis are renewed.

8. Hymn[c]

(Thomas of Capua, Cardinal of Santa Sabina)

I. In that celestial company
Are honors for a comrade new;
Where sanctity and beauty grows,
There flourishes the freshest rose.

II. There Francis, burgeoning with grace,
Paragon for all the lowly,
Is blessed with joy and happiness
And fellowship with the holy.

III. Ripe harvest of the scattered seeds
Provides him with the sheaves he needs, Jn 4:35,36; Ps 126:6
As beneath the morning soil
He did our adversary foil.

IV. The carnal self of proud conceit
He bade the spirit's laws obey, Rom 7:25; 8:13
Brought to a world of sin defeat, Jn 16:33
And by self-conquest won the day.

V. The hand, forerunner of the tongue,
Prepared the path words run along, Mt 3:3
And so, the ages saw diffused
Doctrine by acts and deeds produced.

VI. In field of poverty he sowed[d]
The vine of the Minors, Is 5:1,2

a. The ancient monastic practice of nocturnal prayer or vigils became known as Matins or the prayer recited before dawn. It was composed of three distinct sections or nocturns each of which was inspirational in nature and offered participants three psalms, readings and scriptural responses in preparation for the celebration of the day's feast.

b. The invitatory was an invitational chant sung together with Psalm 94. It took on the nature of a prelude to the celebration of the Divine Office by always expressing an invitation to praise in an antiphonal way, that is, as a refrain.

c. The hymn following the Invitatory generally took up its same theme and was usually energetic, necessarily so, given the hour at which it was sung.

d. Cf. Hymn of I Vespers III.

And by a living lesson showed
Their course and way of life's design.

VII. To riches of eternity
He drew his pauper company
Whom to unearthly charms untold
His conduct was the voice that called.

VIII. Splendid in conduct as in creed,
Resplendent still in miracles;
In doing good he took the lead,
Was a lamp-lit route for peoples.

IX. In the Most High King's palace hall,
Teacher, your pupils now install;
Secure the grace that they be saved,
For those who Jesus Christ have served.

X. From shadows of our cheerless plight
We keep a guiding star in sight,[a]
Seeking the Father's grace, we might
At last have part in glory bright. Amen.

First Nocturn

9. Antiphons[b]

I. This man was raised in vanities
And shameful was his rearing;
Outstripping those that nurtured him,
His ways were overbearing.[c]

Ps 77:11 II. By favor of the Most High's hand,
Amazingly converted,
He helped the lapsed for pardon hope,
Since Christ's bliss he now enjoys.[d]

a. A passage from the hymn of the Epiphany, *Stellam sequentes praeviam.*

b. Julian of Speyer uses the liturgical psalmody to highlight the life of Francis, the details of which would be spelled out in the three readings of each nocturn.

c. Psalm I, *Beatus vir* [Blessed is the man] was used as the first of the three psalms of the First Nocturn. The Chapter of Narbonne in 1260 changed the last two verses of this antiphon to read: *Divinis charismatibus/Praeventus est clementer* [Through divine gifts/Was mercifully delivered].

d. This antiphon introduced Psalm II, *Quare turbulantes gentes* [Why do the nations].

III. He was made mild, though not at once:
First, by ailments he was taught;
Then, equipped with heaven's weapons,
Moral change he fully wrought.[a]

10. V/ The Lord loved him and adorned him.[b]
R/ He clothed him with a robe of honor. Sir 6:32

11. Responsories[c]

I. R/ As soon as Francis ceased to deal
In civic merchandising
Into the Lord's field he withdrew
To meditate in quiet;
1C 6-7 The gospel treasure he found there Mt 13:44
Would henceforth be his trading.

V/ No one but God would he consult
On what to do; and so, he heard
The heaven-given signal.

II. R/ Fervid in the work of God,
Now, his property once sold,
To the poor he purposed to give Mt 19:21
The money thereby acquired;
Its heavy weight would be a hurt
To the freedom of the heart.

V/ A priest, though poor, would not in fear
Accept the gift; so then, Francis
Threw it away as worthless.

1C 10 III. R/ During his father's harassment
He hid till wrath abated; Rom 12:19
Then undertook audaciously
To face the public waiting:
1C 11 Oh, what a sordid face was seen!
They considered him quite crazed.

a. This antiphon introduced Psalm III.

b. The versicles and responsories of each of Matin's three Nocturns were used as responses to the three psalms. In this instance, they are taken from the Common of a Confessor-non-Pontiff.

c. This more elaborate form of response took place after each of the three readings and usually synthesized the thought of the reading. Inevitably the responsory or the verse cited or alluded to some passage of Scripture.

V/ While mire and stones were flung at him,
The man of patience strove to pass away with unhearing
Ps 38:14 ears.

Second Nocturn

12. Antiphons

IV. Dragged home and sorely beaten by 1C 12
The angriest of fathers;
Acts 12:6 Reproached, subdued, confined, until
Slyly by his mother freed. 1C 13

V. Released, no longer will he yield
To such unbridled fury;
Of his own free choice, he cried out, 1C 13
Acts 5:41 For Christ he will suffer woes.

VI. Before the local bishop brought,
All his father's claims disowned:
Standing naked, himself he called 1C 14-15
A banished man in this world.

13. V/ The mouth of the righteous utters wisdom.
Ps 37:30 R/And his tongue speaks justice.

14. Responsories

IV. R/ The rags upon his back were few,
As songs of praise in French he sang,
1 Mc 2:26,58 Championing a charter new.
Thieves, accosting him in woods,
Are answered in prophetic tones:
Ps 47:3 "The Great King's herald am I."

V/ Thrown into freezing snow, he heard,
Ez 34:8,12 The future shepherd of his flock,
"Lie down there, you rustic boor!" 1C 16

V. R/ Maltreated in a monastery,
He searched out now a former friend,
Who gave him a tunic. 1C 16

Glad to receive human contempt,
1C 17 He lovingly the lepers served,
Whom he'd formerly despised.

V/ Foreshadowing his Orders three
From God the inspiration came
Francis built up churches three.

VI. R/ He listened to the Gospel words,
Those Christ spoke to His disciples
On sending them out to preach. Mk 3:14
"This is," he said, "what I desire."
He rested happy in these words,
Keeping them in memory.

V/ No use had he for staff, or shoes,
1C22 Or scrip. A rope around his waist, Mt 10:10
No spare tunic would he wear.

Third Nocturn

15. Antiphons

1C 23 VII. In the word of renewing grace
Earnestly he set his heart,
And the message of repentance
With simplicity pronounced.

1C 24 VIII. The peace of salvation he preached Is 52:7
In the power of the Spirit, Lk 1:17; Rom 15:13
And made the friends of lasting peace
Those exiled from saving grace. Is 57:19; Eph 2:17

1C 26 IX. As merits of the holy man
Were honored with new offspring,
Instruction fresh he gave these sons:
The way of simplicity. Prv 10:29; 11:5

16. V/ The law of his God is in his heart.
R/ His steps shall be saved from stumbling. Ps 37:31

17. Responsories
(Author: Thomas of Capua)

Dt 23:24 VII.R His flesh Francis flailed like an ear of corn
Upon the threshing-floor of this dire world;
And with chaff removed, he, like purest grain,
Mt 3:12 Enters and goes through to the High King's barn.

Jn 6:41 V/ Death joined him to the Living Bread;
2 Mc 9:28 True Life began when life was dead.

(Author: Gregory IX)

VIII.R/ From granary of poverty
Saint Francis drew supplies to feed
The famished throng that followed Christ,
Mt 15:32 Lest on their journey they grow weak.
The road to glory he spread out,
Mt 7:14 Enlarged the way that leads to life.

V/ For being poor in this world's goods
He reigns rich in his true homeland,
And constitutes his kingly heirs
Those poverty on earth enriched.

IXa.R/ Seventh now with a group of six,
Their father, rapt in heaven-light,
What the future held foresaw.
Humblest Friar Minor of them all,
What ensured for his tiny flock
He gazed at with clear vision.

Mt 5:26 V/ And lifted was that last of weights, 1C 26-27
When, for the sins he ever did,
Revealed was full forgiveness.

IXb.R/ Telling his sons these secret things, 1C 27-28
An either son he received at length.
Then, he gathered them to send
Mk 6:7; Lk 10:1 In pairs, to peoples far afield,
Bidding them to humble themselves
1 Thes 5:14 And ever to be patient.

1C 29 V/ The flock all fell upon their knees;
The shepherd raised them up again;
And for gladness they embraced.

1C 29 IXc.R/ "Go now upon your way," he said,
"And on the Lord who cares for you
Cast all consideration." Ps 55:23
He then forbade the brothers take
Any errant and endless track
Of craving anxiety.

V/ Thus would the heart that's free of cares
Not for tomorrow then provide Mt 6:34
With money strapped in purses. Mk 6:8

1C 31 IXd R/ The friars whom he had sent returned
And reached the complement of twelve.
Giving ratification
1C 32-33 To the rule the saint had written,
Pope Innocent gave directives
About the task of preaching.

V/ Francis his mina traded off,
Motivated to use that gift Lk 19:13
Lucrative returns to gain.

Lauds[a]

18. Antiphons

1C 35 I. Saint Francis set out to obtain,
Through many an attentive prayer,
Directives on what to do:
He would not live just for himself
But for the good of everyone,
Influenced by godly zeal.[b]

---

a. *Laudes* [Praises] were sung upon rising, that is, at the beginning of a new day, in order to turn immediately to God with a prayer of thanksgiving, praise, and joy. It consisted of five psalms of praise or, on feasts, four psalms and the Canticle of the Three Children, (Dn 3:57-88, 56) a brief reading from Scripture, Hymn, the Canticle of Zachary, and a final prayer.

b. As dictated by the rubrics, the psalms of the feast of a Confessor-non-Pontiff were those of Sunday. This first psalm, then, was Psalm 92 *Dominus regnavit* [The Lord reigns]. Once again Julian of Speyer develops the refrains or antiphons by referring to 1C.

Mt 9:35 II. He wandered round about to preach 1C 36
And, by no human teacher taught,
Left the learned struck with awe.
Of valor were the words he spoke,
So that a fresh militia came
To follow their new captain.[a]

III. Three were the Orders he arrayed: 1C 38
The Friars Minor he called the first;
And the Poor Ladies were next,
Becoming the middle order;
Then thirdly came the Penitents,
Comprising men and women.[b]

IV. He studied in the school of grace, 1C 38-41
He learnt in the school of trial
All matters of perfection,
Jn 14:26 All the things that he taught the friars,
As much through acts as in many
A honey-flowing discourse.[c]

V. He bade us praise as praise he did, 1C 58
For praise was ever on his lips,
The praise of his dear Savior;
And he invited bird and beast
And every other creature, too,
To praise their Lord and Maker.[d]

19. Hymn[e]
(Cardinal Ranieri Capocci)

I. Poor little cluster, clap your hands,
Your wealth comes from your father poor;
Hold up the cup that's filled with praise,
Cup full of his pressed richness blest.

---

a. The psalm in this instance is Psalm 99 *Jubilate Deo, omnis terra* [Make a joyful sound to God, all the earth].

b. The psalm is Psalm 62 *Deus, Deus meus* [O God, You are my God].

c. *The Canticle of the Three Children,* Dn 3:57-88, 56.

d. The final psalm is Psalm 148 *Laudate Dominum de caelis* [Praise the Lord from the heavens].

e. The Hymn of Lauds followed the spirit of the liturgical hour, that is, it is laudatory in tone. In this instance, the hymn composed by the Cistercian Cardinal, Ranieri Capocci, expresses his understanding of and praises the Gospel spirituality of Francis, especially his embrace of poverty.

II. He was simple, upright, humble, Jb 1:1,8; 2:3
The endearing champion of peace;
A light in an earthen vessel 2 Cor 4:7
Burning, bright in a vessel frail.

III. Though wretched were the clothes he wore,
He was warmed by a holy flame;
Both cold and heat he overcame
Whilst stigmata of Christ he bore.

IV. Crushing the carnal and mundane,
And trampling the malignant foes,
As victor crown of gold he won,
As doctor coronet he gained.

V. Poor and naked he departed,
Endowed richly heaven entered,
To strew sovereign benefactions,
For the sick destroy their heartbreak.

1C 76 VI. O father of the true poor,[a] Jb 29:16
Help us to be in spirit poor; Mt 5:3
Partners of those that dwell above
Make us who have been snatched from ruin.

VII. To Father, Son, and Paraclete
Beauty, honor and glory be; Rv 5:12,13
And, by the merits of this Saint,
To us eternal happiness. Amen.

20. V/ Pray for us, Blessed Francis.
R/ That we may be made worthy of the promises of Christ.

21. Benedictus Antiphon[b]

1C 107 O Francis, martyr by desire,
Feeling His pain, with all your soul
You followed in the steps of Him
Whom suffering you found in the book
You took and opened wide.
While you were gazing at the sky

a. Cf. The Sequence of Pentecost, *Veni Sancte Spiritus* II, 1.

b. The singing of the Canticle of Zechariah was a stable element of Lauds undoubtdly because of its reference to the light illumining "those in darkness and sitting in the shadow of death."

The Seraph on the cross you saw,
And thence you bore on hands and side
And felt the image of the wounds
Of Christ the Crucified.
Tend still the flock you left behind;
For after you had passed away,
Though hard and dark your flesh till then,
To all appearance you displayed
A body glorified.

The Small Hours[a]

Terce

21a. Short Responsory

V/ The Lord loved him and adorned him.
R/ The mouth of the righteous utters wisdom. Ps 37:30

Sext

22. Short Scripture Reading

Peace and mercy be upon all who walk by this rule, upon the Israel of God. Gal 6:16

R/. Thanks be to God.

22a. Short Responsory

V/ The mouth of the righteous utters wisdom. Ps 37:30
R/ The law of his God is in his heart. Ps 37:31

None

23. Short Scripture Reading

Henceforth let no man trouble me; for I bear in my body the marks of Jesus. The grace of our Lord Jesus Christ be with your spirit, brethren. Amen. Gal 6:17,18

R/. Thanks be to God

23a. Short Responsory

The law of his God is in his heart.
V/ The Lord guided the righteous on straight paths.
R/ And showed him the Kingdom of God. Wis 10:10

a. There were generally four small hours, Prime, Terce, Sext and None, celebrated, as the Latin words suggest, at the first, third, sixth and ninth hours of the day. The early manuscripts for the feast of Saint Francis do not contain any liturgical texts for Prime, suggesting that the friars celebrated Lauds in its place, a practice that was common at this period of history.

Second Vespers[a]

24. Hymn[b]

(Author: Thomas of Capua, Cardinal of Santa Sabina)

I. Flower of Virtue, chief Friar Minor,
Francis holding up the trophy,
Gifted to life, in You, the Vine,
O Christ, Redeemer of us all.[c]

II. Our brother hails, our father reigns,
Dwelling with heaven's citizens;
Let tears recede, let chorus sing,
Let all in heaven their voices raise.[d]

III. When earth lost him the heights gained him,
As all those works of wonder prove;
Therefore he lives, for he attained
The gifts of Christ that never fail.[e]

IV. For a lifetime's deep desiring
Now he reaps glory's endowments;
You gave him grace, gave him favors,
O God of boundless mercy free.[f]

V. Let all him follow, all him join
Ps 114:1 Who march out of Egypt;
With him as lead, in broad daylight
"The standards of the King draw nigh."[g]

VI. Regal seals on our worthy guide
Are imprinted on hand and side;
The light surmounts the dark's domain,
The star of day begins to reign.[h]

---

a. For the most part Second Vespers was an echo of the First and was the conclusion of the feast. The psalms and, therefore, the antiphons were taken from First Vespers.

b. The antiphons and reading are taken, as usual, from Lauds.

c. The first line of the hymn of the Matins of the Nativity, *Christe, redemptor omnium.* Cardinal Thomas of Capua weaves hymns used for the feast of the Nativity and for the Common of Apostles as means of developing themes of Francis's life and spirit.

d. The first line of the hymn of Vespers for the Common of the Apostles, *Exultet caelum laudibus.*

e. The first line of the hymn of Matins for the Common of the Apostles, *Aeterna Christi munera.*

f. The first line of the hymn of Matins for Saturday morning, *Summae Deus clementiae.*

g. The beginning of a hymn of Passion Sunday, *Vexilla Regis prodeunt.*

h. The beginning of the hymn of Prime of Sunday, *Iam lucis orto sidere.*

VII. A trusty leader, bright lodestar,
Escorts, glistens, rambling pathways
He steers clear of, while displaying
To us again those blessed joys.[a]

VIII. Drive the flock, captain, to the King, Ex 3:1
You crusher of the crafty foe;
Escort us and lead us into
The supper of the caring Lamb.[b]

24a. V/ Pray for us, blessed Francis.
R/ That we may be made worthy of the promises of Christ.

25. Magnificat Antiphon

Oh, marvel at such a man
Of portents and of miracles,[c] Bar 2:11; 2 Cor 12:12
of afflictions and of demons Mt 4:24; Mk 1:35
At hand to drive away.
He made the woodland birds give ear,
1C 58 When he stopped and preached to them,
And heed his every word.
Oh, how worthy was that life,
A life that so enhanced the faith
And even raised the dead to life,
When his life was no more.
Francis, make us to be one day
Citizens with those on high,
To whom you are now joined.[d]

a. The beginning of the hymn of Matins of Pentecost, *Beata nobis gaudia.*

b. The beginning of the hymn of Vespers of the Saturday of the Easter Season, *Ad cenam Agni providi.*

c. Julian of Speyer relies upon the third antiphon for the Second Nocturn of Matins for the feast of Saint Martin of Tours, Bishop: *O ineffabilem virum per quem nobis tanta miracula coruscant.*

d. The final prayer of Julian of Speyer with which he ends his Office for the feast of Saint Francis.

26. Benedictus and Magnificat Antiphons for the Octave and for the Commemoration of Saint Francis

(Ascribed to Pope Gregory IX)

I. Saint Francis, come, do not delay
O father, hasten with your aid:
Here are a people sorely pressed
And crushed beneath their heavy loads
Of straw and clay and building bricks.
But now that the Egyptian lies
Ex 1:14; 2:12; 5:7 In sand, release us from our ties,
Exterminate the flesh of sin.

(Attributed to Thomas of Capua, Cardinal of Santa Sabina)

II. Hail, holy father, light of your homeland,
Mirror of virtue, rectitude's pathway,
Rule for our conduct:
From earthly exile bring us to reach
The uppermost kingdoms.

(Attributed to Pope Gregory IX)

III. Lament, poor little company;
Jb 29:16 To the father of the poor, like orphans cry:
This sorrowful and plaintive sigh,
Father Francis, take up and hear,
And show to Christ those precious brands
Upon your side, and feet, and hands,
That to us orphans He may give
A worthy father in your stead.

(Ascribed to Cardinal Ranieri Capocci)

IV. The skies above in splendor gleamed,
A new star sprang out of the blue:
Saint Francis was made manifest.
To him the Seraph did appear
Who marked him with his sacred seal

On palms, on soles of feet, on side:
Ever he would the cross display
In heart, in word, in every work.

Masses in Honor of Saint Francis

First Mass

1. Introit[a]

The mouths of the just speak wisdom and their lips say what is right;
Ps 37:30-31 the law of their God is in their heart. Do not fret because of the wicked;
Ps 37:1 do not envy those who do evil.

v/. Glory be . . .

2. Prayer [Collect]

God, by the merits of blessed Francis you enlarge your Church with the birth of new offspring. Grant, that by imitating him we may look away from everything on earth, in order to enjoy forever sharing the gifts of heaven. Through our Lord . . .

3. Epistle
(Gal 6:14-18)

A reading from the Letter of Paul to the Galatians:

Brothers, God forbid that I should glory save in the cross of our Lord Jesus Christ; by whom the world is crucified to me and I to the world. For in Christ Jesus neither circumcision availeth anything, nor uncircumcision, but a new creature. And whosoever shall follow this rule, peace on them and mercy, and upon the Israel of God. From henceforth let no one be troublesome to me; for I bear the marks of the Lord Jesus in my body. The grace of our Lord Jesus Christ be with your spirit, brothers. Amen.

4. Gradual

You came to meet him with the blessings of success; you have set on his head a crown of pure gold.

a. This is the Introit of the Common of a Confessor-non-Pontiff and of Abbots.

v/. He asked you for life and this you have given, days that will last from age to age. Ps 21:4-5

Alleluia, alleluia.[a]

v/. Holy father Francis, show to Christ the stigmata on your body, that He may grant us the glory of His kingdom.[b] Alleluia.

5. Gospel
(I. Mt 19:27-29)
or
(II. Mt 11:25-30)[c]

A reading from the Gospel of Saint Matthew:

At that time Jesus answered and said: I confess to you, Father, Lord of heaven and earth, because you have hidden these truths from the wise and the prudent and have revealed them to little ones. Yes, Father, for so it seemed good in your sight. All things have been delivered to me by my Father. And no one knows the Son but the Father; neither does anyone know the Father but the Son and he to whom it shall please the Son to reveal Him.

Come to me, all you who labor and are burdened and I will refresh you. Take my yoke upon you and learn from me, because I am meek and humble of heart. And you shall find rest for your souls. For my yoke is sweet and my burden light.

6. Offertory

My truth and my love shall be with him; by my name his might shall be exalted.[d] Ps 89:25

7. Prayer over Gifts

Make holy, Lord, the gifts presented to you, and, through the intercession of the blessed Francis, purify us of all our lapses into sin.

---

a. Thus far the Gradual has been taken from the Common of Abbots.

b. This prayer is similar to that of 1C 118, 119, as well as that of Gregory IX in the antiphon attibuted to him, *Plange, turba paupercula,* cf. supra.

c. This is the Gospel of the Common of Abbots. It was the Gospel used at least until the year 1253, as Thomas of Celano reflects in 3C 111.

d. This Offertory verse is that of the Common of a Confessor-non-Pontiff.

8. Communion [Antiphon]

Lord, you have given me five talents: behold I have gained another five. Mt 25:20

9. Postcommunion [Prayer]

Lord, we pray that heavenly grace may expand Your Church, which it was Your will to illumine with the glorious merits and examples of the blessed Francis.

Second Mass

1. Introit

Let us all rejoice in the Lord as we celebrate this feast day in honor of the blessed Francis; it is a solemnity which causes the Angels to rejoice, and to praise together the Son of God.[a] Exult in the Lord, you righteous; praising befits those who are upright. Ps 33:1

2. Prayer (See First Mass)

3. Epistle (See First Mass)

4. Gradual

The mouths of the just speak wisdom and their lips say what is right.

v/. The law of their God is in their heart, their steps shall be saved from stumbling.[b] Ps 37:30-31

Alleluia, alleluia
v/. O Patriarch of paupers true,
Francis, amplify by your prayers
The number of those who are yours,
In the charity of Christ;
Whom, crossing your hands and growing
Blind, like Jacob on his death-bed,
You gave your benediction.[c]
Alleluia

v/. Francis, once poor and meager, enters heaven enriched, and is honored with celestial hymns.

a. The Introit is similar to that of the Mass for the Feast of All Saints.

b. The Gradual is taken from the Mass of Common of a Confessor-non-Pontiff.

c. Cf. 1C 108, a reference to Francis's own death and its similarity to that of Jacob.

5. Gospel (See First Mass)

6. Offertory (See First Mass)

7. Prayer over gifts (See First Mass)

8. Communion [Antiphon]

A faithful and wise servant, whom the Lord set over His household
Lk 12:42 to give them their allowance of food at the proper time.

9. Postcommunion [Prayer] (See First Mass)

Third Mass

1. Introit

Beloved by God and humanity, his memory is held in benediction. See, he departs for the heavenly kingdoms; for, tried in virtue, he was found faithful in his words; therefore, his heritage lasts for ever. Psalm: For his loyalty and gentleness God sanctified him, and chose him out of all humankind. Sir 45:4

v/. Glory be . . .

2. Prayer [Collect] (See First Mass)

3. Epistle (See First Mass)

4. Gradual

Christ took away his sins and exalted his power and gave him the covenant of life and a throne of glory on high. Sir 47:13

v/. In the multitude of the elect he will have praise, and among the blessed he shall be blessed for ever.

Alleluia, alleluia.

v/. True light, enlightening all humanity, Christ our God, at the prayers of Saint Francis, pour into our hearts the light of your truth. Rejoice, Jerusalem our mother, founded on sapphires and crowned with roses.

Alleluia.

5. Gospel (See First Mass)

6. Offertory

My servant, see, I have made of you a witness to the peoples, a leader and a master of the nations. My Spirit that is in you and the Is 55:4
words I have placed in your heart, shall not depart from your lips nor from the lips of your descendants, says the Lord, now and for ever. Alleluia.

7. Prayer over Gifts (See First Mass)

8. Communion Chant

Is 49:5 The Lord has become my strength, and with his great love has had
compassion on me; therefore, magnify him, you who love the Lord, for
Ps 106:1 he is good, for his steadfast love endures for ever. Alleluia, Alleluia,
Alleluia.

9. Postcommunion [Prayer] (See First Mass)

Sequences in Honor of Saint Francis

Laetabundus [Fully Gladsome]

(Ascribed to Cardinal Thomas of Capua)

I. Fully gladsome[a]
To Francis let the chorus sing:
Alleluia!

II. He was fastened
With nails new-made by True Love:
O wondrous thing!

III. Soul in body suffered pain,
Now gleamed newly with pure light
Sunbeam from star.

IV. He, of such new florescence,
To the very birds had preached,
Ever clear-toned.

V. Just as it was taught by Christ,
He held fast to poverty
In equal form.

VI. He did not wish his children
Ever to possess those things
That perish here.

VII. As he in heaven sings for joy,
With more and more marvels glows
This vale of ours.

VIII. Eyes that were blind get new sight;
A child's tongue grew normally
With added flesh.

IX. The mouths of the dumb are loosed;
Many are to life restored;

a. The author of this liturgical sequence uses a hymn of the Season of the Nativity as the foundation. Thus the opening verse, *Laetabundus/exultet fidelis chorus/Alleluia*, is changed to *Laetabundus/Francisco decantet chorus/Alleluia*.

Heresy is now convinced
How blind it is.

X. Leprosy is gone; the lame
Leap, and fevers fly away;
Many kingdoms stand amazed
At all these things.

XI. Sultan's favors and rough
Places he spurned, and yet
Was by him unscathed,
Unhappy race.

XII. The wounds he has show forth
Gifts of a newer kind,
Bestowed by that Son
The Virgin bore.

Caput Draconis [The Dragon's Head]
(Author: Gregory IX)

I. Last of the evil dragon's heads,
Holding aloft its vengeful sword,
Against God's people now stirred up
The seventh of its savage wars. Rv 12:3; 13:1

II. Against the skies it took its stand
And strove mightily to drag down
The greatest portion of the stars,
To match the number of the damned.

III. But yet, from Christ's own side was sent
A legate with a mission new,
Upon whose holy body marked
The ensign of the Cross was seen.

IV. Protected by the shield of faith,
And helmeted with hope, he bore 1 Thes 5:8; Eph 6:16-17
The sword of the Word, and for belt
He was girded with chastity. 2 Kgs 1:8

V. Francis, chieftain of great renown,
Carried the regal banner forth,
Assembled a council of war Ps 89:8; 110:1
To move throughout the whole wide world
Against the rifts the dragon wrought.

VI. He marshaled three full battle-lines
Of soldiers readied for action,[a]
To put to flight and rout that force
And that threefold demonic band
The dragon ever kept at strength. Rv 16:13

VII. On the King's orders he hastened
To those joys that last for ever;
Saint Francis putting in his claim
For his well-earned soldier's wages.

VIII. Bequeath to us, kindest Father,
The grace our father had from You;
So may the sons he fathered be
Partakers of his glory too. Amen.

---

a. The three Orders of the Franciscan Family.

Sanctitatis Nova Signa [Sanctity's New Signs]
(Attributed to Thomas of Celano)

I. Sanctity's novel emblems came,
Signs that were worthy of acclaim,
Awesome, and yet with warmth aflame,
To Francis's hands entrusted.

II. A new flock to be led and ruled,
With a new set of laws imbued;
Thus were the King's commands renewed,
By Francis's hands transmitted.

III. An order new, a life-form new
Appeared on earth out of the blue;
Its sanctioned rule was to renew
The pattern the gospels teach.

IV. In the image of Christ's decree,
Law is remodeled perfectly;
The purpose of the rule must be
The apostolic peak to reach.

V. With simple cord his austere wear
He bound, to vesture gave no care;
Bread he carried in measure spare,
And barefooted, shoes he spurned.

VI. As poverty alone he sought,
To earthly goods he gave no thought;
Underfoot all these Francis trod,
And a purse for money scorned.

VII. Places he sought in which to weep
And voice a heartfelt sorrow deep,
Lament upon sad lament heap
For those worldly years of waste.

VIII. Caved in seclusion on the Mount,
He wailed and prayed upon the ground;
And when serenity he found
In those confines hid encased.

IX. In that place with rock for shade,
Absorbed in godly things he stayed;
To slight things here wise judgment made
And espoused the world above.

X. He curbed his flesh and made it tame
Until transfigured it became;
The food he took, from Scripture came,
Food of earth away he drove.

XI. Then from on high a hierarch
Came down on low, the royal Monarch;
Struck with fright was that patriarch
By the sign on which he gazed.

XII. Bearing the marks of Christ the Lord,
He on Francis those scars conferred,
Who stayed the while, with grieving heart,
Silent, by the Passion dazed.

XIII. Thus was that holy body signed;
To hand and foot were wounds consigned;
Transfixed appeared the right-hand side,
That all the while blood had dyed.

XIV. Words exchanged, much the future hid
Was clear; the saint could see amid
So much the meaning of things said,
By mystic breath of insight.

XV. Now awesome nails came into sight,
Outside black-hued, flame-hued inside;
Fierce piercing pain did him betide,
As sharp points excruciate.

XVI. No instruments of skill were used
To carve out those limbs' apertures;
Nor were the dug out holes nature's,
Nor from mallet's cruel weight.

XVII. By the signs of the Cross you wore,
Through which the world you triumphed over,
Through which you quelled the carnal foe
In a victory renowned,

XVIII. Let us, Francis, be safeguarded,
Shield in hardship be afforded,
So that we may be rewarded,
In celestial glory crowned.

XIX. Loving father, holy father,
Devout people, with your succor,
Companioned by throngs of brothers,
May they gain their longed-for prize.

XX. Partners make in life supernal,
Those who formed through your example;
May the flock, your own Friars Minor,
Reach those sempiternal joys.

Fregit Victor [Valiant Victor]
(Sometimes attributed to Thomas of Celano)

I. Fracted has the valiant victor
This man Francis, triumphantly
Left the cross's enemy.

II. Hearty carrier of the cross,
In spiritual battle, chief;
Peerless among those that love.

III. Whom the king to come, who would
Combat, who would care, sent ahead
With a massive assembly.

IV. He fortified him till secure
He would amass his store of arms,
To provide a sound defense.

V. Tell us, tell us why, O Francis,
To the cross why were you fastened?
In that the Cross contemplating
And my sinful flesh supplanting
Always was my constant care.

VI. Tell us, tell us why, O Francis,
To the cross why were you fastened?
In that this world abdicating
And the Cross by imitating,
Of Christ's life I was conveyor.

VII. Tell us, tell us why, O Francis,
To the cross why were you fastened?
Love of Jesus within me burned
And its sweetness absorbed my heart,
Amplifying its desire.

VIII. Tell us, tell us why, O Francis,
To the cross why were you fastened?
Keeping the mind fixed firm on high,
My heart, at sight of Jesus like
A Seraph, was all on fire.

IX. Tell us, Francis, how did you fare
When you had looked on Jesus there?

Good Jesus, for whom my heart yearned,
Now so near me, I could discern
So visibly resplendent.

X. Tell us, Francis, how did you fare
When you had looked on Jesus there?
With pleasure were my looks aglow,
And more deeply than speech could say,
I felt this love stupendous.

XI. Tell us, Francis, How did you fare,
When you had looked on Jesus there?
Six great wings around Him mantled,
Five cuts from which He was wounded,
All cruelly besmirched with blood;
In such wise was He endued.

XII. Tell us, Francis, How did you fare,
When you had looked on Jesus there?
At once by love animated,
And with nails to sorrow fastened,
Into the Loved One transmuted,
My whole spirit was renewed.

XIII. Tell us, Francis, What met your eyes
Contemplating those scars of Christ?
The soul so strangely set aflame
And sealed and signed the body's flesh,
As to change to my Love's image
In all its fulgent brightness.

XIV. Tell us, Francis, What met your eyes
Contemplating those scars of Christ?
These hands and feet were fixed with nails,
This right side pierced as with a lance,
This servant of Christ transfigured
Into His very likeness.

XV. O Francis, crucifer, you show
The Cross's signs, we truly know.

XVI. You bore, all arguments accord,
The form of our Redeemer Lord.

XVII. Tell us, Francis, tell us,
What saw you upon the cross?
Son of the living God by birth,
Crucified for love of all here on earth.

XVIII. Tell us, Francis, tell us,
What saw you upon the cross?
Christ affixed with nails to the cross,
And upon His head a crown of thorns.

XIX. Credence is due Francis on his own as more veracious
Than crowds of worldlings that sound loquacious.

XX. We know that Christ suffered death upon the cross verily:
Therefore, King benign, show us your mercy.

THE LIFE OF SAINT FRANCIS

BY

JULIAN OF SPEYER

(1232–1235)

Introduction

Shortly after writing liturgical texts for the feast of Saint Francis, Brother Julian of Speyer composed a second piece on Saint Francis, *The Life of Saint Francis* [*Vita Sancti Francisci*].[1] Drawing on *The Life of Saint Francis* by Thomas of Celano, Julian wrote both of these texts within a few years of one another. The dates of 1232 for the liturgical texts and 1234/5 for *The Life of Saint Francis* are generally accepted.[2] Julian advanced the nascent literary tradition on Saint Francis in liturgical texts for use in the Divine Office; he then developed a new life of Saint Francis, shorter in length than that of Thomas of Celano, and better adapted to public reading during meals and gatherings of the brothers.

The Life of Brother Julian

Julian was born at the end of the twelfth century in Speyer, the imperial city in the upper Rhine valley, south of today's Frankfurt am Main. As a youth he went to Paris for an education in music and it was there that his talents were recognized, earning him a place in the choir of the royal court chapel. He was promoted to *magister cantus* [master of song] at the court of the French King.[3] Thus, early in his life Julian exercised responsibility for composing, directing and organizing music for social and liturgical functions at the French court.

The date of Julian's entrance into the Franciscan Order is unknown, but it would have been before October, 1227, when he was in Assisi for the General Chapter. After that Chapter, he accompanied his Provincial Minister, Simon the Englishman,[4] to Germany and spent some time at his hometown of Speyer, most probably until 1229 when another provincial chapter was held at Worms. When Simon was released from the office of Provincial Minister and appointed lector of theology, his successor, John of Pian di Carpine, sent Simon to Magdeburg "with good, upright and learned men" to begin a school of theology. Julian may have accompanied Simon to Magdeburg, but his stay was probably brief for *The Life of Saint Francis* indicates that he was an eyewitness to the translation of Francis's body from the Church of Saint George in Assisi to the new basilica of Saint Francis on May 25, 1230.[5] Thus Julian may have returned to Assisi with the new Provincial Minister, John of Pian di Carpine, for the General Chapter which was held that same year, shortly after Francis's body was moved to the new burial site.[6] After the General Chapter Julian may have returned to Germany but he did not stay long. For reasons that remain unknown, later in 1230 Julian moved back to Paris.[7]

By the time of Julian's arrival in Paris in 1230, a center of studies sponsored by the Order as a whole was well established. Although the first brothers arrived in Paris in 1218 or 1219 with little intention of becoming involved in academic activities, the situation changed in 1226 when four doctors of the University of Paris entered the Order.[8] Within a few years, the brothers moved from outside the city at Saint Denis into the university quarter. By 1229 the brothers and other students were attending lectures and the academic importance of the Parisian fraternity was established. Its growth was so notable that in 1236, when Alexander of Hales, the leading theologian of the university, joined the Order, the pope appealed to the citizens of Paris to help the brothers build a larger structure to house the school of theology. Completed in 1240, it became known as the "Grand Couvent des Cordeliers."

From 1230 until his death in 1250, Julian participated in the development of this center of learning. He was able to tend to his passion of organizing, teaching, and composing music. During these twenty years, he served his brothers as "*cantor Parisiensis et corrector mensae,*"[9] whose responsibilities were to oversee the proper singing of the Divine Office, to teach music to the students, and to correct any mistakes that were made in the public reading during the Divine Office, meals or other community gatherings.

During his first decade in Paris, according to Jordan of Giano, ". . . Julian . . . wrote the offices of Blessed Francis and Blessed Anthony in a lofty style and beautiful meter, [and] ordered a provincial chapter to be held at Cologne on the Feast of the Apostles Simon and Jude (October 28, 1227)."[10] Julian also may have been the author of a lost work on musical theory, *Mensurae et Modi Canendi Divina Officia.*[11]

During his second decade in Paris Julian lived with Parisian theologians like Haymo of Faversham, Alexander of Hales and John of La Rochelle and certainly influenced new students such as John of Parma and Bonaventure of Bagnoregio, both of whom were subsequently to become General Ministers. There is also evidence that the Dominicans had asked Julian for an office of Saint Dominic, but Julian's death prevented the project.[12]

The Life of Saint Francis: Context and Purposes

Julian's biography of Saint Francis was written in Paris by someone who had never met Francis and had no first-hand experience of the early days of the new fraternity. Unlike Thomas, from the small Italian mountain town of Celano, Julian was formed with experiences of the German Speyer and French Paris, both emerging urban centers. The Speyer of Julian's youth was involved in founding a league of cities during the wars of imperial succession and was usually at odds with the pope. Paris was the setting of the ritual and pomp of the French court and, because of the University of Paris, was quickly becoming one of the centers of European learning. The contexts of the two writers could not have been more diverse. Julian's work, for example, contains little or no mention of the details of Italy's rural geography, Roman ecclesiastical personalities, nor of the early companions or associates of Saint Francis.

In general, Julian follows the textual development of *The Life of Saint Francis* by Thomas of Celano. However, he omits blocks of material that are either editorial or interpretative.[13] In his immediate interest "to narrate briefly the various deeds of Francis,"[14] Julian leaves aside the monastic and ascetical motifs that characterize Thomas of Celano's work. His interests were not to capture the breadth of the hagiographical tradition nor the promotion of the cult of the saint. Rarely does he use Thomas of Celano's vocabulary; yet he does not simply copy and abbreviate.[15] The explicit textual connections between the two lives are found notably in the quotations of Francis's sayings and in the use of Scripture. The fourteen times Julian quotes Francis's own words in his text, the quotations are exactly identical to ones found among Thomas of Celano's more than forty citations. While Thomas of Celano's use of Scripture is much more extensive, more than half of Julian's Scriptural references and citations are found in the same context in which they appear in Thomas of Celano's text. This is especially true in his use of the psalms, which provide a common framework for these two diverse texts. As *corrector mensae* and *magister cantus,* Julian would have been particularly sensitive to dramatic biblical quotations, especially those from the Psalter. He would have been eager, therefore, to see his readers understand them in their context.

Julian did not hesitate to depart from the "official" text approved by the still-living Pope Gregory IX. He moved in a new direction to write for his brothers a biography of Saint Francis that would be brief, clear, direct, and formative. To meet the needs of his own fraternity, Julian began what was to become a significant trend in the rest of the thirteenth century, namely, attempting to provide a better account of Francis's life primarily for use by the brothers.

Theological and Spiritual Themes

As Julian writes about Francis, he differs from Thomas of Celano in his theological and pastoral approach. Whereas Thomas of Celano writes of Francis using a contemplative Christological motif drawn from the earlier ascetical and hagiographical tradition, Julian writes to move the figure of Francis forward toward a practical and pastoral application of Christology. Thomas of Celano writes to edify the whole church, while Julian writes to encourage his younger brothers in their way of life.

Concerning the brothers, Julian identifies them as the "poor ones" who are miraculously cared for by Divine Providence.[16] Their life is a call to "evangelical perfection."[17] Francis's rebuilding of three churches prefigured bringing " 'three famous Orders' to perfection."[18] As the brothers identify with Francis, they are connected to the mystery of grace operative in Francis's life.

It is not surprising that Julian emphasizes the stigmata as a practical and immediate reality. Francis is the "Confessor of Christ," a title not used by Thomas of Celano.[19] The stigmata are not emphasized as enabling Francis "to fly away to the highest order of spirits";[20] rather Francis is "bearing the emblems of Christ's own wounds."[21] Although Julian's text is much shorter, he mentions the stigmata throughout his text more often than Thomas of Celano. Already, then, in the early 1230's the stigmata were increasingly important.

The development of the text indicates that Julian wished to teach his audience that Francis was an evangelist and a follower of Christ. Francis's way of life was a way of gospel perfection. For his hearers and readers, Julian explains that Francis experienced Christ concretely and this experience is founded on the gospel. Moreover, in Julian's context, the call of Christ in the gospel is heard in the worship of the Church.

The story of Francis hearing the gospel at the Portiuncula exemplifies the underlying liturgical motivation which Julian develops in *The Life of Saint Francis.* He writes: "Now one day at Mass, he heard those things which Christ in the gospel spoke to his disciples who were sent out to preach."[22] Thomas of Celano had earlier written: "One day the gospel was being read in that church about how the Lord sent out his disciples to preach."[23] Julian is not satisfied to report that the "gospel was being read" at the time of Francis's visit in the Portiuncula. Instead he makes explicit that it happens not only within the church building but in the liturgical context of the Mass. Francis hears not just the gospel, but "Christ in the gospel." This is the vocabulary of a liturgist, one whose understands the dynamic presence of the living Word in the proclamation of the gospel.

Notes

1. This introduction should be read in conjunction with the introduction to *Liturgical Texts,* where much of Julian's other work is to be found.

2. Scholars maintain that the liturgical texts are the source of LJS, and not vice-versa. See Jason Miskuly, "Julian of Speyer: Life of St. Francis" in *Franciscan Studies,* v.49 (1989) 93-117; Hilarin Felder, *Die Liturgischen Reimofficien auf die heiligen Franciscus und Antonius gedichtet und componiert durch Fr. Julian von Speier* (Freiburg, Schweiz: Universitaets-Buchhandlung, 1901).

3. Julian served under Phillip II (1180-1223) and/or Louis VIII (1223-26). Bartholomew of Pisa states: "*Hic ante ordinis ingressum fuit magister in aula regis Francorum* [Before his entrance into the Order, this man was a teacher in the court of the king of France]," Bartholomew of Pisa, *De Conformitate Vitae Beati Francisci ad Vita Domini Jesu, Analecta Franciscana* IV (Quarracchi: Collegium S. Bonaventurae, 1906) 308. Felder also maintains Julian had influenced the early formation of Saint Louis IX. See Felder, 140-141.

4. Cf. Jordan of Giano, *Chronica fratris Jordanis*, ed. Heinrich Boehmer, *Collection d'Etudes et de documents sur l'histoire religieuse et litteraire du moyen age* 6 (Paris: Librairie Fischbacher, 1908) 54. Jordan identifies Simon as simply "the Englishman" and provides little information concerning his earlier life prior to his ministry in Magdeburg.

5. Cf. LJS 76

6. Cf. Jordan, 57.

7. Cf. Miskuly, 96; J.E. Weis, *Julian von Speyer (+1285) Forschungen zur Franciscus- und Antonius kritik, zur Geschichte der Reimoffiziums und des Chorals,* (Munich: Verlag der J.J. Lentner'schen Buchhandlung, 1900) 8-10.

8. See Stephen J. P. van Dijk, *Sources of the Modern Roman Liturgy. The Ordinals of Haymo of Faversham & Related Documents (1243-1307),* Volume 1 (Leiden: E. J. Brill, 1963) 7.

9. Ibid.

10. Jordan, 53. Other early chroniclers are consistent in indicating that Julian is not only the author of offices for Saint Francis and for Saint Anthony but also of lives of the two. Bernard of Besse by 1283 (or 1297) wrote: "In France, Brother Julian . . . wrote a life of Saint Francis along with the night office of the saint in words and music, with the exception of some hymns and antiphons, which are the work of the most high pope and certain cardinals." Bernard of Besse, *Liber de Laudibus, Analecta Franciscana* III: 666. In 1398, Bartholomew of Pisa, added: "Brother Julian the German . . . wrote histories of Blessed Francis and Blessed Anthony, including the chant, antiphons, versicles and responsories." Cf. *De Conformitate Vitae Beati Francisci ad Vitam Domini Jesu, Analecta Franciscana* IV: 308, 544. Nicholas Glassberger in 1506 or 1508 was more specific about Julian's work: "He later composed a history of Blessed Francis and Blessed Anthony in a noble style and beautiful melody . . . and a *Legenda* of Saint Francis which begins *Ad hoc quorundam.*" Cf. Nicholas Glassberger, *Chronica, Analecta Franciscana* II 91. See also *Chronica XXIV Ministrorum Generalium O.F.M.,* AF 3: 381. This chronicle dates from around 1369; Delorme, "Catalogus Friburgensis Sanctorum Fratrum Minorum," *Archivum Franciscanum Historicum* 4 (1911): 553 (hereafter AFH).

11. See Lothar Hardick, "Julien de Spire," *Catholicisme,* 26: 1240-41.

12. See Vatican codex 4354, fol.112, partially edited by Franciscus van Ortroy: Julien de Spire, biographe de S. François d'Assise," *Analecta Bollandiana* 19 (1900): 328-29.

13. In contrast to the 27,411 words contained in 1C, that of Julian contains only 12,493.

14. Cf. LJS Prologue.

15. This led John R. H. Moorman to raise the possibility that the works of Thomas of Celano and Julian may be based on an earlier common source. Current scholarship does not confirm his thesis. Cf. John H.R. Moorman, *The Sources for the Life of St. Francis,* Publications of the University of Manchester, Historical Series 79 (Manchester: University Press, 1940) reprinted (Ridgewood NY: Gregg Press, 1966).

16. Cf. LJS 22.

17. Cf. LJS Prologue, 16, 73; Francis is identified as an "evangelist" who embraced the "counsels of evangelical perfection."

18. Cf. LJS 14.

19. Cf. LJS 32.

20. Cf. 1C 115.

21. Cf. LJS 36.

22. LJS 15.

23. 1C 22.

Prologue

IN THE NAME OF THE LORD.
INTRODUCTION TO THE LIFE OF SAINT FRANCIS.

The weaknesses of some of the holy people
the Lord was pleased to endow with a special prerogative of merit
are for a particular purpose mentioned in the Scriptures.[a]
Although the innocent may praise and marvel
at the inscrutable depths of that divine plan,
according to which some of the fallen have been raised
by more excellent merits
above many of the just,
they should not,
Ez 33:13 by *trusting in their own righteousness*
despise those laid low in the depth of vice;
nor should sinners, in despair because of their shameful deeds,
fear to approach the fountain of mercy to ask forgiveness.
As a respectful humility moves the just to fear the Lord as judge,
lest the ruinous growth of presumption destroy them,
so the firm and equally determined hope of the fallen
calls for the kindness of a loving Father,
lest the horrible whirlpool of despair drag them down.
Thus the laudable and altogether marvelous *glory*
Ps 145:12 *of the Lord's magnificence* is proclaimed
which, by gratuitous love, sustains the just lest they stumble
Ps 145:14 and, by kind compassion, *lifts up those who have been struck down*
lest they perish.
Hence,
we read that Christ was denied by his first vicar,[b]
and that even his vessel of election persecuted the Church.[c]
We read also about the publican

a. For example Moses and Aaron doubted God's mercy (Nm 20:8ff) and David sinned with Bathsheba and murdered Uriah (2 Sm 2ff).

b. Peter. See Mt 26:69ff.

c. Paul. See Acts 9:15 and Gal 1:13.

who came to be both an apostle and evangelist,[a]
and about that special disciple of Christ
who was possessed by seven demons.[b]
Therefore,
as we begin to narrate briefly the various deeds of Francis,
that glorious confessor and Levite of Christ,
we will first set forth certain of his weaknesses,
so that when his final manner of life,
which we cannot fully or worthily explain,
is compared to his early life,
the Author of his conversion may be splendidly praised by all,
the proper humility of the innocent increased,
Off 9:ii and a firmer hope of pardon given to those who have fallen from grace.[c]

End of the Prologue.

a. Matthew. See Mt 9:9 and Lk 5:27ff.

b. Mary Magdalene. See Mk 16:9.

c. References on the inside margins point out passages from other writings that influenced Julian in the composition of this work. Rather than quoting passages from 1C directly, Julian carefully rewrites them in similar words.

Chapter I

How he was converted and sold his goods, and how he suffered because his father persecuted him.

[1]In the city of Assisi, in the region of the Spoleto valley, there was a 1C 1
certain man named Francis, a businessman by profession, who was
Ti 3:5 very rich in passing wealth, but poor *in the works of justice.* From the
time of his earliest youth, he was disgracefully raised in the vanities of Off 9:i
the world, and became even more extravagant than his parents. Why
say any more?[a]

He devoted himself completely to the most miserable glory and 1C 2
happiness of the world, and having tried to outdistance the rest in these
things, he showed the wantonness of a restless heart in jokes and
games, bearing and dress, lewd words and songs. And although he was
the most careful acquirer of money, he did not keep his largess in balance. In fact, in keeping or dispensing money, he was more inclined to
prodigality than avarice. And so, because of the senseless dissipation
of his wealth, he seemed affable and obliging, but he *dragged* behind
Rv 12:4 him as an evil *tail* many who clung to him for this reason, and they followed him as their guide and leader headlong into ruin.

Thus, surrounded by ranks of confederates, he walked the way of
perdition until almost his twenty-fifth year, when it pleased the Lord to
Ps 111:4 declare the glory *of his wonders,* so that the marvelous *change* wrought
Ps 77:11 in him by *the right hand of the Most High* might be a wondrous example to posterity and hold out hope of recovering grace to sinners.[b]

[2]Thus, the divine mercy first began—for his own benefit and for 1C 3
many others—to call back the vagabond with physical troubles and
forced him, worn down by a lengthy illness, to think differently about
things than he had been accustomed.[c] And so it happened that he began

a. Julian omits the material of 1C 1 which elaborates the educational errors of Francis's age.

b. In this and in the preceding paragraph, Julian uses vocabulary that reflects some scattered similarity to 1C 2. With the exception of the reference to Psalm 77:11, Julian, at this point uses different allusions to the Scriptures.

c. Julian writes that it was divine mercy (*divino miseratio*) rather than the divine vengeance (*divino ultio*) or the divine unction (*unctio*) that came upon Francis to move him to conversion, cf. 1C 3.

to grow somewhat tame under the whip, something of which he was ignorant in prosperity. For when he recovered a bit of his strength, but still needed the support of a staff to move about, he found that everything around him, which he used to find beautiful and desirable, was now the source of a certain loathing—and those who were fond of such things seemed foolish.[a]

But because prosperity after a danger has been wont to deceive the
1C 4 reckless, this man, since he had not yet fully *shaken from his neck the*
yoke of perverse servitude, when prosperity smiled again, began to Gn 27:40
promise himself even greater worldly vanities than before.

Now a certain nobleman of Assisi, eager to increase his reputation and wealth, armed himself to go to Apulia. Francis, now having recovered his former strength of body and no less desirous of riches and glory, wanted to join this nobleman, like one who, light-headed, does not remember the fatherly correction he had received. But in this is wondrous proof of the divine plan, that he who had previously begun to
Off 9:iii grow gentle through infirmities and had already deserved, having been beaten, to be corrected to the full, now more miraculously began to be called back a second time from his purpose. So it might seem reasonable that he should have been even more enthusiastic.

1C 5 [3]Now on a certain night, when he had directed all his attention to completing the trip to Apulia,[b] he was shown a vision of his house filled with military equipment, although it was usually filled with piles of cloth for sale. Amazed at this unusual scene, he was told that these things were to belong to him and his soldiers.[c] Waking up, however, although he saw a vision of this kind as approving his intention and interpreted it as a portent of successful accomplishment of his purpose, he nevertheless suddenly, amazingly began to grow lukewarm toward that which he had intended, to the extent that he had to force himself to accomplish it, until in the end, he refused entirely to go to Apulia. Thus, the future leader of a new army, from this change in himself, deter-
1C 6 mined that the above-mentioned vision meant something far different

---

a. In this last sentence, Julian uses two three-word phrases that are found in the last sentence of 1C 3: *quidquid visu pulchrum* and *amatores stultissimos reputabat*. Otherwise there is scant similar vocabulary between the two texts. Julian also omits Thomas of Celano's description of the Umbrian countryside.

b. Julian's first sentence of LJS 3 is remarkably similar to the first sentence of 1C 5. Julian writes: *Nam quadam nocte, cum ad iter Apuliae consummandum tota se deliberatione dedisset* . . . Thomas of Celano writes: *Nocte igitur quadam, cum ad haec consummanda tota se deliberatione dedisset* . . . Phrases of such similarity in these two texts are infrequent.

c. Here is a section of the text which is remarkably similar to a passage in 1C. Julian writes: *responsum est, haec omnia fore sua militumque suorum*. Thomas of Celano writes: *responsum est ei, omnia haec arma sua fore militumque suorum* (1C 5). This combined with the text identified in the previous note constitutes the first consistent textual similarity of Julian with Thomas of Celano.

than he had believed.[a] Thus he accepted the heavenly arms which he Off 9:iii
later used manfully against all temptations, and from then on began to
change fully his earlier ways.[b]

Francis then removed himself from the tumult of business and made Off 11:i
himself a *salesman* of the gospel. He sought *good pearls,* as it were, un- 1C 6
til *he came upon one precious one, and while he was coming to see
what was more pleasing to God, he meditatively entered the workshop
of various virtues. And when he went away to meditate on the Lord's
field, he found* there and hid the Lord's *hidden treasure,* and, *having*
Mt 13:44-46 *sold everything,* he proposed to buy it along with the *field.*[c]

[4]Now he sought a new counselor of this new purpose: he sought counsel only of God for what he did, and he revealed to no mortal what he intended. Wanting someone who was more familiar to him than others to share his joy, or rather seeking an opportunity to express his joy of soul in words, from time to time he summoned just such a person to secret places. In fact, he spoke to him mysteriously, but did not reveal his secret purpose entirely, only saying he had discovered a great and precious treasure. This man congratulated himself not a little, joyfully came to Francis whenever he was called, and conversed most freely whenever Francis spoke about the treasure. Moreover, flooded with a new spirit, Francis frequently entered a certain cave, while his companion waited outside, completely ignorant of what Francis was doing
inside. There, *in secret,* Francis prayed with tears to his heavenly *Fa-*
Mt 6:6 *ther* that, as his guide on his way, he might show him his will more
clearly.[d] Thus praying at great length, he harshly afflicted himself, and until he knew by divine inspiration how he should begin, the distraction of his changing feelings would allow him no rest. There alternated within him happiness for the sweet taste of the spirit, the gravest sorrow for sins of the past, not a little fear of the future, and a fervent desire to complete what he had begun.

[5]Finally, more fully invoking divine mercy, he merited being heard 1C 7
for what he wanted and being taught infallibly by a heavenly sign what he should do. Then he was flooded with so much joy that, unable to

---

a. In Julian's account, Francis is more explicit about what the vision does not mean than he is in Thomas of Celano's account.

b. In 1C, the arms in Francis's dreams are for combatting the devil and the enemies of Israel. In Julian, they are used to fight temptation.

c. Like Thomas of Celano, Julian concludes the story of Francis's decision not to go to Apulia with the same reference to Matthew 13:46.

d. With the same Scriptural allusion of Matthew 6:6 used by Thomas of Celano, Julian condenses the story of Francis seeking God's will in the solitude of the cave.

contain himself, even against his will, he spoke publicly of certain things. He refused to go to Apulia, but promised that he would do grand things in his own native land. He answered all those who wondered and inquired whether he wished to marry that he would take a wife of great wisdom, and even greater nobility, altogether more lovable and beautiful than they had ever seen.[a]

1C 8 [6]Now confirmed with a divine mission, the man of God did not fail to fulfill the pious desire of his mind. Instead, when the right time presented itself, he rose with joy and confidently strengthened himself with the sign of the cross; taking expensive cloth with him to sell, he went to a nearby city which is called Foligno. Having sold in Foligno everything he had with him, including the horse he had been riding,
Off 11:ii he returned to Assisi laden with money. Then, suddenly fervent for the work of God, he decided to give it to the respectful uses of the poor and the grateful discharge of other needs. But the money itself so vexed his heart, which he was striving to free of such cares, that he hastened to unload it as quickly as he could, just as he would a load of sand.

1C 9 He came upon a church near Assisi, which had once been built in honor of Saint Damian, but which was now close to ruin because of its advanced age. Pitying its poverty right away, he entered it reverently. Inside, he came upon a certain poor priest to whom he first showed reverence by kissing his hands, and then offered the money to repair the walls of the church. The priest, however, seeing this man he knew to be completely given over to the world just a little while before, was much amazed by this deed. And, thinking that he was being ridiculed, he refused to accept the money. Scarcely believing Francis's purpose even when he explained it to him more fully, the priest finally consented to his incessant request to stay with him. Still, he absolutely refused to receive the money out of fear of Francis's parents. When he saw that it was refused, that true despiser of money scorned it as if it were dust by tossing it onto a window ledge.[b]

1C 10 [7]And so Francis's father, not knowing what had happened to him, did not stop being deeply upset until, after a long search, he learned that

a. Without Thomas of Celano's use of dialogue and without his interpretive development (cf. 1C 7), Julian simply states that Francis would take a "wife of great wisdom."

b. This paragraph combines the incidents presented in 1C 8, 9. However, in the narration of these events, there is little similarity in style. For example in regard to throwing the money on the window, Julian writes: *Quam ut refutari verus ille pecuniarum contemptor aspexit, in quadam fenestra deiectam veluti pulverem vilipendit.* Thomas of Celano writes:... *quam verus pecuniarum contemptor in quamdam fenestram proiciens, de ipsa velut de pulvere curat.* Julian heightens the drama.

his son was living wretchedly in hiding in the aforesaid place. Quite
disturbed at this unexpected outcome, *he gathered his friends* and ac-
Lk 15:9 quaintances *together* and ran to the place without delay. But the new
soldier of Christ, hearing the arrival and threats of his pursuers, was
Rom 12:19 pleased to *leave room for wrath.* To avoid being seen by his father, he
hid himself in a certain cave which he had prepared for the purpose. So,
for about a whole month, he was helped by only one person who
chanced to know the hiding place. He emerged from there rarely,
hardly compelled even by necessity, and did not stop imploring the
Jn 2:12 divine mercy there with *tears and fasting* to rescue him from the
Ps 31:16 *clutches of his persecutors.*

While praying in darkness, he was flooded with an amazing and unfamiliar joy. Because of this, he was suddenly filled with such great
constancy of mind that he not only went out in public, spurning his per- Off 11:iii
secutors, but also seriously accused himself of laziness and apathy because he had been inactive in hiding. His acquaintances, seeing him 1C 11
entirely changed from his former state, thin and dirty, did not attribute
this to supernatural grace, but rather to insanity; and they miserably insulted him and threw mud and stones at him. Nevertheless, the man of
God passed through their midst uninjured as if with a deaf ear and gave Off 12:iv
thanks to Him who comforted him from above. When his father heard 1C 12
that Francis had appeared in such a condition, he quickly ran after him
in an inhuman, rather than a fatherly way, and even more than all the Off 12:iv
others, began to rage at him.

[8]Francis's father thought that once he had dragged him home in disgrace, he could, through opposition, be turned back from what he had already begun. So he first cruelly afflicted him with blows and insults, but finally abandoning all mercy, he threw him into a cell in chains. But the more he raged against the knight of Christ by afflicting him with sufferings, so much the more did he render him powerful and strong;
Ps 32:7 nor could he, who had the Lord as his *shelter in distress,* be turned
away by adversity from the state of virtue.

It happened, however, that once when his father was absent from the 1C 13
house on account of family matters, his mother, who did not approve of her husband's actions, tried to call her son back from his purpose by speaking to him with flattering words. But when she saw that she could not, having been moved by motherly piety, she secretly broke the chains and allowed her son to go free. But, as one tried in temptation, he became more composed than ever, and giving thanks to Almighty God,

he returned, in great freedom of spirit, to the place where he had earlier stayed.

When his father returned home and learned what had been done, he
Off 12:v angrily assailed his wife with insults, not stopping until, in a frenzy, he
ran after his son. He was determined that if he could not turn him away
1C 13 from his purpose, he would at least drive him out of town. His son
freely and fearlessly met his father and did not yield to his fury as he had done before; but he shouted that he was willing gladly to endure even more for the sake of Christ.

His father saw that he was inflexible in his constancy, and at last turned to demanding the money. When he found and recovered it where the holy man had thrown it, he began to soften toward his son.
1C 14 The thirst of his avarice was temporarily quenched, and this cooled his anger.

Off 12:vi [9]Then he led him to the bishop of the place so that before him, he
might return all he had and surrender all his wealth into his hands. But
1C 15 before he was even asked, Francis cheerfully showed himself ready,
and taking off all his clothes, including his undergarments, he returned them to his father. Thus he stood completely naked in front of everyone, and presented himself as an exile in the world.

The bishop, truly admiring the man's great fervor, knew that this could only have been done by divine inspiration, and from then on he was prepared to help him with fatherly love. He took him in his arms, and covered him with the mantle he was wearing. Thus the naked man of God had conformed himself to the naked one on the cross, and had perfectly fulfilled the counsel of renouncing all his possessions.[a] He was now separated from the contemplation of God by no earthly thing except the barrier of the flesh.

---

a. Julian, like Thomas of Celano, emphasizes that Francis stripped himself completely naked. Thomas of Celano interprets this event in the ascetical tradition pointing out that Francis was now "naked to wrestle with the naked . . . putting aside all that is of the world" (. . . *nudus cum nudo luctatur*). Julian interprets this differently. He sees that Francis "conforms himself to the naked one on the cross" (. . . *nudus in cruce nudato conformat*). Both authors however conclude that this event has unitive-contemplative dimensions opening for Francis insight and vision into the mystery of God. Thomas of Celano writes: *et solus carnis panes ipsum a divina visione interim separaret.* Julian concludes: *quem a divino contuitu iam nil terrenum, nisi solus carnis paries, separabat.*

Chapter II

THE THINGS HE SUFFERED WHEN HE WAS
FIRST FREED FROM THE HANDS OF HIS FATHER,
AND WHAT HE DID WHILE IN SECULAR GARB,
AND ON HIS FIRST CHANGE OF HABIT.

[10]After Francis had escaped the inhuman persecution of his father,
it happened that one day this zealot of the new law was walking along Off 14:iv
half-naked in a forest, singing the praises of the Lord in French, when
Lk 10:30 he suddenly *fell among robbers.* When they asked him gruffly who in 1C 16
the world he was, he responded prophetically without fear: "I am the
Ps 48:3 herald *of the great King!* What is that to you?"[a] But they indignantly
whipped the servant of God, threw him into a snow-filled ditch, and
insulted the future shepherd of the Lord's flock saying, "Lie there,
stupid herald of God!"[b] When the brigands departed, he jumped out
of the ditch joyfully, and more energetically sang praises to the Creator of all.

[11]When he finally arrived at a monastery, this fellow who had been 1C 16; Off 14:v
used to wearing expensive clothing was wearing only a ragged shirt. Not surprisingly, since he was neither regarded nor even known there, and in want of food, he was rudely sent to the kitchen. After several days, when no one mercifully took note of his nakedness, he was obliged by necessity alone to leave. Later, however, when the report of his sanctity spread abroad everywhere, the prior of the place came to him, deeply sorry for the neglect of such a great man and humbly asked him to forgive him and his monks.

After he left that monastery, the little poor man of Jesus Christ[c] came to the city named Gubbio where he sought out an old friend who, for the sake of friendship, covered his nakedness with a short tunic.

[12]After this, humbly holding himself in low esteem and now not 1C 17

a. The quotation of Francis's response to the robbers is exactly the same in both Thomas of Celano and Julian: *Praeco sum magni Regis! Quid ad vos?*

b. Likewise, the response of the robbers is exactly the same: *Sace, rustice praeco Dei.* Otherwise the language varies in the narration of this same story.

c. Julian's identification of Francis as "little poor man of Jesus Christ" (*pauperculus Jesu Christi*) is not in 1C.

caring that he was despised by others, he moved to the lepers.[a] He
served them devotedly by humbly washing their sores, not even
shrinking from wiping away the pus. Previously, such things were so
disgusting to him that he used to hold his nose, not only when he saw
lepers themselves nearby, but even their homes at a distance. But when
he was still wearing secular clothes, the Lord had visited him with his
grace, when a certain leper happened to meet him. As usual, he was
1C 17 horrified by the sight, but doing violence to himself, he conquered himself, and straightaway *went up and kissed him.* From then on, he fer- Mk 14:45
vently glowed with contempt of self, and began to wage constant war
against himself until it was granted him from above to win perfect victory over himself. Therefore, as he himself later testified, he showed
mercy to the lepers whom he was unable even to look at while he was
living in sin.[b]

While he was still given over to the world, he always looked upon other afflicted and poor people with affectionate compassion, and most readily extended a hand of mercy to those who asked it for God's sake. However, he once, uncharacteristically, reproached a certain poor man who was asking for an alms for the sake of God, but soon afterward, remorseful, he felt most deeply sorry for doing this. He decided that it was most unworthy to refuse anything to one asking in the name of such a great King. Therefore, from then on he decided not to refuse poor people who asked him for anything for God's sake.[c] He carefully strove to carry out this decision to the best of his ability.

His spirit of compassion for the poor after his conversion, though it can be sufficiently gathered from this instance, will be more fully explained a little further on.

13 Although, up to this point, the holy man did not know clearly what
1C 18 was to happen to him; among other things, he undertook as his first pious work the repairing of the church of San Damiano where he had first
stayed. Just as he began this work out of pious concern for the danger of
its imminent collapse, so, *with the Lord's cooperation,* he completed it Mk 16:20
in a short time.

1C 18 This place is worthy of renown, for it was here that the Order which
is endowed with the fullness of so many virtues, namely the religion of

a. Both Thomas of Celano (*se transtulit ad leprosos*) and Julian (*ad leprosos se transtulit*) accent Francis's going to lepers as a movement in humility.

b. In this story Thomas of Celano (1C 17) quotes Test 2. Julian only alludes to it.

c. In placing this story of the poor man asking for alms after the leper story, Julian follows 1C. Both place it in the context of compassion and respect for the name of "a great King."

the Poor Ladies and holy virgins, was happily founded by the same holy man about six years after his conversion. Today, the Lord has greatly extended this praiseworthy religion with the privilege of considerable perfection throughout various regions of Italy.[a]

[14]Meanwhile, the servant of God changed the style of his habit and moved to another place not far from Assisi. There he began to rebuild another church, similarly in ruins, and did not stop until he finished what he had begun. 1C 21

After this, he moved to a third place called the Portiuncula, not far from the city mentioned above, where at one time a church had been built to the honor of Mary, the Most Glorious Mother of God, but was now equally desolate and demolished. He pitied the ruins, and, moved especially by his devotion to the Blessed Virgin, he remained there continuously until the third year of his conversion when the repairs to the Church were completed.

I do not think that this labor of building up the three churches mentioned above lacks a mysterious ulterior significance. Rather, I think that, according to God's will, it prefigured what this simple man marvelously fulfilled: he founded three famous Orders and, by his life and words, carried them to perfection.[b] These things we must treat, though briefly, in their proper place. Off 14:v

a. While Julian omits Thomas of Celano's list of the virtues of the Poor Ladies, he identifies Clare and her sisters as possessing the "privilege of considerable perfection." While 1C does not mention Italy in this context, Julian notes the spread of the Poor Ladies throughout Italy.

b. The comparison of rebuilding the three churches to the founding of the three Orders is not in 1C. This is a new contribution by Julian.

Chapter III

HOW, UNDERTAKING EVANGELICAL PERFECTION;
HE CHANGED HIS HABIT A SECOND TIME,
PREACHED AND BEGAN TO HAVE BROTHER COMPANIONS;
AND HOW HE FOREKNEW HIS AND THEIR FUTURE,
SENT THEM TWO-BY-TWO THROUGHOUT THE WORLD,
AND ARRANGED THEIR COMING TOGETHER AGAIN.

1C 21 15 Blessed Francis had completed his work on the three churches, as has been said, and he had, up until that time, worn the habit of a hermit, carrying a staff in his hand, with shoes on his feet and a leather belt around his waist.

1C 22; Off 14:vi Now one day at Mass, he heard those things which Christ in the gospel spoke to his disciples who were sent out to preach: that they should not possess *gold* nor *silver,* nor *carry a wallet along the way or a purse, or a walking stick or bread, nor have shoes or two tunics.*[a] And later, Mt 10:9-10; Mk 6:8-9; Lk 9:3, 10:4
from the priest, he understood these instructions more fully and was
Off 14:vi soon filled with indescribable joy. "This," he said, "is what I seek, this is what I desire with all my heart." And so, after committing to memory everything he had heard he joyfully applied himself to carrying out these commands and removed his extra clothing without delay. From this moment on he never used a walking stick, shoes, purse, or wallet. Accordingly, he made a very cheap and plain tunic, and throwing the belt away, tied the tunic with a cord.

Off 15:vii; 1C 23 16 Applying all the care of his heart, to fulfill the words of the new grace he had heard, he became, by divine inspiration, the proclaimer of evangelical perfection and began publicly to preach penance with simplicity. Moreover, his statements were neither hollow nor ridiculous,
Off 15:viii but filled with the power of the Holy Spirit. They penetrated the marrow of the heart and provoked stunned amazement in those who heard them. But, as he himself later testified, he also learned by the Lord's
Test 23 revelation a greeting of this sort, that he should say: "May the Lord give you peace." Thus, in all his preaching, he greeted the people at the 2 Thes 3:16; Nm 6:26

a. Julian here follows 1C 22 combining the three gospel accounts of Jesus' instructions to his disciples when sending them out to preach.

beginning of his talk with the proclamation of peace. Filled with the Off 15:viii
Is 52:7 spirit of the prophets, *he proclaimed peace and preached salvation,* as
the prophet said. And it happened that by counsels about salvation, he
brought to true peace many who had previously lived at odds with
Christ and far from salvation.[a]

[17]As the truth of Blessed Francis's simple teaching and life became
known to many, some men soon began to be moved to penance by his
Lk 5:11 example, and *leaving all things,* joined him in habit and life.[b]

Moreover, as the merits of the saint began to be rewarded with new Off 15:ix
sons, he himself became even more filled with a new *consolation of*
Acts 9:31 *spirit,* and began to keep watch over their salvation more diligently.
Hence, soothing and fostering them with fatherly affection, he never
ceased instructing them with new advice, teaching them to walk un- 1C 26
swervingly in the way of holy poverty and true simplicity.

Now the father rejoiced in the joyful company of six brothers, he be- Off 17:ix,a
ing the seventh; and in all things he behaved not as someone greater,
but as the least among the lesser.[c] Since he was still altogether ignorant
of how things would turn out for him and his brothers, he longed to
Lk 12:32 know the future of *the little flock.*

[18]So one day, when he had given himself over to prayer with greater
Mt 15:36 devotion than usual, *giving thanks* for the rich favors bestowed on him
Is 38:15 by God, he recalled, *in the bitterness of* his soul, the years he had
Zec 4:14 wasted, and *stood trembling* before the Lord. His mind was flooded
throughout with a wonderful sweetness and joy to the extent that he lost
himself, until at last, the heavy darkness from his sins was utterly dis-
pelled, and he was made certain that the debt for his offences had been
Mt 5:26 forgotten down to *the last penny.*

From then on, he was transported beyond himself and totally ab- 1C 26
sorbed in the brightness of a wonderful light. His inmost soul was
opened wide and he was granted certainty about the things which he
had desired, and clearly foresaw the multiplication of his brothers com- 1C 27
Acts 2:5 ing *from all nations.* Contemplating not only this, but also many other
Lk 15:17 things hidden in the future, and finally, *coming back* to himself, he re-
Est 15:9 lated *all of these things in order* to the brothers. Totally *renewed in*

a. Julian adds to Thomas of Celano's mention of the "power" of Francis's words that this was the "power of the Holy Spirit." Also, those who "hated peace" in 1C are presented as "at odds with Christ" in Julian.

b. This one sentence summarizes 1C 24-25, which provides further details about Francis's first six companions.

c. Julian's reference to Francis as the "least" of the "lessor" is a word-play on the name of the Order, the "Lesser Brothers." See LJS 23 below.

spirit, he warned them not to mistrust his or their own simplicity, and Ps 51:12
he comforted them *in the Lord,* as those who were to be spread abroad Eph 6:10
to the ends of the earth.[a]

1C 29 19 At that time, another man *was added* to them, and their number Gn 35:29
Off 17:ix,b was brought to eight.[b] Then, calling them all together and pairing them
two-by-two to send them forth into the diverse parts of the world, the
saint kindly and earnestly explained many things to them about the
reign of God and contempt of the world and of self. Among other Acts 1:3
things, he especially instructed them about patience and humility. The
humble flock rejoiced at the voice of the shepherd, and, gladly submitting to him, humbly prostrated themselves at his feet to receive the
mandate of saving obedience. Their most kind shepherd raised them up
and kissed each of them as affectionately as a mother embraces her
1C 29 sons,[c] and strengthened each of them with the words of the prophet:
Cast your cares upon the Lord and he will sustain you. He frequently Ps 55:23
pronounced this word whenever he sent anyone forth. Thus, he wished
to direct the brothers to cast their cares on God and took care to close
Off 17:ix,c the false and fruitless way of cupidity to them. He provided them not
with an extra coin *in their belts,* but with a heart free of worry for tomorrow. Mk 6:8

1C 29 20 The six of them went in pairs into various regions to announce
peace with penance. He himself, however, went to another part of the
world, keeping one of them with him. But, his fatherly affection did not
allow the absence of this new offspring to be prolonged, and not much
1C 30 later he began to be moved by a great desire to see them. Therefore, he
sought his usual refuge of prayer in order to obtain what he desired. He
so merited a hearing from the Lord, that in a short time they were unexpectedly and miraculously *gathered into one.* Having been brought together in this manner, it was not surprising that the pious father Jn 11:52
rejoiced in his sons. They, too, rejoiced in the joy of their father;
equally marveling and rejoicing, they glorified with one heart the magnificence of the Savior. He told them, in his turn, *how the Lord fulfilled
his desire.* They, too, told of the benefits God bestowed on them, and Ps 127:5
humbly accused themselves of any instances of ingratitude.

a. Julian has omitted most of Francis's sermon to his disciples, which is found in 1C 27-28.

b. It is difficult to determine who this may have been, as he is not named in 1C 29.

c. Unlike Thomas of Celano, Julian introduces the notion of "mother" in the relationship of Francis to his brothers, although Thomas of Celano does mention that Francis chose Elias to serve in place of a mother for him. See 1C 98, and LJS 65 below.

After these things, it happened that four other suitable men were 1C 31
Lk 12:32 joined to the *little flock,* and so the number of the brothers was in- Off 17:ix,d
creased to twelve. Thus the fame of the holy man and of his compan-
ions now began to spread more widely, and inasmuch as they rejoiced
1 Pt 1:17 over the conversion of sinners *without regard to persons,* their joy in
the Lord increased daily.

Chapter IV

How he received a rule and permission to preach from the pope, was refreshed in solitude, determined to be perpetually poor and to help his neighbors, and how he guarded himself and his own brothers with strict vigilance.

1C 32 21 Seeing that the number of brothers was gradually increasing,
Blessed Francis explained more fully to them his heart's purpose, not
1C 30 to mention the hidden design of divine revelation. He wrote a rule in
simple language, including words from the holy gospel, for the perfection of which he strove as much as he could. He wanted what he had
written to be confirmed by the supreme pontiff, so he *took* the eleven
brothers that he had *with him,* himself being the twelfth, and made his Mt 12:45
way with them to Rome.[a] When he arrived, he went to one of the cardinal bishops, an esteemed and discreet man, and explained fully and in
an orderly manner the cause of his coming to Rome. The cardinal carefully heard the business of the poor man of Christ and, even though he
justly commended the plan as praiseworthy, he nonetheless first sug-
1C 33 gested to Francis that he enter the eremitical or monastic life. But the
servant of Christ stuck firmly to what he had begun and, as modestly as
he could, refused to agree to suggestions of this sort. But, *with the*
Lord's cooperation he persisted until, thanks to the arrangements of Mk 16:20
the same bishop, the matter came to the hearing of the supreme pontiff.

Divine Providence was with the blessed man in everything he was
doing, and its clear revelations and visions made him confident. At that
time he saw a vision that promised the Lord Pope's assent to his plan: *a*
mighty tree, wondrously tall, whose top he easily bent down to the Dn 4:7
earth with his hands.[b] Later on, when the most excellent and magnani-
mous Lord Pope Innocent III, who was then ruling the church, deigned

a. Julian, unlike 1C, omits any mention of Guido, Bishop of Assisi. Julian mentions "one of the cardinal bishops," but he does not identify him as Cardinal John of Saint Paul as Thomas of Celano does. At the same time, he omits any description or praise of Francis's early followers.

b. In an unusual twist, Julian places the vision of the tall tree *before,* not after, the visit with Innocent III as 1C does. At the same time Julian expresses the pope's approval in a more immediate and direct way.

to give his assent to the poor man, the meaning of this vision became evident.

The supreme pontiff gave the twelve brothers his kind consent concerning the confirmation of their rule and also gave them his mandate Off 17:ix,d
concerning the preaching of penance. With joy, he blessed and dismissed them, but he promised that later, when their number had increased, 1C 33
he would give them even more.[a]

[22]Therefore, it was not without reason that Blessed Francis thought 1C 34
it a wondrous thing that he had obtained such great benefits from the Vicar of Christ, and so he gave thanks to divine mercy for all. Completing his visit with a prayer at the tomb of the Prince of the Apostles, he joyfully left the city with his brothers.

The purpose of the gift moved him to act immediately, lest perhaps Off 17:ix,d
he remain ungrateful, and he dutifully began to make plans with the brothers: first, how by observing the rule they could make progress in 1C 34
virtue; and second, how by edifying their neighbors they might earn in-
Lk 19:13 terest for the Lord on the *silver piece* entrusted to their care.

As they were dutifully discussing these and other similar things, it
Mt 14:15 happened that they came, *late in the day, to a deserted place* where they seemed to be bereft of all human aid, though they were in need of bodily refreshment because of the hardships of their journey. But divine providence, which was with these poor ones, provided bread through a man who came up unexpectedly and disappeared all of a sudden.[b] They ate the bread, marveled at the manner it had been provided, and, returning thanks to the Lord, continued their journey much comforted. Then they came to a solitary place near the city of Orte, where they remained for almost forty days in great lack of necessities. Some of their number went begging in that same city. There they renewed the beginnings of holy poverty with great joy and confirmed it with a per- 1C 35
petual covenant.[c]

[23]These zealots of a new justice next entered the Spoleto valley, and a pious discussion arose whether in the future they should live in solitary places or among people. But truly, the holy man of God, as if de-

a. Julian here briefly summarizes Thomas of Celano's extended development of the oral approval and commission given by Innocent III.

b. Julian writes, "divine Providence" is at work in this story. Thomas of Celano writes, "God's grace" is operating. Julian, unlike Thomas of Celano, hints at the miraculous. Thomas of Celano writes the man who gave them bread simply left. Julian writes that the man disappeared.

c. In both 1C and Julian, this deserted place has significance for the brothers' bond to poverty. Thomas of Celano writes: *coeperunt propterea cum sancta paupertate ibidem habere commercium.* Julian writes: *ibique cum ingenti gaudio sanctae paupertatis initia renovantes, pacto illam perpetuo firmaverunt.*

Off 18:i spairing of his own efforts, anticipated every undertaking with devout
prayer—through which he infallibly learned what he was to do—and,
impelled by a zeal that came from God, chose to live for the gain of his
neighbors rather than for himself alone.

1C 36 Then, comforted *in the Lord,* Saint Francis began *to speak out more* Eph 6:10
boldly owing to the apostolic authority he had been granted, and going Acts 9:28
around through *cities, towns and villages,* he steadfastly preached pen- Mt 9:35
ance. He was particularly careful *to show himself blameless in all*
things, lest he be thought to gloss over the truth with flattering words. Tb 10:13; 2 Cor 6:4
Off 18:ii Educated men marveled at the power of the words of him who had not
been taught by man, and seeing the noble and lowborn, rich and poor
crowd around him in bands, they astutely made their way to him as
1C 36 though to a new star rising in the darkness. In fact, he provided a plan of
salvation to persons of every state and condition, age and sex, giving
them all a rule of life. Today, the church rejoices that his felicitous
1C 37 leadership of both sexes has brought about a threefold army of those
who are to be saved.

1C 38; Off 18:iii As we mentioned above, he founded three Orders, the first of which
he prized above all others by profession and habit, and which, as he had
LR I 1 written in its Rule, he called the Order of Lesser Brothers.[a] The Second
Order, the Order of the Poor Ladies and virgins of the Lord, also mentioned above, likewise took its fruitful origin from him.[b] The Third,
also an order of considerable perfection, is called the Order of Penitents, which profitably brings together clerics and laity, virgins, un-
married, and married persons of both sexes.

24 Who will be able to tell in detail just how Blessed Francis himself magnificently served the Order of Lesser Brothers in the perfection of every virtue by going beyond what was asked, or how he instructed his brothers and sons concerning all matters of true religion?[c]

Off 18:iv Now sufficiently taught in all things perfect by his tutor, the grace of the Holy Spirit, he wished to come to know in himself every kind of perfection by experience. And so, he first taught his brothers by his example those things which he later urged on them by frequent sweet words.[d]

a. See LJS 14, above.

b. See LJS 14 above and 1C 18 which refer to the Second Order, or Poor Clares.

c. See 1C 38-41, which speaks of the virtues of the first brothers. Julian alludes to this material here and also in LJS 26 below.

d. Here Julian summarizes 1C 41.

How these brothers, personally serving as knights under such a
leader, became more proficient in all perfection by his teaching and example, must, I think, be kept secret rather than described in detail with
profuse words. For the blessed man *stood watch* with the highest vigi- 1C 42
Is 21:8; Hb 2:1 lance *over* himself and his brothers. He continually forewarned them
most diligently not only lest they suffer some obvious attack of sin, but
also lest a secret thought grow into a vice, lest any deceit, under the
guise of virtue or the occasion of necessity, rush upon them, or death 1C 43
penetrate their inner selves through the unguarded openings of the exterior senses.

He did not allow in himself or others, any punishable offense to pass
with impunity, lest perchance a lax hand bring on the sluggishness of
neglect. In fact, he exercised the rigor of justice in himself so greatly
that if ever, as sometimes happens, a temptation of the flesh stole over 1C 42
him, if it was winter, he would throw himself into a place full of ice or
snow to drive away the illicit impulse.

[25]Seeing him hold himself under such great restraint, the other 1C 43
brothers were moved to do similar things. Thus, as has been said, the
man of God not only uncompromisingly repressed the urgings of the
flesh, but also secured his bodily senses with bars of the greatest caution, lest they cling to any vanity.

While he was staying at a place called Rivo Torto near Assisi, it 1C 42
happened that the Emperor Otto, with much pomp and a great reti- 1C 43
nue, was passing on the way to Rome for his coronation. Blessed
Mt 13:19 Francis, who was residing *beside* the *road* with his brothers in their
hovel, wished that neither he nor any of his brothers go out or even
look out to see the emperor, but he instructed one of them to proclaim
to the emperor continually that this sort of glory would endure only a
little while.

[26]That most true zealot of poverty settled himself, together with his 1C 42
brothers, in an abandoned dwelling, in the area noted above, that they
might protect themselves there as best they could from the heat and
rain. This dwelling was so confining that they were unable to rest comfortably in it. But the narrowness of the place did not constrict the *wide-*
Ps 119:45; Jer 17:1 *ness of their hearts.* Quite the contrary, they lived happily in this
Is 51:3 extreme want and persisted in *giving thanks and praise to God* continually. The holy man wrote the names of the brothers on the beams of the 1C 44
little house so that no one could disturb in the slightest another who

wished to rest or pray, and that each brother might know the place assigned to him.

One day a man came to the place with an ass, maybe looking for shade, and wanting to enter freely and without rebuff said to the ass: "Get in there. We'll do this place a favor yet." But the man of God liked neither the words nor intentions of this fellow who believed that the brothers had come together there to build houses and enlarge or appropriate the little spot for themselves. So the saint soon left the little house and moved to the place called the Portiuncula, where he had rebuilt a church of the Glorious Virgin.

Chapter V

HOW HE TAUGHT THE BROTHERS TO PRAY,
AND ALSO WHAT TO BELIEVE AND OBSERVE;
ABOUT THE BROTHERS' OBEDIENCE AND SIMPLICITY
AND THE CONSOLATION THEY HAD THROUGH HIM;
AND ABOUT HIS TRANSFIGURATION AND PROPHETIC INSPIRATION.

[27]The brothers then asked Blessed Francis to teach them how to pray. Speaking simply, he passed on to them this formula saying, "*When you will pray, say 'Our Father'* and 'We adore you, Lord Jesus Christ, in all your churches throughout the whole world, and we bless you, because by your holy cross you have redeemed the world.' " The brothers, humbly carrying out these instructions and regarding these simple words as having the force of a mandate of obedience, even bowed toward churches they could only see in the distance, and lying prostrate on the ground, adored as they had been instructed. 1C 45 Lk 11:2; Mt 6:9 Test 5

The brothers did not then have priests of the Order, so they confessed to secular priests, whether good or bad and, showing all priests the greatest reverence in accordance with the example and teaching of the holy father, they did not consider sin in any of them.[a] 1C 46; Test 9

[28]He himself, a Catholic and totally apostolic man, especially recommended in his preaching that the faith of the Roman Church be inviolably maintained, and the order of priests be regarded with the highest reverence, because of the dignity of the Lord's Sacrament which is made present by the ministry of priests.[b] He also taught that teachers of divine law and all ecclesiastical orders were to be given the highest reverence. Off 1:i 1C 62 1C 46 Off 1:i

There was such simplicity among the brothers that when a certain priest, who was known as disreputable, told one of the brothers, "Watch out that you're not a hypocrite," that brother believed himself to be a hypocrite for sure, because he did not think a priest could lie.

a. In 1C 46 Thomas of Celano speaks of a specific incident involving a priest of notorius reputation "*qui meritis valde infamis erat*" to whom the friars nonetheless confessed. Julian changes this occurrence into a generalization, and in the following section joins it to Francis's teaching on reverence for priests as stated in 1C 62.

b. Julian, unlike Thomas of Celano, adds the reason for reverence due to priests, namely, the Lord's Sacrament.

Later, this brother was gravely troubled for some time on this account,
but the *burning eloquence* of the holy father, which frequently used to Ps 119:140
drive all clouds from the brothers' hearts, won him consolation and
wisely excused the words and intentions of the priest.
1C 47 29 At this time, the brothers' simplicity was consoled by frequent
revelations, which they merited to receive because of the presence of
so great a father. One night Blessed Francis was absent from the brothers, and some were sleeping and others praying, behold, about midnight, *a fiery chariot* came through the door and passed through the 2 Kgs 2:11
little house back and forth a number of times. Above it, a large ball,
which looked like the sun, drove away the darkness of the night with its
brightness. As they all came together and asked one another, in great
confusion, what this meant, something memorable occurred: owing to
the power of that wonderful light, their consciences were revealed to
one another.[a] They therefore understood that this was the soul of the
most holy father, which, because of its outstanding purity, was made
worthy of being shown transfigured for the solace of the brothers. This
holy man truly merited to be called *the chariot and charioteer* of the 2 Kgs 2:12
Off 5 threefold army that was spoken of before, because, borne by a fiery
chariot in the form of the sun, while still living, he has won in mortal
flesh the privilege of a transfiguration.[b]
1C 51 Returning physically to his brothers, the man of God delicately be-
1C 48 gan to probe expertly the secrets of their consciences, which, as they
often experienced, did not escape him. Oh, in our times it is truly a mat-
Off 5 ter full of wonder and joy that a frail human being discerns the secrets
of the minds of others! This holy man again and again revealed many
things *hidden* in the *hearts* of his own brothers. Many times he knew 1 Cor 14:25
the actions of absent brothers, in dreams forbidding some to do this or
1C 48 that, and ordering others to perform some action. With foresight, he revealed the damnable evils committed by many who appeared good,
and predicted the gift of future graces to those who were perceived as
evil. Truly the *double spirit of prophecy* which rested on him became 2 Kgs 2:9
manifest in his lifetime by reason of great miracles (as will be clear below). He also made momentous predictions about the future, a few of
which we will describe.

a. Cf. LJS 18, above.

b. In 1C 47 Thomas of Celano writes that Francis's soul was made most radiant [*maximo radiantem*] Julian writes his soul was transfigured [transfiguratam ostendi]. Julian makes the same point in Off. See also LJS 23 above and LJS 71 below.

[30]Rather often, too, the man of God, *absent in the body,* but *present in* 1C 48
1 Cor 5:3 *the spirit,* gave the solace of spiritual joy to the brothers. I will recount briefly one of many such incidents. Once when Brother John of Florence was celebrating a chapter in Provence, where he had been appointed minister by Blessed Francis, the venerable Brother Anthony, who is now a saint and glorious confessor of Christ, was also present.[a] There, while that saint, *full of the wisdom of the Spirit,* was expounding
Jn 19:19 the Scripture passage, *"Jesus of Nazareth, the King of the Jews,"* he affectionately proposed a word of exhortation to the brothers who were gathered there. A certain Brother Monaldo, a priest, who was a simple man and known to be adorned with many virtues, turned his face to the door of the house. There, with his bodily eyes, he saw Blessed Francis, lifted up in the air with his hands spread as on a cross, blessing the brothers who were present. Suddenly, the infusion of spiritual joy was so great in each one that the very experience made worthy of belief, to the astonishment of all, what that priest afterwards told them about his vision.

[31]Let it suffice to narrate one of many examples of how he often laid 1C 49
bare the secrets of others' hearts. A brother, Riccerio by name, as noble in his deeds as in his birth, presumed so much on the merits of Blessed Francis that he believed a man certainly merited divine grace if he possessed as a gift the good will of this saint, but that if he was cut off from that gift, he deserved nothing less than the wrath of God. And though he very much wanted to obtain the gift of friendship with him, he
Gn 32:8 *greatly feared* that the holy man would discern some hidden fault in him, as a result of which it would happen that he be further distanced from his favor. Therefore, this brother was continually and gravely afflicted by such fear and did not reveal his thoughts to anyone.

It happened one day that, while deeply troubled as usual, Riccerio 1C 50
came to the cell in which Blessed Francis was praying. The man of God, knowing of his arrival and his state of mind, kindly called him to his side and said: "My son, from now on let no fear or temptation disturb you, because you are most dear to me, and among those especially dear to me, I love you with a special charity. Come to me confidently whenever it pleases you, and leave whenever you like."[b] He was greatly amazed and joyful at the words of the holy father, and from then

a. Julian acknowledges the canonization of Brother Anthony, which occurred at the behest of Gregory IX on May 30, 1232. Anthony had died on June 13, 1231 at Arcella near Padua, Italy.

b. Though there are some variances, this is another instance in which Julian incorporates a full quotation from Francis as found in 1C.

on, sure of Francis's love, he grew, as he believed in *the grace of the Savior.*[a] Ti 2:11

a. Julian omits the prayer to Francis which follows this incident in 1C 50.

Chapter VI

HIS KEEPING OF POVERTY, HIS ABSTINENCE,
AND THE ADMIRABLE RIGOR OF HIS LIFE;
AND HOW HE FLED PEOPLE'S PRAISE AND WISHED
TO BE THOUGHT OF NO ACCOUNT.

[32]Francis, the holy confessor of Christ, took every precaution that, crossing over the bounds of holy and highest poverty, he would not drift in any way toward superfluous things. The result was that, tending always more to being in need than to abundant sufficiency or excess, even to the point of wanting basic necessities, he would scarcely leave even a dish in the house.

What shall we say about delicate foods or the drinking of wine, or 1C 51
even the abundance of other cheap foods, since, on the very rare occasions he ate cooked foods, he mixed them with ashes or cold water and did not even drink enough water? For he claimed it was most difficult to satisfy need and not become a slave to pleasure. Quite often, when he was going around preaching penance, he took refreshment at the homes of secular people who invited him. On account of the words of
Lk 10:7 the gospel about *eating and drinking what was set before them,* he would put his hand to his mouth, appearing to be eating the meat, but rarely tasting even a little bit of it, he would unobtrusively put the rest in his lap.

When he was forced to sleep, the bare ground was his bed, with only 1C 52
his short tunic in between, and he would more often sleep sitting than lying down, with his head on wood or stone.

It once happened that, because of an illness, he ate some chicken, but after his strength returned, he strictly ordered one of the brothers to lead him through the center of the city of Assisi with a rope tied around his neck like a robber, and to cry out like the town crier: "Behold! Look at the glutton who has fattened himself with the flesh of poultry which he has, unknown to you, eaten in secret."[a] It so happened that many,

a. Julian offers another quotation from Francis which is first given by Thomas of Celano. Julian here follows 1C closely but not exactly. Julian writes: *Ecce, videte glutonem, qui se gallinarum carnibus impinguavit, quas secreto vobis ignorantibus manducavit.* Thomas of Celano writes: *Ecce, videte glutonem, qui impinguatus est carnibus gallinarum quas vobis ignorantibus manducavit.*

struck by this spectacle of remorse, lamented with tearful voice and proclaimed themselves most worthless for having given themselves over to daily pleasures.

1C 53-55 [33]He quite often did many things in this manner to despise himself perfectly and to provoke others to despise him. But when this most genuine despiser of self *was* justly *praised by all,* he alone still re- Lk 4:15
garded himself as most vile, and marvelously used to ward off the people's favor in public. Truly, when he heard that people were extolling him with their praise, taking this amiss, he would order, in strict obedience, one of the brothers at his side to speak abusively to him with insulting words, in order to express words of truth against the lies of those praising him. When this brother, against his own will, called him a boor and a useless hired-hand, the most holy man would applaud agreeably and smile, responding to the brother who reproved him: "*May the Lord bless you,* my dearest son, because you have spoken the Ps 128:5
truth, things that the son of Pietro di Bernardone ought to hear!"

Wishing to be considered perfectly vile by all, he did not shrink from confessing his sins in his public preaching. But if even a fleeting evil thought about someone crept up on him, he humbly asked that person's forgiveness, confessing the very thought he had entertained. This shows, even in regard to fleeting thoughts, how this holy man avoided
1C 55 grumbling and back-biting. What more can be said? Seeking to attain the highest level of every kind of perfection, he used to avoid human favor by every means, so that, with his conscience as witness, he might
1C 53 possess the vessel of sanctification internally, and externally become,
to himself, *like a broken vessel.* Ps 31:13

Chapter VII

HOW HE LONGED TO BE A MARTYR,
SAVED SAILORS FROM THE SEA'S DANGER,
AND HOW HE BEHAVED BEFORE THE SULTAN.

[34]Blessed Francis, burning with a most ardent longing for mar- 1C 55
tyrdom, in the sixth year of his conversion, wished to set out to the region of Syria to announce there the gospel of Jesus Christ to the Saracens. Therefore he eagerly began his journey to Syria, but the ship in which he was a passenger was forced by ill winds to dock in Slavonia. Hearing, moreover, from the sailors that transit on that ship to Syria was not possible that year, unable to fulfill his vow, he went on board another ship which was making for Ancona, although he was barely permitted to board it by sailors who feared that could not pay his way.[a] *And so, through him the Lord recalled*
Ps 111:4 *to memory his miracles.* A long and severe storm arose at sea, and when, after their long labors, the sailors were in need of food, it was the help of the one to whom they had refused entry into the ship because they feared he lacked food that saved them from death. For certain things Blessed Francis, supplied by the Lord, had secretly brought provisions on board, although not enough to feed many people. They were increased by divine intervention on account of his merits, so that there was more than enough to fulfill the needs of everyone all the way to the port of Ancona, although many more days of the journey still remained. Seeing this, the sailors gave immeasurable thanks for the kindness of the Savior of all who had freed them from the danger of death through his servant Francis.

[35]Having left the sea for land, the holy man began again to scatter 1C 56
the seeds of the divine word, and gathered its fruit in the form of many worthy followers.

a. Julian here adjusts the story. In 1C, the sailors stubbornly refuse to allow Francis on board since he cannot pay, but Francis secretly boarded anyway: *Verum illis hoc agere sertinacius recusantibus propter expensarum defectum, sanctus Dei confidens plurimum de Domini bonitate, navem latenter cum socio introivit.* Julian, on the other hand, writes that Francis was barely allowed to board: . . . *a nautis expensarum defectum timentibus vix permissus intravit.*

But the desire for martyrdom had not cooled within him. A little later, hurrying to Morocco to preach the faith of Christ to Miramamolin and his court, several times he rushed on so impetuously that, intoxicated by the Spirit, he left his traveling companion behind, racing ahead all by himself. He reached Spain in a fever of eagerness, but because the Lord, who for the sake of the salvation of many others ordained otherwise, afflicted him with serious ailments so that he returned to Italy.

1C 57 [36]On arrival there, he stayed a little while at Saint Mary of the Portiuncula. At that time, too, he received certain educated men and nobles into the Order. These he treated with the care and decency they deserved and with that outstanding discernment he showed to others. Moreover, although the holy man was unwillingly compelled to put off his project, he did not abandon the desire for martyrdom until at last, in the thirteenth year of his conversion, he crossed over to Syria. Although at the time battles were being fought between the Christians and the unbelievers every day, *trusting in the Lord* he was not afraid to Ps 10:2; 125:1
approach the sultan even at clear peril to his life. After being afflicted with numerous heavy blows and insults, he finally gained a personal audience with the sultan. But it would take too long to narrate how with great steadiness he withstood the sultan and with great eloquence he neutralized the arguments of those railing against the Christian faith. The sultan accepted him with enormous honor and offered him many precious gifts, but when the holy man of God scorned these gifts as if they were filth, the sultan himself was even more amazed at this man unlike any other, and listened more intently to his words.

But in all these things *the blessed man* did not *find his desire fulfilled; for the Lord had wonderfully reserved for him the privilege of a* Ps 127:5
unique grace: bearing the emblems of Christ's own wounds.[a]

a. This express reference to the stigmata in this context is not found in 1C.

Chapter VIII

HOW HE PREACHED TO THE BIRDS,
HOW DUMB ANIMALS WERE OBEDIENT TO HIM
AND FLED TO HIM CONFIDENTLY
AND THE WATER THAT WAS CHANGED INTO WINE FOR HIM.

[37]Blessed Francis was a man completely filled with a dovelike simplicity. Once, when he was going through the Spoleto valley, it happened that near a town named Bevagna, he saw a huge multitude of various kinds of birds all flocked together. He had a great fondness for all creatures because of his special love of the Creator. Leaving his companions on the road, he quickly ran to the spot where the birds had gathered, and, as was his custom, greeted them as though they had human reason. Observing, moreover, that they did not leave the place on his account, he marveled and drew near to them, but even then, when he got there, none of them withdrew, which filled him with great joy. With great care, the man of God urged them to pay attention to the Word of God. Among many other things, he set forth for them in simple fashion things like these: "My brother birds, you who are noble among all creatures are especially bound to love and praise your Creator who clothes you in feathers, lifts you up from the earth by your wings, and provides purer mansions for you in the air. Though you neither sow, reap, nor *gather into barns,* he nourishes you without any trouble to you, and abundantly provides you with everything that's good for you." The little birds themselves opened their beaks, and stretched out their wings and necks, wonderfully exulting after their own fashion and gazing upon the holy man of God who propounded such things to them, seemed to be paying careful attention to his words. Saint Francis, *passing through their midst and returning, touched them at will with his tunic, but they did not move from the spot, until he gave them leave by blessing them with the sign of the cross, and himself departed.*

1C 58; LCh 7 — Off 18:v — Mt 6:26 — Lk 4:30

Then he began to accuse himself of great negligence before the brothers because he had previously neglected to preach to the birds. From that time on, then, the man of God, on whose lips there was al-

1C 81

Off 18:v ways praise, especially praise of the Savior, while himself praising God, not only advised people to praise him, but also earnestly invited birds, beasts and all other creatures to do the same, calling them by the names "brothers" or "sisters," to the praise of the Maker of all.

Off 1:v 38 But he who had totally subjected himself to the will of the Creator, with good reason used to give orders also to creatures inferior to him-
1C 58 self, *invoking the name* of the Most High, and he knew from frequent Acts 22:16
and personal experience that they would be obedient to him.

To refer to a few of many such incidents, it happened that one day
1C 59 while at the town of Alviano, though he wished to explain the Word of God to the people who had assembled there, he was unable to do so because he heard all the noise coming from a flock of swallows nesting there. To the chattering swallows he spoke as follows: "My sister swallows, now *it is time* for me to speak my piece, because up to now you Tb 12:20
have spoken enough indeed; from now on, until *the word of the Lord is*
finished stop your talking altogether!" They, as though they had rea- 2 Chr 36:21
son, immediately quieted down, and did not leave the place until the preaching had been completed. At this marvelous sight, all those present glorified God, and wished at least to touch the blessed man's garments.

1C 60; LCh 7 39 Again and again, the beasts of the forest also ran to Blessed Francis as to the safest port, as though, led by reason, they knew his kind feelings towards them.

Once while he was staying at the town of Greccio, he saw a rabbit caught alive in a snare brought in by a brother. Moved by great pity at this sight, that most gentle man said to the hare, "Brother rabbit, come to me! Why did you allow yourself to be deceived like this?" When he was released by the brother, the rabbit, as if confident, immediately ran
to the man of God and rested *in his lap* just like a tame animal. As often Lk 16:23
as it was placed on the ground by the blessed man so it could run away, it returned to him, not seeking any other freedom, until at last Francis commanded that it be carried away to a nearby woods by the brothers.

While he once stayed on an island in the Lake of Perugia, Francis did something similar to a little wild rabbit.

1C 61 40 Similarly, once while he was sitting in a boat on the Lake of Rieti, a large fish, commonly called a *tinca,* was given to him while it was still alive. The holy man received it joyfully and kindly, not to eat it, but to set it free. He called it "Brother Fish," and while praying and blessing the *name of the Lord* he put it back into the water. While he was per- Ps 113:2

sisting in his prayer and praise, the fish played in the water and did not leave until Blessed Francis, after finishing his prayer, gave it permission.

The glorious confessor of Christ gave orders not only to sensate 1C 77
creatures, such as beasts and birds, about which it would take too long to tell in detail, but also out of consideration for him, the Lord changed even insensate elements into another nature.

Let us briefly narrate another such incident. Once, when the holy 1C 61
man was gravely ill with some disease at the hermitage of Sant'Urbano, water was miraculously changed into wine for him. He so easily regained his health at its taste that no one would doubt that this was a miracle worked by God.

Chapter IX

HIS LOVE FOR ALL CREATURES
ON ACCOUNT OF HIS LOVE FOR THE CREATOR;
AND HOW HE SHOWED GREAT REVERENCE FOR THE NAME OF THE LORD AND HIS WORDS;
AND HIS COMPASSION FOR THE POOR.

1C 77 [41]The mind of Blessed Francis was filled with such great sweetness of divine love that, because he saw the marvelous work of the Creator in all things, he abounded in the greatest tenderness of piety towards all creatures.[a] Yet, among those creatures, the ones he especially loved were those like sheep, which he saw to be of a simpler and gentler nature, and whose names he had heard in the Scriptures, representing Christ because of their likeness to him.[b]

Once, while he was going through the Marches of Ancona with Brother Paul, whom he had *appointed minister,* he saw a lone little Acts 26:16 lamb grazing among a large flock of goats. At the sight of this, he sighed deeply and said to Brother Paul: "Do you not see that little sheep walking alone and simply among the goats? Thus did Our Lord Jesus Christ, innocent, meek and humble, walk among the scribes, Pharisees and the chief priests. Let us, my dear son, pay the price and *lead* this lamb from the *midst* of that flock of goats."[c] Ps 136:11

1C 78 [42]While they stood troubled, since they had nothing but their mean tunics with which to buy the sheep, a passing merchant freely offered to do so and, having paid the price, he left the sheep with the holy man. Joyfully, he took the sheep with him to the city of Osimo, to which he was making his way and where he stopped as a guest of the bishop of the place. To the bishop who was wondering why he was leading a lamb, he narrated a long parable about it, until the bishop, who was mightily struck by the purity of this simple man of God, gave thanks to the Most High. The following day the man of God went to a cloister of the Ladies at San Severino, where he left the lamb with these servants

a. In this chapter, Julian passes over 1C 62-76 that lists miraculous cures from illnesses. He takes up the animal narratives in 1C 77-80. In this way, the current chapter flows more consistently from the previous chapter.

b. See Is 16:1 and 53:7; Jer 11:19; Jn 1:29; and Rv 5:6.

c. Again, Julian quotes Francis in a manner similar to 1C.

of Christ. Devotedly receiving it out of reverence for the holy man, they diligently fed it for a long time, until at last weaving a tunic from its wool, they sent it to the blessed man: a most acceptable gift from "Brother Lamb."[a]

[43]Another time when he was traveling with Brother Paul through the same Marches, he came upon a man who was carrying two lambs on his shoulders to sell. When the pious father heard their bleating, he was *moved to the core of his being* and, approaching them in a kindly manner, he petted them as a mother would stroke her crying children. Moreover, he said to the man: "Why do you torture my brother lambs by tying them up and hanging them?"[b] The man answered that he was taking them to market to get money that he needed. When the saint asked what would become of the lambs, and was told they would be slaughtered, he said: "Perish the thought! Better that you should take the mantle that is covering me, and release my brother lambs to me!" The man readily agreed. The mantle was of much greater value than the lambs. The man of God had been forced to borrow it that same day from a faithful friend on account of the cold. Accepting the lambs, he became troubled about what to do with them, and, finally, talking it over with his brother companion, he gave them into the care of the same man from whom he had obtained them, and strictly ordered him never to sell or harm them.[c]

1C 79] · 1 Kgs 3:26

[44]He was drawn with the same compassion not only to these kinds of beasts and other worthier creatures, but also to vile and lowly creatures. Because we read of the Savior *I am a worm, not a man,* he would frequently pick up even worms from along the road that they might not be crushed, and would serve strong wine or honey to bees in winter, so they would not die. He diligently noted the virtue of these and all other creatures, and whatever he was able to judge as admirable, delightful or of value in any of them, he referred totally to the glory of the Maker of all things. What do you think he drank in of true knowledge, sweetness and grace in the sun, the moon, the stars and the firmament, in the elements and in their effects or embellishments? What, I ask, did he drink in when he contemplated the power, wisdom and goodness of the Creator of all in all things? Surely, I do not think that it would be possible for any mortal to express this in words.

1C 80 · Ps 22:7 · Off 1:v

a. Julian, unlike Thomas of Celano, identifies the lamb as "brother."

b. This quote is taken almost exactly from 1C.

c. Although not identical, this number is one of the closest to 1C 79.

1C 81 Since he traced all things back to their one first beginning, he called
Off 18:v; CtC every creature "brother," and, in his own praises, continuously invited
all creatures to praise their one common Creator.

1C 82 *Calling upon the name of the Lord,* he was profoundly moved be- 2 Tm 2:19
yond the understanding of humanity, was totally joyful, and seemed to be totally from a different age.[a] Because of this, he showed such great reverence for the name of the Savior that anything he found written and set in an unseemly place, he respectfully gathered up and set in a worthy place, in case it contained sacred words or names, or even the letters in which these are written.

1C 77 [45]With how much fire of compassion do you think he, who
abounded in such sweet piety, not only for brute animals but even for insensate and lowly creatures, burned towards the poor? This true patriarch of the poor, wishing to be the poorest of all, sought no posses-
1C 76 sion beyond a mean tunic.[b] But even in regard to this one necessity, he
was unwilling to be easy on himself. On the contrary, many times he most readily wished to give even that to some poor person.

In winter, he would ask wealthy people for all sorts of clothing and, accepting them in such a way that he would not be bound to repay those who had given most freely, he would bestow them on the first needy person he happened to meet. He took it hard if he saw any harm done by word or deed to any of the poor. Once, upon hearing that one of the brothers had scolded a poor man saying, "Watch out that perhaps you're only falsely pretending to be poor," he chided him severely and had him fall naked before the man, kiss his feet and humbly ask his pardon. "Anyone who insults a poor man," he said, "does an injury to Christ, whose noble sign he carries, who voluntarily made himself poor for us in this world." Even though he had little bodily strength, he lent his own shoulders again and again to lighten the burdens of the poor. Out of pious zeal for them he frequently did many other things of this sort, which, if we were not striving after brevity, would not have been unworthy to write.

a. The scriptural quotation can also be translated as "pronouncing the name of the Lord." Julian refers to the manner in which Francis was affected when he pronounced the Lord's name. See LJS 54 below.

b. See the Gradual of the Second Mass in Honor of Saint Francis: *O Patriarcha Pauperum*, cf. supra, p. 349.

Chapter X

THE FRUIT OF HIS PREACHING AND
THE DEVOTION OF THE PEOPLE TOWARDS HIM;
AND SOME OF HIS MIRACLES,
AND THE SOLEMNITY OF THE MANGER
AND THE VISION CONNECTED WITH IT.

46 At the time when the holy man of God, Francis, preached to the birds, as has been said, he *went around* far and wide *through towns and villages.*[a] By divine power he moved the hearts of so many to penance that several times he received some thirty men together into the habit of religion.[b] The desire of those who streamed around him was so great that anyone, who, with deep devotion, was able to touch *even his clothing,* considered himself happy. When Francis entered any city or village, the bells were rung solemnly to greet him; unanimously applauding his coming most joyfully, people sometimes went out in procession with tree branches to meet him. Heretical depravity was confounded and the Catholic faith, which the holy man proclaimed not only by his life and words but also by many miraculous prodigies, was extolled.[c] He cured every illness by invoking the power of the Divine Name, he magnificently drove out demons by his word, and no difficulty of want or peril was able to resist his prayer. Though we reserve his miracles for a longer treatment, nevertheless in this work we shall briefly insert a few.[d]

1C 62

Mt 9:35

Mk 5:28; Mt 9:20-21

47 In the city of Toscanella, Blessed Francis was offered warm hospitality by a certain knight whose *only son,* though he had been weaned, still lay in a cradle, lame and enfeebled physically. The knight humbly prostrated himself at the feet of the blessed man and tearfully asked him to cure his son. But the servant of God, thinking himself unworthy of such a task, at first did not accede until, overcome in the end

1C 65

Lk 7:12

a. See LJS 37 above.

b. See LJS 23 above. In these paragraphs (46-52), Julian moves backward in 1C catching references to numbers he had passed over, considerably rearranging the material.

c. See Prologue and LJS 28 above.

d. Beginning with the next section, Julian omits the miracles mentioned in 1C 63-64, transposing them to LJS 51-52.

by the knight's incessant pleading, he betook himself to prayer, and
having made the sign of the cross, *raised up the boy in the name of the*
Lord. The boy, moreover, immediately got up in front of everyone, Acts 4:10; 3:6-7
and, restored to health, walked around the house as he wished.

1C 66 [48]Another time, a man from Narni named Peter lost the use of all his
limbs to such an extent that, for five months lying as immobile as a log,
he could only move his tongue and open his eyes pitiably. Hearing that
Blessed Francis had arrived there, the man immediately requested that
the bishop of the place ask the servant of God come to him for the sake
of Divine Pity, because he believed that by Francis's presence *he*
would be restored to health. Moved by pity, the man of God came up to Mt 12:13
him, and drew the sign of the cross over him from head to foot. When
his sickness had been put to flight, in *the power of the Most High,* Fran- Lk 1:35; Wis 6:3
cis raised him up healthy.

1C 67 In the same city too, there was a certain woman who had lost her vision who joyfully merited to receive her sight from Blessed Francis the
moment that he made the sign of the cross over her eyes.

A certain woman from Gubbio had withered hands, which were utterly useless for any kind of work. When she heard that Blessed Francis
had come there, she ran to him full of sadness to show him why she deserved his compassion. Having seen her, the man of God pitied her,
touched her and cured her so that immediately, with her own hands, she
made a cheesecake and offered it to the servant of God; he accepted
only a little of it on account of the woman's devotion.

1C 68 [49]A certain brother was being tortured by the miserable pain of
some disease. (I don't know its name.) Many thought he was being tormented by the most evil sort of demon, for at one moment, with a horrible face, he *would writhe foaming at the mouth,* at another, he would lie Mk 9:20
in turn stiff and extended, bent and contracted. Then, in truth, his body
would be raised horizontally to a man's height, only to fall back down
miserably to earth. Knowing about his illness, the holy father went up
to him, first fervently prayed for him to the Lord, and then made the
sign of the cross over him. At this a miracle immediately occurred: the
brother was freed from that terrible suffering so that from then on he
felt not the least twinge of pain as a result of that condition.

1C 69 [50]Once, while Blessed Francis was *preaching the reign of God* in Lk 8:1
the town of San Gemini, he, along with three brothers, was welcomed
with enthusiasm and entered the home of a certain devout man whose
wife, as everyone in the town *was badly tormented by a demon.* The Mt 15:22

holy man was long entreated on her behalf before he assented, because he feared people's applause. But finally, overcome by her entreaty, he placed his three brothers in three corners of the house to pray for her, and he himself withdrew to the fourth corner, likewise to pray. After this, he confidently went up to the stricken woman and, *in the name of*
1 Pt 4:14 *Christ,* commanded the demon to leave by virtue of obedience. Then the Lord did something to preserve the humility of his servant. So suddenly did the demon leave the woman, hissing horribly, that the man of God believed that he had been mocked, and red-faced, he left the place immediately.

Another time, when he was going through the same town, he refused to look at or address the same woman, but she piously hurried along behind him that she might speak to him and *kiss his footprints.*
Est 13:13 And so, at last, he came with difficulty to believe—although everyone attested to it—that she had truly been a demoniac.

Lk 7:33 In Città di Castello, there was also a woman *possessed by a demon,* 1C 70
who, when Blessed Francis arrived there, was brought to him. A crowd from the city was present to petition Francis on her behalf. They complained that they were sore beset by the recurring insanity of this very demoniac. When he heard the furious clamoring at the door, Blessed Francis, wanting to know whether it was really a demon, first sent a brother into the house. She knew as soon as she saw him that he was not Blessed Francis, and smiling evilly, she treated the brother as insignificant. Meanwhile, however, the man of God had prostrated himself in prayer, and when this was completed, confidently approached the woman. Not being able to endure his presence, she writhed along the ground in front of him snarling. He commanded the spirit by obedience to go forth and, not being able to resist his command even for a moment it left.

51 These, and many more similar things were done by Blessed Fran- 1C 64
cis not only when he was physically present; but also in his absence, things he had touched proved a saving remedy against various calamities.

Once, in the territory of the city of Arezzo, a pregnant woman was 1C 63
Is 37:3 suffering unusually, because, *at the point of birth,* she was not able to deliver, so that all hope of saving her was lost. At the time, however, it happened that, due to an infirmity and weakness of the body, Blessed Francis had been taken to a certain hermitage on a horse, which was being led back by a brother through that same place. When the people of

the place saw the brother, they hoped he was Blessed Francis himself, whom they had heard would pass that way, but who had already passed by. When, to their great sorrow, they discovered that this was not Francis, not completely despairing, they began to search diligently for anything that had been touched by the holy man's hands. Coming upon the reins of a bridle which the man of God had held in his hands, they quickly removed the bridle from the horse's mouth and put it over the woman whom they saw in such danger; and it happened that she immediately gave birth with joy, and experienced no further danger.

1C 64 52 An inhabitant of Città della Pieve, a religious man named Gualfreduccio, devoutly kept in his possession a cord with which Blessed Francis had once girded himself. Now it happened that in the same town, when many men and women became gravely ill, the devout man mentioned above, visited the places of the sick, dipped a part of the cord in water, or mixed a bit of the cord with water, and gave the mixture to those who were lying sick in bed to drink. It had so miraculous an effect that, if any of the ill drank this potion, they immediately
1C 63 recovered the good health that they longed for. They would also often offer bread to Blessed Francis to be blessed, and the sick who ate it recovered from various diseases.

The holy father was often left half-naked by people who used scissors to cut his tunic into small pieces which they kept devoutly as a remedy against various dangers to their health.

1C 84 53 Moreover, something marvelous happened three years before the blessed passing of Blessed Francis and, although many other things have been neglected, I think it is worthy of being recalled.[a] The holy man assiduously meditated particularly on the things that were done in the time of Christ, and did not wish, if he could help it, to neglect even a jot or tittle of what was narrated in the books of the holy gospel. Quite the contrary, he considered everything written about Christ, but above all the vicissitudes of his life, and longed to experience the very sweet
Off 1:iv yoke and light burden of the Master himself.

1C 84 Therefore, desiring to represent as faithfully as possible the lowly poverty of the infancy of the Savior born at Bethlehem, when the Feast of the Nativity was at hand, the man of God sent word to a religious nobleman in the town of Greccio named John, who provided an

a. At this point in LJS 53, Julian skips forward, passing over the descriptive portrait of the Saint (1C 83), resuming 1C's textual order from which he had departed in n. 46 above.

ox and an ass, with a stable, in anticipation of the joys of the coming celebration.[a]

[54]Finally the holy night arrived. Blessed Francis was there with many of his brothers gathered around him. 1C 85

The hay in the manger is prepared, the ox and the ass are arranged around the manger, and the vigil celebration begins with joy. A great multitude of people stream together from various places, the night is filled with an unaccustomed joy and made luminous by candles and torches. And so, with a new ritual, the festival of a new Bethlehem is celebrated.[b]

The brothers also paid their debt of praise to the Lord, and all present acclaimed him with new songs of praise. Blessed Francis, however, was standing before the manger full of sighs of joy and suffused by an indescribable sweetness. Finally, when Solemn Mass was celebrated 1C 86
above the manger, the holy Levite of God, dressed in festive vestments proclaimed the gospel with a sonorous voice and then with a voice flowing with honey he preached to the people about the poor King born in Bethlehem. Truly, he was so overcome by sweet devotion toward the infancy of that King, that whenever he had to speak the name of Jesus Christ, he would, as if stuttering, call him "the babe of Bethlehem," out of an excess of loving tenderness.

[55]Lest it be thought that these things happened without divine ap- 1C 86
proval, a miraculous vision was shown to a certain virtuous man, who saw Blessed Francis go up to the manger and waken, as if from a deep sleep, a child who seemed to be lying there lifeless. It is therefore believed, and not without reason, that the Lord Jesus aptly revealed his infancy in this vision to the one who reflected upon it.[c] He who was asleep or dead in the hearts of many, owing to forgetfulness, was awakened and recalled to memory by the teaching and example of Blessed Francis. The solemnities were completed with great exultation, and everyone happily returned to their homes.

Later, hay from the manger saved both men and women from vari- 1C 87
ous perils and also proved health-giving when applied to stricken brute beasts. Moreover, the place of the manger is consecrated as a *temple of*
1 Kgs 8:63 *the Lord,* and an altar, constructed above that same manger, is dedi-

a. Julian greatly abbreviates Thomas of Celano's narration of the Christmas story, leaving out the extensive quotation of Francis regarding his desire for this celebration at Greccio.

b. Like Thomas of Celano before him, Julian here shifts into the present tense.

c. Julian adds an interpretive observation.

cated to the honor of the holy father Francis, and in memory of the event.

[56]During his life, and even after his death, Blessed Francis shone in miracles so numerous and so momentous that it would require a much longer work to explain them more fully.[a] In addition to the other almost innumerable miracles which he worked in the alleviation of various diseases, necessities or dangers, he also miraculously brought many dead persons back to life. The exact number cannot presently be determined, but we are certain that there were very many such occurrences.
LCh 15 We have learned from trustworthy persons that there were at least eleven.[b]

For now, let it suffice to have touched in one way or another upon these things concerning his miracles, lest the narration of miracles tire those who want to hear briefly the course of his life. Why should we dwell on his miracles, which manifest sanctity more than effect it, since in the interests of brevity, we are compelled to remain silent about many of the signs of his miraculous manner of life, a few of which we touch upon lightly. I think that there are very few virtues in the practice of which this blessed man did not accomplish many things worthy of note which would be more profitably related than his miracles.[c]

---

a. See LJS 46 above.

b. LJS 76 below.

c. For a similar attitude toward miracles, see 1C 70, 93.

Chapter XI

HIS ZEAL FOR PRAYER AND
HIS STRUGGLE WITH THE DEVIL;
THE CONSTANCY OF HIS PREACHING,
THE OPENING OF A BOOK
AND THE VISION OF THE CRUCIFIED SERAPH;
AND THE STIGMATA OF CHRIST APPEARING IN HIM.

[57]Truly, in regard to all those things which the glorious father Francis intended to do and did, his safest refuge was frequent prayer. Although he worked with the most ardent zeal for the good of those around him, he nonetheless most diligently took pains lest he neglect to tend to himself in every pursuit of perfection. To this end, he sought out solitary places and made his abode in the wilderness; but, while living among people, he went alone at night to deserted houses or churches. 1C 71 1C 27 1C 71

O what great terrors he endured in places of this sort, and how many tricks of the devil he overcame! The evil one not only frequently tempted him from within by thoughts that imperiled his immortal soul, but he also fought *hand to hand* against the devil in frightful appearance. 1C 72 Es 21:19

Boldly, he chose such places, I say, so that he might keep guard over himself in prayer; there, he first learned what he later taught others. However, he learned not so that he might painstakingly invent words to speak, but that thus, above and beyond the ways of human learning, he might drink most fully of the richness of heavenly wisdom, in order that he might be full, not so much with words as with the *power of the Spirit* which might sprinkle upon his neighbors when the right time came.[a] Rom 15:13

[58]For even if, when he thought he was prepared to say this or that, it happened that when he came to preach he forgot all those things he had thought out beforehand, and did not have anything at all to say, not even then was he ashamed to admit his failing in front of everyone, and thus, all of a sudden, he began to overflow with a miraculous elo- 1C 72

a. This extended personal commentary is unusual in Julian's text.

quence. Continually dependent, in all hopefulness, on the generous Providence of the Lord alone, he had no confidence at all in his own
LCh 9 works. He spoke with the same constancy of mind to the many as to the few, and preached with as much diligence to one as to many.

1C 73 He had no fear of anyone's status, rather he spoke calmly to the wise and the uneducated, to the great and the small. He preached very tranquilly to a gathering of cardinals before the Lord Pope Honorius, not so much moving them to laughter by the simplicity of his words as wringing from them a sigh of remorse at the marvelous fervor of his inspiration.

1C 91 59 Therefore, that most holy man, who had come to know how to divide his time usefully between himself and those around him, on a certain occasion left the crowds of secular people, sought out a place of solitude, and took a few companions with him, in order to defend his repose from all the tumult of those who thronged to him. For, on occasion, he longed to have time free for God alone, and *to shake off any dust* he had picked up while dealing with men. And after his mind was Lk 10:11
quiet for a little while, he tasted the sweeter fruit of contemplation, then with all his heart he longed to know what to do to be able *to make the sacrifice* of himself more pleasing to the Lord. The man of singular vir- Sir 35:4
tue had already reached the goal when he believed he had scarcely begun. His greatest desire had always been to extend himself to the things which lay before him, and to count the past as nothing.

1C 92 Therefore, he desired still to endure anew all the sufferings of body and all the agonies of mind so that *every wish* of the Divine Purpose might be more perfectly *fulfilled* in him.[a] Is 44:28

1C 92 60 And since his pursuit of this desire was as continual as it was fervent, one day he piously went up to the altar in the hermitage where he was staying and, with reverence and fear, placed on it the book of the Gospels. Then, humbly prostrating himself in prayer before the altar, he *cried out to the Lord* with as much devotion as he was able, that he Ps 3:5
be given a sign of God's purpose about himself at his first opening of the book.

1C 93 Finally, *rising up from prayer* with a *contrite heart,* he strengthened Lk 22:45; Ps 51:19
himself with the sign of the cross, and reverently took the book from the altar and opened it. When he was first confronted with the passion of Our Lord Jesus Christ, he was distrustful lest this might have hap-

a. With this paragraph, LJS 59, Julian begins to use 1C Book Two.

pened by chance. And so he closed the book, opened it once again, and
as many times as he repeated this very act, he found the same or similar
passage as before. The intrepid soldier of Christ was not frightened by
this; in fact, he who had long yearned to be a martyr, at that very mo- Off 21
ment disposed himself zealously to bear all that he could bear for
Christ.

And because, for all these things he brought forth with glad heart songs of joy to the Lord, not much later he was deemed worthy of the revelation of a greater mystery.[a]

[61]Two years before that blessed man happily died in grace, while he 1C 94
was staying in a hermitage called La Verna, in the air he saw *in a vision*
Dn 8:2 a six-winged *seraph,* as it were, fastened to a cross with its arms
stretched out and feet bound together. It kept *two of its wings raised*
above its head, two extended for flight, and with the remaining *two cov-*
Is 6:2; Ez 1:5ff *ered its whole body.*[b] The holy man was stupefied at the vision, and fear
and joy were alternating within him. The marvelous beauty of that appearance was delightful to him, while the horrible crucifixion much
frightened him, but this also gave him joy for he noticed that he was being regarded graciously by the seraph. And though for a long time he
pondered with anxious spirit what this strange sort of vision might por-
tend, he understood nothing about it clearly, until he later saw this most
glorious miracle in his very self—a miracle unheard of, in my judgment, in all the preceding ages.[c]

Jn 20:25 [62]For, lo and behold, the *prints of nails,* as it were, appeared in his 1C 94
hands and feet, and his right side was pierced as though by a lance. Yes,
the palms of his hands and the tops of his feet were swollen as if from 1C 95
something like the heads of nails protruding from his very flesh; while
the backs of his hands and the soles of his feet bore oblong marks, like
the sharp points of nails bent back, which also similarly passed through
the rest of the tissue. Truly, in his right side a wound covered by a scar
appeared, which often dripped sacred blood, stained his tunic and,
sometimes, his undergarments.

---

a. Julian adds the notion of mystery (*maioris revelatione mysterii dignus*) to the meaning of this revelation, which he takes from 1C 93 (*maiore revelatione dignus*).

b. Both visions describe a Seraph with the extended six wings. Also, in both versions there are hands extended and feet joined. Whereas Thomas of Celano writes that Francis saw "in a vision of God," Julian simply states that Francis saw "in a vision." The object of the vision seems to differ between these two authors. Thomas of Celano places in the vision "a man . . . attached to a cross" (*virum unum . . . cruce affixum*) who is (*quasi Seraphim*) like a Seraphim. Julian writes that in the vision Francis saw one "like a Seraph" (*quasi Seraph unum*). It is not clear if the absence of the man (*virum*) in Julian's text is intentional.

c. Julian identifies the La Verna event as a miracle. Cf. 1C 112, 113.

Therefore, with such pearls as these manifest in him, the man of God strove to keep hidden from the eyes of all that most precious treasure with which the Lord, by a special privilege, had enriched him, lest he incur even the slightest loss which might result from those close to him coming to know about the stigmata. And so it happened that, because he was accustomed to reveal only rarely and to a very few the most important mysteries, the mystery of the stigmata, which had been so gloriously manifested in him, remained long unknown, even to his friends.[a]

1C 96 63 Thinking it most dangerous to appear famous in the eyes of men, and believing one's hidden blessings to be greater than those which are brought to public notice, he very often kept this prophecy on his lips: *Your words I have hidden away in my heart so that I do not sin against you.* He also instructed the brothers who were his constant companions Ps 119:11
that if, when he was engaged with strangers, they heard him recite the aforementioned psalm, they should extricate him courteously from the conversation, lest he drift into saying things damaging to himself.

1C 95 Thus only Brother Elias merited to see—and only by chance—the wound in Francis's side, for the man of God carefully concealed it as long as he lived. But Brother Rufino, when allowed to scratch him, felt it palpably with his hand, but only by chance.[b] At his touch, the holy man groaned, experienced most acute pain, and reproved the brother, adding that the Lord would forgive him for this.

a. In addition to the notion of "miracle" used by Julian above, he also introduces the notion of "mystery."

b. Besides Elias and some other ministers or notable personalities, e.g. Paul, minister of the Marches of Ancona (41), John of Florence (30), the newly canonized Anthony of Padua (30) and the troubled Riccerio (31), of the close companions of Francis only Rufino is mentioned.

Chapter XII

THOSE THINGS HE UNDERWENT,
SAID, AND DID BEFORE HIS DEATH;
HIS FERVOR AND PATIENCE;
AND HIS PASSING AND FUNERAL.

64 Eighteen years after his conversion, the most blessed father Fran- 1C 67-68
cis had been going around preaching with great difficulty through diverse parts of the world. He gave not even moderate rest to the flesh,
which he had not ceased afflicting with new and unaccustomed kinds
of discipline. Although in the past he had suffered many weaknesses,
he nonetheless began to be oppressed by much more painful and
chronic infirmities in the two years of his life which remained. But
even though his flesh knew in advance it was approaching its natural
dissolution and necessary failure, yet as much as it could, it still did not
object to being held to the conditions of Francis's accustomed exacting
regimen. To so great an extent had the revered man mastered himself,
and with such great harmony reconciled his body to his spirit, that he
scarcely felt any resistance on the part of the flesh to those things which
his spirit dictated had to be done.

Therefore, the holy man, most ready in spirit for every good, who up 1C 98
until now burned with such great zeal for souls, still did not cease to exert himself in preaching for the salvation of his neighbors. He caused
his half-dead body to be carried around on an ass through *towns and* 1C 97
Mt. 9:35 *villages.*

65 The brothers kept trying to persuade and would beg him with a 1C 98
stream of requests to allow his infirmities to be helped by the care of
doctors, particularly because they were observing him failing more
and more every day. But he altogether refused to agree with the brothers in this matter. As one who had given no care to the body up to this
time, he longed, as for a far better thing, to *depart this life* and *be with*
Phil 1:23 *Christ.* But, even though he *carried the marks of the Lord Jesus in his*
Gal 6:17 *body,* nevertheless, because it was fitting for *those things which were*
Col 1:24 *lacking to the sufferings of Christ to be fulfilled* in him, he began to
have a most grave illness of the eyes over and above his other weaknesses. Then the above-mentioned Brother Elias, whom he had put in
place of a mother, as it were, to be shepherd over his flock even while

he was still alive, compelled him and by arguments persuaded him to permit himself to be treated medically, fearing lest through negligence he might lose his eyesight completely. The holy man was obedient to him as though to a father and from that time on he allowed a number of medicines to be applied to his eyes, though, with the malady getting worse, they were of no help.

1C 99 Finally, on the occasion of treating the above-mentioned malady, he was brought to Rieti, where the Lord Pope Honorius III was then staying, and there he was received with honor and devotion by the Roman Curia. The Lord Hugolino, then Bishop of Ostia, was present. He was more familiar to him than the rest, since the holy man had, with the approval of the same Lord Honorius, chosen him before all others as fa-
1C 100 ther and lord. Into his safekeeping Francis had entrusted himself, together with his whole Order, which he had subjected to the mandate
Off 1:iii of his obedience. Led by a prophetic spirit, he had not only predicted with words that Hugolino would become pope but also with his acts had prefigured it in many ways.[a]

1C 101 [66]Hugolino, therefore, used to feel very keenly a wonderful affection for the holy man; he used to minister to this little poor man of Jesus Christ, as a servant would to a lord. Later Hugolino himself, when he had been promoted to the apostolic dignity, used to bear witness that he was never so perturbed but that every cloud of mind departed at only a glance or a word from the holy man of God, and immediately an agreeable serenity and sweet joy would reappear. As often as he saw him, he would show him reverence as if to an *apostle of Christ.* 1 Cor 1:1; 2 Cor 1:1

And so Hugolino constantly advised blessed Francis to take care of himself; and the saint himself was humbly obedient to Hugolino in this regard, as in all other things. Therefore, his head was cauterized, his veins cut, and salves and plasters applied. Nothing improved his health at all: no, rather, the illness increased as the remedies were multiplied.

1C 102 Truly, he bore up under so many troubles of the body in all patience and thanksgiving; he made little of his body's members and directed all his attention to God with his spirit comforted. And, so that he could more freely direct his attention to interior consolation, the four brothers, *men of virtue,* appointed to watch over him, most solicitously de- 1 Mc 5:50
voted themselves not only to provide for his every bodily necessity, but also to preserve the peacefulness of his soul.

a. Thomas of Celano's discourse of extended praise of both Honorius III and of Lord Hugolino is omitted, as is the detail that Hugolino was also bishop of Velletri.

67 The glorious father, greatly perfected in the grace of so great vir- 1C 103
tues, thought that he had spent his days to no purpose; and though he
was altogether unfit for physical exertions, he still continued to drive
himself toward the triumphs of a new struggle. Truly he used to say:
"Let us begin, brothers, to serve God. Let us begin," he would say.
"And let us make progress, because up to now we have made too little
progress." He wished to turn back again to his early simplicity, abjectly
to serve the lepers anew, and remove himself from human contact to
the most remote places.

He wished also to remove himself from all the cares of administra- 1C 104
tion, because he maintained it was dangerous for many reasons, particularly at this time, to hold a place of authority; he thought it more useful
to the greater number of people to be ruled than to rule.[a]

Mt 25:5 When he *was staying* at Siena, about six months before his death, 1C 105
his whole body wasted away even more gravely than previously; he
was obviously near the end. And so, Brother Elias came hurriedly from
afar, and when he arrived he took Francis, who had recovered a little,
with him to Le Celle di Cortona. When he had stayed there for a while,
his illness became even worse, and he asked to be taken to Assisi. After
Eph 5:20 he got there, the whole city exulted greatly and, *giving thanks,* they
unanimously praised the Lord because they hoped so great a *treasure*
Tb 12:8 was being *put back again* in their care.

68 Therefore, having been led into the palace of the Bishop of Assisi, 1C 108
he began, not long after, to lack the strength in his whole body and to be 1C 107
so atrociously tormented in every part of his body that, when asked
whether he would rather bear martyrdom at the hands of an executioner, he replied that, suffering of that kind for three days, although accepted and pleasing to him as being God's will, was more painful than
any martyrdom.

Seeing, therefore, that the last day of his life was very near (for this 1C 108
he had learned two years before through a revelation), he *summoned*
Mk 3:13; Jn 19:11 the brothers *he wanted,* and as had been *given* to him *from above,*
blessed them one by one. And since he could not see, his eyes being
weak, as once the patriarch Jacob, he crossed his *hands,* placed his
Gn 48:14 *right hand* on the brother who was sitting on his left, and asking who he
was, and finding out that he was Brother Elias (who, as we mentioned,
he had placed in his stead), he responded that so he had wished.

a. The condemnation of ambitious brothers found in the corresponding paragraph of 1C is omitted.

First he blessed him and, in him, all the brothers; and, after praying for a great number of things for him, he confirmed many kinds of blessings in him. After this he added: "Be strong, my sons, all of you, *in the fear of the Lord,* and always abide in him, because tribulation ap- Tb 2:14; 6:22
proaches you and a mighty temptation will be upon you. Happy, however, are those *who will have persevered* in the good works they have Mt 10:22
begun."[a]

Then he asked to be taken immediately to Saint Mary of the Portiuncula, wishing to return his soul to the Lord there in that very place where, first, as we have said, he had come to know the *way of truth* perfectly.[b] He had counseled the brothers to guard that place with Ps 119:30
all reverence and honor. He maintained that it was especially suitable
1C 106 for prayer and divine services and he said that it was visited by a multitude of spirits from above.

1C 109 69 He rested for a few days in the place he longed for, until, knowing that the hour of death was finally near, he called two brothers to him,
CtC whom he instructed quickly to proclaim loudly in song the *Praises of the Lord* for his nearing death. He himself, as much as he could, broke forth into this psalm: *With my voice I have cried to the Lord, with my voice I have beseeched the Lord.* One of the brothers, standing by and Ps 142:2-8
troubled on the part of everyone, said to him: "Ah, kind father, behold your sons who remain here without a father! Be mindful of the *orphans* Jn 14:18
whom you are deserting and, forgiving all our faults, deign to console with your holy blessing those present and those absent." The most pious father answered him: "Behold, my son, I am now being called by the Lord. Truly, I remit all the offenses and faults of my brothers, present and absent; and, as much as I can, I absolve them. Do you, when you report these things to them, my son, bless them all for me."

1C 110 Then he asked that the Gospel according to John be read to him, with the passage that begins . . . the day before the Passover.[c] Then he Jn 13:1
instructed the brothers to cover him with a hair shirt and sprinkle him with ashes. Thus, with his sons standing around him and mourning, the holy father happily *fell asleep in the Lord.* Acts 7:60

1C 110 70 One of them, a special disciple of his, a man of no little fame, whose name is kept silent because he did not wish to be glorified by

a. Julian greatly abbreviates the story of the blessing of Brother Elias, but he concludes quoting Francis's admonition in much the same way.

b. Cf. LJS 15 above.

c. Here Julian with the phrase, *ante diem festum paschae* corrects Thomas of Celano's use of *ante sex dies paschae* in 1C 110 where Thomas of Celano confuses John 13:1 with John 12:1.

public proclaiming while he was still alive, saw that glorious soul,
freed from the flesh, in the form of a great and radiant star *ascend* di-
Jos 8:20; Ps 29:3 rectly to *heaven* as though borne *over many waters,* on a *small white*
1 Kgs 18:44; Rv 14:14 *cloud.* No doubt, he who with contempt had *crushed the husk* of his Off 17:vii
Dt 23:26 flesh by *grinding* it on the earthly threshing floor of his troubled life,
after the *chaff* had been threshed away, entered as pure grain *into the*
Mt 3:12 *granaries of the most high King.* Having no more to do with mortal life,
Jn 6:41 and about to triumph forever, he was joined to the *living bread* which,
from the granary of poverty, had satisfied the hungry crowd of Christ Off 17:viii
Mt 15:32 so *that it would not perish along the way.*

Well was he seen to ascend *over many waters* in the form of a star, 1C 110
Rv 14:14; Ps 18:16 borne on *a little white cloud! Claimed* as one cleansed *from the waters*
of earthly delight, he shone upon the multitude of peoples as much by
his miracles as by his life and teaching. For people, as though blind,
Mt 7:13; Ps 107:40 *wandering in the wide way of perdition,* for all those following him in
Mt 7:14 bands he enlarged the *way of life,* the bright way toward glory which Off 17:viii
previously was feared to have been narrowed to the few walking along
it. Therefore, he reigns rich in his homeland due to the abundance of
passing poverty. The kings of this world lie beneath him, those enriched here by the wretched want of things that perish.

Acts 21:30; Lk 2:13 [71]The *people* of the city of Assisi *came together praising God* with 1C 112
unanimous joy because He had stooped to commend to them so great a
trust. At first, there was great weeping by the sons for having had so
great a father taken away, but, not long afterwards, this was changed
into a song of joy! They saw a *new* thing which the *Lord had made*
Jer 31:22 *upon the earth;* they saw, I say, a miracle worthy not of mourning but
of cheering: the sacred body decorated with the stigmata of Christ. 1C 113
They looked at his limbs, previously diseased and rigid, now bending 1C 112
easily to the will of anyone touching them. His flesh, too, hard and pur- Off 21
ple before, now shone with marvelous whiteness as if it had regained
boyhood softness and as if it were displaying the appearance of the glorified flesh on account of the greatness of its honor.

It was then glorious to see in such white flesh the likeness of the 1C 113,114,118
Jn 20:25 *print of nails*—nails as black as iron, formed from his very flesh,
placed in the middle of his hands and feet; and his right side, red with
Lam 5:15 sacred blood.[a] His sons therefore cried for *joy of heart* and kissed the LCh 13
marks of the most high King on their father.

a. See LJS 62 above. Julian and Thomas of Celano indicate that only the wound in Francis's side bled.

72 The night on which the saint died was made solemn by the bright
torches of a great multitude of people praising God *until morning,*
1C 116 when the entire commune of Assisi came together with all those who
had gathered in great numbers from the surrounding areas. Then the sa- Jn 21:4
cred body was raised aloft and honorably carried to the accompani-
ment of hymns, praises and the sound of trumpets. Carrying out the
sacred funeral rites in solemn fashion, they *took tree branches* in their
hands.

His sons, moreover, carrying their devoted father, stopped at the Jn 12:13; Mt 21:8
Church of San Damiano, which, as we have said, was the first he had
built.[a] They showed him to his daughters, that is, the Poor Ladies and
holy virgins, whom he had planted there. Behold their pious mother,
the first seedling of that Order, "Clare" in fact and in name,[b] after
she—together with her daughters—was allowed to see the body of the
most dear father began to *weep* pitiably *over him.* For her, among all
mortals, the solace of which she was deprived was so certainly irre-
1C 117 placeable. But the rest also lamented, as much as was allowed their vir- Zec 12:10
ginal modesty; and finally, one by one they kissed his hands which
were adorned with the most precious gems. Thus, with the greatest
grief, they released him to be carried out, as was proper.

Then the most sacred body was carried into the city and buried in the
place where he had first learned his letters as a little boy and where he
1C 23 had later preached for the first time, with the result that it was clear that
a happy beginning, an even happier middle, and the happiest end had
suitably come together through this body into one single height of
glory.

---

a. See LJS 13 above.

b. Following 1C 116, Julian here presents a word play on the name "Clare," which means "bright." See also 1C 18.

Chapter XIII

HOW MANY YEARS HE LIVED AFTER HIS CONVERSION;
ON WHICH DAY HE DIED;
AND UNDER WHICH ROMAN PONTIFFS HE LIVED;
AND THE MANNER AND THE TIME OF HIS
CANONIZATION AND TRANSLATION.

73 A span of twenty years had passed since the glorious confessor 1C 109
and Levite of Christ had first embraced the counsels of evangelical per-
Ps 119:32 fection and *had run along the way of the mandates* of the divine law
with steady footsteps. Now, this same venerable father left the shipwreck of this world in the year of the Lord's Incarnation 1226, on 1C 88
Sunday, the fourth day of the nones of October, and was buried, as has
been said, in the city of Assisi.

This blessed man had begun his *course* under the illustrious Lord Off 1:ii
2 Tm 4:7 Pope Innocent III, and he happily *completed it* under his successor,
Honorius. Just as the former, as has been said above, agreed with the
man of God in all things concerning the institution of the Order, so did
the latter, as is touched upon in the Rule, later kindly confirm all things
for the same saint. They were happily succeeded by the Lord Pope Gregory, who, of course, while established in a lesser office, had defended the
planting of this same religious Order from the out-of-season onslaught
of those plucking it. He had nourished it until it took root more firmly,
and just like a most faithful gardener had encouraged it to a manifold
harvest, with the help of God. Gregory had come to know the most holy
father personally, not only as famous for his innumerable and proven
miracles, but also for his miraculous manner of life, and had concluded
that Francis should be praised the more on earth, as no one doubted he
was already glorified in heaven.

74 In the year of the Incarnation of the Lord 1228, he held a discus- 1C 123-126
sion on the canonization of this same saint with the cardinals and many
other prelates of churches. With the assembly of the whole Roman Curia and all the prelates who were then residing at the Curia, not to mention earthly princes and a countless multitude of the people, the pope
personally came to Francis's tomb from Perugia. Then, with the common consent of all, he gloriously enrolled him in the catalog of the

saints with the mysteries of the Mass, the exhortation of a sermon, the recitation of his miracles, the glory of vestments, the glittering of lights, the sound of bells, the blare of trumpets, the songs and hymns of those praising him, the applause and jubilation of those rejoicing, not to mention the most solemn rites, which would be too long to narrate. He also instituted and ordered that on the day of his death, that is the fourth day of the nones of October, his feast be solemnly celebrated throughout all the regions of the earth, just as he himself later declared
LCh 17 in writing. This famous solemnity of the canonization of Blessed Francis was held on Sunday, seventeenth of the calends of August.[a]

75 In the year of the Lord 1230 a great multitude of brothers from diverse parts of the world gathered at Assisi to celebrate the translation of the same saint as well as a general chapter. The Lord Pope Gregory, their aforementioned most special father, whose personal presence for the celebration of this translation was anticipated as certain, at that time was prevented owing to certain other urgent business of the church. He
LCh 15 sent nuncios for the purpose with a personal letter which not only explained as necessary the cause of his unexpected absence, but also announced for sure to his sons, whom he comforted with fatherly affection, that a certain dead man had been brought back to life by blessed Francis.[b] Also, through the same nuncios he sent a gold cross, priceless owing to its work in gems, but containing wood from the cross of Our Lord more precious than all the gold and gems. Besides this, he sent ornaments and several vessels which pertained to the ministry of the altar and also vestments which were most fitting for solemn uses. He bestowed all these most precious things upon the Basilica of Blessed Francis, which was being constructed by his authority, and which was exempt from all jurisdiction lower than his own, whose first
LCh 17 foundation stone he himself had laid. He also sent other considerable donations for the expenses connected with the construction of the same building and for the coming celebration.[c]

a. Julian here refers to the bull of canonization *Mira circa nos* issued by Gregory IX on July 19, 1228, and the bull *Sicut phialae aureae* of the same pope dated July 9 and 26, 1228, *Bullarium Franciscanum*, I:44-45(hereafter BFr), cf. infra pp. 565-569.

b. See LJS 73 above. Julian here alludes to the bull of Gregory IX, *Mirificans misericordias suas* of May 16, 1230 (BFr I:64-65).

c. The description of the transfer of Francis's body from the church of Saint George to the newly constructed church in his honor is not in 1C. In his bull *Speravimus hactenus* of July 16, 1239, Gregory IX attests that he laid the cornerstone of the new church, a deed accomplished on July 16, 1228. See BFr I:66-67. The lively description of the transfer of Francis's body in LJS 75-76 indicates, according to some scholars, that Julian may have been present for the event.

[76]The most holy body was translated to that same most holy church which had been constructed outside but near the walls of the city, on Saturday, the eighth of the calends of June, 1230 with such great solemnity that it cannot be briefly described. So great a multitude of people had come together for the celebration of this translation that the city was not able to contain them, and they camped all around the fields like sheep.[a] LCh 13

Just as this glorious holy man
had become illustrious in life by his many marvelous miracles,
so also at his patronage from the day of his passing
until the present,
not only in the place
where the precious treasure of his bones is kept,
but also in whatever part of the earth
that patronage is piously and fervently implored,
the church rejoices that she shines with innumerable miracles.
Remedies for all sicknesses, dangers, or exigencies are conferred
through his merits upon the blind, the deaf, the mute and the crippled;
to the dropsical, the paralyzed, the possessed and the lepers,
the shipwrecked, and the captive.
But also many dead are miraculously brought back to life;
all these things are the magnificent work of the *power of the Most*
Lk 1:35 *High,*
to whom alone is all honor and glory
Rom 16:27; 1 Tm 1:17 *forever and ever. Amen.*

a. When Francis's body was transferred, it was placed in a stone sarcophagus embedded in solid rock beneath the main altar of the lower church.

THE VERSIFIED LIFE OF SAINT FRANCIS

BY

HENRI D'AVRANCHES

(1232–1239)

Introduction

As Julian of Speyer was writing his own life of Saint Francis, re-casting that of Thomas of Celano according to the nuances of the liturgical texts, a literary genius, Henri d'Avranches, was re-casting the same text according to the laws of poetic verse. This was an enterprise undertaken to delight Pope Gregory IX and the members of his court. *The Versified Life of Saint Francis,* written between 1230 and 1235, provides no new biographical data than that of Thomas of Celano. It simply took the basic facts of the life of the pope's friend, Francis of Assisi, and made them more acceptable to a more sophisticated audience. While seeming contrived to the contemporary reader, Henri's versified interpretation of Thomas of Celano's text was a genre quite popular in the thirteenth century, especially in more literary circles.

Life of Henri d'Avranches

Henri was born in the Norman city of Avranches between 1180 and 1200. Little is known of his early years beyond the name of his father, "Trotemen." Even his sacerdotal status is uncertain. His education, the social circles he frequented, and the patronage he enjoyed suggest a clerical and, above all, a literary education of unusual stature.[1] By 1219 he had already moved to England where his literary skills were polished and an epitaph he had written for William Marsahl (+ 1219), the first Earl of Pembroke, became well known.[2]

At Henri's time, the art of disputation as well as competitions in putting prose texts into verse were activities important in the life of the university. They became equally important in the cultural and public life of the royal courts and of the clergy. This development flowed from the liberal arts education fostered by the cathedral, monastic and court schools which emphasized a study of Latin based on Latin verse. Thus diligent students committed verses to memory and learned the art of recitation, an important element in the curriculum for it facilitated accentuation and pronunciation. As texts from many fields of study were put into verse, the recitation and memorization of these verses as memory aids opened doors to the study of law, theology, medicine, philosophy, and, in religious circles, to the study of the lives of saints.[3]

By necessity Henri was quickly drawn into the life of the English court and into sympathy with bishops and abbots, the principal patrons of public poetry.

The subject matter of Henri's poetry became extensive and diverse as the many interests of his patrons. The hierarchy petitioned him to honor the English saints by re-casting the accounts of their lives into verse. For Peter des Roches, the Bishop of Winchester, he placed the life of the Saxon Saint Birinus (+ 650) into verse, for the monks of Crowland Abbey the life of Saint Guthlac (+ 714) , and for those of Peterborough Abbey that of Saint Oswald (+ 641). His most significant attempt, however, was a versified life of Saint Thomas Becket (+1170), which he wrote under the patronage of Thomas's successor as Archbishop of Canterbury, Stephen Langton (+1228). These early years in England were important for establishing Henri's reputation, increasing his skills, and refining his art. His *Comoda gramatice,* the first comprehensive metrical grammar, was poetically designed to be "memorable." Its publication in the English court only enhanced Henri's reputation.

In 1228, Henri was at the court of Pope Gregory IX where he became known for his poetry of "the courtroom debate." After familiarizing himself with the main books of canon law, especially the second part of the *Decretum* of Gratian and the *Decretals* of Gregory IX, the poet put them into in verse. His poetic summaries quickly became popular not only among law students but among the growing class of educated clergy who could easily memorize these texts and use them to their advantage. Placing legal cases into verse that was pleasing to the court could influence its decisions. Thus Henri's talent at such undertakings led him to attract a number of litigants who were undoubtedly pleased with his entertaining tactics. Four of his debate poems were used in actual cases at the papal court.[4] The most important of these was that in which Henri argued before Pope Gregory IX in favor of the attempt of John Blund, to secure papal confirmation of his election to be Archbishop of Canterbury.

This may well have brought the poetic skills to the attention of the pope who commissioned him to put Thomas of Celano's *The Life of Saint Francis* into verse. Henri's earlier hagiographical attempts demonstrated that, especially with poetic interpretations of saints about whom enthusiasm was current and intense, his poetic passion could soar. Although he had little or no contact with Francis's followers as they increased in number and began to move about Europe, by placing Thomas of Celano's text in a new form, Henri enhanced its contents and made the image of Francis even more endearing to the audience of the papal court. Upon completion of his manuscript, the poet, as was expected, recited all fourteen books of his poem before the papal curia, an important forum for public poetry and competitive verse.

Energized by his success, Henri left the papal court in 1239 to travel to that of Emperor Frederick II and, later, to that of King Louis IX. By 1243 he returned to England and the court of King Henry III for whom he composed a verse in honor of Saint Thomas the Apostle, whose relic was being enshrined in Westminster Abbey. During this same period he put into verse the lives of two popular English saints, Edward and George. After 1245, however, Henri left England once more, possibly to teach and dispute in poetry contests in Angers. Six years later he returned to the English court and perfected the art of flyting—a dispute or exchange of personal abuse written with play-on-words, puns, and extravagant insults.[5] Since flytings were commonly performed before a judge and an audience in a mock-trial setting, they were well adapted to the flamboyant personality of the Norman poet. At the time of his death, sometime between January 26, 1262, and April 2, 1263,[6] Henri had composed for one Pope, two emperors, three kings, six archbishops, more than twelve bishops and for a number of abbots and lesser dignitaries. Over one hundred and sixty of his poems have survived,[7] but the Norman poet and grammarian will undoubtedly be remembered best for his *The Versified Life of Saint Francis.*[8]

The Versified Life of Saint Francis

The oldest manuscript of Henri's *The Versified Life of Saint Francis* is that found in Codex 338 in the library of Assisi's Sacro Convento, the friary of the Basilica of Saint Francis. Scholars date the manuscript as mid-thirteenth century, rather close to the composition of Henri's work. Curiously, it does not provide any indication of the author's identity. Antonio Cristofani, who published the text in 1882, thought the author might have been John of Kent, an English Franciscan, while others proposed Julian of Speyer or Henri of Pisa, a friend of Salimbene.[9] Andrew G. Little discovered the poet's name in a manuscript of the University of Cambridge in which there was an inscription: *Super vita beati Francisci versus magistri H. Abrincensis ad Gregoriam papam nonum* [A Verse on the Life of Blessed Francis of Henri d'Avranches for Pope Gregory IX].[10] Although Henri's work has been known and available to modern scholars through these manuscripts, surprisingly little attention has been paid to it.

The first eleven books of the work follow the story as it is found in the first book of Thomas of Celano's *The Life of Saint Francis* (n. 1-87). In most of these books, however, Henri freely interprets the significance of events in various poetic digressions.[11] The first of these digressions (I: 70-142) turns to a discussion of disease and an exhibition of medical terminology. It provides a taste of the frequent digressions that follow, some short, some long, as the poet makes ample use of literary license. In the second book, Henri shows himself something of a moral theologian as he digresses into a long discourse on morality (II: 9-111). A similar moralistic approach follows in the third book as the author places on the lips of the young Francis a seething rebuke of his father's scolding of his son (III: 25-75, 87-126) and again in the fourth book in a denunciation of the laxity of the monks (IV: 92-105) and in hyperbolic descriptions of the ruined churches (IV: 179-184,218-225). Henri lets his imagination run freely in Book Five as he describes Francis's first attempts at preaching (V: 46-78) and his exhortations to live poorly in which the vindication of poverty is contrived and weak (V:180-230). The seventh book contains a commentary on the contemporary church and civil dissent (VII: 151-75). In both the seventh and the eighth books Henri again gives free reign to poetic license as he describes storms at sea in terms that are reminiscent of the classical poets (VII: 176-181; VIII: 15-17). The last of Henri's digressions, found in Book Eight, flows completely from the poet's imagination as he describes the content and the tenor of Francis's preaching before the Sultan, a description in which the saint appears as more of a philosopher than as an evangelist (VIII: 90-180).

The remaining three books are considerably shorter and manifest a selective synthesis of Thomas of Celano's final second and third books (n.91-126). In these last three chapters, the author attempts to bring things to a conclusion and only briefly summarizes the canonization and miracles. However, at the very end of the poem, Henri sings the praise of his patron, Pope Gregory IX, but is far more subdued than Thomas of Celano.

Henri was primarily interested in transforming the text of Thomas of Celano's *The Life of Saint Francis* into a dramatic poetic recitation. As such it would be safe to presume that Francis of Assisi was not Henri's primary interest; poetry was. He was more eager to use his poetic skills in pleasing his new patron, Pope Gregory IX, than in discovering any new details or insights into the newly canonized saint. This is evident from the acrostic, *GREGORIUS NONUS,* with which Henri opens each chapter. The first letter of the first word of each of the fourteen chapters taken together will spell out the name Gregory the Ninth.

Theological insight and historical information were not among Henri's goals. From that perspective, *The Versified Life of Saint Francis* is of lesser value than other subsequent lives. Its value is in its poetic drama as Henri portrays the new saint as a new Aeneid and stirs the imagination of his readers. In the language of the Roman classics, the poet attempts to open the inner struggle of the saint's heart, the mystery within his soul, and the heroic spirit that animated him. Although Henri follows the lines of Thomas of Celano's original prose, he rarely transports a continuous statement from his *The Life of Saint Francis* and only sparingly does he use Thomas of Celano's vocabulary. Curiously, Henri quotes scripture in a manner different than other religious writers of the period, such as Thomas of Celano. Whereas Scriptures are integral to the flow of contemporary lives of the saints, undoubtedly influences of a spirituality centered on the monastic *Lectio Divina,* Henri's use of Scripture is more reflective of his poetic attempts to embellish the text.

A brief paragraph of four verses introduces the theme or content of each chapter, and these verses reflect his poetic intention for the chapter. In the first chapter, for example, the first line echoes Vergil's *Aeneid.*[12] Henri's interpretation focuses on Francis's sanctity and miracles and, because of them, makes him a hero of epic proportions. Employing citations from the ancient poets, Henri presents a Francis who is a hero greater than Alexander the Great and greater than Caesar. He most frequently turns to the works of Ovid and then to Vergil, Horace and other classical Latin authors. These citations are short and cryptic, apt phrases and sayings. Innumerable classical images flow into Henri's text challenging the reader to be cognizant of Roman and Greek mythology and stretching the imagination beyond stereotypical concepts of holiness.

Notes

1. Henri is one of the first poets known to have received direct payment and preferment for his poems. Cf. David Towsend-Rigg, "Medieval Latin Poetic Anthologies (V): Matthew of Paris's Anthology of Henri of Avranches (Cambridge University Library ms Dd. 11.87)" *Medieval Studies* 49 (1987) 352.

2. Cf. Josiah C. Russell, "Master Henri of Avranches as an International Poet" *Speculum* 3 (1928) 34; Josiah C. Russell and John Paul Heironimus. *The Shorter Latin Poems of Master Henri of Avranches Relating to England.* The Medieval Academy of America: Studies and Documents 1. (Medieval Academy of America: Cambridge MA) 1935; Konrad Bund, "Mittelrheinische Geschichte des 13. Jahrhunderts in Spiegel der Dichtung: Untersuchungen zum Gedichtfragment Nr. 116 und zur des mittellateinischen Dichters Magister Heinrich von Avranches," in *Archiv fur Frankfurts Geschicte und Kunst* 59 (1985) 9-78.

3. Henri's own versification of Aristotle's *On Generation and Corruption* would be an example of the diverse and extensive reach of versified texts. Cf. Russel and Hieronimus, 101-104.

4. These debates were: 1) the Bourges-Bordeaux conflict; 2)the defense of John Blund, Archbishop-elect of Canterbury; 3) the seizure of Starkenburg castle by the Archbishop of Mainz; 4) the expulsion of the Dean of Maastricht. For a review of these four cases, the poetry and the historical context, see Russell and Hieronimus, 127-136.

5. Cf. Jan. Ziolkowski, "The Medieval Latin Beast Flyting" in *Mittellateinishces Jahrbuch* 20 (1985) 49-65.

6. Shanahan places the death of Henri in 1272. Cf. Gregory Shanahan, "Poem on the Life of Saint Francis *(Legenda sancti Francisci versificata)," Franciscan Studies,* 48 (1988) 128.

7. The poems ascribed to Henri survive in two main manuscripts: Cambridge, University Library, Dd.xi.78 and in London, British Library, Cotton Vespasian D.v, fol.151-184. Full descriptions of both manuscripts have already appeared. Cf. David Townsend and A. G. Rigg, "Medieval Latin poetic anthologies (V): Matthew Paris's anthology of Henri of Avranches (Cambridge, University Library MS Dd. 11.78)" *Medieval Studies,* 48 (1987), 352-390; Peter Brinkley, "Medieval Latin poetic anthologies (VI): the Cotton anthology of Henri of Avranches (B.L. Cotton Vespasian D. v., fols. 151-184)" *Medieval Studies* 52 (1990) 221-254.

8. For fuller appreciation of Henri's *The Versified Life of Saint Francis,* it would need to be compared to the other texts of versified saints' lives authored by him and/or others, an enormous task that has yet to be done.

9. Antonio Cristofani, *Il piu antico poema della vita di San Francesco d'Assisi, scritto inanzi all'anno 1230* (Prato: 1882). Cristofani's edition of the poem was the first; he used the then only known manuscript (Assisi Bibl. Comm. 338) in which the poem's author is anonymous.

10. Codex Cambridge University Library Dd. 11.78. Cf. Andrew G. Little, *A Guide to Franciscan Studies* (London: 1920) 12-13.

11. Shanahan, 130. See also Fernando Uribe, *Introduzione alle Agiografie di S. Francesco e S. Chiara d'Assisi* (Roma: Pontificio Atheneo Antonianum, 1996) 167-171.

12. An epic is introduced by the opening line—*Gesta sacri cantabo ducis*—echoing Vergil's "Arma virumque cano." This is to be the saga of Francis—the "Francisciad" (like an Aeneid, an Iliad). Cf. Shanahan, 131.

The First Book

FIRSTLY, A DESCRIPTION OF FRANCIS IN PURSUIT OF
THE EARTHLY, TILL THE DIVINE HONOR INFLICTS ON HIM
GRAVE FEVER, THEN COAXING HIM WITH GLEAMING ARMOR,
CONVERTS HIM, AND KINDLES HIS LOVE FOR THE TRULY GOOD.

GREAT feats of a godly captain are the theme of my song:
For mastery over monsters foremost[a] was he and gave those
Called Minor the skill he acquired.[b] And lest shining for
Jn 5:35 Others, he lose his own lamp and brandish the torch, himself
Be rejected, his lessons he led off with actions,[c] and his
Words with example. The flesh he curbed with the soul's
Commands, the foe brought down by orders derived from within,
And on the world he trampled barefooted.
Let fame more sparingly extol
For triumphs of yore, by savagery wrought and with weapons
Physical: those won in our day have out-shone them all!
For what, compared with Francis, did Julius Caesar,
Or the great Alexander, that we can recall?
Julius vanquished a foe, Alexander a world;[d] Francis did both.
1 Jn 5:4,5 Nay, Francis not only overcame a world and a foe,
But also himself: victor and vanquished in the same war.
2 Tm 2:3 O soldier of Christ, you alone, Francis, bore the scars
Of Life-triumphant-in-death; hid in your soul when living,

a. Namely the devil and vices; cf. Below Book II, 15ff.; IV, 99; v, 98, 142, 147; See Sir 45:2 "Foremost" with respect to his Lesser brothers.

b. In order to maintain the author's images, the translator had made certain adaptations. In this instance, he has chosen to translate *minor* [lesser], a reference to the "Lesser" Brothers according to the more traditional Friars "Minor."

c. This is the only word that Henri borrows from 1C, Prologue 1 (where it is the first word of the Prologue), while utterly disregarding the rest that is written there.

d. Versified lives of saints other than Francis came from the pen of Henri. He wrote similarly in other lives of saints, whose prologues follow a certain pattern: brief presentation of theme in which past heroes may be referred to, invocation of the saint, tribute to the patron to whom the poem is dedicated. From the outset of this poem, and in the invocation in line 16, Francis is treated as a soldier engaged in a spiritual war. Minerva in line 19 is the mythical patroness of the arts. The references are to Julius Caesar and Alexander the Great. This is Henri's brief presentation of theme, invocation of the Saint, tribute to the patron, that is, the person to whom Henri dedicated his lives in meter.

And displayed in your flesh when dying.[a] Accept for yourself
This work of your poet, and deign to hear humble Minerva
Do the honors in song to your princely campaign!
Moreover you, holy father, good shepherd, Gregory Ninth[b]
Making orison for gregarian sin, watching over congregational Sir 3:4
Pastures, you fill the measure of so great a name[c]
Prithee be gentle with me[d] and deign to accept in your kindness
This smallest of gifts, O greatest of mortals![e]
Francis's native soil bathes in his light like the sun,
Shining in new refulgence[f] as she glories in her great scion,
Veteran Assisi,[g] in the upper reaches of Spoleto vale,
Clings to a rocky peak's sloping flanks,
With serried ranks of olive-trees
All covered from head to toe.[h] Mt 27:51
1C 1 The boy's mother was upright, unpretentious and kind;
His merchant father violent and sly.[i]
O what a monster we've fashioned! Fickle nature's bad, consisting
Of opposing factors. Not to be excused as though it were rhetorical
Verbal inversion,[j] our perverted state of affairs is such it upsets
And confuses everything. Honor is subjected to might;
Honor dominates to become liegeman in us;
The irresolute overrides the courageous,
The earthy, the celestial, the mortal, the durable.

---

a. Henri will explain this below, XII, 37ff.

b. We attempt to reflect in English the play on the syllables of *Gregorius Nonus*, if in a somewhat archaic and quaint manner. In this dedication verse, the first of the very many quotations from the works of Ovid occurs. "You fill the measure of so great a name." *Epistulae ex Ponto*, I, II. 1. These are numerous and in each case consist of no more than a couple of words, and so they will not be noted. The same applies to Vergil and other authors. A similar play on words is found in 2C 63; cf. Sir 3:4.

c. From Ovid, *Epistulae ex Ponto*, I, II. 1.

d. Ovid, *Fasti*, I, 17.

e. Ovid, *Heroides*, IX, 107.

f. Cf. The Easter *Exsultet* and the words "O earth, in shining splendor."

g. Assisi, usually called Asisi of old, is mentioned by Strabo, *Geographica* V, 227; Ptolemy, *Geographica universalis: vetus et nova;* C. Pliny and the Elder, *Naturalis historia* III, 113; S. Aurelius Propertius, *Elegy*, IV [V] 1, 125.

h. The city was built on the slope, but not on the peak, of Mount Subasio, and is surrounded by olive groves and vineyards. The poet must have visited Assisi at some point.

i. The character of neither parent is described in 1 C 1. The poet introduced the distinction from the different behavior of each; cf. Below, I, 200ff. And II 85ff.; III, 57.

j. This is a figure of speech, the inversion of words; cf. Quintilianus, *Institutio* VIII 6, 62; IX 4, 26.

Sentiment is stronger than reason.[a]
The boy sees his parents' contrasting characters;
From the two ways he decides to follow the wrong one;
Choosing his father's lead,[b] off he goes to the left on a crooked

And rambling track, instead of a straight course rightward
Along those clear lines of living,
traced by his mother's sound footprints.
Our senses are bent on the worse;[c] too easily
Downward we slide; any skyward ascent is with effort.[d]
Ps 78:57 So, for long the youth is like a crooked bow[e]

With no thought for his soul and indulging his flesh,
Judging naught with his head, but all with emotion;
Never striving for virtue, nor testing aught with light of his mind,
Distinguishing nothing with rational aid. He pursues what's unreal
And what appears to be good; he loves food more than life,

What he possesses more than his own self;
though in fact he has no love
For food, life, possessions, or self.
It must be love-gone-astray, or just plain perverse,
When one is led to hate what one loves,
Or to love what one hates.

Now spoilt by his father's first lessons in greed, 1C 2
With a nose for the import of gain, well up in deceit,
He piles up his stocks, pulls off many a swindle, conducts
Himself haughtily, directs his thoughts to enticements,
Fritters his time away. Yet his character, naturally good,

Was by evil unalloyed; still his behavior made good habits
Ugly, rather than the ugly conform to the good.
But being gentle, generous, kindly and affable,

a. Here (vv. 34-41 and below 47-59) Henri in his own manner re-writes rather than imitates what is written in 1C 1 reducing in some places and expanding in others, temporizing (or omitting) some things, expanding others, without delineating any particular fact, but speaking in general.

b. That is, he naturally imitated the character of his father. Cf. Plautus, *Pseudolus* I, 5, 27 (434); Terentius, *Adelphoe* 4, 2, 25.

c. The word *deteriora* occurs in 1 Celano 1.

d. Cf. Vergil, *Aeneid* IX 641.

e. For the most part biblical quotations (Vulgate) are adapted in the original poem for the purposes of poetic rhythm, etc. Since they are recognizable, most will not be specially noted.

Despite these failings so knavish he maintains
Certain traces of virtue that fail to see practice.

For near years five and twenty his youth passed in such wise.
1C 3; 1C 1 A rascal, however, "a whipping" deserves;
So, the way of the Most High changed and would halt Ps 76:11
This evil course: He cuts down him who would not surrender,
Reins in the unbridled one, tames the wild man.

Like a long-lost coin that is found,
With its surface buried in rust and scarcely seeming a coin,
That should be thrown not away, but have its rusty blemish
Purged in the forge's fire.
Even so did mischief close in from all sides on the young

Man's soul, immersed in murky mist till a shade of the divine
Image therein could scarce be seen; yet it should not be damned
But have its cloud of darkness Ps 97:2
Purged in the fever's fire.
Clement sweetness of God, sweet clemency! Ps 31:20; 25:8

A worthless slave he would deign to spare,
One in vice enveloped, to excesses given, by smiting him
In righteous wrath, frightening, striking down, bringing anguish.
Yet in correcting him so, God's wrath is for love of him,
He smites him to heal him, He frightens to teach him,

Strikes down to lift up, brings him anguish for unction;[a]
The fire of His burning is one that is soothing,
The wound He inflicts is a wound that cures him,
The pain He sends is a physic for pain.
Thus when the Doctor Above comes to cure the disease

Of the soul, measureless scourges justly fall
On an uncoaxable slave.[b] A burning strange to him
Drives his natural heat[c] through the body and it rages

a. Cf. 1C 3 *ultio vel potius unctio* [vengeance or, more appropriately, unction].
b. Cato, *Disticha* IV 40.
c. Cf. 1C 3.

About the heart.[a] In his small veins a fluid is produced
By the burning heat of fever;[b] while an inside warmth melts
An exterior phlegm. Over sensitive nerves spreads
A freezing sensation, that bristles his head[c] and brings on a tremor.
The patient trembles whilst seething, seethes whilst trembling,
Numbed are his nerves as they bear the unusual cold.
But once the numbness ends its customary lingering stay,
The nerves settle down and the trembling also is stilled.
But the raging heat still persists; so violent in its first stages
It hastens to melt rather than consume, and in its last stages
To consume rather than melt. Thinned is the blood in that body,
Scarcely enough to hold vital energies. Francis, sore pressed
By such troubles, is losing all hope in this life, and all but all
Hope in the next. When in his struggle, the fear of both hits him,
He knows not what to do. He repents of an ugly past life
And his tears are mixed with his sighs.
Ps 38:9 He who looks on the sigh of the heart with fatherly pity,
Ps 51:19 Who rejects not the crushed heart, lifts up the sick man,
Ps 145:14 Raises the fallen and consoles him who cries.
Gone are the slave's troubles at a nod from the Lord.
There is nothing that withstands the divine will.
At once to the heart all vital energies are mustered,
On a determined day, nature with violent onslaught
Slays morbid symptoms, warms limbs with its heat,
Regulates pulse and tone to urine restores.[d]
The sick man grows enlivened and, seeing he's emerged
From a perilous crisis, he gladly praises the Doctor Above
And acclaims life's Author and Lord.
Then one day he goes out through the fields round his house;[e]

---

a. Henri reveals himself as an expert in medicine and gives detailed descriptions of diseases. It is another matter whether his descriptions are true of actual ailments, particularly those of Francis. Henri has inserted the description of fever on his own (vv. 95-109). About fevers see Aristotle, *Parva Naturalia,* I, 8ff; Hippocrates, *De morbis* I, 1, sect. 2 & 3; Galenus, *Commentum in Aphorisma Hippocrates* IV, 35ff.; especially Avicenna, *Liber Canonis* IV, 1, tract. 1-4.

b. *Chymosis* an excretion of the stomach, a juice; *kauma* is heat; *phlegma* is pituitous slime.

c. Cf. Avicenna, *Liber canonis* I. C. IV 1, tract. 2, c. 6.

d. Cf. *Ibid.*, I. C IV, II, tract. 1, c. 1-13.

e. Cf. 1C 3,

Gleaming streams and fair meadows he sees, green woods, palaces high.[a]
The philosopher in him questions why we enjoy these things,
Since the heart's true fatherland is in heaven, not in the world.
He judges it unfitting and wicked that mundane creation
Should have such a pull upon human minds.
Why are we such fools to hanker after the earthly?
If its loveliness flourishes and its pleasure gives joy,
If its good surfeits our sense and its use intoxicates,
Still, our soul is not made to be drawn by its lure.
For fair is false there, and pleasures bring pain,
And there a goodness that's bad exists, and use is no use at all.
Troubles, fears, sorrows, all have their origin there. Who without toil
Carried things earthly? Who's not afraid when he owns them? Who
Doesn't moan at their loss? None! Be he ever so sharp,
Daring or brave. None but he who's learnt to spurn the world
And fix his whole mind on things of eternity.
1C4 Whatsoever these arguments prove,
Rating low what is cheap, rating high what is best,
He cannot forget the staff of the Lord which, when he sinned Is 10:24
Knocked him down, and in pity in his illness raised him up.
He changes his ways of living and begins curbing the flesh
And sets his heart on purging the sins of the past.
Despite his new thinking, old questions come back to his mind.
His soul's simple nature is upset by various conflicts within him.
He has a kind of debate with himself: Do more things exist in the mind
Than what he perceives with his sense? There's an unequal strife
In his soul, as sense-perception from beneath assaults the peak of
His reasoning. Sense looks to what may be done, reason to what soon
May occur.[b] Sense proceeds not to the end of reality; reason decides
Things beforehand.[c] Sense holds out feasts, allurements of love,
Wealth and high honor and human approval—but cannot go on any further.

a. Cf. above, vv. 30-31.

b. Cf. Aristotle, *De sensu*, c. 1.

c. Compare this with what is written in vv. 162ff.

Reason holds out life without end, delights in that City Above,
Paradise joy, mysterious song, unspeakable light.

Between those two offers there is no proportion: people are mad
When they hesitate between the eternal and transient things,
Between heaven and earth,
between measureless joys and insignificant things![a]
Clear evidence[b] may be shown for the case of contempt of the world;
For love of it, no cogent proof is advanced without quibbling.

Francis, as yet an unwise judge, easily side-tracked,
Makes no intervention for the right in the testimony's favor,
But leans towards the unfavored party. But praise or blame
Should not fall till after the outcome
And the judge's last word reveals all that was wished for.

One moment his mind is up in the air
and again it is down on the ground;
New suggestions he proffers, but falls back on what he's used to.
No firm proposal he makes. Like a ship in a headwind
One moment it is the wind of sense,
The next the wind of reason.

He is carried in different directions;
By a northerly blowing its pleasures,
Or a southerly breeze of good fortune.
Light is the labor in sinking; but if the strong
Take a long time getting used to recovering

Strength, even they can hardly resurface:
What one is used to is hard to relinquish.[c]
Meanwhile the richest citizen in town[d]
Yokes up his wagons and pairs, piles on his wares,
And toward Apulia makes ready to travel;[e] no matter

a. Cf. Ovid, *Metamorphoses*, V, 416-17.

b. Cf. Aristotle, *Analytica Prior* II, 18; *Analytica Postereiora* I, 2.

c. Cf. Ovid, *Remedia Amoris*, 92.

d. The poet not only exaggerates here, but also just below attributes another primary purpose for the journey of this noble military man of Assisi; see 1C 4.

e. From 1C 5.

What happens he'll not return without making plenty of money.[a]
Francis on hearing of his going for the purpose of gain,
His habitual fire of cupidity fanned all the more,
Wants to join him on the journey and be his partner
In wealth. All things set up for traveling, retiring

Hour comes, and twilight leads into the night.
1C 5 One purpose persists in the pair: to go to Apulia
With the dawning of day. To bed they betake themselves,
Drowsy sleep takes over their limbs, while the eyes
Of their minds are fixed on their fortune.

As to that citizen, God only knows what befell him.
As for Francis, celestial grace carries on the merciful work
It began, healing his hardness of heart, the distress Mt 19:8
In his brain. Seeds spring up, left by that rooted-out
1C 5 Sickness, scars reappear in the wounds. But He who poured

Wine in, now applies oil.[b] So the one He tested with Lk 10:34
Violence, He might now tempt with sweetness, to move him
By coaxing when He could not by scourging, and that he who
Resisted when pressured, of his own will now might obey.
   As sleep dulls his feelings, and his unhampered

Mind examines his venture, Francis is carried out 2 Cor 12:2
Of himself. His own house he sees filled with divers
Weapons: breastplates, axes glittering for use, polished
Swords, pointed spears, jeweled helmets, shields
With golden sheen. Astonished delight is his

As in gladness he looks upon objects so many and precious.
For a wonted sight in his home
Weapons of might never were,
But articles only of apparel soft and unwarlike
That either Flanders or fair Britain delivered.[c]

---

a. There is no evidence to suggest that Henri was privy to any special information beyond the basic account of Thomas of Celano. He exaggerates much, perhaps to heighten the drama of events; but he also omits or compresses parts of Thomas of Celano's original, sometimes unaccountably.

b. The *wine* was a (harsh) disinfectant, the *oil* was a (soothing) healing agent.

c. The cloth from Flanders and Great Britain was highly prized at the time and therefore known of by the poet. The term "fair" (*flava*) refers to the British race as "fairskinned," "fair-haired" or "blond."

With a heart that is still[a] he is wondering who
The panoply's possessor may be,
When from heaven he hears a reply: "God with these arms
Shall you and your comrades array."
Up he gets with exceeding rejoicing to interpret

The glad expedition he was on. But the more keenly run
His inner reflections, the more he comes to consider
These gifts to belong, not to laurels mundane,
But rather to triumphs that are true to their name.
From now on it is for spiritual battles

He prepares himself, so he changes his plan and decides
Not to go to Apulia. Why indeed should he work to gain money,
Since gaining money is a thing to be scorned? Now
With a different mind, what he valued so much he rejects,
From what he eagerly sought he escapes, all he once loved

He abhors. "Using force on himself"—for, he recalls, 1C 5; 1C 6
Mt 11:12 The kingdom of heaven has opened to force—he resolves
Not to go. He discards the fixed ways of so many years
And as refuse regards the goods to which he was used.
An old grotto, abandoned for years (you find them in Italy),[b]

Stood a short distance away from the town.
In secret Francis used to betake himself thereto;
And once with more than usual ardor[c] and more prolonged
Lk 22:43; Lam 5:21 He makes his prayer that the Lord convert him and not let
His mind, clinging now to things above, fall back to things of earth.

His plea goes up to heaven high, is inscribed
Dt 9:10 By the finger of God's right hand, stamped with the seal of the holy
And life-giving Cross, so that he is enabled to manfully subdue
His foe, and no longer crave for transient things.

a. Ovid, *Heroides*, XXI, 201.

b. This is the poet's insertion—he saw them himself.

c. From 1C 5.

The Second Book

THIS SECOND PART GOES ON TO DEAL WITH THE FORCES
STANDING BY HIM, THE WAR HE FOUGHT, THE ENEMY HE FACED,
THE WEAPONS WITH WHICH HE SUBDUED THEM, HOW HE GAVE AWAY
HIS POSSESSIONS FOR CHRIST, AND WAS MALTREATED BY FOES UNEXPECTED.

RINSING dew the Holy Spirit moistens his faithful heart with;
Compunction, like a broom, sweeping the house makes it fit Mt 12:44; Lk 11:25
For that Guest. He can hardly believe that what was always
A robbers' den is now the Lord's House. It was He Jer 7:11; Mt 21:13

On His gracious coming, would permit nothing improper
Within his servant, but instead brightly adorn the rooms
Of the heart, transforming pig-sties into shrines.
Yet what was not removed was the scruple that the uncertain desires
Of the flesh might not return, tickling, as it were, the soul's fancy.

Lest they come back to pervert anything spiritual,
That first of virtues, Fear of the Lord, renders him strong
With her counsel, knowledgeable with her piety, wise
With understanding. Thus does the Spirit[a] equip him with seven shields.
And seven monsters stand over against him supported
by hell's fiery hordes.

From whatever bold stock came swelling Pride, ungrateful
For supernal gifts, she'll regard none as her peer.
For company she's got Pomp, Disdain, and Haughtiness,
With Arrogance, presenting the others with her acquisitions,
And Braggadocio, by defaming making her name;

Then there is Mundane Glory—her contemplation is not of heaven!
Then flowery Hypocrisy, huntress of human praise, hateful to God
And world, nibbling her fatty fare in her false fasting,[b]

a. The following verses until verse 149 are the poet's comments on morality. On the vices and their offspring, see for example Aurelius Clemens Prudentius, *Psychomachia* in PL 60, 11-90; Saint Gregory the Great, *Moralia* I, 31, c. 44-45 (PL 76, 620-22); Hugo of Saint Victor, *De fructibus carnis et spiritus*, c. 1-19 (PL 176, 997-1010).

b. The verb comes from infants' pap; cf. Plautus, *Epidicus*, V, 2, 61; Persius, *Satire*, III, 46.

Disgusting is her cunning power.
Successor to the kingdom where such excellence holds sway

Is the spirit of Envy; kindling minds with her evil fire,
Sparing no friend, sad to gladden relations, glad to sadden them.
Nor does she lack comrades: Detraction the biter, Judgment the liar,
Calumny the false, wrinkled-nose Mockery, and Malice the critic
Of valor, censuring the praiseworthy, lauding the blameworthy.

Should Envy meet with little success, Anger
Is roused, to whom control is unknown, by whom the devil
Himself scarcely is spared. Behind her banner march
Violence, Ferocity, lurking Hatred with wicked intent,
Calamity that mothers all crime and will hear no complaint,

Frenzy the fuel of anger, and Rage the fuel of frenzy;
Dare-devil also that stirs up cruel plots, arming the mind
For facing its dangers, the hand for its wars,
The tongue for insulting.
An evil is Anger all of us reproach ourselves with.

But whatever be the origins from which anger sprang,
It finally turns into the vice of Acedia,[a] that finds
Everything boring and nothing of worth ever achieves.
Acedia's comrades are these: Chatter, knowing no shame,
Dawdling Torpor and Gossip perverse, Somnolence too,

That turns day into night; Wantonness for whom waste
Of time is a laugh; Dreams foreboding the judgment to come,
Fear that pries into proofs of what happens in death,
And sorry Despair, afraid not on herself
To inflict her own gory death.

This dolorous Acedia seeks the first solaces
Of avarice, her sister, that to doleful ones deals out
Wicked allurements: she supplies to the senses what
Is lacking in reason, compensating with transient lucre
For eternal damnation; one that of heaven despairs she bids

Covet the earth, and the soul, for whom the very Creator
Himself denied, with goods created amuse itself.

a. *Accidia, acedia, accidie* an indolent indifference and depressing slothfulness especially in regard to the spiritual, was looked on in the Middle Ages as a peril peculiar to monks—see IV, 94.

And in the wake of Avarice comes this treacherous faction:
Fraud, Guile, Treason, Murders, Stratagems, Robberies,
Wicked Love-of-gain, Double-dealing,
Grasping Ambition and time-selling Usury,
And scandalous Simony that markets the heavenly.
Thus as she tries to check the depression Acedia brings,
Avarice profits by delighting the eye.
Plasters on the outside do no good if hidden forces
Are reeking havoc within! For inside you have Gluttony
Attracting the palate to her delights, she whom no amount
Of provisions can sate. Gluttony's attendants are these:
Eating-too-much, a mouth that works like a mill, grindstone teeth,
A bottomless belly that's like a sack where we throw all our rubbish.
Meals upon meals; gross face; crude belch. And when ready to burst,
The maw still hankers for more. Drunk to the loss of all reason,
Thirsting whilst drinking, drinking whilst thirsting, filling up
Cups and finishing those that are filled. Things end with
Stammering speech, reeling steps and dullness of sense,
Swollen stomach, languid heart, withered look. Then a loathing
For drinking brings the first weary sleepishness[a] into heavy limbs.
Despite all the demolishing Gluttony did, she did not get as far
As the soul's own proper recesses.
Is there no way then of comforting
The inward sorrow of the mind? To this end, up jumps her sister
Nearest in line, Lust, who tampers with the senses of humans
And gets them to sin within, not outside, their own hearts.
As soon as she's sorry, she is glowing with eager desire;
Ready to be a slave, she turns into a savage; she starts off to play
And soon turns to blows;
if she wishes to soothe someone she smears him,
To make one contented she wounds him; at first she's like Venus
But she's actually venomous. Vast is the horde that rushes past
The quarters of Lust: Pleasure, who will loathe sick souls

a. Lethargy in Greek is indolence or fatigue which induces sleep accompanied by wandering of mind and forgetfulness.

A thousand times over, and has as many ways with her to placate them.
Her sighs are interrupted by deep inflections; there is shameless talk
As well as little nods and low whispers
as of a beggar asking a favor.
A mild irritation helps to form more weighty alliances.
A different look and fresh tears get rid of aversions;
The face of simplicity, real or apparent, touches the soft heart;
Her constant airy appearance and yearning to please
Are endowments nature denied mortals to devise,
though they put their mind to it.
While anxious Love draws source and cause out of all these,
Out springs crazy anxiety, with embraces and kisses, tender allurements,
Incitements, furious furnace of fornication, Adultery, ruin
Of lawful wedlock, and Incest that loosens nature's relationships.
And what's called Abuse, more ugly than those.
As Francis conducts his plans for war,
They lead in these plagues[a] against him:
Alecto, Megaera, and Tisiphone.
But they are opposed by as many in Aglaia, Pasithea, Euphrosyne,[b]
Sisters bred from better stock, defending the side of Francis.
These join him and cause him to become humble and gentle.
From them he learns to be patient in any adversity,
To be fervent and bounteous, to be sober and modest.
Within him the Virtues gain mastery of the vices,
The Graces of the Furies; Pride yields to Humility;
Envy is wiped out by Kindliness, and Patience eliminates Anger;
Fervency kicks from her feet the contagions of Sloth, as does
Bounteousness with Avarice; Gluttony falls by Sobriety, Libido
By Purity. And the holy army of the divine sisters
Against that flaunting host fought the war to the finish.
Charity, head of the virtues, to her hero hands heaven-made weapons;
Unerring Modesty tightens the reins on the steed of his flesh,

a. Vergil calls the three terrible Furies, Alecto (Unceasing Anger), Tisiphone (Avenger of Murder), and Megaera (Jealous), who punished the doers of unavenged crimes, are called "plagues." Cf. *Aeneid* XII 845ff.

b. *Aglaia* (Splendor), *Pasithea* (Mirth), and *Euphrosyne* (Good Cheer), three Graces, were the triple incarnation of grace and beauty. The gods delighted in them and whomever they visited was happy.

Upon which two spurs, Love and Fear, their full vigor impose;
Action and Contemplation form the double greave protecting his legs;
On his breast is the cuirass of Justice; by his left flank
Hangs the "shield of Faith"; Patience makes sure his helmet[a]
Is securely strapped round his neck; and the crest of that helmet
Is Hope,[b] that shines with the brightness of a host of stars.
The first movement of battle is made with his spear; the shaft
Of that spear is right Judgment, and its point is fervent Devotion.
When at last the spear falls broken from so many throws, in the thick
Of the fight that still furiously rages, there flashes from his right
Flank the sword of the Cross for cutting to pieces those savage hordes.
Thus was he equipped; and from that time forward, nothing could he
Accomplish that did not bring him military honors,
And nothing stood in the way of his fierce valor.
  Sacred was the inspiration that endowed him with this sacred office;
So, this knight spiritual, lest perchance pride extol him for his virtues,
Or one who shared his secrets should, by exalting him, suppress
The vigor he had received, is trying, through a contradiction, to play
A double part; on his character he casts a mantle, for though he has set
His heart on being good, he fears lest that be seen.
1C 8 Lest his purposes turn his parents against him—for they were
Giving them thought—he makes ready as though he meant to do
Some lucrative deal; he gathers together some stock and sets off
For Foligno. There he sells not only the wares that he carried
But the horses and wagons as well;[c] and with effort brings
Back so much money on foot.
  And now rid of his mercantile empty cares,
On the way back he thinks of what use he will find
For this big heap of money: where is one, who is to be conformed
To the figure of Christ, to deposit this useless load?
1C 9 These worries occupy him, when lo! he comes upon the church
Of Saint Damian, in a sorry state, threatening to fall any moment.

a. These images are found in another context in 1C 11.

b. On the crest, that is, the upper part of the helmet, a tuft was affixed; as to the "shining," Cf. Hab. 3:11.

c. 1C 8 mentions one horse and no wagons; Codex V corrects Henri's error.

He approaches, he enters, a new guest into this ancient house.[a]
He falls at the feet of the priest and offers to have the chapel,
Now ruined, rebuilt. The priest suspects bluff, for he had seen him
Hard at his trading, blazing with zest to make profit; nor was it
Seemly so much acquired through hard work
      be given away on a sudden impulse.

Francis is insistent and refuses to take back his offer,
      says he will stay;
On to a window his bundle he throws, and the money
Rings as it strikes the stonework.
   So, rid of his riches, under a poor roof his dwelling he makes;
None otherwise than just to be fed there perchance,

And continue his life in those sparing confines.
   Strange rumors by now do the rounds in Assisian streets.
His true friends are sad; his false friends are smiling;
His father, too, is hearing the whispers,
And he hardly needs to be told to suppose

That the laughs of the crowd are on Francis.
   O tongues of humans![b] As you hasten to revile,
Rage it is, or malice, gives you edge!
Francis won honor and fame by his virtue,
For modesty makes bold to shoulder the "burden of honor."[c]

But you with reproach have replaced his fame,
      his virtue with vice;
Nor will you say he is mistaken; rather will you say he is mad.
Not a friend of his spares him disparagement; all declare him insane,
And opinion conjures up reasons: some think he drank of the poppy[d]
Of Lethe,[e] some that he tasted slick brain-dulling hemlock.

   Nor think they that sorcery had no act in what's happened—
So that he whom the "glory of the world" was wont to ensnare
Is now in ignominy of his own contriving. It seems to some

a. This highlights Francis's influence on renewal. The new/old antithesis occurs often in 1C, Henri's source. See also IV 175, 205.

b. Another of Henri's poetical flights begins with this verse (vv. 166-183).

c. Ovid, *Tristia*, V, IXV, 16.

d. *Lethe*, the river of the underworld, means sleep and oblivion.

e. This refers to the river of the underworld whose waters had a narcotic effect [On the narcotic effects of the poppy, cf. Vergil, *Georgies* IV, 545. See below III, 28 and XIV, 3].

He could never be preferring things vile to things precious,
What's sad to what's happy, losses to gain, unless put up to it
By infernal Furies, or else that he lacked the use of his reason.
Some also said[a] he was never cured, as he ought, from that fever,
But that a rear-chamber frenzy was begun,[b] as fluids were fetched
Up to the brain by the violent beat of his heart.
1C 10 The father, hearing his son is everywhere mocked,
In no wise checks his already burning anger
Till he asks his relations and kin to join in his rage;
His ferocious attempt to upset mild people dwelling in peace.
Nor, with fire flaring inside him, does he rage any less
Than when by Apollo's arrow Python was pierced,
Or when Pallas tore asunder
what victorious Arachne[c] had wrought.
When the son gets to know his father is coming,
He goes and hides in a hole sought out for such need.
He spent a month there without coming out, and grew used
To prayer, for which he was free, and to fasting, in which
He'd no choice. To a bad father some reverence is due;
And it's not for the child to contend with his parent;
Nor is one wise to trust a quick-tempered man.
1C 11 But when he remembers those weapons divinely bestowed,
He fears he'll have been unworthy by recoiling from
Such great endowments, and recovers his scattered incentives.
1C 4 Shame on the one who would do "mighty deeds" and had lain hid
In such a hole for so long! Divine love drives out human fears;
And with that love in his heart, out he comes to the light
And presents himself to his parents.
When relatives and kin see him in serious mood,
with downcast face,
Grim brow and flesh thin, pale looks and hair tossed, untidy clothes,
They see him so different, they're sure he's someone else

a. Indeed Henri himself is one of these.

b. The poet returns to the fevers described above, I 96ff. On the cells of the brain and heart, cf. Alfred Anglicus de Sareshel, *De motu cordis* 5, 10, a work written between 1210-17.

c. Python was a monstrous snake killed by the god Apollo. Pallas Athene destroyed a web woven by Arachne, and transformed the girl into a spider. Cf. Ovid, *Metamorphoses* I, 438ff; VI, 1, 145.

And inquire: "Who is this!" This shadow of his former self[a]
They can hardly make out. They're in a sort of pitiful amazement
At something that's worthy to relate, but harder to credit:
Francis, changed utterly, who once shone so brightly.
It is clowns and fools who now laugh at a man
Who is doing things wisely; and they call him a fool.
And bereft of all gentleness, they fling the mud off the street
In that gentlest of faces.

a. Cf. Vergil, *Aeneid* IV, 28.

The Third Book

AN EXPLANATION OF THE SHOW HE WAS FOR THE COMMON CROWD,
CHAINED, AS HE WAS, IN A PRISON LIKE A MADMAN,
HOW NO ADVICE COULD DISSUADE HIM, UNTIL DISOWNED THROUGH
HIS FATHER'S WICKED DECISION, NAKED HE ABANDONS HIS CITY.

1C 11 ESTRANGED is he in the city that once was his.
Where but late they worshiped his footmarks Is 60:14
The cobblers and the victualers now buffet his head. 2 Cor 12:7
Whom would such a wrong not annoy, with no guilt as its pretext?

Do what they would, Francis is steady and calm; no hurt,
No wrath can flex him; no suffering inflicted is as great
As the patience he has to endure it.
1C 12 His father rushes to the scene and, adding thrashing to railing,
Binds him like a thief or a maniac, locks him up at home,

And treats him harshly as an enemy. Although he has no mind
Thus to harm him, only to correct him, this is where he errs,
For blind man that he is, he guides a sighted one right
Into the ditch. Two things hurt most: an enemy's trick Mt 15:14
And a friend's error. To Francis leaving the world of the vain,

The worse block is the deception of friends, who to one
Who's been through every peril, close the way to his homeland
And the port of salvation. It was his father, more than all else,
Strove with words and with blows to call him back from his soaring
Course, from entering the starbound[a] ways of the Lord. Acts 13:10

He pledges penalties for virtue, and for wrongdoing payment.
But no talking moves Francis, no trouncing crushes him;
And his father's proposal he refutes in these words:[b]
"What do you want of me, father? You are so wrong.
Return to the vortex I once escaped from?[c] With life

a. Cf. Ovid, *Fasti* II, 496.

b. A prayer composed by the author.

c. Cf. Vergil, *Aeneid* III, 420ff.

Held out to me, shall I undergo death? Celestial freedom
I could enjoy; shall I be damned in some Lethean dungeon?[a]
Ill it becomes you begetting for hell one you begot for this life.
Too high is the cost of carnal paternity, if it generates also
The soul's corruption. We are all in an exile, you surely must know,

Heb 11:14 And from here is our journey as we seek our true homeland.
The world is our exile, our roadway is time, our fatherland heaven.
What a crime on your part to prefer exile to home and journey to goal!
Why store up treasure, you who will live but an hour? What profit
Seek you from this profusion of wealth? With old age coming on

And your life near its close, you're a fool to pile up travel supplies.
What was a help once to have, will shame you to have had;
For "having" is a boon that is brief, while "to have had'" will mean
Perennial penury. So, lest you do things and miss your salvation,
Give up these false doctrines and become a learner once more.

Flee the world and its fortunes before the day they fly away;
Gal 6:10 While there is time, remember you can't have the world
As well as God to enjoy. As you walk away from the world, trip it up,
Gn 27:36; Ps 17:13 Or it'll trip you up. A shaky believing merits no glory,
And everything's shaky in this world of ours;
so let your trust in it be nil.

Ps 11:2; 1:1; Jer 17:7 Rather, trust in the Lord, for happy is the one who trusts in him,
For he will suffer no loss and will go on living for ever.
For this, to abandon the mundane was my own wish; at least be said
By that example of mine. Should the world's glory be yours,
The whole globe on its knees before you alone, so that you could tell

Flintstones to talk and magpies be silent[b]—none of that would bring
You salvation. The day of reckoning's at hand, that will all of a sudden
Eccl 5:14 Grab and make off with all you have got. And you shall end up naked,
And your fall will be all the lower, for having flown so high.
Mt 11:30 Maybe you'd find the Lord's yoke not easy, nor his burden light—

---

a. "Celestial" and "lethean" are opposites. Cf. M. Quintilianus, *Institutio* I, 6, 36. Cf. 1C 71.

b. Pica is the Latin for a magpie. It is not clear whether the poet knew and is playing on the name of Francis's mother, sometimes given as "Pica." The reference is improbable on the grounds that the proverbial chattering of magpies is derogatory, whereas the poet consistently praises the mother and contrasts her with her husband. Cf. Ovid, *Metamorphoses* V. 294ff.; Isidore of Spain, *Etymologiae* XII, 7, 46 (PL 82, 465) who cites the phrase of martial, *Epigrams* SIV, 76: "the talkative magpie . . . "

Especially since you are so delicate? But perish the thought!
You can stop being used to mundane delights, if you accustom yourself
To the ways of Christ: 'One familiarity is forgotten by another.' "[a]
The unrestrained harshness of the stern father did not loosen its grip
But fastened all the more tightly on the one that told him these things;

Nor would he listen to any more of such holy advice. It is the worst
Of errors to try to teach a crude ignorance; wisdom will never make Wis 1:3,4
Its way into a crafty soul. Evil power overtops its own bounds;
It doesn't want what is right, but forces the one who does to be the same
As itself. But in this it sows seed in the sand; for a nature

That's kindly takes care to guard against such, lest
Coercion alter its purpose.
A shining example of this is Francis,
1C 13 against whom all things conspire:
His fellow townsmen's derision, the wrath of his father, the hardship
Of beatings, the horrors of prison, the tears of his mother.[b]

Against all these troubles one man makes a brave stand;
So many attempts to drag him back captive to earth and keep him
From soaring to celestial freedom. But the Four Virtues,
Standing squarely together, prevent all assaults being made on his soul.[c]
And all those adversities affect him no more

Than can ants set about moving a mountain as great.
Beyond his powers no one is allowed to be tempted; 1 Cor 13
So, at God's bidding, his mother with pity for her son
Sets him free from his bonds while her husband is absent.
He comes forth, but no longer a fugitive; not far away does he go,

But feeling secure, he returns in joy to the room close by
From which an angry father had thrust him in shame.
The father returning learns that his wife had loosened his bonds.
Hers was an open act of pity, but he condemns it as an occult crime.
The air is filled with his noisy shouting, as he loads filthy curses

On his good wife. Suddenly rushing inside the sacred precincts,
The chains he fastens on Francis
and threatens him with dire punishment.

---

a. Cf. Ovid, *Remedia Amoris, 503.*

b. Here the poet exaggerates what is written in 1C 13.

c. These are the so-called four cardinal virtues: prudence, justice, temperance, fortitude.

He, devoid of fear, speaks up:[a] "Father—or rather, stepfather—
Why fix me in chains, and why do you threaten me with torture?
Your shackles or your torture instruments I shall not smash;

They are hammers that strike in vain upon ice-cold iron!
O what foolishness in a savage father! Are you trying to fool me,
Hoping to seduce me with dire threats? I cannot be fooled,[b]
Jn 14:6 Or lured, or yield to your threats. Christ the way, truth, and life
Ps 16:8 Stands on my right, so that I shall not be moved. Nor will I beg you

To spare me. So fight like a man, so I can fight you fairly.
I owe more to God than to you; shall I neglect God's commands
For you? You have given me human birth; but God did more
Ps 100:3 In endowing me with life: He made us, we belong to Him.
Hanging on the cross it was God who redeemed us; and He who reigns

In the heavens will save, not all, but only those that prove
Themselves faithful. Human faith is something owing to God,
And we are of His fashioning. Everyone who believes in him
Rom 9:33; 10:11 Will be saved from shame—though it depends on how he believes.
A man could have faith on his lips but not in his soul; or

The other way round; but he should have both. He may not conclude
He has faith that is real, till he makes it complete in the two.
If you want to be faithful fully, you must hold your soul
In your hands and prove your faith by your works. What do you advise
Me to do? Through what works can I show I am a believer?

Shall I carry on outside and cheat all the faithful in my usual way,
Now as buyer, now as seller? As buyer, running down goods;
As seller, exalting their merits. The art of a merchant is all
Cheating and fraud; he makes his money as others lose out.
Even a friend is not spared, no, nor a kinsman. Him whom

Our neighbor, then, knows is a fraud, shall we regard as faithful
Eph 2:8 To God? Since no one is saved without faith, let me then have faith
Jas 2:2 That is perfect, that perfects my salvation. But keep far from me
Things acquired through deceit! When the talent of perfect faith
Ps 119:127; 23:1 Comes my way, no topaz, no gold, no silver will hold any delights

a. This reproach (vv. 87-126) is totally the creation of Henri.

b. Cf. Ovid, *Metamorphoses* I, 376.

For me; since more than gem or gold and more than silver I desire
That talent. As for you, if you've the will for it, believe!
Or stay, if you wish, incredulous still! As for me, who have tasted
The honey of divine goodness, from the love of God, whose true
Perfection is in Christ Jesus, neither human nor angel will snatch me;

Neither prince nor power, neither hope nor fear, neither height
Nor depth, neither death nor life, neither present nor future!" Rom 8:38-39
1C 14 It was a stiff-lipped Francis that delivered this speech.
The father, seeing his firm and final resolve, switches to other matters.
He cannot win the man; instead he will extort his money.

The cash, which he values less than dirt[a] and which he'd thrown
On the window, Francis takes and returns to his greedy father.
But the father in his violence has not finished yet.
Forgetting a father's love, to his son he denies the basest
Because he begs for the greatest things of all; since he longs to have

God as father, he refuses any longer to be called his father;
And since his heart is set on Christ and on being his co-heir, Rom 8:17
He cannot have him succeed him as heir. He then compels him
To go to the bishop's house, with all the townspeople there,
That in their presence he shall all rights renounce

To property, grounds and paternal home.
1C 15 The virtuous Francis, aggrieved by his father's fury,[b]
Goes even further with his thorough renouncing:
Lest he appear to keep anything he gave him as gift,
He feels for his belt and unties it,[c] and stripped of all

His clothes, he lays them down, including his trousers.
Without a stitch, stark naked he stands, for all the world like Adam.[d]
But he differs from Adam in this: he suffers freely what Adam
Was forced to endure; he suffers by merit what Adam endured for sin;
And yet he is penalized as Adam was—though in a different way:

Exposed was the shamefulness of Adam, while no shame
Is discovered in him. Where is the shame in a naked body
When the vesture of its soul is honor? Wherein did this

---

a. Cf. 1C 14.

b. The words "father" and "fury" are found in 1C 14.

c. Thomas of Celano does not expressly recount this.

d. Cf. Gn. 3:7ff. The poet's comparison continues to v. 157.

Manliness lie? In scorning the world, in making himself disdained
By the world; in caring not a whit for his property or person,
In putting up with derisive taunts, in leaving an earthly father
Mt 19:29 For his Father in heaven. Is there one word to describe the virtue
In the man who accomplished so many arduous tasks?
The bishop rises in admiration of such daring courage
And, clasping those fine shoulders, takes off his mantle
And puts it round them.
Moreover he pledges support for his intentions
And follows up promises with help. Thus Francis, in giving up resources
And garments, will keep nothing
by which his opponent might hold him.
Besides heaven, in the world he seeks nothing
And, though still on earth, he belongs not here, but to a city
Beyond this earth; of the upper world, he yet languishes here;
Of the earthly world, his real life is beyond; and his soul dwells
More truly in heaven than his body does on earth. Now he sees God
1 Cor 13:12 In a mirror, and should see him face to face, if the hull of flesh
Intervening would but allow clear vision to the soul inside.
Naked he takes his departure under the eyes of father, prelate,
And all his fellow citizens of Assisi.[a] But by reason of the fact
That the air on a height,
being moist and having no force to withstand,
Is moved away by all things opposing it, there is no doubt
But that it transforms bodies that are naked, in accordance
With the patterns by which it is itself transformed; nor does
Our constitution suffer its continuous motions.[b] Hence, albeit
He was fervent, he gives some thought to this theory,
And knowing he could not go on long thus exposed,
He accepts some old clothes offered him by a pauper.
He goes on his way with nothing but himself; and just as an exile
Would return to his country, he lives in exile in his own,
Nobody forcing him and of his own will. He has come

a. From here to the end of Book III (including v. 178) Henri adds material from his own store, freely expanding on a few words from 1C 15, 16: *cum semicinctiis involutus pergeret* [dressed in half-girdles he went].

b. Namely, of the air. Cf. XI 15-22.

From fortune to misery, from riches to poverty;
Or is it from misery to fortune and from poverty to riches?

The coverings of sackcloth[a] he wears are full of holes,
He who used to wear ornamented new clothes of soft wool
And change with the seasons his plumed ones for silken
And the silken for plumed.

a. Sackcloth was low class cloth made from coarser wool, which Francis wore in tatters.

The Fourth Book

AN EXAMINATION OF HIS CRUEL TREATMENT AT THE HANDS, NOW OF THIEVES AND AGAIN OF MONKS, OF THE GREAT ZEAL WITH WHICH HE TOOK CHARGE OF LEPERS, OF HIS CARE IN REPAIRING FOR CHRIST OLD CHAPELS AROUND ASSISI.

GRACE from on high accompanies the wretch[a] on his way. 1C 16
Infinite his woes, such as would weigh, O Job,
On your patience, if not break it!
He has become like a "wandering jester"[b] with no fixed abode,

Poor, needy, neglected and freezing, fatigued and famished.
He is to others a burden and despised by himself,[c] a wanderer
And exile on his own native soil. In that better country he'd belong
To a household and be a free man and would know a house
Where he could lay down his head. For so many misfortunes

There must be some recompense.
The winter season now, as a slanting sun lengthens the nights
And shortens the days; when the earth, once dotted with a thousand
Hues, gleams with only one color, as her bareness is swathed
Ps 148:16,17 In the snow's woolen robe and adorned with crystals of ice;

When travelers are happy at the shimmering roads,
and all pathways
Are white, and no foot is moistened; the north wind congeals all
Waters; warmth from walking tempers the winter's cold, and the cold
Mt 5:12; Lk 6:23 Tempers the warmth. Francis, traversing the woods, rejoices
And exults with all his heart, and his gladness makes him sing.

He delights at the thought that he is free of his wicked
Father's control, with his fraudulent gains; that he walks now
1 Cor 7:2 As Christ's slave and a free man himself; that being naked

---

a. The word *verna* means servant or wretch; Cf. Horatius, *Epodes* II, 65.

b. Horatius, *Epodes* I, XV, 28.

c. Cf. 1C 4: *vilescere sibi.*

Makes the fierce cold almost soothing. For who is so rigid
He would not rejoice at the change from a worse to a better condition?

So many reasons for rejoicing transacting within his breast,
Francis opens up in song in the language of the French.
It resounds through the woods and reaches the ears of some robbers.
They leap forth and see a fellow with nothing. Their hopes disappointed,
They think they've been fooled, and they throw out their query:

"Who are you?" And he replies: "The herald of Christ, why ask?"
Fanned by no stronger a breeze their anger flares up
And they lay hands on one who's in no wise afraid of them.
Alas! Before the ferocity of thieves no traveler may sing,[a]
Though harmless and purseless he be. Indeed he pays dearly,

Our moneyless songster, thrown into a trench full of snow.
What if his pockets were full and he'd sung!
Francis lies in the snow and the robbers deride him:
"There's your bed, lie in it, silly herald
Of Christ. For your song, these are the bed-clothes

You're getting." But he answer makes none.
As they go off, out he comes from his snowy cave,
The tomb he lay in almost buried up to the hair
Of his head. But no hostile force gets the better Ps 89:23
Of him whom divine pity keeps safe in its keeping.

Shaking off the snow, stuck in lumps in all parts of him,
All stiffened his clothes, his beard and his hair,
He feels glad to have escaped the rage of the robbers.
Then finding the lost route, taking up his unfinished song,
With praise of the Creator he pierces meandering hollows

And trains the woods to re-echo the mysteries of Christ.[b]
Singing away, he arrives at the edge of the forest
And goes to a monastery a short distance away,
Where for some peaceful lodging he asks and obtains.
And[c] as the night's rest is soothing the day's turmoil,

a. Henri plays on the line from Juvenal, *Satire* X, 22: *Cantabit vacuus coram latrone viator* [It's the empty-headed traveler who sings before the thief]. There is a further allusion in v. 36.

b. See to Vergil, *Eclogues* 1, 5: *Formosam resonare doces Amaryllida silvas* [. . . teach the forest to resound the beautiful Amaryllis].

c. The poet himself here digresses on snowy regions already affected by spring and the south wind (See v. 56).

A humid and pore-opening wind exposes the ground's surface,
And a south wind melts the snow and the ice
The north wind piled up all around.
Torrents are everywhere,[a] and water from the mass
Of snow and ice spreads over all the fields; crashing

Stones are dragged along, and logs and uprooted oaks
From the woods are afloat.[b] There is no walking on ground
Soggy to the core; all pathways are foul,[c] all roads
Obscure; bridges are covered by floods or carried away
By the currents. Rushing rivers show no signs of subsiding

Soon: their constant motion melts objects compressed,
And water gushes from these as they melt. No rapid recession
Is there; rather does the flooding for long fill the land.
What is Francis to do as he lacks food and clothes, and
Neither monks let him stay nor weather move on? He is

In dire straits from the two in his moment of need: he has
Against him an inflexible host and furious weather. Hard
Enough is the host, but harsher still is the bout of the weather.
For the prior of the cloister as though forced
To conceal it, puts up with the annoyance, but permits

The wretched guest, caught in the rain with no place to go,
There to shelter till the storm should pass.
While Francis stays on, the south wind still blowing hard,
His poor time-worn hair coat falls to pieces, not a thread
Holding another together. Content with a shroud[d]

For a shirt he sits like a clown at the fire:
If he warms his front his back is like ice, and the same
When the other way round. Distressed more by hunger
Than cold, of the bread that he gets he'd eat ten times
As much. Nor[e] has he hope of some broth with which

---

a. Cf. Ovid, *Metamorphoses* I, 285.

b. *Ibid.*, I, 304.

c. See above, vv. 15-16.

d. The original is for *vili camisia* Cf. 1C 16.

e. What follows in vv. 84-102 is Henri's denunciation, contrary to the mind of Thomas of Celano and more so of Francis.

To season his morsels; for the devout brethren
Would rather fatten their sows with it. So how could he hope
They would give him something a human being might wear,
When the supper they gave to a pig they denied him?
Every kind of sin a greedy monk commits:

For when one that strictly professes religion
Inclines to acedia, there is nothing he will shrink from.
He will go on to all manner of crime,
After but one offence. Perfection is safe in the hands
Of no creature; but more horrific is the fall

Of one that is nobler and higher. Lucifer once
Was the glory of angels; now he is the one at whom shudder
The demons. And Adam the first of all mortals, when death
Was his earning none could be uglier, as human death
And its dread still testify. The same for the monk,

Whom holy profession puts above other Church members,
When he stoops to the lowest he is more crooked
Than others who believed him more upright than they!
The snow, melted by sun and wind, flows off into rivers
And the ice begins to crack up.

And Francis, seeing the swollen rivers subside,
Resumes his journey, which is more like his flight,
For he flees like a wounded deer, not caring which way
He goes so long as he moves. No more gladly did Paul
Flee from Hebrew synagogue, or Peter from Herod's prison.[a]

He wasn't as happy even in his recent release from his
Father's mastery or the hands of the robbers. Nor did he
Strive less from these false brethren to flee, than if they
Were the Lotus-eaters or the inhospitable Cyclopean monsters
Or the songs of the Sirens from which long ago Ulysses fled.[b]

---

a. Acts 13:51; 14; 12:9. The wandering poet himself, a secular priest, availed of the hospitality of many an abbey, for which he wrote poems; though if denied a welcome, he could use his pen in resentment.

b. The *Lotophagi* or Lotus-eaters, the Cyclopean giant, and the Sirens (half-bird, half-woman) were among the hazards encountered by Ulysses (Odysseus) on his wanderings. By eating the lotus plant, his mariners lost all desire to return home; the Cyclopes held them captive; the song of the Sirens lured them to destruction. Cf. Vergil, *Aeneid* III, 614ff; V, 863ff; Homer, *Odyssey* 12, 39ff.

By the time he hoped he was a fair distance from the monastery,
He found himself coming to Gubbio without a stitch on;
There an old friend has a new garment to put on him, so he can
Go about more decently and take more easily whatever
The weather might bring.

Acts 5:41 Through suffering so much destitution for Christ's name
He always and constantly kept the same steadfast countenance;
The poorer outwardly, the more stalwart was he within.
What spread his good name in the first place was his patience,
In virtue of which he is given care of the lepers; no one 1C 17

Was more zealous than he in looking after them, even if
At one time he could not bear to watch their houses even
At a distance. Now he makes beds, wipes away venom, soothes ulcers,
Touches mouths, washes feet, strokes corroding rotten limbs,
And forces to the task his fugitive feelings.

Nor should we omit the fire of blessed love that flared in him
When by chance he meets a leper on the road; and seeing he was
A leper goes to him and, "made stronger than himself,"
He presses kisses to those canker-eaten lips.
Nor were lepers his sole concern, for indeed he was full of pity

For all beggars, so that he saw no one go in want while he had
Plenty. Something of what he had, even little, the hungry, thirsty
And the naked got; there was something good for the lonely,
The needy and the wanderer; the orphan and the widow
And the drifter felt his help. He was like a waiter to the hungry,

Mt 25:25-44 Like a wine-steward to the thirsty,[a] like a garment to the naked,
Like solace to the lonely, like riches to the needy, like asylum
Ex 22:22 To the exile, like a father to the orphan, like a spouse
To the widow, and like good fortune to the drifter. He was making
Himself one for all, spreading the means he had beyond all limits.

But contrary to his custom it happened that once, by a *felix culpa,*[b]
He upbraided a certain poor man; then he was sorry not to have

a. These were the officials of the courts of nobles of that time. The waiter (*dapifer*) was in charge of storing, preparing, and serving food; the wine steward (*pincerna*) was the purveyor of wine.

b. A reference to the Exultet, the Paschal Enconium sung on Holy Saturday.

Granted his request, recalling that the beggar had asked him
For so little in the name of so great a King. And that such a sin
Might not become habitual, he resolved in his heart and vowed
That henceforth should he have anything, he would rebuff no one
Who begged in the name of Christ. Never would he let that promise
Slip from his heart, nor should hand resist the dictate of heart,
For the desires now inscribed in his mind he would seal with his acts.
Thus[a] does a divine call lead forward a just man capable of learning
From misfortunes; for the just one profits from his mistakes.
Daring to fall, contemptuously going to excess, he becomes a criminal:
As soon as he is contrite, his rash daring becomes application,
His lapse becomes rising, his contempt admission, his excess merit,
His crime goodness. Thus did obstacles work in Francis, whose
Double strength derived from falling—like that of Antaeus—[b]
Fought the better when it seemed it was already defeated.
And by his own example
Francis taught those whomsoever one mishap
Confuted that they should throw every fault to the ground.
1C 18 Meanwhile that chapel that offered Francis shelter when he first
Set about leaving the world, was not destined to last long,
Due to the extreme poverty of its incumbent, the crumbling old age
Of the fabric, and the inaction of its first builder. The
Foundations subside, dampened by constant flowing of rain off the roof;
The walls, their joining loosened, fall apart; part of the roof
Hangs aloft, another part lies on the ground. As it threatens
To suddenly collapse, the priest is minded to abandon it completely.
So as not to have been his useless lodger once, and have made void
His own words in not keeping his promise,
remembering the money he'd
Given[c]—the first thing he does is to carry out his first intention
And renovate that aged chapel, lying ruinous, poor and pitiful.
Francis comes to prop up the ruinous, enrich what is poor, renew
The time-worn, raise what is fallen low.

a. However upright, this editorial comment is the poet's.

b. Hercules, wrestling with the giant Antaeus, found that when the giant was thrown to Earth (his mother) he redoubled his strength.

c. Cf. above II, 150ff.

This is the place that honorable Ladies make radiant;
Where widows in the company of virgins rejoice in offering
Jn 16:12 Fitting worship to God. This, the woman named Clare—
Clearer in likeness, clearest in life—precedes in praise,
Excels in merit, surpasses in mode of life, as a torch
Outshines its sparks, and as Cynthia the stars.[a]
It is with another light the credit of the others shines:
If such as their frail sex, slow perception, dignity of nature
And beauty of form have placed them in the world's first rank,
Yet frailty rules not out their being strong, nor slowness
Their being well-informed, nor dignity their humility, nor beauty
Their chastity. Through Francis's mediation these the Lord called
Jn 17:15 Out of the world: a frail sex but valiant in heart, serpents 1C 19
Mt 10:16 In shrewdness but doves in simplicity, who deem themselves reeds
3 Kgs 4:33 Though their origin matches the cedars; a particular beauty
Is theirs, but they are modest in every respect.
When Francis had brought his plan to a happy end and seen flourish 1C 21
Inside, a temple of the Spirit, and outside, the work of his hands,
He turns to a chapel near Assisi, that lay well-nigh destroyed,
And not wishing to leave unfinished what he had started on
He restores the sundered building.
Near unto those churches is a chapel called Portiuncula
Under the title of Saint Mary. Now in a state of great decay,
It was all fissures, and was a stable for oxen, a sty for pigs.
It was a hostess to rain, a passage for hail showers, and a home
To all winds.[b] But Francis in his total and loving esteem
For the Mother of the Lord, makes his visit to her chapel
To raise it as new out of its time-worn state. And so
To the faulty and aged the prime of youth returns; beauty
Springs forth from the ugly, and profit is made from loss.

---

a. Cynthia was another name for Diana, the moon goddess. Cf. Cicero, *De Natura Deorum* II, 68ff; Horatius, *Carmen Saeculare* III, 22, 4; 28, 12.

b. This description by Henri uses hyperbole. See above, vv. 170ff.

The Fifth Book

On his fulfilling Christ's injunction, content with a tunic;
girded with tri-knotted rope, his appearing
an unexpected master, with no instructor,
and his instilling gladsome newness in his followers.

Of all places this was his favorite; nor are they frequent
His departures from it. He lingers on, settling there quietly,
Repairing the building, planting the gardens, sustaining life
On meagre fare, not clothed in his usual garb,

But in such as hermits wear.
1C 22 During his sojourn there, longing to set his mind upon the Gospel
That was read one day: Jesus sent out his disciples—after Mt 10:5
The service was duly celebrated, in humble supplication he asked
The priest to deign to clarify the Redeemer's words and the Gospel

Of the day. Expounding the Gospel, the priest goes through all
The injunctions one by one: how, sending out the disciples
The Lord bade them be content with one tunic, and to walk unshod,
Nor to carry gold or silver, neither purse nor money, neither wallet Mt 10:9-10
Nor staff. As Francis is lending him an attentive ear, the Spirit

Of the Lord comes down on him and fills his breast full with the gift Mk 6:8-9; Acts 2:4
Of grace, and shows him the secret pathway to heaven. No one till now
Had sought heaven by that path[a]
which Francis in his new fervor discovers,
Intending, as he does, with heartfelt desire to fulfill all righteousness. Mt 3:15
Nor will he gloss over anything, but follow the text and faithfully cling

To every word. Allegory may in much prevail; but the literal sense
Surpasses it, when no metaphor cloaks the author's mind
And his words mean what they say.[b]

a. See the similar expression in 1C 36. These are omitted by Henri below, VI, 148-60.

b. Cf. Gregory the Great, *Homiliae in Evangelia* II, 40 (PL 76, 1302); Isidore of Spain, *De fide Catholica* II, 20 (PL 83, 528-9).

Jas 1:23 Having listened therefore to everything demanded of him,
As his own interpreter he knows better than to be of the word
A hearer only and not a doer.[a] He says: "What Christ commands
I must now do. This is my wish, my vow, what my whole soul desires."
What garments he wore he takes off, save the tunic; he will have
No staff in hand, no shoe will grace his feet, no girdle round
His middle. He makes for himself a cross-shaped tunic, for in
That sign he will crush his defeated foes. He will do with a halter
Jdt 7:17 To wear as a belt; for he'll not make bold to leave his sins to
The vengeance of God. He himself is his own prosecution and defense!
As witness and as plaintiff and as judge—no legal statute barring this[b]—
After he's gone through the case and weighed it he convicts himself!
And his loins that have exposed themselves to seduction's fires
Like robbers he dispatches them
by hanging with his triple-knotted rope![c]
Reverently fulfilling Jesus' injunctions to his disciples, 1C 23
Jn 9:27 Jesus' disciple in his turn he will be, willing to be master
For the people and take up the contest against the Furies.
This will be a new campaign, and its pay will go to Christ,
Where ruthless dedication strips the flesh, and wondrous wisdom
Invests the mind afresh. Lest Jesus' bidding he should do in vain
He wants to use the mind in making good the lost condition
That his body lacked. So, though he not know the Pegasean spring[d]
Or ever see Parnassus's twin-peaked heights,[e] he is not slow
Ps 94:12 To master sacred truth. The Holy Spirit's stronger flame ignites him,
Whence the knowledge of all words proceeds. He who had no doctor
Teach him, teaches now a multitude. Those who know him stand
Astonished as he speaks on things transcending human ken;
A pupil they had never seen him, now they listen to a teacher.

a. Cf. Juvenal *Satire* 1, 1: *Semper ego auditor tantum* [I'm always just a listener].

b. *Decret*. um II, causa II, qu. 2, c. 18 and *ibid*, causa IV, qu. 4, c. 1.

c. Henri is witness that at least in the early 1230's the cord with three knots was worn by the Friars Minor. In the preceding lines, with imagery a little too *recherché*, he employs terms of criminal court procedure, the cord being the hangman's noose!

d. The winged horse Pegasus caused the Font of the Muses to flow by unearthing it with its hoof. Cf. Ovid, *Fasti* III, 449ff; *Metamorphoses* IV, 783-4; V, 256ff.

e. Twin-peaked Mount Parnassus was sacred to Apollo and the Muses. Ovid, *Metamorphoses* II, 221.

1C 25 "Nothing has he ever learnt,[a] nothing will he ever teach":
So supposes the common saying,[b]
and it holds in the natural run of things;
But let the common rule be broken, as when miracles occur,
that saying
Is no longer true. Presumptious human often cloak the true meaning
Of things.[c] Needs he a teacher from outside whom within the Spirit
Instructs? By his courtesy Francis receives the doctrines he imparts
With skill. The more graciously God instructs the heart, the more
Clear the message of the tongue. O secrets of God, hidden from all
Mortal beings! Here is one who earthly interests left for his sake,
And now the obdurate converts, when from being obdurate turned
But a while away himself. Behold a distinguished master now,
While townsfolk and companions gaze,
and wonder how their simple[d] friend,
Whom they had thought quite out of mind, true wisdom
meanwhile Has acquired!
On entry to any house, his first greeting is:[e]
"Peace to this house." Lk 10:5
His peace goes out to all. It becomes his mode of greeting, to
Good and bad alike, to citizen and pilgrim he announces it,
And for the faithful, both men and women, it is his prayer.
A man of discretion in Assisi sees the great man's
Footmarks worth imitating, and begins to shoulder
Poverty's ignoble burden.[f] He spurns the world with its
Fleeting opulence, subjugating himself lest he fall prey
To the enemy, and now a pauper, joins the man of poverty.
One that was host to Francis did the same, Bernard,

---

a. Cf. below, v. 117.

b. That is, a *locus communis* of rhetoricians: cf. Cicero, *Topica* 2ff; *De Oratore* 27, 35.

c. Cf. Vergil, *Georgies* II, 490.

d. Henri exaggerates a bit; see also his "out of his mind" in the next verse. No one should conjecture that the poet has taken the rhetorically opposite word "idiot" from Test. The word "idiot" occurs also in 1C 25.

e. Henri substitutes his own version for the greeting found in 1C 23: "The Lord give you peace (which is certainly genuine because it is recorded in Test, fits his poetic hexameter, and certainly not because it would sound authentic and evangelical (cf. ER XVI and LR II 3). Note that this new greeting sounds out of context, and the other ("The Lord give you peace") fits the following verses. Regarding the form of greeting, cf. Rom 5:1: "peace . . . to God."

f. The poet follows Thomas of Celano (1C 24) in mentioning this anonymous disciple as the first to follow Francis.

A man of importance in the city of Assisi, rich in 1C 24
Provision and lands. Watching the holy doings of Francis
And his peerless life, he ponders the peril to salvation
His own pursuit of the earthly brought. Him he hears, not
Merely now and again but often and, you might say,

All the time, attentively saying psalms and wrapped up in
His works of devotion. Meal-times, and the very night that
Ought to be given to sleep, keep him not from the praise
Of God and the Blessed Mary. Full of God's power by which
Mt 10:16 Demons are routed, shrewd as serpent, alert as dragon,[a]

Francis the prudent fights the serpent, Francis the watchful
Assaults the dragon. His host is in awe to see him unrelenting
And in bed never yield to slumber. The common bedroom
Wards off fumes and rising vapors,[b] and a small room allows
No sleep-producing agent to fill it.[c] And when at last his eyes

Are from long exertion forced to yield, his drowsy tongue
Goes on to mutter prayers and is scarcely still when overcome
By sleep. Captivated by this picture of good example,
Eph 6:14-16 Bernard makes his soul secure with the breastplate
Of faith and the weapons of justice, and as a fresh

Soldier in the camp of Francis,[d] militates with fervor
Against the ancient foe. No wonder, then, that great
Mt 19:21 Captain's rival he becomes in selling all and giving
To the poor. And wearing the clothing revealed by the Gospel,[e]
He cleaves to him like a loyal comrade. Victory over

The world[f] thus wrought is an example spurring many
To have a love for this spiritual war, and such virtue
Attracts others as followers of what was done in their sight.
Another from the city is converted by his zeal, 1C 25
Jb 1:1 A simple[g] and God-fearing man, who fought bravely

a. Cf. the "watchful dragon" in Ovid, *Heroides* XII, 101; VI, 13 and *Metamorphoses* VII, 149.

b. On the workings of the brain and sleep-inducing substances, cf. Aristotle, *De somno* 4-5; *De partis animae* II, 7; *De historia animalium* I, 16; Avicenna, *Liber canonis* I, I, 3, c. 1.

c. The words "allows . . . sleep" are found in Ovid, *Metamorphoses* XV, 321.

d. Cf. Ovid, *Metamorphoses* V. 128.

e. See above, vv. 10-12.

f. Cf. Ovid, *Metamorphoses* III, 348.

g. Henri here originates an unfortunate confusion because this word and others in vv. 103-6 are applied to Br. Giles in 1C 25, and not to this third disciple who is likewise unnamed by Thomas of Celano.

For long until victory was sure, and then to others
Left an object lesson on how to abandon the worthless.
The fifth[a] to grasp the banner in the fight
Against the Furies is Aegidius[b] with a variegated aegis[c]
Shielding his breast, for the day of the light of the new sun Is 9:2
Rising, whereon will shine forth the dazzling gold of the cross
And of faith, his linen-white[d] purity, and the hyacinth-red[e]
Of his tribulations.
One other still having joined the group,
The seventh to take up arms is Friar Philip, transformed utterly
Within from his very arrival;[f] he speaks secret words and teaches 2 Cor 12:4
Things he has never studied. All whose hearts he warms, whose ears
Intoxicates, stand awed: for he learnt none of this
And but lately lacked it all.
1C 26 Francis, protosoldier and commander, orders to battle
His recruits, and shows them the course by actions
And the strategy by words. But by neither word nor act
Will he let valor be proven, till the soul so check old passions[g]
—Which the supreme Judge must scrutinize—that it not produce
New ones from the old. To his men on fire with love for
The heavenly wreath he teaches all the types of war they'll need
To triumph over monsters of the spirit world. Supported
By the saints of old and by his model virtue, the troop of brothers
Advances under their great leader, and little do they reck
Their efforts in relation to the joys to come. Sir 35:21
Yet few are the men he can draw into the lists
Against such hordes of Furies and of devils.
The holy captain asks of heaven to be shown if many are to join

a. The fifth, includes Francis; otherwise Giles is the fourth companion.

b. The Latin name for Giles is retained to preserve the play on "aegis."

c. Cf. Ovid, *Metamorphoses* VI, 79; IV, 798 and Vergil, *Aeneid* X, 181.

d. Cotton or linen is white. The word *munditiae* [cleanliness] occurs in another context in 1C 25.

e. The color red was as the hyacinth to the ancients (Cf. Vergil, *Eclogues* III, 63). The story goes that Hyacinth, a youth beloved of Apollo, was changed into the flower by the god when the youth was accidentally struck by the discus thrown by the god. Cf. Ovid, *Metamorphoses* X, 162-219, especially vv. 211-2: "a flower is born brighter than purple . . ."

f. For the phrase "transformed in his breast," see Ovid, *Fasti* II, 798; VI, 538. For his "teaching," see 1C 26.

g. These things occur in another context in 1C 31. Cf. Peter Lombard, *Collectanea in epistolas Pauli* on Rom 7:15, 20, 23 (PL 191, 1423, 28, 20).

His ranks. In all-out pleading,[a] the prayer he makes pierces
The heavens, and his simple soul gazes on God present to him.

As his keen-edged soul remains thus fixed, the Holy Spirit pours
Light in him, and he sees and hears, as though beside him,
The unnumbered brothers that are to come from every race.[b]
Bearing the arms of Francis, they all call him master and guide,
And confess him as their liege lord and their father.

In the gladness of the vision of so huge a cohort, he comes back 1C 27
Acts 10:10 From the trance, and to the brothers of here and now gives careful
Account of how he saw brothers of prefigurement
behind his standard
And, others yet that were to follow. So many will make
Profession in his holy Order, that no part of the world

Will be without them.
Glad[c] are the lips of the gentle[d] father as he tells these things.
A certain close connection of soul in him still clings
To the images of the vision, and he senses the various shapes
1 Kgs 3:11 Returning, and his ears ring to the loud sound of their marching.

As against thinking this was all a dream, he forgets not ideas
Impressed upon two of his senses; rather is allowance still made
Concerning the sense called common.[e]
Greater joy[f] than they usually have fills the hearts of the Minors: 1C 28
They rejoice in their present father, rejoice in their future brothers.

Gn 41:11 But lest they'd think forecasting the future means it's arrived,
Many predictions of future events does he lay out before them,
And these deep thoughts on their destiny does he announce to them:
"At first, my little sons, fruit that is very sweet is put before us,
Then a kind that is less sweet, and last of all the sour.

a. Cf. Ovid, *Metamorphoses* VII, 590; IX, 159.

b. A fuller account is found in 1C 27. Even vv. 148-9 recount the matter too narrowly.

c. This whole section (vv. 146-52) is the poet's creation.

d. Ovid, *Metamorphoses* XIII, 555.

e. This refers to the "common sense" of the philosophers; cf. Aristotle, *De anima*, II, 6, text 136-40; 147-9. Wherefore, *mutatio* [allowance] means *passio* [passion]: Francis continues the revelation made to him in vv. 158-64.

f. Cf. 1C 27.

The sweet fruit is the praise we get when the Order is young;
The less sweet is when we suffer the scandals of false brothers;
Finally, the sour fruit, even that which smells good, is when
Friars, scattered throughout the world,[a] make themselves loathsome
To people."

1C 29 Meanwhile another good man of acceptable life, so that he'd be
A better Christian and his life be still more acceptable,
Comes to take up arms and engage in brave battles under Francis,
That "wager of brave wars,"[b] and consecrate himself a soldier
Under a holy commander.

Their number reached eight, Francis calls them together
And sends them in twos throughout the world, to pass on Lk 10:1
What they learned of the art of combat. He commands them to show
Courage in battle, be patient in affliction, whatever might happen, Heb 11:12
And be constant in purpose, not to seek easy ways nor fear opposition,

To cast a wary eye on successes, and all the more readily accept
Adversities. Without opposition no one is toughened; no one fights
A war without being tough; but there is no triumph if there's no war,
And the kingdom of heaven comes not, unless it is won. Mt 11:12
And, directing his words towards them, he said:[c]

"Note well the situation you are in, and know that life here
Is but a military campaign, and sides now eager for battle Jb 7:1
Have declared an unending war, each against the other.
Souls belong to the side of heaven,[d] bodies to the side of earth.[e]
Now composed of these natures are humans; and the soul levitates

To the sphere of heaven, while the body gravitates down
To the middle of the earth. But any move forward awaits
The composite's decision as to which must be the progression
That will bring it to either region; whichever is favored
Is stronger, and will draw the other one with it.

As either component stands within the composite, so shall it be
Outside it. If the soul's progression is decided for, both take

---

a. Cf. 1C 27.

b. Ovid, *Consolatio ad Livians* 368.

c. From here to the end of this Book is Henri's expansion.

d. Cf. Isidore, *Etymologiae*. m III, 32-5 (PL 82, 171).

e. Aristotle, *Problema* I, 18; XIV, 6.

Their place above; if the body's, both go downward. The two are yet
One human being; so, it might be hoped they would agree on certain
2 Cor 6:15 Things. But, what accord has Christ with Belial? Each side here
Has its own special thrust; neither can be drawn unless overcome.
Strive we must therefore to give the mastery to our better self
And bring our worse self to heel, and compel, not the spirit
Rom 7:6; 8:6-7 To serve the flesh, but the flesh to render service to the spirit.
The body has five attendants,[a] and in their desires, reason,
Most loyal partner of the soul, hardly shows interest. It is hers
To raise our downcast consciousness, not to pamper
the taste of the senses.[b]
Jb 36:8 But drawn along is the body by the rope of poverty,[c]
Once it loses its turgid fleshiness and adopts the soul's vigorous gait;
Once it sets its course on interests celestial and is not bound
For the things of earth. For there is a freedom in poverty
That makes her the seat of frugality; she is the untroubled rest
Where virtues lie. She does not sink under weighty worries,
Nor fear the hand of the thief; nor does she hunt for vanities.[d]
And yet she is much suspected. But still, in one committed to the war
Christ wages, forbearance is not strong
if fortune presses him hard.
She is mild; though poverty may be harsh to the eyes of some.
If he but willingly carry it, no one will falter under her load.[e]
If he have the will for it, he can be glad with even a little.
This is hard at the outset; but we are left with the habit
Of frugality, and then practice makes it something we are used to.[f]
When the timid complain about poverty
It is not poorness, but poor persons themselves, they offend:
Unless there be one who poverty freely accepts, no one unhappy
In want will ever accept her. If people in need had more toleration,

a. Cf. Ovid, *Epistulae ex Ponto* I, IV, 45.

b. Cf. Ovid, *Epistulae ex Ponto* I, III, I: "downcast mind"; 27: "downcast soul"; 35: "with delight."

c. Horatius, *Epodes*, I, X, 47-8.

d. Horatius, *Ars poetica* 230.

e. Cf. D. Cato, *Disticha de moribus* I, 24: "Remember to bear the burden of poverty patiently."

f. Concerning this whole praise of poverty, cf. Matthew Vind (died after 1174), *Paraghrasis merica in librum Tobiae* 4 (Pl 205, 950).

Need itself, however great, we could well tolerate.
And no pauper exists who puts up with so much
That poverty cannot offer him still more to bear.
For liberal is the rest she gives and quiet is her freedom;
Nor is she torn apart by fickle fortune.[a] Instead she contemplates
And prays, her gaze only on the only supreme good,
And solely supernal are her thoughts.
Have her to lead you, choose her to guide you,
And your faces shall not be abashed. For just it is Ps 34:6
And from God himself, that for whom mundane glory
Holds no delights, the glory of heaven will bring enjoyment."

a. Cf. Ovid, *Tristia* V, VII, 15, 18: "fortune" in her fickleness.

The Sixth Book

A DESCRIPTION OF HIS CALLING BACK IN, THROUGH HIS POWERFUL PRAYERS, THE BROTHERS DISPERSED THROUGH THE WORLD'S CLIMES, OF HOW THE NEW ORDER GREW, UNDER APOSTOLIC CONFIRMATION OF ITS STATUTES, AND RECEIVED ITS NEW NAME.

RECTIFYING directions for the resisting of evils, taught them by Francis, 1C 30
And, ordered, as they were, to open their souls to heaven's will, they
Set out, two by two, for three of the world's regions.[a]
Francis gave them his blessing, and betook himself, content

With but one of his soldiers, to a fourth area.[b]
Who will give account of the divers combats they marched into,
Planting the foot of virtue upon the neck of vices,
Gn 3:15 And everywhere they went, crushing the head of the serpent
Prv 5:22 That was dragging all towards death by the halter of sin?

It was painful for Francis, who tenderly loved them, to abide
Their absence for long. He prays that He who brought the disciples,
Scattered through the countries of the world, back home for
Their Mother's obsequies, might gather these dispersed ones too.[c]
And what he, a mere man, did ask, God was moved to grant:[d]

For at one and the same time, and without appointment,
Do they return: it was the same Spirit calling them back
In the twinkling of an eye, from away in the wide world.[e]
Amazed they stand and still their wondering grows
What cause impelled them to return so quick.

Even Francis is awed at the effect his praying had.
They look at one another and rejoice;
They are glad for him and he is glad for them,

a. Cf. 1C 29 and 30.

b. Ibid.

c. A gathering of the Apostles for the death of Mary is mentioned, for example in Pseudo-Melito, *De transitu Virginum* c. 3. (PG 3, 1233); in Gregory of Tours, *Liber miracularum*. 1, 4 (PL 71, 708).

d. Ovid, *Epistulae ex Ponto* III, 1, 100.

e. Cf. Ovid, *Fasti* I, 544.

And they talk of all that happened in their departure and return.
Innocent living and spiritual cheer marked the life

Of the brothers, and no turmoil disturbed them.[a]
1C 31 Then they were joined by four other zealous men.
These take up arms under the same commander;
Rejecting the world with its destructive enticements,
They wage war upon the malicious demons and impose

Silence on the stupid ranting of the flesh.
When Francis had brought the number of his comrades
To equal the Apostolic assembly,[b] some noised it
Abroad that at hand were the last days of the world 1 Tm 4:1; Jude 18
Of whose end an unknown Order would be herald.[c]

But as for Francis, gladness filled his heart Ps 119:32
At the coming of each one to undertake to join his war on sin.
Whate'er a man's condition, fortune, age, none is turned away.
Admitted is every man that comes, nor is he ever levied:
The good man and the bad, the lofty and the lowly,

The rustic and the knight, the commoner and man
Of noble blood, the cleric and the layman, the raw
And the refined, the pauper and the rich man,
The freeman and the serf, the healthy and the sick.
And Francis to them all a loving welcome gives.

What draws them is the doctrine he taught, his exemplary life, Ti 2:7,8
Lending weight to the spotless word he speaks.[d]
1C 32 Lest his teaching come to grief as roundabout and vague,
The brothers of his company he instructs in such wise
That for brothers of the future there would be clear rules of action.

He puts it all in writing, bidding everything contain
The tenor of the Gospel. Yet lest he who was the founder
Of an Order that was novel appear arrogant in attempting Jd 6:15
The impossible, he would have the apostolic records
Give permanence to whatever came from his dictation.

---

a. In these two verses the poet compresses texts from 1C 30.

b. Twelve in number.

c. In this passage, Henri alludes to the work of Joachim of Fiore (+1202), *Concordantia Novi ac Veteri Testimenti* and to other works attributed to him. Similar ideas can be found in 1C 8; 18-23; 37.

d. Ovid, *Metamorphoses* I, 20; *Heroides* III, 98.

It was a most illustrious father then governed the wide world:
Innocent not only was he, but earned to be called
The Church's beneficial father.[a] Nothing was there so arduous
He did not tread under foot, nothing so bowed down
He did not lift up; the mere shadow of his name

Ps 2:2 Struck terror[b] in the kings of the earth, as he subjected
The world to the Church, taming with Peter's the sword of Caesar:[c]
For ever should his name be remembered.
Happy Francis would be to have the advice and favor
Of so great a father, and have him give lasting

Authoritative weight to the statutes he had compiled.
So, he sets out for Rome to petition that father that the new
Order, under his examining, obtain the Apostolic See's favor.
As he takes to the road he brings some of his brothers
Along as companions. And as they arrive in the City,

2 Kgs 4:9 There already is a holy man, by the name of Guido,
Assisi's bishop, who asks them what was their urge
In visiting Rome.[d] And having heard them he is pleased
With their reasons. For he'd feared they were going elsewhere. 1C 33
With that he gives them his counsel about their affairs.

Then there was the father and priestly president of Sabina,
John of Saint Paul: great and good men in those days had the curia,
But none greater nor better than he. Kindly encouragement he gives
Them, open-armed welcome; he treats them with warm compassion
And graciously pays them respects.

Yet he is afraid some human weakness may bring them down,
Perhaps may make their Order's newness and fervor die
And vanish into thin air.[e] He strives to dissuade them
From wandering about in this corrupting world of ours,[f]
Instead of entering the shelter of monastery or hermitage.

a. Pope Innocent III, 1198-1216.The name "Innocent," from *in-nocuous*, not harmful, becomes improperly "useful." Cf. 1C 33.

b. Cf. Ovid, *Epistulae ex Ponto* III, VI, 50: "frightened by the title of the name." See also Lucanus, *Pharsalie* I, 35; "the shadow of a great name," and above, I, 23.

c. Cf. Innocent III, *Regesta sive epistolae* I, 171, 401, 404; II, 209; IX, 130; SV, 189 (Pl 214, 227, 377, 387, 758; 215, 947; 216, 709); and *Decretum* I, tit. 33, c. 4-6; II, 1, 12; III, 17, 13.

d. From Vergil, *Eclogues* I, 27.

e. Cf. Vergil, *Aeneid* IV, 278; IX, 658.

f. Cf. Ovid, *Tristia* V, V, 25.

O man of great renown," replies Francis,[a] "would you
Advise to cling to cloister or hermitage men asked
To heal a whole world? We feel obliged to carry weapons
Not alone for ourselves but to guard all who are brethren to us.
Would you have us neglect to bring medicine

To a plague-ridden world—while merely wishing it well?
Surely it is wicked to prefer our own saving to that of all men.
To bring back the guilty and stoop down to the fallen—
That is my work.[b] This is the cross that I shoulder. Lk 14:27; Jn 19:17
I earnestly yearn to follow Christ thus; and I think I can

Follow him no otherwise; so do I learn
from the very words of the Gospel."
Moved by such great fervor in Francis, John
Leads him in to face the Pope he wished to consult.
The brothers bear him company on his way.[c]
And of the good purposes for which he had come

The Pope readily grants in favor. Everything yields
Ground to the requests and nothing whatever is refused.
Thus having obtained all that they came to petition,
The time comes to go. The Pope gives them license and leave
And imparts them his blessing. He bids them take once again

To the paths they had started out on, and throughout
Every land to publish the doctrine of Christ, and bring back
To safe haven those swamped by the billows of vices,
in the ship of the virtues.
Verily following Francis is grace of the highest divine favor;
Endowed with it he is filled with amazement

As it brings him so many and such speedy triumphs.[d]
An oath God did swear to make him increase. His like Sir 44:22
Was not found in furthering the law of the Most High, Sir 44:20
In serving God, in contemning the world, in mastering
Himself, in fostering his fellows, in converting the crooked,

a. This whole response (vv. 85-95) was fittingly composed by Henri, representing 1C 35. Note that these are missing below in v. 144.

b. Cf. Vergil, *Aeneid* VI, 129.

c. Ovid, *Metamorphoses* IV, 483.

d. Henri omits the vision of the tree in 1C 33. What follows in vv. 110-115 is his own embellishment.

In improving the good, in performing all seemly things.
 It cheered Francis to have set eyes on that great father, 1C 34
And departing, he visits the places sacred to Peter
And Paul, and leads away his happy brothers.
Conversing one with another they lighten the toil

Of the journey: how kindly the gentle Pope had treated them;
How mad one must be to break with his guidance;
Ps 133:1 How pleasant for brothers to dwell as one under him.
And as they while time away,[a] talking so much as they walk,
Unknown to them passes much of the day.

Walking and heat combine to increase their fatigue
And balmy airs all round bring languor to limbs.
Jaded they sit on the ground, weary at the late hour
And from toil; and more than all, hunger calls them
Lam 1:11 To refresh themselves. But there are no means

Of refreshment in a place so remote.
 But God cannot leave his loyal ones uncared for;
And so there happens to come a man from whose bounty
They gladly receive some bread: and lo! the unknown one is gone!
They stand astonished, and one another admonish

In trusting words to place their hopes in still more gifts
From the supernal goodness. Sure is their confidence
In that supreme good, their past experience creating their future hopes.
Jn 6:12 A cave keeps in its ample lap the left-over bread 1C 35
And the gathered broken pieces, and there together they dwell

Some days, nor thence would they fain depart.
But the place has a perilous beauty, adorned as it is
With dense evergreen verdure, patterned with flowers[b]
Of a thousand hues; and lest allurements of sense stifle
Their wits, much as they might wish to, they must not stay there.[c]

 The beloved vale of Spoleto welcomes its chosen ones.

---

a. Cf. Ovid *Tristia* III, III, 12.

b. Namely, similar to vermiculate work, as in mosaic (see Quintilianus, *Institutio* IX, 4, 113), made up of minute strands, multi-colored and distinct.

c. Henri reduces to these few lines the section of 1C 35; the rest (10-15) were touched upon above (vv. 85-95), together with the ideas of poverty, above, V, 202-230.

Here the Patarene error had led many astray[a]
But Francis leads back the sheep of Christ to the fold.[b] Acts 10:16
1C 36-37 While he instructs the unschooled, the Lord's word sits nobly Acts 6:7
Upon his lips: like jasper on gold, like the dew
On the fields, a flower[c] in thickets, a glowing fire in some
Palace hall.[d] With divine faith he adorns souls like a jasper,
Like dew he moistens them, delights them like a flower,
And capturing human feelings, soothes them with sweet savor,
And reaches into the heart's deepest core.[e]
And now those whose souls he pierced the more, prevail on him
Who learned from God such honored skill,
To let them join him as brethren; let them share
The onus he carries, share, too, the honors that are his.
These he enrolls under his banner;[f] the Order
Grows greatly in numbers.[g] Yet up to now it lacks a name.[h]
1C 38-41 Therefore its craftsman must give it[i] a definite name,
And decides to call it the Order of Minors.
How right! For who was minor or lesser than he,
Meager in victuals and drinking, uncluttered with mantle or toga,
Not puffed up with grandeur or sway; that reckoned
All above himself and self to none preferred; that valued
What the world calls cheap and the costly learnt to scorn;
That lest he lose what was Christ, let himself go in want?
And so, Francis was right in calling them Minor—

a. Thomas of Celano makes no mention of Cathars in the Spoleto Valley. In 1C 62 Thomas of Celano speaks of the "confusion" of "heretics" in the Marches of Ancona, though not of their conversion. Henri may have known from his own experience and from contemporary reports of Cathars in the Spoleto region, but possibly exaggerates their following.

b. Henri contributed this from his own poetic source; no such thing is found in Thomas of Celano. Henri transferred this mention from there (and omitted it from its place, below, IX, 70) for the sake of meter, substituting *Paterinorum* [Cathars] for *haereticorum* [heretics]. Not even Gerard Gilberti, whom Innocent III excommunicated, and whom the people of Assisi elected their *podesta*, was a Cathar or a heretic. Cf. the Bull of Innocent, June 6, 1204, in his *Regesta*, VII, 83 (PL 216, 365-6). There was a small number of Cathars in the valley of Spoleto in about 1230, but they were no threat. Cf. below, VII, 159.

c. Cf. 1C 37.

d. That is, gleaming and glowing, but not out of control.

e. In these few words Henri freely compressed what is said in 1C 36 and 37.

f. Cf. 1C 37: "the threefold army of the saved." Henri usually delights in metonymy—here he passed it over.

g. Cf. Ovid, *Fasti* V, 537.

h. Cf. Vergil, *Aeneid* II, 558; IX, 343.

i. In 1C 38: "he wills;" in 1C 37 "the originator."

The gate of heaven is too narrow for anyone larger.[a]
After[b] this new Order became known by name, 1C 42, 44
Shelter for Francis and comrades was a derelict hovel
With rotten straw for a roof, its scrawny timbers
Jutting out, destined to stand but a few more days:[c]

Its very poverty was comfort to men that loved her.
Till there came this peasant leading his laden ass
And annoyed them by passing a silly remark.
Forced by a heavy downpour to shelter,
He turns to his beast and this does he say:

"In you go, to be sure, my little brown donkey;[d]
We'll lend a hand in this house in due time."
As much as to say: These brothers are starting to build
Themselves houses. His notion and hidden meaning are hateful
To Francis, who betakes himself to places not vexed

By travelers' pert words, where habitual peace finds a home.

a. In these verses (161-70) Henri compresses what 1C 38-41 had more expansively and beautifully related.

b. Here Henri incorporates the few things narrated in 1C 42, leaving aside the whole of 1C 43 concerning the Emperor Otto.

c. This is Henri's supposition, founded on 1C 42.

d. The adjective is of vulgar origin, taken from its tawny color.

The Seventh Book

HE IS SHOWN TEACHING THE BROTHERS TO PRAY;
HOW, AS THEY KEEP WATCH, HE APPEARS, THOUGH ABSENT;
HOW HE STROVE IN THE WORLD'S EYES TO BE VILE;
HOW FERVOR FOR MARTYRDOM SENDS HIM OVER THE SWELLING WAVES.

1C 45 IN the meanwhile the brothers were all heart in pressing Francis
To give them instruction in the way they should pray.
Kindly he answers their honest request in these terms:
"We are all of us caught in the snare of vices and sins.[a] Nm 16:26

Prayerfully turn then to the help of the powers above you;
For, unaided you durst not ascend to your heavenly goal.
1C 21 No, let the Virgin blest be your mediatrix with Christ,
And Christ with the Father be your mediator.
'To the Virgin let his be your salutation:

O loving Mother, *hail Mary, filled* with the Spirit's gift, Lk 1:42
The Lord be with you, *you who are *blessed* among *women,* *Lk 1:28
And blessed the fruit of your womb.' And say those words
For as long and as often as your devotion lasts.
For through these you ponder the first joys of Christ's mother;

So may he help you reach the joys of the future.
His mother greeted, prayed unto Christ in this vein:
'We adore you, O Christ, ruler of all above and on earth,
We bless you, O you who were crucified.
By the cruel cross you healed our wounds, by your death

Restored our mortal race.' Supported by these intercessions,
Send up this prayer to the highest Father:
'O fatherless *Father* of *ours,* heaven's radiant halls Mt 6:9-13; Lk 11:2-4
Bow down before you. *Hallowed be the name* of your Godhead,
And your *kingdom come,* and *your will be done on earth as in heaven.*

Give us this day our daily bread, and remit *our debts,*
Just as we remit the debts of others, and *lead us not*

a. Henri himself inserted these grounds for prayer, and of prayer to the Blessed Virgin (vv. 4-15).

Into trial, but let *evil* be kept far from us
By that Goodness in which you created all things.' "
Through these and other prayers, which implore the most high 1C 46
Father's clemency, were the brothers taught devout simplicity,
Of which they had so much, it would never occur to them
That the words of a priest meant anything else but the solemn truth.
For it happened once there went a certain friar to a priest
For confession, when that priest to him did say: "Brother,
Take care would you be a hypocrite." Believing this to be
More a true statement of his condition than a mere
Caution offered him,[a] he sighed with sorrow sore,
Nor could the solace of a friend his grief remove.
For he held for sure he was nothing but a hypocrite,
Since that is what he thought the priest had put in words.
Till ready words from Francis put closure to his scruple,
And assured him there was nothing to it and no call for fear.
A word of his could soften and get through to hardest hearts,
Could lift again the fallen, give hope to those in misery,
Give light to those in blindness, consolation to the sad.
As to how he stood with the Lord were his brothers to ever 1C 47
Waver in opinion, they learned the truth by this supernal sign.
About the mid-hour of night, when the lofty sun draws
The shades from the nether earth,[b] while their master was away,
Some brothers slumbered,[c] some stayed at prayer. When, lo!
2 Kgs 2:11 A fiery chariot is seen being let down from the sky above.
Resting on it is a globe that shines like the sun,
A ball of light, all glittering, that dazzles and flashes
Its intense flame on the eyes of those brothers in full view.
They rouse one another; they bestir themselves to see
The wondrous spectacle. They are curious as to what the chariot
Might mean. Opinions vary at first, then at last they come
To see it stands for the soul of Francis—perfect
Like the sphere, fleet as the chariot, blissful as the radiance.

a. Cf. Cato, *Disticha* I, 14.
b. Cf. Ovid, *Metamorphoses* III, 144.
c. Cf. Ovid, *Metamorphoses* IX, 470.

Their fear was that perchance his soul had vacated his body.
1C 48 The spirit of prophecy was given him. 1 Cor 12:9,10
In unearthly manner he was aware
Of those predestined and of those foreknown
In Destiny's eternal and unbreakable chain[a]

As she earnestly studies with every care
How she will damn the damned and choose the chosen;
Rejoicing to join to herself those like her, careful
To avoid those unlike her; and while guiding mistress of both,
Spurning neither, the first she cares for, the others nurtures.

1C 49, 50 Friar Riccerio[b] was one who noticed that hidden from Francis
Was no plan of fate, no mind's dark secret.
He pondered his own excesses, things he once did,[c]
And dreaded his knowing of them. What hope had he
Of gaining his favor which he so much longed for?

Let us not imagine Francis knew nothing of Riccerio's fears.
"Why, my Riccerio," said he, "are you afraid?
I bear you no hate. For whatever you did,
Your sin is mourned and pardon is yours. Lk 17:4; Gn 4:13
Doubt not that you are very dear to me."

1C 48 To draw his followers all the closer to him
The power used was the same, though different the sign given.
Many brothers gathered again, this time for chapter, the master
Away. Friar Anthony, bidden to preach, took as his theme:
"Jesus of Nazareth, King of the Jews." And *focusing Jn 19:19; *Acts 7:55; Ps 123:1

His entire heart on heavenly things, his eyes he lifts up high
Francis to see, his hands extended as though on a cross.[d]
To prove it was no illusion, no horrible fraud,
An unearthly sweet aura was there, and the souls
Of the brothers standing around with exultation were filled. Tb 3:22

a. The formulation of Ovid, *Metamorphoses* XV, 152 is less rigid: "fate's evolving chain." Concerning such matters, cf. *Boëthius, De Consolatione Philosophica*. IV, prosa 6 (Pl 63, 814-20); Alexander of Hales, *Summa Theologica* I (Quarracchi, 1924) 304-14.

b. In 1C 48 he is called "Riccerius." Henri inverts the order of 1C 49, 50 and 48.

c. The accusation and unjust assumption of guilt are the poet's own; the same for vv. 77-8. The verb "fears" is found in another context in 1C 49.

d. Mention of Monaldus (1C 48) is omitted and his vision is attributed to Saint Anthony.

That was once; but oft and again in different signs
His presence returned; though not like a poor earthly man,
But already as one whose own was the kingdom above.
1 Chr 17:18 It was God's loving kindness honoring his servant
In whose eyes nothing is fouler than the mundane, 1C 52

And whose special possession means owning nothing at all.
Although indulgence in meat was never his wish, once
A mighty fever forced him to feed on flesh meat.
As soon as he was well, the blood-red feast he regretted
Ever tasting, and assigned himself a penance: to a lay friar

Strict orders he gave to tie a rope round his neck
And drag him through the city of Assisi,
Crying out like a herald: "Behold, ye citizens,
Mt 6:16 A parasite glutton, a glum-looking fraud;[a]
To you he talks well about fasting—but he hates it.

Into his hungry maw fat chickens he's packed."[b]
The friar under orders carried out all he was told.
The townsfolk are awestruck and say: "For just once
Eating meat, is that treatment he gets? What of us, then,
Whose diet is blood all the time,[c] whose cravings

Stop short at this earth? Holy men must be fools, 1C 53
Or else we are a race of perdition."
Francis again gave orders to one of the brothers
That whenever he was wined and dined by people

With high notions, the friar was to heap insults on him
And call him a dealer and mountainman.[d] Hard though it was
To exactly fulfil these commands, the brother spared him
Not a whit, as he sat among the distinguished.
Rewarding him with approval for the bad things he'd said,

With honor for abuse, with praise for the insults,
It was usual for Francis to say: "Brother, I sanction

a. Henri added this phrase.

b. Cf. Ovid, *Metamorphoses* XIV, 209; XV, 105.

c. Perhaps with Genesis 9:4; Leviticus 3:17; 6:26-7; Acts 15:20 in mind. Thus Henri inappropriately renders the passage from 1C 52: "whose whole life is carried on in blood."

d. Henri contents himself with these titles of contempt; compare with those in 1C 53: "bumpkin, dealer and useless."

All that you said. In all honesty, the son
Of Peter Bernardone ought to put up with that without demur."
By these means and others, unabashed and forthright,

He puts to flight all that flatters the human mentality.
As he waits for the day of the Lord which reveals the secrets 1 Cor 3:13; 4:5
Of hearts, he cannot be drawn to perform any good
For some day of human approval. Thus disentangled 1 Cor 4:3
He completed six years of his soldierly deeds.[a]

His resolve aimed only at heaven. And if one fortune remains
To try his courage, no power has it to make him waver
From coming through all that befalls, with flying colors.
Brief moments are ages to the eyes of the saintly man,
And small he counts his achievement for all his days.[b]

Albeit unceasingly for him mirth was moan
And moan was mirth, feeding meant fasting, fasting was food
To him, toil was rest to him, rest was an effort—
Unsatisfied still was he till he'd start further attacks
On his carnal self, and at the cost of his own blood

1C 55 Be willing to fight for the name of Christ. Acts 15:26
A noble impulse within him restlessly burned with desire
Of death, and wearied of waiting. But so as to find
An angry prince,[c] a savage sergeant, or a worthy cause,
He makes up his mind to cross the sea, and for the saving

Of idolaters preach to them what must be believed. Thus Heb 11:6
Either they, who only live for this world in a kind of death,
Will be won for Christ, or he himself, who is dead to this world, 1 Cor 9:19, 22
Will share life with Christ, the only true life worth living. Gal 2:20; Phlm 1:21
With a martyr's death, therefore, longing to crown his labors,

He sets his mind on making for Parthian regions.[d]
But with the Church's house in flames within, what is its Ps 127:1
Watchman looking outside it for? Italians, more than Parthians,

a. From 1C 55. The following verses (130-37), in some way deriving from the same passage, are Henri's own; he skipped over n. 54, with a couple of verses expanded upon.

b. These matters are found in 1C 103; below (XIII, 29) Henri omits them.

c. Ovid *Tristia* I, I, 33; IV, X 98.

d. 1C 55 says "to the Saracens . . . in the region of Syria." See also *ibid,* 57. Parthians, Syrians and Persians are mentioned sporadically below.

Need a good preacher to teach them the faith—the populace,
I speak of, not of the nobles. Just one error made the Parthian

Slip; not one but every error made Italy slip.
The Parthian preserves a schism taken up from of old;[a]
The Italian rebuffs the precepts of faith he embraced.
To one foundling heresy the Parthian is guardian;[b]
The Italian is founding father of thirty-two![c]

And this gives the latter more license to sin.
While freedom belongs to Italians, Syrians are slaves;
It was not they that owed God the first fruits or the tithe[d]
Prescribed in the law: they sin, but without an avenger.[e]
For should the Holy Father excommunicate them

Or an irate Emperor threaten war on them,
They couldn't care less, as for neither have they any respect;
They've already consigned them to the yoke and the tax!
Rv. 7:9 Out there there are countless millions of people
And there a knight is the same as a boor:

The knight for his muscle, the boor for his hatred of lords.
But enough! Certain things may be true but can't always be told.
1 Cor 13:7 Yet the holy simplicity of Francis sustains to the last,
And has no eyes for sins or for faults.
Meet he the crafty, he will take them for wise citizens

Of Italy; nor will he believe they need a schoolmaster.[f]
And so, he embarks, with his heart in converting the Syrians.
Mk 6:48 There rises a contrary wind; the level sea is turning

a. This assertion fits the Greeks better than the Saracens, since the latter were never united with Christians. The poet here relies on a popular notion of the time that Muhamed was once a Christian (Nestorian). Cf. Emicho Prefect of Mainz (about 1040), *Historia de Mahumete* c. 1-16, which is found falsely attributed to Hildebert, a Celtic bishop (died 1133) in Pl 171, 1343-66. (This history in verse is obviously fictitious.) Cf. also Guibertus Abbot of Novigneti (died 1124), *Gesta Dei per Francos* I, 3-4 (PL 156, 689-95); it is he who ineptly wrote: "The Kingdome of the Parthians, whom we by linguistic corruption call Turks."

b. Cf. Saint John Damascene, *De Haeresibus* 101 (PG 94, 763-74); Peter Alfonsus, *Dialogus* 5 (PL 157, 597-606). See Guibertus, cited above, note 21 and Peter Venerable (died 1156), *Adversus sectam Saracenorum* II (PL 189, 661-720); Alan of the Lille, *De fide Catholica contra haereticos sui temporis haereticorum* I, IV: *Contra paganos seu Mohometanos* (PL 210, 421-30).

c. This number (as those in VIII, 23 and 59) appears to be arbitrary. Even according to Rainerus Sacconi, once, as he says, a heresiarch, now a Dominican, *Summa de catharis* (*sive patarenis*) about 1230: "the total of Cathar churches," within and outside Italy, was 16, among which "the church of Tuscany and the Valley of Spoleto (had) about 100" adherents.

d. *Decretum* II, c. 16, qu. 1; c. 55-7, 65-8; *Decretales* III, c. 1-34.

e. Ovid, *Heroides* VIII, 7; *Metamorphoses* I, 93.

f. The real reason that moved Francis to travel in v. 176 can be found in 1C 55.

Rough; the voyage is no longer benign,
While the weary travellers are blown on to the Slavic coast.[a]

There Francis waits for a westerly, is held up by an easterly,
And in the end he senses the rise of a northerly.
And now he prepares to return, since he cannot proceed.
Christ was recalling his servant, albeit his purpose
Was sound, for more useful purposes still; the evangelic

Master he denies the Parthians, he now gives back to Ausonians.[b]

a. According to 1 C 55, to *Sclavonia* that is, to Illyria or Dalmatia. These shores Henri calls *Geticas* following Ovid, *Epistulae ex Ponto* I, I, 2; *Tristia* I, X 14, who in a distant part of the "Getic shore" near the Black Sea languished as an exile.

b. Ausonia: Italy or rather Lower Italy.

The Eighth Book

His fervor at Damietta in crossing the Nile to convert the enemy, his speech to the birds upon return, releasing their sylvan song in praise of their Lord.

Unfinished initiatives withstood by the elements, and his wings 1C 55
Being clipped, Francis suffered with only the greatest grief.
He now spots a ship making ready to give her sheets to the winds,[a]
And sailors preparing hastily to voyage to Ancona.

When he asks the seamen for passage they refuse to let him
On board, not because he can't pay the fare, nor for the weight
In the ship, nor for any wild weather, but for shortage
Of food, of which they'd scarce enough to be brought in the stern
For themselves. As for him, he'd no worries, as Christ lends

A hand, and he secretly enters the ship as the sailors are absent
And hides down below in among horses. There for the needy pair[b]
A rich man had stored up provisions and instructed his vassal
To the effect that as often as meal times came round
He was to give out to them as much as they needed to eat.

The seafarers[c] return, the anchor is weighed, ropes
Are hauled, cables are loosed and hoisted the sails;
First the plank to the stern is away, lastly that to the prow.
The breeze fills the great fold of sail;[d] under increasing
Pull the mast is groaning and threatening to fall.

Steering-oar straight at the stern follows the flying
Prow, and swifter than any bird the ship sails over the waters[e]
And is almost swallowed up in her own slip-stream.
Two hundred leagues[f] it seemed traversed when all at once
A pall of darkness covers all the sky.

---

a. Vergil, *Aeneid* IV, 516.

b. Francis and his companion.

c. Vergil, *Aeneid* II, 207.

d. Ovid, *Fasti* V, 609.

e. Ovid, *Metamorphoses* IV, 706.

f. The number is undoubtedly arbitrary.

Fast roll on the clouds, winds rise out of every quarter,
Waves build up and crash against one another, nowhere
Is there level sea, all is rough;[a] billows foam with rage.
There's a rush for the ropes, the sailors release the sea-anchor.[b]
But the storm-wind hisses at the mast enmeshed with ropes,

And a wave more violent than any wind brings it down.
Water is baled, and the jettisoned anchor bites the sand.[c]
All the winds that are, still harass this single ship.
She is driven on now by a hurricane easterly,
By sou'wester next, by southerly then, by northerly next.

One minute she's high over the clouds, another down in the depths.
She is sighing for some haven, yet dreading every harbor.[d]
No end to that driving tempest as it stirs the sea, and curdles
The atmosphere, scares the sailors and whirls the ship
In circles. But what shall they do when on the whole ship

No means of subsistence remain to stave off their hunger?
Long is the way that stretches ahead, food for the journey
Is nil; shipwreck looms near, land is far, certain death gazes
From all sides. The fear of shipwreck, even if it ends not
In death, makes seem but slight the sufferings of famine.

Every kind of death the nearer it approaches, the more
Fear of it is struck; it is then a man peers into
His innermost heart, and bids cares begone.
Yet there is no tempest that can conceal so long a fast
From food. But all that remains is the portion of food

Given Francis and his brother; and it is this that now
Sustains them all and feeds all, as Francis distributes
It to everyone. So little suffices to relieve the hunger
Of so many;[e] it lasts, to the amazement of all,
Nor is it finished by continuous eating.

Just as it resulted from divine power that Jesus Mt 14:19-21;
Would feed the five thousand, handing them only five loaves Jn 6:10-13

a. See above VII, 178.
b. Cf. Ovid, *Fasti* III, 587; *Metamorphoses* XI, 477.
c. Ovid, *Metamorphoses* IX, 61.
d. Ovid, *Tristia* I, XI, 25.
e. Ovid, *Metamorphoses* XI, 129.

And two fish and the portions (leaving Euclid bewildered)[a]
Exceeded the whole, while with the fragments
Left over one and twelve baskets they filled,[b] none of which
Would be full with only two fish and five loaves;
So thanks to this same divine work of his
The store of his servant shared among many
Was never used up, and still more was left over.
Already the winds are checked, their quarrels are silent,
Clouds roll away,[c] mists abate, all gloom dissolves.
A fairer sky for mariners now, and clearer air;
Surer their sailing, easier steering, on a friendly level sea.
The sheets swell to the breeze over placid waters, and quicker
Than thought, the ship comes to rest as they land in the port
Of Ancona. To touch land was joy to the tempest-tossed, long
Gripped by fear. Rescue from storm and starvation they ascribe
To the merits of Francis; their thoughts and their words
Prv 16:7 Do him honor as guardian and savior of lives,[d] as they avow
That through him they came safe through all that befell.

The whole city is alive with the fair name of Francis: 1C 56
Jn 20:30 Just to look on the face of this world-famous worker
Of wonders, just to hear him speak, the citizens gather.[e]
Many of them he arms and enlists to follow his banner.
Still, that popular love, or the comforting company
Of brothers, or yet sweet love of country,[f] can't banish his wish
For martyrdom, with which all his devotion flares like a fire.
Ready to cross to Morocco, he takes to the road. The God
Of power, while lauding his move, blocks his first mighty stride.
He who'd made him sure guide to many, halts his dead-end trip
With a useful fever: although he is peeved he forces him

a. Cf. Euclid, *Elementa* I, I, con. 9.

b. All four Evangelists give "twelve" as the number of baskets (Mt 14:21, Mk 6:43, Lk 9:17, Jn 6:13) for metrical reasons the poet substitutes *tredecim* for *duodecim.*

c. Cf. Vergil, *Aeneid* V 820 and X 358.

d. Henri borrowed this half-verse from Ovid, *Metamorphoses* IV 736.

e. Henri here introduces the citizens of Ancona; Thomas of Celano however relates this of "the land," that is, the region of Ascoli and of Umbria, Cf. 1C 56.

f. From Ovid, *Fasti* V 653.

Back,[a] and he detains him although he's reluctant.
1C 57 Compelled to return to Assisi, he fits out all he can
Of recruits for Christ's army. With unerring command
He shows the way to the trophy to all who will carry his banner.

All this, however, cools down not the passion for virtuous
Death that was born in his heart. Far from it;
For he boards ship, and the ship he commits to wind and wave,
And wind and wave unto God, who as steersman,
Carries him safe to Damietta's coveted harbor.[b]

Christ's faithful and Gentile, the one in turn against the other,
Were locked in great conflict there: Damietta was the constantly
Shifting hub of the war,[c] and the prize in a future of triumph.[d]
With neither savage close combat[e] nor hand-to-hand fighting
Could they take it; but only with long-distance bow,

With sling and with engines of siege: blows fell like hail.
Nor could they attack it at a much closer range,
For between flows the seventh of its river's branches:[f]
Its source must be none, or else torrid zone hides it
From every explorer, and eyes of ours may never reach it.[g]

Midway between the armies the waters flowed,
And they grabbed the missiles raining down from either side.
But though the water moved, it never spread out in rings,
And there was no measuring by circles the strokes

a. Ovid, *Epistulae ex Ponto* IV, III, 49.

b. The city is not named in 1C 57. Damietta was indeed the "hub of the war" (v. 97). Henri could have obtained information from contemporary chroniclers and from Crusaders who bore arms in the 5th crusade. Cf. Jacques de Vitry *Historia Orientalis;* several of the same author's Epistolae, cf. supra; Oliverus, scholar of Cologne and Cardinal (died 1227), *Historia Damiatina;* various contemporary accounts, *Libri duelli Christ in obsidione Damiatae or Gesta obsidionis Damiatae 1218-1220; Chronique d'Ernoul* (up to 1229) *et de Bernard le Trésorier.*

c. Ovid, *Amores* I, X, 2: II, XII, 17; Vergil, *Aeneid* VII 553; XII, 567.

d. Damietta had, therefore, not yet been captured.

e. Ovid, *Metamorphoses* III 119; the "long distance bow" also occurs there.

f. The ancients already numbered the Nile's channels as seven; these formed the Nile Delta. Cf. Ptolemaeus, *Geographike Huphegesis* IV, 5; Pliny, *Naturalis historia* V, 11, 5 who names these seven mouths Canopicum, Bolbitunum, Sebennyticum, Phatniticum, Medessicum, Taniticum, Pelusiacum. Damietta was (and still is) situated on the right bank of the Nile on a narrow strip of land between the Phatniticum and Lake Menzaleh.

g. Cf. Lucanus, *Pharsalia,* or *De bello civili,* X, 189-92: "Nothing would I prefer to know than the sources of the river hidden for so many centuries, and its unknown origin."

That came, for their points of entry were everywhere.[a]

What manly courage in a man to cross that great river
In a tiny skiff! Alone and unarmed he moves towards
The weaponed and hostile host, through darts, through
Unquenchable "Greek fire,"[b] through a thousand mortal perils![c]
A thousand dangers strewed his path, yet more the menace

At journey's end. Fears he neither till the greedy river
He crosses and, nothing daunted, reaches the enemy's midst.[d]
But before he can advance further to reach the presence
Of the king of the Persians, to whose ears
Acts 6:7 The word of the Lord he intended first to convey,

He must take furious treatment in plenty,[e] with cruel club
Be smitten. His flesh is livid, his blood pours out;
Violet is his body from violence, and rose-red his wounds
Within. Nor does the soul within him any sorrow feel
For those tortured limbs now all swathed in purple.

While the flesh is hostile to the soul, why should
Its wounds be pitied? Anyone who boosts his foe
Leaves himself in a weaker position. Hence the inner
Francis sought nothing of outer honors, through the losing
Of which he has his will set on salvation's gaining, on

---

a. Concerning the circle and its mid-point, cf. Euclid, *Elementa*, I, Def. 14-15; III, 1ff. Henri, therefore has in view the Phatniticum channel or branch of the Nile near where Damietta sits, and that period of time in which the Christian and Saracen armies fought fiercely from opposite sides, the former on the left bank and the latter on the right. Either he had heard about the site of Damietta and the siege of the city from some Crusaders who had fought there, or he had read about them in trustworthy authors, e.g. in *Gestis obsidionis Damiatae, loc. cit.*, 671ff., or in Ernoul, *Chronique* c. 36-37. These authors narrate how Christian attacks and battles tried in vain to cross that channel of the Nile several times in 1218; they had landed there already on May 29, 1218. The Christians crossed to the right bank in the Month of February, 1219, after Sultan Melek-el-Kamel, there having arisen a conspiracy in his ranks, moved his camp to the upper Nile Delta, and built the city of Mansura for them on the southern Mendesic branch of the Nile. Thus the Christian soldiers were able to tighten the siege on Damietta and finally took it during the night between November 4 and 5, 1219. But by September 8, 1221, the Saracens had again occupied Damietta.

b. So-called incendiary missiles of the time.

c. In these verses the poet embellishes the moment in which Francis crossed the Nile (the Phatnitic channel) in order to praise the saint's intrepid spirit. Those battles were already over when Francis arrived in the camp of the Christians in the Summer of 1219. (See 1C 57 and 1C 30). Besides, he could not have crossed over to the Saracens during such fierce combat. An eyewitness at Damietta, Jacques de Vitry in his *Historia Orientalis* 32, openly intimates this. Clearly then, Henri is playing the part of the poet, not the historian. This same is apparent in his whole approach to 1C 55-57, although little is taken from Thomas of Celano; much is Henri's poetic adornment. Since other contemporary authors do not mention the crossing of the Nile, it remains doubtful.

d. Cf. Ovid, *Metamorphoses* VIII 338; XIII 121.

e. These things (vv. 120-24) can be read in 1C 57, but more briefly and more restrained.

Reaching heights through being brought low, on winning
Through losses, on living through dying, on delights
Through pain. For the flesh's woes cheer the soul, groans
Are comfort, wounding brings healing, agreeable are insults,
Hurts are helpful, distress spells relief.

When the fair name of the holy man who was indomitable
Under every affliction had spread through the Persian camp,
Such was a kingly king's admiration for his great spirit
That he gave him a great reception and offered him precious gifts.
He, content with what he has, declines the king's

Offer, and asks for that gift of gifts, to be given a hearing.
So as to hear him, the king himself bids the crowd be silent Acts 13:16
And orders every noise to cease, while to his attendants
He said: "Fetch me my sages; let them be the judges
If this man's teaching be genuine, or if he's not minded

Rather to lead multitudes astray."[a] And so, as he speaks Jn 7:12
To the wise ones gathered together, this wise man
Proves the source out of which he has drawn his philosophy.
All of his reasoning he hastens to carry onto celestial things;
He discourses on things unheard before, as though beyond

Mere human ken: here is one to whom nothing's unknown.
He reasons matters which few mortals have ever perceived,
Or on the origins of the universe manifest only to God.[b]
Whence he introduces reflections upon the first cause;
Then he condemns the perverse school of Mohammed, proves

That God is one, and that a host of gods has no existence;[c]
How it is that all things come from one source, how a moment
Of that first principle is simple substance, a simple
Moment in the present, a substance simpler than
A mathematical point; how its essence is wondrously present

a. This preaching Henri could have drawn from 1C 57 or from Jacques de Vitry, *Historia Orientalis*, c. 32 and from his *Epistola VI* written at Damietta in March of 1220. Ernoul relates much about this preaching in his *Chronique* 37 where he narrates that the "most wise" Saracen "clerics" refused to engage Francis in debate.

b. For the phraseology, cf. Ovid, *Metamorphoses* XV 67.

c. A useless doctrine to argue with Muslims, since they profess one God, the creator of all (but not a Triune God), as the Koran asserts (c. 1; c. XX, 7-14). It appears, therefore, that Henri was ignorant of Muslim beliefs.

Wholly, always and everywhere outside of place and time.
Where pride comes from, and how Lucifer, once "morning star,"
Is now laden with murky mud; at what price the world's
Redemption was wrought, and what reasons brought
2 Cor 11:3 The incarnation; how it was the ancient *serpent seduced*

Eve, Eve the first man formed, the first-formed man
His posterity, how that posterity betrayed Christ, how Christ
Outwitted the serpent, death now driven back whence it sprang.
How not only is Christ's body glorified,
But while it glorifies other bodies,

His living flesh adorning the soul with gifts,
He is fully at one and the same time in divers churches,
And how Christ assembles all his holy people into his Church;
How Baptism is a spiritual cleansing power
That purifies souls of the stain of the first parent.

While he thus teaches the articles of faith with skillful
Tongue, he impresses sages and king, and nobody dares
To harm him. Indeed heralds are bidden to make this
Their cry: "Often may he come and go among us."[a] Yet on his own
He is unable to convert so many Persians; and as ministers

Which his plan badly needed are missing, he is forced to give up
The venture, and is borne over the seas by a homeward wind.[b]
Returning to his native soil[c] with only one friar, 1C 58
He urges not alone humans but the very beasts of the field
To utter the divine praises. And oft did the wonder occur

That though they lacked the power of reason they would obey
His words to them and understand him when he spoke.
His delight was to visit the various parts of his land
And while near Bevagna he espies an assortment of birds
Congregated in a closely knit flock;[d] a mild bravery

Was making them await his kindly approach. Yet he wonders
Why, and how they could come to know the secret

---

a. Ovid, *Metamorphoses* II 409. Both the expression and the substance are merely poetic. Cf. note 30 above.

b. This is not the real reason for returning, but rather that the preaching to the Saracens took place, for his desire for martyrdom was not fulfilled. Cf. 1C 57.

c. Ovid, *Metamorphoses* VII 52; *Epistulae ex Ponto* I, III, 35.

d. Vergil, *Aeneid* II 450; IX 788; XII 442.

Of his gentleness. Up he comes, calling them brothers,
Said to them: "O noble product of the First and Powerful One
How right and proper for you to ring out his praises!

Up above the world he placed your bodies, covering you
With wings and plumage.[a] He made straight tracks for you,
With nothing to strike against, there in the heavens,
And set you in the pure air, where you are not weighted
Down like us, although out of the same element.

He produced the fish and yourselves, your nobility
Is the greater, your course is swifter, your range
Is wider, greater your freedom, and more delicious your fare.
Together, then, praise the Lord, bless his name, Ps 96:2; 116:1
Who has marked you with so much distinction and beauty."

O creative force present to nature, O glory not hidden
From creatures, though transcending our senses!
Sylvan hearts respond to the voice of humans
And are gladly mild for the servant of their Maker.
Since he himself is his Creator's perfect subject,

Every creature bows before him; there's none that's deaf
To word of his, who always the divine voice obeys.
A discernment human comes upon the birds: you would think
They could tell with minds whatever he bade them do.
Of divers kinds are they, yet all one song they sing;

Or as one and with one accord mounting up the sky,
They melodiously praise the name of God, in the way Ps 69:31; 112:1
That nature gave them;[b] the air is loud with the chorus,
Re-echoed by the hills, resounding in the woods.[c]
Delighted with their singing more than with harp or lyre,

And skywards raising his hands for joy,[d] Francis moves
In among the birds, still singing on both sides of him,
Remaining still and allowing themselves to be handled,
And he loves to touch them with the hem of his long tunic.
And then he blesses and with dulcet voice gives them leave to go.

a. Cf. Ovid, *Metamorphoses* V 546.

b. Cf. Vergil, *Georgies* II 20.

c. *Ibid.*, III, 223 and IV, 50.

d. Vergil, *Aeneid* IX 16; Ovid, *Metamorphoses* VI 368; *Tristia* I, XI 21.

Free to depart they rise, their legs kicking back the ground,[a]
And convey their soaring bodies on poised wings.

a. Cf. Ovid, *Metamorphoses* VI 511; VIII 201-2.

The Ninth Book

THE MAN WHO RESTRAINED CHATTERING SWALLOWS
AND MADE THEM STAND STILL; WHAT HE DID FOR A HARE
AND A FISH; WATER BY MIRACLE CHANGED TO WINE
AND CURING HIM, AND HIS HEALING THE MALADIES AND MORALS OF THE SICK.

1C 58 SURVEYING the sky, he is full of wonder that wandering birds[a]
Of space could hold his sermon's weight,
Could allow him to touch them, and give forth
A pleasant song and heedfully chant supernal praises.

1C 59 The footsoldier, happy that miracles sparkled at his command,
Completes his planned march, and end of day finds him
In Alviano. There on the following morning[b] he is ready
To address devout words to the crowds assembled from everywhere.
But the tiny place itself is filled with so many swallows

Flying all about[c] and making such rustling sounds
And plaintive murmurs,[d] that no one saying something
Can be heard by those that stand beside him.
He, bothered by such great chatterers, said: "Sisters,
You have said your say and it is quite enough for now;

It is now my turn, so you give ear to what I have to say. Ps 78:1
Nor should I presume to order you about like this,
But that you ought to be moved by reverence for your Maker
Whose holy praises I am announcing to the people." Ps 51:17
His admonition finished,[e] all of them kept silence

And remained in their places nor dared make a stir
Until he had said the last word of his sermon. Dn 4:30
Those present, staring at the spectacle, say among

a. Cf. Ovid, *Metamorphoses* IV 717.
b. 1C 59: "one day" not on the same journey.
c. Cf. Vergil, *Georgics* I 377.
d. Cf. Ovid, *Metamorphoses* XI 734-5.
e. Ovid, *Metamorphoses* II 103.

Themselves: "This man is a saint, we ought to revere him;
His word has authority; why, even a flock

Of winged creatures dares not ignore his orders." 1C 58, 28
Thence[a] he makes his way to Greccio,
a town named after Greece.[b] 1C 60
Welcomed there and during his stay by chance
A live leveret was given him: it had been caught
Not by a coursing hound, but by means of a treacherous snare.

With pity for it he says: "Why, little Brother Hare,
Did you get yourself shackled like that, and you so fleet
A fellow? Why didn't you fly and not get trapped by that vile
Hunter, who tricked you with his net? The examples
Of many should have taught you to be cautious,

And the lesson is: 'Once bitten, twice shy.'
Now let your own experience make you more careful."[c]
Having said this first, he calls it to him. And with that
It takes refuge in his bosom and, feeling completely at home,[d] 1C 60
Even though it was at liberty to go where it liked,

Now freed of its bonds it takes not to the open field,
But goes back to the covert, and would lief return
In servitude to Francis, rather than run away free.
Thus was it that the holy man's remarkable mildness
Brought both bird and quadruped a similar mildness.

Nor did his fervent kindness stop at restoring the birds 1C 61
To the air, or the beasts to the woods, but put back
The fish in the water. For "beyond belief"[e] and marvellous
To relate is what happened the time a kindly fisherman
Presented him with a big fish. Taking it more gratefully

Than if it were gold, and calling it his brother, he said:
Ps 30:10 "Your blood, Brother, could profit me little. Far be it
From me, then, that I should enjoy a moment's tasty pleasure

a. The place can be attributed to poetic license; the source reads: "at one time."

b. An etymological word-play on *castrum Graecium*.

c. The Saint gave this warning not to the hare, but to fish; cf. 1C 61. The warning is omitted in v. 55.

d. In 1C 60 said of a rabbit.

e. Ovid, *Fasti*, II, 113; *Metamorphoses* XIV 406.

By depriving you of the enjoyment of a long life.
Go back free and unharmed to your ancestral home."

With that, he threw it back out into the safety of the waters.[a]
Although it had suffered loss of liberty
And had feared for its life, it comes out nonetheless unafraid
From the deep recesses of the river; it plays on the edge
Before its rescuer, and never minds

Being approached or touched: such great trust
Derives from the experience of kindness. Nor does it give up
Its playing until Francis at length bids it be off.
And not daring to ignore the command,
It hides its silvery form[b] far in the flowing stream.

On leaving there Francis is forced to take to bed
With a serious bout of sickness. But so to provide
For his servant a medicine, Christ's clemency changes
Water to wine. A draught of this
By its sweet taste upon palate and its boosting of natural

Warmth, all the malady's causes eliminates.
1C 62 The grace of God is a cure not only for Francis,
But through him bestows a double healing on many.
On his way through the lands, the farms, the cities,
He is entering the city called Ascoli, when all

The sick come to him; and a struggle there is
To see if they can touch even the hem of his garments. Mt 14:36
1C 63 For they regard his very garments as relics,
And they so tear them off him that he goes around
In tatters. And they offer him loaves which he blesses;

A crumb of which, seasoned with faith, mitigates pains,
Alleviates ailments and brings riddance to injuries.
A woman of Arezzo laboring in childbirth,
Has for ages to the saints been praying and none of her pleas
Have been answered. Nor is she aided by herbs,

a. Cf. Ovid, *Fasti* II 111.
b. Ovid, *Metamorphoses* X 735; XI 500.

Precious stones, or incantations.[a] Oft but in vain
Has she tried the various cures of skillful physicians.
And now she lies lifeless and like one that senses
The hand of Fate cutting the threads of her hope.[b]
Over the bed of the dying woman friends place reins:

Since they were reins Francis, riding in the region, had handled,
They credit what they had in them something of power.
At once the woman gives birth: the imprisoned fetus
Breaks its bars, and issues from the womb's dark chamber.
Likewise with regard to a rope Francis,
from the Order's beginnings 1C 64

Used to wear as a belt,[c] one Walfried had, who lived
In Città della Pieve: guilty he'd feel to hold on
To that sacred possession if he didn't oft place it
Upon the persons of women that were sick,
For by mere contact with it much solace did they derive.[d]

There is report from Toscanella, evidence from Narni, 1C 65-67
An account from Gubbio: of a sick weakling child,
Of a color-blind woman and a paralytic man;
Of a woman both of whose hands were crooked
From a contraction inflaming the finger sinews,

Allowing her to do no manual work whatever.
The kind support of Francis brought it all to an end,
Curing by brief word and brief touch longstanding ailments.
A terrible affliction troubled a certain friar: 1C 68
Mk 9:19 Often he foamed at the mouth, writhing, and torn;

It ripped and disjointed his limbs, making his mouth
Twist and gape. Now it bundles him up, again
It stretches him out; he turns savage with a furious
Roll of the eyes,[e] and frightens bystanders with menacing
Shouts. In his suffering, the right hand of Francis makes 1C 69

a. Ovid, *Metamorphoses* X 397 on incantations; concerning the powerful force of gems for healing, cf. Marbodus, Bishop of Rennes (dies 1123), *Liber lapidum or Carmen de gemmis* (PL 171, 1737-60).

b. Cf. Ovid, *Metamorphoses* VIII 453.

c. See above, V. 12, 36, 39.

d. Henri wrongly interprets his source, 1C 64.

e. Cf. Ovid, *Metamorphoses* V 241; VII 579.

The exorcizing sign of the cross and blesses him.
Such holy exorcisms by such a holy one the devil cannot bear,
So that, seeing the divine emblem, he comes out sad,
Never, once thrown out, to return to his resting-place.
1C 62 While[a] the saint thus wiped out the furies of the ancient foe
And everything that stood against human salvation,
His zeal takes root in the souls of thirty men
Who follow after his banner in the spiritual warfare.
1C 69 Entertained in the faithful city of San Gemino,
His host came knocking on his door with earnest pleas
That he might deign with his holy prayers to come to the help
Of his poor wife who for long had been possessed by a fiend.
He hears the enticing prayers[b] of the honest pleader
And, calling three brothers, says: "No corner is to be
Unoccupied; each of you three take a corner, I will stand
In the fourth. Let the cross we thus form[c]
Be a sort of obstacle device, to prevent that evil spirit
From thinking he can escape from our hands."
Having arranged things accordingly, "What, wicked demon?"
He cries, "Are you pretending or do you not know that bodies
Baptized for God only must let him reside in them?
Therefore, come out, you that are an unclean spirit; Mk 9:24
Under penalty I command you, devil, never to dare
Lay claim in your madness to godly bodies."
As he flung him these threats and promised him a lashing,
So suddenly and as though by stealth did the demon depart
That Francis thought he had tricked him and the woman
Hadn't recovered. But in fact there was a happy ending:
Any of his utterances were not to have been made in vain;
For after a not very long time had passed, he happened
To be heading once more to the place, though not the house,
When by chance he saw her. In possession of senses

---

a. Henri transferred these verses from 1C 62.

b. Cf. Ovid, *Metamorphoses*, X 642; Heroides III 30.

c. Francis and the friars forming an X, or sign of the Tau or the Cross, is the poet's ingenious and not improbable explanation of 1C 69. Perhaps Henri also had in mind the rhetorical figure called "chiasm" named from the letter X.

And reason, she gives thanks for her full health
In her devotion to one she'd not known; and is clear
In her telling of his making the demon depart

And how it dared not return after his forbidding it.[a]
Città di Castello was next to warmly welcome him 1C 70
Who far and wide performed mighty acts of healing.
They plead with him for an obsessed woman whose loud
Screams and horrible sounds disturbed the peace of the people.

He sends a friar on ahead of him to investigate with all
Care if it is by volition or compulsion, if it be
By a confusing human or devilish the city is being upset.
He complies with the orders he is given, and comes
To probe the occurrence. But the obsessed when she sees

The one coming isn't Francis, jeers at him,
And sticks out her tongue, and wrinkles her nostrils,
And with twisted mouth starts making various spookish
Faces, and gives the thumb-between-fingers sign.[b]
He goes away as though baffled, and tells all about

The jeering of the obsessed woman that he'd endured.
Francis approaches her. Both the demon inside
Est 7:6 And the woman possessed cannot bear to look at his face;
Mk 9:19 It was on the ground she was, writhing. A word
Of command from him has the woman on her feet, unpossessed.

The demon thrust out departs, and makes no venture to return.
Jn 11:47 As he is in such wise driving the Furies away, performing 1C 72
Mk 6:13; Jb 12:21 Signs round the world, healing sick, relieving the burdened,
Francis the preacher is wont to explain all things[c]
With sure method, to be constant and steadfast,

Wis 8:12 To scorn no one's face, nor any fear.
Why, in his eyes a thousand potentates are no more
Than a single pauper; or a thousand experts than a simple soul.
He minds not that it is to one he must preach
Or to many; he works at a sermon intended for one

---

a. Henri here neglects Elias and his intervention.

b. Still a vulgar and filthy gesture of disrespect and derision.

c. Henri skips over 1C 71 and 72 and continues from there.

As he would if for many; and is as spontaneous before many
As he'd be before one.[a] And yet, his attentive eloquence
Is not uniform for all; no, to the unschooled his instruction
Isn't the same as his word of advice to the learned:
For the unschooled some common practices apt to invigorate

The mores of men; followed by something on vices, something
On virtue, the Lives of the Fathers too,[b] together with
Positive proofs of life after death for the holy; of Christ's
Miracles, deeds and commands, of the torture-marked courage
Of the Saints that earned them their crown;

Of just acts and wrongdoing and what they consist in; and of
What punishment awaits the guilty, what rewards the just.
But then, from these twenty-four means,[c] developed further
By repeated teaching, deeper reflection and sharper
Perception, he weaves one art of living.

He also shows what links the virtues together,
And the order of descent of them all from the principal four;[d]
How hard it is to find the golden mean,[e] how the slippery paths Prv 15:24
Of life and, though with what effort, extremes can be shunned.

---

a. Verses 181-98 are to be attributed to Henri's rhetorical and poetic expansion.

b. The *Lives of the Fathers*, namely of ancient monks and hermits, which were much read at that time (PL 73 & 74).

c. This number, like others, is arbitrary; see above, VII, 159; VIII, 23 and 59. Concerning the variety of arts, cf. Hugo of Saint Victor, *Eruditio didascalica* II 7ff. (PL 176, 751-65); III, 1, where the computation is of 21, or if ranked, 38.

d. See above the note on II, 13. In addition, v.g. Isidore, *Sententiae* II, 32-44 (PL 83, 634-54); the work entitled *De conflictu vitiorum et virtutum*, among the spurious works of Isidore (PL 83, 1131-44), now attributed to Ambrosius Autpertus.

e. Cf. the axion *in medio stat virtus* founded in Aristotle, *Ethica Nicomachea* II, 8; see also Ibid., II, 6 and *Ethica Eudaemonica* II, 3 and 5. Ovid *Metamorphoses* II, 137: *medio tutissimus ibis* Horatius, *Satire* I, I, 106-7.

The Tenth Book

THE EFFECT OF HIS SPEAKING UPON WISE MEN AND POPE;
HIS PREDICTION CONCERNING A FUTURE POPE, HIS
LIGHTENING THE LOADS OF THE BURDENED, HIS PITY
FOR A SHEEP, AND HIS RESCUE OF SOME PITIABLE LAMBS.

NAME brought him renown, but every virtue still more, 1C 73
The man who in those days was holy father to the City
Of Rome and to the world: that pinnacle of honesty
And honor, Honorius.[a] To him Francis comes, bidden to preach

Upon a theme. Though he must speak before so many
Of the purpled brethren[b] and the reverend Father,[c] he consults
None of the textual masters, opens up no volumes, nor his own
Mental resources. Instead, pouring forth at once with never
A break, and aptly forming them into sentences,

Delivers each single one of his choicest thoughts.
And also making use of rhetorical gesture he involves
Not only his tongue but his total body in speaking.[d] 1C 97
With inclinations and signals, his external motions keep pace
With those of his mind, each articular move expressive

Of his articulate skill. Lest his peculiarly elegant discourse
Lose flow, wander off course, in among his own words
He plants, like flowers in grass, sayings from the ancients.
  And to create coherence between what's from himself and what
He brings in, he unlocks prophetic mysteries, explores

The fathomless depths of law and Scripture, as well as
The finer points of faith, the profundity of the Gospel,

---

a. Another example of the poet's often apt and elegant play on proper names. Honorius III was Pope 1216-1227.

b. Henri, writing at the Roman Curia, refers to Cardinals in his poem as "the brethren," the manner in which the Pope himself addressed them (see also line 25). To distinguish them from "the friars" which *fratres* elsewhere in the poem means, we adopt the terms "the purpled brethren" for Cardinals.

c. From 1C 74.

d. In 1C 97 it says, "Of his whole body he made a tongue." Cf. Jerome, *Epistolae* 108 (al. 27) in PL 22, 878; 1 Cor 12:14-23.

And the world of God's own hidden secrets.
His sermon goes down so well with the audience
That he to whom it meant more admired him all the more.

The purpled brethren to a man are in awe of him;[a] so too
Is the Pope; who all have their silent question: What spirit Mt 10:20
Is it speaks through the lips of this layman? It is their
Devoted listening that is vocal; for lips are silent, faces
Fixed,[b] it is their hearts that are moved; understanding

Is alive, senses are stilled and, as they lift the eyes
Of their thought, they gaze on the face of an angel!
1C 74 The bitter foe, however, is not far off, with calumny
Instead of praise.[c] But Ostia's bishop, the lord Hugolino,
Is Francis's shield, and heaven-sent grace

Made him promoter of the holy man's plans.
He now extols his virtues, vindicates what he says,
And with his personal authority restrains all detractors.
Francis had known him for a while and obtained first place
In his heart as a father when, on his way to the people

Of France, he had to increase the brothers minor in number.[d]
When Florence was host to our footsore traveler,[e]
He learned that that bishop was there as Legate,
And went to see him. And he receives him with fatherly
Welcome—star that he was, flower, splendor and jewel:

Star of probity, flower of rectitude, splendor of clerics,
Jewel among priests. He asked him where he was headed
And to what purpose; and since to go beyond the Alps was his aim,
He persuaded him to return, and ordered him to visit the brothers.
Then they commended themselves to each other's prayers.

From that moment they were joined in an unbreakable bond,
A bond of friendship that had the strongest knot in the

---

a. Ovid, *Fasti* V. 275.

b. *Ibid.*, IV, 317-8.

c. Notice that 1C 74 said the same more at length and more specifically.

d. The notions that Francis had had long acquaintance with Hugolino and that he had expansionist ideas concerning the Order as such, are the poet's own.

e. *Pedes* means "footsoldier" or "walker." It is translated as "footsore traveler" to honor the "military" tone of the poem as a whole.

World; no two were ever more powerfully united.[a]
To the holy the holy are known and the true know who to trust; 1C 75
To this great priest's guardianship Francis commits

Lk 10:34 The care of all the Order and the brothers.
He took the onus on, and never made a single slip.
Great the need that lay in store for him,[b]
Often would Francis say, as with prophetic utterance
He would call him "Bishop of the Whole World."

What he said proves now to be true: he who then was Hugolino
Now is Gregory; head of one city was he then,
Now head of the wide world, where the Order of Minors thrives.
Well did he merit the honors reserved for the great, 1C 76
Since his gracious devotion respected them that were little!

Ps 10:8; 111:4 God who is just, in secret rewards each one for his acts;
And he is deserving of reward all the greater
Who offers himself to those that are lesser.
Now, his compassion was beyond measure.
For after he'd given away everything, with no means left

With which to satisfy his own desires, he is bold enough
To shame his own head with modest mien
Begging from the rich to give to the needy.
And not alone does he feed them, but pays them respect,
And forbids all talk that would cause them annoyance.

No one must dare hurt Christ's little ones with ranting words:
He corrected one friar for this and in him he corrected us all.
He, seeing a man without means, said: "Make sure, my dear man,
You're not feigning poverty." Francis when he hears him
Say it, bids him beg forgiveness for the remark,

Naked and prostrate at the feet of the poor man.
Reverence for the poor to Francis meant that anything said
Of a pauper was scandal uttered against Christ.
And if he saw anyone carrying stones or timber
Or with some other load that was difficult to bear,

a. Thomas of Celano treats these matters at greater length especially in 1C 100 and 101. Recall that this Legend in meter was dedicated to Gregory IX. Cf. above, I, 21-25.

b. Ovid, *Epistulae ex Ponto* II, VIII, 11.

He would put it on his shoulders, which were far from robust,
Sooner be laden himself than overburden the pauper.
1C 77 His devotion was such that the dishonored are honored,
The burdened relieved; he would pity not alone humans
But even dumb beasts in any wretched condition.

So, while in the Ancona region, accompanied
By Paul who was over the brothers in those parts,
He is going through woods and over rivers, ravines and fields,
Till in a flock of she-goats, surrounded by ill-smelling
He-goats, he spies this sheep, and calling Paul, says:

"Paul, look; do you see how it walks among she- and he-goats?
Even so did Jesus go among the scribes and Pharisees.
Hence I wish we'd pay the price and lead her out
1C 78 Of this foul flock." Paul agrees. But the pair
Can lay their hands on nothing whatever to pay

With, save their poor tunics. But then a traveler
Who happened to pass paid the price of the sheep they want to buy.
Into the city they go: a surprise for the bishop:
As to why two sensible men like these should want
To go around like two fools, a sheep behind them.

After leaving the city, a hospitable house, called
San Severino, received them; it is an abode fit for those
Ladies that dedicate to God their chaste bodies and gracious
Souls. Francis gives them the sheep to be tenderly cared for.
All joy to accept it, they keep it for a long spell;

And a tunic made from its wool they send on to Francis.
At a chapter held in Assisi, a minister comes in to say:
"Father, you are to have this, it is from your daughters;
A tunic made from the wool of that sheep you had."
Francis takes it as a most acceptable present, telling

The brothers of what happened. Happy are the brothers
That the very simplicity of their father resulted in such great fruit.
1C 79 Nor was this once the only case of Francis's piety:
He shows it every time he sees a wretched animal
Whose pain he might dispel through prayer or payment.

From countless examples I choose but one:[a]
Once again we find him in the company of the aforesaid friar
In the same Marches of Ancona, where he meets a man
Carrying two small lambs; they are hanging downwards
By their weight, tough shackles binding the tender little

Feet, and are opening their mouths[b] in that piteous bleating[c]
Nature gave them, the cry of pain in every sound they make.
Francis, seeing their dreadful state and fearing the worst
Of fates for them, asks the man that was carrying them
Why he should be inflicting hurt on the poor things.

He replies: "I'm off to the market and I'll sell them
To the butcher for slaughter." "Don't do that," cries Francis,
"But be mild with mild creatures, do no harm to the harmless.
If you're willing to spare them, whatever your bidder would
Give you to kill them, I'll give you as much so they'll not

Have to die." It was his kindly devotion praying for lambs
In misery. And so as not to waste his words on the air,
Taking off his cloak he gives it to the countryman,
With strict instructions and asking for solemn promises[d]
Mk 5:4 That he release the lambs from bonds and give them a rearing.

a. Cf. Ovid, *Epistulae ex Ponto* II, III, 11. The number is obviously exaggerated.

b. Cf. Ovid, *Metamorphoses* VII 190.

c. Ovid, *Heroides* XIX 107.

d. In the source, only "he commanded that . . ."

The Eleventh Book

How he would exhort all things to praise God and call them his brethren. What his human appearance was like. How he celebrated the feast of Christ's birth represented with special figures.

1C 80 Of virtues best, piety, is infused in his fair soul
In such wise that he brings all help to pitiable creatures,
Permitting cruel treatment none, any savage attack
Preventing, dreading the very thought of bloodshed.

Simple he is no less than clement; it is as though
He emitted a fragrant amber resin,[a] a mixture
Of two elements: clement simplicity, simple clemency.
With these for wings, high he soars,[b] above the lofty stars,
Yet beneath his own self, every created thing companioning,

Leading, tutoring to climb to where true bliss lies.
Regarding things beneath him with comrade courtesy,
In the manner of Ananias, Azarias and Mizael, and conferring
The name of brother on each of the creatures,[c]
He addresses them in dulcet tones and eagerly invites them

To proclaim the praises of the Highest Good: the heavens Dn 3:59ff
And stars, sun and moon, darkness and light, seasons and years,
Shower-bearing clouds and the many-splendored rainbow,[d]
The thunder and the lightning, the storm-clouds
And rains, the winds and winter weather, the cold and heat;

And atmosphere, circling round the world's center,
Reaching to the vault of heaven, freshening all
With its moistening, itself refreshed by all things else;

---

a. Ovid, *Metamorphoses* II 363-6.

b. Vergil, *Aeneid* X 664.

c. In verses 14-39 Henri freely paraphrases that *Canticle of the Three Youths* more at length than in Thomas of Celano's offhand citation in 1C 80. The poet nowhere makes specific mention of the *Canticle of the Creatures*. See below, XIII, 109-12. The "name of brother" in v. 13 is taken from 1C 81; the names are not found in the *Canticle of the Three Youths*.

d. Cf. Ovid, *Metamorphoses* XIV 830-51; Aristotle, *Meteorolgica* III, II, 4.

Then the winged kind[a] and every species of bird; 1C 77
The land-encircling sea, under the secret stir of the moon,

And at nature's pivot creating the whirlpool;
The scale-bearing fish and the swimming shellfish shoals,
And the poised land masses, anchored far and wide,[b] 1C 81
That heaven's courtesy keeps harnessed at fair distance;
Mountains, too, and valleys, plains and meadows, metals

And stones, and the sands that are beyond all number;
Springs and rivers, flowers and grasses, woods
And cornfields, gardens and vineyards, and a kind
Yet nobler than all of these, and, beneath it,
Gn 1:20, 21 The numberless creeping species, and another more energetic

Than those, the quadrupeds, some tame, some wild;
Then the human race, on which all the rest attend;
Next, distinguished in its ninefold rank, the noble host
Of heaven; and all of nature's works he calls to raise
Their eager praise to God Who first caused things to be.

Nor does he revere solely what nature made, but also things 1C 82
Wrought by skillful hands: for writings, wherever found, he
Shows the greatest honor, and ones cast aside puts in a proper
Place. And if perchance sometime an extra letter be written in,
His simple reverence for written words was such

That he would not suffer it to be deleted.
The verses above paint you a picture of Francis; 1C 83
But lest a foggier image of him stay in your mind than that
Which you'd rather remember, here is a bodily portrait:[c]
Of medium height, though closer to shortness,

Was Francis; but his frame held the heart of a giant.
Black in color, pliant in texture was his hair,
His head sat straight and was round, upward and short his ears,[d]

---

a. Cf. Vergil, *Aeneid* IXX 249.

b. Cf. Ovid, *Metamorphoses* I 13.

c. From 1C 83 with the sections inverted.

d. In 1C 83: "moderate (in size) and round." Nothing in Thomas of Celano's text suggests that his head was "erect, straight" whatever that might indicate. In 1C 83 has "upright (*erectae*) ears" while Henri has "lifted, raised (*subvectas*)." Perhaps in v. 61 ("upright" again) Henri has in mind Ovid, *Metamorphoses* I 86: "to raise upright looks to the stars."

His temples were deep and flexuous,[a] his forehead
Was small and smooth, shallow and linear the arc of his brows,

The pupils of his eyes were dark and attentive,[b] like
Quiet and lambent torches; cheerful and pleasant was his
Countenance,[c] his nose-line natural and unbent, his cheeks
Were hollow and lean,[d] his lips thin and of moderate size,
Set closely together were his snow-white[e] teeth,

Black was his beard but sparse, his throat drooping and gaunt;[f]
His deep shoulders were on an upright neck,[g]
Small were his arms, thin his hands, slender his legs,
His feet were little, while his fingers and toes were long;[h]
And as for his flesh, it was enclosed in the roughest of garb.

That was to think of appearance; now you should look at his
Character:[i] in mentality he was suppliant and simple, in body
Chaste and celibate, in both he was clear and pure; as to
Things above he was rich and noble, poor and lowly in things
Of earth. His waking hours meant thirst and fast, his resting

Hours meant prayer and vigil, he battled on through both heat
And cold.[j] Dear and true was his affection, his heart benign[k]
And thoughtful, he was ever ready and eager to help;
His perception was sharp and agile, well-expressed was his
Speech and lively, warm and keen was his temperament,

Compassionate and lenient to everyone,[l] on himself he was harsh
And austere. He was clever and shrewd in things he said,
1C 83 Foreseeing and wise in things he did; in coming to decisions
Deep-browed and serious, he was swift and prompt with pardon;

a. Here the poet rather disfigures the image, since 1C 83 has "smooth forehead."
b. 1C 83 has "moderate eyes, black and simple." Cf. 1C 83: "circumspect in choosing."
c. 1C 83 has "his face a bit long and prominent;" Henri is less accurate, but embellishes the picture.
d. Thomas of Celano nowhere notes this feature. Henri drew his description from the "oblong face" of Thomas of Celano (note 12 above), or from another passage of 1C 83: "very spare flesh," from the traditional look of ascetics.
e. This adjective Henri borrowed from Ovid, *Heroides* XVIII 18.
f. That is, like the drooping of cut flowers; Thomas of Celano writes of a "slender neck." Cf. 1C 83.
g. In Thomas of Celano, Francis has "straight shoulders." Cf. 1C 83.
h. Cf. Ovid, *Metamorphoses* VII 77. Thomas of Celano does not mention toes.
i. In 1C 83.
j. Cf. Horatius, *Ars poetica*, 413.
k. The same adjective is found elsewhere in 1C 83.
l. Cf. Ovid, *Tristia* III, XI, 20.

Slow and cool when it came to anger, he adapted with prudence to every case.

Perhaps you think it futile to depict the features and temper
Of a holy man. But it was only right to describe them,
For thereby good reasons and a useful purpose are served.
The rather complete description which fills a few verses
Contains the Francis of my reflections or the image I have
Of him. Moreover, it deposits in the mind ideas of a
Partly similar kind, even if not exactly the same.[a]
Monstrous foes by now long tamed, a world plowed underfoot, 1C 84
Francis's flaming valor still fights for the stars, no mortal
Thing draws his heart. The mysteries of Christ are ever
Enough for his meditation: the Word incarnate
And the heart-stirring passion of his nature assumed,
He never allows himself to forget; these sear the core
Of his heart and make it catch fire with desire for heaven.
It gives him joy to present these mysteries in appropriate
Figures, and share out his pleasure to other people.
Again, one time wishing to celebrate the Birth of Christ, 1C 84; 1C 85
He orders a manger made. An ox and an ass draw in hay
For their fodder; and things are provided whereby to
Becomingly represent the mysteries of the virginal birth.
The people that gather for the holy festivities fill
The church, bring candles and torches, while incense breathes
Forth its scent. After matins, the Mass of the Feast
Is celebrated. •Francis it is who reads the Gospel •1C 86
In sweet-toned melody; and then when the people are seated,
Jn 12:40 He gives them a sermon, and softens hearts that were hardened
And out of hard rock causes rivers to flow.
There leaps forth a compunction mixed with gladness; clapping
Of hands dries up the tears, a tear moistens the hands that clap.
All the night, till the new day dawns, passes in festive song 1C 85
And in praise of the Child that was born of the Virgin.
Accepting the mysteries celebrated in his honor, Christ, 1C 87

a. All the more because Henri, as we have had occasion to note, both uses and abuses his poetic license; cf. Horatius, *Ars poetica* 9-11.

For his part, gives rewards: eating the hay left over,
Beasts swollen by ailments are eased and cured.
Through contact with the same, women with child and those long
In labor are enabled to give birth with ease,
As their weary wombs release the children waiting to be born.
The place of the crib is now, to the joy of the people,
A little chapel dedicated in honor of the blessed Francis.

The Twelfth Book

THE TIME OF HIS DEATH IS PREDICTED,
CRUCIFIED CHERUB APPEARS, CHRIST'S PASSION,
STIRRING HIS SOUL, IS SHOWN IN HIS LIMBS,
SADLY SUFFERING WITH HIS EYES, HE RELUCTANTLY SEES A DOCTOR.

NO cessation for him in a warfare that presses hard 1C 109
The proud necks of the haughty, as he holds back injurious
Attacks, brings monsters to heel, over fifteen years and three.[a]
And once while spending the night in Foligno, purging it of

Fuliginous sin and brightening it with the fulgent word[b]
Of God, there appears to Brother Elias
This venerable priest with white hair all over his temples.[c]
On seeing him, the brother is filled with wonder. "Go,"
Says the priest, "tell Francis he must prepare for his hour:

Fate[d] stands at the door; in two years she will knock.
This is the span he has left, and no more time remains."[e]
What he was told to say Elias relates to Francis.[f]
He, giving thought to the fact that the last days of his life[g] 1C 91
Had arrived, betakes himself to a secluded place to reside

Lk 9:5; 10:11 In quiet. There he might shake from his feet earth's clinging
Dust, where Martha's ministrations would not distract
His unsullied soul, but contemplation would wholly engage it,
And where he could spend the remaining years on things above.
Mt 25:5 Sojourning there he contemplates and prays,

a. A total of 18, as stated in 1C 88 and 109.

b. The introduction of an additional "i" in *Fulgineum* (Foligno) makes possible the play with "fuliginous" (sooty, dark).

c. Cf. Ovid, *Metamorphoses* VIII 567.

d. One of the three goddesses, "the spinners of fateful threads" to the ancients. Cf. Ovid, *Tristia* V III, 25. See above, IX, 88.

e. Ovid, *Metamorphoses* VI 284.

f. See below, XIII, 83. Henri omits 1C 88-90.

g. Cf. Ovid, *Metamorphoses* XI 757-8. Not the last moments of his life, but two years before death. Cf. 1C 94.

Nothing save Christ being in his heart or on his lips.
God inspires him, as it is love that spurs him, to seek
To know what destiny may have in store for him,[a]
And which track he must take when he makes his starbound[b]
Journey. Anxious is his watch and ward. And what no human art

Could tell him, he looks for in a divine revelation.
•1C 92 •The next thing[c] he does is to place upon the altar a great
Volume containing the Gospels. He falls down in adoration,
And begs the Lord to show him what must be, on a first
Opening of the book. And when he opened up the book,

•1C 93 •The first thing offered was the passion of Jesus Christ
The Lord. Lest it be thought this occurred by accident,
Again and again he looks into the freshly opened book,
And is amazed to find the same thing happens always:
The same message, even if not always the selfsame words.

From this, man of discernment that he was, he learns Prv 11:12
That before he dies, great afflictions must come his way.
1C 94 Very probable his interpretations seem,
And the dark doubts in his heart are blotted out
By a second vision that followed. Disclosed to him in this

Is the sight of a Seraph with six wings, Is 6:2; Ez 1:6ff
His feet close together, the palms of his hands extended
On a cross, and two of the wings above his head for going
Upward, two to cover his body, and two with which he flew,
Or with which he was ready[d] and set to fly.

His gaze is fixed on the sight: the presence of such a great
One from the city beyond rejoices a future fellow-citizen.
Yet he is puzzled and is worried as he strives to think
What marvel such a vision might convey, and how it is
That a simple impassible being should wish to be seen

To undergo pain. Troubled much he is to know; but it is
In his own self he is to find the pain he queries in the

a. See above, VII, 64.

b. Vergil, *Eclogues* V 50 and 51.

c. Having nicely digested 1C 91, Henri borrows very little from 1C 92.

d. Ovid, *Epistulae ex Ponto* I VIII, 10.

Seraph. So does Jesus' passion remain implanted in his heart,
So imprinted right through the marrow of his soul,
That it cannot be hid, but must flood outwardly

And mark its likeness on his partnered flesh, 1C 95
Becoming visible, as it were, through transparent limbs.
The five wounds of the Redeemer appear impressed
In their separate places: •Hard to believe a lance •1C 95
Did not pierce that very side; and there to be seen

On hands and feet are nails, raised up over the flesh,
And the appropriate scars shown by their special marks.
Rm 6:5 For closely fitted to the pattern of the Lord's death[a] 1C 97
Is flesh of his, altogether subject to soul's command,
1 Cor 9:9; Dt. 25:4 Laboring without eating, threshing with muzzled mouth;

Scarred by hair-shirts, crushed by hard work, eaten
By little worms,[b] petrified by cold, melted by heat,
Emaciated by hunger. At length after so much combat,
Wasted by so many woes, he feels the advance of divers
Diseases, and knows his spent vigor has lost its resistance.

Those jewels that adorn the brow, those windows of the soul, 1C 98
Are shut off by cloud, distressed by a misty veil,
That is to say, an unbearable pain grieves the optic nerve.[c]
A fluid reddens the pupils,[d] and thickened eyelids derange
The vision, and irritation distorts the eye's keenness.

The very pain invites the hands, and scratching fingers
Undo the relief they bring; for noxious is that touching
And it is even aggravating to the existing harm.
Visual power by this is weakened, and as it begins to be
Often done, the inner core of the eyelids itch,

---

a. See 1C 119; see above, II, 146-7.

b. These things occur nowhere in 1C, nor do the sicknesses the Saint had at that time involve such. Henri also composed a legend in verse of Saint Thomas, Archbishop of Canterbury. The poet seems to have imported the hair shirt and worms from *Vitae S. Thomae*. Cf. John of Salisbury, *Letter on the Killing of Saint Thomas:* "the body was found to be wrapped in goat's hair full of lice and worms." (PL 199, 358); see also his *Vitae S. Thomae* in Pl 190, 59, 207, 311. This Saint Thomas's hair shirt was for a long time greatly admired by all who saw it. The hair shirt of Saint Francis is nowhere mentioned in 1C.

c. Here again (cf. above, I, 90-125; II, 181-3; V, 87-90) Henri presents himself an expert of medical arts. It is not at all apparent that his descriptions and accounts (which, for the rest, describe any sort of inflammation of the eyes) correspond to Francis's disease of the eyes.

d. See above, I, 98-9. Avicenna, *Liber Canonis* III I 1-14.

And in the eye's sevenfold skin the fluid is infected.
He is in pain worse than one might credit
A man could feel; he bears in patience all the weariness
Of his bodily frame. And lest he seem not to bear with
A divinely sent affliction, he refuses to call in doctors.

But moved with the greatest compassion for him, Brother Elias[a]
Presses him with many reasons to receive medical aid
For his bodily ills, proving from Solomon that for the sake
Of our mortal race, lest there be on earth no easement Sir 38:1
Of pain, the Most High himself it was that created

The art of healing, as well as curative herbs.
1C 99 Coaxed by the good words of Friar Elias
1C 101 He permits the doctors to come.[b] But all of them fail to bring
Any improvement. Not alone can a malady attaching to healthy
Roots not be removed by plasters, but in fact

It rages at anything adverse and rebounds
At the touch of an obstacle, like flame hid in a fresh sconce,
As it tastes liquids poured in, flaring up all the more
Briskly, leaps forth and blots out lights with a sudden puff of smoke.
Seeing that plasters did him no good, but that the very cures

Only made him worse, he yields to his comrades who urge him
1C 99 To go to Rieti. There an excellent physician was supposed
To be found; for him there sets out a sick man
Wanting healing, who himself had healed so many sick people.

a. Not surprisingly, Henri, who here greatly contracts 1C, passes over the brief praise of Elias in n. 98. Even greater omissions of this sort occur below relating to Gregory IX (XIII, 29) and to Elias (XIII, 80-83).

b. In these verses (91-6) Henri connects the last sentence of n. 98 with the first of n. 99.

The Thirteenth Book

OF NO BENEFIT TO HIM ARE ALL MEDICAL SKILLS;
CARRIED INTO THE CITY OF ASSISI, HE IS NOT AFRAID
OF THE HOUR OF DEATH, AND HE SINGS
HIS OWN FUNERAL RITES, AS HIS SWAN-SONG.[a]

UPON his entry to the city, the papal court residing 1C 99
There, greets his arrival with solemnity. All speedily
Come running; not one of them gives thought to his own
Affairs, and no matter what loss of rights of their own

They incur, to have seen Francis is gain enough.[b] There is
No bargaining one with another: this one chance is sufficient
For all.[c] Great may it have been to set eyes on two-bodied
Chiron,[d] or the bull of Minos that ravaged the Athenians,[e]
Or the lynxes of Bacchus with their all-piercing stare,[f]

Or rejuvenated Phoenix after momentary death,[g]
Or the wild boar let loose in Calydon,[h] or the Emperor's
Elephant,[i] or the wild asses whose nostrils spouted

---

a. Ancient poets reported that the swan uttered a melodious sound, the nearer to death, the sweeter the song; Ovid, *Fasti* II 109-10: "The doleful swan, pierced by an arrow, sings of harsh times played out as if in harmony"; *Metamorphoses* VII 372ff; *Heroides* VII, 1-2: " 'when the fates fly' the white swan sings in harmony." Others deny such song, e.g., Pliny, *Historia naturalis* X, 32 (al. 23).

b. There is not even a word in 1C 99 of such a gathering of people, only "the whole Roman Curia received him kindly and honorable."

c. Vergil, *Georgica* IV, 184.

d. Chiron was a Centaur, son of Saturn, Ovid, *Metamorphoses* II 630ff: "Chiron, half-man mixed with horse of golden body."

e. Minos, King of Crete, waged war on the Athenians who killed his son; seven boys and seven girls, whom the Athenians were forced to send him in place of tribute, were thrown to the Minotaur (half-man, half-bull) to be devoured. Ovid, *Metamorphoses* VI 456ff; VIII, 152ff; AA, II, 24. Of Minos it was said: "The crowds rushed and longed to know a man of such renown."

f. Lynxes, tigers and panthers were captured in India by Bacchus who yoked them to his chariot; Ovid, *Metamorphoses* III 668; IV 25; XV 413.

g. The Phoenix was a bird that arose fresh from its ashes. Ovid, *Metamorphoses* XV 393-4; 401-2.

h. The story is that Diana sent a giant boar to Calydon in western Greece to destroy crops and slaughter cattle, and the strongest men of Greece launched a famous hunt to capture and kill it. Ovid, *Metamorphoses* VIII 260ff.

i. Henri here recalls the elephant of Emperor Frederick II (1212 - 1250), which Salimbene admired in 1235. The poet makes that wonder and spectacle contemporary. Salimbene reports: "Frederick sent an elephant to Lombardy along with many camels, and with many leopards and many falcons and hawks. They passed through Parma, and I saw them with my own eyes"; *Cronica*. It appears that the same elephant of Frederick II had made an appearance in Ravenna in 1231 or 1232.

The swamp of Maeos on to hostile shores,[a]
Or all the secrets in the sea's far corners

That we in our clime are not wont to see:
How far more wondrous this man to behold
Here now—though not here, for he is totally in a realm above— Prv 8:28
And on earth to have sight of a celestial citizen.
Although he is distraught by a world of cares

The pope receives him fain, and all of the purpled
Brethren graciously bid him welcome; yet none more kindly
Than Hugo, under whom in those days flourished happy Ostia.
His was it to fill the role of bishop to the whole wide
World, and hold the leading-strings of the human race.

Such qualities of character, the utmost height of honor,
And so many more endowments, did God and nature confer
Upon one man, that he alone was recipient of
An entire world's share, and through his mediation
The fountain of religion flows forth for all.[b]

Since the aforementioned physician is unable to produce
Any remedy, everything he thought up having been tried,
·1C 105 ·Of yet another doctor there is rumor in town,
One that was practised in aiding eyes that were ailing;
Prudent he was, urbane, senior in years, and dwelt in urban

Siena.[c] To him, also, Francis goes; but none of his cures
1C 101 Will relieve the pain. Suffering instead his entire body
Pervades, and produces the symptoms that accompany death.
The liver fails, the stomach swells, and by dint of both
Ills, blood, nature's seat and food digester,[d]

Is vomited, the veins within the diaphragm being ruptured.
When news of these great woes reaches the ears of Friar

---

a. Henri knew the name of wild asses also from Scripture (see margin cit.). Cf. Vergil, *Georgica* III 409; Martial, *Epigrammatjca* XIII, 97 and 100; Pliny, *Historia naturalis* VIII, 69, 4; Isidore, *Etymologiae* XII 1, 39 (PL 82, 429-30). But he seems to have considered them a species of elephant! The swamp of Maeos is a lake in the Crimea. Cf. Ovid, *Tristia* III, XII, 3; *Epistulae ex Ponto* III, II, 59.

b. This praise of Gregory IX (vv. 23-29) is much shorter than that in 1C 99-101, even counting what Henri had borrowed in X, 33-62. The praises of the Pope are generic, as befits Henri, who was a member of the secular clergy. After this notice, he thoroughly omits 1C 102-4.

c. The doctor is said to be "urbane" and "senior" or old (*senex*) merely because he lived in the city (*in urbe*) of Siena (*Senensi*)—a play on words, not special information.

d. Concerning blood as the "seat of nature" and its feeder, cf. Aristotle, *De historia animalium* III, 19.

Elias, he hastens to visit his beloved father.
On seeing his disciple, Francis is so comforted
His spirit must find unfettered joy, and to his heart

Ps 119:32 This rejoicing lends freedom. His freed heart
Releases his spirits, and this supply of spirit checks
The malady and has a rebounding effect on his nature.
Somewhat safely thence he can manage to go to Cortona.
But then, rejoicings of soul may be impetuous emotions,

And cannot once and for all have effect on the soul.
Aware is Francis that little by little those same joys
Recede and are annihilated because the effect they had
Is ruined. Once his spirited vigor ceases, disease
Is back and nature suffers her old attacks:

His legs refuse to move, enfeebled is every sinew,
And his weak stomach now all food rejects,
And no amount of endurance alters his weakened powers.
So when for the very great sorrows his soul was bearing,
Struggling in the last agony of dying, Francis 1C 105

Lk 3:9; Mt 3:10 Is aware that the axe has been put to the roots of the tree,
Rv. 3:20 And aware of the advent of Christ knocking on the door,
He begs to be brought to Assisi, not out of love for
His native place, but in order that he might leave
This earth from the spot where he relinquished earthly things,

And make his way towards Christ whence first he clung to Christ.
Carried thither (for by now no power of movement of his own
Has he), the life that hung by so thin a thread,[a] and which he
Cannot salvage for earthly time, he saves for endless ages.
O soldier brave and vindicator invincible! 1C 93

Misfortune masters him not, for he draws energy out of
His very weakness, and that which renders him lifeless
Is that which enlivens him; for the battles he waged
Unwearied in life, more gallantly still he completes in death!
•Sprinkled with ashes, and a goatskin garb on him,[b] •1C 109

a. Cf. Ovid, *Metamorphoses* IV 178-9.

b. According to Thomas of Celano it is a "hair shirt" (*cilicium*) not a goat- (or sheep-) skin (*melote*). This latter was proper to monks and made of goat or sheep skin. Cf. Jerome, *Praefatio in Regulam Sancti Pachomii* 4 (PL 23, 64); Isidore, *Etymologiae* XIX 24, 19 (PL 82, 691).

1 C 107 And although seeing final destiny appear,
Naught dreads he who for aught mortal never craved;
Scorns he the sadness of dying, since he had but scorn Sir 37:1
For the pleasures of living.[a] Then those he loved as partners Jn 4:36; Rm 8:17
In work he prays will share also his wages on high.

And that his soul may bless them before he dies, Gn 27:4
He calls them all[b] together around him,
And through those present he sends to the absent a message
Of all that seems goodly, and prays upon both his farewell.[c]
Meanwhile as the father's sad departure approaches,

Grief runs free as for a funeral, and touches hearts 2 Chr 34:27
With emotion and to faces brings rivers of tears. Is 41:18
He, wishing not that there be cause for his friends to mourn,[d]
Says: "Why weep for me, when I for you instead Lk 23:28
Should weep? For I go back to my fatherland,

Whereas exile detains you still. After the torments I've
Been through, I rest; but you toil on. I am in the city Heb 11:13
Where I belong, but you are pilgrims still. Led through
Fire and water, I am brought relief, and a bright horizon Ps 66:12
Makes up for dangers on the way. Was not the life I lived

A death, and what but life shall my death bring? This life Mt 10:39
I have reckoned loss for Christ, who his life lost for us; 1 Jn 3:16
And payment he will kindly give me for the loss, salvation
For the ruin. Long have I fought and sighed and gone
Without food. And now at last these many struggles 2 Tm 4:7

Ended, I march on triumphant, after all the sighing
I walk in gladness, all fasting finished I go full fed.
Why should I detain you and say much more?
Wretched was I here, a pity to behold, lowest of the low,
Death's own, tired out. But summoned now to the kingdom,

---

a. Vergil, *Aeneid* XI 180.

b. Not "all," but some of whom "he wanted," according to 1C 108 and then Francis gave a special blessing to Elias and through him to all the brothers. Henri here notes neither the special blessing nor the name of Elias. Then he passes immediately to the other blessing and forgiveness given to all the brothers. See the note above to XII, 85.

c. 1C 108 has this "last farewell" directed to all the brothers. Henri passed over the means by which the dying saint was transported from Assisi to the Portiuncula (1C 108).

d. Cf. Ovid, *Metamorphoses* I 738.

A happy wretch is on his way, a sad one heads for gladness,
The lowest of creatures reaches stars; marked for death,
He shall seize on life, a tired one takes his leisure.
Rm 8:17 So let no one be my friend, I pray, that pities me;
1 Cor 13:6 It is joy he must share with me. Rejoice with me

For I am called from pain to pleasure, a prisoner in a mundane
Cell to liberty celestial. As a finishing touch to my work
For Christ so gracious, sing ye a song of joy,[a]
And hymn your praises on my behalf."[b]
He said his say. The brothers about begin the psalms.

And now, while they continue singing, he sings himself,
Though dying, and with what voice he has, breaks into
Ps 142:2 This psalm: "With all my voice I cry to the Lord."
•Next he asks for this Gospel reading: Jesus was certain 1C 110
Jn 13:1 Before the day of Passover that his hour had come

When he should pass to the kingdom of the Father
From the prison of the world and the rest.
On this instruction, the minister brings the book, opens it,
And amidst the various lessons in the big volume
This is the one that first appears.

---

a. Ovid, *Epistulae ex Ponto* III, IV, 46.

b. We find this prayer somewhat less than marvelous. It consists of more hackneyed contrasts than one near to death would ever be able to gather, even if he were a poet, as Francis was. But the genius of his hero escaped Henri. Even the allusion to CtC contained in 1C 109 moved him not at all.

The Fourteenth Book

FINALLY, THE DEATH WITH WHICH HE CLOSED
HIS LAST DAY, THE MARKS ON HIS FLESH,
THE HONORS HE WAS RAISED TO AND BY WHOM,
HOW HE CAME TO LIVE HAPPY WITH CHRIST FOREVER.

SOARS that hale spirit now to skies above,
For weighty woes no longer hold it here.[a]
And passing by Lethe, no draught of oblivion shall it taste,[b]
But equal and free, its starry abode revisit and paternal
Home, to take up on high one day its partnered flesh.
Marvel at the contrasts in these events![c] The same that lies
On earth takes his stand amongst the stars; just now
He sleeps, but wakes to live for ever there; death claims
Him here, life there; here dies he in time, alive is he
There for an endless age; not really human here, nor spirit;
A spirit human is he there, a human of the spirit, a saint
In realms both. Here his mark was of one accurst,
But kindly consecration there.[d]
1C 114-115 All present observe the signs that show the death of Christ,
1C 114 As they look at five wounds rose-red with blood
In the flesh of the blessed Francis:
The feet and the palms with the nails, the right side
As with a lance transfixed, as on a cross
The body spread. And the passion of Jesus had left
1C 112; 114 Every mark, entirely present here in this man.
O new and marvellous thing! Who heard tell of it ever before?
Who, beside Francis, in actual parts of the body

a. Cf. Vergil, *Aeneid* VI 128; Ovid, *Metamorphoses* III 101.

b. Lethe is the river of Hades; cf. Vergil, *Aeneid* VI 703ff., where he says the dead "drink of untroubled waters and prolonged forgetfulness." Cf. Ovid, *Metamorphoses* XI 603; see above, II 174; III 26.

c. At this point Henri intends only distantly to follow the unfolding of events in 1C 111 and 114.

d. *Almus* is said to be the title Francis enjoys in heaven. The word means "kind" or "beneficent" and is frequent in Christian hymnody in the invocation of Saints. Cf. 1C 111 *almitas gloriosa*. *Sacer* is taken in its sense of "accurst" to respect the contrast in this passage. "Kindly consecration" renders *dicitur almus*.

Bore five wounds in the image of Christ in his dying?
On many, to be sure, was the Lord's death laden; in him 1C 116-118
It was bred in the bone. Many were forced to carry the cross;
He bore it so in his soul, cherished it in his heart,
So eagerly made it his own, that what was revealed
And printed on his very flesh was a deep secret of soul.
People convene, as do the brothers hasten out of all parts 1C 116-118
To their father's laying to rest. And he is buried
In Assisi, in the church called Saint George:[a]
There he is honored with a tomb of pure stone.[b]
Mt 11:5 At his sacred tomb[c] time and again are lepers
Cleansed, the sick recover, dead bodies arise,
Shaking paralysis from many departs, as do
The swelling of dropsy and the flaring fever,
Lethargy's cramping cold epileptical shiver.
The blind and the lame and the deaf and the mute
Lie down at his grave. There it is normal for blind
To see cripples leap, for deaf to hear dumb people speak.
Pope Gregory the Ninth hears tell of these wonders, 1C 121
And witnesses prove what he hears, as repute acclaims
What is proven. •To Assisi he comes with his purpled •1C 123-124
Brethren,[d] and there are not enough rooms for the crowds
That foregather; the very fields can't contain such
Thousands of folk. There are nobles and counts there
And dukes, and even royalty takes its place. Dense
Is the throng of abbots and pontiffs: every rank
In the Church flocks to that head whom the clergy admire,
Gregory, that is, as he pours out the wine of his heaven-born words.
Sir 50:6-7 He took for his theme: As the star of morning gives forth 1C 125
Splendor in the midst of a cloud, as a full moon

a. Saint George's is not named in 1C 116; 118 but is named in *The Legend for Use in the Choir* 13.

b. Nowhere in 1C is the material of the tomb mentioned. *The Legend for Use in the Choir* 13 says "a stone coffin."

c. In verses 33-40 Henri recounts the miracles of 1C 127-50 only by the type of miracle.

d. Here *fratres* again means "Cardinals." See above, XIII, 20-21.

In his days, like the sun in its brilliance, even so did he
Shine in the Lord's temple. To the end a true saying 1 Tm 1:15
It was, a penetrating sword-like sermon, kindling men's
Hearts like flame, like honey filling the innermost core.
The miracles, which were wrought by Christ to bring Francis
Honor, and with which he wished to highlight his everlasting
Name, are read in clear tone by Octavian for the common
Benefit. More profuse is the speech by lord Rayner.[a]
The latter in years mature, the former in nature, and lower
In rank as prelate; plainly the latter was senior as prelate.
The former, though junior in age, came of lineage nobler.
1C 126 The holy father spoke with heart broken and voice serene: Ps 109:17
"To the praise of the Trinity, of Christ and of Mary,
His Mother, and of Saints Peter and Paul, it is our duty
To canonize on earth the blessed father Francis
Whom Christ already glorified in the realm above."
It was a case of a holy father having the sole right
To inscribe a holy father in the list of the Saints.
Let us illustrate more clearly his quality and stature
Among apostolic pontiffs.[b] This man is a fiery-red gem,
A laurel, a vine, or a balsam-tree. The others
Were crystal or myrtle or wild-vine or olive.
Amongst them then he is like a gem amid crystals,
A laurel in a grove of myrtles, like a true vine Is 5:2,4
Amid wild vine, a balsam-tree amid olives. Sir 24:20
Right was it that such a great father
Should canonize such a great father: one that had learnt
What rewards after death
Were owing to his merits in life; one that revered
Him when living, and when buried should honor him still.
And so, that mirror of ancestral magnitude, chief
Of the Minors, though minor on earth, his standing is major Lk 9:48

a. Octavianus Ubaldi was the Pope's subdeacon and was made a Cardinal in 1244 (died 1273). Rainerio Capocci was made a Cardinal in 1216 and died in 1250.

b. "The Apostolics" was the title by which the Roman Pontiffs were known at the time. In the Prologue of his *Vita Oswaldi* the poet eulogized Martin de Ramsey, Abbot of Peterborough in England, in a similar vein: "Martin, flower of the clergy . . . who are to Abbots what your patron is among Pontiffs . . . The sun among stars, the flower among grasses . . ."

2 Cor 6:10 Above. Here of his own he had nothing, now he possesses all.
He that was scorned by worldlings and in his turn spurned
The mundane, now traverses as victor celestial space,
Rv 2:17; 10:9 Where he feeds on honey and manna and is crowned with jewels
And gold.[a] He thrives on delights and on praise; hale

And happy is he and blest with repose. May we to his company
Be led by Christ, to whom with the Father and Holy Spirit
Is 2:10; Sir 41:16 Be majesty and glory, both now and forever.

Amen.

a. Cf. Ovid, *Epistulae ex Ponto* III, IV, 103.

THE SACRED EXCHANGE

BETWEEN

SAINT FRANCIS AND LADY POVERTY

(1237–1239)

Introduction

The Sacred Exchange between Saint Francis and Lady Poverty[1] is one of the richest texts of the early Franciscan movement, "the single most brilliant example of the simple but lapidary allegory which was to become a major mode of spiritual writing in the later Middle Ages."[2] An allegory offering insights into Francis's vision of poverty, the *Sacred Exchange* weaves a luxuriant tapestry of images held together by the strong threads of a biblical theology. For all of its richness, however, no text of these first hundred and fifty years is more mysterious. Like the weaver of an undated tapestry, the author of the *Sacred Exchange* is content to hide obscurely making sure that the ends and threads are in their proper place that the beauty and exactness of his work may be seen. Although there are many names suggested, the author of the *Sacred Exchange* still remains unknown. The same holds true for the date of its composition.

The allegory is an exhortation written to encourage Francis's followers to live in an authentic way the saint's biblical vision of poverty. The central figure of the work is Lady Poverty, the personification of biblical Wisdom and, at times, of the Church. Much of its content is taken up with her story, one that she weaves together with that of salvation history to secure the confidence of those desiring her embrace.[3] Lady Poverty's narrative becomes a critique of the practice of poverty (a) in the history of monasticism and (b) in the brief history of the friars themselves. And many of its insights echo similar exhortations and cautions of ancient or newly found religious movements struggling to live the Gospel ideal of poverty.[4]

Examination of early manuscripts of the *Sacred Exchange* provide two possibilities for dating its composition. The first comes from seven manuscripts which end with the following statement: "This work was completed in the month of July after the death of blessed Francis, in the year one thousand two hundred and twenty-seven after the incarnation of Our Lord and Savior Jesus Christ."[5] The other comes from six manuscripts which do not contain this claim, leaving unresolved the question of dating. In his critical edition of the text, Stefano Brufani meticulously examined each of these thirteen manuscripts and discounted the date 1227 since it comes from the weaker of the two branches of manuscripts.[6] Brufani leaves the question open and attempts to arrive at an answer through the internal evidence of the *Sacred Exchange.*

The same line of investigation must be followed in attempting to identify the author of the work. The principal manuscripts offer two different possibilities: Saint Anthony of Padua and Blessed John of Parma. The others, the majority, prefer to leave the author anonymous. After examining the manuscript evidence, most scholars, including Brufani, conclude that the identity of the author of the *Sacred Exchange* is as hidden as the date of its composition.[7]

Answers to these questions of the date of the work's composition as well as of its author, then, must be derived from the text itself. In his introduction to the work, Placid Hermann notes that "some authors have attempted to read between the lines of the work to see a certain bitterness that would be characteristic of the later *Spirituals* and hence would likely assign a date later than 1227 . . ."[8] Following this line of reasoning, the *Sacred Exchange* emerges as a polemical work expressing the more reactionary ideals promoted by the more zealous friars. This would place the work sometime after the death of Saint Bonaventure (+1274) when division within the Order became more pronounced. Hermann rejects this position since he accepts 1227 as the date of composition. Consequently, he maintains that the *Sacred Exchange* has "no connection whatsoever with that sharp spirit of controversy that arose in the succeeding years over the matter of poverty."[9] Hermann proposes that it was written by "a Franciscan whose identity is shrouded in mystery."

While not denying this intra-Franciscan interpretation, Brufani does not judge it "sufficient to explain the great, rich theological undertaking of the author."[10] Instead, he suggests as the "soil in which the work was conceived" the controversy that raged at the University of Paris from the 1250s to the 1270s over the mendicant life of the Friars Preacher and the Friars Minor and, in particular, over their choice of poverty.[11] Such a hypothesis enables the Italian scholar to see Bonaventure's *Epistola de tribus quaestionibus* and *Questiones de perfectione evangelica* as containing passages akin to those of the *Sacred Exchange.* Brufani also focuses on the polemical nature of the *Sacred Exchange* in the same vein as those authors highlighted by Hermann, but he places it in the larger context of the teaching friars and secular masters at the University of Paris. The *Sacred Exchange* lacks, however, the refined, subtle polemics of the late thirteenth century secular masters such as William of Saint-Amour. Although it suggests underlying challenges to its ideals, there is no easily identifiable protagonist at whom the allegory is directed, none, that is, beyond ordinary human nature.

Is the work a product of the controversies of the University of Paris as Brufani suggests? This seems possible. As Brufani suggests, the *Sacred Exchange* represents an attempt to develop "a theology and an ecclesiology on the foundation of poverty to legitimize the right of the mendicant friars to live in the Church."[12] Not only do certain phrases of Bonaventure's defenses resonate with the *Sacred Exchange,* but its theological identification of the cloister with the world (cf. *Sacred Exchange* 30) is a refutation of religious life as separation from society and as a negative view of earthly reality.[13] Nevertheless, the biblical character of the work is not typical of the scholastic style of argumentation that favored the use of dialectic reasoning. There is nothing argumentative or disputatious about the text. Nor is any of the acerbic rhetoric of the later literature of the Franciscan tradition in which the rival standpoints of the Community and the Spirituals became pronounced. *The Sacred Exchange* seems to be more of an early encouragement to follow the spirit of Francis's love of poverty and to avoid the failings of many who had seen poverty as an ideal but had compromised their vision.[14]

Is there a solution that has been overlooked? Michael Cusato has examined the question in the context of the tumultuous period after Francis's death.[15] Three significant events stand out: the promulgation of Pope Gregory the Ninth's *Quo elongati* in 1230, the election of Brother Elias of Cortona as General Minister in 1232, and the construction of the magnificent basilica in honor of Saint Francis carried out by both Pope Gregory and Brother Elias. All three points affected the Gospel vision of poverty embraced by Francis and his brothers.[16]

In his *Reform and Division in the Franciscan Order (1226-1538),* Duncan Nimmo provides insights into a papal initiative that exacerbated tensions already present among Francis's followers: Gregory IX's papal decree, *Quo elongati* (September 28, 1230). This was the first papal clarification of Francis's *Rule* undertaken by one who relied not only on his position as pope but on his friendship with Francis and his own role in helping him articulate his vision. One of the more troublesome aspects of the document was its declaration that the brothers were bound only to the evangelical counsels, poverty, chastity and obedience. In essence, the pope broke the identification of Gospel and Rule with which Francis began his Rule. Another disconcerting declaration was that Francis's *Testament* was commendable but not binding in nature. Nimmo sees that this became "a wedge between the friars and by itself, perhaps, made certain the fraternity's future disintegration."[17] The document not only set aside Francis's dying wishes for his brothers, it unleashed a debate about the obligation to the Gospel as their "rule and life" and about the practice of poverty as its foundation. As discussions over *Quo elongati* emerged, they did so between those preferring a more urban way of life to those preferring one more eremitical, a discussion that originated as early as 1209 when Francis and the first brothers returned from receiving papal approbation for their way of life.[18] All of these discussions were no doubt aggravated by the building of the lavish basilica in honor of Saint Francis and, in 1232, the election of Brother Elias. In his *Chronicle or History of the Seven Tribulations of the Order of Minors,* Angelo Clareno places in the mouth of Caesar of Speyer words that undoubtedly express the tensions felt by many friars:

"I ask you for one favor. If during my days it should happen that the brothers draw distant from the pure observance of the Rule . . . and because of their opposition I cannot freely observe it in conformity to that holy and perfect intention revealed to God by you, I ask you, with your obedience and permission, can I withdraw alone or with a few brothers to observe it perfectly?"[19]

While admittedly Clareno's work represents the prejudices of the later Spirituals, it suggests tensions that encouraged the composition of the *Sacred Exchange,* tensions that grew during the decade after Francis's death.[20] These same tensions may well have encouraged those desiring to observe more purely the Gospel life proposed by Francis to "withdraw alone or with a few brothers," that is, to observe the founder's *Rule for Hermitages.* Just as Lady Poverty fled from the cities and the plains, places where she had been spurned and then neglected, and gone to the mountain (cf. *Sacred Exchange* 5-10), so those desiring to live Francis's Gospel vision perfectly went to those mountain hermitages known for regular observance, LaVerna, Greccio, and Montecasale.

This may also have prompted Pope Gregory IX to re-issue on March 24, 1238, the papal decree, *Cum secundum consilium.* The initiative of Gregory's predecessor, Honorius III, aimed at stabilizing Francis's followers by establishing a year of probation, the novitiate, and by prohibiting them from wandering about without permission. Gregory's renewal of that decree may have been aimed at achieving these same objectives, most especially at discouraging those who chose the eremitical way of life as a means of side-stepping *Quo elongati.*

In light of this, could this be the more appropriate *sitz-im-leben* of the *Sacred Exchange* and could Caesar of Speyer be the author of the *Sacred Exchange?* Ubertino da Casale provides a clue in his *Arbor vitae crucifixae Jesu,* when he writes that the author of the *Sacred Exchange* was "a certain holy doctor, a professor and vigorous enthusiast of this poverty." Angelo Clareno describes Caesar of Speyer as "a great teacher of holy theology," one whom Jordan of Giano had portrayed as "learned in sacred scripture." (It was Caesar who, according to Jordan, assisted Francis by adding Scripture passages to the *Earlier Rule.*) Caesar, according to Clareno, was clearly caught in the dilemma of the authentic observance of the *Rule* and received Francis's blessing to retire to a hermitage.[21] Having led the first successful mission to Germany in 1219, Caesar undoubtedly knew Thomas of Celano; he definitely would have known of his *The Life of Saint Francis* and been inspired with his concept of the "sacred exchange" that the brothers had with holy poverty.[22]

If Caesar of Speyer is the author of the *Sacred Exchange,* this would suggest an earlier context than those proposed by scholars who see it coming from the later division of Francis's followers and by Brufani who maintains that it emerges from the debates over Mendicant poverty in the University of Paris. The work would have to have been written before 1238 or early 1239 when

Caesar died.[23] Its biblical idealism is far more understandable, as is its positive, exhortatory nature and a difficult period of the history when, because of death, the first generation of Francis's followers were decreasing. Emerging from a period of history in which poverty and the poor were seen differently, the *Sacred Exchange* is an important early expression of the self-understanding of those who, with Francis, strove to ascend the mountain of Lady Poverty.

NOTES

1. The translation of *commercium* as "exchange," while expressing the general meaning of the word, does not capture its full sense. Auspicius van Corstanje underscored its biblical implications by using "covenant," cf. *The Covenant with God's Poor. An Essay on the Biblical Interpretation of the Testament of Saint Francis of Assisi,* translated by Gabriel Ready (Chicago: Franciscan Herald Press, 1966). In light of his interpretation, *commercium* might also be translated as "covenant." Yet this biblical emphasis overlooks the "commercial" or marketplace vocabulary that Lester K. Little sees in the mendicant literature of the period. Little refers to the work as "The Holy Commerce" and refers to a fourteenth-century author who called it "The Business of Poverty." Cf. *Religious Poverty and The Profit Economy in Medieval Europe* (Ithaca, Cornell University Press, 1978), 200.

2. Cf. John V. Fleming, *An Introduction to the Franciscan Literature of the Middle Ages* (Chicago: Franciscan Herald Press, 1977), 78. Kajetan Esser, "Untersuchungen zum 'Sacrum commercium beati Francisci cum Domina Paupertate,' " in *Miscellanea Melchor de Pobladura,* tom. I, (Roma, 1964), 1-33.

3. Thirty-three of its sixty-nine numbered paragraphs are taken up with the account of Lady Poverty's life.

4. It is most important to view this work in light of the movements of religious poverty contemporary with the first Franciscans. Invaluable works are: Michel Mollat, *The Poor in the Middle Ages,* translated by Arthur Goldhammer (New Haven and London: Yale University Press, 1986); and Lester K. Little, *Religious Poverty and the Profit Economy in Medieval Europe* (Ithaca, NY: Cornell University Press, 1978).

5. *Actum est hoc opus mensae iulii post obitum beati Francisci anno millesimo ducentesimo vigesimo septimo ab incarnatione Domini Salvatoris nostri Iesu Christi.*

6. *Sacrum commercium sancti Francisci cum Domina Paupertate,* a cura di Stefano Brufani (S. Maria degli Angeli: Edizioni Porziuncula, 1990), 59-122.

7. Commentators have suggested names other than Saint Anthony and John of Parma: Thomas of Celano, John Parenti, Crescentius of Iesi and John Pecham.

8. Placid Hermann, "Sacrum Commercium or Francis and His Lady Poverty," *Saint Francis of Assisi: Writings and Early Biographies, English Omnibus of the Sources for the Life of St. Francis,* edited by Marion A. Habig (Chicago: Franciscan Herald Press, 1973) p. 1534.

9. *Omnibus,* p. 1534.

10. *Fontes Franciscani,* 1700.

11. Stefano Brufani, *Sacrum commercium sancti Francisci cum Domina Paupertate,* "Introduzione," *Fontes Franciscani,* a cura di Enrico Menestò e Stefano Brufani (S. Maria degli Angeli: Edizioni Porziuncula, 1995), 1700.

12. *Fontes Franciscani,* 1700.

13. Brufani notes: "This conclusion seems to be at the same time a response to the alternative posed by William of Saint-Amour to the Franciscans: either be monks living apart from the world by the fruit of their own work, or clerics responsible for the *cura animarum* who benefit from the offerings of the faithful." Cf. *Fontes Franciscani,* p. 1702.

14. Michel Mollat, *The Poor of the Middle Ages: An Essay in Social History,* translated by Arthur Goldhammer (New Haven and London: Yale University Press, 1986) 117-157.

15. Cf. Michael Cusato, *La renonciation au pouvoir chez les Freres Mineurs au 13e siècle,* Thesis (Paris: Université de Paris-Sorbonne, 1991).

16. During this same period Pope Gregory was challenging the observance of poverty undertaken by the Poor Ladies of San Damiano, that is, of Clare of Assisi and her followers. Cf. *Clare of*

Assisi: Early Documents, 2nd revised, edited and translated by Regis J. Armstrong (St. Bonaventure, NY: Franciscan Institute Publications, 1986).

17. Duncan Nimmo, *Reform and Division in the Franciscan Order (1226-1538)* (Rome: Capuchin Historical Institute, 1987) 56.

18. 1C 35: "conferebant . . . utrum inter homines conversari deberent, an ad loca solitaria se conferre." Cf. Grado G. Merlo, "Eremitism in Medieval Franciscanism," in *Franciscan Solitude,* edited by Andre Cirino and Josef Raischl (St. Bonaventure, NY: Franciscan Institute Publications, 1995).

19. Angelo Clareno, *Chronicon seu Historia septem tribulationum ordinis Minorum,* edited by Alberto Ghinato (Rome, 1959), 50.

20. Duncan Nimmo, *Reform and Division* 150.

21. The passage quoted above continues: "Upon hearing these words, blessed Francis was filled with immense joy and, blessing him, said: 'What you have asked for has been granted by Christ and by me.' "

22. Cf. 1C 38.

23. Cusato maintains that Caesar's death was prior to May 1239, the deposition of Brother Elias as General Minister, and probably after March 28, 1238, the promulgation of Pope Gregory IX's *Cum secundum consilium* directed at those living in hermitages. Since Caesar had been given permission to "live alone," he was one of them.

The Sacred Exchange between Saint Francis and Lady Poverty

[Prologue]

[1] Among the other outstanding and exceptional virtues which prepare in us an abode and a dwelling for God and which show *an excellent* and unencumbered *path* of going to and arriving before Him, holy Poverty 1 Cor 13:1
shines with a certain prerogative before them all.[a] By a unique grace, it excels the claims of the others. For it is the foundation and guardian of all virtues and enjoys a principal place and name among the gospel virtues. As long as they have been firmly placed on this foundation, the others need not fear *the downpour of rains,* the rush *of floods, and the blast of winds* that threaten ruin. Mt 7:25

[2] This is certainly appropriate since the Son of God, *the Lord of virtue and the King of glory,* fell in love with this virtue with a special af- Ps 24:10
fection. He sought, found, and embraced it while achieving our *salvation in the middle of the earth.* At the beginning of his preaching Ps 74:12
he placed it as a light of faith in the hands of those entering the gate, and even set it as the foundation stone of the house. While the other virtues receive the kingdom of heaven only by way of promise from Him, poverty is invested with it by Him without delay. *Blessed,* he said, *are the poor in spirit, for the kingdom of heaven is theirs.* Mt 5:3

[3] The kingdom of heaven truly belongs to those who, of their own will, a spiritual intention, and a desire for eternal goods, possess nothing of this earth. It is necessary for those who do not care for the goods of the earth to live for those of heaven. Just as it is necessary for those who renounce the things of the earth and consider them *all as dung* to Phil 3:8
taste with pleasure during this present exile *the* sweet *crumbs which fall from the table* of the holy angels. Thus might they merit to savor Mt 15:27
how *sweet* and *delightful is the Lord.* Ps 34:9; 100:4; 1 Pt 2:3

---

a. Stefano Brufani in his critical edition of this text, *Sacrum commercium sancti Francisci cum domina Paupertate* (S. Maria degli Angeli: Edizioni Porziuncula, 1990), numbers the paragraphs differently. However, to avoid confusion, the editors have chosen to remain with the numbering of the Quaracchi edition, *Sacrum commercium sancti Francisci cum domina Paupertate* (Quaracchi: PP. Collegii s. Bonaventurae, Ad Claras Aquas, 1929).

This is the true investiture of the kingdom of heaven, the assurance of an eternal possession in that kingdom, and a kind of holy foretaste of future beatitude.[a]

4 At the beginning of his conversion, therefore, blessed Francis, as
the Savior's true imitator and disciple, gave himself with all eagerness,
all longing, all determination to searching for, finding, and embracing
holy poverty. He did so neither wavering under adversity nor fearing
injury, neither shirking effort nor shunning bodily discomfort, in order
to achieve his desire: to reach her to whom the Lord had entrusted *the*
Mt 5:3; 16:19 *keys of the kingdom of heaven.*

Blessed Francis Asks about Poverty

5 He eagerly began to go about *the streets and piazzas of the city,* as a
Sg 3:2 curious explorer diligently *looking for her whom his soul loved.* He
asked those standing about, inquired of those who came near him:
Sg 3:3 *"Have you seen her whom my soul loves?" But that saying was hidden*
Lk 18:24 *from them* as though it was barbaric. Not understanding him, they told
him: "We do not know what you're saying. *Speak to us in* our own *lan-*
2 Kgs 4:31 *guage* and we will answer you."

2 Kgs 4:31 At that time there was no *voice and no sense* among Adam's children of being willing to converse with or to speak to anyone about poverty. They hated it with a vengeance, as they do even today, and could
Gn 37:4 not *speak peacefully* to anyone asking about it. Therefore, they answered him as they would a stranger and declared that they did not
know anything of what he was seeking.[b]

6 *"I will go to the best and to the wise,"* blessed Francis said, *"and I*
will speak with them. For they have known the way of the Lord and the
Jer 5:5 *judgment of their God,* because those others *are poor and stupid, igno-*
Jer 5:4 *rant of the way of the Lord* and *of the judgment of their God."*

After he had said this, these men answered him more harshly: *"What*
Acts 17:19-20 *kind of doctrine is this you are bringing to our ears?* May the poverty
Gn 13:15 you seek always be with *you,* your children *and your seed* after you. As
for us, however, let it be our good fortune to enjoy delights and to

a. Investiture refers to the feudal ceremonial conferral through symbols of office and subsequent rights and duties. In this instance poverty gives Francis—and his followers—a claim on the kingdom of heaven.

b. This reluctance of city dwellers to speak of poverty reflects their rich status, a phenomenon that was not uncommon in the early thirteenth century. The urban poor were not that numerous and lived a type of poverty different from those of the countryside. Cf. Lester K. Little, *Religious Poverty and the Profit Economy in Medieval Europe* (Ithaca: Cornell University Press, 1978) 19-30.

abound in riches for *the duration of our lives is tedious and demanding, and there is no remedy at one's final hour.* We haven't learned anything better than *to rejoice, eat and drink while we live."* Wis 2:1 Eccl 3:12,13; Is 22:13; 1 Cor 15:32

7 While he was listening to these things, blessed Francis marveled in his heart and, thanking God, declared: *"Blessed* are you, *the Lord God,* who *have hidden these things from the wise and prudent and have revealed them to little ones! Yes, Father, because such was your pleasure!* Lord, father and ruler of my life, do not abandon me to their counsels nor let me fall in that condemnation. Through your grace, let me, instead, find what I seek *for I am your servant and the son of your handmaid."* Lk 1:68; Mt 11:25-26 Ps 116:16

8 After he left the city, then, blessed Francis quickly came to a certain field in which, as he looked from afar, he saw two old men wasted away *from great sorrow.*[a] One of them spoke in this way: *"Whom shall I respect except the one who is poor and contrite in spirit and the one who trembles at my words?" "We brought nothing into the world,"* the other said, *"and, without a doubt, we can take nothing out of it; but having food and whatever covers us, we are content with these."* Lam 1:13 Is 66:2 1 Tm 6:7-8

He Asks To Be Shown Where Poverty Lives

9 When blessed Francis reached them, he said to them: "Tell me, I beg you, where does Lady Poverty dwell? *Where does she eat? Where does she rest at noon,* for *I languish with love* of her?" Sg 1:6; Sg 2:5; 5:8

But they answered: "Good brother, we have sat here *for a time and for times and for half a time.*[b] We have frequently seen her pass by for there are many searching for her. Sometimes many accompanied her, but she returned alone and naked, not *adorned with* any *jewels,* nor graced with any companions, nor wearing any clothes. She used to weep bitterly and say '*The children of my mother have fought against* Dt 7:25; 12:7; Rv 12:14 Is 61:10

a. These two elders may well reflect the monks of religious orders who originally fled the cities for the poverty and simplicity of the "desert," i.e., the countryside, or who had more recently returned there to renew their religious traditions. A more common interpretation sees the two elders as Isaiah and Paul speaking for the Old and New Testaments.

b. Since he does not yet have brothers, it is curious that the elders call Francis "brother." This raises the question: is this because they consider him one of them in their appreciation of Lady Poverty or is this simply an anticipation of the author that Francis will have brothers and will not be alone?

Sg 1:5; Mt 18:26; Sg 1:3 *me.*' And we said to her: '*Be patient,* for *the upright love you.*'[a]
[10]"Brother, *she has* now *gone up to a great and high mountain*
Rv 21:10; Mt 28:16 *where* God *has placed* her. She is dwelling *in the sacred mountains be-*
Ps 87:1-2 *cause* God *loved her above all the tabernacles of Jacob.* Giants have
Est 13:13 not been able to touch *the footprints of her steps* and eagles cannot fly
even to her shoulder. Poverty is the only thing that everyone condemns
Jb 28:21 so that *it cannot be discovered in the land of those living comfortably.*
She is hidden from their *eyes,* then, and *concealed from the birds of the*
Jb 28:21; Jb 28:23 *sky.God understands her path and He knows her place.*[b]

[11]"If, then, you wish to reach her, brother, take off your *clothes of*
Jdt 10:3; Heb 12:1 *rejoicing,* and put aside *every burden and sin clinging to* you for, unless
you are naked, you will not be able to climb to her who lives in so high a
1 Cor 13:4 place. Yet, because *she is kind, she will easily be seen by those who love*
Wis 6:13 *her and be found by those who search for her. To think about her,*
brother, *is perfect understanding, and whoever keeps vigil for her will*
Wis 6:16 *quickly be secure.* Take faithful companions so that during the mountain's ascent you will have their advice and be strengthened by their
help. For *woe to the one who is alone! If he falls, he will have no one to*
Eccl 4:10 *lift him up. For if anyone falls, he should have someone help him!*"

Blessed Francis Encourages His Brothers

[12]After receiving the advice of such men, then, blessed Francis
came and chose some faithful companions for himself with whom he
hurried to the mountain. He said to his brothers: "*Come, let us climb*
Is 2:3 *the mountain of the Lord and the dwelling* of Lady Poverty *that she*
Mi 4:2 *might teach us her ways and we might walk in her paths.*"

Because of its great height and difficulty, they studied the ascent of
the mountain from every angle. Some of them said to one another:
Ps 24:3 "*Who can climb this mountain* and who can reach its summit?"

[13]Blessed Francis understood this and said to them: "*The road is*
difficult, brothers, *and the gate that leads to it is narrow. There are few*

a. The reference seems to be to religious such as the Cistercians whose eventual success in providing for their needs brought them great wealth and weakened their reform by taking them away from the poverty of their beginnings. (cf. Little, Lester K., *Religious Poverty and the Profit Economy in Medieval Europe* [Ithaca: Cornell University Press, 1978] 90-96.) Hence the subsequent comments of the elders reflect their disappointment with the failure of the idealism of older religious movements to maintain their ideal of poverty.

b. These passages weave together a variety of images in which Poverty is referred to in terms of the Church, (Rv 21:10) Jerusalem (Ps 88) and Wisdom. (Jb 28:21) All of the ScEx frequently uses passages or allusions to the Wisdom literature of the Old Testament suggesting the strong resemblance of Poverty to Wisdom.

who find it. Be strengthened in the Lord and in the power of his virtue Mt 7:14
for everything difficult will be easy for you. Cast off the burdens of Eph 6:10
your own will, get rid of the weight of your sins, and *gird yourselves* as
powerful men. Forgetting whatever is in the past, *stretch yourselves as* 1 Mc 3:58
much as you can for what lies ahead. I tell you that *wherever you place* Phil 3:13
your foot will be yours. For *the Spirit* is before your face, *Christ the* Dt 11:24
Lord, Who *draws* you to the heights of the mountain *in bonds of love.*[a] Lam 4:20
The espousal of Poverty, brothers, is wonderful, yet we will be able to
enjoy her embraces easily because *the lady of the nations has been*
made as it were a widow,[b] the queen of the virtues worthless and con- Hos 11:4
temptible to all. There is no one of our region who would dare to cry
out, no one who would oppose us, no one who would be able to prohibit
by law this salvific exchange.[c] *All her friends have spurned her and*
have been made her enemies." Lam 1:1

After he said these things, they all began to follow the holy Francis.

Poverty Marvels at the Ease of Their Ascent

[14]While they were hastening to the summit at a very easy pace, Lady
Poverty, standing at the top of the mountain, looked down its slopes.
She was greatly astonished at seeing these men climbing so ably, almost flying. *"Who are these men,"* she asked, *"who fly like clouds and*
like doves to their windows? It has been a long time since I have seen Is 60:8
such people or gazed upon those so unencumbered, all their burdens set aside. Therefore I will speak to them about what engages my heart so that, when staring down at the abyss that lies about them, they do not, like others, have second thoughts about such a climb. I know they can-

a. The translator has attempted to remain as faithful to the Latin as possible because of the rich Pneumatology of the text: *Etenim est spiritus ante faciem vestram, Christus Dominus, qui trahet vos ad montis cacumina in vinculis caritatis.*

b. This passage, "*Mirabilis est, fratres, desponsatio Paupertatis* . . . [The espousal of Poverty . . . is wonderful . . .], is a subject of controversy. Six of the eight early manuscripts contain the word *dispensatio* [design, plan, covenant, management] rather than *desponsatio* [espousal]. These manuscripts suggest a more Pauline interpretation of living within the design or stewardship of Poverty, cf. 1 Cor 9:17; Eph 1:10; 3:2,9; Col 1:25. According to the interpretation, Poverty is closely linked with God's plan of salvation and is the spouse, the Lady of Christ. In the tradition of medieval chivalry, it is she who prepares the way to her lord. The translation has chosen to follow the text of the critical editions by using *desponsatio*, because it seems to fit the context which speaks of embraces and of Poverty being made a widow. Thus the terminology is more espousal in nature.

c. This is the only use of the word *commercium* in this work. It appears only once in these early texts, 1C 35, where it is used to refer to an "exchange" between Lady Poverty and the brothers. Those favoring the use of the word *dispensatio* over *desponsatio* see *commercium,* a word suggesting a business mentality, as reflective of the Pauline concerns for the "economy of salvation." One fourteenth century translation of this work entitles it The Business of Poverty (cf. Lester K. Little).

not take hold of me without my consent, but there will be a reward for
me before my heavenly Father if I give them saving advice."

And behold a voice was heard: "Fear not, daughter of Sion, be-
cause these men are the seed whom the Lord has blessed and chosen *in*
Lk 1:44; cf. Jn 12:15; Zep 3:16; Cf. Is 61:9; 2 Cor 6:6 *unfeigned love."*

15 And so Lady Poverty, resting on a throne in her nakedness, *wel-*
Ps 21:4 *comed them with blessings of sweetness.* "Tell me, brothers," she asked
them, "what is the reason for your coming and why have you come so
quickly from the valley of misery to the mountain of light? Are you,
perhaps, looking for me who, as you see, am *a poor little one tossed*
Is 54:11 *about by storms and without any consolation?"*

Blessed Francis Praises Poverty

16 "We have come to you, our Lady," they answered, "and beg you:
receive us in peace! We wish to become servants of the Lord of hosts,
Ps 24:10 because *He is the King of glory.* We have heard that you are the queen
of virtues and, to some extent, we have learned this from experience.
Casting ourselves at your feet, then, we humbly ask you to agree to be
with us. Be for us the way of arriving at the King of glory, just as you
were for Him when He, *the Daybreak from on high,* agreed to visit
Lk 1:79, 78 *those sitting in darkness and in the shadow of death.* For we know that
1 Chr 29:11 *yours is the power, yours is the kingdom.* Established as queen and lady
1 Chr 29:11 by the King of kings, *you are above all powers.* Simply make peace
with us and we will be saved. In that way, He Who redeemed us
through you may receive us through you. If you decide to save us, immediately we will be set free. For He, *the King of kings, the Lord of*
Rv 19:16 *lords,* the Creator of heaven and earth, *desired your splendor* and
Ps 45:12; Sg 1:11 beauty. Even though *the king was reclining at table,* rich and glorious
in his kingdom, *he left his house and gave up his inheritance: for there*
Jer 12:7; Ps 112:3 *were glory and riches in his house.* And so, coming *from his royal*
Wis 18:15 *throne,* he sought you with the greatest courtesy.

17 "How great must be your dignity, then, and how beyond compare
your stature! He left behind all the ranks of angels and the immense
powers—of which there is a great abundance in heaven—when He
came to look for you in the lowest regions of the earth—you who were
Ps 40:3; Ps 88:7 lying in *the mud of the swamp, in darkness, and in the shadow of death.*
All living beings held you in great contempt. All people ran from you

and, as far as they could, cast you aside. Even though there were some who couldn't escape from you, you were no less contemptible and despicable to them.

18"But after *the Lord of lords came,* taking you as His own, *He lifted up your head* among the tribes of the peoples. He adorned you *as a bride with a crown,* exalting you *above the heights of the clouds.* Yet, even though any number of people, ignorant *of your power and glory,* still hate you, this takes nothing away from you because you live freely *on the sacred mountains,* in *the strongest dwelling-place* of Christ's glory.

Mal 3:1
Ps 110:7
Is 61:10; Is 14:14
Ps 63:3; 2 Chr 6:33

The Dignity of Poverty

19"The Son of the most high Father, *enamored of your beauty* and clinging only to you in the world, proved that you were most faithful in everything. For before he came to earth from his radiant homeland, you prepared an appropriate place for him, a throne upon which he would sit and a dwelling-place in which he would rest, that is, a very poor virgin from whom his birth would shine upon this world. At his birth you certainly greeted him with faithfulness so that in you, not in luxuries, he would find a place that would please him. *He was placed in a manger,* the Evangelist said, *because there was no room* for him *in the inn.*[a] Thus, always inseparable from him, you accompanied him so that throughout his life, *when he was seen upon earth and conversed with human beings, while the foxes have dens and the birds of the air nests, he* nevertheless *had nowhere to lay his head.* Then, when he opened his own mouth to teach—he who once had opened the mouths of the prophets—among the many things that he uttered, he first of all praised you, he first of all exalted you: *Blessed are the poor in spirit because theirs is the kingdom of heaven.*

Wis 8:2
Lk 2:7
Bar 3:38
Mt 8:20
Mt 5:3

20"Moreover, when he chose some of the indispensable witnesses to his holy preaching and to his glorious manner of living for the salvation of the human race, he surely did not choose rich merchants but poor fishermen, to show by such esteem that you were to be loved by all. Finally, to reveal to everyone your goodness, magnificence, dignity

a. The Latin text has *non erat ei locus in diversorio* [there was no room for him in the inn]. The Latin Vulgate, meanwhile, has *non erat eis in diversorio* [there was no room for them in the inn]. In his Office of the Passion, Francis wrote *positus in praesepio quia non habebat locum in diversorio* [because he did not have a place in the inn], which reflects the reading in Francis's Gospel Book which has *quis non erat ei locus in diversorio.*

and strength, how you surpass all other virtues, how nothing can be a
Jn 18:36 virtue without you, and how your *kingdom is not of this world* but of
heaven, you alone clung to the King of glory, when all the chosen and all his beloved abandoned him filled with fear. You, most faithful spouse, most sweet lover, did not abandon him for a moment. Moreover, the more you saw him despised by everyone, the more you clung to him. For if you were not with him, he could never have been so despised by all!

21 "You were with him in the mockery of the Judeans, in the insults of the Pharisees, in the curses of the chief priests. You were with him in the slapping of his face, in the spitting, in the scourging. He who should have been respected by everyone was mocked by everyone, and you alone comforted him. You did not abandon him *even to death, death on*
Phil 2:8 *a cross.* And on that cross, his body stripped, his arms outstretched, his
hands and feet pierced, you suffered with him, so that nothing would appear more glorious in him than you. Finally, when he went into heaven, he left you the seal of the kingdom of heaven to mark the elect, so that whoever yearns for the everlasting kingdom would come to you, ask from you, [and] enter through you. For no one can enter the
Sg 8:6; Rv 7:3 kingdom except the one *signed with* your *seal.*

22 "Lady, have compassion on us, therefore, and mark us with the seal of your grace. For who is so dull, so ignorant as not to love with a full heart you who have been chosen by the Most High and prepared from eternity? Who would not revere and honor you when he, whom all the powers of heaven adore, has adorned you with such honor? For
Is 60:14 who would not willingly *adore the footprints of the feet of you* to whom
the Lord of majesty so humbly stooped, to whom he so intimately united himself, to whom he clung with such love? Lady, we beg you through him and because of him: 'despise not our petitions in our necessities, but deliver us always from danger, [you who are] glorious and blessed forever.' "[a]

a. Cf. Marian antiphon: *Sub tuum praesidium confugimus, sancta Dei Genetrix, nostras deprecationes ne despicias in necessitatibus: sed a periculis cunctis libera nos semper, Virgo gloriosa et benedicta.* [We fly to your patronage, O holy Mother of God; despise not our petitions in our necessities, but deliver us always from all dangers O glorious and blessed Virgin.]

The Response of Lady Poverty

[23]At this Lady Poverty responded with a joyful heart, a radiant face,
and a gentle voice: "Brothers and very dear friends, I admit that, from
the moment you began to speak, I was filled with joy, with an overflowing happiness, as I observed your fervor and learned of your holy
intention. Your words became *more desirable to me than gold and a*
very precious jewel and sweeter than honey and the comb. For it is not Ps 19:11
you who have spoken, but the Holy *Spirit who has spoken in you.* That Mt 10:20
anointing teaches you everything you have uttered about the most high 1 Jn 2:27
King Who, by his grace alone, took me as his beloved, *taking away my*
reproach from the earth, and glorified me among the most celebrated Lk 1:25
in heaven.

[24]"Therefore, if it is not too much of a burden for you to hear, I want
to tell you the long but no less useful tale of my condition. In this way
you might learn *how you should walk and please God,* being careful of 1 Thes 4:1
any hint of looking back, you who want *to put your hand to the plow.* Lk 9:62

"I am not uneducated, as many think, but I am quite old and abounding in days, knowing the nature of things, the varieties of creatures, the changes of times. I have known the fluctuations of the human heart, in part by the experience of time, in part by the insight of nature, in part through the nobility of grace.

A Recollection of Poverty in Paradise

[25]"I was once *in the paradise of God,* where *man* was *naked.* In fact I Rv 2:7
was in man and was *walking* with *naked man* through that entire splen- Gn 2:25; 3:8
did paradise, fearing nothing, doubting nothing, and suspecting nothing amiss. I thought I would be with him forever, because the Most High created him just, good and wise and placed in the most delightful
and beautiful place. I was so happy *playing before him all the while* be- Prv 8:30
cause, possessing nothing, he belonged entirely to God.

[26]"Unfortunately, however, an unexpected evil arose, one utterly
unheard of from the beginning of creation. That unhappy one, who *in*
his splendor long ago *lost* his *wisdom,* encountered *a serpent,* who Ez 28:17
couldn't remain in heaven. [The serpent] approached him with deceit
so that, like himself, he would become a transgressor of the divine Gn 3:1

command. The miserable one believed the evil counselor. He agreed,
Dt 32:18 consented and, *oblivious of God his creator,* imitated the first trans-
gressor. At first *he was naked,* as Scripture says about him, but *he was*
Gn 2:25 *not ashamed* because in him there was complete innocence. Once he
had sinned, however, he knew he was naked and, running for *fig leaves*
Gn 3:7 out of shame, he made *a covering for himself.*

[27]"When I saw, therefore, that my companion had become a transgressor and was covered with leaves because he had nothing else, I distanced myself from him. Standing at a distance, I began to look at him
with tears in my eyes. *I awaited him who would save me from such an-*
Ps 55:9 *guish and turmoil.*

"Suddenly there was a sound from heaven shaking all of paradise
and with it a brilliant light sent from heaven. As I looked about, I saw
Gn 3:8 the Lord of majesty *walking in paradise in the cool of the day,* brilliant
with indescribable and exquisite glory. Multitudes of angels accompanied him shouting and saying in a loud voice: *'Holy, holy, holy Lord*
Is 6:3 *God of hosts, all the earth is full of your glory.' Thousands upon thou-*
sands were ministering to him and ten thousand times a hundred thou-
Dn 7:10 *sand were assisting him.*

[28]"I confess, I began to shake and tremble terribly, to faint with
complete amazement and fright. My body was shaking and my heart
was beating wildly: 'Lord, have mercy! Lord, have mercy!' *I cried out*
Ps 130:1 *of the depths,* 'Do not enter into judgment with your servant, because
Ps 143:2 no living being is justified in your sight.' And [God] said to me, *'Go*
Is 26:20 *away for a moment and hide yourself until* my *anger has passed.'*

"Immediately [God] called my companion. *'Adam, where are*
you?' But Adam said, *'Lord, I heard your voice and was afraid be-*
Gn 3:9-10 *cause I was naked and hid.'* He was truly naked because, as *he went*
down from Jerusalem to Jericho, he fell among thieves who robbed him
first and foremost of his good nature, causing him to lose his likeness to
Lk 10:30 the Creator. That most high King was, nonetheless, very kind, longed
for his repentance, after giving him an opportunity to return to him.

[29]"But the miserable man *turned away his heart,* breaking out *in*
Ps 141:4 *malicious words to make excuses for his sins.* And so he even aug-
mented his guilt and increased his punishment, *storing up wrath* for
himself *on the day of wrath* and indignation *of the just judgment of*
Rom 2:5 *God.* He did not spare himself or his seed after him, casting everyone to
the terrible curse of death. Condemned by every bystander, *the Lord*

cast him out of the paradise of delight with a judgment that was just but no less merciful. And that *he might return to the earth from which he was* taken, [God] passed his sentence, or curse, though greatly tempered. After the garment of innocence had been stripped away, *[the Lord] made him a garment of skin,* signifying with it his mortality. Gn 3:23 Gn 3:19 Gn 3:21

[30]"Seeing my companion, therefore, clothed with the skins of the dead, I drew completely away from him because he had thrown himself into increasing his work to become rich. I went then *as a wanderer and an exile on earth,* weeping and lamenting greatly. From that time *I found no place to rest my foot,* while Abraham, Isaac, Jacob and the other just ones received as a promise riches and *a land flowing with milk and honey. In all* these *I sought rest* and *found none,* while *the Cherubim* stood before the gate of paradise with *a fiery sword turning every which way,* until the Most High, Who sought me so very graciously, came to earth from *the bosom of the Father.* Gn 4:12 Gn 8:9; Ex 3:17 Sir 24:11; Jer 45:3; Gn 3:24; Jn 1:18

The Covenant of Christ

[31]"He accomplished everything you said. And when he wanted to return to his Father who had sent him, he left me as a covenant to his faithful chosen ones and confirmed it with a clear-cut directive: *'Do not possess gold, silver or money,'* he said to them. *'Do not carry a bag, wallet, bread, staff or shoes. You may not have two tunics. Whoever wishes to contend with you in court and to have your tunic, give him your cloak as well. Whoever forces you to go a mile, go with him another two. Do not store up treasure for yourselves on earth, where rust and moth consume and where thieves break in and steal. Do not be anxious saying: 'What shall we eat?' or 'What shall we drink?' or 'With what shall we clothe ourselves?' Do not be anxious about tomorrow, tomorrow is a day anxious about itself. Sufficient for the day is its own trouble.* Unless *someone renounces all that he possesses, he cannot be my disciple.'* [The Lord said these and] other things written in the same book." Mt 10:9-10; Lk 9:3 Mt 5:40-41 Mt 6:19-20 Mt 6:31 Mt 6:34 Lk 14:33

The Apostles

[32]"The Apostles and all his disciples observed this with the greatest care. They did not neglect anything of all they had heard from their

Gal 2:5 Lord and Teacher, *not even for an hour.* These most brave soldiers, judges of the whole world, fulfilled the mandate of salvation, *preaching it everywhere, while the Lord was working with them and con-*
Mk 16:20 *firming their word with his signs.* They burned with charity and gave themselves to the needs of all, overflowing everywhere with a feeling of piety and with a thorough vigilance, careful that no one would say
Mt 23:3 of them: *'They spoke but did not do!'* One of them, therefore, spoke very confidently: *'For I do not dare to mention anything except those things which Christ has accomplished through me in deeds and*
Rom 15:18,19 *words by virtue of the Holy Spirit.'* While another said: *'Silver and*
Acts 3:6 *gold I have not!'* So all of them lifted me up with the highest praises in life and in death.

"Their listeners strove to fulfill everything that had been proclaimed to them by their teachers. *Selling* their *possessions and goods,*
Acts 2:45 *they divided them among all as each one needed. All were together and held everything in common, praising God and they were held in favor*
Acts 2:44, 47 *by all the people.* Therefore *day by day the Lord added to their number such as were to be saved.*

The Sucessors of the Apostles

33 "The truth of these sayings remained among many for a long time, especially as long as the blood of the poor Crucified was still warm in their memory and the wonderful cup of his suffering inebriated their hearts. In fact, if there were any who were sometimes tempted to abandon me because of excessive bitterness, as they remembered the Lord's wounds which revealed the bowels of piety, they would punish themselves severely for this temptation, cling to me more strongly, and embrace me more fervently. Therefore I was always with them, deepening the sorrows of their memories of the eternal King's suffering, so that, because they were comforted not a little by my words, they willingly accepted the iron tearing at their bodies and enthusiastically saw the sacred blood flowing from their flesh.

"That victory lasted for a very long time, so that *the seal* of the most
Rv 7:2-3 high King *sealed* thousands upon thousands day by day.

The Peace Contrary to Poverty

34"Unfortunately, a short time later, peace was made and that peace was worse than any war.[a] At its beginning few were sealed, in its middle fewer, and at its conclusion fewer still. *My bitterness is* now *certainly most bitter during* a peace in which everyone flees from me, drives me away, does not need me, and abandons me. This is a peace Is 38:17
crafted for me by enemies not by my own, by outsiders not by my children. Indeed, *I have brought up and exalted my children, but they cast me off.* Is 1:2

35"At that time, when the Lord's *light shone upon my head and I walked in darkness by his light,* the devil was raging in many who were Jb 29:3
with me, the world was alluring and the flesh was lusting. Thus many began *to love the world and whatever was in it.* 1 Jn 2:15

Persecution: The Sister of Poverty

36"The consummation of all virtues, however, that is Lady Persecution to whom God gave *the kingdom of heaven* as he did to me, was with me as a faithful helper, a strong support, and a prudent councilor in all things.[b] Wherever she saw that some had become lukewarm in Mt 5:10
love, or a little forgetful of heavenly matters, or were setting their hearts on material goods, she immediately lifted her voice, immediately mobilized her army, and immediately filled the faces of my children with shame so that they would seek God's name.

"But now *my sister has left me. The light of my eyes is no longer with me.* For, when there was a cessation of persecution among my children, war, domestic and internal, tears them apart with greater cruelty. *They envy one another and provoke one another* in acquiring riches and luxuriating in delights. Lk 10:40; Ps 38:11; Gal 5:26

a. This is a negative interpretation of the peace of Constantine in 315 understood as an enrichment of the Church which weakened its sensitivity to poverty.

b. History is filled with examples of victims of war who suffered arson, pillage, deportation, and imprisonment as the Burgundian, Frankish and Gothic kings waged frequent war. In his works, *The History of the Franks, Miracles* and *The Book of the Glory of Confessors*, Gregory of Tours (+594) describes the miseries of these victims of war, the poor, and evoked sympathy for their plight.

The Praise of the Good Poor

37 "After awhile, in fact, some began to breathe and willingly to walk the right path which for some time they had walked out of necessity. All those who came to me begged me sincerely with many prayers and tears to enter into a covenant of perpetual peace with them, and to be with them as I once was *when I was a girl when the All-powerful was*
Ez 16:60; Jb 29:5 *with me and my children were about me.* They were men of virtue,
2 Pt 1:7 peaceful, *blameless before God,* constant *in their love of fraternity.* As long as they were in the flesh, they were poor in spirit, needy in material things, [yet] rich in life and holiness, endowed with the gifts of the heavenly charisms, *fervent in spirit, joyful in hope, patient in trials, meek and humble of heart,* maintaining peace of spirit, a harmony of
2 Pt 1:7; Rom 12:11,12; Mt 11:29 manners, kinship of spirits, unity of lifestyle, and a joy of unity.

"Finally, they were men dedicated to God, pleasing to the angels, beloved of all. They were strict on themselves, merciful to others, religious in deed, modest in stride, cheerful in look, serious in heart, humble in prosperity, generous in adversity, restrained in feasting, sparing in wardrobe, seldom in sleep, mortified and retiring, and conspicuous by the brilliance of all goods. My soul was bound to theirs and there
Eph 4:4,5 was in us one *spirit and one faith.*

The False Poor

38 "Then there arose among us some *who were not of [our company], certain children of Belial,* speaking vanities, doing wicked things. They *called themselves* poor when *they were not,* and they spurned and maligned me whom the glorious men about whom I have
1 Jn 2:19; cf. Dt 13:13; Rv 2:9; 3:9 already spoken had loved with their whole heart. *They followed the*
2 Pt 2:15 *path of Balaam of Bosor who loved the reward of wickedness,* men cor-
1 Tm 6:5 rupt *in mind, deprived of truth, supposing their quest to be one of piety.* They were men who took up the habit of holy religion but did not *put on*
Eph 4:24 *the new man* and only covered over the old. They detracted from their elders and sniped in secret about the life and conduct of those who founded their holy way of life. They call them undiscerning, merciless,
Jer 50:42 and cruel. They accused me, whom they had accepted, of being lazy, crude, depraved, uncultured, lifeless, and dead. It was my rival who did this with the greatest zeal—my rival who, putting on a lamb's clothing, hid the voracity of a wolf with the cunning of a fox.

Greed

[39]"This is Greed whom people speak of as an immoderate desire to
acquire or retain riches.[a] They call her a holier name that they do not
seem to have completely abandoned me by whose largesse they have
arisen from the dust and been lifted from the dung heap. *They spoke*
civilly to me about these things, *but they thought* about wrath *with*
guile. Although the desolation of *a city placed on a mountain cannot be* Ps 35:20
hidden, they, nevertheless, *bestowed upon her the name* of Discretion
or Foresight, although such discretion would better be called confusion
and [such] foresight the destructive forgetfulness of all good. Mt 5:14; Dt 22:17

"And they said to me, '*Yours is the power, yours the kingdom,* don't
be afraid. It is good to continue in works of piety, to have time for good, 1 Chr 29:11
fruitful deeds, to provide for the needy, and to give something to the
poor.'

Poverty Warns False Religious

[40]"I said to them: 'I am not contradicting the good that you have
said, brothers, but I beg you: *look at your calling.* Do not look back. Do 1 Cor 1:26
not *come down from the housetop to take something from the house.* Mt 5:14
Do not *turn back from the field to put on* clothing. Do not become in- Dt 22:17
volved *in the business world.* Do not become entangled in the world's 1 Chr 29:11
initiatives and the corruption you have fled through knowledge of the
Savior. For it is inevitable that those who are again entangled in these
affairs will be overcome and *their last state will become worse than*
their first, for under the appearance of piety, they withdraw from that
which was given them by a holy commandment.' 2 Pt 2:20; Mt 12:45

Their Response

[41]"Whenever I placed those matters before all of them, *dissension*
arose among them. Some were saying: '*She is good and speaks well!*' Jn 7:43; 10:19
Others, however, said 'No, rather she wants to *seduce* us into imitating
her. She is miserable and wants us to be miserable with her.' Jn 7:12

a. Traditionally most authors wrote of pride as the worst vice. In the eleventh century, Peter Damian maintained that "greed was the root of all evil" and saw the primary problem of monasticism to be "the love of money." (Ep I 15, *PL,* CXLIV, 234) Writers such as John of Salisbury, Bernard of Clairvaux, Peter Lombard and Alan of Lille were equally vehement in their condemnation of greed or avarice.

Poverty Speaks about Good Religious

[42]"My rival was unable at that moment to drive me from their midst, for there were many among them still at the beginning of their conversion imbued with great zeal and charity. They were pounding upon heaven with their cries and were penetrating it with the persistence of their prayers, stretching themselves in contemplation and condemning all earthly things. *Then the Creator of all things, the one who created me, commanded me: 'Let your dwelling be in Jacob, your inheritance* Sir 24:12-34 *be in Israel and take root among my elect.'* In fact, I was doing all these things with great diligence. Whenever I was with them in this way and we proceeded together along the royal road, they possessed *an aura among the crowds because of me and they were admirable in the sight* Wis 8:10-11 *of the powerful.* People honored them and called them holy. They began to put up with the name of holiness with difficulty. Remembering Jn 5:41 what the Son of God taught—'I do *not* receive glory *from the people'* —they completely refused the glory offered to them.

Greed Assumes the Name Discretion

[43]"But while they were walking in such zeal out of love for Christ, Greed, assuming the name Discretion, began telling them: 'Do not show yourselves to people as rigid or as scorning their honor. Show yourselves, instead, as affable to them. Do not reject outwardly the glory offered you; at the most, do so inwardly. It is good to have the friendship of royalty, the acquaintances of princes, and a familiarity with the great. For, when they so honor and respect you, when they get up and come to meet you, it will be an example for many. Those who see this will be more easily converted to God.'

[44]"But seeing profit, these men accepted the advice offered to them. They did not protect themselves from the trap placed along the way but, with all their heart, they embraced glory and honor. They considered themselves to be inwardly what they proclaimed outwardly, placing their glory in the mouth of those praising them as *the foolish virgins* Mt 25:8; 25:30 in the merchants and *the useless servant* in the ground.

"But people who thought them to be inwardly what they saw outwardly freely offered their goods in remission of their sins. At first these men looked upon these goods *as dung* and said: 'We are poor and Phil 3:8; 2 Cor 12:14 we always want to be such. We want *you, not your goods. Having food*

and clothing, with these we are content. For vanity of vanities, all 1 Tm 6:8
things are vanity.' Therefore, each day people's devotion to them in- Eccl 1:2; 12:8
creased greatly, so that many of them loved less the goods which they
saw scorned by the holy men.

Greed Calls Herself Foresight

[45]"Meanwhile that savage enemy of mine, seeing this, began to become violently angry and *to grind her teeth.* Distressed *at such grief of* Ps 35:16
heart, she said: *'What shall I do? Behold, the whole world has gone af-*
ter her. I will assume the name 'Foresight,' " she said, '*and I will speak* Gn 6:16; cf. Lk 16:3; Jn 12:19
to their *heart, if only they will listen and acquiesce.*' Ez 2:5

"She did this, addressing them in humble words: '*Why do you stand*
all day idle, without providing for your future? What does it profit you Mt 20:6
to have the necessities of life while you abstain from luxuries? For you
could work out your salvation and that of others with great peace and
leisure if everything you needed were readily available. *While you*
have time, provide for yourselves and your offspring, for people will Gal 6:10
withdraw their hand from their initial generosity and from their customary gifts. It would be good to remain always as you are, but you
cannot always achieve that since daily *the Lord adds to your number.* Acts 2:47
Since [the Lord] says *"It is more blessed to give than to receive,"*
wouldn't it be acceptable to God if you had something to give to the
needy and were *mindful of the poor?*'[a]

"After that fierce enemy said these and similar things to them, some
of those whose conscience was corrupt immediately gave their assent.
Others, however, turned a deaf ear and refuted the arguments she
brought forth *in their midst* with shrewd answers, and rested them no Lk 4:30
less than the others on the testimonies of the Scriptures.

---

a. The religious of the twelfth and thirteenth centuries responded to the needs of the poor by ministering to them from their surplus. Hospitality, building and maintaining hospices, distributing alms: these were some of the charitable institutions adopted by monks. Caring for the poor was guaranteed by income from the common canonical property, which was used to build hospices for the sick and for pilgrims as well as to support the monk responsible for distributing alms to the poor. Thus foresight had to be practiced in order to continue this apostolic outreach. (Cf. Michel Mollat, *The Poor in the Middles Ages: An Essay in Social History*, translated by Arthur Goldhammer [New Haven and London: Yale University Press, 1986].) (Cf. Acts 20:35; Gal 2:10) "Why don't you accept the goods that are offered to you so that you do not defraud those giving to you of an eternal reward? It is not that you should fear sharing riches, since you consider them nothing. Vice is not in things but in the soul, for God saw all that he had done and that it was very good. To the good everything is good, everything is useful, and everything is made for them. O how many have goods and use them poorly! While if you had them, you would put them to good use because your intention is holy, your desire is holy! Your wish is not to enrich your relatives for they are rich enough! If you had what is necessary, however, you could live more respectably and properly!"

Greed Seeks the Help of Sloth[a]

46 "But Greed, realizing that by herself she could not accomplish her desire through these men, changed her strategy in order to fulfill her plan. She summoned Sloth who neglects to initiate good deeds and to complete initiatives. [Greed] entered into an agreement with her and made a pact against them. She was hardly acquainted with [Sloth] nor even connected with her, yet *they* willingly *came together* as one for an
Acts 4:26,27 evil purpose, as *Herod and Pilate* had once done *against* the Savior.

"Once the agreement was made, Sloth growled and, after she had launched her attack, advanced her cohorts against the territory of these men. As she drew her weapons with all her strength, she extinguished the charity of these men, and turned them toward apathy and laziness. And so little by little, shriveled up by faintheartedness, their hearts became dead.

Religious Overcome by Sloth

47 "Then they began to pine with misery for what they had left behind in Egypt.[b] What they had once scorned with magnificent heart, they now sought with shame. They walked in sadness *the way of God's commandments* and, with arid hearts, they ran after his precepts. They grew weak under the burden and were hardly able to breathe for want of spirit. Sorrow was rare among them, contrition non-existent, obedience full of complaint, thought animal-like, joy dissipated, sadness fainthearted, speech unguarded, laughter easy. There was giddiness on their face, vanity in their manner of walking; their clothes were soft and delicate, carefully cut and even more carefully stitched. Their sleep was plentiful, food abundant, drink intemperate. They tossed their trash, foolishness, and words to the winds. They told stories, changed laws, administered provinces, and eagerly manipulated people's deeds. There was no care for spiritual exercises, no eagerness for

---

a. *Acidia,* more commonly called sloth through confusion with its most notable effect, is a disgust with the spiritual because of the physical effort involved. Following the earlier monastic tradition, John Cassian saw *acidia* as one of the principal vices of religious life and devoted one of his *Conferences* to a study of its spirit (cf. John Cassian, *Conferences* 10, PL 49: 359-369).

b. The description of *acidia* [sloth] that follows parallels those of monastic authors who list six "daughter-sins:" malice, rancor, pusillanimity, despair, torpor concerning commandments, and a wandering of the mind around forbidden things. The author of this text clearly sees this vice as encouraging religious to look elsewhere, i.e., to the rich, for satisfaction of their desires.

their soul's salvation; conversations about heavenly matters were rare, and the desire for eternal things was lukewarm.

[48]"Obdurate as they were, they began to envy one another, to provoke one another, and to dominate one another. One brother would accuse *another of the worst crime* with a gesture. They avoided what was Gn 37:2
sad while hungering to rejoice in what was vain for they were truly incapable of rejoicing. As they maintained the appearance of holiness in whatever way they could, lest they become entirely worthless, and while they spoke of holy matters, they, nevertheless, concealed their miserable way of life among the simple. But the corruption of their inner being was such that, while they were unable to restrain themselves, they became evident through clear, blatant signs.

[49]"They finally began to fawn upon those of the world and to enter into marriage with them that they might drain their purses, enlarge their buildings, and multiply what they had thoroughly renounced.

"They sold their words to the rich, their greetings to matrons, and frequented the courts of kings and princes with all-out zeal that *they might join house to house and unite field to field.* Now they are magnif- Is 5:8
icent and rich, the powerful of the earth, because *they have gone from evil to evil, and have not known the Lord.* They fell *when they had been* Jer 9:3
lifted up, had fallen upon the earth before their birth, yet they still say to me: 'We are your friends!' Ps 73:18

The Poor Who Had Become Rich Persecute Poverty

[50]"In grief, I was sorry more for those who, when they were sufficiently miserable and contemptible in the world, *became rich* after they had come to me. *Lazy* and *fat they were* more *recalcitrant* than the rest Rv 18:19; 1 Cor 1:5
as they derided me. They were surely considered *unworthy of life itself,* Dt 32:15
sterile from want and hunger, eating herbs and the bark of trees, disfigured by calamity and misery. Now they are not content with common Jb 30:2-4
life, but *segregate themselves shepherding themselves without fear.* Jude 19, 12
Their way of life is sufficiently annoying to others as they seek superfluous things and strive to achieve honor among Christ's disciples when, in the world, they were held in contempt even by those of note. Those who frequently lacked barley bread and water, who *considered it a delight to be under briars; children of the foolish and the ignoble and, not appearing at all upon the earth, have rolled themselves down*

to my miseries. They despise me, run far from me, and are not afraid to
Jb 30:7-8; 30:14; 30:10 *spit in my face.* I suffer *abuse and frightening things* from them. Those
Jer 20:10 who *used to be my friends and stood at my side* insulted me. They were
ashamed of me and the more they knew themselves to be enriched by
my kindness, the more strongly they spurned me. And so they even felt
contempt at hearing my name.

Poverty Warns Them to Return to Her

51 "In grief, I was sorry and said to them: *'Return, you children* who
Jer 3:22 are withdrawing, *and I will heal your aversions. Beware of all greed*
which is the service of idols, for *the greedy will not be filled with*
Lk 12:15; Eph 5:5; Eccl 5:9 *money. Remember those first days when you, enlightened as you were,*
Heb 10:32 *endured a great struggle of sufferings.* Do not become *children of a*
Heb 10:39 *withdrawal into perdition but of faith in the salvation of your soul.*
Whoever violates the law of Moses without mercy of any kind will die
before two or three witnesses. How much greater do you think will be
the punishment of one who has trodden the Son of God underfoot and
let the blood of the Testament in which he was made holy to be de-
Heb 10:28-29 *graded, and affronted the spirit of grace? Return to your heart,* therefore, *you transgressors, for one's life does not depend in the*
Is 46:8; Lk 12:15 *abundance of the things he possesses.'*

"But becoming angry they said: 'Go away, *depart from us,* you
Jb 21:14 wretched one! *We do not want knowledge of your ways.'*

"I said to them: '*Have mercy on me, have mercy on me, at least you,*
Jb 19:21-22 *my friends. Why are you persecuting me* without reason? Did I ever tell
you that my ways and yours would ever agree? Look, it pains me to
have seen you.'

The Lord Speaks to Poverty

52 *"Then the word of the Lord came to me: 'Return, return,*
Jer 13:1; Sg 7:1 *Sulamite, return, return that we might behold you.* These children are
instigators and do not wish to hear you because they do not wish to hear
Ez 2:7; 3:7 me. *Their heart has become incredulous and irritating to them. They*
Jer 5:23 *have departed and gone away, for they have not rejected you, but me.*
In fact, you have taught them against your own interest and have in-
structed them against your own good. If they hadn't accepted you, they

would never have become so rich. They pretended to love you that they would depart enriched. They have, therefore, turned away with stubborn contempt and, *as they cling to a lie refused to return.* You should Jer 8:5
not believe them when they tell you good things, because *they have despised you and sought your life. You should not take up praise and* Jer 4:30
prayer for them, because I will not hear you, for I have rejected them because they have spurned me.' Jer 7:16; 1 Sm 15:23

Lady Poverty Admonishes Blessed Francis About Progress and Regression in Religious Life

[53]"Behold, brothers, I have told you a long parable that *your eyes might precede* your *steps* and that you might see what you should do. It Prv 4:25
is very dangerous to look back and to mock God. *Recall Lot's wife* and *do not believe every spirit.* Nevertheless *I trust you, dearly beloved,* Lk 17:32; Gn 19:26; 1 Jn 4:1; Heb 6:9
because in you, more than in others, I see things better and closer to salvation. For this reason you seem to have completely rejected and unburdened yourselves of everything. In all these things, the most convincing proof for me is your ascent of this mountain that few have ever been able to approach. But *I tell you, my friends:* the malice of many has made me suspicious of the virtue of the good. I have fre- Lk 12:4
quently experienced *ravenous wolves in sheep's clothing.* Mt 7:15

[54]"I surely want each one of you to become an imitator of the holy ones who have inherited me in faith and in patience. Yet, because I fear that what happened to others might also happen to you, I am giving you salutary advice, that is, that, in the beginning, you should not want to reach what is more lofty and more hidden. Instead, with Christ as your guide, as you slowly make progress, may you finally reach the summit. Watch that, after the dung of trivia has been placed at your roots, you may be found barren, for then there is nothing else than for an ax to be used upon you. Do not believe all of the impressions you now have, because *human senses* are more prone to doing *evil* than good and the spirit easily returns to what it is accustomed, even though it may have been considerably distanced from it. For I know that in an excess of fer- Gn 8:21
vor everything seems very easy to you. But remember what is said: *'Behold those who serve God are not steadfast and he has found defects in his angels.'* Jb 4:18

55 "At first everything will seem very sweet for you to bear, but after a little while, once you have accepted security, you will tolerate negligence of the blessings you have received. At that hour you will think you want to return to that state and to rediscover the first consolation, but negligence once allowed is not easily uprooted. Your heart will then turn to other things, but reason will call you back to the first.[a] Thus turned in spirit to laziness and sloth, you will offer thoughtless words of excuse. 'We cannot be as strong as we were in the beginning,' you say, 'times are now different.' And so you do not know what is said:
Sir 18:6 *When a man has ended, he is only just beginning.* There will always be an inner voice, however, which will say: 'Tomorrow, tomorrow we
Hos 2:7 will return *to that first husband* for it was better *then than now.'*

"*Behold I have predicted* many things to you, brothers, and *I have*
Mt 24:25; Jn 16:12 *many things to say to you* which *you cannot bear now. The hour will*
Jn 16:25 *come when I will explain to you clearly* everything mentioned above."

Blessed Francis Together with His Brothers Responds to Poverty

56 At these words the blessed Francis and his brothers fell flat on the ground and gave thanks to God. "What you say pleases us, our Lady," they said. " There can be no fault in anything you have said. What we heard in our land about your words and your wisdom is true. Your wisdom is so much greater than the rumor we had heard. Your men and your servants are blessed, those who are always before you and listen to your wisdom. May the Lord God be blessed forever whom you have pleased and who has loved you forever and placed you as queen to show mercy and judgment upon His servants. O how good and sweet is your spirit, correcting the erring and admonishing sinners!

57 "Lady, by the eternal King's love with which he loved you and by the love with which you love him, we beg you not to cheat us of our desire. Deal with us, instead, according to your kindness and mercy. For your deeds are great and ineffable. For this reason those who lack discipline have strayed from you! Because you march over rocky ground, like an army of soldiers set in array, the foolish cannot stay with you. But we are your servants and the sheep of your pasture. For all eternity and age upon age we promise and resolve to keep the judgments of your justice."

a. Another reading of this passage, based on one collection of manuscripts, has: "Your heart will then turn aside to other things, but *rarely* will it cry out for you to return to the first things."

The Consent of Poverty

[58]*These words deeply moved* Lady Poverty. Always accustomed to 1 Kgs 3:26; Gn 42:30
be merciful and forgiving, she ran, incapable of containing herself any
more, and embraced them. She placed a kiss of peace on each one.
"Look, I am coming to you, my brothers and sons," she shouted. "I Rv 22:7,12
know many will acquire me as profit because of you."

Blessed Francis, unable to contain himself out of joy, with a loud
voice began to praise the All-powerful Who did not abandon those *who
hope in him. "Bless the Lord,"* he said, *"all you his chosen ones. Keep* Jdt 13:17
days of joy and confess to him because He is good, because His mercy Tob 13:10
is forever!" Ps 106:1; 135:1

As they came down from the mountain, they led Lady Poverty to the
place where they were staying, for *it was nearly the sixth hour.* Jn 4:6

The Banquet of Poverty with the Brothers

[59]After they had prepared everything, they persuaded her to eat with them. But she said: "First show me your oratory, chapter room, enclosure, refectory, kitchen, dormitory and stable; your beautiful chairs, polished tables and large houses. I do not see any of these. I only notice that you are cheerful and happy, overflowing with joy, filled with consolation, as if you expect that everything will be given you at your request."

They answered: "Our Lady and Queen, we, your servants, are tired from the long journey and you, coming with us, have expended no little effort. Let us first eat. Once we are strengthened, if you direct, we will do everything as you wish."

[60]"I am pleased at what you say," she said. "But bring some water that we might wash our hands and some towels to dry them." They brought her immediately a cracked earthen bowl—because there was not a whole one—filled with water. Pouring the water over her hands they looked here and there for a towel. When they couldn't find one, one of them offered her the tunic he was wearing that she could dry her hands with it. Accepting it with thanks, she then gave in her heart glory to God Who had brought her into association with such men.

[61]Then they led her to where they had prepared the table. When they had led her there, she saw that there was nothing more than three or four crusts of barley or bran bread set upon the grass. She was greatly aston-

ished and said to herself: "Who has ever seen *in past generations* such
Is 66:8; 51:9 things as these! Blessed are you, Lord God, Who cares for all things! Everything is possible when you wish. You have taught your people to please you through such deeds." They then sat down together, thanking God for all His gifts.

[62]Lady Poverty gave the order to bring the cooked food on dishes. Behold a single dish was brought filled with cold water for all of them to dip bread. There was neither an abundance of dishes nor a variety of cooked foods.

She asked that at least uncooked, aromatic herbs be brought to her. Since they did not have a gardener and knew nothing of a garden, however, they gathered wild herbs in the woods and placed them before her.

"Bring me a little salt," she said, "to season the herbs for they are bitter." "Wait, Lady," they responded. "We will go to town for some. If they are offered to us, we will bring them to you."

"Bring me a knife," she said, "and I will cut away what is superfluous and slice the bread which is hard and dry." "Lady, we don't have a blacksmith to make us swords. For now use your teeth in place of a knife. Afterwards, we will provide one."

Jn 2:3 "Is there a little wine among you?" "Our Lady, *we have no wine,"*
they responded. *"At the beginning of human life there was only bread*
Sir 29:28 *and water.* It is not good for you to drink wine because Christ's spouse
must avoid wine like poison."

[63]When they were satisfied more by the glory of such want than by an abundance of all things, they blessed the Lord in whose sight they found such grace and led her to a place where she would rest because she was tired. And so she laid down naked upon the naked earth.

She even asked for a pillow for her head. They immediately brought a stone and placed it under her head.

After enjoying a very quiet and healthy sleep, she quickly arose and asked to be shown the enclosure. Taking her to a certain hill, they showed her all the world they could see and said: "This, Lady, is our enclosure."[a]

a. Whereas poverty in the monastic world was limited to its pursuit in the confines of the enclosure and demanded their stability, that of the friars envisioned no barriers and enabled them to travel throughout the world. Commenting on this new approach to religious life and subsequent evangelization, Matthew Paris made a similar statement of the Friars Preacher: "The whole earth is their cell and the ocean is their enclosure." Cf. Lester K. Little, *Religious Poverty and the Profit Economy in Medieval Europe* (Ithaca: Cornell University Press, 1978), 218.

Lady Poverty Blesses the Brothers and Urges Them to Persevere in the Grace They Have Received

64 She ordered all of them to be seated about her and spoke to them
the words of life. "You are blessed by the Lord God *Who* made *heaven* Jn 6:69
and earth, my sons. You who have received me into your home with Jd 13:23, 24
such a fullness of charity that it seems to me that today I am with you as
in God's paradise. I am, then, *filled with joy. I overflow with consola-* Ez 31:8,9; Rv 2:7
tion, and I ask pardon for having so delayed in coming. Truly the Lord 2 Cor 7:4
is with you *and I did not know it.* I see what I have yearned for; what I Gn 28:16
have desired I now possess, for I am joined on earth to those who bear
the image of Him to Whom I am espoused in heaven. May the Lord
bless your *strength* and receive *the work of* your *hands.* Dt 33:11

65 "I ask and greatly beg you as dearly beloved children to persevere in what you have begun by the teaching of the Holy Spirit, not abandoning your perfection as is the custom of others. After you have avoided all the snares of the dark, however, may you always strive for what is more perfect. Your profession is very lofty. It shines with a more brilliant light above humanity, above the virtue and perfection of the ancients.

"Let there be no doubt about your possession of the kingdom of heaven. Let there be no hesitation among you! For you already possess a promise of a future inheritance and have received the pledge of the Spirit. Signed with the seal of Christ's glory, you respond in everything, by His grace, like those of that first school which He established upon coming into the world. For what they did in His presence, you have thoroughly begun to do in His absence. Isn't it what you dare to
say: *'Behold we have left everything and followed you?'* Mt 19:27

66 "Let the length of the race and the immensity of the labor not deter
you for you will have a great reward. *While focusing on the author and*
goal of all good, the Lord Jesus Christ, who, after he condemned its
shame, endured the cross for the sake of the joy that awaited him, hold
onto the unwavering confession of your hope. Run in love *to the race* Heb 12:2; 10:23
that is set before you. Run with the patience which is especially neces- Heb 12:1
sary for you, that, while you are doing God's will, you may receive
what is promised. *For God is able* to bring to completion with joy what Heb 10:36
you have begun with his grace beyond your powers, because He is
faithful to His promises. Rom 11:23

67 "Let *the spirit that works within children of unbelief* not find any-
Eph 2:2 thing pleasing in you. Let it not find anything doubtful. Let it not find
anything fainthearted so that it will not have in you reason for exercis-
ing its perversity against you. For *that spirit is exceedingly proud* and
Is 16:6 *its pride and arrogance are more than its strength.* It will show *great*
anger toward you, will turn the arms of its universal cunning on you,
and attempt to pour out the venom of its wrath. It will be like the one
who, in warring against the rest, has conquered and cast them down and
Rv 12:12 is now sad to see you looking down on it.

68 "At your conversion, dearly beloved, the citizens of heaven have
been celebrating with great joy and have *sung new songs* before the
Rv 5:9 eternal King. The angels rejoice in and about you for through you many
will preserve virginity and will shine with chastity. The ruins of the
heavenly city will be filled, where the virgins are more wonderfully
gathered since those who *neither marry nor are given in marriage will*
Mt 22:30 *be like God's angels in heaven.* The Apostles exult at seeing their life
renewed, their teaching proclaimed, and their examples of outstanding
holiness shown through you. The martyrs rejoice in expecting that their
own constancy in pouring out their sacred blood will be repeated. The
confessors dance with joy at knowing that their frequent victories over
the enemy will be remembered in you. The virgins *following the Lamb*
wherever he goes are jubilant at sensing that their number is growing
Rv 14:4 each day through you. Finally, the entire heavenly court is filled with
exultation and will celebrate the daily solemnities of new inhabitants
and will be continually refreshed by the fragrance of the holy prayers
rising up from this valley.

69 *"Therefore, I beg you, brothers, through the mercy of God which*
has made you so poor, do that for which you have come, that for which
Rom 12:1 *you have risen up from the waters of Babylon.* Humbly receive the
grace offered you. Always use it worthily for the praise and glory and
honor of Him Who died for you, Jesus Christ, our Lord, Who lives and
reigns, conquers and rules with the Father and the Holy Spirit, God
Rv 4:9 eternally glorious, forever and ever. Amen."

RELATED DOCUMENTS

(1215–1237)

Introduction

In addition to Francis's own writings and the hagiographical documents which came from within his own brotherhood, there are a wide variety of other sources which provide some additional data and interesting perspectives on the life of Francis.[a] Most of these do not focus much attention on the personality of Francis himself, but saw him mainly as the founder of the radically new movement of gospel life which they were encountering. Some of these witnesses were captivated by the new Order, others were threatened or indifferent. But taken together, they form a rich tapestry of impressions, letting us see how Francis's contemporaries viewed him and his Order of Lesser Brothers during the first three decades of their existence.

a. Many of these were collected by Leonard Lemmens. O.F.M., *Testimonia minora saeculi XIII de S. Francisco Assisiensis* (Quaracchi, 1926).

Papal Documents

A) *Cum dilecti* of Honorius III (1219)

This brief letter is the first known official document of the Papal court concerning Francis's brotherhood.[a] It is essentially a "letter of introduction" assuring bishops and pastors that members of this highly untraditional group did in fact belong to an approved religious community. Such letters were especially necessary in light of the fact that the Fourth Lateran Council (1215) had taken strong measures against unauthorized wandering preachers.[b]

Honorius, Bishop, Servant of the servants of God, to our venerable brothers, the archbishops and bishops; and to our beloved sons, the abbots, deans, archdeacons, and other prelates of churches: health and apostolic benediction.

Our beloved sons, Brother Francis and his companions of the life and religion of the Lesser Brothers have rejected the vanities of this world and have chosen a way of life deservedly approved by the Roman Church;[c] after the example of the Apostles they go throughout different regions sowing the seed of the word of God.

We therefore beseech and exhort all of you in the Lord, and by these apostolic letters command you, when members of the aforesaid brotherhood present themselves to you bearing these letters, to receive them as [true] Catholic faithful, showing yourselves favorable and kind to them out of reverence for God and us.

Given at Rieti, the eleventh of June, in the third year of our pontificate (1219).[d]

---

a. BFr, 1, p. 2. n. 2.

b. Especially canon 3: "There are some who *holding to the form of religion but denying its power,* as the Apostle says, (1 Tm 3:5) claim for themselves the authority to preach, whereas the same Apostle says, *How shall they preach unless they are sent?* (Rom 10:15) Let therefore all those who have been forbidden or not sent to preach, and yet dare publicly or privately to usurp the office of preaching without having received the authorization of the Apostolic See or the Catholic bishop of the place, be bound with the bond of excommunication and, unless they repent very quickly, be punished by another suitable penalty." Cf. also canon 62. *Decrees of the Ecumenical Councils,* 1: 234-35, 263 (hereafter DEC).

c. We have literally translated the word *religio* used by Honorius here, as it was the usual term for a religious order. He here is apparently recognizing the oral approval of the primitive Rule by Innocent III and the subsequent on-going approbation of the Roman court as giving full legal foundation to the Lesser Brothers.

d. Both the town and, more importantly, the date of issuance of this bull differ in the manuscripts. Sbaralea (Bfr 1, p. 2) gives 1219, from Rieti. In 1919, Delorme was persuaded to assign the letter to 1218, and from the Lateran; his opinion was followed in a number of studies. We have followed the argument of Williel R. Thomson ("Checklist of Papal Letters Relating to the Three Orders of Saint Francis: Innocent III—Alexander IV," AFH [1971]: 379), who views the 1219 date as preferable.

B) *Pro dilectis* of Honorius III (1220)

This bull, reinforcing the previous one, was sent to the prelates of France, where apparently fears about unauthorized preaching were especially prevalent.[a] Indeed, legislation for the diocese of Paris in 1213 approved by the Papal legate, Robert Courçon, which was extended to the whole province by the Council of Rouen the following year, specifically outlawed wandering preachers, especially those who were also collecting alms.[b] Jordan of Giano is most likely referring to this letter, when he relates in his Chronicle: "When the brothers went to France, . . . they were put down as heretics. But when the bishop[c] and the masters read their Rule . . . , they took counsel about the matter with the Lord Pope Honorius. The Pope, however, declared in a letter that the Rule was authentic, since it had been confirmed by the Holy See, and that the brothers were in a very special way sons of the Roman Church and true Catholics."[d]

> Honorius, bishop, Servant of the servants of God, to our venerable brothers, the archbishops and bishops; and to our beloved sons, the abbots, priors, and other prelates of churches, established throughout the kingdom of France, health and apostolic benediction.
>
> We recall that we sent you a letter on behalf of our beloved sons of the Order of Lesser Brothers in order that you might consider them as having been recommended in the sight of the love of God.[e] But, as we now understand, some of you seemingly have a doubtful conscience about this same Order. We also gather from other reports, in which we can place full trust, that others of you do not even allow these brothers to stay in their dioceses, although the very fact that we have granted these brothers our letter shows that you should not consider them suspect in any way.
>
> Therefore, we want all of you to take note that we hold their Order [to be] among those approved by us, and that we regard the brothers of this Order as truly Catholic and devout men. We therefore take this occasion through these apostolic letters to warn and exhort you, indeed we prescribe and command you, to admit them into your dioceses as

a. Text from BFr, I, p.5, n.4.

b. Cf. references in Richard H. and Mary A. Rouse, *Preachers, Florilegia, and Sermons* (Toronto: Pontifical Academy of Mediaeval Studies, 1979), 45-46.

c. Probably Peter of Nemours, 1208-19.

d. Jordan, 4 [*Thirteenth Century Chronicles*, pp. 21-22]. Although some friars were sent into France in 1217, Franciscans probably did not reach the Paris region until a second mission following the chapter of 1219, which was led by Brother Pacifico.

e. The letter *Cum dilecti* cited above, or perhaps other letters sent to the bishops of Paris and Sens. Cf. BFr 1, p. 5, note e. It is also interesting that the Pope here employs the precise canonical term: "order."

true believers and religious and to hold them, out of reverence for God and for us, as having been favorably recommended.

Given at Viterbo, the twenty-ninth day of May, in the fourth year of our pontificate (1220).

C) *Cum secundum* of Honorius III (1220)

With this bull,[a] the Papacy moved to correct what it saw as deficiencies in a yet highly unstructured religious brotherhood. Francis was known for accepting all who wished to join him; the simple act of distributing one's goods to the poor and putting on the habit of penance made one a Lesser Brother. There was no stage of "formation" which could test those who may have made a hasty, unconsidered decision to follow this demanding radical Gospel life, a point which drew criticism from even enthusiasts of the new brotherhood.[b] Furthermore, the total freedom of movement which characterized the itinerant life of the early brothers also came at the cost of undisciplined or idle brothers causing scandal rather than edification. Accepting the minimum structures contained here also helped the Lesser Brothers gain recognition as a true religious Order. The provisions of this bull were incorporated by Francis when he prepared the 1221 revision of the Rule.

Honorius, Bishop, Servant of the servants of God, to our beloved sons, the priors and custodians of the Lesser Brothers:[c] greetings and apostolic benediction.

Prv 13:16 The Wise One tells us that *the clever do all things intelligently,* lest
they come to regret it later on. So it is important that anyone proposing
to undertake a higher way of life look before he leaps, that is, take prudent stock of his own [inner] resources. Otherwise—which God forbid—he might aspire to things that are beyond his strength and his
Gn 19:26 steps waver and turn back, only to be turned into a pillar of salt, because
he did not know how to season the sacrifice which he intended to offer
to the Lord—his very self—with the salt of wisdom. For just as a prudent man becomes stale should he lack enthusiasm, so the enthusiastic man will be covered with confusion if he is not prudent.

a. Text in BFr, I, 6, n.5.

b. For example, see "Letter VI" of Jacques de Vitry infra, p. 580.

c. One sees here the lack of familiarity of officials at the Roman Curia with the terminology used among the Lesser Brothers, i.e., the use of priors [the Dominican term for the major superiors] instead of ministers.

For this reason practically every religious order has wisely ordained that those who propose to undertake a life of regular observance should first test it and be tested in it for a certain length of time so that they will not later have reason to regret their decision, which cannot be excused under pretext of levity. Therefore, by authority of these present letters,[a] we forbid you to admit to profession in your Order anyone who has not first completed a year of probation. And once he has made profession, let no brother dare to leave your Order. It is also forbidden for anyone to receive [into another religious community] any brother who has left your Order.[b]

We further forbid anyone to wander about clad in the habit of your Order outside obedience, corrupting the purity of your poverty. If anyone should presume to do this, it is lawful for you to bring ecclesiastical censure upon such a brother until he has come to his senses.[c]

No one, therefore, is in any way permitted to tamper with this decree of our prohibition and concession or rashly dare to oppose it. If anyone shall have presumed to attempt this, let him know that he will incur the wrath of Almighty God and of his holy Apostles Peter and Paul.

Given at Viterbo, the twenty-second day of September, in the fifth year of our pontificate (1220).

D) *Solet annuere* of Honorius III (1223)

For the text of this bull, see the *Later Rule* among the writings of Francis.

E) *Quia populares* of Honorius III (1224)

The first itinerant Lesser Brothers attended liturgical services in parish churches like other lay people, where they also preached when invited to do so. As permanent dwellings or "places" gradually became established, they simply

a. This bull was reissued by Gregory IX shortly after his election, 13 May 1227 (BFr, 1, p. 27, n.2).

b. In other words, promising to observe the life of the Lesser Brothers was equivalent to profession in one of the old approved orders, another step in the recognition of the new brotherhood as an official religious order.

c. Honorius III followed this up with the bull, *Fratrum Minorum*, in December, 1223, demanding that bishops recognize such censures imposed on brothers by their ministers as canonically binding (BFr, 1, p. 19, n. 15).

had oratories for private prayer; only a few churches were given to the brothers.[a] But as the number of clerics in the Order grew, it was only natural that the brothers would want to celebrate their own services, instead of having to go out for them. This bull granted them the privilege of celebrating the full choral Eucharist and Divine Office in all of their houses, effectively letting them carry on liturgical prayer independently of the local church in the manner of monastic communities.[b] It is a clear testimony to an increasing clerical orientation in the Order.

Honorius, Bishop, Servant of the servants of God, to our beloved sons, the brothers of the Order of Minors: greetings and apostolic benediction.

Fleeing the tumult of the crowds as something that impedes your proposed way of life, you eagerly seek separate places so that you can give yourself more freely to the sacred quiet of prayer. Because of this, we are most attentive to this opportune request of your many prayers. For your intercession before God will be all the more efficacious to the extent that, living perfectly, you become all the more worthy of graces from him.

We consider that what does not take away from anyone else's rights should not be denied to you, while genuine religion entreats us to concede to you even those things which are a special favor. Furthermore, since you have professed and embraced holy poverty, you are not seeking any temporal favor from us, but a spiritual one for your devotion. Therefore, favorable to your petitions, by authority of these present letters, we concede to you this privilege: that in your places and oratories you may celebrate solemn Masses with a portable altar, as well as the other divine offices, without prejudice to the rights of parochial churches.[c]

No one, therefore, is in any way permitted to tamper with this decree of our concession and indult or rashly dare to oppose it. If anyone shall have presumed to attempt this, let him know that he will incur the wrath of Almighty God and of his holy Apostles Peter and Paul.

---

a. For many years, the only church in the Order was the Portiuncula. The number of actual churches continued to be very small even at this time. A previous bull of Honorius had exempted the brothers from an interdict, allowing them to celebrate Mass "in your churches, should you happen to have any" [*Devotionibus vestrae,* March 29, 1222, BFr 1, p. 9, no. 10]. The first church officially granted the Order by Papal provision was not until 1227 [*Licet Sacrosancta,* 20 October 1227, BFr, 1, p. 34, n. 13].

b. Text in BFr, 1, p. 20, n.17.

c. In a subsequent bull, Gregory IX specified that parochial churches had rights to the offerings, tithes, and first fruits of the faithful [*Nos attendentes,* May 26, 1228, BFr 1, p. 41, n.23].

Given at Rieti, the third day of December, in the ninth year of our pontificate (1224).[a]

F) *Vineae Domini* of Honorius III (1225)

With this bull,[b] the Papacy gave its full support to the missionary initiative among Muslims, so dear to Francis's heart, but by singling out roles that only an ordained brother could perform, Honorius is subtly redefining that mission in a more clerical direction. This bull was followed up by two others which further accentuated this trend. One, to the archbishop of Toledo, empowered him to consecrate one of these brothers as a bishop.[c] Another dispensed them from some of the prescriptions of the Rule in view of the demands of their mission; they did not have to wear the habit and tonsure and were allowed to use money.[d] We see that acceptance of a pastoral mission on behalf of the church is beginning to determine the Franciscan way of life.

Honorius, Bishop and Servant of the servants of God, to the brothers, Preachers and Minors, designated by the Apostolic See to go to the Kingdom of the Miramamolin:[e] greetings and apostolic benediction.

Set up as guardians and cultivators of the vineyard of the Lord, though without any merit of our own, we are bound to send workers into the harvest, distributing tasks to each of them according to their ability, so that all might better fulfill their mission.

We are mindful that, denying your very selves, you wish to surrender your own souls to Christ, in order that you might win over the souls of others for him. Since no sacrifice is ever more pleasing to God than seeking to gain souls, we confer upon you who are going into the Kingdom of the Miramamolin, the authority of the Apostolic See, so that proclaiming the Gospel of Jesus Christ there, insofar as he grants, you might convert the infidels, regain those who have fallen away from the faith, strengthen those who are weak, console the fearful, and encourage the strong.

a. The same bull was re-issued by Gregory IX, May 4, 1227, shortly after his election [BFr 1, p. 27, n.1], thus renewing this privilege. This was soon expanded by giving the brothers the right to bury their own dead in their places [*Ita vobis*, 26 July 1227, BFr 1, p. 31, n.8].

b. Text in BFr 1, p. 24, n. 23.

c. *Urgente officii*, February 20, 1226, BFr 1, p. 24, n. 24.

d. *Ex parte vestra*, March 17, 1226, BFr 1, p. 26, n. 25.

e. Miramamolin, "Ruler of many nations," was an appellation of the rulers of the Almohad empire of Morocco and Southern Spain.

So that you might exercise this ministry with greater confidence, we concede to you all that we can, so that in the aforementioned region you will have our authority to preach, to baptize the Saracens who have just come over to the faith, to reconcile apostates, to impose penances, and to absolve those who are excommunicated and who cannot travel easily to the Apostolic See. You are also permitted to pronounce a sentence of excommunication in that land on all those who pass over into heresy.

Furthermore, we prohibit any Christian from expelling you from that land by force. We also command you, under virtue of obedience, to in no way presume to abuse these faculties, but as indefatigable laborers for Jesus Christ, to conduct yourselves there in a manner beyond reproach, so that you might merit a just wage from the divine Father of the household and so that we ourselves might be able to assign you to even more important tasks.[a]

Given at Rieti, on the seventh of October, in the tenth year of our pontificate (1225).

G) *Recolentes qualiter* of Gregory IX (1228)

Even before the process of Francis's canonization had been completed, his friend and protector Hugolino, now Pope Gregory IX, made plans to construct a basilica in his honor. The commune of Assisi had already donated a hill outside the walls as a site for the church. In this bull he requested donations from the faithful of the Catholic world to assist in this project.[b] The following year he sent another bull under the same title to the Minister General, John Parenti, taking the basilica under his protection as the property of the Apostolic See.[c]

Gregory, Bishop and Servant of the servants of God, to all the faithful who may read these letters: greetings and apostolic benediction.

We recall how the sacred plantation of the Order of Lesser Brothers began and grew marvelously under blessed Francis of holy memory, through the favor of Christ spreading far and wide the flowers and perfumes of a holy way of life, so that in the desert of this world the beauty

a. The Papacy soon utilized Franciscans for other sensitive missions, for example to bear a threatening letter from Gregory IX to the Emperor Frederick II (*Ascendit ad nos*, 7 May 1228, BFr 1, p. 41, n. 22).

b. One Simone Puzarelli had donated the land on March 30, 1228; see notes to the bull *Is que ecclesiam*, April 22 1230, BFr 1, p. 60-62.

c. This bull has the same incipit *Recolentes;* text in BFr, 1, p. 46, but for the correct date (April 29, 1229), see Thomson, p. 385.

of holy religion seems to come from the aforesaid Order. Thus it seems to us both fitting and opportune that for the veneration of the same Father, a special church should be built in order to hold his body.

For such a work, the assistance of the faithful is needed, and we believe that it is beneficial for your salvation if you show yourselves to be devoted children and extend a helping hand. Therefore, we beg all of you, we admonish and exhort you in the Lord, and, for the remission of your sins, we enjoin you, that for this work you donate pious alms from the riches bestowed on you by God and subsidies imposed from the gratitude of love, so that through this and other good works which you perform through God's inspiration, you might be able to arrive at the prize of eternal happiness.

And we, invoking the mercy of almighty God and by the authority of his holy Apostles Peter and Paul, graciously grant to all the benefactors of this work the remission of forty days of penance imposed upon them.

Given at Rieti, the twenty-ninth of April, in the second year of our pontificate (1228).

H) *Mira circa nos* of Gregory IX (1228)

With this document, the Pope proclaimed Francis as a saint of the Church. While the actual ceremony of canonization took place in Assisi on July 16, 1228, this document was promulgated three days later in Perugia.

Gregory, Bishop, Servant of the servants of God, to our venerable brothers, the archbishops and bishops; and to our beloved sons, the abbots, deans, archdeacons, and other prelates of churches: health and apostolic benediction.

1 "O wondrous condescension of the divine mercy for us! How boundless the depths of God's love, which sacrificed a Son to ransom a slave!"[a] Yet God does not withhold the gifts of his compassion, but still protects with his continual care the vineyard *which* his *right hand has planted.*[b] Even *at the eleventh hour,* God has sent workers to cultivate Ps 80:14; Mt 20:1-7

a. From the Proclamation at the Easter Vigil, the *Exultet* (*Liber Usualis* [New York: Desclée, 1952], 740).

b. It is helpful to keep in mind the renewal and reform imagery found in many works of medieval ecclesial and religious literature for it permeates this papal document. Agricultural images, such as the vineyard, as well as eschatological ones, such as "the eleventh hour," are common here as they will be in the works of Thomas of Celano, Henri d'Avranches, and Bonaventure of Bagnoregio.

it, rooting out briars and thorns with hoe and *plowshare,* with which
Jgs 3:31 *Shamgar slew six hundred Philistines.*[a] These workers have cut back the overgrown branches and pulled up the brambles and shallow-rooted offshoots so that the vines might produce sweet, delicious fruit. Such fruit, when purified in the winepress of endurance, can be stored in the cellar of eternity. For the vineyard has been laid waste by ungodliness as if by fire, and the charity of many has gone cold; they are destined to be destroyed in the same catastrophe as that which befell the Philistines, who were overcome by the poison of their earthly sensual pleasures.[b]

[2]But just as when the Lord destroyed the earth with the waters of the
Wis 10:4 flood, he saved *the righteous man by a paltry piece of wood,* so even now he has not allowed *the scepter of wickedness . . . (to) rest on the*
Ps 125:3 *land allotted to the righteous.* For behold, *at the eleventh hour,* he
1 Sm 13:14 raised up his servant Francis, *a man* truly *after his own heart.* He was a beacon whom the rich viewed with contempt, but whom God had prepared for the appointed time, sending him into his vineyard to root out the thorns and brambles after having put the attacking Philistines to flight, to light up the path to our homeland, and to reconcile people to God by his zealous preaching.

[3]For when Francis heard the voice of his beloved calling within him, he rose up without delay. Like another Samson,[c] with God's help he broke the bonds that tied him to the seductive world. Filled with the zeal of the Holy Spirit, he *took up the jawbone of an ass,* preaching in simple words, *not with the plausible words of human wisdom,* but with the mighty strength of God, *who chose what is weak in the world to*
1 Cor 2:4-5; 1:27 *shame the strong.* With this weapon, through the grace of the one *who touches the mountains and makes them smoke, he slew,* not just *a thou-*
Ps 104: 32 *sand,* but many thousands of Philistines, bringing back to spiritual ser-

a. Two references in the *Glossa ordinaria* help us to understand this cryptic reference to the obscure Biblical figure. In his *Questiones in Heptateucum,* Augustine writes: "You ask: why did Shamgar fight for Israel after Aod and why is he described as having rescued it? He had not been taken prisoner or made a slave. But he rescued Israel not because the enemy had harmed him, but because he prevented him from doing evil since it should be maintained that his adversary sought to begin a war and was prevented by his (Shamgar's) victory." Origen, commenting on the same passage in his *Homilia IV in Liber Judicum,* writes: "I see here another motive for praising Shamgar. This man fought with a plow, while Aod won with a sword and subdued the Philistines. After this, therefore, it happens that a judge of the Church does not always avail himself of a sword, that is, he does not always have recourse to severe discourses and the use of the goad of correction. But, more than anything else, he imitates the farmer as he plows the field of our earth with his plow and often breaks it open with a kind of admonition, so that it may be more receptive to the seed. So here, the Philistines are killed when we do not go against our adversaries with arguments and subtleties, but with simple admonitions for the souls of our hearers to avoid vice."

b. A second allusion to the book of Judges, this time to the destruction of the temple of the Philistines by Samson in the midst of their feasting (Jgs 16:23-30).

c. This paragraph is another extended allusion to the story of Samson (Jgs 15:14-16).

vitude those who had previously been enslaved by the pleasures of the
flesh. Once they were dead to their vices and could live for God and no
longer for themselves, from the moment that their old selves were
killed, there flowed forth for them *from that same jawbone* [of Fran- Jgs 15:19
cis's preaching] abundant waters, which refreshed the fallen, cleansed
the filthy, and irrigated the dry. This *spring, gushing up to eternal life,* Jn 4:14, Is 55:1
could be purchased without money and without price; its stream spread
far and wide, watering the vineyard, *sending out its branches to the sea*
and its shoots to the river. Ps 79:11

[4]Finally, following the footprints of our father Abraham, this man
not only left spiritually his *country and* his *kindred,* but even his *fa-*
ther's house, to go *to the land which* the Lord, by divine inspiration, Gn 12:1
had shown him. And that he might more readily *press on for the prize of* Phil 3:14
the heavenly call and more easily *enter by the narrow gate,* he dis- Mt 7:13
carded the baggage of worldly possessions. He conformed himself to
the one who, *although rich, became poor for our sake; he distributed* 2 Cor 8:9
his goods *freely, giving to the poor,* so that *his righteousness* might *en-*
dure forever. Ps 112: 9

As he approached *the land of vision, on one of the mountains* that had
been shown him—namely the height of faith—he offered as *a holocaust* Gn 22:2
to the Lord his own flesh. As it had previously deceived him, like Jgs 11:34-35
Jepthah he offered this only-begotten daughter, laying it on the fire of
love, mortifying his flesh by hunger, thirst, cold, nakedness, fasting, and
countless nights of prayer. When he had thus crucified his *flesh with its*
passions and desires, he was able to say with the Apostle: *It is no longer I* Gal 5:24
who live, but Christ who lives in me. Truly, he no longer lived for him- Gal 2:20
self, but rather for Christ, who died for our sins *and was raised for our*
justification, so that *we might no longer be enslaved to sin.* Rom 4:25; Rom 6:6

Uprooting his vices and courageously taking up *the struggle*
against the world, the flesh, and *the spiritual forces of evil,* he utterly Eph 6:12
renounced *wife, farm,* and *oxen,* the things which had prevented *those*
who had been invited from attending the banquet. Rather, when the Lk 14:15-20
Lord commanded him, he rose like Jacob. Having received the Gn 35:1-15
seven-fold gift of the Spirit, and with the aid of the eight Gospel beatitudes, he went up by these fifteen steps of virtue, mystically contained
in the Psalter, to *Bethel, the house of God,* which he himself had prepared for him. There he made an altar of his heart for the Lord and offered upon it the fragrance of devout prayers. These the angels brought

into the sight of the Lord by their own hands, as he was soon to join
their angelic company.

[5]But not wishing to benefit only himself by remaining on the mountain, clinging to Rachel's embraces alone, that is to a contemplation
that is beautiful but sterile, he came down to Leah's forbidden bed-
Sg 4:2 chamber, to lead his flock, now fertile with twins, to the interior of the
desert to seek the pastures of life.[a] There, where the manna of heaven
refreshes by its sweetness, and separated from the din of worldly concerns, he scattered his seed with many tears so that he might *carry his*
Ps 126:6 *sheaves rejoicing* into the storehouse of eternity. Thus he would be
Ps 113:8 placed *with the princes of his people,* and crowned *with the crown of*
2 Tm 4:8 *righteousness.*

Phil 2:21 Certainly, he did not seek his own interests, but those of Christ,
serving him zealously like an industrious bee. *Like the morning star*
among the clouds, like the full moon in its days, like the sun shining on
Sir 50:6-7 the Church of God,[b] he took into his hands a lamp to attract the humble
to grace with the example of his shining deeds, and a trumpet to recall
the shameless from their baneful excesses by striking fear into them
with his stern reproaches.

In this way, impelled by the virtue of charity, he rushed fearlessly
Jgs 7:18-22 into the camp of the Midianites, those who were contemptuously disregarding the teaching of the church. With the help of the one whose authority encompassed the entire world even while enclosed in the womb
of the Virgin, Francis took away the weapons on which the strong man
relied while guarding his house, dividing the spoils which he had
Lk 11:21-22; Eph 4:8 seized and leading his captivity captive, submitting it to Jesus Christ.

[6]Therefore, having overcome even while here on earth the
three-fold enemy, he entered *the kingdom of heaven* violently, *taking it*
Mt 11:12 *by force.* After many glorious combats in this life and triumphing over
the world, he passed happily to the Lord. He, who was knowingly
ignorant and wisely unlearned, entered before many who were endowed with knowledge.

---

a. Gregory here is making an extended allusion to the story of Jacob and his two wives in Genesis 29, as interpreted by medieval spiritual authors. This tradition was succinctly summarized by Richard of Saint Victor in his *Benjamin Minor*: "For we read, Jacob is known to have had two wives. One was called Leah, the other Rachel. Leah was more fruitful; Rachel, more beautiful. Leah was fruitful but with poor eyesight. Rachel was nearly sterile, but of singular beauty . . . Rachel is teaching of truth; Leah, discipline of virtue. Rachel is pursuit of wisdom; Leah, longing for justice." *Richard of Saint Victor: The Twelve Patriarchs,* trans. Grover A. Zinn, Classics of Western Spirituality (New York: Paulist Press, 1979), p. 53.

b. The Biblical image in this passage is a reference to Simon "the Just," son of Jachanan, high priest from 219 to 196 BC. In those days, the temple of the Chosen People was fortified. The author, most likely a contemporary of Simon, uses these images to describe the impact of the presence of the renovator of the temple.

[7]Clearly, a life like his, so holy, so heroic, and so outstanding, was sufficient to win for him a place in the Church Triumphant. Yet because the Church Militant sees only outward appearances and does not presume to judge by her own authority those things not in her domain, it does not presume to venerate people for their way of life alone because sometimes *even Satan disguises himself as an angel of light.* But 2 Cor 11:14
the almighty and merciful God, by whose grace the above-mentioned servant of Christ served him in such a worthy and admirable manner, has not permitted such a marvelous *lamp* to remain hidden *under a bushel basket.* Rather, God has shown that he wishes it to be placed *on a lampstand to give* the consolation of *light to* those *in the house* by de- Mt 5:15
claring through numerous and outstanding miracles that Francis's life was pleasing to God and that his memory should be venerated by the Church Militant.

[8]Therefore, since the marvelous facts of his glorious life are fully known to us because of the great familiarity that he had with us while we were placed in a lesser position, and since we have been convinced by reliable witnesses of his many splendid miracles, we are confident that, through the mercy of God, we and the flock committed to us will be helped by his prayers, and that we will have as a patron in heaven him who was our close friend on earth. And so, with the advice and consent of our brothers [the cardinals], we have decided to inscribe him as worthy of veneration in the catalog of the saints.

[9]We decree that his birthday [into heaven] be celebrated devoutly and solemnly by the whole Church on the fourth of October, the day on which he was freed from the prison of the flesh and reached the heavenly realms.

[10]Therefore, we ask, counsel, and exhort all of you in the Lord, commanding you by this apostolic letter, that on the day aforementioned, you intently dedicate yourself to the divine praises, to honor his memory and humbly implore his protection, so that, through his merits and intercession, we may attain fellowship with him by the help of God, who is blessed forever and ever.

Given at Perugia on the nineteenth day of July (1228), in the second year of our pontificate.

I) *Quo elongati* of Gregory IX (1230)

This document was destined to be one of the most influential in Franciscan history. As Gregory states, he composed it at the request of the general chapter of 1230, where growing divisions and some confusion were apparent among the brothers as to how they should interpret various provisions in their Rule. One particularly poignant issue was the juridical authority of Francis's *Testament:* was it simply an exhortation or did it establish an interpretive context for the observance of the Rule? But this was only one of a number of issues generated by the Order's rapid numerical growth, geographical expansion, and increasing involvement in the pastoral ministry of the church.

The brothers undoubtedly appealed to Gregory not simply because he was the Pope, but because he had been Francis's close advisor and the Cardinal Protector of their Order. But Gregory was first and foremost a jurist: for him the Rule was a legal document, which now had an existence independent of its original author. His decisions, ultimately those of a pragmatic if principled administrator, paved the way for the increased accommodations of the Order to the demands of its pastoral ministry and for succeeding Papal expositions of the Rule.[a]

Gregory, Bishop and Servant of the servants of God, to our beloved sons, the general and provincial ministers, the custodians, and the other brothers of the Order of Minors: greetings and apostolic benediction.

[1]The further you have flown away from the world, above your-
Ps 55:6 selves, having taken wing like a dove into contemplative retreat, the more clearly you perceive the darts of sin; the more too can the eye of your heart scrutinize those things which you recognize to be obstacles on the road to salvation. Thus at times the Spirit discloses to your consciences what lies hidden to others. Still, because the darkness of human weakness beclouds the splendor of spiritual understanding, occasionally the anxiety of doubt presents itself, and thus difficulties that are almost insurmountable begin to pile up.

[2]And so, beloved sons, there recently arrived at our court a delegation whom you, provincial ministers, dispatched as you met in general chapter, and whom you, beloved son, as General Minister,

a. This translation is based on the critical edition of the document by Herbert Grundmann, "*Die Bulle 'Quo elongati' Papst Gregors IX*," AFH 54 (1961): 1-25. This also contains a careful study of the bull. Cf. BFr, 1, pp. 68-70, n.56.

personally accompanied.[a] It has thus come to our attention that your Rule contains some doubtful and unclear passages as well as certain phrases which are difficult to comprehend. But the holy confessor of Christ, Francis of blessed memory, did not want to have his Rule interpreted by any of the brothers. So towards the end of his life he commanded—and this command is called his *Testament*—that the words of his Rule should not be glossed: that no one should say, and here we use his own words, "that they should be understood in this or that way." Furthermore, he added that the brothers are in no way to seek any letter
Test 38-39, 25 from the Apostolic See. He also included several other directives that are impossible to observe without considerable difficulty.

[3] Since you are doubtful in regards to your obligation to observe this *Testament,* you have asked us to remove the uncertainty from your conscience and that of your brothers. For as a result of the long-standing friendship between the holy confessor and ourselves, we know his mind more fully. Furthermore, while we held a lesser rank, we stood by him both as he composed the aforesaid Rule and obtained its confirmation from the Apostolic See. And so you have petitioned us for a clarification of the doubtful and obscure points in the Rule, together with a response to the difficulties.

We certainly believe that in the *Testament* the confessor of Christ demonstrated a single-hearted purpose and that you therefore aspire to conform to his just longings and holy desires. Nevertheless, we are aware of the danger to your souls and of the difficulties you could incur because of this. And so, wishing to remove all anxiety from your hearts, we declare that you are not bound by the *Testament.* For without the consent of the brothers, and especially of the ministers, Francis could not make obligatory a matter that touches everyone.[b] Nor could he in any way whatsoever bind his successor because an equal has no authority over his equal.

[4] In addition, as we gather from your messengers, some of the brothers are entertaining doubts about whether they are bound by the counsels of the Gospels as well as by its precepts. For your Rule has as its beginning: "The Rule and life of the Lesser Brothers is this: to ob-

a. Besides the General Minister, John Parenti, members of this delegation sent by the Pentecost chapter of 1230 included Anthony of Padua, outgoing Provincial Minister of Lombardy; Haymo of Faversham, later General Minister; Leo of Milan, later Provincial Minister of Lombardy and Archbishop of Milan; Gerard of Modena, a companion of Francis and celebrated preacher during the Great Alleluia of 1233; Gerard Ruscinol, a Papal penitentiary; and Peter of Brescia.

b. Cf. Gaines Post, "A Roman-Canonical Maxim, '*Quod omnes tangit,*' " in *Traditio* 4 (1946): 197-251, esp. 197-209 and 249-51.

serve the holy Gospel of our Lord Jesus Christ by living in obedience, without anything of their own, and in chastity." And it concludes with these words: "[so that] we might observe the poverty and humility and the holy Gospel of our Lord Jesus Christ which we have firmly promised." So the brothers want to know: are they bound to the other Gospel LR I 1; XII 4
counsels besides those which are expressly contained in the Rule by way of precept or prohibition? This question is of special moment since they did not intend to oblige themselves in this way; furthermore, it is only with great difficulty, if at all, that they can observe all of the counsels literally.

Our answer is brief: you are not bound by the Rule to observe the counsels of the Gospel, other than those explicitly contained in the Rule to which you have committed yourselves. As for the rest of them, you are bound in the same way as other Christians, although even more so by virtue of the goodness and integrity with which you offered to the Lord a total holocaust by your contempt of all that pertains to this world.

[5]Likewise, in the same Rule the brothers are forbidden to "in any way receive coins or money, either personally or through an intermediary." Since they desire to observe this prohibition always, they seek a LR IV 1
clarification. Dare they, without violating the Rule, present to God-fearing people some of the faithful through whom the former might relieve the needs of the brothers? Furthermore, dare they with a sound conscience have recourse to these same faithful for their necessities, even though they know these faithful have accepted coins or money—coins or money, to be sure, which on their own authority the brothers have no intention of causing to be held or demanding from them—in the name of the donor?

We are led to respond to this matter as follows. If the brothers want to buy something necessary or make payment for something already purchased, they may present to those persons who wish to give them a [monetary] alms either an agent of the person from whom the purchase is being made or someone else, unless perchance these donors prefer to make payment themselves or through agents of their own. The one presented by the brothers in this way is not their agent, even though he may have been designated by them; rather, he is the agent of the person on whose authority he makes the payment, or of the one receiving it. Such an agent must promptly make payment, so that none of the donated money remains with him. If, however, this same agent is presented for other imminent necessities, he may deposit the alms committed to him, as though they were his own, with a spiritual friend or familiar acquaintance of the brothers, and through such a one, dispense the alms as he judges expedient according to the circumstances and time of the brothers' needs. The brothers may also have recourse to this agent for necessities of this kind, especially if he is negligent of or simply unaware of such needs.

[6]Furthermore, the Rule clearly states that "the brothers shall not appropriate anything as their own, neither a house nor a place nor any-
LR VI 1 thing at all." But as time goes on the brothers fear that the poverty of the Order will be compromised, especially since some people have been maintaining that moveable property belongs to the brotherhood in common. And so in this matter also you have humbly requested us to give attention to these threats for the sake of your consciences and for the purity of the entire Order. Therefore, we decree that property may be possessed neither individually nor in common. However, the brotherhood may have the use of equipment or books and such other moveable property as is permitted, and that the individual brothers may use these things at the discretion of the general and provincial ministers. Dominion over places or houses is excepted; this is the right of those to whom you know they belong. Nor may the brothers sell or exchange or alienate moveable goods outside the Order in any way, unless the Cardinal of the Roman Church who is the governor of the brotherhood authorizes the transaction or gives approval for it to the general or provincial ministers.

[7]Another chapter of the same Rule says: "If any of the brothers, at the instigation of the enemy, sin mortally in regard to those sins about which it may have been decreed among the brothers to have recourse only to the provincial ministers, such brothers must have recourse to
LR VII 1 them as soon as possible, without delay." The brothers conscientiously question whether this means only public sins or both public and private sins. We therefore reply that the chapter in question refers only to manifest public sins. We wish that the general minister appoint, or have appointed, from among the more mature and discreet priests, as many confessors as the ministers deem suitable for the provinces. Let these priests hear the confessions for private sins, unless the brothers choose instead to confess to their ministers or custodians who happen to be visiting their places.

[8]Furthermore, the Rule forbids any of the brothers to preach to the people "unless he has been examined and approved by the general minister and received from him the office of preaching." You wish to know LR IX 2 whether, in order to assist the work of the brothers and for the sake of avoiding hazardous travel, the general minister may delegate to other discreet brothers the said examination, approval, and authorization for the office of preaching, and if so, whether he may delegate universally for examining brothers assigned to the provinces or delegate only for certain brothers in particular. To this we respond as follows. The general minister may not delegate these matters to any brother in his absence. Let the brothers who are judged ready for examination be sent to him; or let them accompany their provincial ministers to the general chapter for this purpose. Now, if they do not require an examination, on the basis of having had training both at a school of theology and in the office of preaching, and if they are of mature age, and if they possess all those other qualities that are expected of such men, then they may preach to the people in the approved manner, unless the provincial minister decides otherwise.

[9]Furthermore, the brothers are wondering whether the vicars of the provincial minister, whom these latter appoint to act in their stead when they are traveling to the general chapter, may receive postulants into the brotherhood or dismiss them once they have been received. We declare that they may not. Even the ministers themselves may not do this unless they have been specially authorized. And just as the general minister has power to authorize them, so may he deny the authorization. According to the Rule, the reception of brothers may not be delegated to others besides the provincial ministers. Much less, then, do LR II 1 these ministers have the power to subdelegate. For this authority has been entrusted to them alone, not to others.

[10]Then again, the Rule states that "upon the death of the general minister, the election of a successor should be made by the provincial ministers and custodians at the Pentecost chapter." You are asking LR VIII 2 whether all of the custodians in the entire Order have to assemble at the general chapter. Or, in order to conduct business with greater tranquillity, might it suffice that from each province a few attend who know the mind of the others? This is our reply: let the custodians of each province designate one of themselves to send together with their provincial minister to represent them at the general chapter, advising him of their

views. Once you yourselves shall have passed this statute, we consider it approved.

[11]Finally, it is written in the Rule that "the brothers should not enter the monasteries of nuns, except those to whom special permission has
LR XI 2 been granted by the Apostolic See." Up to now the brothers have interpreted this passage as referring to the monasteries of the Poor Cloistered Nuns for whom the Apostolic See exercises a special concern.[a] This interpretation is believed to have been handed down by the provincial ministers in general chapter through a statute at the time when the Rule was approved and blessed Francis was still alive.[b] Nevertheless, you have asked for a clarification. Does this mean all monasteries without exception, since the Rule excepts none, or does it refer only to the monasteries of the aforesaid [Poor Cloistered] Nuns? We respond: the prohibition affects communities of nuns of every description. And by the term monastery we mean the cloister, the living quarters, and the inner shops. Those brothers to whom the superiors have granted permission by virtue of their maturity and suitability may go into the other areas to which lay people also have access in order to preach or beg alms, with the exception always of the monasteries of the aforesaid Cloistered Nuns. No one has any access to them without the express permission of the Apostolic See.[c]

Given at Anagni, the twenty-eighth day of September, in the fourth year of our pontificate (1230).

J) *Quoniam abundavit* of Gregory IX (1237)

During the 1230's Gregory IX's letters to local church leaders recommending the Franciscans and defending their ministry increasingly emphasized the role of the ordained brothers. The simple penitential preaching which characterized the early brotherhood was downplayed more and more in favor of the doctrinal and moral sermons demanded by the pastoral needs of the church. Gregory was viewing the Franciscan Order, at least in terms of its ministry, as a twin of the Dominicans. This decree provides perhaps the clearest statement of Gregory's view which identified the very *raison d'être* of the Lesser Brothers as a task force to implement the pastoral provisions of the Fourth Lateran Council

a. The name given by Gregory to the communities of Clare's Damianite movement in his "Form and Manner of Life" of 1219, 1 (Text in *Clare of Assisi: Early Documents* translated and edited by Regis Armstrong [St. Bonaventure, NY: Franciscan Institute Publications, 1993] 90).

b. There is no extant record of such a regulation.

c. "The Form and Manner of Life" 10, p. 96.

by providing the "suitable men, powerful in word and deed," to assist the bishops as preachers and confessors of the people.[a]

Gregory, Bishop and Servant of the servants of God, to our venerable brothers, the archbishops and bishops; and to our beloved sons, the abbots, priors, deans, archdeacons, pastors, archpriests, and other prelates of churches to whom these letters may arrive: greetings and apostolic benediction.

Because iniquity has abounded and *the charity of many has grown*
Mt 24:12 *cold,* behold, the Lord has raised up the Order of his beloved sons, the
Lesser Brothers, who, not seeking the things that are their own but
Phil 2:21 those which are Christ's, have dedicated themselves to preaching the
Good News of the Word of God in the abjection of voluntary poverty, overthrowing heresies and expelling other fatal vices.

As we desire to favor their holy proposal and indispensable ministry, we are led to affectionately commend them to all of you; we exhort you in the Lord, and through these Apostolic letters command you, kindly to strive to receive our beloved sons of this noted Order out of reverence for God and us for the office of preaching, for which they are assigned by profession in their Order, so that the people committed to your care might devoutly receive the seed of the Word of God from their lips. We admonish you to assist them in all their needs, nor should you impede any [of your people] who might wish to draw near to their preaching or to confess to the priests among them. Instead, by your exhortations let the people be prepared to receive their preaching, so that as fruitful ground they might begin to sprout forth virtues instead of the thorns of vice, and that the aforesaid brothers through your cooperation might more happily reap the fruit of the ministry they have taken on.

Now since vices can sometimes secretly gain entry under the guise of virtues, and an angel of Satan can often transform himself into an angel of light, we order you in virtue of these present letters, that if any [preachers] in your territory claiming to belong to the aforesaid Order of brothers should preach that money should be turned over to them-

a. The text of the bull clearly alludes to canon 10 of the Council: "Among the various things that are conducive to the salvation of the Christian people, the nourishment of God's word is recognized to be especially necessary . . . we therefore decree that bishops are to appoint suitable men to carry out with profit this duty of sacred preaching, men who are powerful in word and deed and who will visit with care the peoples entrusted to them. . . . The bishops shall suitably furnish them with what is necessary . . . [These men should help]. Not only in the office of preaching, but also in hearing confessions and enjoining penances and in other matters which are conducive to the salvation of souls." DEC, 1: 239-40. The text of this bull is in BFr 1, p. 214-15, n. 224.

selves, and thus defame their Order, which professes poverty, you should seize them as impostors and condemn them.

Given at Viterbo, the sixth of April, in the eleventh year of our pontificate (1237).

Writings of Jacques de Vitry

Letter I (1216)

Jacques de Vitry (c.1160/70-1240) noted preacher, historian and church leader, was a keen and often critical observer of religious life in the early thirteenth century. His writings form a uniquely valuable witness to the early Franciscan movement. An enthusiastic promoter of church renewal, he was impressed by what he saw as the radical "apostolic life" of the first Lesser Brothers. Furthermore, history placed him in a position to witness closely key aspects of the Order's development for more than two decades.

A native of Vitry, near Rheims, Jacques was educated at Paris; after his ordination to the priesthood he worked in the diocese of Liège. There he came to be deeply influenced by Marie of Oignies, one of the early leaders of the Beguine movement; in 1211 he joined the canons regular of Saint Augustine in that town and, at Marie's urging, took up a career as a popular preacher. His fame caused the Papal legate to commission him in 1213 to preach the Crusade against the Albigensians, and eventually led to his election as Bishop of Acre in the Crusader States. In the summer of 1216, Jacques proceeded to Italy to be consecrated by the Pope; he arrived in Perugia just after the death of Innocent III and was ordained bishop there on July 31 by Honorius III. This first selection is from a letter he wrote from Genoa in October of that same year to his friends in Liège before departing Europe to assume the care of his diocese. In it he described his stay in Italy, especially the new religious movements among the laity he encountered there.[a]

> . . . After this, I came to the city of Milan, which is a cesspool of heretics. I remained there for some days and preached the Word of God in a number of places. In the whole city I scarcely found anyone who opposed the heretics, except for certain holy men and religious women, whom malicious lay people call "Patarines,"[b] but whom the Supreme Pontiff designated the "Humiliati." He gave them the right to preach and resist the heretics and approved them as religious.[c] They have renounced all their goods and have gathered together in various places,
> Tb 2:19; 1 Cor 4:12; Eph 4:28 *living by the work of their hands.* They frequently preach the Word of God and gladly listen to it, remaining perfectly founded in the faith and

a. Latin text from RBC 72-76.

b. The name often given to the Cathars in Northern Italy. Cf. canon 27 of the Third Lateran Council, 1179 [DEC, 1: 224].

c. Innocent III approved the way of life of the Humiliati in 1201.

productive in good deeds. Already this order has so multiplied that in the diocese of Milan there are over one hundred and fifty communities, some of men and others of women, not counting those who still live in their own homes.

Departing from there, I arrived at Perugia. There I discovered Pope Innocent dead, but not yet buried. During the night some thieves had stripped his body of all the precious vestments with which he was to be interred, and left it there in the church virtually naked and already decaying. I went into the church and saw with utter faith how fleeting and empty is the deceitful glory of this world. The day after the funeral, the cardinals elected Honorius, an elderly and devout man, quite simple and humble, who had distributed almost all his patrimony to the poor. He was consecrated as Supreme Pontiff the Sunday after his election; I myself received episcopal ordination from him the following Sunday. . . . I received permission from him for the devout women, not only of the diocese of Liège, but also of the Kingdom [of France] and of the Empire, to live together in community and to encourage one another to do good through mutual exhortations . . .[a]

. . . After I had been at the Curia for a while, I encountered a great deal that was repugnant to me. They were so occupied with worldly affairs, with rulers and kingdoms, with lawsuits and litigation, that they hardly let anyone speak of spiritual things. I did find, however, one source of consolation in those parts. Many well-to-do secular people of both sexes, having left all things for Christ, had fled the world. They were called "Lesser Brothers" and "Lesser Sisters." They are held in great reverence by the Lord Pope and the Cardinals. They are in no way occupied with temporal things, but with fervent desire and ardent zeal they labor each day to draw from the vanities of the world souls that are perishing, and draw them to their way of life. Thanks be to God, they have already reaped great fruit and have converted many. Those who have heard them, say: "Come," so that one group brings another.

They live according to the form of the primitive Church, about whom it was written: *The community of believers were of one heart and one mind.* During the day they go into the cities and villages giving Acts 4:32
themselves over to the active life in order to gain others; at night, however, they return to their hermitage or solitary places to devote themselves to contemplation. The women dwell together near the cities in various hospices, accepting nothing, but living by the work of their

a. This was the first Papal approval of the Beguine movement.

hands. They are grieved, indeed troubled, by the fact that they are honored by both clergy and laity more than they would wish.

With great profit, the brothers of this Order assemble once a year in a designated place to rejoice in the Lord and eat together; with the advice of good men they draw up and promulgate holy laws and have them confirmed by the Lord Pope. After this they disperse again for the whole year throughout Lombardy and Tuscany, Apulia and Sicily. Not long ago, Brother Nicholas,[a] a provincial administrator for the Lord Pope and a holy and religious man, left the Curia and took refuge with these men, but because he was so needed by the Lord Pope, he was recalled by him. I believe, however, that the Lord desires to save many souls before the end of the world through such simple and poor men in order to put to shame our prelates, who are like *dumb dogs not able to*
Is 56:10 *bark.*

Letter VI (1220)

Jacques de Vitry arrived in Acre to assume his new bishopric in November, 1216. His activity was soon affected by larger events; in the fall of 1217 the armies of the Fifth Crusade began assembling in Acre, setting sail the next May to launch an attack on Egypt. In the fall of 1218 Jacques himself accompanied a subsequent expeditionary force there to assist in the siege of Damietta, which was finally conquered by the Crusaders in November, 1219. Jacques remained in Egypt until the end of the campaign in 1221. This selection is from a long letter he wrote from Damietta in February/March, 1220 to friends at home.[b] It is interesting that Jacques did not include this section in the version of the letter he sent to Honorius III.

Lord Rayner, Prior of Saint Michael,[c] has entered the Order of Lesser Brothers. This Order is multiplying rapidly throughout the world, because it expressly imitates the pattern of the primitive Church and the life of the apostles in everything. But to our way of thinking, this Order is quite risky, because it sends out two by two throughout the

a. Nicholas was a monk of the Cistercian abbey of Casamari and a Papal penitentiary. Cf. M. Bihl, "Nicolaus de Romanis (+1219), fueritne primus Cardinalis O.F.M.," AFH (1926): 286-89.

b. Hinnebusch, p. 6; Latin text in Huygens, pp. 131-33.

c. A church in Acre.

world, not only formed religious, but also immature young men who should first be tested and subjected to conventual discipline for a time.[a] The head of these brothers, who also founded the Order, came into our camp.[b] He was so inflamed with zeal for the faith that he did not fear to cross the lines to the army of our enemy. For several days he preached the Word of God to the Saracens and made a little progress. The Sultan, the ruler of Egypt,[c] privately asked him to pray to the Lord for him, so that he might be inspired by God to adhere to that religion which most pleased God. Colin, the Englishman, our clerk, also has joined this Order, as well as two more of our company, namely, Master Michael and Lord Matthew, to whom I had committed the care of the Church of the Holy Cross. I am having a difficult time holding on to the cantor[d] and Henry and several others.

Historia Occidentalis (c.1221/25)

The Historia Occidentalis is the second volume of Jacques de Vitry's *Historia Hierosolimitana Abbreviata,* which he intended to be a vast narrative of the Crusading movement. The first book is the *Historia Orientalis,* which includes a detailed topographical description of the Holy Land and an account of the early Crusades. *The Historia Occidentalis* then turns to a consideration of the Latin West, the bulk being devoted to the current state of Christendom, especially recent movements of renewal in the various orders of the Church. Jacques also projected a third book, which would return to the Orient and describe events there from the Fourth Lateran Council to the capture of Damietta, but he never had an opportunity to complete it.

The Historia Occidentalis is one of the most important commentaries on church life in the early thirteenth century. The work was begun by Jacques at Damietta; this section on the Franciscans, which comprises chapter 32 of the History, was traditionally thought by most scholars to have been written in

a. This sentence was omitted by Lemmens in his *Testimonia Minora,* p. 80, but is included in the critical edition of Huygens, who defends its authenticity with convincing reasoning. The sentiments expressed are similar to those voiced by Jacques at the end of the following selection.

b. The text in Lemmens's version includes after the words "who also founded the Order" the phrase "who is called Brother Francis, loved by God and venerated by all." This appears to be an interpolation in some of the manuscripts, taken from the following *Historia Occidentalis.* Francis probably arrived at Damietta late in August, 1219. For references to Francis and the Crusades, see the notes in the following section, "Chronicles of the Fifth Crusade."

c. Malik al-Kamil (1180-1238), nephew of Saladin, who became ruler of Egypt in 1218.

d. A certain Jean de Cambrai, mentioned in an earlier letter (Huygens, p. 110).

1221, although there is evidence which would indicate that, like other parts of the work, it may not have been completed until 1223/25.[a]

[1]As we have seen, [up to now] there have been three religious orders: hermits, monks, and canons. But in order that the state of those living according to a rule might rest firmly on a solid foundation, the Lord in these days has added a fourth form of religious life, the embellishment of a new order, and the holiness of a new rule.

[2]But if we carefully consider the form and condition of the primitive Church, the Lord has not so much added a new way of living as renewed an old one; he lifted up one that was being cast aside, and revived one that was almost dead. Thus, in the twilight of this world that is tending to its end, at a time when the son of perdition is soon to arrive, he might prepare new athletes to confront the perilous times of the Antichrist, fortifying and propping up the Church.

[3]This is the religious way of life of the true poor of the Crucified One and of the order of preachers whom we call Lesser Brothers. They are truly Minors, for they are more humble than all present-day religious in their habit, in their poverty and in their contempt of the world. They have one general superior, whose commands and regulations the lesser superiors and the other brothers of the same Order obey; he sends them throughout the various provinces of the world to preach and to save souls.

[4]They diligently strive to renew in themselves the way of life of the primitive Church, its poverty and humility. They drink in the pure waters of the fountain of the Gospel with such thirst and ardor of spirit that they work hard at carrying out not only the evangelical precepts but the counsels as well, thus imitating more explicitly the life of the apostles.
Lk 14:33 They *renounce everything they possess;* they *deny themselves and take*
Mt 16:24 *up their cross* and, naked, follow the naked Christ. Like Joseph, they
Gn 39:12; Jn 4:28 leave their cloak behind, like the Samaritan woman, their water jar.[b]
They run their race unburdened. They walk before his face and do not turn back; forgetful of the past, they are always straining with tireless

a. For the dating, see Armando Quaglia, "*Sulla datazione e il valore della 'Historia Occidentalis' di Giacomo Vitry,*" *Miscellanea Francescana* 83 (1983): 177-92, revising the judgment of Hinnebusch, pp. 17-20; the critical Latin text of this passage is in Hinnebusch, pp. 158-63.

b. The expression "naked to follow the naked Christ" goes back to the letters of Jerome, but beginning in the late eleventh century was increasingly utilized to state the goal of reform movements, referring especially to the ideal of the "apostolic life." For background, see Jean Châtillon, "*Nudum Christum Nudus Sequere:* A Note on the Origins and Meaning of the Theme of Spiritual Nakedness in the Writings of Saint Bonaventure," trans. Edward Hagman, *Greyfriars Review* 10 (1996): 293-310.

gait towards what is ahead, *flying like clouds, and like doves to their* Phil 3:13
windows, on guard with all diligence and caution lest death enter in. Is 60:8

[6]The Lord Pope confirmed their Rule and gave them authority to preach at any church they came to, although out of reverence having first obtained the consent of the local prelates. They are *sent two by two* to preach as if before the face of the Lord and before his Second Coming.

ER XIV [7]These poor men of Christ carry *on their journey neither purse nor*
pouch nor bread, nor money in their belts; they possess *neither gold*
nor silver, nor do they have *shoes* on their feet. Indeed, no brother of Mt 10:9-10; Lk 9:1-3; Lk 10:1-4
this Order is allowed to possess anything; they have no monasteries or
churches, no fields nor vineyards, no animals, no houses, nor any other
possessions, and they have no place to lay their heads. They do not use Mt 8:20
garments made from linen or pelts, but only woolen tunics with a hood.
They use neither capes, nor cloaks, nor hats, nor any other such clothing.

[8]If anyone invites them to dinner, they eat and drink what is set before them. If anyone out of kindness should donate something to them, Lk 10:7
they do not hold on to it for future use.

[9]Once or twice a year, at a predetermined time and place, they gather together to celebrate a general chapter, except those who are a long distance away or are across the sea. After the chapter, they are sent again in twos or more by their superior to various regions, provinces and cities.

[10]Not only by their preaching, but also by their example of a holy life and perfect conversion, they invite many men, not only of lower station but also high-born nobles, to a contempt of the world, to leave behind their estates, their castles and their very ample possessions, and in a blessed exchange to trade their temporal wealth for spiritual treasure. These take the habit of the Lesser Brothers, that is, a cheap tunic with which they are clothed and a piece of rope by which they are girt.

[11]They have so multiplied in such a short time that there is not a province of Christendom which does not have some of these brothers, who exhibit in themselves to the eyes of all who see them, as in a most clear mirror, the contempt of worldly vanity. Their growth is due especially to the fact that they refuse no one entry into their Order, except those bound to marriage or to another Order. Such men they do not wish to nor should they accept, as is right, without the consent of their wives or religious superiors. But the more confidently they receive

everyone else into the fullness of their Order regardless of obstacles, the less they are worried about what source the Lord might use to support them, for they commit themselves totally to the munificence of divine Providence. All that they give to those who come to them is a cord and a tunic, and the rest they leave to heavenly care.

[12]And so the Lord has given back a hundredfold to his servants in
Mt 19:29 this world; on this road they are traveling he keeps his eyes fixed on them, so much so that we ourselves have seen fulfilled to the letter in them what has been written: *the Lord loves the stranger, providing him*
Dt 10:18 *food and clothing.* Indeed, people consider themselves fortunate if these servants of God do not refuse to accept alms or hospitality from them.

[13]Not only Christ's faithful but even the Saracens and people in the darkness [of unbelief] admire their humility and virtue, and when the brothers fearlessly approach them to preach, they willingly receive them and, with a grateful spirit, provide them with what they need.

[14]We have seen the founder and master of this Order, Brother Francis,[a] a simple, uneducated man beloved by God and man, whom all the others obey as their highest superior. He was so moved by spiritual fervor and exhilaration that, after he reached the army of Christians before Damietta in Egypt, he boldly set out for the camp of the Sultan of
Eph 6:16 Egypt, fortified only with *the shield of faith.* When the Saracens captured him on the road, he said: "I am a Christian. Take me to your master." They dragged him before the Sultan. When that cruel beast saw Francis, he recognized him as a man of God and changed his attitude into one of gentleness, and for some days he listened very attentively to Francis as he preached the faith of Christ to him and his followers. But ultimately, fearing that some of his soldiers would be converted to the Lord by the efficacy of his words and pass over to the Christian army, he ordered that Francis be returned to our camp with all reverence and security. At the end he said to Francis: "Pray for me, that God may deign to reveal to me the law and the faith which is more pleasing to Him."

[15]In fact, the Saracens willingly listen to all these Lesser Brothers when they preach about faith in Christ and the Gospel teaching, but only as long as in their preaching they do not speak against Mohammed as a liar and an evil man. When they did speak in such a manner, the Saracens irreverently put them to the lash and savagely expelled them

a. The critical text actually reads *Francinum* rather than *Franciscum* (Hinnebusch, p. 161).

from their city; they would have killed them, if God had not miraculously protected them.

[16]Such is the holy Order of Lesser Brothers, a religious way of life which should be admired and imitated. These are the men whom, we believe, the Lord has raised up in these last days to oppose the son of perdition, the Antichrist, and his unclean henchmen. *Surrounding the litter of Solomon* as valiant soldiers of Christ and going *from gate to gate* with swords, they are posted as *watchmen upon the walls* of Jeru- Sg 3:7; Ex 32:27
salem. For day and night they do not cease to express their divine Is 62:6
praises and holy exhortations. Courageously they lift up their voice
like a trumpet liberating the nations and rebuking the people; they do Is 58:1
not withhold their swords from bloodshed: slaughtering and devour- Jer 48:10
ing, they *go round about the city suffering hunger like dogs.* They are Ps 59:7
like *the salt of the earth,* transforming its food into the sweet nourish- Mt 5:13
ment of salvation: they preserve the meat, removing the decay of
worms and the stench of vices. They are like *the light of the world, illu-* Mt 5:14
minating many towards the knowledge of truth, inflaming and enkindling many to the fervor of chastity.

[17]However, this Order of perfection and the extent of its spacious cloister do not seem to be suitable for the weak and imperfect; these, in
fact, *going down to the seas in ships and trading on the mighty waters,* Ps 107:23
might well be overcome by the waves, if they do not first *stay in the city*
until they *are clothed with power from on high.*[a] Lk 24:49

Sermon I to the Lesser Brothers (1229/40)

Apparently disappointed with the situation in the Near East, Jacques traveled to Europe on an embassy in 1225 but never returned to his see, engaging in various activities as an auxiliary to the bishop of Liège. Gregory IX finally accepted his resignation as bishop of Acre in 1228, but in 1229 called him to Rome, where he was made Cardinal Bishop of Frascati (Tusculum). Jacques served as a key advisor in the Papal court until his death in May, 1240.[b]

During these years as a Cardinal at the Curia, he preached two sermons to assemblies of brothers, probably at chapters. Jacques had great renown as a

a. This quotation is Jesus' command to his disciples to wait in the upper room until the Spirit comes upon them, a reference to Jacques's conviction—also expressed in the previous letter—that Franciscans should institute a novitiate year based on the traditional monastic/canonical model before going out to engage in their life traveling about the world. This demand was at least partially fulfilled by the Bull *Cum secundum* of 1220, requiring the brothers to institute a year of probation.

b. Hinnebusch, pp. 6-7.

preacher in his own time. The seemingly forced Biblical and nature imagery, which seems so foreign to us, was precisely what attracted contemporary audiences. Although too lengthy and diffuse to reproduce here in their entirety, these sermons are not without interest for both the history and the spirituality of the Order during this critical decade.[a]

[1]Our theme today is taken from Proverbs: *Four things on earth are exceedingly little, yet they are wiser than the wise: the ants are a people without strength, yet they provide food for the harvest; the rabbits are a weak people, yet they make their bed in the rock; the locusts have no king, yet all of them march in rank; the lizard supports itself on*
Prv 30:24-28 *hands, yet dwells in kings's houses.*

[2]. . . Since the dignity and richness and splendor of clothing usually generate pride, just as disdain, poverty, and meanness of clothing generate humility, the less you keep of the goods of this world, the humbler and lesser you appear. Now I notice that you possess nothing in this world but a habit and a cord, nor do I see that you could have anything less. And thus, even though there are many *little ones* in this world, you are truly lesser [*minores*]; even though there are many who are wise, you are *wiser than the wise.* . . . For they are *wiser,* who wish to imitate Christ more closely, that is, to draw closer to the divine wisdom in labors and abjection, in humility and poverty, and make themselves more closely conformable to Christ. It is they who strip themselves of
Phil 2:5-7 majesty to take on the form of a slave; of riches, to [embrace] poverty; of rest, to [endure] struggles and labor; of life, to [prefer] death. Thus it is that the humility and wisdom of the saints is likened to these four little animals, which are *the wisest of the wise ones* of this world, that is, *the ant, the rabbit, the locust, and the lizard.*

[3]Through these four animals, we can point out the four different types of brothers who lead a religious life in the friary. For some among you are simple lay brothers, who help the work of the others by the labor of their own hands or by collecting alms from the faithful. They are compared to *ants,* because the ant is a tiny animal but one that works very hard to gather and prepare its food.

Others are weak and infirm; they cannot work with their hands, or carry the burdens of others, or perform great penances. But they should not mistrust divine mercy: the less they have of their own, the more

a. Text edited by H. a L. (Hilarin Felder), "Jacobi Vitriacensis (1180-1240): Sermones ad Fratres Minores," *Analecta Ordinis Minorum Capuccinorum,* 19 (1903): 22-23, 114-122, 149-158.

they can benefit from the labors of others. For this is exactly the purpose of the Communion of Saints, and especially of those who serve the Lord in one brotherhood, because the merits of each are the common property of all, just as all [the soldiers] share equally in the spoils—whether they marched in the first rank of battle or whether they were exhausted and had to remain behind to guard the baggage. Therefore the *rabbit,* a weak people, cannot fittingly represent those who fast, keep vigils, and perform other works of penance, but those [weak ones] who do not despair or lose hope, but make their bed in the rock and rest in the mercy of Christ, who did penance for all of us on the cross and thus supplied for our weaknesses.

Others are able to labor much in meditating, reading, and praying, thus elevating themselves with the wings of reason and understanding to heavenly things. These are compared to the *locusts* because of the leap they make in contemplation and the flight of their sublime way of life.

Finally, others go out to preach and actively strive through their works for the salvation of their neighbors. These *support themselves by hands* in the manner of *lizards, yet dwell in the house of the* heavenly *king,* for they have their hearts in their heavenly dwellings and yet labor for the reward of eternal life . . .

[4]And since it is written, *How are they to preach, unless they are sent?* a brother should not claim this office for himself, but should wait for the Rom 10:15 command of his superior . . . They should not be quick to go out [of the friary], but leave only when compelled by obedience. For to the scandal of many people, the town squares, the waterfronts, the palaces of princes, the residence of prelates, are at times full of religious, without any compelling necessity save the urge of curiosity and their stomach.

[5]We do not call those people poor who are able to live by the work of their hands and yet beg. They are not thought of as poor but as robbers. If they ask others to give them bread, may not these justly reply: "Give us your ability, so that you might thus work for us"? . . . Since these wanderers are not in the bed of contemplation, nor in the field of preaching, nor in the mill of physical labor —for they have no orderly Lk 17:34-35 life—what is left for them save that place *where the shadow of death, and no order, but everlasting horror dwells?* Jb 10:22

[6]Some, miserable and senseless, seeking an excuse for their laziness, say that they should not study, but that it is better for them to remain brothers in the humility of their simplicity, because *knowledge*

1 Cor 8:1 *puffs up* and much learning makes them foolish. To them we can respond that the other virtues can also occasionally make one proud. In fact, without charity, none of them are profitable, but for the most part are an obstacle. For if they disdain to learn and fill themselves with the words of Scripture, how will they be able to ruminate? . . .

If therefore a simple brother is not gifted with much cleverness, let him make up for his lack of brilliance with the ardor of study. Let him not be ashamed to beg the bread of the word of God where he can, and commit to memory each day at least one good passage. I have seen many who were slow in wit make more progress than those who presumed on their abilities and their intelligence and refused to learn from others. . . .

[7]We read of a certain king, who said to one of his soldiers: "Let's go out tonight through the streets of the city and see what is going on." When they came to a certain place, they saw a light coming from the window of an underground dwelling. There a poor man sat, covered with filthy and torn clothing, beside his wretched little wife. She was dancing near her husband, singing and exulting with great joy. Then the king began to wonder how these people, who were surrounded by such squalor, not having decent clothing or even a real house, could lead such a happy and secure life, indeed seemingly a rich one. And he said to his soldier: "It is truly amazing that you and I are not more pleased by our life, surrounded as we are with so many pleasures and so much glory, while these stupid people rejoice in their miserable life which seems to them sweet and gentle, when it is really bitter and harsh." The soldier replied very wisely: "How much more stupid and miserable does our life seem to the lovers of true life and of eternal glory. When compared with heavenly treasure, they would judge our splendid palaces and clothing and riches as dung and our glory as wind, nothing when compared to the ineffable beauty and glory of the saints which is in heaven. For just as these people we've seen appear crazy to us, in the same way and more do we, who wander about in this world and think we have fulfillment with this false glory, appear worthy of tears in the eyes of those who enjoy the delights of eternal goods."

Sermon II to the Lesser Brothers (1229/40)

[1]Our theme today is taken from the prophet Jeremiah: *Jonadab the son of Rechab, our father, commanded us, saying: "You shall drink no wine, neither you nor your children, forever. Neither shall you build houses, nor sow seed, nor plant vineyards, nor have any, but you shall dwell in tents all your days."* Jer 35:6-7

[2]This promise, in the spiritual sense, is directed to those who obey the commandments of God and of their spiritual fathers. For our spiritual father was Saint Francis, who could truly be called Jonadab the son of Rechab. For Jonadab means "the spontaneity of God," and Rechab "chariot" or "ascent." And so Francis spontaneously undertook things far over and above those he was bound to do by the precepts of the law of God. He, with the chariot of the four Gospels and the four cardinal virtues, ascended ceaselessly from perfection to perfection, so closely following the Crucified that at his death there appeared in his feet, hands, and side the traces of the wounds of Christ. For this reason his sons have been so multiplied throughout the world that in them has been fulfilled spiritually what the Lord said through Jeremiah: *There shall not be wanting a man of the race of Jonadab the son of Rechab, standing before me forever. . . .* Jer 35:19

[3]. . . The Rechabites observed these precepts according to their literal sense, just as you do, who are the descendants of the heat of your father Rechab, that is to say, of blessed Francis. For you literally *do not build houses,* even if others build them for your use, and you live in them as guests; you do not possess them, but the Church does, in whose name they were constructed. Likewise, you do not sow or plant vines. . . .

[4]. . . Therefore, brothers, have at the same time caution and compassion. For you are standing in a more sublime state, following the example of the Apostles, not *having a staff, nor a traveling bag, nor a purse, nor money in your belts, nor bread in your baskets, nor two tunics, nor shoes on your feet.* Therefore, so much more scandalous and shameful would be any fall from it—which the Lord forbid. Following the example of your father Rechab, namely blessed Francis, as true Rechabites, *forgetting what lies behind,* always *stretch out to what lies ahead,* so that fighting bravely you might attain the crown of eternal happiness.

Mt 10:9-10; Lk 9:1-3; Lk 10:1-4

Phil 3:13

Other Chronicles and References

Boncampagno of Signa (c.1215/20)

Boncampagno (c. 1170-after 1240), a native of the town of Signa near Florence, was for many years a leading master of rhetoric at the University of Bologna. [a] His witty, boastful personality is vividly captured by Salimbene.[b] These two brief, passing comments about the Lesser Brothers are from his most important work, the *Rhetorica antiqua sive Boncampagnus,* a major contribution to the medieval *ars dictaminis* (the craft of composing letters and legal documents).[c] The final written redaction of this work dates from 1220, but these remarks could well have been in the first draft, read publicly at Bologna in 1215. They reveal clearly the ambivalence felt by many observers toward the new movement.

> The Lesser Brothers are truly able to be counted among the disciples of the Lord, because by spurning worldly desires they torment and mortify their flesh and they follow Christ on bare feet and clothed in a hairshirt. . . .
>
> The Lesser Brothers in part are mere youths or boys. If, then, the pliability of their years makes them inconstant and easily led, that is only to be expected; but they have already gone to an extreme of madness, since they wander through cities and towns and solitary places without any discretion, enduring horrible and inhuman sufferings.

Odo of Cheriton (1219/47)

Odo of Cheriton (1180/90-1246/47) took his name from the ancestral manor of his prosperous family in Kent.[d] Although the heir, he became a priest and studied theology at Paris, becoming a master by 1219. Odo never seems to have become a faculty member at a school however, but returned to his estates in England to lead the life of a "gentleman cleric," devoting himself to study, writing, and extensive travels. Odo composed three sermon cycles, several treatises, and

a. See E. J. Polak, "Boncampagno of Signa" *Dictionary of the Middle Ages,* 2: 320 (hereafter DMA).

b. *Chronicle,* trans. Joseph Baird et al. (Binghamton, NY, 1986), pp. 54-55.

c. Latin text in Lemmens, *Testimonia minora,* p. 92.

d. H. Riedlinger, "Odo v. Cheriton," LdM, 6: 1358-59; for more detail, see Albert Friend, "Master Odo of Cheriton," *Speculum* 23 (1948): 641-58.

a celebrated collection of fables. All of his works were designed for the aid of preachers and enjoyed a wide circulation.

The following is a story or "exemplum" included by Odo in his collection of Sunday Sermons, first published at Paris at the end of 1219.[a] Would Odo have heard this story from the first brothers to reach France at just about this time? We do know he was also very interested in the new Dominican Order, and he refers to Francis as "Brother," an indication that he probably composed this story before Francis's canonization.[b] On the other hand, there is reason to believe that Odo oversaw revised editions of his Sunday Sermons years afterwards, so a dating after 1219 may well be possible.[c]

> Brother Francis, asked who was going to take care of his brothers, since he received all [who came to him] indifferently, answered: "A certain king made love to a woman who lived in the woods and she bore a son. After she had raised him for a time, she came to the gate of the king, so that he might take care of her son from then on. When this was announced to the king, he said: 'So many evil and useless men eat food at my court; isn't it only right that my own son should be fed among them?' " After he told this story, Francis said that he was the woman whom the Lord had impregnated with his word, and that he had borne these spiritual sons. "And so, if the Lord provides for so many unjust people, you should not wonder how he is going to supply nourishment for his own children along with the others."

Chronicle of Lauterberg (c. 1224)

We do not know the identity of the author of the chronicle of the Premonstratensian abbey of Lauterberg (Montis Sereni), near Halle, then in the archdiocese of Magdeburg. But he clearly echoes the traditionalist attitude of many members of the existing orders, manifest in canon 13 of the Fourth Lateran Council, which required founders of new religious communities to take

a. Text in Michael Bihl, "S. Francisci parabola in sermonibus Odonis de Ceritona an. 1219 conscriptis," AFH 22 (1929): 584-86.

b. It certainly seems that Odo heard the story by word of mouth, as it was not included in a Franciscan source until 2C 16-17, which was not published until 1247.

c. Friend, pp. 657-58. Also cf. J. Th. Welter, *L'exemplum dans la littérature religieuse et didactique du moyen âge* (Paris, 1927), pp. 124-27.

one of the existing rules with their proven customs.[a] For him renewal of the church could only lie in the restoration of tried and true observances.

This entry is under the year 1224; the chronicle itself ends in 1225. Its report corroborates that of Jordan of Giano (ChrJG 36), who recalled that the Franciscans had arrived in Magdeburg in 1223.[b]

> Two orders having a new way of religious life began to settle in the province, especially in the city of Magdeburg. One of them was called the Holy Preachers; the other, the Lesser Brothers. It is reported that they were founded about twenty years before this time and were confirmed by Pope Innocent. The first of these is made up only of clerics; the second receives both clerics and laymen, and it is said that it was begun by a merchant.
>
> But why are such novelties introduced, if not as a kind of reproach against the neglected and indolent manner of religious life of those [of us] living in orders on which the Church was first founded? In fact, the most blessed Augustine and Benedict lived as they taught, and it is known to what great heights of sanctity they climbed by living their way of religious life. Certainly if anyone had the will to follow their precepts obediently, it would seem that he would need no new institutions.[c] For if these new institutions are seeking after holiness, then that holiness at which those two most holy fathers arrived by living according to their rules should be enough. It is not easy to believe that anyone from the Order of Holy Preachers or from the Order of Lesser Brothers will become holier than Augustine or Benedict!
>
> Now far be it from me, when I say these things, to disparage anyone's zealous endeavors. But I am saying that one must deplore, yes vigorously deplore, the fact that the ancient orders have been led into such disrepute by the disordered way of life of those who profess them, that they are no longer believed to suffice for salvation by those wishing to renounce the world. For if they were still considered sufficient, new ones would never be sought.

---

a. "Lest too great a variety of religious orders lead to grave confusion in God's church, we strictly forbid anyone to found a new religious order [*religionem*]. Whoever wants to become a religious should join one of the already approved ones. Likewise, whoever wishes to found a new religious house should take the rules and institutes from already approved religious orders." DEC, 1: 242. As the chronicler goes on to say here, the "approved orders" were the monastic [following the Rule of Benedict], the canons regular [following the Rule of Augustine], and the eremetical.

b. Latin text in Lemmens, *Testimonia minorum*, pp. 18-19.

c. The Premonstratensian (Norbertine) canons professed the Rule of Augustine.

Burchard of Ursperg (c.1228/30)

Burchard (before 1177-1231) was a canon of the Premonstratensian abbey of Ursperg, in the diocese of Augsburg.[a] He visited Rome twice: first in 1198, the year of Innocent III's accession, and again in 1210/11. It was during this latter visit that he witnessed the first beginnings of the Lesser Brothers. He was elected provost of his abbey in 1215, and eventually composed a vast "world-chronicle" towards the end of his life. His account there of the early Franciscan movement is based on the reminiscences of his Roman stay.

Burchard's attitude towards the Lesser Brothers is decidedly more favorable than that of his confrere of Lauterberg. For him the "novelty" of the new brotherhood demonstrates that the church constantly renews itself to meet new challenges; he shared the attitude of those in the hierarchy who viewed the Franciscans as a providential orthodox alternative to heretical groups. Burchard's is the only source which attests that Francis's brotherhood originally went by another name.[b]

> At that time, when the world was already growing old, there arose two religious orders in the Church, whose youth is [continually] renewed like the eagle's, and which were approved by the Apostolic See, namely the Lesser Brothers and the Friars Preachers. Perhaps they were approved at that time because two sects, which had previously sprung up in Italy, were still around: one was called the Humiliati and the other the Poor Men of Lyons. Pope Lucius had not long before listed them among the heretics, for among them had been found superstitious teachings and observances.[c] Furthermore, in their clandestine preaching, which for the most part took place in their secret haunts, the Church of God and the priesthood were disparaged.
>
> At that time we saw some of their number, who were called the Poor Men of Lyons, at the Apostolic See with one of their ministers whose name, I think, was Bernard. He was seeking to have his sect confirmed and given privileges by the Apostolic See.[d] In fact, they went about through towns and villages, saying that they were living the life of the apostles, not wishing to possess anything or to have a definite place to live. But the Lord Pope took them to task for certain irregular practices

a. See W. Maleczek, "Burchard v. Ursperg," *Lexikon des Mittelalters*, 2:952 (hereafter LdM).

b. Latin text, *Testimonia minorum*, pp. 17-18.

c. Burchard is referring to the synod of Verona (1184) which had proscribed both these groups.

d. Burchard's memory is correct; he is referring to the visit to Rome in 1210 of Bernard Prim, a reconciled Waldensian. But contrary to the impression one might gain from these remarks, Innocent did eventually grant the group his approval. [*Cum inestimable* (*PL*, 216, 289).]

in their way of life, namely, that they cut off their shoes above the foot and went about walking as if barefooted. Besides, while they wore mantles like religious, they had their hair cut just like the lay people. But what was most shameful about them was that men and women would walk together on the road and often stay in the same house, even—so it was reported of them—sleeping together in the same bed! Nevertheless, they claimed that all these practices came down from the apostles.

In place of these the Lord Pope approved certain others then on the rise who called themselves "Poor Minors." These rejected the above-mentioned superstitious and scandalous practices, but traveled about both in winter and in summer absolutely barefoot; they accepted neither money nor anything else besides food, and occasionally a needed garment that someone might spontaneously offer them, for they would not ask anything from anyone. However, later on these men realized that their name could possibly lead to self-glorification under the cover of great humility and that, as many bear the title "poor" to no purpose,[a] they could boast in vain before God; therefore, obedient to the Apostolic See in all things, they preferred to be called Lesser Brothers instead of Poor Minors.

Caesar of Heisterbach (c.1225-35)

To complete these German references to the early Lesser Brothers, we should include the following incident mentioned in the *Life of Saint Engelbert,* Archbishop of Cologne from 1217 to 1225. This *legenda* was written by Caesar (c.1180-c.1240), a monk of the Cistercian abbey of Heisterbach, of which he was elected prior in 1227. A noted preacher and prolific writer, he left some 36 works, including a life of Elizabeth of Hungary.[b] Caesar dedicated this life of Engelbert to his successor, Archbishop Henry of Cologne (+ 1238).[c] This incident reveals the "wait and see" attitude of even sympathetic ecclesiastics towards the new order.

When the brothers of the new Order of Preachers and the brothers who are called Minors first arrived at Cologne,[d] some of the clergy,

a. As Burchard alludes, the Waldensians were called the "Poor of Lyons"; the reconciled groups led by Durand of Huesca and Bernard Prim were known as the "Catholic Poor" and "Poor Lombards" respectively.

b. See F. Wagner, "Caesarius v. Heisterbach," LdM, 2: 1363-65.

c. Text in *Acta Sanctorum,* Nov., vol. 3, p. 650.

d. For the arrival of the brothers in Cologne about 1221, see the *Chronicle of Jordan of Giano,* 23, 28, 30.

> who were very harsh towards them, betook themselves to the Archbishop [Engelbert] to protest their presence, lodging various complaints against them. But he responded: "So long as things are going well, leave them alone." But the priors and pastors insisted, saying: "We are afraid that they are the ones that the Holy Spirit prophesied through the mouth of Saint Hildegard that would be a cause of grief for the clergy and danger for the city."[a] But he responded with this remark, which is worth remembering: "Well, if it was divinely prophesied, then it has to be fulfilled." And with that they were reduced to silence.

Richard of San Germano (1228)

Richard of San Germano (+1243) was notary of the court of the Kingdom of Sicily; his chronicle contains the following entry under the year 1228. His ruler, the Emperor Frederick II, was opposed to the policies of Gregory IX and this may account for the slightly negative connotation here.[b]

> In the month of July Pope Gregory traveled from Perugia to Assisi where he canonized Brother Francis, the innovator of the Order of Lesser Brothers, because of the two miracles which he had openly performed, one on a blind man and the other on a lame man, to whom he had given sight and the ability to walk.

Luke of Túy (1231-34)

Luke (+ 1249), a native of León, was a canon of the collegiate church of Saint Isidore in that city; he is best known to history for a great "world chronicle," which he began around 1236. Its fourth book is one of the major sources for Spanish history of the period. He was named bishop of Túy in the kingdom of León and Castile in 1239.[c]

---

a. Hildegard of Bingen (1098-1179), "the Sybil of the Rhine," was celebrated for her visions of events that would befall the church. It is difficult to know if the clerical critics here were referring to the works of Hildegard themselves, most likely her predictions to Cologne [*PL*, 197: 250-53], or to their popularizations, such as one put into circulation around 1220 by the Cistercian Geben of Erbach in his *Speculum futurorum temporum.*

b. *Testimonia minora*, pp. 15-16.

c. Cf. O. Engels, "Luca v. Tuy," LdM, 5:2152-3.

In an earlier treatise, dating from the early 1230's, "Against the Errors of the Albigensians," Luke mentions the Stigmata of Francis in the context of refuting "the errors of those who believe there were only three nails fixed in the hands and feet of the Savior." This work, which cites Thomas of Celano's *The Life of Saint Francis,* is a testimony to the rapid diffusion of that work.[a]

> As is found in his holy *legenda* and in the witness of many religious, clerics, lay people, and seculars who merited to see them five years ago with their bodily eyes, and to touch them with their hands, pious testimony is set forth that in the hands and feet of blessed Francis four marks of nails appeared in this soldier of Christ. These demonstrated his perfect victory over the struggle of the world and that by the sign of the four nails of our Lord's Passion he was a imitator of his King, Jesus Christ. Passages are found in his *legenda,* that after a certain beatific vision of a crucified Seraph, "the marks of nails began to appear in his hands and feet." 1C 94

Roger of Wendover (c.1225-35)

The monastery of Saint Albans, one of the largest and best endowed abbeys of England, was noted for a series of able chroniclers, the most distinguished of whom was certainly Matthew Paris, whose detailed *Chronica majora* was composed between 1236 and his death in 1259. However, Matthew's famous work is actually a revised edition and continuation of the Flores historiarum of his predecessor as chronicler at Saint Albans, Roger of Wendover, who died in May, 1236. When composing his own annals, Matthew simply incorporated Roger's, offering a number of improvements.[b] Thus the records for the years prior to 1236 are largely Roger's work.

Knowledge of Roger is extremely scanty; for some time he was prior of the dependent house of Belvoir. He apparently began composing his chronicle around 1217, but was working on revisions until the end of his life. The first entry cited below, under the year 1207, was undoubtedly composed after the arrival of the brothers in England (1224).[c] Roger's chronicle offers a striking testimony of how Francis had become a religious "celebrity" only a few years after his death. Roger does not betray the same strong prejudice against the

a. *Testimonia minorum,* pp. 92-93.

b. See Richard Vaughan, *Matthew Paris* (Cambridge: University Press, 1958), pp. 1-34.

c. Text of Roger's work is in *Rerum Britannicarum Medii Aevi Scriptores* (Rolls Series), no. 84, vol. 2, pp. 35-36, 328-333, partially cited in Lemmens, *Testimonia minora,* pp. 26-32.

mendicant orders that characterized his successor, Matthew Paris, who incorporated these accounts in his Chronica majora with only minor changes.

[1]About that time (1207), there sprang up, under the auspices of Pope Innocent, the preachers called Minors, who quickly filled the earth. They dwelt in cities and towns in groups of ten or seven, possessing no property at all, living according to the Gospel, displaying the most extreme poverty in both food and clothing, walking about barefoot, and giving to all the greatest example of humility. On Sundays and feast days they went forth from their dwellings, preaching the Word of the Gospel in the parish churches, eating and drinking whatever they found among the people to whom they preached. They seemed all the more devoted to the contemplation of the things of heaven, the more they proved themselves strangers to the concerns of this present world and the pleasures of the flesh. No sort of food in their possession was kept for the morrow, so that the poverty of spirit which reigned in their minds might show itself to all in their habit and actions. . . .

[2]*The Death of the brother who first established the Order of Minors.*

About that time (1227) a certain brother of the Order of Minors, named Francis, who had been the founder and master of this Order, marvelously departed this life at Rome.[a] Now this Francis was noteworthy for the nobility of his birth, yet he was even more illustrious for the integrity of his morals. From his boyhood, spent in a simple way, he began to reflect more and more upon the allurements of this world and the mutability of worldly things, and constantly to ponder how vain and ephemeral are all temporal goods. For he had learned this from the books and theological studies which he had pursued from his childhood, until he had reached such a perfect knowledge that he scorned the mutability of perishable things, and with all his strength he yearned with desire for the kingdom of heaven.

[3]In order that he might more freely carry out the resolves of his mind, he renounced his considerable paternal inheritance with all its

a. Matthew Paris's re-working of Roger's chronicle more accurately has a separate entry for the year 1226, correcting some details: "This same year (1226), on Sunday, October fourth, at Assisi, where he was born, blessed Francis departed for the contemplation of heavenly things at Saint Mary of the Portiuncula, where he had begun the Order of Lesser Brothers, having completed twenty years in which he most perfectly clung to Christ, following the life and footprints of the Apostles . . . his life and behavior and rule are more fully described under the year 1227" (*Monumenta Germaniae Historica*, Scriptores, 28, p. 120).

worldly pleasures, clothed himself with a sackcloth garment with a hood, discarded his shoes, and mortified his flesh with vigils and fasts; in order truly to choose voluntary poverty, he determined to have nothing at all of his own; he would not even accept bodily nourishment unless he received it as alms from the faithful under the title of charity; if he had any food left over after his meager meal, he would keep nothing for the next day, but give it all to the poor. At night he slept in his clothes, having a mat in his cell for a bed and a stone under his head for a pillow, and for a blanket he was content with only the hood and sackcloth that he wore during the day.

[4]And so to prepare a way for the Gospel, he went about barefooted and, embracing the apostolic life, he fulfilled the office of preaching on Sundays and feastdays in parochial churches and in other assemblies of the faithful. The more he became detached from the desires of the flesh and the debaucheries of high living, the more efficaciously was he able to impress the Gospel on the hearts of his listeners.

[5]In order to carry out his salutary purpose this man of God, Francis, had the above-mentioned norms set down in writing, together with some others which are most faithfully observed by the brothers of this Order up to the present time, and presented this document to Pope Innocent, who was sitting in consistory at Rome,[a] requesting that his petition be confirmed by the Apostolic See.

[6]*How the Lord Pope confirmed this Order by his favorable response.*

The Pope attentively considered the brother standing before him: his strange habit, his ignoble countenance, his long beard, his unkempt hair, and his dirty and overhanging brow, and once he had Francis's petition read, which was so difficult, indeed impossible in common estimation to carry out, he despised him and said: "Go, brother, and look for some pigs, to whom you are more fit to be compared rather than to human beings, and roll around with them in a slough; give them this Rule you prepared and fulfill there your office of preaching."

When Francis heard these words, he bowed his head and left immediately. He finally found some pigs and rolled with them in the mud until he had covered his body and habit with filth from head to toe. He then returned to the consistory and presented himself to the gaze of

a. Innocent III was accustomed to hold a public "consistory court" three times a week at which he, together with the cardinals and canon lawyers present, examined and resolved cases presented to him.

the Pope: "My Lord," he said, "I have done as you ordered; I beg you, now hear my petition." When the astonished Pope saw what Francis had done, he deeply regretted having treated him with contempt. When he composed himself, he ordered Francis to wash himself and then return to him. Francis swiftly cleansed himself from the filth and returned immediately. Overcome with emotion because of this, the Pope granted his petition; after confirming his Order and, through a privilege of Roman Church, the office of preaching which he had requested, he dismissed him with a blessing. Then Francis, the servant of God, built an oratory in the city of Rome where he might reap the fruit of contemplation and, as a noble warrior, take up the spiritual battle against evil spirits and carnal vices.

[7] *The preaching of Francis and the remarkable end of his life.*

Francis thus devoutly fulfilled the office of preaching throughout the whole of Italy and other nations, and especially in the city of Rome. But the Roman people, who are hostile to all that is good,[a] so scorned the preaching of this man of God that they would not listen to him or even be present at his holy exhortations. Finally, after they had refused to accept his preaching for very many days, Francis severely rebuked their hardness of heart: "I grieve very much," he said, "over your unhappy condition, because you are spurning not only me, the servant of Christ, but you are also despising him in me, since I am announcing the Good News of the Redeemer of the world to you. So now I am leaving Rome, invoking upon your desolation the testimony of him who is the faithful witness in heaven; and to your shame I am going to preach the Good News of Christ to the wild animals and the birds of the air, that they might listen to the healing words of God, obey them, and find peace."

[8] He then left the city, and on the outskirts he found crows sitting among the carrion, as well as kites and magpies and many other birds flying about in the air. He said to them: "I command you, in the name of Jesus Christ, whom the Jews crucified and whose preaching the miserable Romans have scorned, to come near to me and listen to the word of God, in the name of him who created you and preserved you in the ark of Noah from the waters of the flood." As soon as he gave the command, that entire multitude of birds drew near and surrounded him;

a. The two Saint Albans chroniclers have a strong anti-Roman bias.

keeping quiet and ceasing all their chirping, those birds did not move from the spot for the space of half a day, but remained intent on the words of the man of God, never turning their gaze away from the face of the preacher.

This remarkable incident was soon discovered by the Roman citizens and by those entering and leaving the city, and when this was repeated for three days by the man of God when he called the birds together, the clergy, together with a crowd of people, went out and with great veneration led the man of God back into the city. And then by the oil of his supplicatory preaching, hearts that had been fruitless and consistently hardened were softened and changed for the better.

[9]As a result, the fame of his name began to be so spread throughout all of Italy, that many nobles, following his example, left the world with its vices and concupiscences and subjected themselves to his leadership. In a short time this Order of Preachers increased throughout the world: dwelling in cities and towns in groups of seven or ten, they went forth during the days, preaching the word of life throughout the villages and parish churches, planting young shoots of virtue among the field laborers, and even bringing forth much fruit from usurers. It was not only among the faithful that they scattered the seed of the word of God and the dew of heavenly doctrine, but they also went among the Gentile nations and those of the Saracens, bearing testimony to the truth, and by this means many of these brothers attained the glory of martyrdom.

[10]*The concourse of people at the death of this celebrated brother.*

At length, after this friend of God, Francis, had with his brothers preached the Gospel of peace for many years in the city of Rome and in its environs, thus returning the talent entrusted to him by the Lord with multiple interest, like a good money-lender does for his investor, the hour came for him to pass from this world to Christ and to receive as a reward from his labors the crown of life which God has promised to those who love Him.

[11]And so on the fifteenth day before his death there appeared wounds on his hands and feet, which continually emitted blood, just as had appeared in the Savior of the world as he hung on the Cross when he was crucified by the Jews. His right side also seemed to be laid open and so besprinkled with blood so that even the intimate secrets of his heart were plainly visible. And what else? A great crowd of people

flocked to him, marveling at such an unusual happening; among these were Cardinals themselves coming to inquire from him what this appearance meant.

To this he replied: "This manifestation has been revealed in me so that you, to whom I have preached the mystery of the Cross, may believe in him who, for the salvation of the world, bore on the Cross these wounds which you see here, and also that you may know that I am a servant of him whom I have preached to you, as crucified, dead and risen; and that, with all doubt being removed, you may persevere in constancy of faith until the end. These wounds in me which you now see open and bloody will become closed and healed as soon as I am dead, so that they will appear like the rest of my flesh."

[12]And very soon, without any bodily distress or suffering, he was freed from the flesh and returned his spirit to his Creator. After he had died, no marks of the wounds in his hands or feet or side remained. The man of God was buried in his oratory, and the Roman Pontiff inscribed him in the catalogue of the saints and ordered the day of his burial to be observed as a solemn feast.

[13]. . . [At that time (1234)] the Preachers and the Minors, who have freely chosen poverty and humility, were raised to such heights, not to say arrogance [by Pope Gregory IX] that they sought to be received in religious houses and cities in solemn procession, with standards, lighted candles, and festive vestments; it was conceded to them to grant an indulgence of many days to their hearers; they signed people with the crusader vow one day, and on the next, when they gave money, they absolved them from the vow . . .[a]

Alberic of Trois-Fontaines (c.1227-35)

The author of yet another monastic chronicle, Alberic (+ after 1252), of the Cistercian abbey of Trois-Fontaines, near Chalons-sur-Marne, also gives some attention to Francis and his new brotherhood. The brief reports, under three different years, are quite matter-of-fact. These sections of the chronicle seem to

a. This section is in Matthew Paris's emendation, not in Roger's original. It reveals his hostility to the mendicants, associating them with the greed and authoritarianism of the Papal court. (Text in *Monumenta Germaniae Historica*, Scriptores, 28, p. 128.)

have been composed between 1227 and 1235;[a] the entry for the year 1207 already refers to Francis as "blessed," so it is hardly contemporary.

Although Alberic was a countryman and admirer of Jacques de Vitry, his references to the new Order are sober, containing none of Jacques's enthusiasm.[b] He focuses on the elements of novelty that distinguished the Lesser Brothers from the structures of his own Cistercian life, but says little about their spiritual values. He also intimates that novelty carries with it the risk of aberrant preaching.[c]

> . . . There also began around this time (1207), another order in Tuscany near Assisi; it was the work of a certain religious man by the name of Francis. They are called "Lesser Brothers" because of their humility and their bodily austerities. They have their own rule which was approved by Pope Innocent III, which blessed Francis composed with the help of religious and expert men. As for their custom of reading [Scripture] and chanting the Psalms, he selected the form of the Roman church. They have one superior, whom they call the general minister. . . .
>
> . . . On the fourth of October (1226), blessed Francis, founder of the Order of Lesser Brothers, happily passed on to the Lord; his body was honorably buried in Lombardy in the city of Assisi . . .
>
> . . . In Tuscany, in Assisi, which is near Perugia, the canonization of blessed Francis, the father of the Lesser Brothers, was held (1228). One [brother] of this Order, who publicly preached some heresies in Paris, was seized and imprisoned.[d]

The Life of Pope Gregory IX (c. 1240)

The biography of Gregory IX, composed about the year 1240, is the work of an anonymous author who was obviously familiar with the Roman court,

---

a. These references are partially cited in Lemmens, *Testimonia Minora*, pp. 19-20, but this translation contains the full text from the critical edition, *Monumenta Germaniae Historica, Scriptores*, 13, pp. 887-888, 918, 922. According to the editors, Alberic wrote the work in two distinct stages; the entries for the years prior to 1235 were composed between 1227 and 1235; then he returned to this project during the years 1250-52, composing the entries for the years 1235 to 1241, when the chronicle ends (*Ibid*, pp. 641-47).

b. He has full entries on Jacques's ordination to the episcopate (*Ibid.*, p. 905), his death (p. 948), and burial at Oignies (p. 950).

c. Evident not simply in his remark cited below, but in his report of Peter of Boreth, a brother who predicted the imminent coming of the Antichrist (*Ibid.*, 920).

d. It is not clear to whom Alberic is referring here. Lemmens thought it might be Gerardo of Borgo San Donnino, but this seems unlikely in light of the chronology given above by the editors. Gerardo was active more than a decade after the chronicle ends in 1241.

possibly one "John of Campania, subdeacon and our notary," whom Gregory referred to in a letter of 1240. This might well be the same "John, notary of the Apostolic See," who according to Bernard of Besse, composed a life of Francis, *Quasi stella matutina,* now lost.[a]

The author clearly exaggerates the role of his patron in the foundation of the Franciscan movement, as is evident from the writings of Gregory IX himself.

> [1]At the time of his office [as bishop of Ostia] he [Pope Gregory] established and brought to completion the new orders of the Brothers [and Sisters] of Penance and of the Cloistered Ladies. He also gave form to the yet unorganized Order of Minors, which in its early stages was wandering about without definite bounds, by providing them with a new Rule and by designating Francis as their rector and minister. Under his leadership those limits were increased, so that by God's power there is hardly a hamlet throughout the whole world that now may be found without their venerable brotherhood.
>
> [2]Besides the many things, to be noted with great admiration, which he with dutiful liberality contributed for the necessities of these brothers, for the above-mentioned [Cloistered] Ladies he had constructed through the resources of his office and at incalculable expense a monastery in Rome, that of Saint Cosmas, and [others] in Lombardy and in Tuscany, afterwards providing for the necessities of each one. These are the Ladies who, divinely inspired by the zeal of his preaching to leave parents and homeland and not dissuaded by the tears of their own children, had exchanged the pride of the world and temporal wealth for the rigors of extreme poverty, and the weave of their costly garments for the smarting prickle of rough wool. After he ascended the throne of the Supreme Pontiff he gathered them together as daughters, venerated them as mothers, and helped their indigence with more abundant aid. . . .
>
> [3]. . . At that time blessed Francis shone in the city of Assisi like a new star in the firmament of the Church because of the splendor of his miracles. After these miracles were verified by means of a diligent, thorough examination of the truthful reports of witnesses, the most holy Pope Gregory on the advice of his brothers (the cardinals) went to Assisi with a prestigious group of venerable cardinals and prelates. There on the fourth of October, in the second year of his pontificate

a. Lemmens, *Testimonia minora*, pp. 11-14.

[1228],[a] wearing ornate and costly vestments, and with a multitude of people gathered from all parts of the world, carrying palms and candles, he delivered a profound discourse for which he chose this beginning: "He shone in his days as the morning star in the midst of a cloud,
Sir 50:6-7 and as the moon at the full. And as the sun when it shines, so did he shine in the temple of God." Then, after the miracles were related and diligently explained, the most blessed pontiff decreed with an abundance of tears that Francis, the servant of the Crucified, whose heart and body bore the marks of the Stigmata, be added to the catalogue of the saints. After three days the pontiff returned to Perugia.

a. The chronicler's memory is in error here; the date of Francis's canonization was July 16, 1228, not October 4, which was the date established for the liturgical memorial.

Chroniclers of the Fifth Crusade

Chronicle of Ernoul (1227/29)

Francis's dramatic crossing of the Crusader-Egyptian lines to visit the Sultan at Damietta captured the imagination of later generations and the scene was often depicted in art, yet there are only two contemporaries who recorded the visit: Jacques de Vitry and the so-called *Chronicle of Ernoul*.[a] The reputed author of this work, which is considered the most accurate of the several attempts to continue the classic twelfth-century Crusade chronicle of William of Tyre, was one Ernoul, the shield-bearer of Balian II of Ibelin, one of the great feudal lords of the Crusader states. Late in life this Ernoul apparently either wrote or dictated his reminiscences, and these were combined with other, anonymous accounts to complete the narrative. The chronicle was written in Old French in a direct and artless style.[b]

> [1]Now I am going to tell you about two clerics[c] who were among the host at Damietta. They went before the Cardinal,[d] saying that they wished to go preach to the Sultan,[e] but that they did not want to do this without his leave. The Cardinal told them that as far as he was concerned, they would go there neither with his blessing nor under his orders, for he would never want to give them permission to go to a place where they would only be killed. For he knew well that if they went there, they would never come back. But they responded that, if they were to go there, he would have no blame, because he had not commanded them, but only allowed them to go.
>
> And thus they begged the Cardinal insistently. When he saw that they were firm in their resolve, he told them: "Sirs, I do not know what is in your hearts or in your thoughts, whether these be good or evil, but if you do go, see that your heart and your thoughts are always turned to

a. On this work, see M. R. Morgan, The Chronicle of Ernoul and the Continuation of William of Tyre (London, 1973). For a good analysis of Francis's visit to the Sultan, see James Powell, "Francesco d'Assisi a la Quinta Crociata: Una Missione di Pace," *Schede Medievali* 4 (1983): 68-77. Cf. also Benjamin Kedar, *Crusade and Mission: European Approaches towards the Muslims* (Princeton: University Press, 1984), pp. 119-131. The best brief history of the Fifth Crusade is James Powell, *Anatomy of a Crusade, 1213-1221* (Philadelphia: University of Pennsylvania Press, 1986).

b. Text in G. Golubovich, *Biblioteca Biobibliografica della Terra Santa*, vol. 1 (Quaracchi, 1906), pp. 10-13.

c. Ernoul apparently did not know the identity of Francis; the first Franciscan sources also report that Francis took a companion on his mission to the Sultan (*Cel.* 57); later sources identify him as Brother Illuminato [*LM* 9.8].

d. Pelagius, Cardinal-bishop of Albano, Papal legate accompanying the Crusade.

e. Malik-al-Kamil (1180-1238), nephew of Saladin, who became Sultan of Egypt in 1218.

the Lord God." They responded that they only wanted to go [to the Sultan] to accomplish a great good which they longed to carry to its conclusion. Then the cardinal said it was indeed good for them to go if they wished, but that they were not to let anyone think that he had sent them.

[2]And so the two clerics left the Christian camp and headed towards that of the Saracens. When the Saracen sentinels saw them coming they thought that they were messengers or perhaps had come to renounce their faith.[a] When they met them, they seized them and led them to the Sultan.

When they were brought into his presence, they greeted him. The Sultan returned their greeting and then asked if they wished to become Saracens or perhaps had come with some message. They responded that they never would want to become Muslims, but that they had come to him as messengers on behalf of the Lord God, that he might turn his soul to God. "If you wish to believe us," [they said], "we will hand over your soul to God, because we are telling you in all truth that if you die in the law which you now profess, you will be lost and God will not possess your soul. It is for this reason that we have come. But if you will give us a hearing and try to understand us, we will demonstrate to you with convincing reasons, in the presence of the most learned teachers of your realm, if you wish to assemble them, that your law is false."

The Sultan responded that he had archbishops, bishops, and good clergy of his law,[b] and that he could not listen to what they had to say except in their presence. "Very well," responded the two clerics, "order them here, and if we cannot demonstrate with solid arguments that what we tell you is true, that your law is false—that is, if you are willing to listen and understand—then you can have our heads cut off."[c] So the Sultan ordered them to join him in his tent. And so some of the highest nobles and wisest men of his land and the two clerics were gathered together.

[3]When they had all assembled, the Sultan explained the reason why he had called them together and brought them into his presence, and what the two clerics had said, and the purpose they had in coming to his court. But they answered him: "Lord, you are the sword of the law: you

a. Francis crossed the lines during a time of truce while negotiations were being conducted, early in September, 1219 (Powell, *Anatomy of a Crusade*, p. 159); also, there is evidence of both Muslims and Christians crossing the lines at Damietta to join the faith of their adversaries (Kedar, pp. 121-22).

b. Ernoul uses Christian terms to attempt to describe Muslim religious leaders for his readers.

c. From at least the ninth century, it was a capital offense under Islamic law for Christians to attempt to convert Muslims; those who did so were motivated by a desire for martyrdom. See Kedar, pp. 9-18.

have the duty to maintain and defend it. We command you, in the name of God and of Mohammed, who has given us the law, to cut off their heads here and now, for we do not want to listen to anything they have to say. We also warn you not to listen to them, because the law forbids giving a hearing to preachers [of another religion]. And if there should be someone who wishes to preach or speak against our law, the law commands that his head be cut off. It is for this reason that we command you, in the name of God and the law, that you have their heads cut off immediately, as the law demands."

[4]Having said this, they took their leave and departed, without wanting to hear another word. There remained only the Sultan and the two clerics. Then the Sultan said to them: "My lords, they have told me that in the name of God and of the law that I should have your heads chopped off, because it is so prescribed. But I am going to act against the law, because I am never going to condemn you to death. For that would be an evil reward for me to bestow on you, who conscientiously risked death in order to save my soul for God." After saying this, the Sultan said that he wished they would remain with him, and that he would give them vast lands and many possessions. But they replied that they did not want to stay, from the moment they saw that he did not want to listen to them or understand their message, and that they would like to return to the Christian camp, if he would permit them.

The Sultan replied that he would gladly have them returned safe and sound to the Christian camp. Furthermore, he brought great quantities of gold, silver, and silk garments and invited them to take whatever they wanted. They said that they would not have taken anything once they saw they could not obtain his soul for the Lord God, for they considered this the most precious thing they could give to God, rather than the possession of vast treasure. They said it would be sufficient if he would give them something to eat, and then they would be on their way, since they couldn't accomplish anything else there. The Sultan gave them plenty of food to eat, whereupon they took their leave of him, and he had them escorted safely back to the Christian army.

Bernard the Treasurer (1229/30)

Another Old French chronicle, this is highly dependent on the Chronicle of Ernoul. It was translated and edited into a more elegant Latin style about 1320 by the Dominican Francesco Pipino of Bologna.[a] This passage is in a work entitled *The Death of Coradin, Sultan of Damascus.*

[1]Regarding the humanness and clemency of the same Sultan, Coradin,[b] this Bernard gives the following example. During the siege of Damietta, there were in the Christian camp two clerics who, burning with zeal for the faith, proposed to go to the Sultan to preach the faith. But when they sought permission from the Cardinal legate, he replied: "I do not know whether you are led by zeal, moved by the Spirit of God, or if a temptation of Satan has possessed you. As for whether you go or not, I will not encourage or dissuade you. But if you decide to go, strive that your actions bear fruit in the sight of God."

[2]When they drew near the camp of the Saracens, they were led into the Sultan's presence, who sought to know from them whether they had come on some embassy or perhaps wished to become Saracens. They replied: "We are ambassadors of the Lord Jesus Christ, and have come here for the salvation of souls. We are ready to show you convincing arguments that it is only through the observance of the Christian law that one can be saved." And they declared that they were ready to suffer death for that faith. Now since the Sultan was gentle of heart, he listened to them kindly. He called together his archbishops, bishops, and other experts in his law, and also some of the commanders of his army. But when the Sultan had explained to them the reason why he had called them together, one of them replied for them all: "One who is bound to be the defender of our law and who should oppose its adversaries with the sword of vengeance indeed acts most imprudently if he instead grants an audience to blasphemers of the law, such as these are." Having said this, they entreated him, in virtue of the law, to have them put to death. Then they left.

[3]But the Sultan said to the Christians: "Far be it that I would ever condemn to death you who have come for my life." He added that he was ready to entrust them with great possessions if they wished to remain with him, and he ordered gold and silver ingots presented to them; but they refused to take anything, protesting that they had come not for temporal goods but spiritual ones. And so, accepting an escort from the Sultan, they returned to their own camp.

a. Text in Golubovich, 1, pp. 13-14.

b. Either Bernard or Pipino has confused al-Kamil with his brother, Coradin; this was the Crusaders' name for Malik-al-Mu'azzam, Sultan of Damascus. However, the latter may well have been present at this meeting as he was in Egypt with an army assisting his brother at the time of Francis's visit.

The History of the Emperor Eracles (1229/31)

Still another continuation of the Chronicle of William of Tyre is an anonymous Old French work known by its opening words. It does not mention Francis's visit to the Sultan but is interesting in that it does tell us how long Francis remained in Egypt, the reason for his departure, and the fact that he spent some time in Syria afterwards.

> That man, who began the Order of Lesser Brothers—a brother called Brother Francis—who was later made a saint and officially raised to that dignity, so that we call him Saint Francis, came to the army at Damietta. He accomplished many good things and remained until the capture of the distressed. For that reason, he left there and stayed for a space of time in Syria, and from there he returned to his country.

APPENDIX

Explanation of Maps

This geographic supplement is designed to orient the reader—especially those unfamiliar with European geography—to the world of Francis. At its heart is a series of maps, but equally important is the gazetteer, or index of geographic place names, which will allow the reader to find specific locations.

Map one illustrates the European political world in which Francis lived. The political geography of this world was fundamentally different from that of Europe today. That there are many recognizable names of places is deceptive; even though a region may have the same name in the thirteenth century as it does today, its overall political structure was completely different. Nation-states as we know them did not exist in the Middle Ages. Western Europe at this time was organized under a feudal social-political system. Land was controlled by local nobility in the name of a king, or regional ruler. The local nobility swore oaths of fealty to the king, who depended on the cooperation of his nobility to carry out his wishes. No boundaries between regions in Western Europe are shown on Map 1 because they would tend to communicate the notion of a stable, demarked and defended border as is found in Europe today.

Map two illustrates some of these new social realities of the High Middle Ages. The population of Europe had fallen considerably after the fall of Rome and the Germanic invasions, and only began to recover and grow after the tenth century. All population estimates of the Middle Ages can be considered educated guesses at best because the historical data is fragmentary. Geographers estimate that the population between the ninth and fourteenth century doubled, from approximately 45 to 90 million. This increase was not uniformly distributed over the continent, and was frequently interrupted by invasions, wars, plagues, or famines.

The two regions of Europe having the greatest agricultural productivity and the most rapid population increase were the Northern Italian Peninsula and the lowlands of Northwest Europe (modern Belgium, Netherlands, and the Rhine Valley). It is important to distinguish between these regions, however. Although they had suffered a long period of decline in sophistication and population since the fall of the Roman Empire, Northern Italian cities had perdured, and because of their location, when trade with Byzantium and the East began to increase, they were uniquely positioned to become thriving commercial centers.

Located at the southern edge of Western Europe and surrounded by the Mediterranean Sea, the cities of Lombardy, the Po Valley, Tuscany and to a lesser extent, the Duchy of Spoleto, had merchants who traded with Byzantium in the east and the rest of Europe in the north. The port cities of Venice, Genoa, and Pisa were some of the largest and wealthiest cities in Europe at this time.

The population growth in Northwest Europe was furthered primarily by the wool industry. The climate and soils are not well suited for crop production, so the region began to specialize in the production of wool and woolen cloth. From the twelfth century onward, agricultural specialization increased, which in turn led to the revival of fairs as a place to exchange goods. These were huge gatherings of merchants from all over Europe lasting about thirty days each. Eventually a pattern of rotation evolved between the various fairs in the two main geographic areas, Flanders (today's Belgium) and Champagne (northern France). The economies of Northern and Southern Europe linked up at these fairs, which fulfilled commercial functions similar to that of the Italian cities.

Map three shows the region of Italy during Francis's era. What we understand to be the modern country of Italy did not exist until the end of the 19th century. During Francis's era, Italy would have been understood to be the area south of the Alps but not extending beyond Rome (on map 3 this is shown as the Holy Roman Empire, Peter's Patrimony and the Papal States). Strong regional contrasts and variations have characterized the Italian Peninsula. Some of these contrasts can be attributed to physical geography, and some to cultural history. Since the fall of Rome, the Italian Peninsula had been divided into numerous political configurations, and there was little expectation that the whole peninsula could be politically united. Extending 700 miles into the Mediterranean and divided into sub-regions by mountains, the peninsula's population identified much more with a local region than with the political aspirations of political leaders. During the Middle Ages, the Byzantine Empire, Moslems, Normans, and the Holy Roman Empire alternately controlled the southern peninsula and the island of Sicily. Lying at the crossroads of the Mediterranean, the Kingdom of Sicily was one of the richest and most civilized states of Europe.

Lombardy and Tuscany grew to be among the most populous and wealthy regions in Europe during the High Middle Ages. The cities in this region benefited from the fertility of the Po Valley, their location as a natural sea-land transfer point for goods between Northern Europe and Byzantium, and the protection of the Alps.

Map four demonstrates how climate and geology combined to impose sharp natural divisions on the Italian Peninsula. The Alps forms a natural barrier to the North, one impenetrable as much as half the year. Over two-thirds of the peninsula may be classified as hill or mountain, and along most of the 100-mile wide peninsula, these are jumbled together in the Apennines. In Lombardy alone there are more variations of elevation, climate, soil and vegetation than in the whole of Germany. The Po Valley is the only expansive fertile plain; in peninsular Italy, fertile lowlands are limited. The ruggedness of the landscape, the unevenness of soil fertility, and the ease of access to the sea led the residents of the Italian Peninsula to become proficient mariners. Trade was much more easily accomplished along the peninsula by sea than by land. There are several physical regions of the northern Italian Peninsula: the greater Po Valley (including Lombardy, Romagna and Venice), the Arno Valley and Tuscany, the more isolated eastern coast of the Marche, Abruzzi (which has historically been the wildest part of the Apennines), the Duchy of Spoleto and Latium (the upper and lower watershed of the Tiber River, respectively).

Map five describes the transportation, religious and social geography of the northern Italian Peninsula at the time of Francis. There is no reliable way to determine the population of cities during the Middle Ages. Map 5 shows Venice, Milan, Genoa and Florence to be larger than other towns. Historians generally agree that Venice was the largest town, and estimate that it had a population of between 50,000 and 100,000. The other three large towns had slightly fewer residents, and overall, the population density in Lombardy and the Po Valley was twice that of the rest of the Italian Peninsula. Rome's population is estimated to have been 30,000. Assisi is estimated to have between 10,000 and 20,000 people at this time, with Perugia about twice as large.

The rise of the city-states and the movement toward urbanization coincided with the heretical movements that began to appear in Western Europe. A proper geography of medieval religious dissent has yet to be undertaken, and a thorough job may be impossible because of the scattered historical record. At the onset of the thirteenth century, there were several heretical movements in Lombardy and the Italian Peninsula, the most significant being the Waldensians, and the Cathars (they were called several other names, including Albigensians and Patarines). The Catholic hierarchy perceived these movements as grave threats because they challenged the official Church authority. Map 5 shows the cities with established communities of these two groups. Other heretical groups may have been present, and these two groups almost certainly had followers in many other cities, but the historical evidence is missing.

Map six details the regions of the Duchy of Spoleto and the Marche of Ancona. The first Franciscans did much of their preaching in the towns and villages shown on this map. Maps 6-9 show all the towns and villages that Francis or the early friars are reported by the early sources to have visited on the Italian Peninsula. There are, of course, many other villages that existed, but in the interest of clarity, they are not shown on the maps. The spine of the Central Apennines separate the Duchy of Spoleto and the Marche of Ancona, with much of Marche oriented toward the Adriatic Sea. Map 6 can be seen as having three sub-regions: the lower Spoleto Valley, where Assisi and Perugia are located, the Rieti Valley, where Francis spent considerable time, and the less-densely settled region of the Marche of Ancona.

Map seven shows the physical relief of the Rieti Valley and the location of the several places of the friars in that region. This map is a good illustration of the geographic relationship between early Franciscan hermitages and an emerging urban center. Francis spent a considerable amount of time in this region.

Map eight illustrates the territories of Assisi and Perugia, its neighbor to the west. Perugia became a papal city and the empire claimed Assisi. Tensions between the two cities dated back centuries, with the Tiber River forming a historical boundary between peoples. Sometime during the eleventh century, Perugia had occupied a strip of land on the east bank near an area called Collestrada. Violence escalated after 1200, resulting in the Battle of Collestrada in 1202. Francis fought in this battle, and when Assisi lost, he was imprisoned in Perugia (2C 4). It seems that Francis's father, Pietro Bernardone, owned some land near the site of the battle.

Map nine shows the first places of the brothers as well as the first two temporary residences of Clare. Also shown are the approximate location of most of the lands which archival records show as belonging to Francis's father, Pietro Bernardone.

Maps ten and eleven show what the city of Assisi looked like at the time of Francis. The walls on this map are essentially the same as those built by the ancient Romans. The locations of the four most important social powers in Assisi are all shown on this map. The Rocca Maggiore was the symbol of Imperial authority, and it dominated the landscape until it was torn down by the Assisians in 1198. The bishop's palace was the seat of Church power, and it was in the Santa Maria Maggiore Piazza (plaza) that Francis shed his clothes, spurning his father and embracing his vocation in a deeper way. Trade and commerce had grown remarkably in the century before Francis's birth and the Market in the town's center became increasingly important. With the emergence of the *commune*, the lesser nobility and merchants organized themselves and established the *Palazzo del Consoli*, or city hall, across from the Basilica of San Rufino. The *Palazzo del Consoli* moved in 1212 to the Tempio di Minerva.

Although Arnaldo Fortini confidently asserts that the paternal house of Francis lies in between the churches of San Paolo and San Nicolo (site #1), the evidence is circumstantial. Other scholars argue that his family home lay on the site now occupied by the Chiesa Nuova (site #2), or the church of San Francesco Piccolo (site #3).

Gazetteer

Place Name	General Location	Type of Feature	Map	Co-ord
Abruzzi	C Italian Peninsula	Region	5	5F
Acquapendente	Tuscany	Town	5	5D
Acquasparta	Sabina	Village	7	1B
Acre	Holy Land	Kingdom/City	1	5H
Adriatic Sea	N Mediterranean	Sea	3	3E
Alessandria	Lombardy	Town	5	2A
Alexandria	Egypt	City	1	6G
Alife	Kingdom of Sicily	Town	5	6F
Almería	Iberian Peninsula	Town	2	4A
Alps	C Europe	Mountains	4	1D
Alviano	SW Duchy of Spoleto	Village	6	7B
Amiterno	Abruzzi	Village	5	5F
Ancona	Marche of Ancona	Town	6	2F
Antioch	Asia Minor	City	1	5H
Antrodoco	Sabina	Village	7	4G
Apennines	Italian Peninsula	Mountains	4	3D
Apulia	S Italian Peninsula	Region	3	5F
Aquitaine	France	Region	1	3B
Aragon	Iberian Peninsula	Kingdom	1	3B
Arezzo	E Tuscany	City	6	3A
Arles	S France	Town	1	3C
Armenia	Asia Minor	Kingdom	1	5G
Ascoli	S Marche of Ancona	Village	6	5F
Assisi	Duchy of Spoleto	Town	6	4C
Asti	Lombardy	Town	5	2A
Atlantic Ocean	W Europe	Ocean	1	2A
Augsburg	Holy Roman Empire	Town	1	2D
Austria	Central Europe	Region	1	2E
Bagnara	Duchy of Spoleto	Village	6	4D
Bagnolo	Lombardy	Town	5	1C
Bagnoregio	Peter's Patrimony	Village	6	7A
Baltic Sea	N Europe	Sea	1	1E
Barcelona	Iberian Peninsula	Town	1	3B
Bari	Apulia	Town	3	4F
Barletta	Apulia	Town	5	6H
Basel	Holy Roman Empire	Town	2	3D
Bastia	Lower Spoleto Valley	Village	9	2A
Bavaria	Holy Roman Empire	Region	1	2D
Benvento	Kingdom of Sicily	Town	3	5D
Bergamo	Lombardy	Town	5	1C
Bettona	Spoleto Valley	Village	8	5E
Bevagna	Spoleto Valley	Village	8	7G
Biscay, Bay of	Atlantic Ocean	Bay	1	2B
Bishop Guido's Palace	Assisi	Bishop's palace	11	5C

Place Name	General Location	Type of Feature	Map	Co-ord
Black Sea	W Asia	Sea	1	3G
Bobbio	Lombardy	Monastery	5	2B
Bologna	Romagna	City	5	3D
Bolsena, Lake	Peter's Patrimony	Lake	4	4E
Bordeaux	France	Town	1	3B
Bovara	Spoleto Valley	Village	6	5C
Bracciano, Lake	Peter's Patrimony	Lake	4	4E
Brenner Pass	Alps	Mountain pass	4	1E
Brescia	E Lombardy	Town	5	1C
Brindisi	Kingdom of Sicily	Town	3	5F
Bruges	Low Countries	Town	1	1C
Buda Petsch	E Europe	Town	1	2E
Bulgaria	Balkan Peninsula	Kingdom	1	3F
Burgundy	France	Region	1	2C
Cadiz	Iberian Peninsula	Town	2	4A
Cairo	Egypt	City	1	6G
Calvi	Sabina	Village	7	5B
Camaldoli	N Marche of Ancona	Monastery	5	3D
Camerino	W Marche of Ancona	Village	6	4D
Campagna	Peter's Patrimony	Region	5	6E
Campiglia	N Tuscany	Village	5	4C
Candia	Cyprus	Town	1	5F
Cannara	Lower Spoleto Valley	Village	8	6F
Canterbury	England	Town	1	1C
Capua	Kingdom of Sicily	Town	5	6F
Carceri	Monte Subasio	Friars' place	9	2E
Carpathians	Eastern Europe	Mountains	2	2E
Castile	Iberian Peninsula	Kingdom	1	3A
Celano	Abruzzi	Village	5	5F
Celle di Cortona	E Tuscany	Friars' place	8	1A
Cerea	Lombardy	Town	5	1D
Cetona	E Tuscany	Friars' Place	6	5A
Champagne	France	Region	1	2C
Chiascio	Lower Spoleto Valley	River	9	1A
Chiusi	E Tuscany	Castle	6	2A
Città della Pieve	W Duchy of Spoleto	Town	6	5A
Città di Castello	N Duchy of Spoleto	Town	6	3B
Città Castellana	Sabina	Village	7	6A
Civitavecchia	Peter's Patrimony	Town	5	5D
Collestrada	Lower Spoleto Valley	Battle site	8	4F
Collevecchio	Sabina	Village	7	6B
Cologne	Holy Roman Empire	Town	1	2D
Concorezo	Lombardy	Town	5	1B
Constantinople	Asia Minor	City	1	4F
Contigliano	Rieti Valley	Village	7	5D
Coppito	Abruzzi	Village	6	8E
Córdoba	Iberian Peninsula	Town	2	4A
Cori	Peter's Patrimony	Village	5	6E
Corsica	Central Mediterranean	Island	1	3C
Cortona	E Tuscany	Village	8	1A
Cremona	Lombardy	Town	5	2C
Cremona	S Lombardy	City	5	1C

Place Name	General Location	Type of Feature	Map	Co-ord
Cyprus	E Mediterranean	Island	1	5F
Dalmatia	E Europe	Region	1	3E
Damascus	Holy Land	City	1	5H
Damietta	Egypt	City	1	6G
Danube	Hungary	River	2	3E
Denmark	N Europe	Kingdom	1	1D
Dijon	France	Town	2	2C
Durazzo	Bulgaria	Town	1	4E
Egypt	NE Africa	Region	1	6G
Emilia	N Italian Peninsula	Region	5	2B
England	NW Europe	Kingdom	1	1B
Erfurt	Holy Roman Empire	Town	2	2D
Faenza	Romagna	Town	5	3D
Fano	Marche of Ancona	Town	6	1D
Farfa	Peter's Patrimony	Monastery	5	5E
Farneto	Duchy of Spoleto	Friars' Place	8	3F
Fermo	E Marche of Ancona	Village	6	4F
Ferrara	Lombardy	Town	5	2D
Flanders	N Europe	Region	1	1C
Florence	N Tuscany	City	5	3D
Foggia	Kingdom of Sicily	Town	5	6G
Foligno	Duchy of Spoleto	Town	8	6H
Fondi	Kingdom of Sicily	Town	5	6F
Fonte Columbo	Rieti Valley	Friars' place	7	5E
Forano	Marche of Ancona	Friars' place	6	3E
France	W Europe	Kingdom	1	2C
Gaeta	S Italian Peninsula	Town	5	6F
Geneva	Central Europe	Town	2	3C
Genoa	N Italian Peninsula	City	5	3B
Georgia	W Asia	Region	1	3H
Giano	Duchy of Spoleto	Village	6	6C
Granada	Iberian Peninsula	Town	2	4A
Greccio	Rieti Valley	Friars' place	7	4D
Gualdo Tadino	N Duchy of Spoleto	Village	8	2H
Gubbio	NE Duchy of Spoleto	Town	6	3C
Hispania	Iberian Peninsula	Region	1	3A
Hochtor Pass	Alps	Mountain Pass	4	1E
Holy Roman Empire	N Europe	Empire	1	2D
H. of Bernardo di Quintivale	Assisi	House	11	4A
House of Clare	Assisi	House	10	2G
H. Pietro B. (Chiesa Nuova)	Assisi	House	11	3D
H. Pietro B. (Fortini)	Assisi	House	11	2A
H. Pietro B. (S.F. Piccolo)	Assisi	House	11	3D
Hungary	E Europe	Kingdom	1	3E
Iesi	Marche of Ancona	Town	6	2E
Imola	Romagna	Town	5	3D
Ireland	NW Europe	Kingdom	1	1B
Isola Maggiore	Lake Trasimeno	Friars' place	8	3B
Isola Romana	Lower Spoleto Valley	Village	9	2A
Jerusalem	Holy Land	Town	1	6H
Kiev	Russia	Town	1	2G
La Foresta	Rieti Valley	Friars' place	7	4E

Place Name	General Location	Type of Feature	Map	Co-ord
La Verna	N Marche of Ancona	Friars' place	6	2A
Languedoc	France	Region	1	3C
Leon	N Iberian Peninsula	Kingdom	1	3A
Limoges	Touraine	Town	2	3C
Lisbon	W Iberian Peninsula	Town	1	4A
Lisciano	NW Duchy of Spoleto	Village	8	1B
Lombardy	N Italian Peninsula	Region	5	1C
London	England	Town	1	1C
Lubeck	N Germany	Town	1	1D
Lucca	NW Tuscany	City	5	3C
Lugano	Lombardy	Town	5	1A
Lyons	France	Town	1	3C
Machilone	Abruzzi	Village	7	3G
Magliano	Sabina	Village	7	5A
Málaga	Iberian Peninsula	Town	2	4A
Mantova	Lombardy	Town	5	2C
Marche of Ancona	C Italian Peninsula	Region	5	4E
Market (P.d. Commune)	Assisi	Piazza	11	2C
Marseilles	S France	Town	2	3C
Massa Trabaria	N Marche of Ancona	Region	6	2B
Mediterranean Sea	S Europe	Sea	1	4C
Messina	Island of Sicily	Town	3	7E
Milan	Lombardy	City	5	1B
Modena	Lombardy	Town	5	2C
Mogliano	Marche of Ancona	Friars' place	6	4F
Mont Cenis Pass	Alps	Mountain pass	4	2B
Monte Cassino	S Italian Peninsula	Monastery	5	6F
Monte Castrilli	Sabina	Village	7	1B
Monte Gargano	N Apulia	Monastery	5	5H
Monte San Vicino	Marche of Ancona	Friars' place	6	3D
Monte Subasio	Duchy of Spoleto	Mountain	9	3F
Montecasale	W Marche of Ancona	Friars' place	6	2B
Montefalco	Duchy of Spoleto	Village	6	5C
Montefeltro	N Marche of Ancona	Castle	6	1B
Monteluco	Duchy of Spoleto	Friars' place	6	6D
Montenero	Duchy of Spoleto	Village	6	6B
Montenero	Duchy of Spoleto	Village	6	6B
Montepulciano	Tuscany	Town	5	4D
Monteripido	Duchy of Spoleto	Friars' place	8	3D
Monterubbiano	Marche of Ancona	Friars' place	6	4F
Montpellier	Languedoc	Town	2	3C
Morocco	NW Africa	Region	1	5A
Mount Alverna	see: La Verna			
Naples	S Italian Peninsula	Town	3	5D
Narbonne	S France	Town	1	3C
Narni	Duchy of Spoleto	Village	7	3B
Navas de Tolosa	Iberian Peninsula	Town	1	4A
Nera	Duchy of Spoleto	River	7	4A
Nicea	Asia Minor	Kingdom	1	4G
Nocera Umbra	N Duchy of Spoleto	Village	8	4H
Norcia	S. Marche of Ancona	Village	6	6E
North Sea	N Europe	Sea	1	1C

Place Name	General Location	Type of Feature	Map	Co-ord
Nottiano	Duchy of Spoleto	Village	8	4G
Orte	Sabina	Village	7	4A
Orvieto	Duchy of Spoleto	Town	6	6A
Osimo	E Marche of Ancona	Village	6	2F
Ostia	Peter's Patrimony	Town	5	5E
Oxford	England	Town	2	1C
Padua	Lombardy	Town	5	1D
Padua	N Italian Peninsula	City	5	1D
Palazzo dei Consoli	Assisi	Council hall	11	1E
Palermo	Island of Sicily	City	3	7D
Panzo	see: Sant'Angelo di Panzo			
Papal States	Italian Peninsula	Region	5	4E
Paris	France	City	2	2C
Parma	Emilia	Town	5	2C
Pavia	Lombardy	Town	5	2B
Penne	Abbruzzi	Town	5	5F
Perugia	Duchy of Spoleto	Town	6	4B
Peter's Patrimony	C Italian Peninsula	Region	5	5E
Petrella	Sabina	Village	7	6G
Piacenza	Lombardy	Town	5	2B
Piazza del Commune	Assisi	Piazza	11	2C
Piglio nella Campania	Peter's Patrimony	Village	5	5E
Pisa	NE Tuscany	City	5	4C
Po	N Italian Peninsula	River	4	2C
Pofi	Kingdom of Sicily	Village	5	6F
Poggibonsi	Tuscany	Town	5	4C
Poggio Bostone	Rieti Valley	Friars' place	7	3F
Poland	NE Europe	Kingdom	1	1E
Ponte dei Galli	Lower Spoleto Valley	Bridge	9	1D
Ponte San Vettorino	Lower Spoleto Valley	Bridge	9	2C
Porta Antica	Assisi	Gate	10	3C
Porta del Parlascio	Assisi	Gate	10	2H
Porta del Sementone	Assisi	Gate	10	5E
P. Murorupto Inferiore	Assisi	Gate	10	3A
P. Murorupto Superiore	Assisi	Gate	10	2A
Porta Moiano	Assisi	Gate	10	4F
P. qua itur in Marchiam	Assisi	Gate	10	1G
Porta San Giorgio	Assisi	Gate	10	3G
Porta San Rufino	Assisi	Gate	10	3G
Porta Sant'Antimo	Assisi	Gate	10	4D
Portiuncula, S. Maria A.	Spoleto Valley	Friars' place	9	3B
Portugal	W Iberian Peninsula	Kingdom	1	3A
Potenza	Kingdom of Sicily	Town	5	5E
Prague	Holy Roman Empire	Town	1	2D
Preggio	Duchy of Spoleto	Friars' place	8	2C
Provence	France	Region	1	3C
Provins	France	Town, Fair	2	2C
Ragusa	Balkan Peninsula	Town	1	4E
Ratisbon	Holy Roman Empire	Town	2	2D
Ravenna	Lombardy	Town	5	3D
Recanati	Marche of Ancona	Village	6	3F
R. Canons of San Rufino	Assisi	Church residence	10	2G

Place	General Location	Type of Feature	Map	Co-ord
Rhine	Germany	River	2	2D
Rhone	France	River	2	3C
Rieti	Sabina	Town	7	5E
Rieti Valley	Sabina	Region	7	4E
Rimini	SE Romagna	Town	5	3E
Rivo Torto	Spoleto Valley	Stream	9	3D
Rivotorto	Spoleto Valley	Friars' place	9	3D
Rocca	Sabina	Village	7	6F
Rocca Maggiore	Assisi	Castle	10	1D
Romagna	N Italian Peninsula	Region	5	3D
Rome	C Italian Peninsula	City	5	5E
Russia	E Europe	Kingdom	1	1G
Sabina	C Italian Peninsula	Region	5	5E
San Bartolomeo	Lower Spoleto Valley	Priory	9	2C
San Benedetto	Mt. Subasio	Abbey	9	4F
San Bernardo Pass	Alps	Mountain Pass	4	2B
San Damiano	Spoleto Valley	Friars' place	9	2D
San Gemini	Duchy of Spoleto	Village	7	2B
S. Giacomo Murorupto	Assisi	Church	10	2A
San Gimignano	Tuscany	Town	5	4C
San Giorgio	Assisi	Church	10	4G
San Giorgio	Assisi	Piazza	10	4G
San Gottardo	Alps	Mountain pass	4	1C
San Gregorio	Assisi	Church	11	3A
San Gregorio	Assisi	Piazza	11	3A
San Lorenzo	Assisi	Church	10	1G
San Masseo	Lower Spoleto Valley	Church	9	2C
San Nicolo	Assisi	Church	11	2B
San Paolo Abbadesse	Lower Spoleto Valley	Monastery	9	2A
San Paolo di Assisi	Assisi	Church	11	2A
San Pietro della Spina	Lower Spoleto Valley	Church	9	4C
San Quirico	Tuscany	Village	5	4D
San Rufino	Assisi	Basilica	10	2G
San Rufino	Assisi	Piazza	11	1E
San Rufino del Arce	Lower Spoleto Valley	Church	9	3C
San Severino	Marche of Ancona	Village	6	4E
San Stefano	Assisi	Church	10	3D
San Stefano	Marche of Ancona	Village	6	2A
San Verecondo	Duchy of Spoleto	Monastery	8	1G
San Vettorino	Lower Spoleto Valley	Monastery	9	1C
Sansepolcro	E Tuscany	Town	6	2A
Sant' Agata	Assisi	Church	11	2C
Sant' Angelo di Panzo	Spoleto Valley	Church	9	3E
Sant' Annessa	Lower Spoleto Valley	Monastery	9	2D
S. Eleuterio Contigliano	Sabina	Friars' place	7	5D
Sant' Elia	Rieti Valley	Village	7	5E
Sant' Urbano	Sabina	Friars' place	7	4C
S. Maria degli Episcopi	Lower Spoleto Valley	Monastery	9	2D
Santa Maria Maggiore	Assisi	Church	11	4C
Santa Maria Maggiore	Assisi	Piazza	11	4C
Santiago de Compostela	W Iberian Peninsula	Pilgrimage Site	1	3A
Sardinia	C Mediterranean	Island	1	4C

Place Name	General Location	Type of Feature	Map	Co-ord
Sarteano	E Tuscany	Friars' place	6	5A
Satriano	Duchy of Spoleto	Village	8	3G
Saxony	N Germany	Region	1	1D
Sclavonia	E Europe	Region	1	3E
Serbia	Balkan Peninsula	Region	1	3E
Seville	Iberian Peninsula	Town	1	4A
Sicily	C Mediterranean	Island	3	8D
Siena	Tuscany	Town	5	4D
Sirolo	NE Marche of Ancona	Friars' place	6	2F
Soffiano	Marche of Ancona	Friars' place	6	5E
Sora	Kingdom of Sicily	Village	5	6F
Spello	Duchy of Spoleto	Village	8	6G
Spoleto	Duchy of Spoleto	Town	6	6C
Spoleto Valley	Duchy of Spoleto	Valley	9	2B
Spoleto, Duchy of	C Italian Peninsula	Region	5	4D
Subiaco	Peter's Patrimony	Monastery	5	6E
Syracuse	Island of Sicily	Town	3	8E
Syria	Asia Minor	Region	1	5H
Tarano	Sabina	Village	7	5B
Tempio di Minerva	Assisi	Roman temple	11	2B
Terni	Duchy of Spoleto	Village	7	2C
Tescio	Lower Spoleto Valley	River	9	2B
Tiber	C Italian Peninsula	River	4	4E
Tivoli	Campagna	Village	5	5E
Todi	Duchy of Spoleto	Village	6	6B
Toledo	Iberian Peninsula	Town	1	4A
Topino	Spoleto Valley	Stream	9	3B
Torino	Lombardy	Town	5	2A
Torre del Pozzo	Assisi	Tower	11	2D
Toscanella	Sabina	Village	6	8A
Toulouse	S France	Town	2	3C
Touraine	France	Region	1	2B
Tours	France	Town	2	2B
Trapani	Island of Sicily	Town	3	7C
Trasimeno, Lake	Duchy of Spoleto	Lake	8	3B
Trave Bonate	Marche of Ancona	Friars' place	6	4D
Trevi	Spoleto Valley	Village	6	5C
Treviso	N Italian Peninsula	Town	5	1D
Tripoli	Holy Land	Town	1	5H
Tripoli	N Africa	City	1	6D
Troyes	France	Town	2	2C
Tunis	N Africa	Town	2	5D
Tuscany	Central Italian Peninsula	Region	5	4C
Tyrrhenian Sea	C Mediterranean	Sea	4	5D
Valencia	Iberian Peninsula	Town	2	4B
Valfabbrica	Duchy of Spoleto	Monastery	8	3F
Vallombrosa	Tuscany	Monastery	5	4D
Venetian Territories	E Mediterranean	Captured lands	1	5E
Venice	N Italian Peninsula	City	3	1E
Venosa	Kingdom of Sicily	Town	3	5E
Verina	Sabina	River	7	3D
Verona	N Italian Peninsula	Town	5	1C

Place Name	General Location	Type of Feature	Map	Co-ord
Via Aemilia	Lombardy	Roman road	4	3E
Via Antica	Lower Spoleto Valley	Road	9	4E
Via Appia	S Italian Peninsula	Roman road	4	5G
Via Aurelia	C Italian Peninsula	Roman road	4	4D
Via Capobove	Assisi	Street	11	1A
Via d. Ceppo della Catena	Assisi	Street	11	3D
Via dell'Abbadia	Assisi	Street	11	3C
Via di Murorupto	Assisi	Street	10	3B
Via di San Rufino	Assisi	Street	11	2D
Via di Spello	Lower Spoleto Valley	Road	9	4E
Via Flaminia	C Italian Peninsula	Roman road	4	4E
Via Francesca	Lower Spoleto Valley	Road	9	4E
Via per il Collis Infernus	Assisi	Street	10	3B
Via Portica	Assisi	Street	10	3D
Via Sabina	Sabina	Roman road	7	5F
Vicenza	Lombardy	Town	5	1D
Vienna	Holy Roman Empire	Town	2	2E
Viterbo	Peter's Patrimony	Town	6	8A
Volterra	Tuscany	Town	5	4C
Ypres	France	Town, Fair	2	2

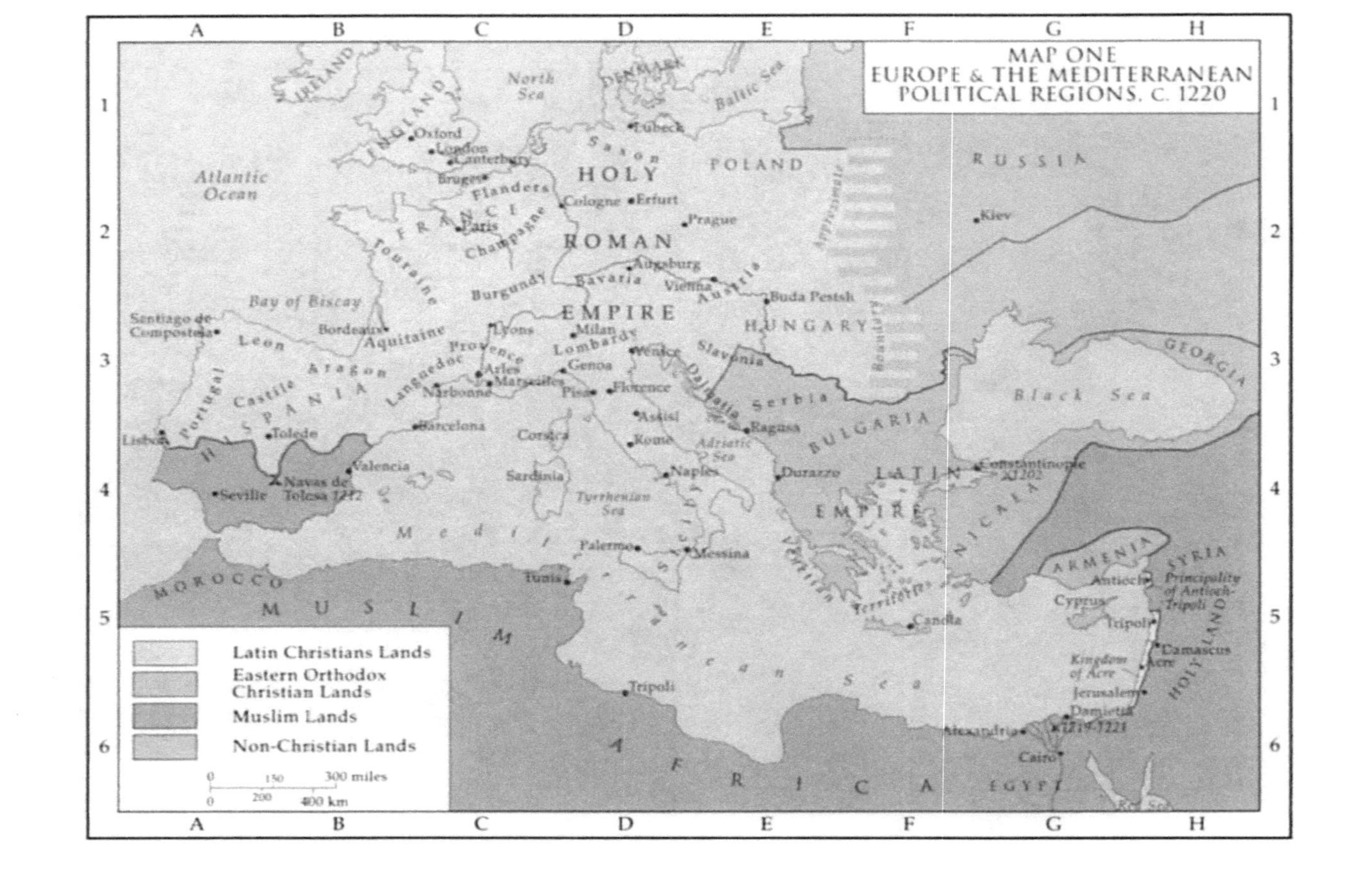
MAP ONE
EUROPE & THE MEDITERRANEAN
POLITICAL REGIONS, c. 1220
Latin Christians Lands
Eastern Orthodox Christian Lands
Muslim Lands
Non-Christian Lands
0 150 300 miles
0 200 400 km
A B C D E F G H
1 2 3 4 5 6
Atlantic Ocean
North Sea
Baltic Sea
Bay of Biscay
Black Sea
Adriatic Sea
Tyrrhenian Sea
IRELAND
ENGLAND
DENMARK
Oxford
London
Canterbury
Bruges
Flanders
FRANCE
Paris
Champagne
Touraine
Burgundy
Bordeaux
Aquitaine
Santiago de Compostela
Leon
Aragon
Castile
Portugal
HISPANIA
Lisbon
Toledo
Seville
Navas de Tolosa 1212
Valencia
Barcelona
Narbonne
Languedoc
Provence
Arles
Marseilles
Lyons
Saxon
HOLY ROMAN EMPIRE
Lubeck
Cologne
Erfurt
Prague
Augsburg
Bavaria
Vienna
Austria
Milan
Lombardy
Venice
Genoa
Pisa
Florence
Assisi
Rome
Naples
Corsica
Sardinia
Palermo
Messina
POLAND
Approximate Boundary
RUSSIA
Kiev
Buda Pestsh
HUNGARY
Slavonia
Dalmatia
Serbia
Ragusa
BULGARIA
Durazzo
LATIN EMPIRE
Constantinople
NICAEA
GEORGIA
Venetian Territories
Candia
ARMENIA
SYRIA
Antioch
Principality of Antioch-Tripoli
Cyprus
Tripoli
Damascus
Acre
Kingdom of Acre
Jerusalem
HOLY LAND
Damietta
1219-1221
Alexandria
Cairo
EGYPT
Red Sea
MOROCCO
MUSLIM
Tunis
Tripoli
AFRICA
Mediterranean Sea

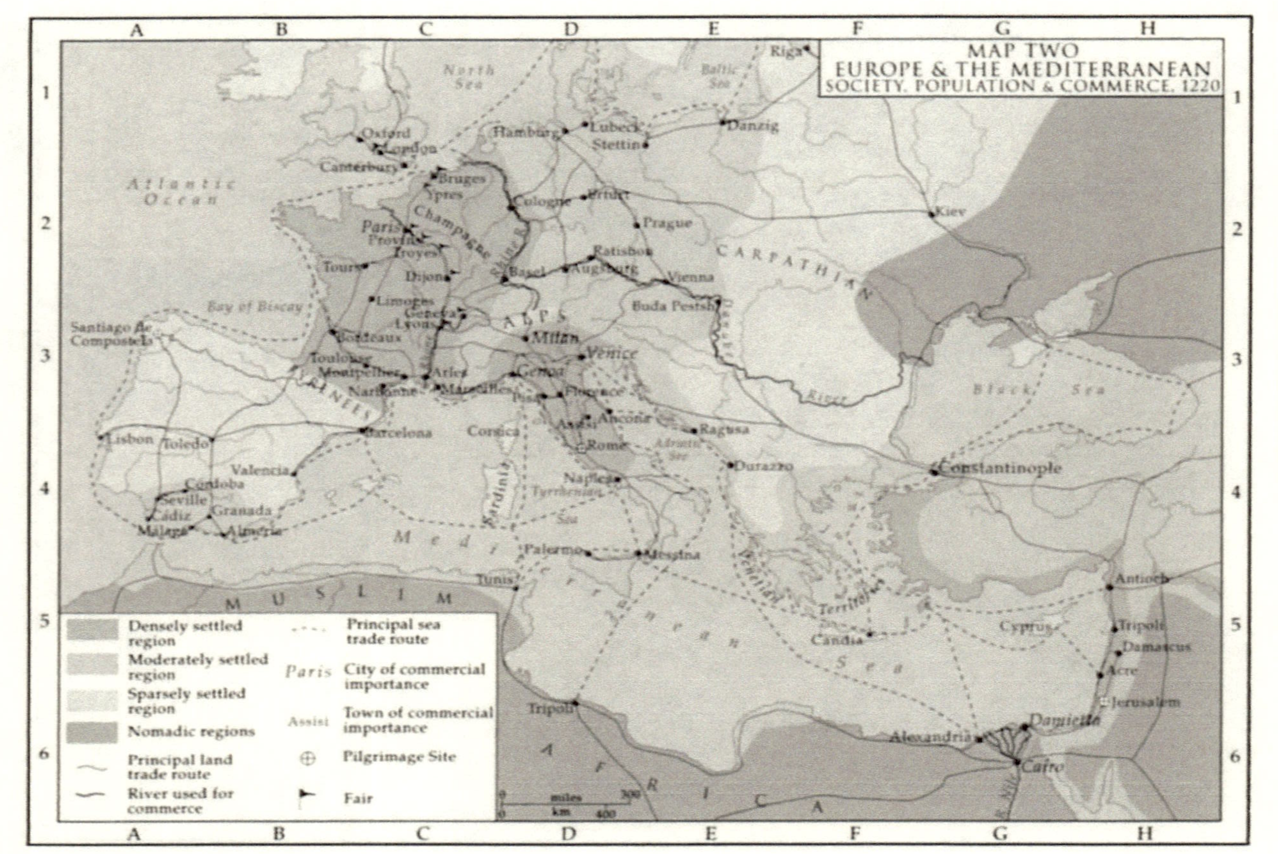
MAP TWO
EUROPE & THE MEDITERRANEAN
SOCIETY, POPULATION & COMMERCE, 1220
Densely settled region
Moderately settled region
Sparsely settled region
Nomadic regions
Principal land trade route
River used for commerce
Principal sea trade route
Paris City of commercial importance
Assisi Town of commercial importance
Pilgrimage Site
Fair
miles 300
km 400
Atlantic Ocean
North Sea
Baltic Sea
Bay of Biscay
Black Sea
Mediterranean Sea
Tyrrhenian Sea
Adriatic Sea
ALPS
CARPATHIAN
PYRENEES
Champagne
MUSLIM
AFRICA
Riga
Oxford
London
Canterbury
Hamburg
Lubeck
Stettin
Danzig
Bruges
Ypres
Cologne
Erfurt
Prague
Kiev
Paris
Provins
Troyes
Tours
Dijon
Basel
Augsburg
Ratisbon
Vienna
Buda Pesth
Limoges
Geneva
Lyons
Bordeaux
Milan
Venice
Santiago de Compostela
Toulouse
Montpellier
Arles
Genoa
Narbonne
Marseilles
Pisa
Florence
Ancona
Assisi
Ragusa
Lisbon
Toledo
Barcelona
Corsica
Rome
Durazzo
Constantinople
Valencia
Cordoba
Seville
Cadiz
Granada
Malaga
Almeria
Sardinia
Naples
Palermo
Messina
Tunis
Antioch
Candia
Cyprus
Tripoli
Damascus
Acre
Jerusalem
Alexandria
Damietta
Cairo

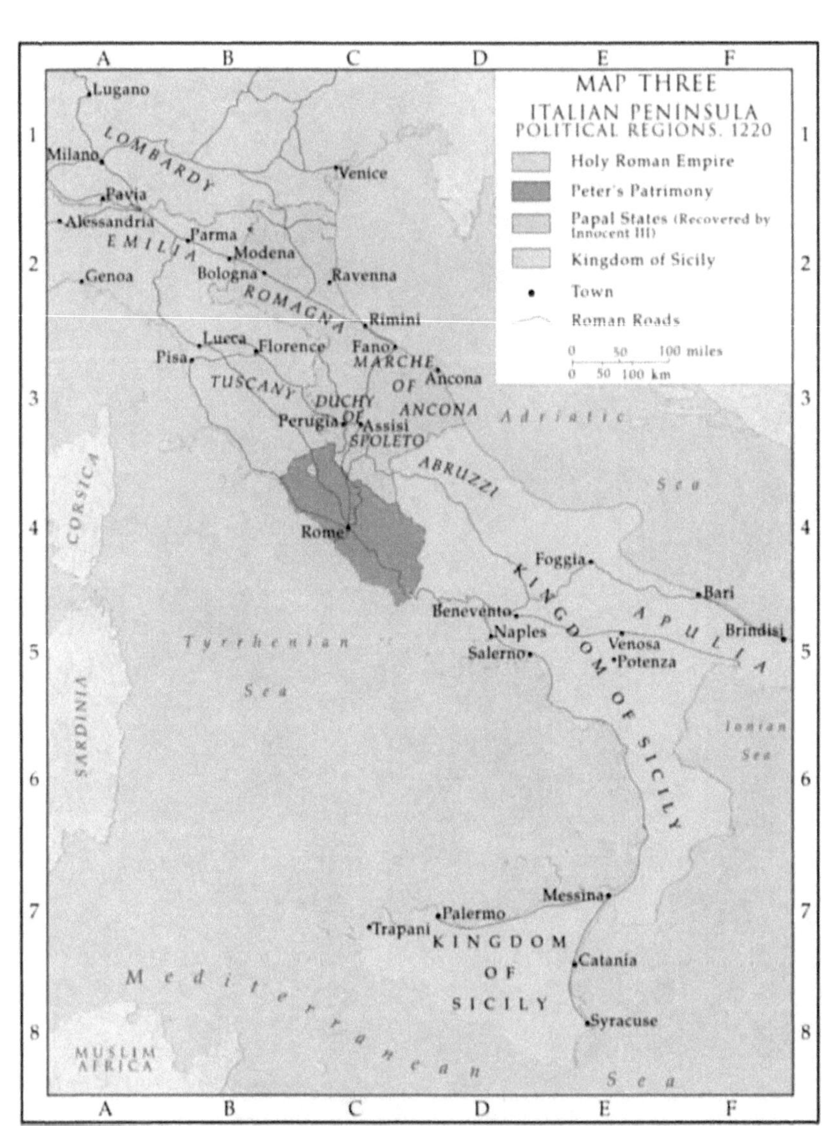
MAP THREE
ITALIAN PENINSULA
POLITICAL REGIONS. 1220
Holy Roman Empire
Peter's Patrimony
Papal States (Recovered by Innocent III)
Kingdom of Sicily
Town
Roman Roads
0 50 100 miles
0 50 100 km
A B C D E F
1 2 3 4 5 6 7 8
Lugano
Milano
LOMBARDY
Venice
Pavia
Alessandria
Parma
EMILIA
Modena
Genoa
Bologna
Ravenna
ROMAGNA
Rimini
Lucca
Florence
Fano
Pisa
MARCHE
Ancona
TUSCANY
OF
DUCHY
ANCONA
Adriatic
Perugia
OF
Assisi
SPOLETO
ABRUZZI
Sea
CORSICA
Rome
Foggia
KINGDOM OF SICILY
Bari
APULIA
Benevento
Brindisi
Naples
Venosa
Tyrrhenian
Salerno
Potenza
Sea
SARDINIA
Ionian
Sea
Messina
Palermo
Trapani
KINGDOM
OF
SICILY
Catania
Mediterranean
Syracuse
MUSLIM
AFRICA
Sea

MAP FOUR NORTHERN ITALIAN PENINSULA:
PHYSICAL GEOGRAPHY WITH ROMAN ROADS & ALPINE PASSES
0 -- 200 meters
201 -- 1000 meters
1001 -- 2000 meters
2001 -- 3000 meters
Over 3000 meters
Permanant Snow Cover
Mountain Pass
Roman Road
0 30 60 miles
0 50 100 miles
A B C D E F G H
1 2 3 4 5
Hochtor Pass
Brenner Pass
San Gottardo Pass
San Bernardo Pass
Mte. Cenis Pass
Geneva
Lyons
Lugano
Milano
Venice
Via Postumia
Via Annia
Torino
Pavia
Alessandria
Parma
Modena
Bologna
Ravenna
Via Aemilia
Genoa
Po River
Rhone River
Rimini
Fano
Ancona
Lucca
Pisa
Florence
Via Flaminia
Via Aurelia
Assisi
Perugia
Lago Trasimeno
L. di Bolsena
L. di Vico
L. di Bracciano
Tiber River
Via Salaria
Rome
Via Latina
Via Appia
Naples
Salerno
Foggia
Via Traiana
Bari
Brindisi
Marseilles
CORSICA
Tyrrhenian Sea
Adriatic Sea
ALPS
APPENINE MOUNTAINS

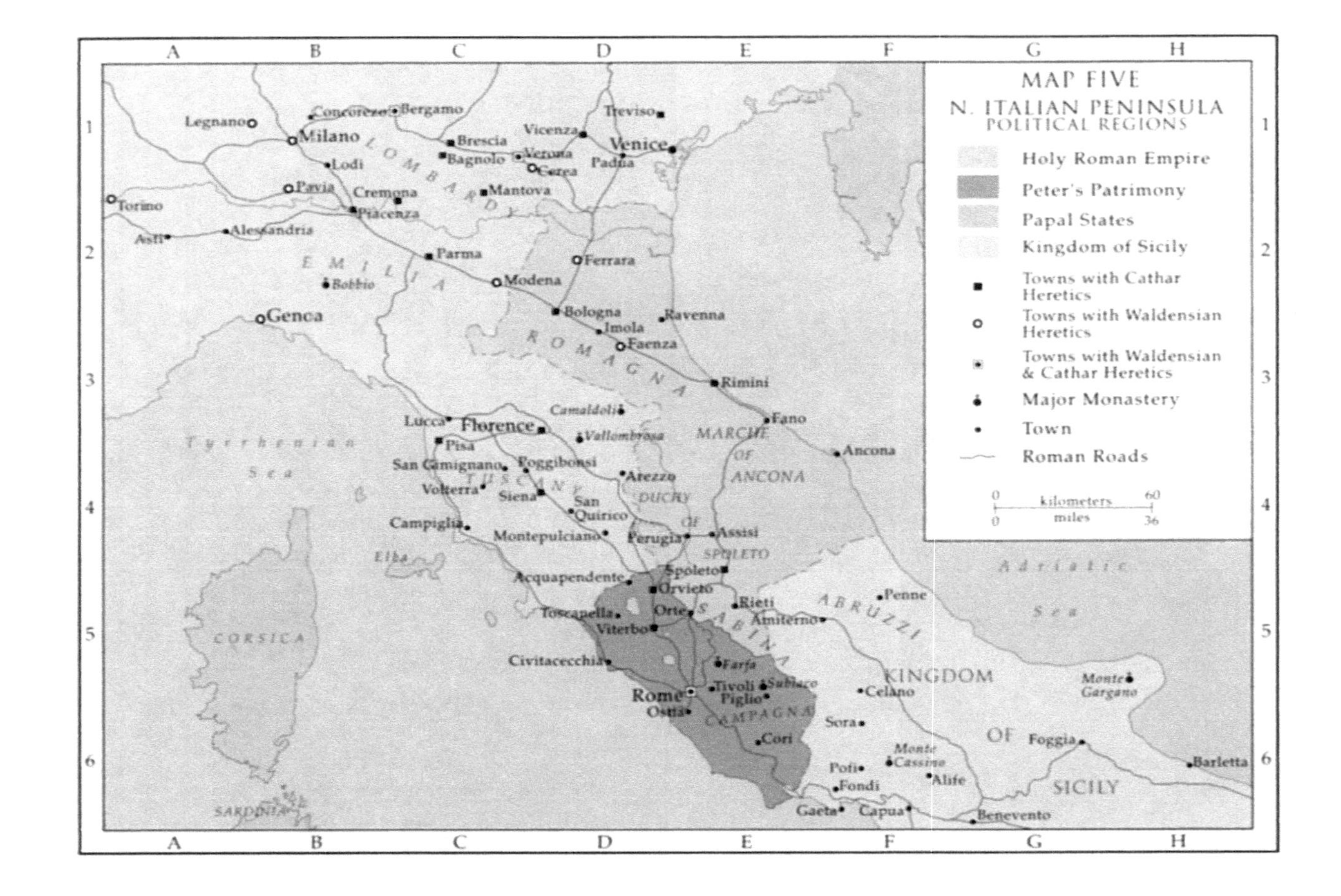
MAP FIVE
N. ITALIAN PENINSULA
POLITICAL REGIONS
Holy Roman Empire
Peter's Patrimony
Papal States
Kingdom of Sicily
Towns with Cathar Heretics
Towns with Waldensian Heretics
Towns with Waldensian & Cathar Heretics
Major Monastery
Town
Roman Roads
0 kilometers 60
0 miles 36
A B C D E F G H
1 2 3 4 5 6
Legnano
Concorezzo
Bergamo
Milano
Lodi
Pavia
Torino
Asti
Alessandria
Cremona
Piacenza
Brescia
Bagnolo
Verona
Cerea
Mantova
Vicenza
Treviso
Venice
Padua
LOMBARDY
EMILIA
Parma
Bobbio
Modena
Ferrara
Genoa
Bologna
Imola
Faenza
Ravenna
ROMAGNA
Rimini
Fano
Ancona
MARCHE OF ANCONA
Camaldoli
Vallombrosa
Lucca
Florence
Pisa
San Gimignano
Poggibonsi
Volterra
Siena
TUSCANY
Arezzo
San Quirico
Campiglia
Montepulciano
Perugia
Assisi
DUCHY OF SPOLETO
Tyrrhenian Sea
Elba
CORSICA
SARDINIA
Acquapendente
Spoleto
Orvieto
Toscanella
Orte
Viterbo
Rieti
Amiterno
Penne
ABRUZZI
SABINA
Civitacecchia
Farfa
Rome
Tivoli
Subiaco
Piglio
Ostia
CAMPAGNA
Cori
Celano
Sora
KINGDOM OF SICILY
Adriatic Sea
Monte Gargano
Foggia
Barletta
Monte Cassino
Pofi
Alife
Fondi
Gaeta
Capua
Benevento

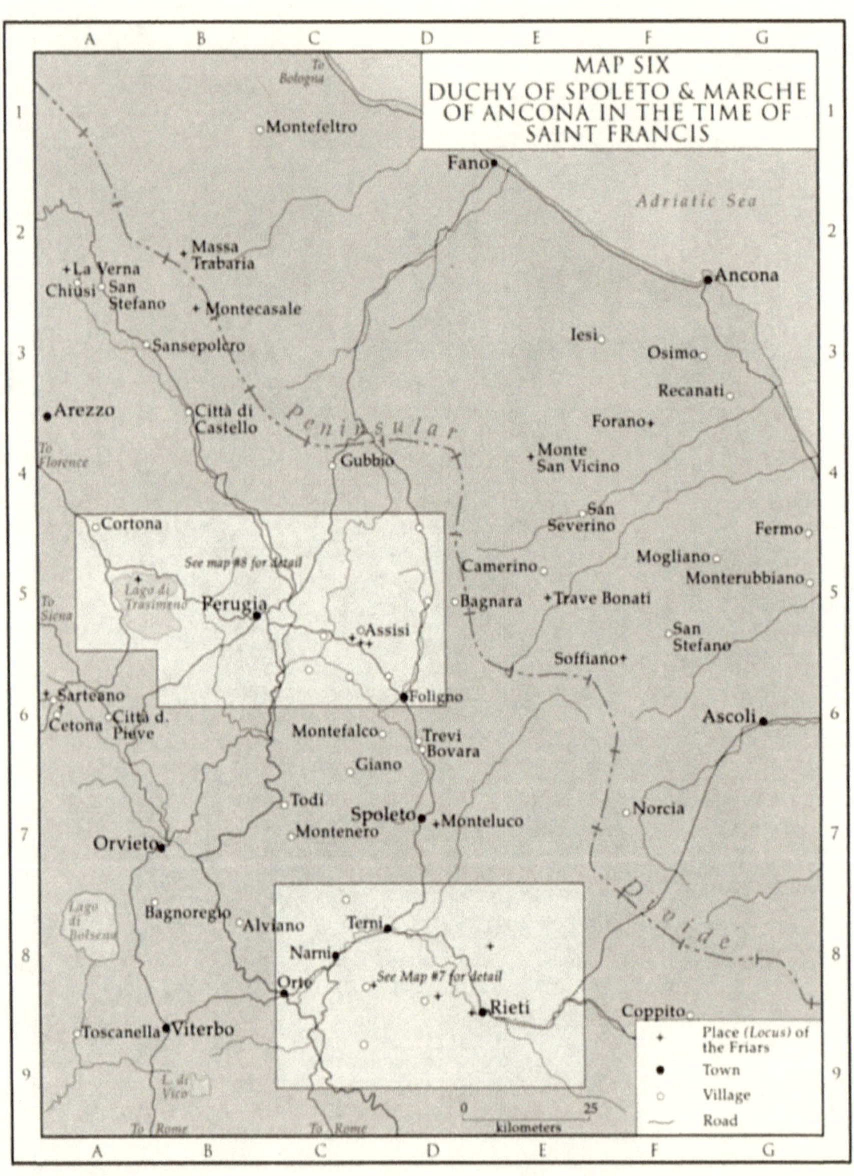
MAP SIX
DUCHY OF SPOLETO & MARCHE OF ANCONA IN THE TIME OF SAINT FRANCIS
A
B
C
D
E
F
G
1
2
3
4
5
6
7
8
9
To Bologna
Montefeltro
Fano
Adriatic Sea
Massa Trabaria
La Verna
Chiusi
San Stefano
Montecasale
Ancona
Iesi
Osimo
Sansepolcro
Recanati
Arezzo
Città di Castello
Forano
Peninsular
To Florence
Monte San Vicino
Gubbio
San Severino
Cortona
Fermo
See map #8 for detail
Mogliano
Camerino
Monterubbiano
Lago di Trasimeno
Perugia
To Siena
Bagnara
Trave Bonati
Assisi
San Stefano
Soffiano
Sarteano
Foligno
Ascoli
Cetona
Città d. Pieve
Montefalco
Trevi
Bovara
Giano
Todi
Spoleto
Monteluco
Norcia
Orvieto
Montenero
Divide
Lago di Bolsena
Bagnoregio
Alviano
Terni
Narni
Orte
See Map #7 for detail
Rieti
Coppito
Toscanella
Viterbo
L. di Vico
To Rome
To Rome
0
25
kilometers
Place (Locus) of the Friars
Town
Village
Road

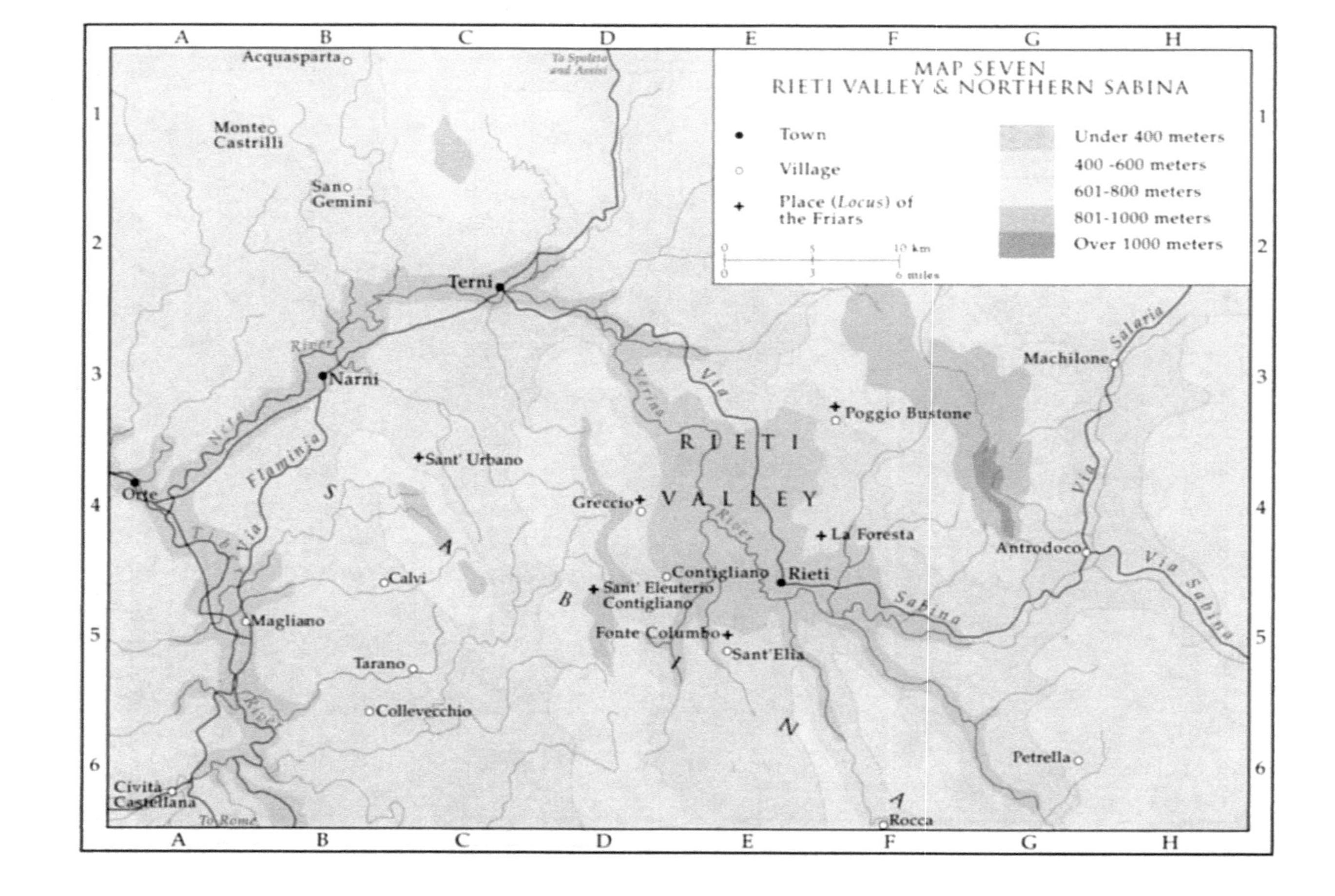
MAP SEVEN
RIETI VALLEY & NORTHERN SABINA
Town
Village
Place (Locus) of the Friars
0 5 10 km
0 3 6 miles
Under 400 meters
400 -600 meters
601-800 meters
801-1000 meters
Over 1000 meters
A B C D E F G H
1 2 3 4 5 6
Acquasparta
To Spoleto and Assisi
Monte Castrilli
San Gemini
Terni
Narni
Nera River
Flaminia
Via Tiberina
Orte
Sant' Urbano
S A B I N A
Calvi
Magliano
Tarano
Collevecchio
River
Civitá Castellana
To Rome
Greccio
RIETI VALLEY
Via Verina
Sant' Eleuterio Contigliano
Contigliano
Fonte Columbo
Sant'Elia
River
Rieti
Poggio Bustone
La Foresta
Rocca
Via Salaria
Machilone
Antrodoco
Via Sabina
Petrella

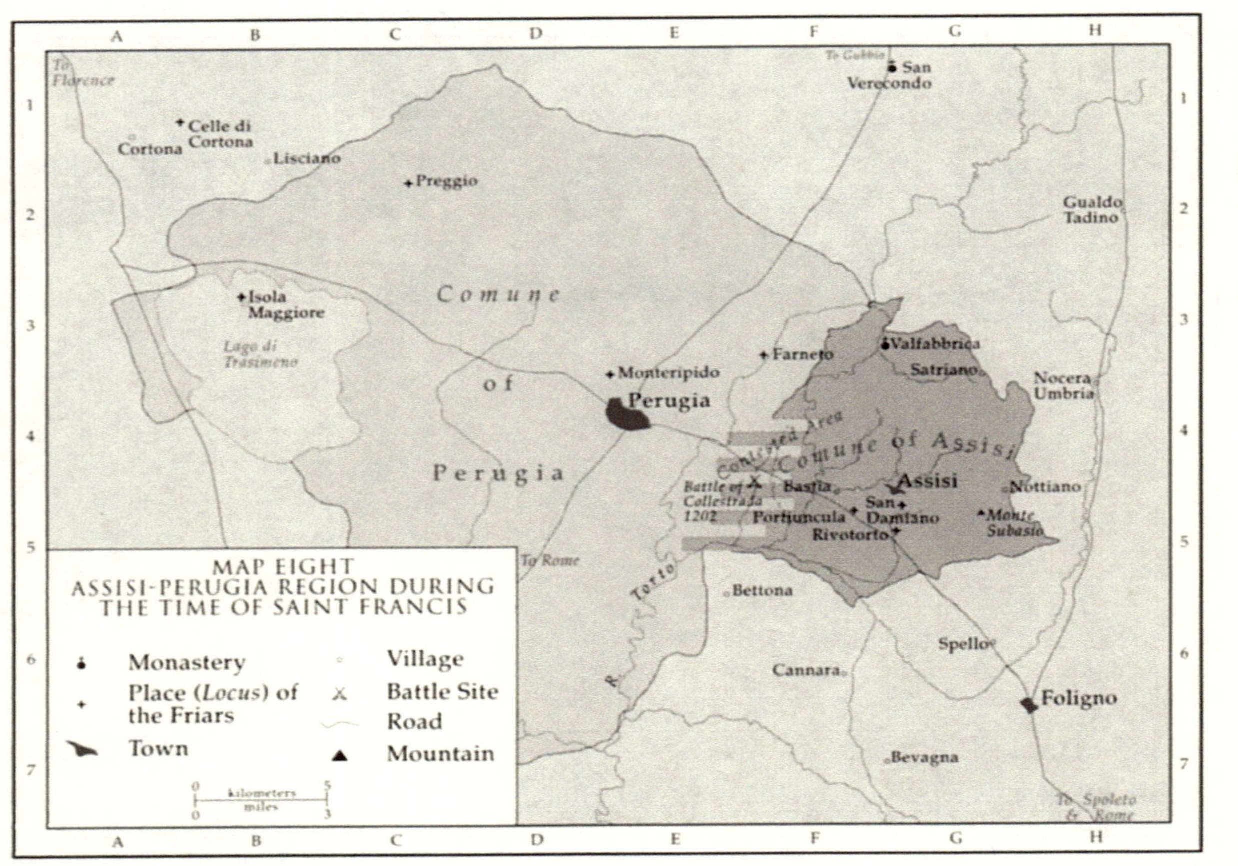
MAP EIGHT
ASSISI-PERUGIA REGION DURING
THE TIME OF SAINT FRANCIS
Monastery
Place (*Locus*) of the Friars
Town
Village
Battle Site
Road
Mountain
kilometers
miles
To Florence
Cortona
Celle di Cortona
Lisciano
Preggio
Isola Maggiore
Lago di Trasimeno
Comune of Perugia
Monteripido
Perugia
To Rome
R. Torto
To Gubbio
San Verecondo
Gualdo Tadino
Farneto
Valfabbrica
Satriano
Nocera Umbria
Contested Area
Comune of Assisi
Battle of Collestrada 1202
Bastia
Assisi
San Damiano
Portiuncula
Rivotorto
Nottiano
Monte Subasio
Bettona
Spello
Cannara
Foligno
Bevagna
To Spoleto & Rome

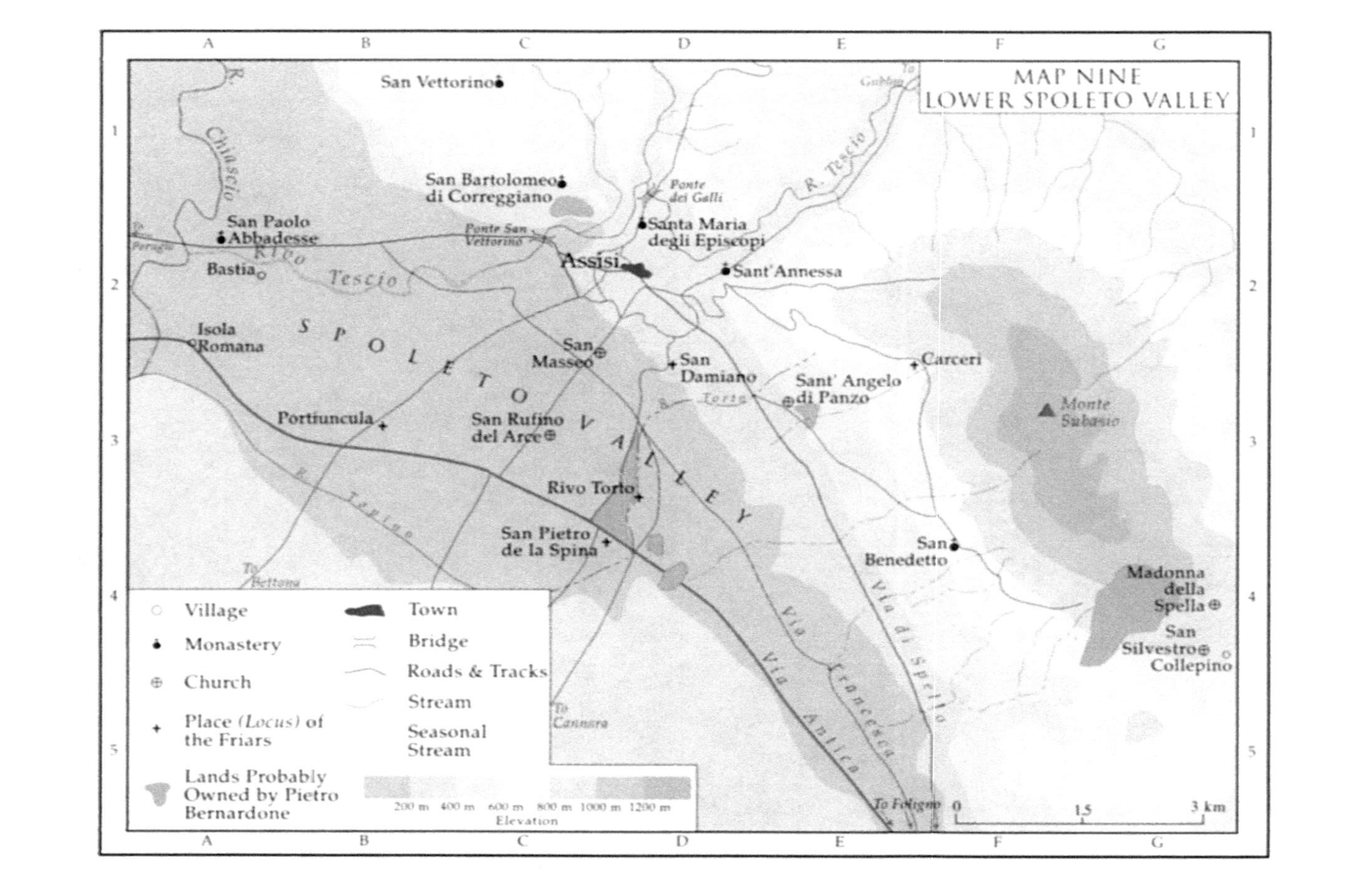
MAP NINE
LOWER SPOLETO VALLEY
San Vettorino
San Bartolomeo di Correggiano
San Paolo Abbadesse
Bastia
Isola Romana
Ponte San Vettorino
Ponte dei Galli
Santa Maria degli Episcopi
Assisi
Sant'Annessa
R. Tescio
R. Chiascio
Rigo Tescio
SPOLETO VALLEY
San Masseo
San Damiano
Sant' Angelo di Panzo
Carceri
Monte Subasio
Portiuncula
San Rufino del Arce
Rivo Torto
San Pietro de la Spina
San Benedetto
Madonna della Spella
San Silvestro
Collepino
R. Topino
Via Francesca
Via Antica
Via di Spello
To Gubbio
To Perugia
To Bettona
To Cannara
To Foligno
Village
Monastery
Church
Place (Locus) of the Friars
Lands Probably Owned by Pietro Bernardone
Town
Bridge
Roads & Tracks
Stream
Seasonal Stream
200 m 400 m 600 m 800 m 1000 m 1200 m
Elevation
0 1.5 3 km
A B C D E F G
1 2 3 4 5

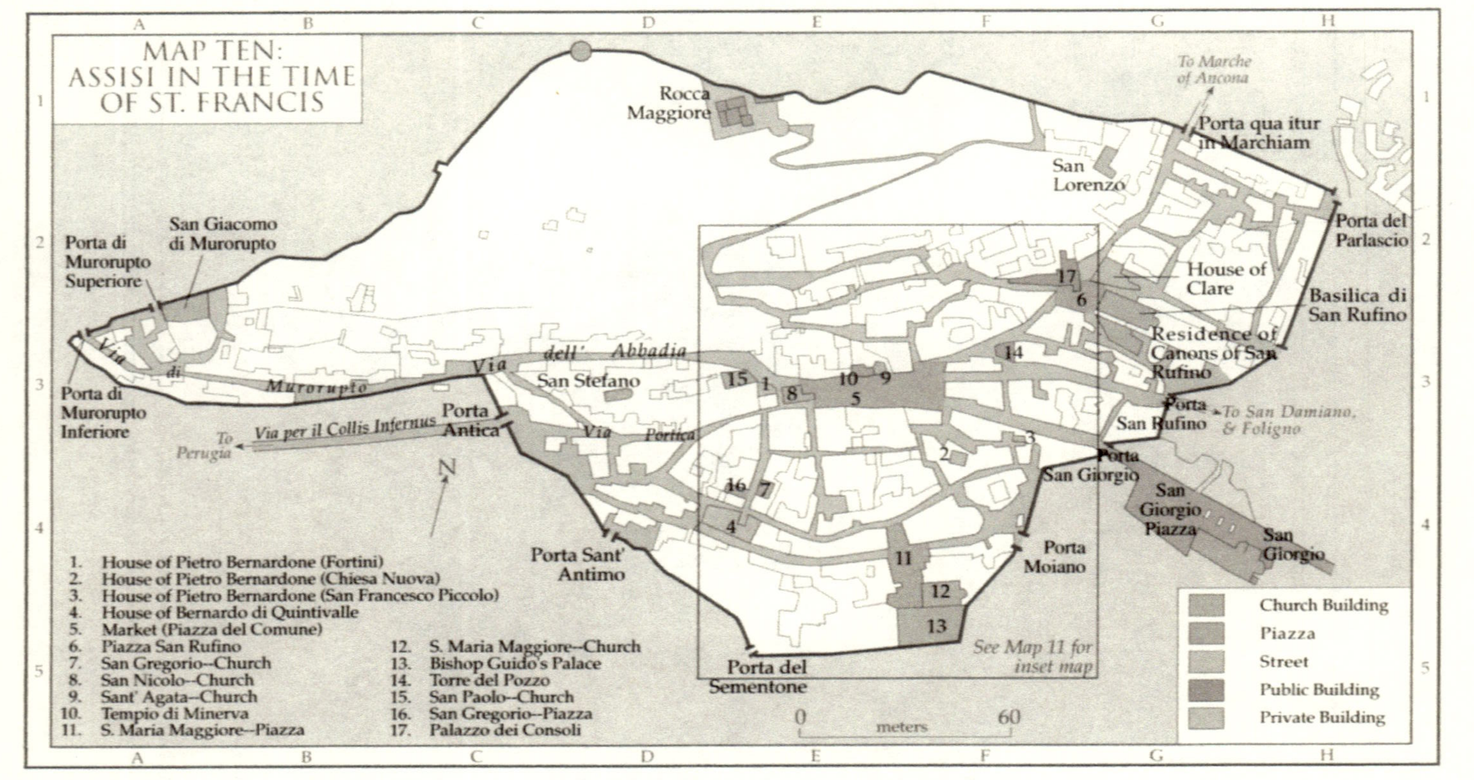
MAP TEN:
ASSISI IN THE TIME
OF ST. FRANCIS
Rocca Maggiore
To Marche of Ancona
Porta qua itur in Marchiam
San Lorenzo
Porta del Parlascio
San Giacomo di Murorupto
Porta di Murorupto Superiore
House of Clare
Basilica di San Rufino
Residence of Canons of San Rufino
Via di Murorupto
Via dell' Abbadia
San Stefano
Porta di Murorupto Inferiore
Porta Antica
Via per il Collis Infernus
To Perugia
Via Portica
Porta San Rufino
To San Damiano, & Foligno
Porta San Giorgio
San Giorgio Piazza
San Giorgio
N
Porta Sant' Antimo
Porta Moiano
Porta del Sementone
See Map 11 for inset map
0 meters 60
1. House of Pietro Bernardone (Fortini)
2. House of Pietro Bernardone (Chiesa Nuova)
3. House of Pietro Bernardone (San Francesco Piccolo)
4. House of Bernardo di Quintivalle
5. Market (Piazza del Comune)
6. Piazza San Rufino
7. San Gregorio--Church
8. San Nicolo--Church
9. Sant' Agata--Church
10. Tempio di Minerva
11. S. Maria Maggiore--Piazza
12. S. Maria Maggiore--Church
13. Bishop Guido's Palace
14. Torre del Pozzo
15. San Paolo--Church
16. San Gregorio--Piazza
17. Palazzo dei Consoli
Church Building
Piazza
Street
Public Building
Private Building

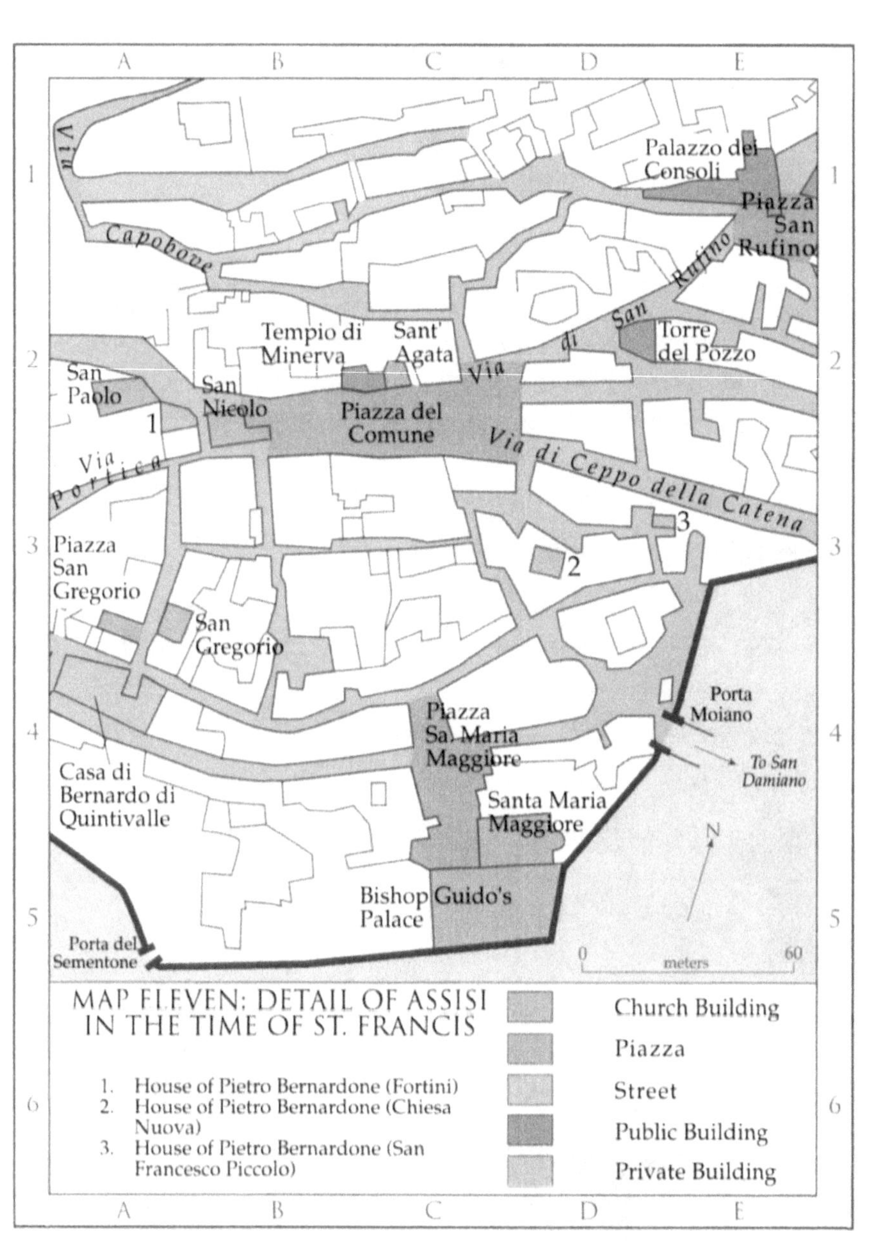

MAP ELEVEN: DETAIL OF ASSISI IN THE TIME OF ST. FRANCIS

New City Press is one of more than 20 publishing houses sponsored by the Focolare, a movement founded by Chiara Lubich to help bring about the realization of Jesus' prayer: "That all may be one" (John 17:21). In view of that goal, New City Press publishes books and resources that enrich the lives of people and help all to strive toward the unity of the entire human family. We are a member of the Association of Catholic Publishers.

www.ingramcontent.com/pod-product-compliance
Lightning Source LLC
Chambersburg PA
CBHW030102010526
44116CB00005B/56